LAW & REGULATION OF INVESTMENT MANAGEMENT

AUSTRALIA
Law Book Co.
Sydney

CANADA and USA
Carswell
Toronto

HONG KONG
Sweet & Maxwell Asia

NEW ZEALAND
Brookers
Wellington

SINGAPORE and MALAYSIA
Sweet & Maxwell Asia
Singapore and Kuala Lumpur

LAW & REGULATION OF INVESTMENT MANAGEMENT

DICK FRASE (ed.)

LONDON
SWEET & MAXWELL
2004

Published in 2004 by Sweet & Maxwell Limited of
100 Avenue Road
London NW3 3PF
Typeset by J&L Composition, Filey, North Yorkshire
Printed by MPG Books Ltd, Bodmin, Cornwall

No natural forests were destroyed to make this product: only farmed timber was used and replanted.

A CIP catalogue record for this book is available from the British Library

ISBN 0 421 83570 2

All rights reserved. Crown copyright material is reproduced with the permission of the Controller of HMSO and the Queens' Printer for Scotland.
No part of this publication may be reproduced or transmitted in any form or by any means, or stored in any rerieval system of any nature without prior written permission, except for permitted fair dealing under the Copyright, Designs and Patents Act 1988, or in accordance with the terms of a licence issued by the Copyright Licensing Agency in respect of photocopying and/or reprographic reproduction. Application for permission for other use of copyright material including permission to reproduce extracts in other published works shall be made to the publishers. Full acknowledgment of author, publisher and source must be given.

ISBN 0-421-83570-2

9 780421 835702

© Sweet & Maxwell 2004

FOREWORD

Investment management occupies a central position in financial markets both in the United Kingdom and globally. It provides the essential means by which private individuals and institutions can participate in financial markets which might otherwise be inaccessible to them. Nearly everyone has some kind of stake in the healthy functioning of the investment management industry.

Those who look after and undertake to manage the assets of others are subject to obligations derived from the general law as well as the regulatory framework under the Financial Services and Markets Act. This is apparent both in the context of the management of portfolios for individuals and collective management of investment funds and other schemes. The regulation of investment managers engages both of the FSA's overall aims of maintaining efficient, orderly and clean financial markets and helping consumers to achieve a fair deal. This book provides some very useful insights into the legal and regulatory issues which affect investment managers. It is a subject which deserves more attention from legal writers and practitioners and this is a very timely and welcome contribution.

Andrew Whittaker
General Counsel
Financial Services Authority

v

TO SARAH, JAMES AND AMELIA

ACKNOWLEDGMENTS

The publishers would like to thank the Investment Management Association for their kind permission to reprint the Pension Fund Disclosure Code, and the Institutional Shareholders' Committee Association for their kind permission to reprint The Responsibilities of Institutional Shareholders—Statement of Principles.

PREFACE

Not that long ago, investment management was barely recognised as a distinctive activity. Lots of people did it, but it was usually seen as something incidental to their "real" business, which was likely to be banking, broking, or insurance. Now, in the first years of the twenty first century, the position is very different. Investment management is now recognised as a leading industry and skills' set in its own right – and bankers, brokers, and insurers are keen to present themselves as high quality, specialist, investment managers.

As yet there is relatively little legal analysis of this new industry. This book is intended to help fill that gap.

The investment management service, in its general legal structure and related service functions such as custody and order execution, is described in Chapters 1 and 5. The conceptual basis for the service is the subject of Chapters 2 and 8, while current contract practice and case law are reviewed in Chapters 7 and 11. The controversial but crucial concept of the "fiduciary" is discussed in Chapter 9, and the position of occupational pension schemes, the largest single UK investor group, is the subject of Chapter 13.

The increasing prominence of the investment management sector has also attracted regulatory attention, and the regulatory spotlight, so long focused on the broker dealers on the "sell side" of the market, is now switching to the managers on the "buy side". The regulators' general approach to investment management, and the recent surge of regulatory initiatives in this area, are discussed in Chapters 3 and 4.

While this book is written largely from an English law point of view, one of the most instructive aspects of the common law is the way its common concepts develop in different jurisdictions. The United States has a particularly prominent role in this process. Key analyses of the US approach to investment management regulation and fiduciary duties are provided in Chapters 6 and 10. Chapter 12 discusses the US concept of managed futures – a driving inspiration for much of the current English futures industry.

PREFACE

Investment management is a growing area of practice, and its law and regulation will continue to develop.

A.R.G. Frase,
Serjeants' Inn,
March, 2004.

CONTENTS

	page
Foreword	*v*
Dedication	*vii*
Acknowledgments	*viii*
Preface	*ix*
Contents	*xi*
Table of Cases	*xv*
Table of Legislation	*xxvii*
Table of Statutory Instruments	*xxxiii*
Table of FSA Rules	*xxxv*
Table of Abbreviations	*xxxviii*

		para.
1	**Elements of Investment Management, Dick Frase**	**1–001**
	The Elements of Investment Management	1–001
	The Clients	1–002
	The Investment Portfolio	1–003
	The Investment Managers	1–005
	Managing the Investments	1–008
	Related Services	1–023
2	**The Legal Nature of the Client Services Relationship, Dick Frase**	**2–001**
	Introduction to Client Service Relationships	2–005
	Service Standards—Care and Skill and the Scope of the Service	2–014

CONTENTS

3 Regulation and the Promotion of Investment Management Services, Stuart Willey **3–001**
    Overview of FSA Regulation of Investment Management.... 3–001
    The Regulatory Regime for Investment Management Services... 3–002

4 Efficiency, Conflicts of Interest and Governance: Regulatory Developments for Investment Managers, Ashley Kovas **4–001**
    Introduction.. 4–001
    The *Myners Review*................................. 4–002
    Investment Research and Conflicts of Interest............. 4–014
    Bundling and Soft Commission Arrangements............. 4–020
    Best Execution..................................... 4–026
    Polarisation **4–030A**
    The *Sandler Review* 4–034
    Hedge Funds: Marketing, Regulation and Short Selling...... 4–049
    CIS Reform 4–068
    Conclusion.. 4–076

5 Custody—The Regulatory and Legislative Regime, Nick Doe **5–001**
    Introduction and Definitions 5–001
    The Legal Pre-Requisites and Regulatory Requirements 5–007
    Issues for Consideration.............................. 5–019

6 US Regulation of Investment Management, Michael McDonough and Maureen Magner **6–001**
    Introduction....................................... 6–001
    US Federal vs State Regulation 6–002
    Who Must Register Under the Advisers Act 6–003
    Adviser Registration Process 6–011
    Ongoing Requirements for a Registered Investment Adviser .. 6–016
    Advisory Contracts 6–036A
    SEC Inspections.................................... 6–041

7 Some Contractual Issues, Dick Frase **7–001**
    The Investment Mandate 7–001
    Commencement of the Mandate 7–009
    Client's Instructions 7–011
    Delegation 7–018
    Know Your Customer and Suitability 7–028
    Risk Warnings 7–031
    The Trade Execution Process 7–035
    Liability 7–039
    Conflicts of Interest 7–043
    Confidentiality..................................... 7–056

xii

CONTENTS

Default and *Force Majeure* Clauses 7–060
Termination 7–062

8 Judgment and Implementation—A Commentary, Dick Frase.... 8–001
The Exercise of Skilled Judgement..................... 8–002
The Basics of Implementation—Agency and Principal
Dealing, and Arranging 8–013

9 Investment Management and Fiduciary Duties, Stuart Willey 9–001
Introduction.. 9–001
Are Investment Managers Fiduciaries?................. 9–003
Comparison With Other Investment Firms 9–007
What Fiduciary Duties Do Investment Managers Owe?..... 9–008
Fiduciary Duties under FSMA......................... 9–009
The FSA's Principles for Businesses 9–011
FSA Rules—Single Capacity for Certain Investment
Managers 9–012
Secret Profits 9–013
FSA Rules—Self-Dealing in Fund Assets............... 9–016
FSA Rules—Priority and Aggregation of Orders......... 9–020
Duty of Care—Investment Managers As Fiduciaries...... 9–022
The Modification of Fiduciary Duties Through Contract 9–025

**10 US Approach to Fiduciary Duties: General Law, the Investment
Advisers Act, the Investment Company Act, and ERISA,
John F. Cacchione Esq 10–001**
Introduction to the Law of Fiduciaries in the United States .. 10–002
Fiduciary Duties of Investment Advisers 10–005
Fiduciary Duties Under ERISA........................ 10–017
Fiduciary Duties Under the State Law of Business Entities ... 10–027
Additional Obligations of Boards of Directors Under
the ICA 10–030

**11 Developments in Investment Management Accountability—
Benchmarks, Performance Targets and Internal Controls,
Helen Parry and Duncan Black.......................... 11–001**
The Case of Unilever and Mercury Asset Management...... 11–001
The Legal Basis For Claims Against Investment Managers ... 11–010
The *Myners Review*................................. 11–027
Conclusion... 11–028

**12 US Regulation of Managed Futures—Commodity Trading
Advisors and Commodity Pools, Susan C. Ervin 12–001**
The Regulatory Landscape for Derivatives............... 12–002
Regulation of Commodity Trading Advisors 12–013

xiii

CONTENTS

CFTC Regulation of Commodity Pool Operators 12–027
Selected CFTC/NFA Compliance Considerations Relevant to
CPOs and CTAs 12–042

13 Investment Management and Occupational Pension Schemes,
   Andrew Powell and Fraser Sparks 13–001
   Introduction 13–001
   Particular Investment Vehicles 13–012
   Trustees' Investment Powers 13–021
   Delegating Decision-Making Powers 13–045
   Trustee Protection 13–062
   The *Myners' Review* and the Government's Response 13–063
   Ethically and Socially Responsible Investments 13–094
   Other Issues 13–098

Appendix 1: Investment Management Association: Pension Fund
   Disclosure Code App1–001

Appendix 2: Institutional Shareholders' Committee: The Responsibilities
   of Institutional Shareholders and Agents—Statement of
   Principles App2–001

page
Index *402*

xiv

TABLE OF CASES

(All references are to paragraph number)

National Cases

Aas v Benham [1891] 2 Ch. 244, CA 7–050
Allinson v Clayhills (1907) 97 L.T. 709 7–050
Amalgamated Metal Trading Ltd v Department of Trade and Industry, *The Times*, March 21, 1989; *Financial Times*, February 28, 1989, QBD . . . 2–002
Anglo Overseas Transport Ltd v Titan Industrial Corp Ltd [1959] 2 Lloyd's Rep. 152, QBD (Comm Ct) 7–039
Armagas Ltd v Mundogas SA (The Ocean Frost) [1986] A.C. 717; [1986] 2 W.L.R. 1063; [1986] 2 All E.R. 385; [1986] 2 Lloyd's Rep. 109; (1986) 83 L.S.G. 2002; (1986) 130 S.J. 430, HL. 8–022
Armitage v Nurse (Exclusion Clauses) [1998] Ch. 241; [1997] 3 W.L.R. 1046; [1997] 2 All E.R. 705; (1997) 74 P. & C.R. D13, *The Times*, March 31, 1997; *Independent*, April 11, 1997, CA 7–042, 9–023
Arctic Shipping Co Ltd v Mobilia AB (The Tatra) [1990] 2 Lloyd's Rep. 51, QBD (Comm Ct) 8–022
Aston v Kelsey [1913] 3 K.B. 314, CA 7–048
Ata v American Express Bank Ltd *The Times*, June 26, 1998, CA 9–006, 9–023
Attwood v Small *see* Small v Attwood

Bailey & Co v Balholm Securities [1973] 2 Lloyd's Rep. 404, QBD (Comm Ct). 7–039, 8–023
Bankers Trust International v PT Dharmala Sakti Sejahtera (No.1) [1996] C.L.C. 252, QBD 2–036, 2–038, 2–039, 7–034, 8–011
Banque Bruxelles Lambert SA v Eagle Star Insurance Co Ltd; United Bank of Kuwait Plc v Prudential Property Services Ltd; Nykredit Mortgage Bank Plc v Edward Erdman Group Ltd; BNP Mortgages Ltd v Key Surveyors Nationwide Ltd; BNP Mortgages Ltd v Goadsby & Harding Ltd; Mortgage Express Ltd v Bowerman & Partners (No.2) [1995] Q.B. 375; [1995] 2 W.L.R. 607; [1995] 2 All E.R. 769; [1995] L.R.L.R. 195; [1996] 5 Bank. L.R. 64; 73 B.L.R. 47; [1995] E.C.C. 398; [1996] 5 Re.

TABLE OF CASES

L.R. 23; [1995] 1 E.G.L.R. 129; [1995] 12 E.G. 144; [1995] E.G.C.S. 31; (1995) 92(12) L.S.G. 34; (1995) 145 N.L.J. 343; (1995) 139 S.J.L.B. 56; [1995] N.P.C. 32, *The Times*, February 21, 1995; *Independent,* February 24, 1995, CA 11–010

Barclays Bank Ltd v Quistclose Investments Ltd; sub nom. Quistclose Investments Ltd v Rolls Razor Ltd (In Voluntary Liquidation) [1970] A.C. 567; [1968] 3 W.L.R. 1097; [1968] 3 All E.R. 651; 112 S.J. 903, HL 1–025

Barclays Bank Plc v Fairclough Building Ltd (No.1) [1995] Q.B. 214; [1994] 3 W.L.R. 1057; [1995] 1 All E.R. 289; 68 B.L.R. 1; 38 Con. L.R. 86; (1995) 11 Const. L.J. 35; [1995] E.G.C.S. 10; (1994) 91(25) L.S.G. 30; (1994) 138 S.J.L.B. 118 *The Times*, May 11, 1994, CA 2–016

Barker & Sons v Inland Revenue Commissioners [1919] 2 K.B. 222, KBD . . 2–029

Bartlett v Barclays Bank Trust Co Ltd (No.1) [1980] 2 W.L.R. 430; [1980] 1 All E.R. 139; 124 S.J. 85, Ch D 11–024, 13–038

Bath Glass, Re (1988) 4 B.C.C. 130; [1988] B.C.L.C. 329 7–042

Bauman v Hulton Press Ltd [1952] 2 All E.R. 1121; [1952] W.N. 556, QBD 7–064

Bell v Strathern & Blair (Mandatory: Motion to sist mandatory) 1953 S.L.T. (Notes) 23, OH 2–019, 2–025

Bevan Investments Ltd v Blackhall & Struthers (No.2) 11 B.L.R. 78; [1978] 2 N.Z.L.R. 97, CA (NZ) 2–027

Boardman v Phipps; sub nom. Phipps v Boardman [1967] 2 A.C. 46; [1966] 3 W.L.R. 1009; [1966] 3 All E.R. 721; 110 S.J. 853, HL 7–045, 9–017

Bolam v Friern Hospital Management Committee [1957] 1 W.L.R. 582; [1957] 2 All E.R. 118; [1955–95] P.N.L.R. 7; 101 S.J. 357, QBD 2–024, 2–025, 2–028

Bolkiah v KPMG; sub nom.HRH Prince Jefri Bolkiah v KPMG [1999] 2 A.C. 222; [1999] 2 W.L.R. 215; [1999] 1 B.C.L.C. 1; [1999] P.N.L.R. 220; (1999) 149 N.L.J. 16; (1999) 143 S.J.L.B. 35, *The Times*, April 20, 1999; *Independent,* January 12, 1999, HL 2–047, 7–045, 7–048, 7–050, 7–055, 7–058

Booth v Davey (1988) 138 N.L.J. Rep. 104, *Independent*, April 18, 1988 (C.S), CA 2–036

Boyce v Rendells (1983) 268 E.G. 268, CA 7–032, 7–032

Brandeis Brokers Ltd v Black [2001] 2 All E.R. (Comm) 980; [2001] 2 Lloyd's Rep. 359, QBD (Comm Ct) 2–027, 9–007

Branwhite v Worcester Works Finance Ltd [1969] 1 A.C. 552; [1968] 3 W.L.R. 760; [1968] 3 All E.R. 104; 112 S.J. 758, HL 8–020

Brickenden v London Loan & Savings Co [1934] 3 D.L.R. 465, PC (Can) . . . 9–002

Bristol and West Building Society v Mothew (t/a Stapley & Co); sub nom. Mothew v Bristol and West Building Society [1998] Ch. 1; [1997] 2 W.L.R. 436; [1996] 4 All E.R. 698; [1997] P.N.L.R. 11; (1998) 75 P. & C.R. 241; [1996] E.G.C.S. 136; (1996) 146 N.L.J. 1273; (1996) 140 S.J.L.B. 206; [1996] N.P.C. 126, *The Times*, August 2, 1996, CA 2–010, 7–044, 9–003, 9–023, 9–023

Bromley LBC v A Ellis (Luff & Sons, Third Party) [1971] 1 Lloyd's Rep. 97; (1970) 114 S.J. 906, CA 2–043, 7–017

Brown v KMR Services Ltd; Sword Daniels v Pitel [1995] 4 All E.R. 598; [1995] 2 Lloyd's Rep. 513; [1995] 4 Re. L.R. 241, *The Times*, July 26, 1995; *Independent*, September 13, 1995; Lloyd's List, October 3, 1995 (I.D.), CA 2–021, 2–035, 2–036, 2–037, 7–029, 7–034, 8–007

xvi

TABLE OF CASES

Brown v Rolls Royce Ltd [1960] 1 W.L.R. 210; [1960] 1 All E.R. 577;
    1960 S.C. (H.L.) 22; 1960 S.L.T. 119; 104 S.J. 207, HL 2–023
Burns v Kelly Peters & Associates Ltd [1987] 16 B.C.L.R. (2d) 7–044

Calico Printers Association Ltd v Barclays Bank Ltd 1931) 39 Ll. L. Rep. 51,
    CA 7–019, 7–022
Carradine Properties Ltd v DJ Freeman & Co [1999] Lloyd's Rep. P.N. 483;
    [1955–95] P.N.L.R. 219; (1989) 5 Const. L.J. 267, *The Times*, February
    19, 1982, CA 2–036, 2–039
Central BC Planers v Hocker (1970) 9 D.L.R. (3d) 689, Sup Ct 2–031
Chatterton v Gerson [1981] Q.B. 432; [1980] 3 W.L.R. 1003; [1981] 1 All
    E.R. 257; 124 S.J. 885, QBD 7–032
Chaudhry v Prabhakar [1989] 1 W.L.R. 29; [1988] 3 All E.R. 718; (1988) 138
    N.L.J. Rep. 172; (1989) 133 S.J. 82, CA 2–006, 8–021
Cheshire & Co v Vaughan Bros & Co [1920] 3 K.B. 240; (1920) 3 Ll. L. Rep.
    213, CA 7–019
City Equitable Fire Insurance Co Ltd, Re [1925] Ch. 407; [1924] All E.R.
    Rep. 485, CA 2–023
Clark v Kirby Smith [1964] Ch. 506; [1964] 3 W.L.R. 239; [1964] 2 All E.R.
    835; [1964] 2 Lloyd's Rep. 172; 108 S.J. 462, Ch D 2–020
Clark Boyce v Mouat [1994] 1 A.C. 428; [1993] 3 W.L.R. 1021; [1993] 4 All
    E.R. 268; (1993) 143 N.L.J. 1440; (1993) 137 S.J.L.B. 231; [1993] N.P.C.
    128, *The Times,* October 7, 1993; *Independent*, October 12, 1993, PC
    (NZ). 2–038, 9–026, 9–027
Coco v AN Clark (Engineers) Ltd [1968] F.S.R. 415; [1969] R.P.C. 41,
    Ch D. 7–057
Cohen v Kittell (1889) L.R. 22 Q.B.D. 680, QBD 7–015
Coleman v Myers [1977] 2 N.Z.L.R. 225, Sup Ct (NZ) 2–009, 7–044
County Ltd v Girozentrale Securities[1996] 1 B.C.L.C. 653, CA 2–022, 2–039
Cowan v Scargill;sub nom.Mineworkers Pension Scheme Trusts, Re [1985]
    Ch. 270; [1984] 3 W.L.R. 501; [1984] 2 All E.R. 750; [1984] I.C.R. 646;
    [1984] I.R.L.R. 260; (1984) 81 L.S.G. 2463; (1984) 128 S.J. 550, Ch D . . 13–094,
                                                                                  13–096
Cropper v Cook (1867–68) L.R. 3 C.P. 194, CCP 7–039
Crossnan v Ward Bracewell & Co (1989) P.N.103 . . . . 2–032, 2–038, 2–040
Cunliffe-Owen v Teather & Greenwood; Cunliffe Owen v Schaverien
    Habermann, Simon & Co; Cunliffe Owen v LA Seligmann & Co [1967]
    1 W.L.R. 1421; [1967] 3 All E.R. 561; 111 S.J. 866, Ch D 7–015

De Bussche v Alt (1878) L.R. 8 Ch. D. 286, CA 7–018
De la Bere v Pearson Ltd [1908] 1 K.B. 280, CA 7–019
Decro-Wall International SA v Practitioners in Marketing [1971] 1 W.L.R.
    361; [1971] 2 All E.R. 216; (1970) 115 S.J. 171, CA. 7–064
Dickson & Co v Devitt (1916) 86 L.J.K.E. 315. . . . . 2 021, 2–026
Dixon v Hovill (1828) 4 Bing 665. 7–013
D'Jan of London, Re; sub nom Copp v D'Jan [1993] B.C.C. 646; [1994] 1
    B.C.L.C. 561, Ch D (Companies Ct) 7–042
Donoghue v Stevenson; sub nom. McAlister v Stevenson [1932] A.C. 562;
    1932 S.C. (H.L.) 31; 1932 S.L.T. 317; [1932] W.N. 139, HL 2–007, 2–016
Dorchester Finance Co v Stebbing [1989] B.C.L.C. 498 2–028
Drexel Burnham Lambert International BV v Nasr [1986] 1 Lloyd's Rep.
    356, QBD. 2–019, 2–036, 2–039
Duchess of Argyll v Beuselinck [1972] 2 Lloyd's Rep. 172, Ch 2–025

xvii

TABLE OF CASES

Dunbar v A&B Painters Ltd and Economic Insurance Co Ltd and Whitehouse & Co [1986] 2 Lloyd's Rep. 38, CA 7–029
Dunn v Fairs, Blissard Barnes & Stowe (1961) 105 S.J. 932 2–020
Dunne v English (1874) L.R. 18 Eq. 524, Ct of Chancery 7–047

Eagle Trust Plc v SBC Securities Ltd (No.2). sub nom.Eagle Trust Plc v SBCI Swiss Bank Corp Investment Banking Ltd [1995] B.C.C. 231; [1996] 1 B.C.L.C. 121, *Independent*, September 28, 1994, Ch D 7–050
Ellis v Pond [1898] 1 Q.B. 426, CA. 2–017
Enlayde Ltd v Roberts [1917] 1 Ch. 109, Ch D 7–013
Equitable Life Assurance Society v Hyman [2002] 1 A.C. 408; [2000] 3 W.L.R. 529; [2000] 3 All E.R. 961; [2001] Lloyd's Rep. I.R. 99; [2000] O.P.L.R. 101; [2000] Pens. L.R. 249; (2000) 144 S.J.L.B. 239, *The Times*, July 21, 2000; *Independent* October 30, 2000 (C.S), HL 2–011
Erskine Oxenford & Co v Sachs [1901] 2 K.B. 504, CA 8–020
Esso Petroleum Co Ltd v Mardon [1976] Q.B. 801; [1976] 2 W.L.R. 583; [1976] 2 All E.R. 5; [1976] 2 Lloyd's Rep. 305; 2 B.L.R. 82; 120 S.J. 131, CA 2–037
European Asian Bank AG v Punjab & Sind Bank (No.2) [1983] 1 W.L.R. 642; [1983] 2 All E.R. 508; [1983] 1 Lloyd's Rep. 611; [1983] Com. L.R. 128; (1983) 127 S.J. 379, CA 7–013

Faithful v Kesteven (1910) 103 L.T. 56 CA 2–020
Farquharson Bros & Co v C King & Co; sub nom. Farquharson Bros & Co v King & Co, [1902] A.C. 325, HL 8–022
Fine's Flowers v General Accident Assurance Co of Canada (1974) 49 D.L.R. (3d) 641, HC 2–024, 7–029
First Energy (UK) v Hungarian International Bank [1993] 2 Lloyd's Rep. 194; [1993] B.C.C. 533; [1993] B.C.L.C. 1409; [1993] N.P.C. 34, *The Times*, March 4, 1993, CA 8–022
Freeman & Lockyer v Buckhurst Park Properties (Mangal) Ltd [1964] 2 Q.B. 480; [1964] 2 W.L.R. 618; [1964] 1 All E.R. 630; 108 S.J. 96, CA . . . 8–022

Garnac Grain Co Inc v HMF Faure & Fairclough Ltd; sub nom.Bunge Corp v HMF Faure & Fairclough Ltd [1968] A.C. 1130; [1967] 3 W.L.R. 143; [1967] 2 All E.R. 353; [1967] 1 Lloyd's Rep. 495; 111 S.J. 434, HL. 8–020, 8–021
Garside, Re; sub nom; Wragg v Garside [1919] 1 Ch. 132, Ch D 13–021
General Accident Fire and Life Assurance Corp Ltd v Peter William Tanter (The Zephyr) [1985] 2 Lloyd's Rep. 529, CA 2–042, 8–021
Ginora Investments v James Capel & Co Ltd 2–020, 2–025, 2–036, 2–039, 2–043, 7–032, 7–034, 8–010
Gladwell v Sreggall (1839) 5 Bing N.C. 733 2–032
Glynwill Investments NV and Proxyward Limited v Thomson McKinnon Futures Limited unreported 13th February 1992. . . . . 7–051, 8–020, 8–023, 9–006, 9–007
Goody v Baring [1956] 1 W.L.R. 448; [1956] 2 All E.R. 11; 100 S.J. 320, Ch D 2–029
Gorham v British Telecommunications Plc [2000] 1 W.L.R. 2129; [2000] 4 All E.R. 867; [2001] Lloyd's Rep. I.R. 531; [2000] Lloyd's Rep. P.N. 897; [2001] P.N.L.R. 2; [2000] Pens. L.R. 293; (2000) 97(38) L.S.G. 44; (2000) 144 S.J.L.B. 251, *The Times*, August 16, 2000, CA 3–019

xviii

TABLE OF CASES

Great Scottish & Western Railway Co Ltd v British Railways Board
QBENF98/1005/A2, CA. 7–042

Greaves & Co (Contractors) Ltd v Baynham Meikle & Partners [1975] 1
W.L.R. 1095; [1975] 3 All E.R. 99; [1975] 2 Lloyd's Rep. 325; 4 B.L.R.
56; 119 S.J. 372, CA 2–020

Groom v Crocker [1939] 1 K.B. 194; (1938) 60 Ll. L. Rep. 393, CA 2–011, 2–043

Guerin v The Queen (1984) 13 D.L.R. 321 2–008

Guinness, Son & Co (Dublin) Ltd v Owners of the Motor Vessel Freshfield
(The Lady Gwendolen) [1965] P. 294; [1965] 3 W.L.R. 91; [1965] 2 All
E.R. 283; [1965] 1 Lloyd's Rep. 335; 109 S.J. 336, CA. 2–032

Hacker v Thomas Deal & Co [1991] 2 E.G.L.R. 161; [1991] 44 E.G. 173. . . 2–025

Hale v Guildarch [1999] P.N.L.R. 44, QBD 11–010

Hall & Barker, Re (1878) L.R. 9 Ch. D. 538, Ch D 7–064

Hambro v Burnand [1904] 2 K.B. 10, CA 8–022

Hancock v Smith (1889) L.R. 41 Ch. D. 456, CA 7–044

Harmer v Cornelius (1858) 5 C.B. N.S. 236 2–029

Harries v Church Commissioners for England;sub nom.Lord Bishop of
Oxford v Church Commissioners of England [1992] 1 W.L.R. 1241;
[1993] 2 All E.R. 300; (1991) 135 S.J.L.B. 180, *The Times*, October 30,
1991; *Independent,* October 29, 1991; *Guardian*, October 30, 1991,
Ch D. 13–095

Harrods Ltd v Lemon [1931] 2 K.B. 157; 80 A.L.R. 1067, CA. 7–047, 7–055

Hedley Byrne & Co Ltd v Heller & Partners Ltd [1964] A.C. 465; [1963] 3
W.L.R. 101; [1963] 2 All E.R. 575; [1963] 1 Lloyd's Rep. 485; 107 S.J.
454, HL. 2–006, 2–007, 2–008,
2–010, 2–012, 2–019,
2–029, 2–030, 2–042,
2–045, 7–025, 8–021

Henderson v Merrett Syndicates Ltd (No.1); sub nom. McLarnon Deeney v
Gooda Walker Ltd; Gooda Walker Ltd v Deeny; Hallam-Eames v
Merrett Syndicates Ltd; Hughes v Merrett Syndicates Ltd; Feltrim
Underwriting Agencies Ltd v Arbuthnott; Deeny v Gooda Walker Ltd
(Duty of Care) [1995] 2 A.C. 145; [1994] 3 W.L.R. 761; [1994] 3 All E.R.
506; [1994] 2 Lloyd's Rep. 468; (1994) 144 N.L.J. 1204, *The Times,* July
26, 1994; *Independent*, August 3, 1994, HL 2–006, 2–009, 2–010,
2–024, 2–029, 2–042,
7–022, 7–025, 9–023

Hermione, The (Appraisement & Sale) (1921) 9 Ll. L. Rep. 399, PDAD . . . 7–016

Heywood v Wellers (A Firm) [1976] Q.B. 446; [1976] 2 W.L.R. 101; [1976] 1
All E.R. 300; [1976] 2 Lloyd's Rep. 88; (1975) 120 S.J. 9, CA 2–021

Hilton v Barker Booth & Eastwood; sub nom.Hilton v Baker Booth &
Eastwood; Hilton v Bariker Booth & Eastwood [2002] EWCA Civ 723;
[2002] Lloyd's Rep. P.N. 500; [2003] P.N.L.R. 32; (2002) 146 S.J.L.B.
152; [2002] N.P.C. 74, *TheTimes*, June 6, 2002; *Independent*, May 29,
2002, CA 7–045

Hong Kong and Shanghai Banking Corp v Kloeckner & Co AG [1990] 2
Q.B. 514; [1990] 3 W.L.R. 634; [1989] 3 All E.R. 513; [1989] 2 Lloyd's
Rep. 323, QBD (Comm Ct) 8–023

Hospital Products v United States Surgical Corp[1984] 156 C.L.R. 41 7–044,
9–025

Howard Marine & Dredging Co Ltd v A Ogden & Sons (Excavations) Ltd
[1978] Q.B. 574; [1978] 2 W.L.R. 515; [1978] 2 All E.R. 1134; [1978] 1
Lloyd's Rep. 334; 9 B.L.R. 34; 122 S.J. 48, CA 2–009

xix

TABLE OF CASES

Hunter v Hanley; sub nom.Galloway (or Hunter) v Hanley 1955 S.C. 200;
1955 S.L.T. 213; [1955–95] P.N.L.R. 1, 1 Div; 2–025
Hurlingham Estates Ltd v Wilde & Partners [1997] 1 Lloyd's Rep. 525;
[1997] S.T.C. 627; [1997] B.T.C. 240; (1997) 147 N.L.J. 453, *The Times*,
January 3, 1997; *Independent*, February 17, 1997 (C.S.), Ch D ... 2–024, 2–029

Independent Broadcasting Authority v EMI Electronics Ltd; sub nom.IBA
v EMI Electronics Ltd and BICC Construction Ltd 4 B.L.R. 1;
[1955–95] P.N.L.R. 179, HL 2–025
Inglefield Ltd, Re [1933] Ch. 1, CA 8–020
Investors Compensation Scheme Ltd v West Bromwich Building Society
(No.2) [1999] Lloyd's Rep. P.N. 496, Ch D 11–010
Ireland v Livingston (1871–72) L.R. 5 H.L. 395, HL................. 7–013

Jirna v Mister Donut of Canada (1971) 22 D.L.R. (3d) 639, CA......... 2–002
Joachimson (A Firm) v Swiss Bank Corp (Costs) [1921] 3 K.B. 110; (1921)
6 Ll. L. Rep. 435, CA 2–044
Jobson v Palmer [1893] 1 Ch. 71, Ch D 7–018
Johnson v Bingley [1997] P.N.L.R. 392; [1995] N.P.C. 27 *The Times*, February
28, 1995, QBD.. 2–036, 2–037
Johnson v Kearley [1908] 2 K.B. 514, CA 2–043

Kelly v Cooper [1993] A.C. 205; [1992] 3 W.L.R. 936; [1994] 1 B.C.L.C. 395;
[1992] E.G.C.S. 119; (1992) 136 S.J.L.B. 303; [1992] N.P.C. 134, *The
Times*, November 5, 1992, PC (Ber)................. 7–045, 7–048, 7–040,
8–021, 9–004, 9–025,
9–026, 9–027, 9–029
Keppel v Wheeler [1927] 1 K.B. 577, CA 2–043
Kendall & Sons v William Lillico & Sons Ltd; sub nom.Hardwick Game
Farm v Suffolk Agricultural and Poultry Producers Association Ltd;
Holland Colombo Trading Society Ltd v Grimsdale & Sons Ltd;
Grimsdale & Sons Ltd v Suffolk Agricultural Poultry Producers
Association [1969] 2 A.C. 31; [1968] 3 W.L.R. 110; [1968] 2 All E.R.
444; [1968] 1 Lloyd's Rep. 547, HL............................ 2–015
Kennedy v De Trafford [1897] A.C. 180, HL 2–002
Kenney v Hall, Pain & Foster (1976) 239 E.G. 355 2–024
King (Or Fiehl) v Chambers & Newman (Insurance Brokers) [1963] 2
Lloyd's Rep. 130, QBD....................................... 7–032

Lac Minerals Ltd v International Corona Resources Ltd [1990] F.S.R. 441,
Sup Ct (Can) 7–044, 7–045, 7–057
Ladenbau (UK) Ltd v Crawley & de Reya [1978] 1 W.L.R. 266; [1978] 1 All
E.R. 682, QBD... 2–021
Learoyd v Whiteley; sub nom.Whiteley v Learoyd; Whiteley, Re (1887) L.R.
12 App. Cas. 727, HL 2–023, 13–028
Lindsey CC v Marshall; sub nom. Marshall v Lindsey CC [1937] A.C.
97, HL 2–026
Lloyd Cheyham & Co v Littlejohn & Co [1987] B.C.L.C. 303; [1986]
P.C.C. 389.. 2–027
LLoyds Bank Ltd v Bundy [1975] Q.B. 326; [1974] 3 W.L.R. 501; [1974] 3 All
E.R. 757; [1974] 2 Lloyd's Rep. 366; 118 S.J. 714, CA.............. 7–044
London v Shell [1992] A.C. 173,HL................................ 2–001
London Loan & Saving Co v Brickenden *see* Brickenden v London Loan
& Saving Co

xx

TABLE OF CASES

Loosemore v Financial Concepts [2001] Lloyd's Rep. P.N. 235, QBD (Merc Ct) 11–010
Lowe v Lombank [1960] 1 W.L.R. 196; [1960] 1 All E.R. 611; 104 S.J. 210, CA 2–036
Luxmoore-May v Messenger May Baverstock [1990] 1 W.L.R. 1009; [1990] 1 All E.R. 1067; [1990] E.C.C. 516; [1990] 07 E.G. 61; (1990) 140 N.L.J. 89, CA.. 2–031, 7–026

McCann v Western Farmers Mutual Insurance (1978) 87 D.L.R. (3d) 135, HC (Ont) 7–029
McInerny v Lloyds Bank Ltd [1974] 1 Lloyd's Rep. 246, CA 2–002
Mackersy v Ramsays (1843) 9 C.L.& F. 818. 7–022
McNaughton Paper Group Ltd v Hicks Anderson & Co [1991] 2 Q.B. 113; [1991] 2 W.L.R. 641; [1991] 1 All E.R. 134; [1990] B.C.C. 891; [1991] B.C.L.C. 235; [1991] E.C.C. 186; [1955–95] P.N.L.R. 574; (1990) 140 N.L.J. 1311, *Independent*, September 11, 1990, CA............... 2–009
Macoun v Erskine Oxenford & Co [1901] 2 K.B. 493, CA 7–050, 7–058
Maloco v Littlewoods Organisation Ltd;Smith v Littlewoods Organisation Ltd [1987] A.C. 241; [1987] 2 W.L.R. 480; [1987] 1 All E.R. 710; 1987 S.C. (H.L.) 37; 1987 S.L.T. 425; 1987 S.C.L.R. 489; (1987) 84 L.S.G. 905; (1987) 137 N.L.J. 149; (1987) 131 S.J. 226, HL 2–042
Marson (Inspector of Taxes) v Morton [1986] 1 W.L.R. 1343; [1986] S.T.C. 463; 59 T.C. 381; (1986) 83 L.S.G. 3161; (1986) 130 S.J. 731, Ch D.... 13–021
Martin v Britannia Life Ltd [2000] Lloyd's Rep. P.N. 412, Ch D 3–019
Martin v Edinburgh DC 1988 S.L.T. 329; 1988 S.C.L.R. 90, OH......... 13–095
Martin-Baker Aircraft Co v Canadian Flight Equipment; sub nom. Martin-Baker Aircraft Co v Murison [1955] 2 Q.B. 556; [1955] 3 W.L.R. 212; [1955] 2 All E.R. 722; (1955) 72 R.P.C. 236; 99 S.J. 472, QBD 7–064
Merrill Lynch Futures Inc v York House Trading (1984) 81 L.S.G. 2544, CA 2–020, 11–010, 11–019
Midland Bank Plc v Greene [1994] 2 F.L.R. 827; [1995] 1 F.C.R. 365; (1995) 27 H.L.R. 350; [1994] Fam. Law 676; [1993] N.P.C. 152, Ch D....... 2–043
Midland Bank Ltd v Seymour [1955] 2 Lloyd's Rep. 147, QBD.......... 7–013
Midland Bank Trust Co Ltd v Hett Stubbs & Kemp [1979] Ch. 384; [1978] 3 W.L.R. 167; [1978] 3 All E.R. 571; [1955–95] P.N.L.R. 95; 121 S.J. 830, *The Times*, December 2, 1977, Ch D................ 2–006, 2–010, 2–021, 2–023, 2–026, 2–029, 2–043, 7–017
Mint Security v Blair, Miller (Thomas R) & Son (Home) and Darwin Clayton (E C) and Co[1982] 1 Lloyd's Rep. 188, QBD.............. 2–043
Montgomerie v United Kingdom Mutual Steamship Association [1891] 1 Q.B. 370, QBD 7–039
Moody v Cox [1917] 2 Ch. 71, CA.................................. 8–025
Moorcock, The (1889) L.R. 14 P.D. 64; [1886–90] All E.R. Rep. 530, CA .. 7–048
Moore v Moore (1611) 1 Bulst. 7–039
Morgan v Elford (1876–77) L.R. 4 Ch. D. 352, CA 2–009, 8–027
Morgan Crucible Co Plc v Hill Samuel Bank & Co Ltd [1991] Ch. 295; [1991] 2 W.L.R. 655; [1991] 1 All E.R. 148; [1991] B.C.C. 82; [1991] B.C.L.C. 178; (1990) 140 N.L.J. 1605, *Independent*, October 25, 1990, CA 2–009
Morgan Stanley UK Group v Puglisi Cosentino [1998] C.L.C. 481, QBD (Comm Ct).. 7–030
Morris v Duke-Cohan & Co 1975) 119 S.J. 826, *The Times*, November 22, 1975 7–032

xxi

TABLE OF CASES

Morten v Hilton Gibbes & Smith [1937] 2 K.B. 176 (Note, HL 7–015, 7–016

Mutual Life & Citizens Assurance Co v Evatt [1971] A.C. 793; [1971] 2
W.L.R. 23; [1971] 1 All E.R. 150; [1970] 2 Lloyd's Rep. 441; 114 S.J. 932;
[1969] 1 Lloyd's Rep. 535; (1968) 42 A.L.J.R. 316, *The Times* November
17, 1970, HC (Aus). 2–029

National Home Loans Corp Plc v Giffen Couch & Archer [1998] 1 W.L.R.
207; [1997] 3 All E.R. 808; [1998] P.N.L.R. 111; [1997] N.P.C. 100, *The
Times*, October 9, 1997, CA 2–039

Nationwide Building Society v Balmer Radmore, [1999] Lloyd's Rep. P.N.
241; [1999] Lloyd's Rep. P.N. 558, Ch D 9–002

Navarro v Moregrand [1951] 2 T.L.R. 674; [1951] W.N. 335; 95 S.J.
367, CA 8–022

Nestle v National Westminster Bank Plc [1993] 1 W.L.R. 1260; [1994] 1 All
E.R. 118; [1992] N.P.C. 68, *The Times*, May 11, 1992, CA; [2000]
W.T.L.R, *Independent*, July 4, 1988 (C.S.), ChD 11–010, 11–022,
11–0241, 11–025

New Zealand and Australian Land Co v Watson; sub nom. New Zealand
and Australian Land Co v Ruston (1880–81) L.R. 7 Q.B.D. 374, CA. . 7–022

New Zealand Netherlands Society "Oranje" v Kuys; sub nom. New Zealand
Netherlands Society Oranje Inc v Kuys (Laurentius Cornelis [1973] 1
W.L.R. 1126; [1973] 2 All E.R. 1222; [1974] R.P.C. 272; 117 S.J. 565, PC
(NZ). 7–047

Normans Bay Ltd (formerly Illingworth Morris Ltd) v Coudert Brothers
(A Firm) [2003] EWHC 191, QBD. 2–028

North & South Trust Co v Berkeley; sub nom. Berkeley v North & South
Trust Co [1971] 1 W.L.R. 470; [1971] 1 All E.R. 980; [1970] 2 Lloyd's
Rep. 467; (1970) 115 S.J. 244, QBD (Comm Ct) 7–045, 7–054

O'Connor v BDB Kirby & Co;sub nom.O'Connor v DBD Kirby &
Co[1972] 1 Q.B. 90; [1971] 2 W.L.R. 1233; [1971] 2 All E.R. 1415; [1971]
1 Lloyd's Rep. 454; [1971] R.T.R. 440; 115 S.J. 267, CA 2–020, 7–029

Ogden & Co Pty v Reliance Fire Sprinkler Co Pty [1975] 1 Lloyd's Rep. 52,
Sup Ct (ACT) (Sgl judge). 2–019

Parker v McKenna (1874–75) L.R. 10 Ch. App. 96, Lord Chancellor 7–047

Pentecost v London District Auditor [1951] 2 K.B. 759; [1951] 2 All E.R.
330; [1951] 2 T.L.R. 497; 115 J.P. 421; 95 S.J. 432, KBD 7–041

Pilkington v Wood [1953] Ch. 770; [1953] 3 W.L.R. 522; [1953] 2 All E.R.
810; 97 S.J. 572, Ch D. 2–043

Piper v Daybell, Court-Cooper & Co (1969) 210 E.G. 1047. 2–043

Potter v Equitable Bank (1921) 8 Ll. L. Rep. 332, KBD 7–017

Powell v Phillips [1972] 3 All E.R. 864; [1973] R.T.R. 19; 116 S.J. 713, CA. . . 2–027

Prager v Blatspiel Stamp and Heacock Ltd [1924] 1 K.B. 566, KBD 7–016

Primavera v Allied Dunbar Assurance Plc [2002] EWCA Civ 1327; [2003]
Lloyd's Rep. P.N. 14; [2003] P.N.L.R. 12; [2002] Pens. L.R. 513; (2002)
146 S.J.L.B. 222, CA. 11–010

Prince Jefri Bolkiah v KPMG *see* Bolkian v KMPG

R. v Clowes (Peter) (No.2); R. v Naylor (Peter John)[1994] 2 All E.R. 316,
Independent, August 10, 1993, CA 7–013

xxii

TABLE OF CASES

R. v Investors Compensation Scheme Ltd Ex p. Weyell; R. v Investors
  Compensation Scheme Ltd Ex p [1994] Q.B. 749; [1994] 2 W.L.R. 678;
  [1994] 1 All E.R. 601; [1994] 1 B.C.L.C. 537; [1994] C.O.D. 87; (1993)
  143 N.L.J. 1297; (1993) 137 S.J.L.B. 82, *The Times*, August 18, 1993;
  Independent, July 22, 1993; *Guardian*, July 26, 1993, DC.   2–043
Rakusen v Ellis Munday & Clarke [1912] 1 Ch. 831, CA.   7–055
Rayner v Grote (1846) 15 M & W 359.   2–002
Red Sea Tankers Ltd v Papachristidis (The Hellespont Ardent) [1997] 2
  Lloyd's Rep. 547, QBD (Comm Ct)   7–042
Reggentin v Beecholme Bakeries [1968] 2 Q.B. 276; (1967) 111 S.J. 216,
  CA.   7–017
Reeves v Thrings & Long [1996] P.N.L.R. 265; [1993] E.G.C.S. 196; [1993]
  N.P.C. 159, CA 2–036, 2–038
Regal (Hastings) Ltd v Gulliver [1967] 2 A.C. 134; [1942] 1 All E.R. 378,
  HL.   7–045
Reigate v Union Manufacturing Co (Ramsbottom) Ltd [1918] 1 K.B. 592,
  CA.   7–048
Robinson v Mollett; Robinson v Bull; Robinson v Unsworth (1874–75) L.R.
  7 H.L. 802, HL.   8–020
Roe v Ministry of Health;Woolley v Ministry of Health [1954] 2 Q.B. 66;
  [1954] 2 W.L.R. 915; [1954] 2 All E.R. 131; 96 S.J. 319, CA   2–025
Romer & Haslam, Re [1893] 2 Q.B. 286, CA   7–064
Rust v Abbey Life Insurance Co Ltd [1979] 2 Lloyd's Rep. 334, CA   3–019

SCF Finance Co Ltd v Masri (No.2) [1987] Q.B. 1002; [1987] 2 W.L.R. 58;
  [1987] 1 All E.R. 175; [1986] 2 Lloyd's Rep. 366; [1986] Fin. L.R. 309;
  (1987) 84 L.S.G. 492; (1987) 131 S.J. 74, *The Times*, August 12, 1986,
  CA 7–047, 7–048
SNW Commodities v Falik [1984] 2 Lloyd's Rep. 224, QBD 2–005, 7–015
Saif Ali v Sydney Mitchell & Co [1980] A.C. 198; [1978] 3 W.L.R. 849; [1978]
  3 All E.R. 1033; [1955–95] P.N.L.R. 151; 122 S.J. 761, HL   2–025
Samson v Frazier Jelke & Co [1937] 2 K.B. 170, KBD 7–015, 7–016
Seager v Copydex Ltd (No.1) [1967] 1 W.L.R. 923; [1967] 2 All E.R. 415;
  2 K.I.R. 828; [1967] F.S.R. 211; [1967] R.P.C. 349; 111 S.J. 335, CA . . .   7–057
Shearson Lehman Hutton Inc v Maclaine Watson & Co Ltd (Application
  for discovery) [1988] 1 W.L.R. 946; [1989] 1 All E.R. 1056; [1989] 2
  Lloyd's Rep. 570; [1989] 3 C.M.L.R. 429; (1990) 140 N.L.J. 247, *The*
  Times, June 11, 1988; *Independent*, June 30, 1988, QBD.   2–011
Shell International Petroleum Co Ltd v Transnor (Bermuda) Ltd 1987] 1
  Lloyd's Rep. 363, QBD.   2–001
Shell Co of Australia v NAT Shipping Bagging Services (The Kilmun)
  [1988] 2 Lloyd's Rep. 1, CA.   2–002
Simmons v Pennington & Son [1955] 1 W.L.R. 183; [1955] 1 All E.R. 240; 99
  S.J. 146, CA   2–209
Small v Attwood (1838) 3 Y. & C. Ex. 150.   8–010
Smith v Eric S Bush (A Firm); Harris v Wyre Forest DC[1990] 1 A.C. 831;
  [1989] 2 W.L.R. 790; [1989] 2 All E.R. 514; (1989) 21 H.L.R. 424; 87
  L.G.R. 685; [1955–95] P.N.L.R. 467; [1989] 18 E.G. 99; [1989] 17 E.G.
  68; (1990) 9 Tr. L.R. 1; (1989) 153 L.G. Rev. 984; (1989) 139 N.L.J. 576;
  (1989) 133 S.J. 597, HL 2–020, 2–036
Smith v Littlewoods Organisation Ltd *see* Maloco v Liitlwoods Organisation
  Ltd

xxiii

TABLE OF CASES

Sollitt v DJ Broady Ltd [2000] C.P.L.R. 259, CA 8–021
Spector v Ageda [1973] Ch. 30; [1971] 3 W.L.R. 498; [1971] 3 All E.R. 417;
    22 P. & C.R. 1002; 115 S.J. 426, Ch D 7–052
Speight v Gaunt; sub nom. Speight, Re (1883–84) L.R. 9 App. Cas. 1,
    HL 7–018
Spring v Guardian Assurance Plc [1995] 2 A.C. 296; [1994] 3 W.L.R. 354;
    [1994] 3 All E.R. 129; [1994] I.C.R. 596; [1994] I.R.L.R. 460; (1994)
    91(40) L.S.G. 36; (1994) 144 N.L.J. 971; (1994) 138 S.J.L.B. 183, *The*
    Times, July 8, 1994; *Independent*, July 12, 1994, HL 2–009, 2–024
Stafford v Conti Commodity Services Ltd [1981] 1 All E.R. 691; [1981] 1
    Lloyd's Rep. 466; [1981] Com. L.R. 10, QBD (Comm Ct) 2–020, 2–036,
                                        2–039, 11–010,
                                            11–019
Starkey v Bank of England. sub nom.Oliver v Bank of England [1903] A.C.
    114, HL 2–017
Swindle v Harrison [1997] 4 All E.R. 705; [1997] P.N.L.R. 641; [1997] N.P.C.
    50, *The Times*, April 17, 1997, CA 9–002
Sword-Daniels v Pitel and Others [1994] 4 All E.R 385 2–021
Sykes v Midland Bank Executor & Trustee Co Ltd [1971] 1 Q.B. 113; [1970]
    3 W.L.R. 273; [1970] 2 All E.R. 471; 114 S.J. 225, CA 2–021, 2–036

Tai Hing Cotton Mill Ltd v Liu Chong Hing Bank Ltd (No.1) [1986] A.C.
    80; [1985] 3 W.L.R. 317; [1985] 2 All E.R. 947; [1985] 2 Lloyd's Rep.
    313; [1986] F.L.R. 14; (1985) 82 L.S.G. 2995; (1985) 135 N.L.J. 680;
    (1985) 129 S.J. 503, PC (HK) 2–045
Tallentyre v Ayre (1884) 1 T.L.R. 143, CA 2–017
Tate v Williamson (1866–67) L.R. 2 Ch. App. 55, Lord Chancellor 7–044
Transportation Agency v Jenkins 1972) 223 E.G. 1101 7–029
Turpin v Bilton (1843) 5 M.& G. 455 7–017

Underwood Son & Piper v Lewis [1894] 2 Q.B. 306, CA 7–017, 7–064
Unilever v Merrill Lynch 11–001, 11–010, 11–029
United Dominions Trust Ltd v Kirkwood 1966] 2 Q.B. 431; [1966] 2 W.L.R.
    1083; [1966] 1 All E.R. 968; [1966] 1 Lloyd's Rep. 418; 110 S.J. 169,
    CA 2–031

Varden v Parker (1798) 2 Esp.710 7–017
Virgin Group Ltd v De Morgan Group Plc (1994); subnom.Virgin
    Management Ltd v De Morgan Group Plc 68 B.L.R. 26; 45 Con. L.R.
    28; (1994) 10 Const. L.J. 247; [1994] E.G.C.S. 47, *The Times*, March 9,
    1994; *Independent,* March 28, 1994 (C.S.), CA 2–036, 2–038, 2–039
Voisin v Matheson Securities (CI) Ltd (1999–2000) 2 I.T.E.L.R. 907, CA
    (Jer) 11–010, 11–011, 11–013

Warlow v Harrison (1858) 1 El. & El 7–039
Weigall & Co v Runciman & Co (1916) 115 L.T.61 . . . . 7–013, 7–016
Weinberger v Inglis [1919] A.C. 606, HL 2–011
White v Jones [1995] 2 A.C. 207; [1995] 2 W.L.R. 187; [1995] 1 All E.R. 691;
    [1995] 3 F.C.R. 51; (1995) 145 N.L.J. 251; (1995) 139 S.J.L.B. 83; [1995]
    N.P.C. 31, *TheTimes,* February 17, 1995; *Independent*, February 17,
    1995, HL 2–007, 2–045, 7–027
Whiteford v Hunter [1950] W.N. 553; 94 S.J. 758, HL 2–026
Wight v Olswang (No.1) (1998–99) 1 I.T.E.L.R. 783, *The Times*, May 18,
    1999; *Independent*, May 24, 1999, CA 2–023

xxiv

TABLE OF CASES

Williams v Natural Life Health Foods Ltd [1998] 1 W.L.R. 830; [1998] 2 All
  E.R. 577; [1998] B.C.C. 428; [1998] 1 B.C.L.C. 689; (1998) 17 Tr. L.R.
  152; (1998) 95(21) L.S.G. 37; (1998) 148 N.L.J. 657; (1998) 142 S.J.L.B.
  166, *The Times,* May 1, 1998, HL 2–008
Wilsher v Essex AHA [1988] A.C. 1074; [1988] 2 W.L.R. 557; [1988] 1 All
  E.R. 871; (1988) 138 N.L.J. Rep. 78; (1988) 132 S.J. 418, HL 2–024
Wilson v Brett (1843) 11 M. & W. 113 7–041
Woods v Martins Bank [1959] 1 Q.B. 55; [1958] 1 W.L.R. 1018; [1958] 3 All
  E.R. 166; 102 S.J. 655, Assizes (Leeds) 2–010, 2–030, 2–034,
                                                          2–036, 2–039, 2–043
Woodward v Wolfe [1936] 3 All E.R. 529 .... 8–020, 8–023
Wragg Re *see* Garside, Re; sub nom. Wragg v Garside
Wray v Kemp (1884) L.R. 26 Ch. D. 16, Ch D 7–018
Wrightson Group v Crocker 124 S.J. 83, *The Times*, December 19, 1979,
  CA 2–019

Yager v Fishman & Co(1944) 77 Ll. L. Rep. 268, CA ... 2–036, 2–039, 2–043, 7–032
Yonge v Toynbee [1910] 1 K.B. 215, CA 2–017

International Cases

Bertram, Armstrong and Co v Hugh Godfray [1830] 1 Knapp 381;
  12 E.R 364 (PC) 7–012, 7–013
Born v Premier Investments (Victoria) Ltd (1947) 1 W.W.R. 492; (1948) 1
  D.L.R. 596; (1948) 1 W.W.R. 685 (Can) 2–021
Burks v Lasker 441 U.S. 471, 478–79 (1979) 10–030
Bussian v RJR Nabisco, Inc. 223 F. 3d 286 (5th Cir. 2000) 10–022

Dixon & Org. v Jefferson Seal Ltd 1997 J.L.R. 20 11–010
Donovan v Bierwirth 680 F 2d 263 (2c Cir. 1982) 10–022

Eagle Star Insurance Company Ltd v National Westminster Finance
  Australia Ltd (1985) 58 A.L.R. 165 2–019
Eaves v Penn 587 F.2d 453, 457 (10th Cir. 1978) 10–021

Fletcher v Marshall (1946) 15 M & W 755; Ry. & Can. Cas. 340; 10 Jur. 528;
  153 E.R. 1055 2–019

Gartenberg v Merrill Lynch Asset Mgmt., Inc., 694 F.2d 923, 928 (2d
  Cir.1982) 10–015

Kalish v Franklin Advisors Inc., 742 F. Supp. 1222, 1228 (S.D.N.Y. 1990)... 10–016
Kamen v Kemper Fin.Servs., Inc., 500 U.S. 90, 98 (1991) 10–030
Krinsk v Fund Asset Mgmt., Inc., 875 F.2d 404, 409 (2d Cir. 1989) 10–016

Jones v Canavan [1972] 2 N.S.W.L.R 236 (Aus) 7–048
Jones and Marsh McLennan v Crawley Collosso [1966] Lloyds List
  1 August 7–025

MacInnes v Cartwright & Crickmore (1931) 1 D.L.R. 572 2–017
Maillet and Pother v Haliburton & Comeau (1983) 55 N.S.R. (2d) (Novia
  Scotia) 2–020

XXV

TABLE OF CASES

M'Colloch v Maryland 17 U.S. 316, 424 (1819) 10–002
Meinhard v Salmon 164 N.E. 545, 546 (N.Y.1928) 10–005
Mitchell v Newhall (1846) 15 M.&W. 308; 4 Ry & Can Caas 300; 15 L.J.Ex.
    292; 7 L.T.O.S 88;10 Jur. 318; 153 B.R. 867 .... 7–013.
Moodie Co. Ltd v Minister of National Revenue [1950] 2 D.L.R. 145
    (CAN) 8–007

Pankhurst v Gardner & Co (1960) 25 D.L.R. (2d) 515 7–012
Phacelli v Conti Commodity Services Inc., [1986–1987 Transfer Binder]
    Comm.Fut.L.Rep.(CCH)23.250 (Sept 5, 1986) 12–044

Quebec and Richmon Railway Co v Quinn (1858) 12 Moo.P.C. 232 7–018

Rickel v Schwinn Bicycle Co 192 Cal. Rptr. 732 (1983) (CAL) 2–002

SEC v Capital Gains Research Bureau Inc.,375 U.S. 180, 191–92 (1963)... 10–006

Tiffin Holding Ltd v Millican 49 D.L.R. (2d) 216 2–011

United States Securities and Exchange Commission v Capital Gains
    Research Bureau Inc. 375 U.S. 180 (1963) 6–001
United States Securities and Exchange Commission v Fife 311 F.3d 1 (1st Cir
    Nov.6 2002) 6–005
United States v Lopez 514 U.S. 549, 558–59 (1995) 10–002

Volkers v Midland Doherty (1985) 17 D.L.R. (4th) 343 (CAN) 7–017

xxvi

TABLE OF LEGISLATION

(All references are to paragraph number)

National Legislation

1907   Limited Partnership Act (c.24) 1–016
1958   Church Funds Investment Measure (c.1) 4–060
1958   Prevention of Fraud(Investments)Act (c.45) 1–004, 4–068
1961   Trustee Investments Act 11–028
        Sch.1, Pt 1 13–023
1964   Charities Act (Northern Ireland) (c.33)..................... 4–060
1967   Misrepresentation Act (c.7)................................ 3–019
1973   Finance Act (c.51).. 13–008
1977   Unfair Contract Terms Act (c.50).......................... 9–027
        s.3 .... 9–027, 9–029
1978   Civil Liability (Contribution) Act (c.47) 7–026
1985   Companies Act (c.6).......................... 1–015, 7–042, 13–020
1986   Insolvency Act (c.45) 13–025
        s.238(4)... 13–026
1986   Financial Services Act (c.60)............. 4–030A, 5–001, 8–027, 13–029
1988   Income and Corporation Taxes Act (c.1) 13–001
        s.468... 13–016
1992   Taxation of Chargeable Gains Act (c.12)
        s.100(1) 13–016, 13–017
1993   Charities Act (c.10)...................................... 11–029
        s.24.. 4–060
1995   Pensions Act (c.26)............. 13–014, 13–021, 13–022, 13–025, 13–026,
                                 13–029, 13–045, 13–054, 13–101
        s.31.. 13–062
        s.33.. 13–062
        s.34.. 13–048, 13–055
        s.34(1)... 13–021
        s.34(2)............................... 13–013, 13–045, 13–062

TABLE OF LEGISLATION

1995	Pensions Act (c.26)—*cont'd*	
	s.34(4)	13–041, 13–045
	s.34(5)	13–062
	s.34(6)	13–062
	s.35	13–024
	s.35(4)	13–024
	s.36	13–038, 13–055
	s.36(2)	13–023
	s.36(3)	3–023, 13–048
	s.36(4)	3–023
	s.36(6)	3–023
	s.36(7)	13–056
	s.40	13–025
	s.40(2)	13–025
	s.47	13–045, 13–053
	s.47(2)	13–013, 13–053, 13–055
	s.49	13–056
	s.56	13–024
1999	Finance Act (c.16)	13–015
	Sch.,19, para.16	13–015
1999	Welfare Reform and Pensions Act (c.30)	13–006
1999	Contracts (Rights of Third Parties) Act (c.31)	1–012, 7–023, 9–023
2000	Financial Services and Markets Act (c.8)	3–004, 4–031, 4–058, 4–059, 4–060, 5–001, 5–002, 7–008, 9–001, 9–009, 9–022, 13–013, 13–014, 13–017, 3–023, 13–026, 13–027, 13–028, 13–029, 13–035, 13–042, 13–046, 13–062
	s.5(2)	4–058
	s.21	3–008, 13–036
	s.21(1)	3–008
	s.21(2)	3–008
	s.21(6)	3–008
	s.22	13–028, 13–045, 13–053
	s.30	3–008
	s.39	4–060
	ss 129–131	5–001
	s.149	3–017
	s.150	3–017, 9–011
	s.157	4–001
	s.235	3–004, 3–005,13–014
	s.236	3–006
	s.236(2)	13–020
	s.238	3–009, 3–012, 3–016
	s.238(4)	3–009
	s.238(5)	3–009, 3–013, 3–015, 4–060
	s.241	3–009
	s.243(10)(a)	4–074
	Sch.2	13–028
	Sch. 6	4–4–057
2000	Trustee Act (c 29)	2–023, 11–024, 11–025, 11–026, 11–027, 11–028, 13–042
	s.1	9–028, 11–026
	s.4(2)	11–027

xxviii

TABLE OF LEGISLATION

2000	Trustee Act (c 29)—*cont'd*	
	s.4(3)(a)	11–027
	s.4(3)(b)	11–027
	s.11(1)	11–026
	s.15(1)	11–026
	s.15(2)	11–026
	s.15(3)	11–027
	s.18	11–027
	s.37	9–028
	Sch.1	9–028

International Legislation

USA

Commodity Exchange Act	12–002, 12–004, 12–005, 12–009, 12–010, 12–013, 12–032, 12–033, 12–043	
	s.1(a)	12–016
	s.1a(3)	12–004
	s.1a(4)	12–009
	s.2(a)	12–016
	s.4b	12–044, 12–047
	s.4d	12–038
	s.4m(1)	12–013, 12–016, 2–018
	s.4m(3)	12–015
	s.4m(a)(11)	12–016
	s.4o	12–019, 12–039, 12–047, 12–048
	s.4o(1)	12–049
	s.4o(2)	12–049
Glass Stegall Act		9–002
	s.4f(a)	6–024
1933	Securities Act	4–014, 6–001, 10–002, 12–029, 12–034, 12–040
1934	Securities Exchange Act	6–001, 6–008, 10–002, 10–006
	s.13(f)	6–036, 10–008
	s.15	12–038
	s.15(b)(1)	6–024
	s.28(e)	10–011, 10–012
	Rule13(f)-1(c)	6–036
	Rule 15a-6	6–008
	Rule 17a-3	6–035
	Rule 17a-4	6–035
1935	Public Utility Holding Company Act	6–001
1939	Trust Indenture Act	6–001
1940	Investment Company Act	6–001, 6–019, 10–001, 10–002, 10–012, 10–019, 12–035, 12–039
	s.1b	10–030, 10–033
	s.2(a)(3)	10–030
	s.2(a)(19)(A)	10–030, 10–031
	s.2(a)(19)(B)	10–031
	s.2(a)(41)	10–034
	s.2(51)A	12–034, 12–038

xxix

TABLE OF LEGISLATION

1940	Investment Company Act—*cont'd*	
	s.3(a)(1)	10–030
	s.3(b)–(c)	10–030
	s.3(c)(1)	10–030
	s.3(c)(7)	10–030
	s.6	10–030
	s.8	10–030
	s.9(a)	10–031
	s.10(a)	10–031
	s.12	10–030, 10–034
	s.13	10–034
	s.15(c)	10–015, 10–016, 10–033
	s.16(a)	10–031
	s.32(a)	10–034
	s.36	10–014
	s.36(a)	10–031, 10–032
	s.36(b)	10–014, 10–15
1940	Investment Advisors Act	6–001, 6–002, 6–005, 6–007, 6–008, 6–009, 6–010, 6–019, 6–021, 6–029, 6–030, 6–040, 10–001, 10–002, 10–005, 10–006, 10–008, 10–010, 12–008, 12–014, 12–015, 12–018
	s.202(a)(ii)	6–003
	s.202(a)(1)	6–038
	s.202(a)(1)-1	6–038
	s.202(a)(2)	6–024, 12–017
	s.202(a)(11)	6–002, 6–004, 12–017
	s.202(a)(11)(C)	6–008
	s.202(a)(22)	12–039
	s.203(a)	6–003
	s.203A(a)(1)(B)	6–002
	s.203(c)(2)	6–013
	s.203(e)(6)	6–031
	s.205	6–036
	s.205(a)(1)	6–037
	s.205(a)(2)	6–038
	s.205(a)(3)	6–028
	s.205(b)(1)	6–037
	s.205(b)(2)	6–037
	s.205(b)(3)–(5)	6–037
	s.206	6–001, 6–016, 10–006, 10–007
	s.206(3)	6–017
	s.206(4)	6–029
	s.215(a)	6–039
	s.222(d)	6–002
	Rule 17a-7	6–019
	Rule 203A-2(a)	6–002
	Rule 203A-2(b)	6–002
	Rule 203A(b)(1)	6–002
	Rule 203A-2(c)	6–002
	Rule 203A-2(d)	6–002
	Rule 203A-2(f)	6–002
	Rule 203(b)(3)-1	6–009
	Rule 203(b)(3)-1(b)(5)	6–009

TABLE OF LEGISLATION

1940 Investment Advisors Act—*cont'd*

Rule 204(1)...	6–015
Rule 204-2... 6–033,	6–035
Rule 204-2(a)(16)	6–021
Rule 204-2(a)(3)	
Rule 204-2(a)(4)	6–034
Rule 204-2(a)(5)	6–034
Rule 204-2(a)(6)	6–034
Rule 204-2(a)(7)	6–034
Rule 204-2(a)(8)	6–034
Rule 204-2(a)(10)	6–034
Rule 204-2(a)(11)	6–034
Rule 204-2(a)(12)	6–034
Rule 204-2(a)(14)	6–034
Rule 204-2(a)(15)	6–034
Rule 204-2(a)(16)	6–034
Rule 204-2(b)	6–035
Rule 204-2(c)	6–035
Rule 204-2(e)	6–035
Rule 204-2(g)	6–035
Rule 204-2(h)	6–035
Rule 204-2(j)	6–033
Rule 204-3(a)	6–033
Rule 204-3(b)(1),n..	6–033
Rule 204-3(b)(2)	6–033
Rule 204-3(e)	6–033
Rule 204(3)(g)	6–033
Rule 204A	6–032
Rule 205-1	6–037
Rule 205-2	6–037
Rule 205-3	6–037
Rule 205-3(d)(1)..	6–037
Rule 206(3)-2	6–018
Rule 206(3)-2(c)	6–018
Rule 206(4)-1(a)1	6–021
Rule 206(4)-1(a)2	6–021
Rule 206(4)-1(a)3	6–021
Rule 206(4)-1(a)4	6–021
Rule 206(4)-1(a)(5).......................................	6–021
Rule 206(4)-2 5–022,	6–023
Rule 206(4)-2(a)(1).......................................	6–024
Rule 206(4)-2(a)(1)(i)....................................	6–024
Rule 206(4)-2(a)(1)(ii)...................................	6–024
Rule 206(4)-2(a)(2).......................................	6–024
Rule 206(4)-2(a)(3).......................................	6–025
Rule 206(4)-2(a)(3)(ii)...................................	6–025
Rule 206(4)-2(a)(3)(ii)(B)	6–025
Rule 206(4)-2(a)(3)(ii)(C)	6–025
Rule206(4)-2(a)(3)(iii)...................................	6–025
Rule 206(4)-2(a)(4)(5)....................................	6–025
Rule 206(4)-2(a)(5).......................................	6–025
Rule 206(4)-2(c)	6–023
Rule 206(4)-2(c)(2)	6–025
Rule 206(4)-2(c)(3)(i)	6–204

xxxi

TABLE OF LEGISLATION

1940 Investment Advisors Act—*cont'd*
    Rule 206(4)-2(c)(3)(ii).. 6–024
    Rule 206(4)-2(c)(3)(iii) 6–024
    Rule 206(4)-2(c)(3)(iv) 6–024
    Rule 206(4)-3 .... 6–028, 6–029
    Rule 206(4)-4................... 6–026, 6–024, 6–029
    Rule 206(4)-6 6–030
    release 58 6–039
    release 1000 6–011
    release 1092.......................... 6–005, 6–006, 6–007
    release 1105 6–020
    release 1435 6–017
    release 1452 6–017
    release 1504 6–017
    release 1536 6–015
    release 1585 6–017
    release 1594 6–017
    release 1633 6–002
    release 1666 6–017
    release 1732.................................... 6–017, 6–018
    release 2061 6–019
    release 2106 6–031
    release 2176 6–022
1974 Employee Retirement Income Security Act 4–006, 4–008,
                                           10–001, 10–002, 10–012,
                                           10–017, 10–018, 10–019,
                                         10–020, 10–021, 10–024,
                                         10–025, 10–026, 12–014,
                                         12–035, 12–036, 12–039,
                                         13–039
    s.3(21)(A)..................................... 10–017
    s.3(21)(B)............................. 10–017, 12–039
    s.3(32)....................................... 12–036
    s.402(a) 10–017, 10–026
    s.402(a)(1) 10–017
    S.402(a)(2) 10–017
    s.403(a),x1.......................... 10–017, 10–023
    s.403(a)(2) 10–023
    s.403(c)...................................... 10–022
    s.404.. 10–022
    s.404(a) 10–021, 10–026
    s.404(a)(1) 10–021
    s.404(a)(1)(B)....................... 10–023, 10–026
    s.404(a)(1)(C) 10–024
    s.405(d)...................................... 10–023
    s.405(d)(1) 10–023
    s.408(c)(3)................................... 10–023
    s.409.. 10–026
1996 National Securities Market Improvement Act.................... 6–002
2002 Sarbanes-Oxley Act 13–102

xxxii

TABLE OF STATUTORY INSTRUMENTS

(All references are to paragraph number)

1988	Control of Misleading Advertisements Regulations (SI 1988/915) ..	3–019
1991	Retirement Benefits Schemes (Restriction on Discretion to Approve) (Small Self-administered Schemes) Regulations (SI 1991/1614) ..	13–008, 13–100
1995	Public Offers of Securities Regulations (SI 1995/1537) 3–005, 3–006	
1996	Capital Gains Tax (Pension Funds Pooling Schemes) Regulations (SI 1996/1583)....................................	13–018
1996	Stamp Duty and Stamp Duty Reserve Tax (Pension Funds Pooling Schemes) Regulations (SI 1996/1584).....................	13–019
1996	Income Tax (Pension Funds Pooling Schemes) Regulations (SI 1996/1585) 13–018	
1996	Occupational Pension Schemes (Scheme Administration) Regulations (SI1996/1715).......................................	13–053
	reg.3(3)...	13–053
	reg.11...	13–056
1996	Open-Ended Investment Companies (Investment Companies with Variable Capital) Regulations (SI 1996/2627)...............	1–016
1996	Occupational Pension Schemes (Investment) Regulations (SI 1996/3127)	13–024
	Pt 2	13–025
	reg.5 .... 13–025, 13–026	
	reg.6...	13–026
	reg.11A	13–094
1998	Individual Savings Account Regulations (SI 1998/1870)	4–060
1999	Unfair Terms in Consumer Contracts Regulations (SI1999/2083)...	9–027
2000	Stakeholder Pension Schemes Regulations (SI 2000/1403)	13–006
Financial Services and Markets Act 2000 (Carrying on Regulated Activities by Way of Business) Order (SI 2001/1177)..................		13–028
	art.3 .... 13–031, 13–032	
	art.3(1)...	13–032
	art.3(2)...	13–032
	art.4.................................. 13–028, 13–031, 13–032	
	art.4(6)...	13–030

xxxiii

TABLE OF STATUTORY INSTRUMENTS

2001   Financial Services Act 2000 (Regulated Activities) Order (SI 2001/
544) 2–028, 3–002, 8–009, 13–028
      art.15 13–033
      art.16 13–033
      art.25(1) 8–027
      art.28 .... 8–028, 13–034
      art.29 13–034
      art.37 .... 3–002, 13–028
      art.66(3) 13–028

2001   Financial Services and Markets Act 2000 (Promotion of Collective
Investment Schemes) (Exemptions) Order (SI 2001/1060)... 3–009, 4–060
      art.14 3–014
      art.15 .... 3–014, 3–015
      art.21(6) 3–014, 4–060

2001   Financial Services and markets Act 2000 (Collective Investment
Schemes) Order (SI 2001/1062)............ 3–005, 3–006, 9–010, 9–012
      art.3 13–013
      art.13 3–002
      Sch., para.1 13–013
      Sch., para.4 13–013
      Sch., para.10 13–013

2001   Financial Services and Markets Act 2000 (Appointed Representative)
Regulations (SI 2001/1217)............................. 4–029

2001   Financial Services and Markets Act 2000 (Financial Promotion)
Order (SI 2001/1335) 3–008, 3–010, 3–014, 3–016
      art.4, sch.1, para.5 –6 .... 3–008, 13–036
      art.4, para.4–7 3–008
      art.54 13–036
      art.71 .... 3–016, 4–059
      art.73 4–059
      s.28(1) 4–013

TABLE OF FSA RULES

(All references are to paragraph number)

FSA Rules 2–012, 2–026, 3–006, 3–016, 3–018, 4–057, 4–060, 4–061, 5–001, 5–007, 5–012, 5–024, 5–025, 7–006, 7–008, 7–011, 7–031, 7–035, 9–003, 9–014, 9–016, 9–021, 9–022, 9–025, 9–028, 9–029, 13–052, 13–054, 13–056, 13–058

r.5.3.5(3) 1–012
r.21.9(h) 3–016

COB Rules 2–007, 3–015, 4–058

2.1.2R 3–016
2.2.16R 4–025
2.2.3R 4–023
2.2.8R–2.2.12R 9–014
2.2.8(1)R 4–022
2.2.16R 4–023
2.2.18R 4–023
2.5.3 9–028
2.5.4R 9–028
3 3–017
3.2.4R 3–009, 3–009
3.2.5R 3–011, 3–016
3.5.4G 3–018
3.5.5R 3–018
3.6.1R 3–018
3.8.4R 3–017
3.8.5E 3–017
3.8.8R 3–017
3.8.11R 3–018
3.8.15R 3–018
3.9.5R 3–011
3.10.3R 3–012
3.11.2R 3–015, 4–060
3 Annex 5

TABLE OF FSA RULES

COB Rules—*cont'd*

4.1	3–009
4.1.5R(1)	7–023
4.1.9R	3–011, 3–015, 4–060, 4–071
4.2.7	3–011
4.2.10R	4–023
4.2.11E	4–023
4.2.15(23)	7–060
4.2.15(24)	7–063
4.2.15E	4–023
4.2.15E(4)	7–005
4.2.15E(8)(a)	7–011
4.2.15E(13)	7–043
4.2.15E(17)	7–006
4.2.15E(18)	7–006
4.2.15E(19)	7–006
4.2.15E(20)	7–006
4.2.16E	7–006
4.2.16E(1)	7–007
4.2.16E(4)	7–006
4.2.16E(5)	7–006
5	3–018
5.1.6R	4–030
5.1.7R	4–030B
5.1.7R(1)	4–030
5.1.16R	4–030B
5.2	4–035, 4–061, 7–028
5.2R	9–024
5.3	4–035, 4–061, 7–028
5.3.5R	9–024
6.5	3–018
7.1	4–019
7.1.3R	7–043, 9–017
7.1.3	7–046, 7–052
7.1.4E	9–018, 9–018
7.1.5E	9–018
7.1.6E	9–018
7.1.7G	9–019
7.1.8G	9–019
7.1.9.G	9–019
7.3	4–019
7.3.3R	9–019
7.3.4R(1)	4–019
7.3.4R(4)	4–019
7.3.4R(5)	4–019
7.4.3R	9–020
7.4.4R	9–020
7.5	7–035
7.5.3R	9–024, 13–056
7.5.4(3)	7–035, 7–036
7.5.6	4–027
7.7	6–020
7.7.4	9–021
7.7.5R	9–021

TABLE OF FSA RULES

COB Rules—*cont'd*

7.9.10R	3–018
9	5–005
10	2–014

FSA PRINCIPLES

1	9–011
1.1.7G	9–011
2	2–019
5	9–011
6	9–011
8	9–011
10	5–020

FSA SYSC

3.1.1R	4–058
3.2.3	7–021
3.2.4	7–020, 7–021

TABLE OF ABBREVIATIONS

APCIMS	Association of Private Client Investment Managers and Stockbrokers
AUT	authorised unit trust scheme
CEA	Commodity Exchange Act
CFTC	US Commodity Futures Trading Commission
CIS	Collective Investment Scheme
CPO	commodity pool operator
CREST	The central securities depository for the UK market and Irish equities. NB CREST is not an acronym
CTA	commodities trading adviser
DOL	US Department of Labor
DSF	direct sales force
FCM	futures commission merchant
FSMA	Financial Services and Markets Act 2000
FSA	Financial Services Authority
FTSE	FTSE International, a company specialising in UK stock indices and owned by the London Stock Exchange and the Financial Times (the acronym stands for Financial Times Stock Exchange)
FURBS	Funded Unapproved Retirement Benefits Scheme
GAAP	generally accepted accounting principles
ICVC	investment company with variable capital
IB	introducing broker
IFA	independent financial adviser
IMA	Investment Management Association *also* investment management agreement
IMRO	Investment Management Regulatory Organisation
IPO	initial public offering
ISA	Individual Savings Account
LIFFE	London International Financial Futures and Options Exchange
LLP	limited liability partnership
LME	London Metal Exchange
LSE	London Stock Exchange
LTCM	Long-Term Capital Management
MFR	minimum funding requirement
MVA	Market value adjusters
NAPF	National Association of Pension Funds

TABLE OF ABBREVIATIONS

NASAA	North American Securities Administrators Association
NASD	North American Association of Securities Dealers
NASDR	US National Association of Securities Dealers Regulation, Inc.
NFA	US National Futures Association
NYSE	New York Stock Exchange
PEP	Personal Equity Plan
PIA	Personal Investment Authority
PPPV	pension fund pooling vehicles
QEP	Qualified Eligible Person
RFP	request for proposals
OEIC	open-ended investment company
OPRA	Occupational Pensions Regulation Authority
SAI	Statement of Additional Information
SEC	US Securities and Exchange Commission
SFA	Securities and Futures Authority
SSAS	small self-administered schemes
TSA	The Securities Association
UCITS	Undertakings for Collective Investment in Transferable Securities
UURBS	Unfunded Unapproved Retirement Benefits Scheme

CHAPTER 1

ELEMENTS OF INVESTMENT MANAGEMENT

Dick Frase, Dechert LLP, London

The Elements of Investment Management

Investment management has grown out of a range of different practices and businesses, and it is only relatively recently that it has come to be viewed as a distinctive service sector in its own right.[1] The common elements of the service involve: **1–001**

- a *client* granting a mandate;

- over a *portfolio of investments*;

- to a *manager*;

- To *manage those investments*.

The Clients

UK investment management clients are predominately institutional. A survey carried out by the Investment Management Association in June 2002 (the IMA Survey) found that 39 per cent of assets under management in the UK came from pension schemes, and 32 per cent from other institutions. Retail investors accounted for the balance of 29 per cent; which the IMA broke down into unitised insurance policies (9 per cent); private client assets (4 per cent) and other retail funds (16 per cent). In the US, by way of comparison, the much larger retail mutual fund industry is just over 50 per cent the size of the $9,880 billion institutional market.[2] **1–002**

---

[1] The defining moment being perhaps the establishment of IMRO as a discrete regulator for investment management in 1988.

[2] Having said this, the UK retail market is growing at a faster rate than the institutional market. The IMA survey described the retail industry as being $\frac{1}{18}$ of the size of the institutional industry in 1997, increasing to $\frac{1}{15}$ by 2002.

1

Corporate pension scheme clients account for the largest proportion of assets under management, and have had a huge impact on the growth of investment management in the UK.[3] Before the Second World War, most pension schemes collected defined contributions and provided defined benefits to their members. The scheme members' contributions were used to buy an insurance product issued by a life office; which guaranteed to pay the benefits payable under the scheme.[4]

In the post-war period, however, the life offices gradually began to make with-profits schemes[5] available to pension clients. These were first introduced by Prudential in 1950, and allowed the pension scheme to share in any increased returns. But the payment of pension benefits was no longer guaranteed, so a large part of the performance risk moved from the life office to the pension scheme itself. This made it much more important for the scheme to assess which investment manager could be expected to give the best performance. This development also allowed managers with much less capital than traditional insurers to provide management services to the pension schemes. More recently in the 1990s, the switch by many pensions schemes from defined benefit to defined contribution arrangements has put even more emphasis on the importance of the investment manager's role.[6]

The Investment Portfolio

1–003 "Portfolio" is a collective term for the client's assets being managed. It may comprise all the client's investments (often the case with private clients); be a sub-part of a larger portfolio which the client has earmarked of separate management (typical of certain institutional clients such as pension funds, life company portfolios and multi-manager funds); or be the portfolio of a collective investment scheme which the manager has itself established as its own product.

As with other financial services, the core investments tend to be bonds and listed securities. But management services can be applied to other types of asset such as derivatives, foreign currency, short-term money market investment and cash management, commodities, real estate, and private equity. The IMA Survey identified asset allocation in the UK as follows: overseas equities 34 per cent; UK equities 20 per cent, bonds 24 per cent, money market

---

[3] See generally London Business School, "The Competitive Advantage of the Fund Management Industry in the City of London" February 1994.

[4] These insured corporate pensions schemes began to appear in the 1930s and boomed after the Second World War. In 1950 40% of all the Royal Exchange Assurance's ordinary premium income was from pension schemes. Supple, *The Royal Exchange Assurance 1720–1970*, (1970), p.436.

[5] For further discussion of with-profits policies see para.1–006 below.

[6] For a more detailed discussion of current pensions scheme issues see Chap.13.

12 per cent and alternative asset classes (real estate, futures, venture capital, hedge funds, etc) 10 per cent.

This sort of diversified portfolio allocation has developed over a long period of time. 200 years ago investment was heavily focused on government bonds. Jane Austen's contemporaries knew that capital invested in government consols would assure them a steady 4 per cent income for life,[7] and 4 per cent as the standard rate of interest endured right up to the end of the century. But during the nineteenth century there was also growing interest in other products. Corporate bonds and equities became very popular with the advent of the railway company flotations.[8] Foreign government bonds received increasing attention.[9] Collective investment scheme products were marketed to the public as early as the 1860s, achieving a major boom period shortly before the Second World War. [10] Interest in equities grew throughout the twentieth century, with these and other "inflation-proof" investments such as real estate becoming increasingly important in the 1960s and 1970s. Since then innovation has continued, with new products such as financial derivatives appearing in the 1980s and asset securitisations in the 1990s.

A note on terminology

The concept of a "portfolio" is particularly suited to describing a securities portfolio, where the assets have their own independent existence as pieces of property, which can be "put into" the portfolio, and taken out again. The term "account" is also used, though this often indicates the overall business relationship with a particular client—the Smith & Co account—rather than the particular investment portfolio itself. "Account" can also describe management services which are structured in a similar way to a banking relationship, as is the case with managed futures. See further para.1–022 below.

1–004

---

[7] It also enabled them to value each other very precisely: "I am well aware that . . . one thousand pounds in the 4 per cents, which will not be yours till after your mother's decease, is all that you may ever be entitled to" (Mr Collins to Elizabeth Bennett), Jane Austen, *Pride & Prejudice*, Ch.XIX.

[8] The first railway stock boom came in 1835 with the number of officially listed companies (21 in July 1835) almost trebling in 12 months. See Kynaston, *The City of London Volume 1 "A World of its Own" 1815–1890*, (1994), p.102.

[9] See generally Dickson, *The Sun Insurance Office 1710–1960*, (1960), pp.261–263, describing the cautious way an insurance company invested its assets. During the 19th and early 20th centuries the office was overwhelmingly invested in government bonds. It first resolved to allow investments in equities in 1889, though by 1900 there were still no equities on its balance sheet. By 1939, however, equities constituted 11% of its total assets.

[10] The Foreign and Colonial Government Trust first marketed unit trusts to the public in 1868. In this early version the management element was minimal, the composition of the portfolio being fixed at launch by the terms of the trust deed. The product revived in the 1930s with M&G's launch in 1931 of a unit trust which included for the first time an undertaking on the part of the manager to re-acquire units from investors at a price based on the value of the investments held by the trust. Unit trusts were first subject to specialised regulation by the Prevention of Fraud (Investments) Act 1939, the original precursor of the FSMA.

The term "fund" is convenient (only one syllable), but seriously overused in the investment management context. In addition to being used in the same sense as "portfolio", it can also mean money (*e.g.* payment of funds; funding), investments generally (as in funds under management), and particular types of investments (such as government bonds or collective investment schemes). In pensions the term "pension fund" is used both to describe the pension scheme itself and the pool of assets owned by the scheme. To minimise this sort of confusion, in this book the term "fund" is generally used to indicate a formally established collective investment scheme, or occasionally a particular type of asset portfolio—thus it is very standard to refer to the investment portfolio of a pension scheme or life office, taken as a whole, as the "pension fund" or the "life fund".

The Investment Managers

1–005   Who are the investment managers? The IMA Survey categorised investment managers in the UK as being drawn from the following business sectors: insurance companies 34 per cent[11]; investment managers 24 per cent[12]; retail bank 21 per cent[13]; investment banks 15 per cent[14]; pension fund managers 4 per cent[15]; and custodians 2 per cent.[16] This diversity of business origin reflects the way the investment management concept has come together from a range of different sources. Merchant bankers who have helped their clients to raise money on the stock market go on to advise them how to invest it. Stockbrokers providing brokerage execution, and banks accepting customer deposits, have expanded their services in the same way, and firms such as Cazenove, Baring, and Schroder have deliberately developed their investment management specialisations. Other firms such as Gartmore and M&G, which have always operated as specialist investment managers, have provided a model for the specialist manager generally. The IMA Survey estimated total assets under management in the UK by all these firms[17] (at June 2002) at £1,934 billion.

---

[11]   *e.g.* AXA, Legal & General, Royal London and Standard Life.
[12]   *e.g.* Fidelity, Gartmore, Legg Mason, Schroders.
[13]   *e.g.* Abbey National, Barclays and Lloyds TSB.
[14]   *e.g.* Goldman Sachs, Morgan Stanley, Cazenove, Baring, Merrill Lynch, Dresdner.
[15]   *e.g.* Universities Superannuation.
[16]   *e.g.* State Street.
[17]   Note that retail stockbroking managers are usually members of the Association of Private Client Investment Managers and Stockbrokers (APCIMS) rather than the IMA.

Life insurers

The figures in the preceding paragraph show insurers as the largest single **1–006** group of managers. This reflects the volume of investment assets comprised in their core businesses, and also the fact that, unlike pension schemes, they normally manage their own assets. In the modern environment this typically involves the establishment of a separate management company whose main mandate is to manage the group's life fund. It is then also able to take on mandates for other, non-group clients. A leading example of this is Threadneedle Asset Management, established in 1994 by the merger of the in-house investment teams at two major insurers—Allied Dunbar and Eagle Star.

Investment management in the life assurance sector goes back to the early nineteenth century. The original life policies guaranteed the payment of a fixed amount, and any profits were retained by the company, though in the case of mutual offices such as Equitable Life the profits would be available for allocation to the members. From the early nineteenth century onwards, offices began to share their profits with policyholders by distributing policy bonuses. With the development of these "with profits" policies, life assurance increasingly came to be seen as a form of investment.[18] The next major investment development, over 100 years later, was the introduction in the 1960s by Allied Dunbar of unit-linked policies, where the value of the policy was directly linked to an identified pool of assets managed by the life company.

International investment management

While the IMA figures show the biggest players in the domestic market as **1–007** being the insurers and retail banks, the international picture is somewhat different. While assets managed by managers in the UK were £1,934 billion, assets managed outside the UK by those same management groups amounted to £3,501 billion. The managers who dominated in the global figures were investment banks with 33 per cent and investment managers with 23 per cent of the total. In other words the global investment market is dominated not by traditional financial institutions but by specialist international investment managers.

From the UK point of view this international growth can be traced back to factors such as the abolition of exchange controls, and the opening up of

---

[18] The profits were generated initially by the fact that the offices were still using the mortality tables compiled in 1781 by Equitable Life based on death rates in a Northamptonshire village in the period 1735–1780, but by the beginning of the 19th century mortality rates had improved significantly. The Equitable, as a mutual office, paid the profits as bonuses to its members, but the proprietary life offices initially simply sat on their profits or paid them to shareholders. By 1826 however, two out of every three proprietary offices were paying policy bonuses, and by the 1840s "non-participating" policies had all but disappeared. Supple, *The Royal Exchange Assurance 1720–1970*, pp.130–134.

markets to international investment. In the UK it reached critical mass in October 1986 when the London "Big Bang" lifted restrictions on the ownership of LSE brokers and market makers. This immediately prompted the establishment of new, integrated multi-service financial houses, many of them built around investment banks, offering a range of services which included merchant/investment banking, stockbroking, market-making, and of course investment management.

Managing the Investments[19]

Discretionary and advisory management

1–008 Modern investment management services are usually fully discretionary. The manager uses its judgment to decide which investments to buy and sell within the scope of its mandate, and then implements those decisions as agent on behalf of its principal by giving instructions to brokers and custodians.

It is also possible to provide management services on an advisory basis. This type of service is found chiefly in the retail stockbroking sector, and involves the manager first making recommendations to the client, and then obtaining client instructions for the execution of each trade. The labour-intensive nature of this process, compared with discretionary management, means there is usually a much lower level of pro-active management activity. The manager might typically review the portfolio and make its recommendations on a half-yearly or at most a quarterly basis.

Advisory management can also occur at the institutional level, where a firm has a specialist research retainer, such as advising a pension scheme on strategic asset allocation, or a private equity fund or a fund of funds on its monthly investment decisions. In some cases, however, such a service will be occasional or intermittent, without any duty to give continuous advice on portfolio composition.

1–009 Advisory management has historically been seen as allowing the manager to lay off the risk of the final investment decision on the client. This is clearly true for sophisticated clients, but there is increasing recognition that unsophisticated private clients are not necessarily making independent decisions in this sort of situation; and may rather be relying on the firm to give them suitable and appropriate advice.[20]

---

[19] The term "management" is mostly used in this book as shorthand for investment management. But in the case of UCITS funds the "manager" is the entity with overall responsibility for the running of the fund. In such circumstances the manager is usually someone who delegates the specific task of *investment* management to a third party investment manager (who in UK unit trust terminology is called the investment adviser, though the service is a discretionary one).

[20] See paras 2–035—2–040 (Client sophistication).

The advisory/discretionary distinction is discussed further in Chapters 2 and 8.

Individual portfolio mandates

"Mandate" is a fairly loose term which can describe the whole relationship **1–010** generally, the absolute duties contained within the mandate, or, perhaps most specifically, the investment objectives and restrictions which the manager must aim to achieve.

Under a standard portfolio mandate, the manager contracts to manage a defined portfolio of assets according to specific investment objectives and other requirements agreed with that client. The manager will often advise on the investment objectives to be adopted for the portfolio; and on portfolio design generally. This may include advising on factors specific to the manager itself, such as its investment philosophy, its areas of skill or specialisation, and the scope of the services it can provide. The manager discusses issues such as the appropriate/acceptable level of risk for the client's circumstances (the higher the potential return, the higher the associated risk), and the balance between capital and income. For long-term savings, the emphasis is likely to be on capital growth, but private clients may have a particular need for income to meet a particular future need such as mortgage repayments, school fees, retirement, etc.

From these discussions the manager produces a statement identifying the agreed objectives, the way in which they are to be achieved, and any special requirements or constraints. The manager will then match these with its own particular investment skills and produce an optimum set of investment objectives for its management of the portfolio. Appropriate benchmarks and performance standards may be agreed, against which the portfolio's performance could be measured, such as equity or interest rate indices. The IMA Survey found that about 60 per cent of assets are managed with a single tracker mandate and a further 21 per cent are managed against a customised benchmark.

In many cases the manager will be taking over an existing portfolio rather **1–011** than establishing a new one. In this situation the design process described above will be adapted so that the advice is given on any restructuring needed to bring the portfolio into line with the newly agreed strategy.

In other cases, especially with institutional clients such as pension schemes, the client will have already decided what sort of service it wants before it approaches the manager. Thus a pension scheme will first determine with its specialist advisers (typically actuarial consultants) its optimum overall strategy, asset allocation, etc. This will usually involve dividing the overall strategy into a number of separately identifiable mandates, with slices of the pension fund being allocated to each mandate. Tenders from individual managers will then be solicited by issuing questionnaires known as RFPs

ELEMENTS OF INVESTMENT MANAGEMENT

(requests for proposals). The client assesses the manager's ability to meet its required mandate on the basis of the manager's response to the RFPs, as well as interviews, discussions and so on.

When the investment strategy is established and the mandate awarded the investment manager then assumes responsibility for its implementation.

Proprietary strategies

1–012 Some managers do not seek to tailor their service to the client's personal objectives in the way described above. Rather they devise their own proprietary investment strategy, and invite customers to participate in that strategy. At its simplest, such an arrangement can be effected by means of a parallel portfolio structure. The firm establishes a separate account for each client, and runs them in parallel. Trades are executed in bulk and allocated *pro rata* to the individual portfolios. Among other things, this retains the direct service relationship between the client and the manager, avoids the client/client insolvency risk involved in pooling client funds with a single common custodian, and assists the client in preserving any particular tax status attaching to its assets.

In other cases, where the parallel account system would be too cumbersome, the manager establishes a common pooled fund such as a collective investment scheme. The manager's services are then provided to the fund rather than to the underlying investors in the fund.[21] This is particularly clear in the case of an OEIC or life policy, where the fund is itself a separate legal entity, but is also generally considered to apply to a unit trust structure. The investor has bought an investment in the fund vehicle. It has not appointed the investment manager and has no direct legal relationship with the manager.[22]

A second variant is where the manager establishes a proprietary fund but is also prepared to manage separate client portfolios provided they follow the same investment strategy as the manager's main fund. In this proprietary fund-orientated approach, the parallel portfolios are usually described as "segregated accounts".

1–013 The management of a proprietary strategy does not involve any advice on investment objectives to investors. However, the manager should make a proper disclosure of its investment objectives. In the case of a fund this disclosure will be primarily in the fund prospectus. In marketing its fund, the

---

[21] This principle is reflected in FSA, r.5.3.5(3) which provides that "Where with the agreement of the private customer, a firm has pooled his funds with those of others with a view to taking common management decisions, the firm must take reasonable steps to ensure that a discretionary transaction is suitable for the fund, having regard to the stated investment objectives of the fund."

[22] The Contracts (Rights of Third Parties) Act 1999 is normally excluded in the management contract.

manager may also give potential investors generic promotional information on the merits of its investment approach and strategy.

Where the manager also has an established advisory relationship with a particular client, it may also give client-specific advice on the appropriateness of the proprietary strategy to that client. So a broker advising a client on portfolio design may include its own proprietary fund as one of the components of the proposed portfolio.

Legal structures for pooled investment funds

The main legal structures available for a fund are a closed-ended or open-ended company, a unit trust, or a limited partnership. Unit-linked life policies are also sometimes regarded as a form of pooled investment vehicle.

1–014

Closed-ended companies—If a conventional 1985 Companies Act company is used as the investment vehicle, this is described as a closed-ended company or investment trust (though there is in fact no trust element in the structure). The lack of any direct correlation between the value of the underlying assets and the share price of the "trust" means that there is scope for arbitrage between the two prices. As with an open-ended investment company (see below), the investors have no proprietary interest in the underlying assets, save for the usual residual right of shareholders to the distribution of the company's assets on its winding up. A closed-ended company has the advantage in investment terms that it is not subject to any regulatory restrictions as to what it can invest in, or how much it can borrow or leverage. Nor is it subject to the restrictive regulatory regime on marketing.

1–015

Open-ended companies—An open-ended investment company or "OEIC" is a distinct type of legal entity, incorporated under its own special legislation.[23] Unlike a closed-ended investment company, the OEIC can increase and decrease its share capital, and issue and redeem its shares, at will. This means that the capital can expand and contract so as that the value of its shares can be matched exactly with the value of the underlying assets they represent. This will reflect not only changes in the value of the initial investment but the fact that investors will come and go while these changes are happening.

Because the OEIC, like a closed-ended fund, is a distinct legal entity, investors have no direct rights to the underlying assets, and this means that their proprietary rights to the investment are less good than they would be in

1–016

---

[23] OEICs incorporated in off-shore jurisdictions have long been available. The Open-Ended Investment Companies (Investment Companies with Variable Capital) Regulations 1996, in force since 1997, now allow such entities to be established under UK law.

a unit trust or limited partnership. It is widely assumed by both markets and regulators that this is not a material risk issue.

1–017   **Unit trusts**—A pooled investment fund can be constituted as a trust. The trustee holds a portfolio of assets on trust for investors, who have a beneficial proprietary interest in their proportionate share of the portfolio. The only other vehicle which offers investors this level of direct ownership of the fund property is the limited partnership.

When established and operated in accordance with unit trust regulations, such an arrangement constitutes an authorised unit trust, which can be freely marketed to the general public. UK unit trust regulations require the trust's assets to be held by a professional trustee, who is independent of the manager, on behalf of the unit holders. Transfers may be effected by sale between buyer and seller in the market, but are usually achieved by the issue or redemption of units by the manager, or by the manager buying and selling units for its own account or "box".

1–018   **Limited partnerships**—In some cases the fund is established as a limited partnership. Ordinary partnerships can also theoretically be used as investment vehicles, but are unattractive because of the joint and several liability the partners carry for each other's actions. Under a limited partnership structure, the liability of the partners is limited by statute.[24] So long as active management is carried on by the general partner, the liability of the other partners is limited to the value of their original investment in the partnership. Like a unit trust, a limited partner has a direct proprietary interest in the underlying investment portfolio reflecting his proportionate share of that portfolio. As with unit trusts and OEICs, transfers can be effected by market sale or issue and redemption of partnership shares. However, restrictions on these processes, both statutory and under the terms of the partnership deed, are more common than in other pooled investment vehicles.

1–019   **Unit linked life policies**—Unit-linked life policies have been described above in the context of life policies. Like OEICs, their value is directly linked to the value of the underlying portfolio, but without any proprietary interest in that portfolio. They are at their closest to an investment management structure where the life company grants a manager (typically a retail financial adviser)

---

[24] The limited partnership concept can be traced back to the Italian *commenda* of the Middle Ages, and later instances include the French *societe en commandite* established in the Ordonnance du Commerce of 1673. The current UK legislation is still the Limited Partnership Act 1907 but, where tax considerations allow, many funds will establish under the more flexible limited partnership legislation of an off-shore jurisdiction such as Cayman or the British Virgin Islands.

the right both to manage the assets linked to the policy and market the policy to its clients (known as a broker bond or broker fund).

However, a life policy is essentially a contract under which the life office contracts to pay the policyholder a sum of money equal to the money which has been earned on the linked portfolio of assets. As with corporate vehicles, there is no direct right to the underlying assets. There is also a question as to whether the life office owes anyone any particular duty of care and skill in its management of the linked portfolio. Unlike other pooled investment products, policies are not designed to be transferred on a regular basis, and the only ready means of disposal is by cashing in the policy or arranging an assignment.

Ongoing management

The mandate is established once its objectives have been settled and the **1–020** investors have given the manager the necessary control over their assets. In the case of a fund, the fund vehicle must also have been properly established and invested in by the initial investors.

The actual day-to-day management process can now begin. The manager exercises its judgment as to the investments to be made and implements this by instructing executing brokers in the market. The executed trades are settled by the client's custodian, who holds the cash and securities which comprise the clients portfolio. On a purchase the custodian pays cash out of the portfolio and takes delivery of the securities into the portfolio. On a sale it receives the purchase price and makes delivery of securities sold.

The manager will generally have an absolute duty to keep within the scope of the objectives,[25] and a qualified duty (of reasonable care and skill) to manage the portfolio so as to achieve favourable investment returns. See paras 2–016—2–021 (qualified and absolute duties). The performance of the portfolio, and perhaps also the objectives too, will be reviewed by the manager with its client on a regular basis.

For most mainstream managers the ideal duration of the management **1–021** service is at least three to five years to allow their strategy to mature, and short-term losses to be corrected through long term performance (though some managers operating short-term active trading strategies may work to a shorter timescale). But clients may have their own time horizons, and these too need to be allowed for in planning the mandate. Pension funds and life assurers have particularly long time horizons, planning to meet long-term liabilities 20 or 30 years in the future. They can therefore afford to make greater use of illiquid investments, such a real property, and take greater short-term risks. A general insurer, in contrast, needs to work to a shorter time horizon

---

[25] A deliberate and sustained breach of the mandate may also be fraudulent. See *R. v Clowes (No. 2)* [1999] 2 All E.R. 316, CA.

ELEMENTS OF INVESTMENT MANAGEMENT

because the flow of claims made under its policies is less predictable. It will therefore have a greater need for low risk investments and readily availability of funds.

Futures management

1–022 In the specialist area of futures management things work somewhat differently. A carrying broker opens an "account" for the customer in its books to which futures positions are booked. Because of the specialist nature of the market, management services are often provided by the carrying broker itself. In other cases the client may appoint a commodities trading adviser or "CTA",[26] who will have a mandate from the client to give trading instructions to the carrying broker.

The carrying broker role corresponds rather loosely to that of the custodian in a conventional securities market setting. However it differs in various ways. As already noted, it is often combined with the role of investment manager. Moreover, the fact that the broker is carrying its customer's positions on its books (and usually also clearing them through the relevant futures exchange in the role of clearing broker), means that it is personally on risk to the rest of the market for the performance of the customer's futures contracts. To cover the risk of the customer's account moving into deficit, the broker will make margin calls, requiring the customer to pay more money into the account to keep it in credit. Carrying arrangements of this sort are also found in foreign currency and off-exchange derivatives investment.

Related Services

Custody

General

1–023 Custody requires a significant investment in infrastructure. It is increasingly difficult for a manager to provide this infrastructure itself, and nowadays it is usually provided by specialist custodians contracting directly with the client.[27] In some cases the manager may have significant degree of control over the custody arrangements—proprietary funds being an obvious example. In any event the manager has for practical purposes day-to-day "ownership"

---

[26] This term comes from US regulation and practice and is widely used in the UK. See further Ch.12. In UK regulatory terms, however, a CTA would be classified in the same way as any other investment manager as either an advisory or discretionary manager.

[27] Though for domestic broking operations concentrating on a particular exchange it is still possible for the broker to run custody and settlement itself through its membership of the exchange clearing house and the use of a nominee company to hold the assets.

of the custody relationship and therefore needs to understand and be able to deal with the process, ensuring that it has the necessary authority and lines of communication to be able to access the custodian's records, report trades to it and instruct it to settle transactions.

Custody is, at its broadest, any arrangement whereby a firm holds and administers financial assets, particularly securities, for or to the order of a client. At its simplest level the client's securities purchases are settled by the custodian through its membership of the relevant clearing system, acting as either principal or agent,[28] and registered in the name of its special purpose nominee company. The assets are then held in safekeeping by the custodian until it receives instructions to sell or transfer them to another party. Clients dealing internationally will seek a custodian which can provide a centrally-controlled service across the full range of different markets, reflecting the different regulation, dealing and settlement practice, and property laws in each jurisdiction. While some custodians may maintain branches or subsidiaries in each jurisdiction, most will need to sub-contract to a sub-custodian in at least some markets or sectors.

The securities may be held on a segregated or commingled basis. Where one person's assets are commingled with those of another, such that, as a matter of property law, their separate holdings cease to be separately identifiable, the property rights of those persons may be weakened or lost as against each other. Thus, if the custodian were to commingle its own assets with those of its client, they may lose their distinctive identity as the client's assets, and be potentially available to the custodian's creditors on its insolvency.

1–024 Where the client's assets are held separately from those of the custodian, they may still be commingled with the assets of other clients in a common pool. If properly constructed such a pool should enable each client to retain a proportionate proprietary interest in the common asset pool. However a shortfall in the assets of one client (resulting from, *e.g.* trading liabilities incurred by the client and charged against the pool, erroneous trades or transfers, or theft) can still affect the pool detrimentally, with the shortfall being spread proportionately across all the holdings of other clients in the pool.

A firm providing a custody service is usually expected to segregate house and client assets. The commingling of client/client assets, on the other hand, is very common, the only alternative being to set up an individually-designated custody account for each individual client.

---

[28] The usual distinction is that in principal settlement the trade is given up to the custodian who assumes principal liability to third parties for the performance of the contract, while under agency settlement the custodian settles on behalf of the client with the client retaining full liability for performance.

Banking functions

1–025 The role of cash payments in the custody and settlement process means that the custodian will need access to bank account facilities. This means that most major custodians are banks. A non-bank custodian must either take a mandate over its client's bank account, or open a global client account at a bank in the custodian's name, to which all moneys received for or payable by its clients can be credited and debited. This will give rise to segregation issues similar to those which arise in relation to securities. House/client segregation should be achieved if the custodian declares a trust over the money in favour of the clients and ensures that only clients' money is credited to the client money account.[29] There will, typically, still be client/client commingling in such an account.

Typical custody service package

1–026 A standard range of custody services will normally involve:

- Holding those assets in an appropriate manner so as to protect the completeness of the assets, including physical custody of any title documents, and maintaining systems for accessing and communicating with nominees, depositories, and third-party custodians.

- Appointing and supervising sub-custodians.

- Record keeping and reconciliation, including monitoring and advising the client on the status of holdings acquired and disposed of, dividend, interest and other entitlements due and received, valuation of losses and gains, assets available for entering into new transactions, converting foreign currency information into the currency of account where necessary.

- Dealing with corporate actions arising in relation to the securities held. This will include passing on any communications from the issuer, receiving interest and dividends, and exercising any related rights such as voting or subscription rights.

- Implementing instructions to transfer assets to a buyer to take delivery of assets from a seller, and related cash movements

For further discussion of custody see Chapter 5.

---

[29] *Barclays Bank Ltd v Quistclose Investments Ltd* [1968] 3 All E.R. 651, "Nowadays it is considered that the presumption of a debtor/creditor relationship is so well settled that only an express trust direction by the customer or the most compelling circumstances indicating that the bank is not entitled to use the money as its own would be required to displace this presumption", Wood, *English and International Set-Off 1989*, para.9–100.

Broking

General

An investment manager may execute its trades via a broker for many reasons: **1–027**

- the market is (to a greater or lesser degree) opaque, and the customer must rely on the broker to find it a good competitive price;
- the broker has a special expertise in other aspects of the relevant market, such as general trading and market trends, or the fundamentals of particular securities;
- the market is not accessible to the public, but only to its members, and a customer can only access it by employing a broker who is such a member;
- The market is only accessible to persons of a sufficient financial standing or who have made a sufficient financial commitment to the market. (Frequently a broker will guarantee its client's performance to the rest of the market by assuming liability as a primarily obligor to the client's counterparty);
- the market is very illiquid and the broker has a special capacity to search the market for counterparties who can provide liquidity; and/or
- the customer wishes to preserve its anonymity in dealings with third parties.

At the domestic level, stockbroking is till typified by the agency stockbroker, providing an advisory execution service, usually for retail clients, and specialising in UK-listed equities and bonds. Commodities and futures brokers are also long-established on domestic futures exchanges such as LIFFE and the LME. But most securities broking in the UK nowadays is conducted at an international level, typically operating as a division of an investment bank, usually located in the country where the trade is to be executed, and catering for institutional clients.

Trade execution

Broking exists to facilitate customers trading with each other, and specifically **1–028** the execution of customers' orders. The broker may be a mere conduit for its customer's instructions, or it may seek out and negotiate appropriate transactions and counterparties on the client's behalf. Usually, it also executes the trade, though the substantive effect of execution can be achieved where the broker merely arranges the trade between its customer and a third party. The execution normally involves the exercise of a degree of judgment by the broker as to the terms on which it should be executed, and accordingly as to the terms which are appropriate to the client's interests.

For a firm to describe itself as a broker usually implies that it acts as an agent, executing orders on behalf of its client with counterparty, or with another broker acting for that counterparty. The agent deals with third parties for its client, not itself, and has a duty to fill the client's order at the best price possible. In practice many brokers are also prepared take the other side of the trade to their clients, dealing with them as principal. See further the discussion of trade implementation in Chapter 8.

Broking advice

1–029 Most brokers also offer some form of advisory service in conjunction with their execution facilities. At its most basic level, the comments of a broker on the state of the market and how a particular trade is going may be mere commentary rather than any sort of skilled advice. In other cases the broker may go further and actively advise on how to execute a trade, or on which trades to execute. More generalised advice may come in the form of investment analysis reports and market research. It is this advisory service function which brokers have, in many cases, developed into an advisory or even a discretionary management service.

Investment management's near relation—the financial planning service

Background

1–030 Retail packaged product services involve a high level of one-off sales. But there is also a concept of an ongoing service, conducted on an advisory rather than a discretionary basis, whereby the adviser provided ongoing financial advice to a private client on his personal finances. While there are many variations in the way this can be done, the central concept is still that of the full financial planning service which seeks to deal comprehensively with the whole of the client's financial affairs.

Historically this service has evolved in the polarised market operated by the regulators since 1988, where firms are either independent financial advisers (IFAs) or tied to a particular product provider group (tied agents). This particular regime is about to be abolished.[30] In future, firms will notify customers in advance of the product range on which they will offer advice. This may be a single product provider, a specific range of providers, or

---

[30] See FSA, CP 166, *Reforming Polarisation*, January (2003).

"whole-of-market".[31] The requirement to give suitable advice will be by reference to the disclosed product range. If nothing in the range is suitable then no recommendation from the range can be made[32]; but the single and multi-tied firms will be allowed to step outside their declared product range where this is in the customer's best interests. A firm which wishes to hold itself out as independent (*i.e.* as an IFA) must offer both whole-of-market advice and givers its clients the option of remunerating the IFA by payment of a fee instead of by commissions paid by the product provider and deducted from the value of the products sold.

The service

The financial planning service usually involves: **1–031**

- Advising the client on which products to buy to meet his needs. This will normally constitute both investment advice and the provision of a general advisory service; and

- Arranging any subsequent product purchases—typically helping the client to complete the appropriate application form and submitting it, along with payment, to the provider.

The service is orientated towards investment in life assurance, pensions and retail investment funds, but is capable of extending to other areas such as banking and general insurance, broking and investment management. Where the adviser's brief includes direct investment in the securities markets it will often appoint a specialist broker or investment manager, and act as its client's representative in subsequent dealings with the appointee.

The planning process usually begins with a meeting between the client and the financial adviser. This may be the result of "prospecting" by the adviser, a referral from a third party, a periodic call from the adviser to a client with whom it has previously done business, or a call from the client himself. With a new client, the client's personal financial circumstances need to be assessed before giving advice, with the adviser completing a fact find identifying the client's current financial situation, future plans and objectives. With an existing client, whom the adviser has not seen for some time, the process should

---

[31] This does not literally mean that the firm must search the entire market every time it makes a recommendation, as was sometimes suggested in the early days of regulation. An IFA may use a product panel so long as it is properly constituted from a sufficiently large number of product providers and is reviewed regularly, CP 166, para.5.7.

[32] The FSA describes this as introducing the concept of relative suitability for all firms. Under polarisation this has been applied to the tied sector where it requires the recommendation not simply to clear a particular suitability hurdle in absolute terms but to recommend the most suitable product from the available range. CP 166, para.4.13.

be quicker, with the adviser simply checking that the information on the client's existing fact find is brought up to date.

The adviser then studies and analyses the client's needs and objectives shown in the fact find, and designs a solution to meet them. A tied representative will design its solution around its tied products. If none of its principal's products are suitable, it is not allowed to advise his client to buy those products. An IFA in contrast has access to the whole market and should therefore always be able to recommend a suitable product. General suitability considerations include:

- affordability (the ability of the client to maintain any regular premium payments due on a continuing basis);

- acceptable level of risk;

- timing (the right products at the right time to meet the identified need and the client's appreciation of the time horizon—short-, medium- or long-term—of the particular product);

- a demonstrable need (the product recommended is best suited to the client's needs from the available range);

- priority (proper regard is given to each of the client's needs and their relative priority as against each other, the top priority being addressed first).[33]

1–032 The adviser then (often at a second meeting) puts forward its proposals and where necessary refines them with the client before making a formal recommendation. The regulatory expectation is that the adviser should be able to predict fairly accurately the particular *type* of product which is most suitable to the specific client need.[34] Where that product type is available from a number of different providers, the adviser is required to make a recommendation from its available product range. The "whole of market" adviser is not obliged to identify the best product available in the whole market (an impossible task) but to use reasonable care in doing so. Commonly it does

---

[33] The regulators have said that the firm should not simply identify a need and match it with a product. It also needs to consider the priority of that need. For a father, planning for himself, his wife and a young family, the priorities are likely to be capital in the event of death, income protection, and critical illness, followed by retirement planning, savings lump sum and general investment. Someone nearing retirement will have different priorities, orientated more towards income, investment or regular savings products

[34] *e.g.* if the investor is not in regular long term employment it will normally be better for him to buy a single premium pension policy as and when he has funds available, than to subscribe to a regular savings pensions policy. If the adviser is a tied representative, and his principal does not have a single premium pension policy in its product range, the representative is not supposed to sell the investor a regular savings plan as the "next best thing available", but should advise the investor to go to another adviser or provider. In the post-polarisation environment the representative will also be able to make a recommendation outside his product range.

this by carrying out its own evaluation of the products in the market as an independent exercise, using this to create its own "best advice panel" of products and providers. It will then refer to this when giving personal advice to a particular client. In contrast to the tied and multi-tied firms it is free to alter the composition of its best advice panel whenever and in whatever way it pleases, and indeed it will need to keep the panel under review generally to check that its original evaluations do not become out of date.

The adviser's recommendation will be accompanied by some or all of the following:

- a standard, pre-printed key features document, describing the salient features of the product recommended, including the commitment the client is being asked to make;

- for pension products a personal illustration, giving client specific information on benefits and contributions, the effect of charges, surrender values, and the services and remuneration which will be provided to the representative for arranging the sale;

- a "suitability" letter explaining the reasons for the recommendation;

- basic risk warnings as appropriate. Typical warnings might be that the value of investments can go down as well as up, and (in the case of a front-end loaded product) that it is inadvisable to cash it in the early years of the investment and that a guaranteed income product may generate its income by using up the investment's capital elements;

- the application form for the product.

The firm will explain the purpose of the documents and any additional matters relevant to the particular client. If the client accepts the recommendation, the adviser will help him to complete the application form and arrange for this to be forwarded, with the necessary payment, to the product provider.

CHAPTER 2

THE LEGAL NATURE OF THE CLIENT SERVICES RELATIONSHIP

Dick Frase, Dechert LLP, London

A preword on arm's length dealings

2–001 Most commercial and business dealings are not based on the sort of service relationships which are the subject of this Chapter. Rather, they are limited to arm's length or counterparty dealings, and it will be helpful to look briefly at these before going into the detail of the services relationship.

In arm's length or counterparty dealings, the parties operate on a commercially adversarial or *caveat emptor* basis. This is does not mean that they are seeking to defeat or damage each other, as may be said to be the case in adversarial litigation, where the only restraints on the parties' conduct are those laid down by court procedure. Rather, a party to an arm's length transaction must act within the bounds of legally permitted behaviour, performing any contractual obligations it has promised to discharge, and refraining from misleading or defrauding the other party. The counterparty contract will typically cover:

- the precise counterparty obligations to be performed;

- any steps for ensuring performance; and

- The consequences of non-performance.

Within these general constraints, each party is entitled to protect its interests as it sees fit,[1] acting according to its own skill and judgment, whatever they may be, and without any duty to apply such skills for the benefit of the

---

[1] Though there is always the possibility of an exception arising. In *Shell v Transnor* [1987] 1 Lloyds Rep. 363 the court appeared prepared to consider an argument for an implied term that the seller of oil should refrain from driving the price of oil down after selling it to another party. Contrast *London v Shell* [1992] A.C. 173 HL.

counterparty. There is no fiduciary duty to the other party, and (normally) no overlay of a tortious duty of care. The counterparties' duties are to perform their contractual obligations, no more and no less. In financial markets, these duties typically consist of one party paying money and the other delivering a non-money asset such as a security in return, or both parties having money payment obligations to each other.

Where a transaction or relationship fits this general model, the courts are reluctant to impose any additional, service-type duties.[2] However the relationship is a fact-based one, and it is the nature of the relevant obligations, together with their surroundings factual matrix, which establish whether the relationship is arm's length or otherwise. Terms such as "own account", "counterparty", "arm's length", "adversarial", and "caveat emptor" are indicative of arm's length dealings, thought not in themselves conclusive.[3]

2–002

Examples of counterparty transactions are:

- Purchases and sales of financial assets such as securities or foreign currency by one party from or to another;

- The payment of money between the parties according to a formula, as in the case of contracts for differences and other swap or ISDA contracts;

- a loan by a bank or other commercial lender to a borrower;

- a guarantee given by a surety to a creditor for the liabilities of a debtor; and

- a mortgage or charge granted over the assets of a debtor in favour of its creditor.

---

[2] *Amalgamated Metal Trading Ltd v DTI*, The Times, March 31, 1989 *McInerny v Lloyds Bank Ltd* [1974] 1 Lloyds Rep. 246. In *Jirna v Mister Donut of Canada Ltd* (1973) 40 D.L.R. (3d) 303 (CAN) fiduciary duties were denied in a franchising arrangement. In *Rickel v Schwinn Bicycle Co* 192 Cal. Rptr. 732 (1983) (CAL), the test used for a non-fiduciary relationship was whether the contract was designed to promote the non-mutual profit of the parties, each having the right to make a range of decisions adverse to the other's interests.

[3] In other cases someone identified as an agent may in fact be acting as a principal or counterparty. In *Rayner v Grote* (1846) 15 M. & W. 359, a contract showed Rayner as agent for a named principal but because all parties treated the contract as one made with Rayner as principal he was held to be such. In *Shell Co of Australia Ltd v Nat Shipping Bagging Services Ltd (the Kilmun)* [1988] 2 Lloyds Rep., p.1, *per* Lord Donaldson M.R. at p.10 quoting Lord Herschell in *Kennedy v Trafford*, the substance of a contract between Shell and an intermediary was held to be one of subcontract rather than agency, notwithstanding the use of the word "agent" in the contract: "For my part I attach little importance to the use of the word "agent" in the contract . . . No word is more commonly and constantly abused than the word 'agent'".

Pre-contractual dealings

2–003 The execution of a counterparty transaction is often preceded by some form of pre-contractual encounter. This may consist of little more than an invitation to treat, followed by offer and acceptance. But it can also include pre-contractual advertising and promotional activity, face-to-face discussions, and active negotiations.

Frequently, the counterparty nature of the proposed transaction will imbue these pre-contractual dealings with its own *caveat emptor* quality. The parties' dealings will be viewed as arm's length communications rather than as an advisory service so that, for instance, one party will not be under a positive duty to disclose facts to the other, however material those facts would be to the other's decision to contract. But this is not always the case, and sometimes negotiations and discussions can stray into advisory territory; if some element of a reliance relationship is established.

Contractual performance

2–004 A counterparty transaction usually retains its counterparty quality throughout the performance of the contract, with the contract terms determining the continuing nature of the parties' obligations to each other. Contractual obligations to pay money or deliver non-money assets are easily recognisable as counterparty in nature. Where these terms give one party a discretion it can (in a counterparty dealing) expect to be able to exercise this according to its own interest, without any duty to consider or act for the well-being of the other party. Examples are a creditor's discretion to call in an on-demand loan, or to assign the benefit of a debt to a third party.

Introduction to Client Service Relationships

2–005 Service relationships, of the type discussed in this Chapter, are most readily identifiable as a "client relationship", where a firm provides a service to its client. They are characteristic of the services provided by investment managers, brokers, and financial advisers. Historically they have been associated with what may loosely be termed "professional" service providers, such as solicitors, accountants, stockbrokers and insurance brokers; and also with aspects of agency law where a substantial discretion is given to the agent. More recently the concept has had to expand to include the idea of advisory services generally, since these are no longer the exclusive preserve of the traditional professions.

Linguistic indicators of such a relationship include terms such as "client", "adviser", "agent" or (more technically) "fiduciary", "trust", "reliance" and

INTRODUCTION TO CLIENT SERVICE RELATIONSHIPS

"dependence"; the firm is described as acting *for* or *on behalf of,* or providing advice *to* its *client.* Contrariwise, where a firm is described as dealing *with* or trading *with* someone such as a *customer* or *counterparty,* the inference is that there is no client relationship.[4]

The rest of this Chapter discusses the principles underlying the relationship between a firm providing a financial service (the firm) and the recipient of that service (the client), under the following headings:

- The firm undertakes to provide a skilled service;

- The client is dependent on the exercise of skilled judgment by the firm; and

- The firm in its turn has a duty to exercise that judgment in the client's interest.

The firm undertakes to provide a service

The undertaking to provide the service usually takes the form of a contractual promise giving rise to a service contract. Any arrangement where the firm has a right to remuneration is likely to be contractual, since this means that the existence of contractual consideration can then be readily established.[5] The right to remuneration need not be express, and a term that the firm should receive reasonable remuneration for its services is readily implied.   **2–006**

In some situations, the firm may provide a service without remuneration but still be acting by way of business. This typically happens where the firm provides free advice or information with a view to obtaining future business. Occasionally, something similar may arise in the course of an existing contractual relationship, where the firm provides a service which is outside the

---

[4] In some cases the firm acts in both a service and counterparty capacity. In these situations, provided the nature of the relationship(s) is/are clear, the courts have proved very commercially responsive. In *SNW Commodities v Falik* [1984] 2 Lloyd's Rep. 224 at 228, where a future firm trading as principal on a future exchange for its (fiduciary) Webster J. said: "the essential nature of the relationship between a client and a broker in this market is that the broker incurs primary obligations in the market in the client's interest which could put the broker at unlimited risk if that risk is uncovered by the client and if he, the broker, is not free to take action without the client's instructions to protect himself against that risk . . . . In these circumstances, it seems to me that [the clauses allowing the firm to terminate for its own protection] express a code which it might well be necessary to imply in order to give business efficacy to the contract if it were not expressed so that, if he acts in good faith and not arbitrarily, the broker may refuse to carry out an instruction to open any position, so that he may close a position of the client if the broker thinks it necessary for his protection, even if the client is not in default, and so that, if the broker holds insufficient funds or credits of one kind or another of the client to cover his position and if the client is thereby in default he may take any action not limited to but including closing out the position which he thinks necessary for his protection."

[5] *Hedley Byrne & Co Ltd v Heller & Partners Ltd* [1963] 2 All E.R. 575 at 610, [1964] A.C. 465 at 528, *per* Lord Devlin: "Payment for information or advice is very good evidence that it is being relied on and that the informer or adviser knows that it is."

THE LEGAL NATURE OF THE CLIENT SERVICES RELATIONSHIP

scope of its contract but still within a general business relationship with the client. At one time, these services too might have been construed as contractual, but nowadays they are more likely to be viewed as governed by a tortious duty of care arising by operation of law. The mere absence of a contract (typically resulting from the absence of contractual consideration) is irrelevant if all the other features of a service relationship are present:

"A promise given without consideration to perform a service cannot be enforced as a contract by the promisee; but if the service is in fact performed and done negligently, the promisee can recover in an action in tort."[6]

A "service" provided by a private individual, in his capacity as such, without any apparent profession of skill, and without any expectation that the recipient will rely on that advice, ought not to give rise to any service duties.[7] (There remains a residual, rather theoretical, category of a "service" which is not provided by way of business but where the other characteristics of the reliance relationship are still considered to exist.)

The client depends on the firm

2–007 "Dependence" is integral to the concept of a client relationship. The *Shorter Oxford English Dictionary* defines a "client" as:

"A person who is under the protection and patronage of another, a dependent . . . a person using the services of any professional . . .".

This aspect of the financial services relationship arises where the client: (a) depends on the firm to act for his benefit; and (b) involves a material exercise

---

[6] *Hedley Byrne & Co Ltd v Heller & Partners Ltd* [1963] 2 All E.R. 575 at 608. See also *Henderson v Merrett Syndicates* [1994] 3 All E.R. 506 at 521: "If someone possessed of a special skill undertakes, quite irrespective of contract, to apply that skill for the assistance of another person who relies on such skill a duty of care will arise . . ."; and *Midland Bank Trust Co Ltd v Hett Stubbs & Kemp* [1979] Ch.384 at 417, "The case of a layman consulting a solicitor for advice seems to me to be as typical a case as one could find of the sort of relationship in which the duty of care described in the Hedley Byrne case . . . exists".

[7] See *Hedley Byrne & Co Ltd v Heller & Partners Ltd* [1963] 2 All E.R. 575, [1964] A.C. 465 at 610 and 529, *per* Lord Devlin: "Where there is no consideration, it will be necessary to exercise greater care in distinguishing between social and professional relationships and between those which are of a contractual nature and those which are not. It may often be material to consider whether the adviser is acting purely out of good nature or whether he is getting his reward in some indirect form. The service that a bank performs in giving a reference is not done simply out of a desire to assist commerce. It would discourage the customers of the bank if their deals fell through because the bank had refused to testify to their credit when it was good." Contrast *Chaudhry v Prabhaker, The Times,* June 8, CA; [1988] 3 All E.R. 718, CA, (family friend liable for negligently recommending a second-hand car and representing that it had not been involved in an accident).

of judgment by the firm as to what will be beneficial for this purpose. The client may do this because he lacks the skills to make that judgment himself, or because he has chosen as a matter of convenience to delegate this exercise of judgment to the firm, or a combination of the two.

It is to be distinguished from the sort of dependence which may be said to exist in counterparty dealings. A seller of shares may be "depending" on the buyer to pay him the purchase price; but he is not depending on the buyer to decide what price it should pay for them, let alone what price would be most likely to benefit the seller.

Although, as indicated above, the relationship is usually contractual, the case law on the tortious concept of a duty of care gives helpful indicators of how it works. In tortious liability for economic loss the defendant actively "assumes" a particular responsibility. This contrasts with the more usual, passive, tortious responsibility not to interfere with another's well-being. It is this active assumption of responsibility which justifies overcoming the normal tortious inhibition on liability for economic loss.[8] Duties are not externally imposed, but arise because of the relationship in which the parties choose to place themselves.[9]

On this model, the parties place themselves in a relationship to each other **2–008** under which:

(1) The client depends on the firm to provide him with a particular type of service, involving the exercise of judgment by the firm on the client's behalf;

(2) It is reasonable for the client to rely on the firm in this way, bearing in mind in particular the purpose for which the relationship has been established and the circumstances generally[10]; and

---

[8] Tortious liability is based on a close and direct relationship between the claimant and the defendant. In physical damage cases, from *Donaghue v Stevenson* [1932] A.C. 562 onwards, this "nexus" or "proximity" between the act of carelessness and the act of damage is usually self-evident, giving rise to a duty to refrain from injuring another, as distinct from a positive duty to act to their benefit. Tortious liability for economic loss, in contrast, needs to be based on something more than the mere neighbourhood test laid down in *Donoghue v Stevenson*.

[9] Lord Mustill in *White v Jones* [1995] 2 A.C. 207 at 287, [1995] 1 All E.R. 691 at 729, HL, said that *Hedley Byrne* liability arose *internally* from the relationship in which the parties chose to place themselves (such as a client relationship), whereas in other tort cases such as *Donoghue v Stevenson* liability was imposed externally based on the position in which the parties happened to find themselves. The *Hedley Byrne* relationship is established by the parties between themselves as a dynamic factor with consequences over and above those which would otherwise arise. At one point this dynamic principle was equated with a voluntary or intentional assumption of responsibility by the service provider to the recipient, but the courts have since moved away from this. There must, however, still be some objectively identifiable assumption of responsibility by the defendant, even if it does not subjectively intend to assume such liability.

[10] In *Williams v Natural Life Health Foods Ltd*, The Times, May 1, 1998, HL, Lord Steyn said that the touchstone of liability was not the state of mind of the maker. The primary focus had to be on things said or done by the maker or on his behalf in dealings with the plaintiff.

25

(3)   The client actually relies on the firm's judgment in the conduct of his relevant affairs.

The judge in a 1980s Canadian fiduciary case described this sort of dependence relationship as one where:

"the relative legal positions are such that one party is at the mercy of the other's discretion. . .there is a relation in which the principal's interests can be affected by, and are therefore *dependent* on, the manner in which [the firm] uses the discretion which has been delegated to [it]."[11] (Emphasis added)

This general principle was first established in English law in the leading case of *Hedley Byrne*, where Lord Morris said[12] that:

"if, in a sphere in which a person is so placed that others could reasonably rely upon his judgment or his skill or upon his ability to make careful enquiry, a person takes it upon himself to give information or advice to, or allows his information or advice to be passed to, another person who, as he knows or should know, will place reliance on it, then a duty of care will arise."

Lord Reid in the same case said[13] that a duty arises where:

"it is plain that the party seeking information or advice was trusting the other to exercise such a degree of care as the circumstances required, where it was reasonable for him to do that, and where the other gave the information or advice when he knew or ought to have known that the enquirer was relying on him."

2–009   In *Spring v Guardian Assurance plc* Lord Goff expressed the same principle in the following terms,[14] "Where the plaintiff entrusts the defendant with the conduct of his affairs, in general or in particular, the defendant may be held to have assumed responsibility to the plaintiff, and the plaintiff to have relied on the defendant to exercise due skill and care, in respect of such conduct".

Standard examples of this sort of dependence are:

---

[11]   *Guerin v The Queen* (1984) 13 D.L.R. (4th) 321 at 339–341, *per* Dickson J. describing the hallmark of a fiduciary duty, and quoting Professor Ernest Weinreb. See also *Frame v Smith* (1987) 42 D.L.R. (4th) 81 at 98–99 where Wilson J. referred to the fiduciary as having scope for exercise of some discretion or power and the ability to exercise that power or discretion unilaterally.

[12]   [1964] A.C. 465 at 503, [1963] 2 All E.R. 575 at 594.

[13]   [1964] A.C. 465 at 486, [1963] 2 All E.R. 575 at 583.

[14]   [1994] 3 All E.R. 129 at 145.

- An investment manager making and implementing day-to-day investment decisions for its client's portfolio;

- A financial adviser, advising an inexperienced client on the design and structure of his investment portfolio, the general management of his portfolio, or a specific investment opportunity;

- A broker implementing a transaction on behalf of a client by executing or arranging execution on his behalf with a counterparty, where the implementation involves a degree of discretion.

The exercise of judgment or discretion involved in the service normally needs to be as to some material matter, otherwise there is no real discretion involved.[15] A ministerial or administrative service offers little scope for such discretion or materiality.[16]

Dependence is unavoidable and inevitable where the firm is providing a discretionary management service, so that both the decision as to what investments to make and the implementation of that decision is in the exclusive control of the manager.[17] An advisory service can be much more equivocal. Factors which may suggest that a client's reliance on advice or information given (or not given) by the firm is unjustified or unreasonable include:

- The advice was not given for the purpose for which the recipient relied on it.[18]

- Circumstances suggest that the client should have checked the information before relying on it, or should have obtained independent advice.[19]

---

[15] In *Coleman v Myers* [1977] 2 N.Z.L.R. 225, one of the factors relevant to the existence of a fiduciary duty was the significance of the transaction to the parties.

[16] In *Morgan v Elford, and Platt v Rowe (Trading as Chapman and Rowe) and C W Mitchell and Co* (1909) 26 T.L.R. 49, a broker and its customer agreed that the broker would buy for the customer at a specified price. If the broker managed to buy below the price he could keep the difference as a "mark-up" or "commission". The court in *Morgan v Elford* said that this was not a fiduciary relationship. The judge in *Platt v Rowe* referred to *Morgan v Elford* and stressed the fact that the customer had consented to the arrangement. It appears that the terms of the firm's instructions gave it no meaningful discretion to exercise on behalf of the client. The discretion it did exercise (the obtaining of the best price possible) was exercised for its own benefit.

[17] *e.g. Henderson v Merrett Syndicates* [1994] 3 W.L.R. 761, HL.

[18] See *e.g. Caparo* as discussed by Slade L.J. in *Morgan Crucible Co plc v Hill Samuel Bank Ltd* [1991] 1 All E.R. 148 at 159, CA.

[19] In *James McNaughton Papers Group Ltd v Hicks Anderson & Co (a firm)* [1991] 2 Q.B. 113, CA, at 126, Neill L.J. said "the question 'who is my neighbour?' prompts the response 'consider first those who would consider you to be their neighbour'. One should therefore consider *whether and to what extent the advisee was entitled to rely on the statement*, whether he did or should have used his own judgment and whether he did or should have sought independent advice." (emphasis added)

- The advice is not provided as a service, but is given casually, or informally, or in an unconsidered manner.[20]

- The client knows that the advice is wrong or unreliable.

- The advice was not provided to the client specifically, but at large, or to a generalised group of clients, as in the case of advice contained in an advertisement, and was therefore not intended to be specific to a particular recipient's personal circumstances.

- The firm gave no advice, had not been asked to advise, and was not under an obligation to volunteer unsolicited advice in the relevant situation.

The firm's duty to act in the client's interest

2–010 The client depends on the firm because he has entrusted the firm with the conduct of his affairs. The other side of this equation is that the firm has a duty to put itself in its client's shoes, exercising its skill and judgment in a way which it believes to be for the client's good and in his interests.[21]

This duty can also be seen in, while not being synonymous with, the fiduciary duty of loyalty. The fiduciary duty is, on *Hedley Byrne* principles, one instance of a wider more general duty of responsibility owed by a firm to the client who relies on it, and this in turn is closely linked to the standard of care and skill which must be applied in the discharge of that responsibility.[22] The

---

[20] *Howard Marine and Dredging Co v A Ogden & Sons (Excavations) Ltd* [1978] Q.B. 574, CA (no liability for oral off-the-cuff enquiry). Lord Denning M.R. said no duty was owed where the opinion, information or advice was given in circumstances in which it appeared that it was unconsidered and it would not be reasonable for the recipient to act upon it without taking further steps to check it. *Shields v Broderick* (1984) 8 D.L.R. (4th) 96 (estate agent not held liable for telling a buyer not to worry about selling his own home before entering into a contract to buy, as his own home "would sell very easily".)

[21] The term "best interests" is also used. In most cases this can be taken as a slightly more vivid way of describing the same "interests" concept, rather than as representing a higher or more absolute standard.

[22] In *Hedley Byrne* [1964] A.C. 465 at 528–529, [1963] 2 All E.R. 575 at 610, Oliver J. said, "the categories of special relationships, which may give rise to a duty to take care in word as well as deed, are not limited to contractual relationships or to relationships of fiduciary duty, but include also relationships . . . where there is an assumption of responsibility in circumstances which, but for the absence of consideration, there would have been a contract." In *Henderson v Merrett Syndicates* [1994] 3 All E.R. 506 at 543, Lord Browne Wilkinson said: "The liability of a fiduciary for the negligent transaction of his duties is not a separate head of liability but the paradigm of the general duty to act with care imposed by law on those who take it upon themselves to act for or advise others . . . [T]he duty of care imposed on bailees, carriers, trustees, directors, agents and others is the same duty . . . It is the fact that they have all assumed responsibility for the property or affairs of others that renders them liable for the careless performance of what they have undertaken to do." One effect of this is that, post-*Hedley Byrne*, cases on fiduciary duty focus (primarily) on conflict of interest issues, and fiduciary principles are no longer seen as relevant to the performance of a service which, though negligent, does not breach the fiduciary duty of loyalty. Contrast the pre-*Hedley Byrne* case of *Wood v Martins Bank* [1959] I Q.B. 55 where reasonable care and skill were classed as a

INTRODUCTION TO CLIENT SERVICE RELATIONSHIPS

same principles apply where the relationship is contract based, or where there are concurrent duties in tort and contract. See further Chapter 9. In the US in contrast, the picture has become clouded by what looks to an English eye like pre-*Hedley Byrne* reasoning, and by legislators creating statutory duties of care and labelling them as fiduciary duties. See Chapter 10.

Acting in the client's interest frequently goes beyond a mere duty to avoid causing harm to the client (the negative duty found in many torts) to include a positive duty to do right by the client. Oliver J., describing a law firm's tortious duties to its client, said:

> "The relationship of solicitor and client gave rise to a duty on [the law firm] under the general law to exercise that care and skill upon which they must have known perfectly well that their client relied. To put it another way, their common law duty was not to injure their client by failing to do that which they had undertaken to do and which, at their invitation, he relied on them to do."[23]

An equivalent contractual relationship will operate in the same way. In **2–011** *Groom v Crocker*[24] Scott L.J. said:

> "The retainer when given puts into operation the normal terms of the contractual relationship, including in particular the duty of the solicitor to protect the client's interest and to carry out his instructions in the matters in which the retainer relates, by all proper means.[25]

A variation is where the discretion is exercised on behalf of, not one but a group of clients or recipients, as where a firm is acting for a group of investors collectively. The firm's duty would be a general one, to exercise its discretion the interest of the group as a whole. If the interests of individual investors diverge, the firm would not be under a duty to support those conflicting interests against each other. At most it might be under a duty to act

---

fiduciary duty, because the judge wanted to hold the firm liable for the advice it had given and at that time such liability was thought only to attach to fiduciary relationships. *In Bristol & West Building Society v Mothew (tla Stapley & Co)* [1996] 4 All E.R. 698 at 710, CA, Millet L.J. said: "it is obvious that not every breach of duty by a fiduciary is a breach of fiduciary duty." The Court of Appeal went on to hold that an inadvertent failure to give notice of a particular matter was possibly a basis for a claim in negligence but not for a claim of breach of trust/fiduciary duty.

[23] *Midland Bank Trust Co Ltd v Hett Stubbs & Kemp (a firm)* [1979] Ch.384 at 417, [1978] 3 All E.R. 571 at 595–596, *per* Oliver J. (cited with approval in *Henderson v Merrett* [1994] 3 All E.R. 506 at 529).

[24] [1939] 1 K.B. 194 at 222, [1938] 2 All E.R. 394 at 413, CA.

[25] A similar list of a lawyer's general obligations was cited by Riley J. in *Tiffin Holding Ltd v Millican* 49 D.L.R. (2d) 216, approved by the supreme court of Canada (1967) 60 D.L.R. (2d) 469, with the addition of references to the general duty of skill and care, and also to a duty to advise the client on all matters relevant to his retainer so far as reasonably necessary.

THE LEGAL NATURE OF THE CLIENT SERVICES RELATIONSHIP

fairly as between different interest groups.[26] This principle would apply in relation to, for instance, an investment manager investing funds on a collective basis for a common group of investors, or the directors of a life company exercising discretion as to how to allocate bonuses to with-profits life policies. A similar principle applies to the duties of an Investment Exchange to its members.[27]

Regulatory definition of "client"

2-012 The nature of the client relationship has been as described in this Chapter since at least the time of the *Hedley Byrne* case in 1962. When detailed regulation was introduced in 1988, the term "customer" was used to indicate not only client relationships, but also arm's length trading where there was a services element. The rules recognised the special importance of judgmental services for investment management and agency broking, and in these contexts the term customer was synonymous with client. However, practitioners were happy to go along with the regulatory use of the term "customer" since: (a) if anything it downplayed the service element in the substantive client relationship; (b) it was the regulators' decision anyway; and (c) at this point no one saw any need to draw further decisions between a client and a customer. The one place in the rules where the term "client" was prominently used was in the client, money regime, where the term "client" was understood to refer the trust-based nature of the client money concept.

The reasoning described above has not been carried forward into the FSMA regime, which has reversed the normal terminology. In the FSA rules, counterparties are now defined as clients, and clients are defined as customers. In a few places the original logic still seems to peep through—for instance the designation of a "client agreement" is still linked to the idea of special protection being needed where a private client signs up to a service contract.

---

[26] The position would of course be different if the firm had undertaken to look after the individual interests of such persons.

[27] On the common law, quasi-public law duties of investment exchanges see *Weinburger v Inglis* [1919] A.C. 606 at 640; *Shearson Lehman Hutton Inc v Maclaine Watson & Co Ltd* [1989] 2 Lloyds Rep.570; and *Exchanges and Alternative Trading Systems* (Frase and Parry, 2002) paras 1.80—1.100. On the quasi-public law duties of a life company see *Equitable Life Assurance Society v Hyman, The Times*, January 26, 2000, CA, the court of appeal held that directors invested with a discretion to allocate bonuses had been entrusted with powers to be used equitably for the benefit of existing and future policyholders, having regard to the terms of their respective policies and the interests and needs of the Society as a whole. The court could intervene and require decisions taken which were inconsistent with or disregarded those terms to be taken again in much the same way as they intervened in judicial review.

30

Fiduciary duty of loyalty

The dependence relationships described above will often also give rise to a fiduciary duty of loyalty, owed by the firm to its client. This equitable duty requires the firm to avoid conflicts between its own interests and its duty to its client, and between its duties owed to different clients. This duty is tending to be perceived, in modern practice, and with some assistance from the FSA rules, as a duty to avoid any disadvantage to the client as a result of such conflicts, rather than the more punitive black letter view, based largely (though by no means entirely) on private trust case law, that such conflicts can only be overcome by making full disclosure of all material facts and obtaining fully informed client consent.

2–013

Another important but unresolved issue is what happens where the conflict arises, not within the firm itself, but because of the activities of another company in the firm's group. There is no simple answer to this, and the traditional (but clearly inappropriate) answer is that fiduciary conflicts cannot arise where different legal entities are involved. The correct (but difficult to implement) answer should be that where the different legal entities are essentially the same business, they should be grouped together for any application of the conflict of interests test. If however the different group companies genuinely represent separate and unconnected businesses, conflict of interests principles should not be applied intra-group. See further Chapter 9.

Service Standards—Care and Skill and the Scope of the Service

As indicated above, it is implicit in the idea of a financial service that a degree of skill and competence is brought to bear. This tends to be described by reference to two main concepts—the level of care and skill appropriate to the service in question, and the scope of the services the firm has undertaken to provide. The two concepts overlap a good deal. For instance, a profession of skill by an investment manager in relation to derivatives trading implies that it possesses an appropriate level of skill in derivatives and also that it will advise on or invest in derivatives (where appropriate) within the scope of any services provided. The way in which scope can determine the standard of care and skill to be applied is particularly clearly illustrated in the new FSA packaged-product concept of a firm having to provide suitable advice by reference to its declared product range.[28]

2–014

The rest of this Chapter discusses the relevant service standards under the following headings:

- Absolute and qualified duties.

- Measuring the standard.

---

[28] See para.1–030 and FSA CP 166.

THE LEGAL NATURE OF THE CLIENT SERVICES RELATIONSHIP

- Holding out.

- Client sophistication.

- The duration of the service.

Absolute and qualified duties

2–015 The strength of an obligation may be such that it amounts to an absolute duty to achieve whatever object have been laid down, a qualified duty to use reasonable efforts, or some lesser duty.

Absolute duties

2–016 For our financial services purposes, an absolute or strict duty arises where the firm gives a contractual promise[29] that a particular thing will or will not happen, come what may. If the promise is not met, the firm will be liable for breach of contract, irrespective of whether or not it possessed or used appropriate care and skill. A firm which has breached a strict liability obligation may be unable to raise contributory negligence by the other party as a defence.[30] Strict liability may also affect the calculation of measure of loss.

Performance obligations in counterparty transactions are often absolute in this way. The paying party *must* pay the amount specified by the contract on the due date. A seller *must* deliver securities or assets which match the contractual description. It is no good the payer saying that it made reasonable efforts to obtain the money to pay but failed to do so.

A strict obligation may be suspended or varied by other contract terms, as where there is a contractual right for the seller to defer performance on grounds of *force majeure*, or to avoid the contract for breach of a condition. But this does not change the unqualified nature of the basic obligation itself.

2–017 In financial services, strict liability is usually created by an express contractual term, though the court may need to decide how it applies to a particular factual situation. For example, in *Bertram, Armstrong and Co v Hugh Godfray*[31] a broker was given a limit order to sell bonds at 85 or above. It argued that this gave it a right, but not a duty, to sell once the price reached 85. The court held that the firm's "particular" commission was to sell when

---

[29] Strict liability can arise in tort, but usually only in physical damage torts as an absolute duty to avoid physical injury; see *Donoghue v Stevenson* [1932] All E.R. 1. In *Henry Kendall & Sons v William Lillico & Sons Ltd* [1969] 2 F.N. 31 the defendant was held liable for selling contaminated food even though the utmost care and skill might not have detected the defect.

[30] *Barclays Bank plc v Fairclough Building Ltd* [1995] 1 All E.R. 289.

[31] [1830] 1 Knapp 381; 12 E.R. 364, PC.

the price reached 85 and it had no discretion to defer selling till the bonds reached a higher price.[32]

Absolute duties are also sometimes implied, but usually in dealings with third parties rather than as part of the internal client/firm relationship itself.[33]

Qualified duties

The duty of care

Many undertakings involve a more qualified obligation, in which the firm does not guarantee to achieve the desired objective, but only to *try* to achieve it.   **2–018**

The legal value of a mere duty to try to do something, without more, would depend entirely on the whim of the promisor. Such a duty would for practical legal purposes be non-existent. A qualified duty thus usually involves an obligation on the firm to use reasonable care and skill to try and achieve the object. A failure to act with due care and skill is negligence, and where a client incurs loss as a result of such negligence it has a claim for

---

[32] See also *Tallentyre v Ayre* (1884) 1 T.L.R. 143, CA, (broker liable for selling its client's securities in a falling market. The client's instructions were "you may buy 500 Mexican Railway shares: 104–105, provided a recovery from the severe fall is pretty certain; but if Mexicans are going down do not buy at present". Held, that this could not be construed as authority to buy in a falling market); *Ellis v Pond* (1898) 1 Q.B. 426; 14 T.L.R. 152, CA, a broker advanced money for the purchase of railway shares, holding the shares as security for the advance plus interest, on terms that it would not sell the shares before the account of November 26. The broker closed the account by selling the shares on November 19, without instructions and in breach of the agreement not to sell before November 26. If the shares had been sold on November 26 they would have realised a higher price (though still less than the amount owed by the client). Held, that the firm was entitled to the repayment of its advance but the client was entitled to counterclaim for damages reflecting the higher price which would have been obtained if the stock had been sold in accordance with the terms of the mandate on November 26); *MacInnes v Cartwright & Crickmore Ltd* (1931) 1 D.L.R. 572 affirmed (1931) 3 D.L.R. 693 (CAN) (broker instructed to sell certain securities provided he could achieve a certain price or better was liable (in conversion) for selling them at a lower price); *Lambert v Sunshine Mining of London Ltd (formerly SNW Commodities Ltd)*, unreported, May 9, 1988, (Judge Paul Barker Q.C.), a large number of discretionary futures trades booked to the account of an advisory client were held to be unauthorised and invalid. There was no contemporaneous evidence of the day-to-day instructions which had actually been given so the court had to infer this from the surrounding circumstances. Significant factors which led to the finding were that the account executive was unable to give any examples of the limits of discretion which he might have had in any specific trade, his inability to give any explanation of what trading strategy or instructions would have produced the positions which had in fact been were entered into, and the substantial number of day trades, which were inconsistent with the agreed account strategy).

[33] Thus a warranty is commonly implied that an agent that it has proper authority to act on behalf of its principal. In *Yonge v Toynbee* [1910] 1 K.B. 215, solicitors were liable for bringing an action for a client who unknown to them had become incapable (as a result of which their authority had terminated). In *Starkey v Bank of England* [1903] A.C. 114, a stockbroker which transferred government bonds in good faith in reliance on a forged transfer was liable to indemnify the central depository (*i.e.* the Bank of England) against the claims of the true owner.

compensation. The FSA regulatory equivalent, Principle 2 (A firm must conduct its business with due skill, care and diligence), is a regulatory codification of this general principle.

A variety of other expressions are used to express this same qualified duty, such as: "due care and skill", "proper care and skill", "reasonable steps", "best efforts", "best endeavours", and so on. Normally they all mean much the same thing.

2–019   The duty to use reasonable care and skill may be set out as an express term of the contract. But if not it will still normally be implied in any business contract, on grounds of business efficacy.[34] The same conclusion can also be reached in the absence of a contract, as where the firm has provided its services gratuitously.[35]

The principle of qualified duty is the norm for a financial services client relationship. Thus, it has been held that a stockbroker undertakes to use due and reasonable diligence to buy shares for his client, and does not undertake to procure them absolutely and in any event,[36] and an insurance broker must use reasonable care and skill to try to obtain insurance in accordance with its instructions, but will not be in breach of its instructions if the insurance is in fact unobtainable.[37] The responsibilities of a broker do not include a duty to prevent its client incurring losses.[38]

The exercise of judgment

2–020   Where a task is difficult or judgmental, or is subject to factors beyond the control of the firm, or requires the firm, in advising or exercising its judgment, to weigh up imponderables or choose between alternatives which each carry their own particular risks, it will be relatively easy to conclude that even a competent firm might make an error of judgment, or fail to achieve the client's objective for some other reason. Or the judgmental nature of the task may make it difficult to conclude that there has been an error at all. If a lawyer gives legal advice which is wrong on a matter where the law is difficult, he will not generally be negligent so long as his advice is reasonable.[39] If he

---

[34] See *Ogden & Co Pty Ltd v Reliance Fire Sprinkler Co Pty Ltd* [1975] 1 Lloyds Rep. 52 at 68.

[35] See *Hedley Byrne & Co Ltd v Heller & Partners Ltd* [1963] 2 All E.R. 575 at 608, *per* Lord Devlin "The respondents in this case cannot deny that they were performing a service. There sheet anchor is that they were performing it gratuitously and therefore no liability for performance can arise. . .but if the service is in fact performed and done negligently, the promisee can recover in an action in tort."

[36] *Fletcher v Marshall* (1846) 15 M. & W. 755; 5 Ry. & Can. Cas. 340; 10 Jur. 528; 153 E.R. 1055.

[37] *Eagle Star Insurance Company Ltd v National Westminster Finance Australia Ltd* (1985) 58 A.L.R. 165 at 174, PC. "Their duty was to use all reasonable care and skill in seeking to obtain the cover . . . But they did not undertake that cover would be procured."

[38] *Drexel Burnham Lambert International NV v Al Nasr and Another* [1986] 1 F.T.L.R. (Stourton J.).

[39] *Bell v Strathairn and Blair* (1954) 104 L.J. 618 (SCOT); *Wrightson Group Ltd v Crocker* (1979) 124 Sol. Jol. 83, *per* Lord Denning M.R. (error of judgment by a solicitor did not amount to negligence).

interprets a document or statute wrongly he is unlikely to be negligent so long as his interpretation is tenable.[40] Where purely legal considerations are only one factor in the lawyer's advice, an error of judgment on the legal issues is that much less likely to amount to negligence.[41]

Similar examples from the financial services sector would include the failure of a broker or investment manager to spot the precise moment when the market touches bottom so as to shift from a sell to a buy strategy (or vice versa at the top of the market), or to pick the most profitable of a number of different strategies open to him. A corporate finance adviser who follows a reasonable strategy in a takeover bid is not negligent merely because the strategy did not succeed or because its advice relied on unverified factual information which later proved to be inaccurate.[42]

A bad investment is not in itself proof of negligent management.[43] In *Stafford v Conti Commodity Services Ltd* it was held that the fact that an

---

[40] *Laidler v Elliott* (1825) 3 B. & C. 738 (incorrectly construing a rule of court).

[41] *Faithful v Kesteven* (1910) 103 L.T. 56, CA. See also *Dunn v Fairs Blissard Barnes & Stowe* (1961) 105 S.J. 932; *Maillet and Pother v Haliburton & Comeau* (1983) 55 N.S.R. (2d) (Nova Scotia) (solicitor not negligent in advising acceptance of a settlement offer rather than continuing to prosecute the case).

[42] In *Ginora Investments Limited v James Capel & Co Limited*, unreported, February 10, 1995, (Rimer J.), James Capel & Co (Capel) was accused of negligence in the provision of investment advice to Priest Marians Holdings (PMH) in its contested takeover of Local London Group (LLG).

One allegation was that Capel had represented to PMH that the acquisition of LLG would be very beneficial to PMH. Rimer J. found that although Mr Campbell of Capel had not made an express statement to this effect, it was implicit in what he did say that in his view the takeover was potentially beneficial to PMH. This was merely an opinion which he genuinely and reasonably held. Others might have formed a different opinion; as it happened no one in the LLG takeover did.

Another allegation was that Capel was negligent because it had recommended an acquisition price for LLG which was too high. The court found that Capel, though wrong, had used reasonable care and skill in seeking to identify a suitable price.

Capel's principle error was in believing that LLG's residual assets and liabilities balanced out. It made clear that this assumption was based on unverified information and did not give any assurance to PMH that Capel had all necessary information on LLG. PMH was fully aware of the source of Capel's information and the risk that it might be wrong. Capel made clear in particular that its estimate, that LLG's net indebtedness was about £55 million, was derived from third parties (UK Land and Samuel Montagu) who had considered making a bid for LLG but decided not to proceed. The figure had been checked against published accounts, but had not been verified with LLG.

Capel was also alleged to be negligent in failing to advise PMH not to proceed with a hostile bid without first investigating LLG's books records and other unpublished information, and that any bid thereafter should have been made as an agreed bid supported by the board of LLG. Priest Marians said that if such advice had been given it would have followed it. Rimer J. felt that this was highly coloured by hindsight. The hostile bid route was a matter of judgment made by Capel in good faith and a common view endorsed by Samuel Montagu and other professional advisers involved. Capel's choice of strategy reflected a responsible and considered exercise of judgment.

[43] *Clark v Kirby-Smith* [1964] Ch.506 (solicitor); *O'Connor v Kirby* [1972] 1 Q.B. 90 [1971] 2 All E.R. 1415 (insurance broker); *Merrill Lynch Futures Inc v York House Trading Ltd*, (1984) 81 L.S.G. 2544, CA, (futures broker); *Greaves & Co v Baynham Meikle* [1975] 1 W.L.R. 1095 at 1100, *per* Lord Denning M.R. (consulting engineer) *Smith v Eric S Bush; Harris v Wyre Forest DC* [1989] 2 All E.R. 514, HL at 525, *per* Lord Templeman (real estate valuer).

advisory client lost money on futures trading does not mean that its broker's advice was negligent. Mocatta J. said[44]:

> "Losses in the ordinary course of things do occur even if proper care is used when one is dealing with transactions on the commodities futures markets . . . with the best advice in the world; in such an unpredictable market as this, it would require exceedingly strong evidence from expert brokers in relation to individual transactions to establish negligence on the part of the defendants."

The interface between qualified and absolute duties

2–021 Sometimes an obligation will have to be looked at closely to see whether it is an absolute or qualified duty. Setting a performance benchmark in a management agreement might, on a cursory reading, look like a strict obligation. But it is normally a target to aim at, not a performance level which the firm is promising to achieve. The inference is that the client may de-instruct the firm if it fails to match the performance level, not that it must indemnify the client for any failure to meet the benchmark.[45]

A failure to take a necessary step towards achieving the objective is usually treated as a matter of negligence, rather than breach of an absolute duty.[46] But sometimes, negligent delay in performance may be so serious that it amounts to non-performance. This would probably be the case if a manager assumes a discretionary mandate and never executed any trades for the client's portfolio. In *Born v Premier Investments (Victoria) Ltd*[47] a client gave a broker an order to buy shares in a private company. The broker accepted the money and agreed to supply the shares but failed to do so within a reasonable time, and this was held to constitute an entire failure of consideration.

---

[44] [1981] 1 All E.R. 691 at 698. The client had lost £19,000 in trades executed on the commodities markets through Conti, a futures broker. Although the trading was based on advice from Conti, the client usually made his own decision and often rejected the firm's advice. Mocatta J. held (at 697 and 698) that the losses did not of themselves establish negligence on the part of the firm even if it advised on both parts of the transaction which produced the loss. At 697 he said: "A broker cannot always be right in the advice that he gives in relation to so wayward and rapidly changing a market as the commodities futures market. An error of judgment, if there be an error of judgment, is not necessarily negligent."

[45] See the discussion of the *Unilever* case in Ch.11, paras 11–001—11–010.

[46] *Sykes v Midland Bank Executor & Trustee Co Ltd* [1971] 1 Q.B. 113 at 125 (solicitor failed to advise on lease); *Heywood v Wellers* [1976] Q.B. 446 (solicitor fails to carry out certain procedural steps in litigation); *G&K Ladenbau (UK) Ltd v Crawley and De Reya* [1978] 1 W.L.R. 266 (solicitor failed to search commons register).

[47] (1947) 1 W.W.R. 492; affirmed (1948) 1 D.L.R. 596; (1948) 1 W.W.R. 685 (CAN).

SERVICE STANDARDS—CARE AND SKILL AND THE SCOPE OF THE SERVICE

Sometimes basing the service on an absolute duty may operate to limit or exclude the reasonable care and skill duty.[48] In other cases the two duties may exist concurrently. In *Brown v KMR Services Ltd; Sword-Daniels v Pitel and Others*[49] Mr Sword-Daniels was assured that his broker, John Poland, would follow a safety-first conservative approach in recommending the portfolio, and ensure that every syndicate was low risk. Contrary to this assurance, the broker invested his client in a number of high-risk syndicates. The broker was held strictly liable for breach of contract and also, since it had given an assurance as to how the services would be performed, liable for breach of the qualified duty of reasonable care and skill which it had established by that assurance.[50]

It is usually more attractive for a client to bring a claim for breach of absolute duty. All it needs to do is prove that the duty was breached and that loss was incurred as a result. Breach of a qualified duty, in contrast, involves difficult value judgments. **2–022**

In *County Ltd v Girozentrale Gilbert Elliot*[51] County was underwriting a £26 million issue of shares in Richmond Oil & Gas Plc. It appointed Gilbert Elliot as stockbroker to place the shares with institutional investors. It subsequently informed Elliot that the issue would not go ahead unless indicative commitments were obtained for the whole issue. It assumed that this was confidential information which Elliot would not pass on to the market. Elliot, however, informed the market of County's intention. County went ahead with the issue but various indicative commitments failed to translate into share applications.

County now discovered that Elliot had told the market that County would not go ahead without full indicative commitments, As a result it felt obliged to give the market the additional information that not all the indicative commitments had materialised. On hearing this, a number of investors withdrew their applications for shares.

On the facts, the substantive reason for the failure of the placing might well have been that Gilbert Elliot had negligently assumed that it had identified potential placees for the entire issue. In the event unreliable placees accounted for some 17 per cent of the issue. However County was aware of the unreliable nature of those placees as well, which would have made it difficult to sustain a negligence case. Instead, County succeeded in claiming that County had specifically instructed Elliot not to inform the market of County's

---

[48] In *Midland Bank Trust v Hett, Stubbs & Kemp* [1979] Ch.383, Oliver J. found that the firm's duty, to ensure that a grant of an option was properly registered, would be properly performed if the option were registered in time to protect the land from sale to a third party, regardless of whether, in doing this, the firm had delayed excessively, or had otherwise gone about its task in a manner which fell below standards of competent practice.

[49] [1994] 4 All E.R. 385.

[50] See also *Dickson & Co v Devitt* (1916) 86 L.J.K.B. 315 (Aitken J.) (insurance broker liable, both for breach of specific instructions, and failure to exercise reasonable care and skill).

[51] Unreported, December 18, 1995, CA.

37

intention; and Gilbert Elliot's breach of this strict duty rendered it liable for the resulting loss, irrespective of other considerations.

Measuring the standard of skill for qualified duties

Reasonable care—The prudent man standard

2–023 What constitutes the particular legal duty in a given situation is a matter of law.[52] Whether the standard of care and skill necessary to discharge that duty has been attained is a matter of fact.[53]

At its most basic, any individual assuming the responsibilities of an agent or similar must act with the care and prudence which a reasonable man acting in the same circumstances would use. However he is not obliged to exercise a particular level of skill. Rather he is expected to perform his duties with such skill as he possesses or as a person of his knowledge and experience might reasonably be expected to possess.[54] Private trustees have historically been judged by the same low-level prudent man test,[55] though the Trustee Act 2000 has now amplified this to include more specific care and skill standards where appropriate.[56]

Reasonable skill—The competent firm standard

2–024 A firm providing financial services by way of business will usually need to go beyond the mere "prudent man" standard. The expectation is that it is

---

[52] *Midland Bank Trust Co Ltd v Hett Stubbs & Kemp* [1979] Ch.384 at 402, *per* Oliver J.

[53] *Brown v Rolls Royce Ltd* [1960] 1 W.L.R. 210, HL at 214, *per* Lord Keith and at 215 *per* Lord Denning.

[54] In *Re City Equitable Fire Insurance Co Ltd* [1925] Ch.407 Romer J. said at 427 that: "a director need not exhibit in the performance of his duties a greater degree of skill than may reasonably be expected from a person of his knowledge and experience. A director of a life insurance company does not guarantee that he has the skill of an actuary or a physician."

[55] See *Learoyd v Whitely* (1887) 12 App. Cas. 727 at 733, *per* Lord Watson: "As a general rule the law requires of a trustee no higher degree of diligence in the execution of his office than a man of ordinary prudence would exercise in the management of his own private affairs." In *Wight and Another v Olswang, The Times,* April 18, 2000 (Neuberger J.) a solicitor who was the co-trustee of a fund consisting largely of a holding in a public company called Aegis Group plc. The trustees had an absolute discretion in relation to the continued retention of the holding. They sold most of it between 1991 and 1993. The beneficiaries claimed that by reason of alleged breaches of duty they lost opportunities to sell the shares at higher prices. The trustees' were held not liable because the decision made was something which a prudent man in the trustee's position could have made. It was the ultimate decision that mattered, rather than the individual steps by which that decision had been reached.

[56] Under the Trustee Act 2000 a trustee must "exercise such care and skill as is reasonable in the circumstances, having regard in particular to any special knowledge or experience that he has or holds himself out as having and, if he acts as trustee in the course of a business or profession, to any special knowledge or experience that it is reasonable to expect of a person acting in the course of that kind of business or profession". See further paras 11–024—11–026.

SERVICE STANDARDS—CARE AND SKILL AND THE SCOPE OF THE SERVICE

providing a skilled service, because a certain level of skill is inherent to the nature of the service concerned, or because the firm holds itself out as having a certain level of skill, or for both reasons. "Skill" for this purpose can include special knowledge, or a duty to make use of an available source of information.[57]

For a skilled service, the acceptable standard is determined not by reference to the skill which would be brought to bear by the ordinary man in the street, but by the standard of the ordinary *skilled* person—that is to say—the hypo-thetical person possessing the level of competence appropriate to the service in question. In the leading case of *Bolam v Friern Hospital Management Committee*[58] McNair J. said:

> "I must tell you what we mean by 'negligence'. In the ordinary case, which does not involve any special skill, negligence means a failure to do some act which a reasonable man in the circumstances would do, or the doing of some act which a reasonable man in the circumstances would not do . . . How do you test whether this act or failure is negligent? In an ordinary case it is generally said you judge it by the conduct of the man on the top of a Clapham omnibus. He is the ordinary man. But where you get a situation which involves the use of some special skill or com-petence, then the test as to whether there has been negligence or not is not the test of the man on the top of the Clapham omnibus, because he has not got this special skill. The test is the standard of the ordinary skilled man exercising and professing to have that special skill."

A competent firm is expected to recognise when it is unsuited to provide the expected level of skill, and either to warn the client of this or refrain from acting.[59]

Not only must the firm have the necessary competence. It must also take care to use it. So the fact that a firm employs individuals who possess the nec-essary skill is no defence if the particular individual appointed by the firm to carry out the work lacks the necessary qualifications or experience.[60]

It is not normally possible to assess competence by employing some abstract mathematical or statistical model, or by measuring it against the

2–025

---

[57] See *Spring v Guardian Assurance plc* [1994] 3 All E.R. 129 at 145–146, *per* Lord Goff; *Henderson v Merrett Syndicates* Limited [1994] 3 All E.R. 506 at 520, *per* Lord Goff.

[58] [1957] 1 W.L.R. 582 at 586.

[59] In *Fine's Flowers Ltd v General Accident Assurance Co of Canada* (1977) 81 D.L.R. (3d) 139 at 149, Wilson J.A. said: "It goes without saying that an agent who does not have the requi-site skills to understand the nature of his client's business and assess the risks that should be insured against should not be offering this kind of service". See also *Hurlingham Estates Limited v Wilde & Partners* [1997] T.L.R. 15 (solicitor liable for undertaking to provide a legal service for which he knew he did not have the necessary skill).

[60] *Kenney v Hall, Pain and Foster* (1976) 239 E.G. 355 (surveyor); *Wilshir v Essex Area Health Authority* [1987] Q.B. 730 (medicine).

course of action which the claimant personally thinks the firm should have followed. The most reliable formulation is to ask whether any reasonable firm, in the firm's position at the relevant time, and possessing the same information and an appropriate level of skill, would have acted in the way the firm did.[61]

It is axiomatic that there is more than one reasonable course of action in such circumstances. Only if the firm acted in a way which cannot realistically be categorised as one of these hypothetical reasonable courses of action will the firm have been negligent.[62]

In making this sort of assessment it is important to put oneself in the contemporaneous position of the parties, and not to be swayed by hindsight. The question is not whether a firm acted in a way that, in retrospect, is shown to have been undesirable or mistaken but whether, in light of the circumstances pertaining at the time, the firm acted reasonably.[63] In *Duchess of Argyll v Beuselinck*[64]: Megarry expressed this as follows:

> "In this world there are few things that could not have been better done if done with hindsight. The advantages of hindsight include the benefit of having a sufficient indication of which of the many factors present

---

[61] In *Bolam v Friern Hospital Management Committee* [1957] 1 W.L.R. 582 at 586, McNair J. said: "in the case of a medical man, negligence means failure to act in accordance with the standards of *reasonably competent* medical men at the time" and at 587 referred with approval to a statement in *Hunter v Hanley* (1955) S.L.T. 213 that the test for negligent medical diagnosis or treatment was "such failure as no doctor of ordinary skill would be guilty of, if acting with ordinary care." In *Saif Ali v Sidney Mitchell & Co* [1980] A.C. 198 at 220; [1978] 3 All E.R. 1033 at 1041 Lord Diplock said: "No matter what profession it may be, the common law does not impose on those who practise it any liability for damage resulting from what in the result turns out to have been errors of judgment, unless the error was such as no reasonably *well informed and competent* member of that profession could have made." In *Ginora Investments Ltd v James Capel & Co Ltd* Rimer J., referring to *Bolam v Friern* and *Saif Ali v Sidney Mitchell & Co*, said the question was "whether in the light of the circumstances obtaining at the time the defendant acted in a way in which no *reasonable and competent* practitioner could have behaved".

[62] While there are occasional indications that a more mechanical or statistically-based standard might be followed, these usually turn out to have been taken out of context. In *Chapman v Walton* (1833) 10 Bing. 57 at 64 Tindal C.J. appeared to suggest that an appropriate test was that the majority of skilled practitioners would have acted in the same way: "It appears to us, that it is... the most satisfactory mode of determining this question, to show by evidence whether a majority of *skilful and experienced* brokers would have come to the same conclusion as the defendant. If nine brokers of experience out of ten would have done the same as the defendant under the same circumstances, or even if as many out of a given number would have been of his opinion as against it, he who only stipulates to bring a reasonable degree of skill to the performance of his duty, would be entitled to a verdict in his favour". However, in the particular case the point being made was that this was adequate proof of competence, not that it was the only acceptable form of proof.

[63] *Bell v Strathairn & Blair* (1954) 104 L.J. 618; *Duchess of Argyll v Beuselinck* [1972] 2 Lloyds Rep. 172 at 185 (solicitor); *Ginora Investments Ltd v James Capel & Co Ltd* (unreported, February 2, 1995, *per* Rimer J.) (corporate finance adviser); *Roe v Ministry of Health* [1951] 2 K.B. 66 at 84 (medical practice); *Hacker v Thomas Deal & Co* [1991] 2 E.G.L.R. (surveyor); *IBA v EMI Ltd* (1980) 14 Build L.R. 1 at 31 (architect).

[64] [1972] 2 Lloyds Rep. 172 at 185.

Common practice

Reasonable behaviour is not necessarily the same as common practice. Nevertheless, where it is established to the court's satisfaction that a particular practice is commonly followed by practitioners providing a particular service, this will be of considerable significance in determining the standard of the duties owed by those practitioners.[65]

2–026

Standard practice is easiest to establish in a fairly extensive, homogenous and visible market, usually with a high level of regulation or case law in support, such as on-exchange broker-dealing or domestic conveyancing. FSA rules and guidance are themselves a source of common practice. In the most successful cases this is because the FSA rules and guidance have operated to codify good practice and made it more visible. Things have gone somewhat differently in the packaged product markets, where there has historically been much less confidence that common practice can be relied on to establish an acceptable standard. Here, regulatory intervention has gone well beyond mere codification to create a largely artificial market environment.[66]

In cases where practice is not sufficiently standardised to establish the requisite level of care and skill, common practice will often still be relevant by way of background.[67] It may be used as an aid to interpreting a particular contractual obligation, or an analogy may be made with similar practices. Something of this sort is often be implicit in "competent practitioner" tests described above, while acknowledging that general standards of competence need perforce to be applied to the particular facts.

---

[65] Thus, in *Marshall v Lindsey County Council* [1935] 1 K.B. 516 at 540 (a medical negligence case, approved in *Whiteford v Hunter* [1950] W.N. 553, HL), Maugham L.J. said: "A defendant charged with negligence can clear himself if he shows that he acted in accordance with general and approved practice". In *County Ltd and County NatWest Ltd v Girozentrale Securities* (unreported, December 18, 1995, CA), the transaction took place against well established practices of the capital market in London for the raising of additional capital by new issues. This practice (which was not in any substantive dispute as between the parties) played a significant part in the construction of the contract terms.

[66] The major regulatory intervention in the pensions products market of the 1990s involved a loss of confidence by the regulators in the free market for pensions provision, and a (probably correct) regulatory judgment that common market practice did not represent a reasonable standard of care and skill. Since then, expectation has increasingly grown that it is the role of the regulators to design a "perfect" retail market.

[67] In *Midland Bank Trust Co Ltd v Hett, Stubbs & Kemp* [1979] 1 Ch.384 at 403; [1978] 3 All E.R. 612, Oliver J. said: "The test is what the *reasonably competent practitioner would do having regard to the standards normally adopted* in his profession."

Public standards of conduct

2–027 Regardless of what firms actually do in practice, the court is often prepared to look at what it regards as public standards of conduct as an aid to their decisions. Public standards are to be found in codes of practice, guidance, and policy statements issued by trade and public bodies and the like. Some codes are of a purely voluntary nature—the material contained in the Appendices to this book falls into this category.

In other cases a code of practice or similar publication may be viewed as guidance as to standards considered appropriate in the market place As such they usually carry evidential value, rather than constituting actionable obligations *per se*. Thus, in *Powell v Phillips*[68] it was held that a breach of the Highway Code can be relied on in an attempt to show negligence, or contributory negligence, but is not to be elevated into a breach of statutory duty grounding a distinct cause of action. The effect is that if a practice is inconsistent with such a standard this may raise a presumption that the practice is faulty unless the firm concerned can prove otherwise.[69] The FSA rules are persuasive as a standard of this sort, irrespective of whether a breach of the rules gives rise to a right of action for breach of a statutory tort. In *Brandeis (Brokers) Ltd v Black*[70] the court took the rules of the Securities and Futures Authority (SFA) as inflated into a broker/client contract on relatively marginally grounds. There appeared to be an implicit assumption that the SFA rules must be of relevance in any event.

It is submitted that the COB rules are most relevant for this purpose where they represent a codification of good practice. In their more artificial elements, such as the financial promotion rules, a failure to act in line with regulatory requirements is much less likely to constitute a breach of general care and skill standards and would need to be looked at in terms of whether there is any substantive issue involved. This is somewhat similar to asking whether a purely technical breach could ever be sufficiently causative to give rise to a claim for compensation for loss.

Holding out

2–028 The way in which a firm holds itself out is often a relevant factor in determining the appropriate standard of skill and the scope of its service.[71]

---

[68] 116 SJ 713 (CA).
[69] *Bevan Investments Limited v Blackhall and Struthers* (No 2) [1973] 2 N.Z.L.R. 45 at 66 (engineers); *Lloyd Cheyham & Co Ltd v Littlejohn & Co* (1985) 2 P.N. 154 (accountants).
[70] [2001] 2 All E.R. (Comm) 980 (Toulson J.).
[71] "Holding out" is used in this way (though in a different context) in the FSA definition of dealing as principal as a regulated activity contained in art.15 of the Regulated Activities Order 2001, where it may be seen as a "profession" by a firm as to the *scope* of the principal dealing it carries on.

SERVICE STANDARDS—CARE AND SKILL AND THE SCOPE OF THE SERVICE

While it is arguable that this is really just another aspect of the law of misrepresentation, there seem enough distinctive features to treat it as a seperate topic. In particular "holdings out" are:

(a) Often very generalised in form, and not necessarily directed at a particular person.

(b) May depend as much on the way the firm conducts itself as any actual statements which it makes. Many professions of skill are implicit or general in this way.

(c) Operates at one remove from the sort of operative representation/ misrepresentation that would give rise to a cause of action.

As regards this last point, a profession of skill is not itself a service, nor, if the profession is untrue, is this itself a cause of action. Where, however, the firm has undertaken to supply a service to the client, the client may be entitled to assume that any skill professed will be applied in the provision of the service. The profession or holding out is thus a measure of the level and type of skill against which the firm's performance will be judged.[72]

Another feature of such a holding-out is that there is limited, if any, need to show that the client actually relied on the holding out. Either reliance follows implicitly once it is shown that the client relied on the service provided, or the holding out goes directly to the standard of care which the firm owes as a matter of law.[73]

Holding out—the nature of the firm's business

The public profession of an art is (it is said) a representation and undertaking to the world that the professor possesses the requisite ability and skill. Various judicial statements appear to equate a profession by a firm that it carries on a particular type of business activity with a generic form of holding out.[74] Thus, in a discussion of the duties of law firms, Hodson L.J. was

2–029

---

[72] *Bolam v Friern* [1957] 1 W.L.R. 582; *Dorchester Finance Co Ltd v Stebbing* [1989] B.C.L.C. 498 Foster J.; *Normans Bay Limited v Coudert Brothers* Q.B.D. [2003] February 19, lawyers liable because they had held themselves out as specialists in the Russian privatisation process and should at least have investigated that process.

[73] See comments of Oliver J. in *Midland Bank Trust Co Ltd v Hett Stubbs & Kemp* [1979] Ch.384 at 417 and Lord Goff in *Henderson v Merrett* [1994] 3 All E.R. 506, HL at 522; see also *Goody v Baring* [1956] W.L.R. 448 (solicitor).

[74] In *Hedley Byrne & Co Ltd v Heller & Partners Ltd* [1964] A.C. 465 at 529–530; [1963] 2 All E.R. 575 at 610–611, Lord Devlin described the relationships of solicitor and client, and banker and customer, as examples of a general duty relationship. In *Harmer v Cornelius* (1858) 5 C.B. (NS) 236, Willes J. said that if a medical man holds himself out as a person who undertakes the cure or treatment of human ailments there is a limited warranty that he is reasonably competent to the task he undertakes. In *Midland Bank Trust Co Ltd v Hett Stubbs &*

THE LEGAL NATURE OF THE CLIENT SERVICES RELATIONSHIP

able to ask: "Having regard to the degree of skill held out to the public by solicitors, does the conduct of the solicitor fall short of the standard which the public had been lead to expect of the solicitor?"[75]

Making people aware that the firm is a member of a particular exchange or market usually constitutes a holding out of this sort. In *Christopher Barker & Sons v Commissioners of Inland Revenue*[76] it was found as a preliminary matter that the firm were members of the Sheffield Stock Exchange and this was taken as implying a whole range of skills.[77] In *Henderson v Merrett Syndicates*[78] a holding out as to certain matters was implicit in the fact that the firms concerned were Lloyds agents.[79]

The general nature of the firm's business or profession does not necessarily determine exactly what skills the firm is claiming. Rather it sets the scene, by establishing various broad assumptions which can then be tailored to the circumstances of the case.[80]

Holding out—the firm's promotion of itself

2-030   The way in which a firm promotes itself, expressly or implicitly, normally includes a holding out as to its special skills. This may be in the form of sales

---

Kemp [1978] 3 All E.R. 571 at 595–596, [1979] Ch.384 at 417, Oliver J. said: "I would, therefore, hold that the relationship of solicitor and client gave rise to a duty on the [solicitors] under the general law to exercise that care and skill" In *Mutual Life and Citizen's Assurance Co Ltd v Evatt* (1971) A.C. 793 at 805, Lord Diplock described (in the context of *Hedley Byrne*) a concept of duty where the firm "claims to possess that degree of skill and competence and is willing to exercise that degree of diligence which is generally possessed and exercised by persons who carry on the business or profession of giving advice of the kind sought."

[75] *Simmons v Pennington & Son* [1955] 1 W.L.R. 183, *per* Hodson L.J. at 188.

[76] [1919] 2 K.B. 222 at 223.

[77] "For the purpose of their business they required a specialist and intimate knowledge of companies carrying on trade, especially in the case of a number of local companies who did not publish balance sheets and had to have a critical knowledge of accounts generally in order to arrive at a due appreciation of the financial position of companies and corporations (both home and foreign) whose shares and securities were on the investment market; thy had to treat all knowledge of their clients' investing and financial position as strictly confidential; they had to exercise skill and good judgment in buying and selling, and had to be quick and accurate in dealing with figures of a complex character. They were also consulted professionally on the promotion of, and the alteration and adjustment of capital in commercial undertakings, and they made valuations of stocks and shares forming part of the estate of deceased persons which were accepted as evidence by the Commissioners of Inland Revenue . . ."

[78] [1994] 3 All E.R. 506 at 522.

[79] Lord Goff said that agents at Lloyds: "obviously hold themselves out as possessing a special expertise to advise names on the suitability of risks to be underwritten; and on the circumstances in which, and the extent to which, reinsurance should be taken out and claims should be settled. The names, as the managing agents well knew, placed implicit reliance on that expertise, in that they gave authority to the managing agents to bind them to contracts of insurance and reinsurance and to the settlement of claims. I can see no escape from the conclusion that, in these circumstances, prima facie, a duty of care is owed in tort by the managing agents to such names, subject to the impact, if any, of the contractual context."

[80] See *e.g. Hurlingham Estates Limited v Wilde & Partners* [1997] T.L.R. 15, *Crossan v Ward Bracewell & Co* (1989) 5 P.N. 103.

44

talk, or promotional material in written form. Such promotion may refer directly to matters such as the experience which the firm can bring to bear, its past achievements, its areas of special skill and knowledge, and the general standard of service which it provides.

In *Woods v Martins Bank*[81] Mr Johnson, a branch manager at Martins Bank in Newcastle, gave Mr Woods extensive investment advice, which Mr Woods relied and acted on. The bank argued, relying on precedent, that if it provided a service (advice on investment matters) which fell outside the scope of its business as a bank (the handling of the customer's bank account), therefore that service must be provided gratuitously on a non-business footing, and without any duty of care or skill. Salmon J. accordingly analysed the case in terms of whether or not the service came within the scope of the bank's business. He held that the bank had extended the scope of its business from that of mere management of a bank account *because of the additional services which it had held itself out as willing and able to provide*, both in its promotional literature and in discussions with Mr Woods.[82]

Many promotional documents nowadays seek to avoid express holdings out of a particular skill or expertise, and limit themselves to factual statements such as, in the case of an investment manager, the experience of the manager and key individuals, information on the firm's historic performance, extracts from industry league tables, and a description of the investment strategy the manager will follow. The way these facts are presented may of course still constitute some form of holding out but is likely to be a less risky one.

---

[81] [1959] 1 Q.B. 55; [1958] 3 All E.R. 166 (approved by Lord Devlin in *Hedley Byrne v Heller* [1963] 2 All E.R. 575 at 611; [1964] A.C. 465 at 530; and constituting, on the basis of Lord Devlin's comments, a pre-*Hedley Byrne* example of a *Hedley Byrne* duty).

[82] In terms of general holding out, Salmon J. said: "In considering what is and is not within the scope of the defendant bank's business I cannot do better than look at their own publications. I look first at their advertisement. That is in these terms: '. . .We have six district head offices with boards of directors and general mangers, or that the very best advice is available through our managers virtually on your doorstep'; and the advertisement is headed 'We share your problems.' Then I consider their booklet. The material parts read as follows: 'If you want help or advice about investments our managers will gladly obtain for you advice from the best available sources in such matters.' I observe that the best available source in this case was the bank itself. 'You may consult your bank manager freely and seek his advice on all matters affecting your financial welfare. All these advantages are yours as the possessor of a bank account, current or deposit, and in these difficult days, when financial problems of one kind or another always seem to be cropping up, it is a great comfort to know that you have an impartial friend whose help you may seek without obligation.' I hardly think that it would be reasonable to construe these words as meaning 'without obligation to the bank'. At the end of the booklet there is this paragraph: '. . . We shall be delighted to make your acquaintance and to help you with your finances in every possible way.' I find that it was and is within the scope of the defendant bank's business to advise on all financial matters and that, as they did advise him, they owed a duty to the plaintiff to advise him with reasonable care and skill" [1959] 1 Q.B. 55 at 70–71, [1958] 3 All E.R. 166 at 172–173.

Holding out by reputation

2–031 This is a little more controversial since it is unclear to what extent a firm can be regarded as responsible for its own reputation. It may perhaps be characterised as a form of implied holding out—what would a potential client reasonably infer about the firm and its business from what it had learnt about them? In *Central BC Planners Ltd v Kallweit and Bizicki v Hocker*[83] a stockbroker's reputation was referred to as one of the factors (good faith, skill, etc.) which identified the nature of the duty of care it owed its clients. In *United Dominions Trust Ltd v Kirkwood*[84] Lord Denning, discussing the significance of the financial reputation of a bank, said:

> "Like many other beings, a banker is easier to recognise than to define. In case of doubt, it is, I think, permissible to look at the reputation of the firm amongst ordinary intelligent commercial men. If they recognise it as carrying on the business of banking, that should turn the scale."

In some cases "reputation" may operate to limit the firm's liability, as where it is apparent from its circumstances that it will have limited experience or resources in relation to a particular matter.[85] An investor who seeks advice from a firm whose reputation is that of an investment manager providing discretionary portfolio management services should not expect the manager to provide him as part of that service with expert advice on personal financial planning.

Holding out by act of performance

2–032 As noted above, a firm should not undertake to perform a service which it lacks the necessary skills to provide. In such a case and without any express profession of skill, the mere fact that the firm undertakes to provide the service may be enough to constitute a holding out by the firm that it is able to perform the service to the requisite standard.[86] *In Crossnan v Ward Bracewell*

---

[83] (1970) 72 W.W.R. 561; 10 D.L.R. (3d) 689, on appeal (1971) 21 D.L.R. (3d) 639, (CAN).

[84] [1966] 2 Q.B. 431, CA.

[85] *Luxmoore-May v Messanger May Baverstock* [1990] 1 W.L.R. 1009 at 1020; [1990] 1 All E.R. 1067, CA, (country auctioneer in Godalming not expected to have the same standard of skill as a leading London house such as Christies or Sothebys).

[86] See *Arthur Guinness & Co (Dublin) Ltd v The Freshfield (Owners)* [1965] P. 294, *per* Winn L.J. at 350. Guinness had not promised or held itself out to anyone as having any special skill or knowledge as to the handling of ships, but was held liable for failing properly to supervise the ship's master. The law applied a standard which was not relaxed to cater for Guinness's factual ignorance of all activities outside brewing. Since it had become owner of a ship it had to behave as a reasonable shipowner and supervise its ship's master to the same standard as a reasonable shipowner. See also *Gladwell v Steggall* (1839) 5 Bing. N.C. 733 (clergyman practising as unqualified and amateur medical man was liable for causing serious harm to patient).

SERVICE STANDARDS—CARE AND SKILL AND THE SCOPE OF THE SERVICE

& Co[87] the firm, by proceeding to offer advice in a business context on how to obtain funds, were taken to have held themselves out as persons qualified to assist the claimant on the particular matter concerned.[88]

Holding out—common practice and public standards of conduct

These are also relevant to the concept of a holding out or profession of skill. 2–033
See paras 2–026—2–027.

Internal intention of the firm irrelevant

A firm which holds itself out as having a particular skill is duty bound to 2–034
bring that skill to bear, whether or not the holding out was in fact true. The fact that the firm itself knows that the holding out is untrue or unrealistic is of no avail unless this is communicated to the client in some way (for example by means of a disclaimer or by warning the client that it does not possess a particular expertise). In *Woods v Martins Bank*,[89] the bank was liable for the skills its branch manager held it out as having, even though the holding out was prohibited by the bank's own internal procedures.

Similarly, the fact that the firm did not intend to hold itself out in the way it did, or did not intend the holding out to have the effect it did, will not alter the position unless the client realised, or should have realised, this. If an agent holds its principal out as having a particular skill, its principal will be bound by this.

Client sophistication

The nature of the firm's duties is also much affected by the skills of its client 2–035
and there is often a significant difference between the duties owed to sophisticated and unsophisticated clients. See *e.g. Brown v KMR Services Ltd; Sword-Daniels v Pitel.*[90]

---

[87] (1989) 5 P.N. 103 at 106.
[88] "In the present case, in a business setting, across the office desk, Mr McChrystal did, as I find, *hold himself out* as a person qualified to assist the plaintiff as to how he could obtain funds to pay legal costs. He need not have done so, but he chose to do so, without any qualification or disclaimer".
[89] [1959] 1 Q.B. 55 at 71–72.
[90] [1994] 4 All E.R. 385 Gatehouse J. drew a major distinction between the position of Mr Sword-Daniels, an unsophisticated and cautious investor with limited capital resources, investing to pay for his children's school fees, and Mr Brown, a successful businessman investing with a view to general profit, who took a more active and sophisticated interest in his investments and was prepared to take a certain amount of risk.

"Sophistication" is taken here as a global term covering the client's knowledge, experience, and general ability to look after his own financial affairs. In many instances these terms are used interchangeably. However, if we were to be more precise, "knowledge" can be taken as meaning special or expert knowledge relating to (as the case may be) the subject matter of the service: the nature of the services available, and/or the particular market or investment product. A client may have considerable theoretical knowledge of a matter, without much practical experience. Similarly, a client who has been doing business in a market for a long time may have experience, but still be ignorant of how the market actually works.

The client's "general competence" to look after his own affairs is a particularly important issue. In both the case law and the regulatory regime, it is often equated with general business skill and experience; but, importantly, it can also include the ability to obtain appropriate advice from others were necessary, or to make a proper assessment of the information and advice provided to him.

2–036 Factors referred to in the cases as indicators of sophistication include experience, expertise and competence, including the client's skill or experience relative to that of the firm[91]; the fact that the client was a business client and the matter is one which common sense would have told them to do as a simple matter of business[92]; the client is an experienced businessman familiar with the matters in hand who would naturally decide for himself what he wanted to do based on his view of his own interests[93]; the client is a successful business with considerable in-house expertise of the project in hand[94]; and the client has a strong business background and a track record of making own decisions based on own strategy/own investment knowledge/study of the market.[95]

Factors referred to as indicating lack of sophistication include physical and mental capacity: "an elderly widow with failing eyesight and no business experience"[96]; obviously inexperienced, ignorant and in dire need of advice[97];

---

[91] See *Ginora Investments v James Capel* (corporate finance adviser) and probably also *Drexel Burnham Lambert v Al Nasr* [1986] 1 F.T.L.R. 1 (futures broker); *Carradine Properties v DJ Freeman & Co* (1989) (1985) 1 P.N. 41, CA (law firm), *Johnson v Bingley Dyson & Finney* [1997] P.N.L.R. 392 at 408 (law firm).

[92] *Carradine Properties v DJ Freeman & Co* (1989) (1985) 1 P.N. 41, CA.

[93] *Yager v Fishman & Co* [1944] 1 All E.R. 552.

[94] *Virgin Management v De Morgan* [1996] E.G.C.S. 16, CA.

[95] *Brown v KMR Services Ltd; Sword-Daniels v Pitel and Others* [1994] 4 All E.R. 385, *Carradine Properties Ltd v DJ Freeman & Co (a firm)* (1982) 126 Sol. Jol. 157, *Stafford v Conti Commodity Services* [1981] 1 All E.R. 691 *Bankers Trust v PT Darmahla*, unreported December 1, 1995.

[96] *Lowe v Lombank Ltd [1960] 1 All E.R. 611*. The elderly widow in the case had not examined the car she was buying, would not have been able to identify any faults if she had, and did not realise that by signing the receipt she was deemed to be representing that she had examined the car and found no faults.

[97] *Carradine Properties v DJ Freeman & Co* (1989) (1985) 1 P.N. 41, CA, *Sykes v Midland Bank Executor and Trustee Co Ltd* [1971] 1 Q.B. 113 at 130, CA. In *Woods v Martins Bank Ltd and Another* [1959] 1 Q.B. 55 (Salmon J.), Mr Woods was described as having no previous

SERVICE STANDARDS—CARE AND SKILL AND THE SCOPE OF THE SERVICE

wholly unacquainted with the matters in hand[98]; lack of knowledge[99]; inability to understand the subject matter or its implications or the firm's advice[1]; lack of assets proportionate to risk[2]; impecuniosity (unreasonable to expect someone of limited resources engaged in a non-business transaction to pay for additional independent financial advice)[3]; and, generally, a transaction by a private individual without relevant business experience.[4]

Sophistication relative to the particular circumstances

Sophistication (or the lack of it) is relative to the nature of the subject matter, the service, and the parties involved. In general, private individuals of limited means, without any relevant business experience, who are investing their own or their family's personal savings, will normally constitute unsophisticated clients unless they are able to demonstrate a high level of knowledge, experience or business-type skill. A client which is acting in the course of a business, or which has a strong business background, is much more likely to be expected to know what it is doing and take responsibility for him, whether or not he has as a matter of fact the relevant knowledge or experience.

2–037

A client who knows as much as or more than the firm about a particular matter will find it difficult to justify relying on the firm's service to the exclusion of his own skill, knowledge and experience. However, the mere fact that the client is relatively sophisticated in general terms does not exclude the possibility that he is relying on the firm's skill.[5] And even a wholly unsophisticated client will be expected to take responsibility for some matters. A private customer with minimal experience of financial matters may still be treated as sophisticated enough to manage basic bank account or credit card transactions.

---

investment experience of any kind. The only reason he made the investments which he did was because his bank manager Mr Johnson advised him to do so. He had complete confidence in Mr Johnson's knowledge and skill in financial affairs, and followed his advice to the letter.

[98] *Yager v Fishman & Co* [1944] 1 All E.R. 552.

[99] *Crossnan v Ward Bracewell & Co* [1989] 5 P.N. 103; *Sykes v Midland Bank Executor and Trustee Co Ltd* [1971] 1 Q.B. 113 at 130, CA.

[1] *Booth v Davey* [1988] 138 N.J.L.R. 104, CA; *Reeves v Thrings & Long* [1996] P.N.L.R. 265, CA.

[2] *Brown v KMR Services Ltd; Sword-Daniels v Pitel and Others* [1994] 4 All E.R. 385.

[3] *Smith v Eric S Bush; Harris v Wyre Forest DC* [1989] 2 All E.R. 514, HL.

[4] Many cases including *Brown v KMR Services Ltd; Sword-Daniels v Pitel and Others* [1994] 4 All E.R. 385. *Smith v Eric S Bush; Harris v Wyre Forest DC* [1989] 2 All E.R. 514, HL, *Woods v Martins Bank* [1959] 1 Q.B. 55.

[5] In *Esso Petroleum v Mardon* [1976] 1 Q.B. 801, CA at 815 and 818, Mr Mardon was reasonably sophisticated and knowledgeable about the subject matter of the transaction in his own right. Esso's knowledge, experience and skill about the likely throughput of one of its petrol stations was, however, manifestly greater, and in that situation it was quite natural for him to act in reliance on Esso's advice, even though his own judgment was to the contrary. In *Brown v KMR Services; Sword-Daniels v Pitel* a sophisticated client was on same footing as an unsophisticated client because the firm did not tell either of them what it was doing.

Client holding out—an objective test

2–038 The sophistication of the client will depend, as far as the firm is concerned, on what it knows (or perhaps on what it should know) about the client. The cases cited regularly refer to the level of sophistication as being a matter of common sense, or as perfectly obvious one way or the other. However, in cases of doubt, what probably matters most is not that the firm has precisely identified the exact level of the client's sophistication, but that it has formed a view of the client's sophistication which is reasonable in the circumstances. If the firm formed an honest and reasonable view of the client's position, and took proper steps to reflect that position in the services it provided, the firm should not be liable if it subsequently emerges that, despite all this, that view was in fact wrong and the client was less sophisticated or knowledgeable than appeared to be the case.

In *Bankers Trust v PT Dharmala Sakti Sejahtera*[6] Mance J. discussing misrepresentation and duties of care in the context of a counterparty transaction, said:

> "it is necessary to consider the recipient's characteristics and knowledge as they appeared, or ought to have appeared, to the maker of the proposal or presentation. A recipient holding himself out as able to understand and evaluate complicated proposals would be expected to be able to do so whatever his actual abilities. These are problems on which it is commonly not necessary to focus in a commercial context. The assumption on which most business is conducted is that both parties understand, or avail themselves of advice about, the area in which they are operating and the documentation which they use. Business could not otherwise be carried on."

Similarly, in *Virgin Management Ltd v De Morgan Group*[7]; the court held that the scope of the firm's duties depended on the extent to which the client *appeared* to need advice: "The firm was under no duty to give such advice to *apparently* experienced and sophisticated commercial clients." In *Crossnan v Ward Bracewell & Co,*[8] Kennedy J. said, "If, in a business context, a solicitor offers to assist a potential client as to the possible source of funds for litigation, what he should say must depend on many factors including, for example, the knowledge which he can reasonably expect the potential client to possess." In *Clark Boyse v Mouat*[9]; Lord Jauncey said that where a client was in full command of his faculties and *apparently* aware of what he was doing the firm was under no duty to advise outside the scope of its retainer. In

---

[6] Unreported, December 1, 1995.
[7] [1996] E.G.C.S. 16, CA.
[8] [1989] 1 P.N. 103 at 106, *per* Kennedy J.
[9] [1993] 4 All E.R. 268, PC at 275; [1994] 1 A.C. 428.

Reeves v Thrings & Long.[10] Hobhouse L.J. said that a solicitor would have discharged his duty provided the client used language which would lead a reasonable person in the position of the solicitor to believe that his advice was being understood, and there was no evidence that the solicitor should reasonably have observed that his advice was not being understood.

The courts are more likely to treat a business client as bound by an appearance of sophistication than a private client. Business clients may be expected to know how to communicate at a business level. Private clients often do not.[10a]

Significance of sophistication

The client's level of sophistication goes to a variety of factors such as the general scope of the firm's duties[11]; the extent to which it can expect the client to be able to cope with sales-orientated (*i.e.* less than wholly impartial) advice[12] the extent to which the client may be expected to make its own informed decision based on the advice provided to it by the firm,[13] to follow the advice uncritically, or not to know what to do with the advice[14]; the extent to which the firm is expected, as part of its service, to enquire into the client's circumstances, or to explain matters to the client (including any risk warnings)[15]; the extent to which the firm is expected to volunteer advice which the client appears to need; and the extent to which, generally, the client may reasonably be assumed to have (or not to have) relied on the firm's advice or other services.

2–039

Thus, in the case of sales-orientated "advice", Mance J. in *Bankers Trust v PT Darmahla* said:

"A description or commendation which may obviously be irrelevant or may even serve as a warning to one recipient because of its generality,

---

[10] [1996] P.N.L.R. 265, CA.

[10a] *Ginora Investments Ltd v James Capel & Co Ltd*; *Bankers Trust v PT Darmahla*; *National Home Loans Corporation plc v Giffen Couch & Archer* [1997] 3 All E.R. 808, CA; *Omega Trust Co Ltd v Wright Son & Pepper* [1997] 18 E.G. 120, CA; *Carradine Properties v DJ Freeman & Co*; *Virgin Management Ltd v De Morgan Group plc*; *Stafford v Conti Commodity Services Ltd* [1981] 1 All E.R. 691; *Drexel Burnham Lambert International NV v Al Nasr*; *County Ltd v Girozentrale Gilbert Elliot*, CA, unreported, December 18, 1995.

[11] *Carradine Properties Ltd v DJ Freeman & Co* [1982] 126 Sol. Jol. 157; *Virgin Management Ltd v De Morgan Group plc* [1996] E.G.C.S. 16, CA; and probably also *Drexel Burnham Lambert International NV v Al Nasr* [1986] 1 F.T.L.R. 1.

[12] *Bankers Trust v PT Darmahla*, unreported December 1, 1995, and perhaps also *Ginora Investments Limited v James Capel & Co Ltd*, unreported February 2, 1995.

[13] *Bankers Trust v PT Darmahla*; *Ginora Investments Limited v James Capel & Co Ltd*; *Stafford v Conti Commodity Services Limited* [1981] 1 All E.R. 691.

[14] *Woods v Martins Bank Ltd* [1959] 1 Q.B. 55.

[15] *Yager v Fishman & Co* [1944] 1 All E.R. 552.

superficiality or laudatory nature, or because of the recipient's own knowledge and experience, may constitute a material representation if made to another less informed or sophisticated receiver. . . What is fair and adequate presentation in one context between one set of negotiating parties may be unfair or inadequate in another context. Whether there was any and if so what particular representation must thus depend upon an objective assessment of the likely effect of the proposal or presentation on the recipient".

2–040 Exclusion clauses, disclaimers, and clauses which purport to define the scope of the services provided, are likely to be less effective where an unsophisticated client is concerned. Suppose that a firm provides an advisory service to a private client, but advises the client that it is in fact providing a non-advisory service. Further, the firm asks the client to sign a form acknowledging that no advice has been given. The acknowledgement would probably be invalid, but even if it were not, the client arguably would have a cause of action against the firm for misrepresenting that the acknowledgement was a correct reflection of their relationship.

In many cases a client's lack of sophistication is taken into account without being expressly described as such. For instance, in *Crossnan v Ward Bracewell*[16-18] the court took account of the client's ignorance of the ways in which he could obtain money to finance his defence, and lack of understanding of how to make an insurance claim. This was contrasted with the ready knowledge of the firm that the client's insurer was a potential source of litigation funds. It was also implicitly recognised that the client did not have the necessary skill to extract the relevant information from the firm by asking the right questions.

Duration of the service relationship

2–041 "Duration" may be taken as meaning "how long the client relationship lasts". By "relationship" we mean a substantive relationship, and this is not necessarily the same as the contractual duration. Quite apart from the fact that some services may be provided on a non-contractual footing, the existence of a contract may not itself amount to a meaningful relationship. If a firm issues a prospective client with its standard management or broking terms, but the client never gives it any orders or instructions, the fact that the standard terms are notionally in force throughout the relevant period does not really amount to anything, because nothing is happening under them.

[16-18] [1989] P.N. 103 at 106 (Kennedy J.).

"Duration" is not a fixed concept and varies depending on the environment one is working in. For present purposes, the duration of a substantive financial service[19] may be categorised as follows:

(a) **One off or single event**—At its simplest the relationship may be confined to a one-off or single transaction or event, at a particular point in time in the sense that the transaction in question is self-contained and unique in itself, and does not carry over to other unrelated transactions.

A simple example is a customer subscribing for a collective investment scheme or life policy by sending off an application form to the product provider. Other actions that may in their own context be described as one-off include the giving by an adviser of a single piece of advice on one particular matter, or a broker implementing a one-off instruction to buy a particular security.

In futures trading, the opening and closing legs of a futures position comprise, arguably, a single transaction with two linked parts, so that a one-off transaction mandate would not be completed until the open futures position has been closed (or matched with, or netted off, or settled against);

(b) **Ongoing**—A relationship which is not purely one-off can be described as ongoing. The ongoing relationship may consist of:

(i) a single unbroken service performed over a period of time (described to here as "**continuous**"); or

(ii) a series of linked or loosely related transactions or events (described here as "**occasional**" or "**intermittent**").

The duration of the service relationship is important for a number of reasons, most of which are to do with the nature and scope of the firm's duties to its client:

Duty to be proactive

At its very simplest the duty to be proactive usually matches the client's granting of authority to the firm to exercise skilled judgment on the client's behalf. The overall implications of this duty will differ dramatically according to **2–042**

---

[19] This discussion is focused on brokerage or investment management services which consist of a series of one-off dealing transactions which if sufficiently connected will form an intermittent or continuous relationship. In a corporate finance mandate the emphasis would be somewhat different, since there the "continuous" relationship is concerned with a single (albeit long term and complex) transaction.

THE LEGAL NATURE OF THE CLIENT SERVICES RELATIONSHIP

whether the relationship is one-off, occasional or continuous.[20] A single event transaction (though "continuous" within its own limited frame of reference) is usually too specific for the duty of proactivity to hold any surprises—of course the broker must do its best to execute its client's order; but that is pretty much the beginning and end of it. The duty of proactivity is most significant in continuous duration relationships, and intermittent relationships may be regarded as something of a halfway house between the two.

A duty to be proactive requires the firm to anticipate and go beyond specific client instructions and take the initiative to act. This may, at its simplest, consist of deciding the best price at which to fill the client's order. At a more complicated level it may involve soliciting instructions, volunteering advice, or keeping the client advised of the progress of his mandate and any material developments.

This principle is particularly apparent in tort cases, which distinguish between the limited duties in a one-off misrepresentation situation (there is no liability for a mere failure to act[21]) and the more proactive *Hedley Byrne* concept of a firm assuming a positive duty to act because of the existence of a special (client) relationship.[22] See para.2–010 (acting in the client's interest).

2–043 A firm is also under a general duty to keep its client informed of its progress in performing a continuous mandate.[23] This may include drawing the client's attention to matters which are important to the client. An estate agent acting for a buyer must notify its client if a better offer is received than the one he has communicated to his client prior to exchange of contracts[24] or of any new offers received generally.[25] A law firm acting for the buyer of real estate must notify its client if it discovers a defect in title,[26] or a right of way

---

[20] Lord Devlin in *Hedley Byrne* [1963] 2 All E.R. 575 at 611; [1964] A.C. 465 at 529 recognised that a tort duty relationship may be a *general* one, such as that of a solicitor and client (though the situation where a solicitor has responsibility for all a client's legal affairs is less and less common) or banker and customer, or arise specifically in relation to a *particular* transaction. See also *Henderson v Merrett* [1994] 3 All E.R. 506 at 520, *per* Lord Goff.

[21] *Smith v Littlewoods Organisation Ltd* [1987] 2 A.C. 241 at 247, *per* Lord Goff.

[22] In *General Accident Fire & Life Assurance Corp Ltd v Tanter (The Zephyr)* [1985] 2 Lloyds Rep. 529 at 538 Mustill L.J. described liability in negligence as applying to an "obligation to avoid doing something, or to avoid doing something badly . . . doing something badly may often involve *a neglect to carry out an act* which would turn bad performance into adequate performance."

[23] *Groom v Crocker* [1939] 1 K.B. 194 at 222 [1938] 2 All E.R. 394 at 413, CA: Scott L.J., giving a *robust* description of the duties of a solicitor giving professional advice to a private client under a continuous advisory retainer, said: "It is an incident of that duty that the solicitor should consult with his client in all questions of doubt which do not fall within the express or implied discretion left him . . ."

[24] *Keppel v Wheeler* [1927] 1 K.B. 577.

[25] *Johnson v Kearley* [1908] 2 K.B. 514.

[26] *Pilkington v Wood* [1953] Ch.770.

54

over property[27] An insurance broker must inform its client of any changes in the terms of insurance cover on its renewal.[28] It should notify its client as soon as possible, and in unambiguous terms, if the client becomes uninsured.[29]

A firm is not generally required to remind its client of advice it has previously given.[30] However, if the firm has given wrong advice there may be a duty to correct it, particularly while it is still engaged in advising the firm in relation to the same transaction.[31] In *R v Investors Compensation Scheme ex parte Weyell*[32] the court said *obiter* that brokers were under a continuing duty to correct erroneous advice they had given, and that this extended to a duty to correct the mismanagement of an investment fund.

Duty to accept further instructions from the same client

Each instruction which constitutes a single event service or a new phase of an occasional service can be accepted or rejected by the firm on a case by case basis as it sees fit. With a continuous service, however, such as an investment management or a corporate finance mandate, once the basic mandate has been established, the firm may be required to act on any further instructions which are given within the scope of that service, if they are an implicit or necessary part of the performance of the service.[33]   **2–044**

---

[27] *Piper v Daybell Court & Cooper & Co* (1969) 210 E.G. 1047.

[28] *Mint Security Ltd v Blair* [1982] 1 Lloyds Rep. 188 (Staughton J.).

[29] *London Borough of Bromley v Ellis* [1971] 1 Lloyds Rep. 97.

[30] *Yager v Fishman & Co* [1944] 1 All E.R. 552. In *Midland Bank v Hett Strubbs* the fact that, some time after the original advice, the law firm concerned was instructed to advise on new and unrelated matters did not oblige it to revisit previous work, unless there was something in the new instructions which should have caused it to look again at that original work.

[31] See also *Ginora v James Capel* (corporate finance adviser); *Woods v Martins Bank* (investment adviser), *Midland Bank Trust Company v Greene* [1978] 3 All E.R. 555 (solicitor) and duty to correct misrepresentations generally.

[32] [1994] 1 All E.R. 525, PC.

[33] In *Joachimson v Swiss Bank Corporation* [1921] 3 K.B. 110, CA, Aitken L.J. discussed this issue in the context of a deposit-taking relationship. He said at 127: "It is said on the one hand that [a current account] is a simple contract of loan; it is admitted that there is added, or super added, an obligation of the bank to honour the customer's drafts to any amount not exceeding the credit balance at any material time, but it is contended that this added obligation does not affect the main contract. The bank has borrowed the money and is under the ordinary obligation of a borrower to repay. The lender can sue for his debt whenever he pleases. I am unable to accept this contention. I think that there is only one contract made between the bank and its customer." He then went on to list a variety of services implicit in the relationship which included receiving payments into the account, payment out of the account on the instructions of the customer and the need for the customer to demand payment before the bank was obligated to pay out to it. Aitken L.J.'s approach was cited with approval in *Tai Hing Cotton Mill Ltd v Liu Chong Hing Bank* [1986] A.C. 80, PC at 956.

THE LEGAL NATURE OF THE CLIENT SERVICES RELATIONSHIP

Different effects in contract an tort

- *Categorisation of services*

2–045 Duration is a relevant factor in the tort/contract balance in business relationships. A long-term service relationship is usually contractual (though it may also have a tort overlay). Single and occasional relationships may be contractual too, but can also arise outside contract in a purely tortious context, as where a firm gives ad hoc advice as part of a business relationship but without accepting a formal contractual mandate.

- *Compensation claims*

A litigation cause of action, and its related limitation period, can be much affected by the duration of the relationship.

The nature of any claim and measure of compensation involved may vary according to duration.[34] For example, if each transaction is single event, any action for breach of duty must be brought on a case-by-case basis. In a continuous management service the claimant may also be able to assert that, even though individual transactions within of the service were competently executed, the overall service was negligent.

The limitation period within which a claim may be brought differs in practice according to whether the cause of action arises from a single (continuous) contract, or a series of separate contracts with the same party, or the occurrence of a breach of tortious duty (in which case the limitation period will follow tortious principles irrespective of the overall relationship duration). To oversimplify somewhat, a contractual cause of action is actionable for six years after the time of the breach of contract, which may be easy enough to spot in a one-off transaction but much harder in the context of a continuous service. The limitation period for an action in tort, in contrast, runs for three years from the time when the client should reasonably have been aware of the loss giving rise to the cause of action.

---

[34] As regards compensation, The normal tortious assumption is that a successful claimant is to be compensated by being put back into the position he would have been in if the wrongful act had not occurred. However, it may be necessary to distinguish between an act which should never have taken place at all, and one which should have been performed in a different manner. In the latter case it would be illogical to ask what would have happened if advice had not been given, where the substance of the claim is that the firm is liable for *not giving the right advice*. On this line of logic, if no advice had been given, not only would there have been no loss, and no assumption of responsibility either.

This sort of confusion might be avoided if it is first established whether the breach complained of relates to a positive or to a negative duty. If a positive duty has been breached, trying to put the claimant into the position he would have been in if nothing had been done is simply compounding the breach.

It follows from this that, in appropriate cases, compensation can be awarded in tort on an expectation loss as well as on a reliance loss basis. Thus, in *White v Jones* [citation] Lord Goff said: "I do not consider that damages for loss of an expectation are excluded in cases of negligence arising under the principle in *Hedley Byrne*, simply because the cause of action is classified as tortious."

SERVICE STANDARDS—CARE AND SKILL AND THE SCOPE OF THE SERVICE

Duty in an occasional service relationship to take account of previous dealings

A single event transaction is self-contained and therefore unlikely to give **2–046** rise to any subsequent or related duties beyond the obvious scope of the transaction itself.

An intermittent or occasional course of dealing also takes effect on a transaction-by-transaction basis, with the customer choosing each time whether to deal with the firm and without the firm assuming any continuous duties beyond the scope of the particular transaction. In particular the firm has no duty to act on a new matter until it is given (and accepts) new instructions, and no duty to take an active role after the particular matter has concluded.

However, once a new matter is under discussion or entered into, the previous course of dealing between the parties becomes a significant factor. The more regular the relationship, the more likely it is that knowledge and practices will be treated as carried over by implication from one contract to the next one. The scope for the relationship can then extend to include information and matters which each party is aware of from previous dealings, both in terms of looking at the past pattern of the service provided (which may mean that the same pattern will be implied into the current dealings) as well as matters such a disclosures and risk warnings, or the services the firm is capable of providing.

Duties of confidentiality survive the termination of a particular piece of **2–047** business and may become newly significant whenever a situation arises in which previously obtained confidential information may be misused. Fiduciary duties, in contrast, should not normally survive the end of a single event or continuous relationship.[35] The same should be true of the component parts of an intermittent relationship. In the intervals between transactions there should be no possibility of a conflict arising. But an intermittent relationship with one client may be enough in itself to give rise to a potential conflict with a current client.[36]

---

[35] *Prince Jefri Bolkiah v KPMG* [1999] 2 A.C. 222, *per* Millett L.J.: ". . .the Court's intervention [to protect a past client] is founded not on the avoidance of any perception of possible impropriety but on the protection of confidential information . . .. It is otherwise where the court's intervention is sought by an existing client, for a fiduciary cannot act at the same time both for and against the same client . . .. His disqualification has nothing to do with the confidentiality of client information. It is based on the inescapable conflict of interest which is inherent in the situation."

[36] In the Takeover Panel's Ruling of July 1997 relating to Abbey National plc's offer for Cater Allen Holdings, Kleinwort Benson were acting as corporate finance advisers to Cater Allen. The takeover panel expressed some concern that Kleinwort also had a close, recent and continuing advisory relationship with Abbey National, and there was therefore a concern that their advice to Cater Allen might reasonably be thought to have been influenced by their corporate advisory relationship which they might have had, or continued to have, with Abbey National.

Duration in the investment management markets

2–048 Investment management should always be a continuous service, beginning when the firm receives its management mandate, and ending only when the mandate is terminated. During this period the firm is expected actively to manage the portfolio. This is integral to discretionary management.

Execution broking is normally an intermittent but ongoing service of this sort, with often quite extensive elements of continuity between sequences of related transactions. Larger customers with a significant amount of business to place may use a range of different brokers according to factors such as the quality and efficiency of execution, specialist insight into particular sectors or markets, ability to fill large orders quickly, and the quality of the firm's research and other support services.

Advisory services are more prone to uncertainty. One-off advice may occur where a broker approaches an investor with a particular sales idea, or a freelance adviser puts investment proposals to the investment committee of a fund. It will become intermittent if a track record of such dealings builds up. So long as there is no commitment to give ongoing advice, but the service consists merely of volunteering advice as and when the firm sees fit, it is likely to stop short of becoming a continuous service. But beyond a certain point an intermittent advisory service may become a continuous one, with the adviser having a continuous duty to keep the client's investments under review and advise proactively.

2–049 Relevant factors in any transition from one-off, through intermittent or occasional to continuous (in addition of course to the terms of the contractual mandate),will be the relative importance of the firm's understanding of its client, the extent of the client's reliance on the carry over of that understanding from one matter to another; any agency powers (including apparent authority) which the provider holds or appears to hold on a continuing basis for the client; and whether or not the firm has continuing possession or control of the clients' assets.

Continuous advisory management can be difficult to distinguish from intermittent advice. In the early days of regulation, The Securities Association (TSA) specifically stated that its suitability rule did not impose a continuing duty to advise a private customer on suitability.[37] Subsequently TSA identified this as the cause of some confusion, with some brokers, who did not review their client's portfolios on an ongoing basis, still holding themselves out as providing a continuous service. This issue was addressed in the SFA rules adopted in 1991,[38] which make it clear that a firm which had assumed the role of an advisory manager had a continuing duty to keep the suitability of a private client's portfolio under review.

---

[37] *The Securities Association—Synopsis of Conduct of Business Rules,* (July 1987), p.18.
[38] SFA, r.5–31(3)(a).

PIA Regulatory Update 53,[39] looking at same issue, offered the following indicia for the existence of a continuous advisory management relationship:

- the firm accepts responsibility for the composition of the portfolio on a continuing basis;

- there is a clearly identifiable body of assets belonging to the client over which the firm has control; as where such assets are held in the firm's nominee company; and/or

- The firm is proactive in soliciting changes to the portfolio and making recommendations for such changes.

The charging of an annual management fee, or retainer, as distinct from a commission on individual trades, is also a good indicator that the firm has assumed responsibility for providing a continuous management service.

A financial planning adviser may give advice, or arrange the purchase of a contract, on a single event or at best an intermittent basis. Where the advice represents a full financial planning exercise it is probably occasional rather than continuous. The firm is not under a duty to volunteer advice on an ongoing basis, any more than the investor is under a duty to seek advice from that particular adviser to the exclusion of any other. But where there is an ongoing service the adviser will be under a duty to take account of its previous dealings, in giving any subsequent advice. It is possible in some cases where the relationship is particularly developed so that the adviser has, in practice, control of the investor's financial affairs, that this might give rise to a continuous relationship, with previous dealings providing an active context for subsequent advice.

---

[39] July 1998.

CHAPTER 3

REGULATION AND THE PROMOTION OF INVESTMENT MANAGEMENT SERVICES

Stuart Willey, Financial Services Authority

Overview of FSA Regulation of Investment Management

3–001 This Chapter begins by examining the different legal and regulatory controls applied to individual portfolio management on the one hand, and on the other, the promotion of investment funds by which clients participate in pooled or collective investment management. It then goes as to the review the principles which apply to the marketing of such services and products.

The Regulatory Regime for Investment Management Services

Discretionary portfolio management

3–002 Discretionary portfolio management is defined by reference to article 37 of the Regulated Activities Order ("RAO"), and secondary legislation made by the Treasury.[1] This identifies the activity of managing assets belonging to another in circumstances involving the exercise of discretion as a "specified activity" if the assets include securities or contractually based investments. The most obvious example of "discretionary management" is where a firm is appointed to manage a securities portfolio on behalf of a customer. Normally the firm will be appointed as manager with authority to take decisions as to the acquisition or sale of particular securities within the portfolio. Some firms also take custody of the property under management. This will normally involve the firm (or more often its nominee) having legal title to the shares and other assets being managed, but the firm is nevertheless normally

---

[1] Financial and Services and Markets Act 2000 (Regulated Activities) Order 2001 (SI 2001/544) (the "RAO").

THE REGULATORY REGIME FOR INVESTMENT MANAGEMENT SERVICES

regarded as managing investments "belonging to another" given that its customers will beneficially own the property being managed. This can, for example, describe the position of managing trustees who may have legal title to a collection of investments on behalf of a range of beneficiaries with diverse interests in the trust property. As such, discretionary management may embrace arrangements which also involve the type of "collective" ownership of assets under common management which is the hallmark of a collective investment scheme. Where this occurs the collective investment scheme analysis or classification predominates, at least in relation to the way the firm may promote participation in the scheme to potential investors and customers. See paras 3–004 *et seq.*, below.

Discretionary management must involve some degree of authority to deal with the assets being delegated to the manager. That said, regulatory approaches also recognise what is termed as "non-discretionary" management where the firm has no such authority but instead will act on buy and sell orders given to it by its customer,[2] usually based on advice previously given by the firm to its client under the same management arrangement.

Discretionary portfolio management is not confined to management for private individuals but can describe and include management conducted for corporate or institutional clients including the management of investment funds and pension funds. A firm will not be conducting discretionary management where it manages its own assets or, for example, where it manages assets belonging to another company in the group.[3] This is relevant for example in the case of investment trust companies which either manage their own assets or arrange for another group company to do so.

The rights of those clients whose assets are the subject of discretionary portfolio management by a manager are derived from the agreement between the client and the appointed manager (by contrast a collective investment scheme results in investors acquiring a proprietary right in the subject matter of the scheme as distinct from a direct relationship with the scheme manager). **3–003**

Collective investment schemes

A "collective investment scheme" is a wholly statutory and to an extent, artificial, concept and construct. It performs a number of functions. It: **3–004**

- identifies investment vehicles which may fall within a range of authorised fund structures which can obtain regulatory approval;

---

[2] See for example the current FSA definition of *investment manager* in the *FSA Handbook Glossary*.
[3] RAO, art.69(5).

61

- identifies a very wide and flexible range of investment vehicles which, not being companies, are not subject to constraints applicable to the public offering of corporate securities and allows what amounts to a modified public offering regime to be applied instead;

- identifies managers which because they are responsible for the operation of schemes (or because they have custody of the assets) require additional or special regulatory controls to be applied to them.

The term "collective investment scheme" is defined in s.235 of the Financial Services and Markets Act 2000 ("FSMA") as meaning:

"... any arrangements with respect to property of any description including money, the purpose or effect of which is to enable persons taking part in the arrangements (whether by becoming owners of the property or any part of it or otherwise) to participate in or receive profits or income arising from the acquisition, holding, management or disposal of the property or sums paid out of such profits or income,"

"... the arrangements must be such that the persons who are to participate ("participants") do not have day to day control over the management of property, whether or not they have the right to be consulted or to give directions,"

and:

"The arrangements must also have either or both of the following characteristics—

(a) the contributions of the participants and the profits or income out of which the payments are to be made are pooled;

(b) the property is managed as a whole by or on behalf of the operator of the scheme."

The key characteristics of a collective investment scheme are ones which fit the circumstances commonly found in pooled or fund management. The "participants" (the investors) "participate" in "arrangements" maintained by the manager for the "management of property" (the fund assets) with a view to sharing in the profits or losses generated by the fund—the investor's contributions being "pooled". Discretionary management for a single client will not normally involve any pooling of the customer's contributions and nor will there be any collective investment of property. FSMA, s.235 catches a very wide variety of investment funds ranging from conventional "managed" portfolios comprising a mixture of equities, debt securities and other assets through to exotic schemes such as schemes for investment in ostrich farming.

The width of the collective investment scheme definition is cut back by a **3–005**
number of exclusions set out in secondary legislation.[4] This is not the place
to examine the exclusions in any detail but the following exclusions are worth
noting:

- individual investment management arrangements;

- contracts of insurance;

- occupational and personal pensions;

- bodies corporate (other than an open-ended investment company).

The first exclusion for individual investment management arrangements is
directed at what are sometimes termed common or parallel investment
schemes where there is some common management of property insofar as a
firm manages a collection of individual portfolios on the basis of identical
investment decisions. Each individual investor retains a discrete entitlement
to a collection of assets but the composition of that portfolio or fund will be
governed by "bulk" decisions made by the manager affecting a large number
of investors.[5] This exclusion is relevant to, for instance, the management of
PEP and ISA portfolios which are managed on the basis that the investor will
acquire a discrete interest in a set of assets which are then the subject of common management of a kind which would otherwise bring the arrangements
within the CIS definition in s.235 of the FSMA. Taking such arrangements
outside the CIS definition means that the promotion of such services is on
the same footing as individual discretionary management.

The exclusion in the CIS Order of bodies corporate takes out of the CIS
regime (and the consequential promotional restrictions) all capital raising
through companies (other than an open-ended investment company) as well
as operating companies formed for investment purposes.[6] Instead, the
prospectus regime applies, governed by the Public Offer of Securities Regulations (in the case of public offers as defined by those regulations)[7] or the
Listing Rules if a company's securities are to be "listed" as meeting the criteria for official listing. As explained below, this is an important exclusion when
considered alongside the treatment of promotions via prospectuses in the
financial promotions regime (see para.3–016 below). One effect of the new
financial promotion regime is therefore to confer on the promotion of company shares a different, and in some respects lighter, approach than applies in
the case of unregulated collective investment schemes.

---

[4] Financial Services and Markets Act 2000 (Collective Investment Schemes) Order 2001 (SI
    2001/1062) (the "CIS Order").
[5] *ibid.*, Sch.3, para.1.
[6] *ibid.*, Sch.3, para.21.
[7] Public Offer of Securities Regulations 1995 (SI 1995 1537) (the "POS regulations").

3–006 Deciding in any particular case whether an investment fund vehicle is a "body corporate" and, if so, whether it is an "open-ended investment company" is not always easy. Where the vehicle does come within the definition of open-ended company, the vehicle and the means of promoting it fall within the CIS regime rather than the company prospectus regime. In the case of a body corporate formed outside the UK the FSA has said that whether or not any particular overseas legal person or entity is a "body corporate" will depend upon the law applicable in the country or territory in which it is constituted. However, the question of whether the body so constituted is an open-ended investment company must be decided according to the tests set out in s.236 of the FSMA).[8] A non-UK investment vehicle which is a body corporate with a closed-ended investment structure will, when publicly offering its (unlisted) shares for the first time in the UK, need to comply with the POS regulations.[9]

Under FSMA "financial promotion" extends to all forms of promotion including what may be said in the course of conversation with a view to soliciting interest and the attention of potential customers. Financial promotion is not merely restricted to how—in a conventional sense—a firm advertises itself but can, in some cases, go so far as to constrain the ability of advisers to mention in the course of conversation the availability of services and products so called "real time" communications. This aspect of the regime was previously regulated via "cold-calling" restrictions and can, for example, prevent consumers from being approached on an unsolicited basis.

The law and regulation applicable to the promotion of investment management is dependent in particular on whether the management to be carried on for the purpose of:

(a)   Individual portfolio management; or

(b)   Managing a collective investment scheme; and if so whether a regulated fund; or an unregulated fund.

The regulatory controls applied to (a), the promotion of individual discretionary management, are analogous to those which apply in the case of advice and recommendations given to customers in respect of the acquisition or sale of an investment. A firm must, for example, take account of the objectives and risk appetite of the customer in deciding on the parameters of a particular portfolio composition and subsequently in acting with discretion in making buy and sell decisions. At the outset these obligations are reflected in requirements necessitating customer agreements, and as part of this, the delivery of specific and, in some instances, tailored risk warnings. The FSA's

---

[8]   See FSA Authorisation manual, App.2, 2.3.6G.
[9]   This assumes that the vehicle also has "share capital" and arguably is the preferred approach in cases of doubt.

THE REGULATORY REGIME FOR INVESTMENT MANAGEMENT SERVICES

rules contemplate some degree of correlation between the decisions taken by discretionary managers and the needs and objectives of the particular customers whose portfolios are affected by them. The regulatory scheme is therefore one in which the obligations of FSA firms can be classified along with those obligations which relate to the provision of professional services to individual clients. This is a model in which clients are likely to have legally enforceable expectations as to standards of conduct in the delivery of the service, these expectations being generated primarily by the contractual terms entered into between the firm and customer and in particular by the standard of care and skill which the firm professed to have and/or undertook to exercise.

By contrast, the regulatory approach adopted to the promotion of investment management carried on in the context of a "collective" or "pooled" investment scheme (commonly referred to as a "fund") proceeds from the characterisation of any investor's interest in such a scheme as a security or commodity. And from this proceeds the application of promotional controls, which largely focus on the suitability of the security for the investor. The managed fund is "commoditised" such that its promotion, if sold on the basis of advice, is governed by its suitability for the client or, if not, is governed by the need for adequate disclosure as to nature of the fund and any factors which may make it more or less suitable for different types of investor. And, within this approach, regulators have constructed a structural divide between collective investment schemes which can have an "authorised" or "recognised" status, and unregulated funds which cannot. Authorised and recognised funds enjoy the most liberal promotional regime. The regime applied to unregulated funds is, by comparison, complex and restrictive.

3–007

The financial promotion restrictions

The FSMA contains two related schemes for the control of the promotion of investment management services. The financial promotion regime established by s.21 of the FSMA establishes an overarching restriction on making financial promotions by unauthorised persons. A person who contravenes s.21 commits a criminal offence. In addition a controlled agreement entered into in consequence of a breach of s.21 is unenforceable, subject to the discretion of the court.[10]

3–008

A "financial promotion" is a communication made in the course of business involving an invitation or inducement to engage in investment activity.[11] The latter is in turn defined as meaning entering into or offering to enter into an agreement, the making or performance of which by either party constitutes a controlled activity. These are defined in secondary legislation made by

---

[10] FSMA, s.30.
[11] FSMA, s.21(1).

REGULATION AND THE PROMOTION OF INVESTMENT MANAGEMENT SERVICES

HM Treasury[12] to include the activities normally associated with discretionary portfolio management:

- managing investments, safeguarding and administration of investments[13]

- advising on investments and arranging deals in investments.[14]

A person who makes a financial promotion in respect of either of these activities commits a criminal offence unless:

- the person concerned is an authorised person; or

- the content of the promotion is approved by an authorised person; or

- the promotion falls within one of the exclusions specified by the Treasury.[15]

Authorised persons are free of the s.21 financial promotion restriction but the exclusions made by the Treasury are nonetheless important because they are relevant to the scope of the rules made by the FSA. The basic approach is that the FSA does not apply its financial promotion rules (Chapter 3 of the Conduct of Business sourcebook—"COB") to promotions which are excluded by the Financial Promotion Order ("FPO") and which could therefore be communicated by an unauthorised person without contravening s.21 of the FSMA.[16] So a firm should always consider whether a promotion is restricted at all having regard to the list of exclusions in the FPO.

3–009   The second statutory scheme is derived from s.238 of FSMA applicable to authorised persons and provides that an authorised person must not communicate an invitation or inducement to participate in a collective investment scheme. A contravention by an authorised person of this prohibition is not a criminal offence and does render any resulting agreement presumptively unenforceable. A contravention does however confer a statutory right of action for damages for anyone who, as a result of the contravention, suffers loss.[17] This comprehensive prohibition is then lifted in three cases:

- an authorised unit trust scheme;

- a scheme constituted as an open-ended investment company; and

- a recognised scheme.[18]

---

[12] Financial Services and Markets Act 2000 (Financial Promotion) Order 2001 (SI 2001/1335) (the Financial Promotion Order" or the "FPO").

[13] *ibid.*, art.4, sch.1, paras 5 and 6.

[14] *ibid.*, paras 4 and 7.

[15] FSMA, s.21(2) and (6).

[16] COB, 3.2.4 R and Table 3.2.5 R.

[17] FSMA, s.241.

[18] *ibid.*, s.238(4).

66

THE REGULATORY REGIME FOR INVESTMENT MANAGEMENT SERVICES

These three excluded categories of scheme are essentially those which have regulatory approval as to their design, including as to the spread of investment risk and the ability of investors to liquidate their holding by reference to the net asset value of the property in the scheme.[19] A collective investment scheme which is not an authorised scheme or a recognised scheme cannot be promoted by an authorised firm unless the promotion satisfies an exclusion found in secondary legislation made by the Treasury.[20] It is this legislation which governs and fashions the scope within which it is possible for firms to promote unregulated collective investment schemes. It not being possible for the FSA itself to enlarge on the scope of such promotion to the general public.[21] So although the FSA can go beyond the Treasury in permitting authorised persons to promote unregulated schemes, it may only do so in the case of promotions made to relatively limited types or numbers of persons.

The FSA may authorise (and hence allow more or less free promotion of) any collective investment scheme which meets the residual statutory criteria as to form and spread of investment risk,[22] but in practice it has made only relatively limited provision for schemes which extend beyond the confines of the UCITS Directive.[23]

A further general point is that the FSA disapplies many of its conduct of business rules in relation to activities carried on by firms with or for customers who are judged able to look after their own interests. For the most part, this judgment is imposed upon firms and through a mandated system of customer classification which results in so-called private customers (who attract the highest degree of protection) being distinguished from intermediate customers and market-counterparties.[24] So for example, most of the FSA's financial promotion rules are disapplied in the case of promotions to a market counterparty or intermediate customer—with additional provisions for promotions for unregulated schemes and where a firm approves a financial promotion of communication by another firm.[25] The FSA has also made provision whereby a private customer may, if certain criteria are met, be treated as sufficiently expert to enable them to be classified as an intermediate customer.[26] The upshot of this customer classification is that in the case

---

[19] The design and investment criteria will be derived from the UCITS Directive (85/611), FSA for certain non-UCITS schemes or third country law which is considered to afford equivalent or otherwise adequate protection for investors.

[20] Financial Services and Markets Act 2000 (Promotion of Collective Investment Schemes) (Exemptions) Order 2001 (SI 2001/1060).

[21] See the terms of s.238(5) of the FSMA.

[22] The FSA is limited to approving schemes which take the form of a unit trust or which can be registered as an open-ended investment company; in either event the scheme must have as its purpose the aim of spreading investment risk.

[23] Although this is now under consideration by the FSA, see CP 185.

[24] See generally *COB*, 4.1.

[25] *ibid.*, 3.2.4 R and para.(1) of Table 3.2.5 R.

[26] See *ibid.*, 4.1.9 R.

67

of institutional management for clients, who are not private customers, few if any financial promotion rules will apply.

Promotion of discretionary management and collective investment schemes compared

3–010 Distinguishing between discretionary portfolio management and the management of a collective investment scheme is important for the purpose of determining the type and intensity of the regulatory controls applied to those wishing to promote the service to the public or a particular sector of the public. Having considered the classification of investment management services and investment funds it is possible to examine how the financial promotion regime applies in practice to the various forms in which investment management may be offered. The most obvious concern to the investment manager being the extent to which itself and others will be able to approach potential investors and clients and stimulate interest in the service or fund.

Discretionary portfolio management

3–011 The lightest controls are imposed upon investment management which can be classified as individual discretionary portfolio management. As already noted the FSA's financial promotion rules are largely disapplied in respect of promotions made to intermediate customers and market counterparties. Accordingly, few if any controls are applied where a firm promotes its investment management services to potential institutional clients. This will include pension fund trustees where the size criteria (for classification as an intermediate customer) are satisfied.[27]

The promotion of discretionary management services to private customers is not subject to any significant restriction (for example as to the customer's sophistication or net worth) but a management service offered in the form of a broker fund (a fund of a life assurance company or of a collective investment scheme which will be managed by an advisory firm for the benefit of its clients) cannot be promoted via a direct offer financial promotion.[28] A firm must also avoid making an unsolicited "real time" financial promotion in respect of discretionary management services if the firm were to contemplate the portfolio including "non-readily realisable" securities or packaged products which are classified as geared products. Some care is therefore needed

---

[27] The trustee of an occupational pension scheme with at least 50 members and assets under management of at least £10m.

[28] *i.e.* a promotion which includes or comprises a contractual offer by which the customer can commit to acquiring a product or service—COB, 3.9.5 R.

when seeking to speak to potential new clients[29] about discretionary management services if these might reasonably be expected to involve the firm in acquiring securities which are not regularly traded on an exchange, which qualifies a security as "readily realisable".[30] The FSA requires that a firm intending to manage investments on a discretionary basis for a private customer must conclude a client agreement with the customer and must take reasonable care to ensure that the client has a proper opportunity to consider its terms.[31] There are also a number of special terms which are required to be included in the agreement when management terms are being provided. These requirements are primarily to do with the nature of the client service being provided rather than regulation of marketing or financial promotion.

Authorised schemes

The promotion of a regulated collective scheme is also free of any significant restriction. FSMA, s.238 lifts the CIS promotion restriction in respect of authorised and recognised funds. The authorised funds are unit trust schemes and open-ended investment companies which are authorised by the FSA and which fall within the more general classification of "packaged products". There is no restriction on authorised persons making an unsolicited real-time communication provided the packaged product is not what is termed a "higher volatility fund" (a geared futures and options scheme or any other scheme where the investment proposed investment policies as to derivatives is likely to result in significantly amplified movements in unit prices).[32]

3–012

The types of funds which the FSA currently authorises are as set out in s.5 of the CIS sourcebook. They range from funds that satisfy the requirements of the UCITS Directive[33] (securities schemes and warrant schemes) through to non-UCITS funds such as money market and futures and options funds and property funds. The UCITS Directive has recently undergone amendment to increase the range of permissible funds, these changes will take effect in February 2004.[34] A fund which complies with the UCITS Directive can take advantage of a single market passport permitting it to be marketed in other EEA States without having to seek any further authorisation. A UCITS scheme must make a prospectus available to potential investors— although there is no obligation that it be actually supplied to incoming investors.[35] In practice the marketing of UCITS in any EEA State is also

---

[29] This restriction does not apply if the firm is able to take advantage of any of the exemptions offered in the FPO (*COB*, 3.2.5 R).

[30] See FSA *Glossary*.

[31] COB, 4.2.7.

[32] *ibid.*, 3.10.3 R and FSA *Glossary*.

[33] See para.3–009, n.19 above.

[34] Amending Directive (2001/108); and FSA CP 135.

[35] Under the provisions of Amending Directive (2001/107) it will become necessary to distribute a "simplified prospectus".

subject to local promotional rules although these cannot detract from the ability to market with the benefit of the passport.[36]

The scope for regulated or authorised funds to take advantage of relatively freer promotional controls will be extended if the FSA carries through the proposals set out in its Consultative Paper 185. This is because it is proposing to enlarge upon the range of non-UCITS funds which it will be prepared to authorise and which will be capable of promotion to private customers on the same basis as UCITS funds. The FSA also proposes to introduce an entirely new breed of so-called "non-retail" funds which will be permitted a much freer and broader investment policy but such schemes will not be open to subscription by private customers, their promotion will be similar to that described below for unregulated schemes. See the further discussion of this initiative in Chapter 4.

Unregulated schemes

3–013   Unregulated (or unauthorised) collective investment schemes are, by comparison, subject to quite onerous promotional restrictions. These apply not only to unauthorised persons but also to authorised persons—such as the fund manager and third party intermediaries and brokers. It is not possible for the FSA to lift or modify the restrictions in a way which would result in such schemes being capable of being promoted generally to the public.[37]

One general observation is that the financial promotion restriction does not prevent an interested potential investor from undertaking their own research and making an approach to an unregulated scheme. The problem, however, is that the restriction does not make it easy for unregulated schemes to advertise their existence, and left to themselves investors may find it difficult to obtain sufficient information to research the market.

The extent and degree of the restriction imposed by the FSMA in respect of unregulated schemes is perhaps explicable by reference to the very wide range of investment vehicles which may be caught by the CIS definition. In practice, collective investment schemes are used as a means of capital raising for a variety of enterprises. This includes, for example, collective investment in joint venture funds, investment in theatre productions, blood-stock and property investment. The unregulated CIS structure is one means by which small and medium-sized enterprises can gain access to sources of capital outside the conventional senior or junior securities markets. Hedge funds (although mainly constituted outside the United Kingdom) normally fall to be classified as unregulated collective investment schemes.

3–014   The CIS (Promotion Order) ("CIS (PO)") sets out the way in which the regime applies to authorised persons. It does not contain any general

---

[36]   Art.44, see para.3–009, n.19, above.
[37]   FSMA, s.238(5).

permission for the promotion of unrecognised schemes. The restriction is lifted in a number of cases such as any communication which is made only to a person who can reasonably be regarded as an "investment professional".[38] But the prescribed descriptions of such persons is relatively limited. There is an exclusion for "one-off unsolicited real time communications" but the conditions for satisfying this include the communicator believing on reasonable grounds that the recipient understands the risks associated with engaging in the investment activities to which the communication relates; the communication must not be part of any "organised marketing campaign".[39]

With a view to making the regime more accessible to persons who could be expected to look after their own interests, the government, in the course of establishing the new FSMA regime, introduced two relatively novel exclusions in respect of all non-real time communications and solicited real-time communications to "certified high net-worth individuals".

High net worth is put at an annual income of not less that £100,000 or net assets of not less that £250,000. The "certificate" must be signed by the individual's accountant or employer. The scheme which is promoted must not be one which could expose the recipient to a liability to pay or contribute more than he has invested. The scheme must invest wholly or predominantly in shares of an unlisted company[40] so that it is, in effect, aimed at unrecognised schemes with a private equity focus.

Additionally, the CIS (PO) introduced the idea of a certified sophisticated investor. This is a person who holds a certificate which is signed by an authorised person and which confirms that the person holding the certificate is sufficiently knowledgeable to understand the risks associated with participating in unregulated schemes. This corresponds loosely with the "expert customer" categorisation available to authorised firms (see further below). The financial promotion restriction is lifted entirely for such communications to sophisticated investors. However, one practical drawback is that the person operating the scheme which is the subject of communication cannot also be the person who has signed the certificate of "sophistication". Furthermore, authorised persons may be reluctant to take on the risk of signing a certificate, or may charge a prohibitive price for doing so. The net result is that unrecognised schemes may not find it easy to access persons who possess the necessary and qualifying degree of sophistication—in practice the scheme promoter may well not know who they are and for their part authorised firms may be reluctant to entertain the idea of signing a certificate. One possibility might be the creation of a central register of sophisticated and "certified" persons.

---

[38] CIS (PO), article 14—includes "authorised persons" and persons whose ordinary activities involve him in participating in unregulated schemes for the purposes of a business carried on by him.

[39] *ibid.*, article 15.

[40] *ibid.*, article 21(6).

3–015 The FSA's COB rules allow some limited further exemptions from the restriction on the promotion of unregulated schemes, consistent with its power to do so on a basis which does not result in unregulated schemes be capable of promotion to the general public.[41] These further exemptions are found in Annex 5 to Chapter 3 of COB. In particular this Annex permits a firm to promote to limited classes of investor including:

(a) a person who the firm has categorised as sufficiently expert to understand the rules involved and who has consented to this and received a prescribed loss of protections' notice[42];

(b) a person who is or has been within the last 30 months a participant in an unregulated collective scheme of a substantially similar type;

(c) a person for whom an authorised firm has taken steps to ensure that the collective investment scheme is suitable, but only where the person is an established or newly accepted customer of the firm.[43]

The net effect of the restriction and the exemptions in the FPO (Schemes) and the FSA's rules is that it is possible for an intermediary to give advice to a customer who asks for advice about investing in unregulated schemes—the so-called "one-off" exemption[44]; also it is possible for a firm to take reasonable steps to ensure that investment in a particular unregulated scheme is suitable for a customer of the firm and to then give advice pursuant to a customer agreement which satisfies the FSA's requirements.[45]

Listed closed-ended companies

3–016 An investment company, unless it is an open-ended company, is not classified as an unregulated investment scheme[46] and its securities are hence not subject to the promotional restrictions applicable to such schemes contained in s.238 of the FSMA. Further, the FPO contains exemptions for non-real time promotions in respect of listing particulars and any other document required or permitted to be published by the Listing Rules[47] and these exemptions feed through to authorised firms in terms of the scope of the FSA's financial

---

[41] FSMA, s.238(5).

[42] Prosaically termed "a Category 7 person" in COB, 3, Annex 5 referring to an expert private customer reclassified as an intermediate customer in accordance with COB, 4.1.9 R.

[43] COB 3, Annex 5. For the suitability test specifically see COB, 3.11.2 R, Annex 5 and explanatory notes 2 and 3.

[44] FPO (Schemes), article 15.

[45] COB, 3.11.2 R, Annex 5 and explanatory notes 2 and 3.

[46] FSMA Sch., para.21.

[47] FPO, article 71; The Listing Rules are rules that govern the Listing of companies on the Official List and are the responsibility of the FSA.

THE REGULATORY REGIME FOR INVESTMENT MANAGEMENT SERVICES

promotion rules.[48] This is subject to the point already noted arising on COB 3, which prevents a firm from making a wholly unsolicited financial promotion in the case of non-readily realisable securities. However *any* security which is, or which can reasonably be expected to be, admitted to an official list on an exchange in an EEA state is deemed to meet the criteria of being "readily realisable".[49] The criteria for the listing of an investment company under the FSA's rules include the requirement that there should be an adequate spread of risk although in practice this has been interpreted as permitting, for example, funds of hedge funds to list their shares.[50]

Applying the financial promotion standards

The FSA's standards for financial promotions can all be traced to the general overarching requirement in its Principles for Businesses and in particular Principle 7 which provides under the heading "Communications with clients": **3–017**

> "A *firm* must pay due regard to the information needs of its *clients,* and communicate information to them in a way which is clear, fair and not misleading."

This Principle is not restricted in its application to communications with private customers but extends to communications with clients.[51] It is reflected in parallel conduct of business rules which, unlike the Principles, can found an action for damages under s.150 of the FSMA.

COB, 2.1.2 R provides that when an authorised firm communicates information to a customer it must take reasonable steps to communicate in a way which is clear, fair and not misleading. This rule extends to all communications with customers including customer agreements, periodic statements, financial reports, telephone calls and all correspondence. This attaches to anything which a firm does which is not a financial promotion. Financial promotions are subject to two complimentary rules in COB 3. The first, COB 3.8.4 R, provides that a firm must be able to show that it has taken reasonable steps to ensure that a non-real time financial promotion is fair, clear and not misleading.[52] The FSA has included an evidential provision to the effect that to comply with the basic fair, clear and not misleading rule, a firm should ensure that its financial promotion:

---

[48] COB, 3.2.5 R.
[49] FSA *Glossary.*
[50] Listing rule 21.9 (h) which requires that no more than 20 per cent of the gross assets of the investment company may be invested in one company or group.
[51] The term *client* is used here to include private and intermediate customers and market counterparties.
[52] COB, 3.8.4 R.

73

REGULATION AND THE PROMOTION OF INVESTMENT MANAGEMENT SERVICES

- does not disguise the promotional nature of the communication;
- that the statement of any opinion is honestly held;
- that the facts on which any comparison or contrast is made are verifiable and that the comparison is presented in a fair and balanced way.[53]

A second basic provision is at COB 3.8.8 R which provides that a specific non-real time financial promotion must:

- include a fair and adequate description of:

  - the nature of the investment or service;
  - the commitment required;
  - the risks involved.

The purpose behind this and other rules is to ensure that there is, wherever a specific product is being promoted, adequate disclosure both as to the status and nature of the firm issuing the product and as to its qualities.

3–018   If, in the course of making a financial promotion, a firm also provides investment advice to a customer, then the provisions of COB 5 will come into play (the obligation to know your customer and the suitability obligation).

Where a firm communicates the financial promotion (or approves a financial promotion for communication by another person) it must arrange for the financial promotion to be confirmed as compliant with the FSA's rules.[54] This, in effect, means that the firm must have an internal compliance function which is able to sign off, for example, a printed or broadcast advertisement before it is communicated. Note that this confirmation rule does not apply in relation to so called "real time" communications, nor can a firm approve a real time communication made on behalf of another person. Guidance as to what qualifies as a real time and non-real time financial promotion is given in COB 3.5.4 G and COB 3.5.5 R.

A range of other rules apply where the promotion is one which is required to be issued or approved by an authorised person. For instance:

(a)   If a firm wishes to include past performance information in a financial promotion then it must include a warning to the effect that past performance is not necessarily a guide to the future and the information relating to the past performance must be sufficient to provide a fair and balanced indication of that performance.[55] In the case of a packaged

---

[53]   *ibid.*, 3.8.5 E: see s.149, FSMA as to the status and purpose of the so-called evidential provisions.
[54]   *ibid.*, 3.6.1 R.
[55]   *ibid.*, 3.8.11 R.

74

product, the past performance information must cover the period of the previous five years (or the whole period if the packaged product has been offered for less than this) ending with the date on which the firm confirms compliance with the rules for the purposes of COB, Chapter 3. The purpose here is to ensure that firms do not select what may be unrepresentative periods of high investment performance. Also, information about past performance must not be presented in a manner as to suggest that it constitutes a projection illustrating the possible future value of an investment contract or fund.[56] This particular requirement responds to the attempts by life offices and others to get round the constrictions imposed by the projection rules (see section 7) by presenting tables of past performance to consumers under a heading such as "What you might get back today if you had invested £x in the past".

(b) A direct offer financial promotion is a financial promotion which contains an offer by the firm to enter into an agreement with someone who responds to the financial promotion. Typically these appear in newspapers or are sent in the post as mail-shots or are directed at consumers via the internet. The purpose of the FSA's rules is to ensure that direct offer advertisements contain all of the information which a consumer will need before deciding whether to proceed. In the case of a packaged product, a direct financial promotion must contain the information required by COB 6.5 (contents of Key Features).[57] Also, such a promotion must explain cancellation or withdrawal rights and, in the case of a recognised collective investment scheme, give an adequate explanation of the charging structure and make clear whether all or part of the scheme expenses will be taken out of capital or income and the likely long term effect on capital or income.

The general law on marketing investment products and services

The sale of packaged products, whether through advertising or as a result of face-to-face mediation, is subject to a number of legal controls which apply generally. For example, the law of contract provides a basis on which consumers who are the victim some misrepresentation made to them during the sales process can ask the court to set aside the contract and get back what they have paid plus interest. This is the remedy of rescission for a misrepresentation which has induced the consumer to buy the product.[58] Alternatively, the court

3–019

---

[56] *ibid.*, 3.8.15 R.
[57] COB, 3.9.10 R.
[58] The Misrepresentation Act 1967—the remedy being available where one party to a contract has through some misrepresentation induced the other party to enter into it—the misrepresentation must be *a* (but not necessarily the sole) cause of the consumer entering the contract.

may award the recipient damages for consequential loss suffered as result of having bought the product.

Any firm which provides advice and expertise for consumers may be liable to compensate their customers if, in consequence of their advice being faulty and below the standard of competence reasonably expected, the consumer acquires a product which is unsuitable and suffers some financial damage as a result. A firm may incur this liability on the basis that is has been negligent, having regard to its professed level of expertise on which it encouraged its customers to rely. This may apply whether or not the firm giving the advice holds itself as being independent and acting on behalf of its clients.[59] In *Gorham v British Telecom and Standard Life*[60] the case proceeded on the basis that Standard Life Assurance Company owed a duty of care both to the investor who purchased a personal pension and also, in the circumstances, his wife and dependants. Also instructive is *Martin v Britannia Life Limited*[61] where the claim arose out of advice given to surrender a number of existing endowment policies and to replace them with a new one which was also intended to provide collateral security for a re-mortgage transaction. The judge found that no adequate steps had been taken to comply with the know your customer obligation, the investments advised on were unsuitable and no adequate risk warnings had been given. As well as illustrating the importance of the common law and conduct of business requirements in legal claims, the case is also interesting because it confirms that in the case of endowment policies sold in conjunction with a mortgage transaction the courts are prepared to look at the suitability of the entire transaction in order to determine whether the investments had been appropriately sold.

General statute law imposes controls on the publication of misleading advertising. This is achieved through the Control of Misleading Advertisements Regulations 1988[62] which confers on the Director General of Fair Trading (and other consumer bodies) the power to obtain injunctions and to require an advertiser to justify the accuracy of factual claims.[63] The law of misrepresentation mentioned above is also generally relevant in the context of the accuracy and honesty of promotional statements made by firms about their products and services.

---

[59] *Rust v Abbey Life* [1978] 2 Lloyd's Rep. 386 is normally cited as authority for the proposition that a life assurance company selling through its (tied) sales force may incur liabilities if salesmen do not give competent and suitable advice to their customers.

[60] [2000] 1 W.L.R. 2129.

[61] *Martin v Britannia Life Limited* [2000] Lloyds Rep. 412.

[62] SI 915/1988 which in turn give effect to the Misleading Advertising Directive 84/450.

[63] The Regulations do not apply to advertisements which are subject to controls under FSMA but nevertheless the Regulations are indicative of the wider legal environment in which firms operate.

CHAPTER 4

EFFICIENCY, CONFLICTS OF INTEREST AND GOVERNANCE—REGULATORY DEVELOPMENTS FOR INVESTMENT MANAGERS

Ashley Kovas,[1] Business Standards Department, Financial Services Authority

Introduction

The philosopher Heraclitus observed that it is not possible to step twice into the same river, implying that change is the constant and inevitable state of things. Financial regulation demonstrates his point. A significant amount of regulatory change is in prospect and the purpose of this Chapter is to analyse a few of the current hot topics which will impact on investment management.

4–001

Many of the current regulatory issues are closely related—the FSA's work on Best Execution, Investment Research and Bundled Brokerage and Soft Commission Arrangements are an example of inter-relationship. Despite the existence of some linkages, it is not easy to view all present developments as part of a single theme. There are at least three identifiable strands—improvements in efficiency; conflicts of interest and corporate governance. The European agenda for change is motivated principally by the EC Treaty's imperative for economic harmonisation.

This Chapter discusses several of the major regulatory issues currently affecting the UK investment management industry; the Paul Myners review of institutional investment; polarisation; Ron Sandler's review of the retail investment industry; investment research, (an issue given particular prominence following the revelation that some brokers were publicly supportive of certain stocks whilst being privately dismissive of them); FSA Consultation Paper 176, on soft commission and "bundling"; "best execution"; hedge

---

[1] Ashley Kovas writes in a personal capacity. The views expressed herein are those of the author, and do not necessarily reflect those of the Financial Services Authority. This document does not constitute guidance for the purposes of s.157 of the Financial Services and Markets Act 2000.

EFFICIENCY, CONFLICTS OF INTEREST AND GOVERNANCE

funds; and retail investment funds reform (announced in FSA Consultation Paper 185). A concluding section seeks to draw some higher-level lessons from these developments.

The *Myners Review*

Introduction

4–002 Paul Myners' report, *Institutional Investment in the United Kingdom: A Review* was commissioned by HM Treasury and published in March 2001. As is well known, institutions have gradually increased their share of the UK's capital over a period of many years. In 1963 for example, UK institutions accounted for some 30 per cent of the equity market. Individuals themselves directly owned 54 per cent of the equity market (more than £1,500 billion of assets). In 1999, institutions accounted for 52 per cent, with individuals directly controlling around 15 per cent of the market.[2] In addition, there are significant challenges ahead for the provision of pensions—increased quality of health care means that people are living far longer than previously, coupled with the imminent gradual retirement of the post Second World War "baby-boomers". The *Myners Review* was established to investigate whether the framework for institutional investment is efficient and flexible enough to provide for the future needs of investors. In particular, the Treasury was interested in whether there are factors distorting the investment decision-making of institutions, biasing them against investment into small and medium-sized enterprises and other smaller companies. This reflects a concern that current practices in the industry might disadvantage the venture capital industry.[3]

So the Review set out to investigate whether institutional approaches to investment were rational, well-informed, subject to correct incentives and (as far as possible) undistorted.

It has been suggested that the Review was only concerned with the investment activities of pension scheme trustees—recognisably, with insurers, the most significant institutional investors. While it is true that many of the recommendations of the Review are directed at such trustees, the findings of the Review potentially have a much wider application.

---

[2] *Myners Review*, Table 1.1, p.27.
[3] Though the *Myners Review* goes to some length to emphasise that it does not seek to promote venture capital investment at all costs—recognising that there will be some investors for whom such an investment would be unsuitable. See *Myners Review*, p.4, para.5.

Pension scheme trustees

The *Review* found that pension scheme trustees "are not especially expert in investment". In particular[4]:

4–003

(a) 62 per cent of trustees had no professional qualifications in finance or investment;

(b) 77 per cent of trustees had no in-house professionals to assist them;

(c) more than 50 per cent of trustees received less than three days' training when they became trustees;

(d) 44 per cent of trustees had not attended any courses since their initial 12 months of trusteeship;

(e) 49 per cent of trustees spent three hours or less preparing for pension investment meetings.

Although these figures are put forward as representative of pension trustees generally, there is of course a wide spread of practice between different pension schemes—the trustees of the larger schemes are likely to score better than those representing the vast number of smaller schemes.

Some respondents to the *Myners Review* suggested that the perceived deficiencies in pension scheme trustees are already corrected through their use of outside consultants. Quite apart from whether the smaller trustees actually take sufficient advice, the *Review* felt that "advice alone is an inadequate basis for decision-making, if trustees are not in a position critically to examine the information on which it is based".[5] In particular, the *Review* felt that trustees would not query advice *not* given by advisers—for example, if the advisers failed to recommend an appropriate investment into private equity, that failure would be unlikely to be queried by the trustees. The *Review* also found that trustees were involved only in 30 per cent of cases in the setting of the underlying assumptions of their asset-liability model. From this the *Review* infers that trustees may not in fact be exercising genuine decision-making power *vis-à-vis* the trust in their care, and despite their trust law duties.[6]

The *Review* expressed concern that trustees were not as involved as they might be in asset allocation decisions, pointing to academic studies that suggest that investment outcomes are heavily influenced by asset allocation decisions. Trustees should, therefore, be willing to commit more resources to asset allocation decisions.[7]

---

[4] *Myners Review*, p.5, para.10.
[5] *ibid.*, p.7, para.23.
[6] *ibid.*, p.7, para.26.
[7] *ibid.*, p.8, para.32.

4–004 The *Review* noted that there are two ways in which pension scheme mandates are typically run. Under the first method, the favoured investment manager is passed the assets of the scheme and is left to decide both the asset allocation and the security selection. Under the second method, asset allocation decisions are made by the trustees, and various managers are appointed to manage portions of the scheme's portfolio within set parameters. These parameters are tightly controlled, so that the top-level asset allocation decision is not corrupted through the investment managers' security selection decisions.

Unfortunately, the *Review* found problems with both methods. In the first, the scheme monitors the appointed manager by reference to its performance as against its peers. The manager would lose the mandate if it performed badly in comparison with other managers.[8] Yet the pension scheme had an obligation to make payments to beneficiaries when they are due, which meant that the scheme required a rate of return related to its own liabilities. So the objective set for the manager—to exceed the returns available elsewhere—did not match with the pension scheme's own objective. Because of this, Paul Myners considered that "the peer group benchmark model is a mistaken way of managing pension fund investment".[9]

The second method usually results in investment managers being set investment objectives related to an index—they were required, say, to outperform the FTSE 100 index by a set margin. The Review pointed to the arbitrariness of indices by observing that following the acquisition of Mannesmann by Vodafone, the resulting share was officially listed on the London Stock Exchange. This meant that UK managers who were targeted with objectives related to the FTSE 100 index immediately bought the shares. But had the merger resulted in the shares being listed on a non-UK stock exchange, they would have fallen outside the index and the same UK fund managers may therefore have sold the shares. Yet the enterprise in question, and its prospects, remained the same wherever it were listed. The arbitrariness of this effect may not be obvious to pension fund trustees (or, indeed, other investors). In addition, Myners pointed out that where investment manager performance measurement was related to an index, the result might be akin to passive investment management. The manager's incentive was to avoid losing its mandate, rather than to secure outstanding performance. It may therefore hug the index, taking only cautious bets away from it. So, given that active investment management is rather more costly than passive management, the question became whether the active fund management fee is being earned.

4–005 A further theme taken up by Paul Myners concerned "short-termism": the concern that managers perceived a need to defend their mandates on a quarterly basis because the pension scheme trustees might decide at any of their

---

[8] For an example of this see the discussion of the *Unilever* case in Ch.11.
[9] *Myners Review*, p.9, para.44.

quarterly meetings to dismiss the investment manager. This in turn caused the manager to focus strongly on achieving short-term performance for the portfolio.

In order to meet the alleged short-comings of pension scheme trustees, the *Review* recommended that "there should be a legal requirement that, where trustees are taking a decision, they should be able to take it with the skill and prudence of someone *familiar with the issues concerned*".[10] Trustees who could not meet the standard implied by this requirement would be required to undergo appropriate training, or else delegate the decision to a person or organisation that had the necessary skills and expertise.

As mentioned above, the *Myners Review* found that many trustees lacked sufficient expertise in investment and were able to bring only limited time and expertise to the investment decision-making aspects of their work.

The Department of Work and Pensions and HM Treasury subsequently jointly issued a Consultation Document, *Pension Scheme Trustees, "Familiar with the Issues Concerned", A Consultation Document*[11] (the "Issues Consultation"). **4–006**

The Issues Consultation proposed that the UK should enact legislation similar to that in the US ERISA[12] legislation, to increase the standard of care required from pension scheme trustees when making investment decisions. Also, where pension scheme trustees failed to reach that standard, the legislation would provide that the matter could be pursued through the courts.

The Government stated however, that they are not seeking to make pension scheme trustees experts in investment such that they would not need to take any advice from third parties.[13] In addition, it was not the intention that pension scheme trustees should only be drawn from the ranks of investment professionals—trustees are frequently appointed for reasons other than their investment expertise. The Government did not wish to create a system where Member-Nominated Trustees became impossible. However, trustees should be equipped with the skills necessary to evaluate whether the advice they received was complete, up-to-date and based on appropriate assumptions. They should then exercise their own judgment when considering and acting on advice.

The Government's proposal was that[14]: **4–007**

(1) pension scheme trustees should act with the care, skill, prudence and diligence under the circumstances then prevailing that a prudent person

---

[10] *ibid.*, p.14, para.77.

[11] Available on the DWP website at *www.dwp.gov.uk/consultations/consult/2002/myners/trustee.pdf*. This was one of five consultation papers issued by the Department in February 2002. Another of these papers on Shareholder Activism is discussed below.

[12] Employment Retirement Income Security Act 1974.

[13] *Pension Scheme Trustees, "Familiar with the Issues Concerned", A Consultation Document*, p.6, para.12.

[14] *ibid.*, p.7, para.15.

EFFICIENCY, CONFLICTS OF INTEREST AND GOVERNANCE

acting in a like capacity and familiar with such matters would use in the conduct of an enterprise of like character and with like aims.

(2) where a pension scheme trustee has or holds himself out as having special knowledge or experience, he must exercise such care and skill as is reasonable in the circumstances; and

(3) where a pension scheme trustee acts in the course of a business or profession, he must exercise such care and skill as is reasonable in the circumstances, having regard to any special knowledge or experience that it is reasonable to expect of a person acting in the course of that kind of business or profession.

The Government did not believe that it is necessary to set out in any further detail what being "familiar" required, or what must be done to satisfy the proposed duty. The Government propose applying the new duty through amendment to the Pensions Act.

Shareholder activism

4–008 The *Review* noted that investment managers only pursued a limited range of strategies to deliver value to their clients. Managers did not generally intervene in "investee companies" to tackle corporate underperformance. In particular, they were loath to "take pre-emptive action to prevent troubled companies developing serious problems".[15] The natural reaction of a manager to a loss of confidence in an "investee" company seemed to be to sell the holding.

The *Review* recommended that requirements should be placed on managers to intervene in poorly performing companies, for the ultimate benefit of their customers. This recommendation clearly has a greater capture than pension schemes—the requirement, certainly the concern expressed in the *Review*, would seem to apply equally to all managed portfolios.

At the same time as it published the Issues Consultation, The Department of Work and Pensions and HM Treasury also published a Consultation Document, entitled *Encouraging Shareholder Activism, A Consultation Document*.[16] As with the Issues Consultation referred to above this paper raised the proposal that a requirement should be imposed in the UK similar to that in the US ERISA[17] which requires that all fiduciaries concerned with pension schemes act "with the care, skill, prudence and diligence according to the

---

[15] *Pension Scheme Trustees, "Familiar with the Issues Concerned", A Consultation Document*, p.10, para.54.

[16] February 2002, available from the Department of Work and Pensions website, *www.dwp.gov.uk/consultation/consult/2002/myners/shareact.pdf*.

[17] Employee Retirement Income Security Act 1974.

standard of a prudent man".[18] It noted that "fiduciaries" under ERISA includes not only scheme trustees but also scheme administrators and investment managers. This duty falls short of being an express duty on such persons to exercise rights as shareholders, but the US Department of Labor has issued guidance over time to indicate what steps ought to be taken to comply with the ERISA fiduciary duty. The DWP Consultation Document stated:

> "The essence of the guidance is that although within the corporate structure, the primary responsibility to oversee corporate management falls on the corporation's board of directors, active monitoring of and communication with corporate management and the exercise of shareholder votes is consistent with a fiduciary's obligations where the fiduciary concludes that there is a reasonable expectation that such activities by a scheme (either by itself or with other shareholders), are likely to enhance the value of a scheme's investment, after taking into account the costs involved".[19]

Typically, investment managers will consider matters such as the independence and expertise of nominations to an investee company's board; the appropriateness of executive remuneration; financing and capitalisation issues; a company's merger and acquisitions policy and the company's long-term business plan.

The DWP Consultation indicated that the Government believes that, while **4-009** day-to-day management of public companies is not the responsibility of shareholders, broad issues such as the performance of senior management and the company's high level strategy are legitimate interests for shareholders. They have the right to take action where they believe management are not addressing the issues properly. Of course, selling the shares is one such action which the shareholder might take, but the Government observed that this may not always be possible for institutional shareholders—the price impact of a sale of shares might be prohibitive. Also, an institutional investor may need to hold the shares of the company to replicate an index.

In terms of scale, the Government believes that most of the time the best interests of investors do not require the institution to intervene actively in the company's affairs. And it is implicitly accepted that simply selling the shares will usually be an appropriate course rather than intervention.[20] But nevertheless, it is a cause of concern that there is a perceived culture of non-intervention even where such intervention is desirable: "a blanket policy of non-intervention is not compatible with investment managers' responsibilities to clients".

---

[18] *Encouraging Shareholder Activism, A Consultation Document*, Annex B, p.13.
[19] *ibid.*, p.14.
[20] *ibid.*, p.5, para.12.

So, the Government's aim is to secure "appropriate and informed intervention, whether using the mechanism of voting or not". Both pension scheme trustees and investment managers more generally are within the scope of the proposals. Where trustees have delegated investment management functions to an external investment manager, the manager will need to take on much of the responsibility for appropriate intervention. However, the trustees should not be absolved completely from involvement—they have a responsibility to ensure that the duty for active shareholding is carried out on their behalf.

4–010   The Government's proposal is to place an express statutory duty on those persons involved in pension fund management "to use shareholder powers to intervene in investee companies where this is in a pension scheme's best interests".[21]

Although the Government's primary concern in this area is, as has been made clear, with pension schemes, the issue is obviously not one which is restricted to pension schemes. Indeed, if a requirement were applied only to managers in respect of pension scheme investments, the requirement would inevitably have wider application simply because those investment managers which manage money for both pension and non-pension scheme clients would usually find themselves making block investments (or disinvestments) for pension scheme and non-pension scheme clients. The Government asked specifically whether the requirement should apply more widely than pension schemes.[22]

The proposed duty would apply to all pension schemes,[23] of whatever size and whether defined contribution or defined benefit in nature.

4–011   The nature of the proposed duty is framed as follows:

"Any person who is responsible for the investment of the assets of a retirement benefits scheme must, in respect of any company or undertaking (wheresoever resident or incorporated) in which they invest such assets, use such rights and powers as arise by virtue of such investment in the best interests of the members and beneficiaries of such scheme".[24]

The proposed duty would override any contrary provision in the scheme's rules. However, it is proposed that the duty can be varied to the extent that the investment manager is required to follow a specific trustee voting policy.

Breach of the duty would be a statutory tort subject to a civil a claim for compensation for loss.

---

[21] *Encouraging Shareholder Activism, A Consultation Document*, Annex B, p.6, para.21.
[22] *ibid.*, p.7, see the text of question 2.
[23] Though the DWP Consultation Document hints at "some possible minor exceptions", without going into details.
[24] *Encouraging Shareholder Activism, A Consultation Document*, p.8, para.26.

THE MYNERS REVIEW

The Government are open to the possibility that investment managers might need to rely on others to advise them on how to comply with the proposed requirement.

The Department of Trade and Industry's July 2002 White Paper on Com-   **4–012**
pany Law reform has also broached the question of institutional shareholder activism.[25] That document pointed to problems with transparency in the system under which shareholders exercise their votes. It also raised concerns over possible conflicts of interest on the part of institutional investors. Although the White Paper concluded that Company Law might be an inappropriate vehicle to deal with these issues, greater transparency of voting exercised by institutional investors does seem to be Government policy. The White Paper states, "[I]t would be in the public interest for institutional investors to be required to disclose publicly how they have voted in respect of their shareholdings in British quoted companies . . . The Government . . . will set out its position fully in due course".[26]

Private equity

Private equity as an asset class has certain features which make it a more dif-   **4–013**
ficult investment for institutional investors. For example, there are liquidity and pricing problems which are not encountered with other investments. The *Review* noted, however, that overseas investors seem more attracted to the UK private equity opportunities than do domestic institutional investors.[27] This implied there is a problem with the domestic attitude to the asset class. The *Review* has also led to a modification to the FSMA marketing regime, to allow the marketing of private equity to "High Net Worth" private investors.[28]

The *Review* concluded that pension schemes would be better served by an investment philosophy more linked to the funds' liability profiles.[29] This is in turn reflected in the proposed "Principles" of good practice which the Review set out for both Defined Benefit and Defined Contribution Pension Schemes. For further information on these principles, see Chapter 13.

---

[25] *Modernising Company Law*, July 2002, Cm 5553–I, paras 2.42–2.48.
[26] *ibid.*, para.2.47.
[27] *Myners Review*, para.12.107.
[28] Financial Services and Markets Act 2000 (Financial Promotion Order) 2001, s.48(1) (Certified high net worth individuals)
[29] *ibid.*, para.12.9.

Investment Research and Conflicts of Interest

The "US Settlement"

4–014 During 2002 the Attorney-General of the State of New York, Eliot Spitzer, made various allegations against the practices of investment banks operating in New York. The allegations concerned the relationship between investment analysts and their investment banking colleagues. Conflicts of interest had resulted in the analysts recommending stocks as "buys" which the firm privately regarded considerably less favourably (to put it mildly). Spitzer's allegations were various:

(a) *The ratings issued by certain analysts did not reflect the analysts' true opinions of the companies.* Spitzer noted instances where firms' internal communications (mainly email) seem to reveal that a published rating was at odds with the analyst's recorded contemporaneous comment. For example, in the case of one particular firm, a particular stock had a published rating of 1-1, the highest rating implying the firm's opinion that 20 per cent or more price growth was expected.[30] Yet, the same stock was referred to as a "piece of junk" internally.

(b) *There were undisclosed internal policies that no "reduce" or "sell" recommendations would be issued.* Ratings systems operated by analysts typically carried five ratings as follows: (1) Buy; (2) Accumulate; (3) Neutral; (4) Reduce; (5) Sell. It seems that certain firms never rated a stock 4 or 5. Thus, although represented by a five-point system, internally it became a three-point system.

(c) *Analysts' remuneration was linked to their involvement with investment banking work.* Conflicts of interest are not uncommon in financial sector businesses and are frequently addressed through use of "Chinese Walls". Mr Spitzer recognised this, and concluded from it that investment bankers should generally be barred from discussing inside information with a research analyst who is disseminating to the public a research report on the same company. It seems also that the remuneration of analysts was linked to their involvement in assisting the firm's investment banking operations, and how successful they had been.

(d) *The analysts were not independent of the companies they covered.* The same analysts were also giving investment banking advice to the companies they were covering. The analysts violated their firms' own internal policies in disclosing proposed investment conclusions to company management.

---

[30] The stock was also rated, however, as class D ("risky"), as were all of the stocks referred to in that particular case.

INVESTMENT RESEARCH AND CONFLICTS OF INTEREST

(e) *The investment banks allocated shares in "hot" IPOs*[31] *to the top executives of corporations from which the bank sought investment banking business.* This practice has become known as "spinning". A "hot" IPO issue may be defined as one involving the securities of a public offering that trade at a premium in the secondary market whenever secondary market trading begins. There is therefore almost a guarantee of an immediate profit for those allocated the securities prior to the opening of the secondary trading. The investment banks themselves were precluded from holding the securities and so were unable to profit in this way. However, it was alleged that the practice enabled the banks to stimulate investment banking business from the companies whose executives benefited. The arrangement was not disclosed to purchasers of the affected securities, and hence the allegation was that this amounted to a fraud on them.

On April 28, 2003 a joint statement was issued by the Securities and Exchange Commission (SEC), the New York Attorney General, the North American Securities Administrators Association (NASAA), the National Association of Securities Dealers (NASD), and the New York Stock Exchange (NYSE).[32] This announced the settlement of enforcement actions against 10 investment banks. In accordance with common US practice the firms in question neither admitted nor denied the charges brought against them, but paid a total of $875 million in penalties and disgorgement. A proportion of the payment was put into a fund to benefit customers of the firms. In addition, the firms were to make payments totalling $432.5 million to fund independent research, and seven of them also agreed to pay $80 million to fund investor education. The total of all payments amounted to around $1.4 billion.

In addition to the monetary payments, the settlement includes significant changes to existing practices in the firms concerned. This involves the following:

(a) Separation of research and investment banking departments.

(b) The budget for the research department will in future be determined by the firms' senior management, without any input from the investment bankers, and without regard to any revenues which might be derived from investment banking.

(c) The remuneration of investment analysts is not to be based directly or indirectly on investment banking revenues, and investment bankers are to have no involvement in the evaluation of analysts' job performance.

---

[31] In US terms, an "IPO" is the initial public offering of an issuer's equity securities, registered under the Securities Act 1933, as a result of which the issuer becomes a "public company".

[32] See the Joint Press Release on the SEC's website, *www.sec.gov/news/press/2003-54.htm.*

(d) The management in the research area will make decisions on whether to discontinue coverage of companies, without reference to the investment bankers.

(e) Analysts will not be allowed to participate in the solicitation of investment banking business. During the offering period for an investment banking transaction, research analysts may not participate in measures to market the transaction.

(f) Firewalls will be established to restrict interaction between investment banking staff and research analysts, though such interaction may occur in specifically designated circumstances.

In addition, each firm will make its analysts' historical ratings and price target forecasts publicly available.

4–015 The firms also agreed voluntarily to restrict the allocation of securities in "hot" IPOs. This is intended to promote fairness in the allocation of IPO shares and to prevent firms from using these shares as a means of attracting investment banking business. The SEC may yet impose rules in this and other areas. SEC Chairman Donaldson said in his speech at the Press Conference regarding the global settlement, "I view this voluntary initiative as a temporary solution to the problem of spinning. In the months ahead we will explore addressing these issues with revised or new rulemaking".

In some senses the most controversial requirement in the settlement is the requirement that for a period of five years each of the firms will be obliged to provide independent research to their customers from a minimum of three independent research firms. Firms will notify customers of the availability of independent research on customer account statements, on the first page of research reports and on the firm's website.

It seems that the analyst saga in the US has still not ended as yet. The SEC appears to be contemplating possible action against the senior management of at least some of the firms involved in the settlement.[33]

The FSA's work on investment research

4–016 In July 2002 the FSA published Discussion Paper 15 (DP15), *Investment Research: Conflicts and Other Issues*. That Paper was clearly stimulated by the US investigations described above, and concluded that it is likely that the same conflicts of interest are to be found in the UK.[34] DP15 set down and analysed various conflicts of interest as follows. To some extent this analysis

---

[33] See "Regulators Raise Sights In Probe of Wall Street", *Wall Street Journal* (June 4, 2003), p.M1; "Regulators turn up the heat on Wall Street", *Financial Times* (June 4, 2003), p.29.

[34] Discussion Paper 15, para.4.1.

went wider than the conflicts which had been concerning the authorities in the US:

(a) *Analysts are required to become involved in, or influence, other functions within the investment firm.* Essentially the same issue as had been identified in the US—analysts who become involved in investment banking work, in particular IPOs, may be compromised by the resulting conflict of interest.

(b) *Reward and reporting structures.* This also mirrors the US concern that analysts' remuneration could be determined by their corporate finance work instead of in recognition of the quality of their research work.

(c) *The analyst's or his firm's portfolio of investments, or those of clients.* Conflict may arise where the analyst, or his family or friends, or the investment bank itself, have an investment portfolio which includes shares which the analyst will be required to cover. Any research produced by the analyst may be influenced by its likely effect on the analyst's or the connected parties' financial well-being. Or the analyst could produce critical research seeking to reduce the share value of a company prior to buying shares for his own portfolio, or causing others to do so.

(d) *Power of subject companies.* Analysts require co-operation from the companies which they cover in order to produce their research. The subject companies may seek, explicitly or implicitly, to exert power over the analyst to produce unduly favourable research. An understanding that future favourable research will be forthcoming may be required for the investment bank to win corporate finance work.

(e) *Knowledge that is not yet public.* Where Chinese walls are ineffective, information may, for example, flow between the research area, the corporate finance area and the trading/sales area. Involvement in corporate finance work may give the analyst access to privileged information. This may make the analyst an insider for the purposes of the laws relating to insider dealing and market abuse.

(f) *The power of research recommendations.* Research may, when issued, have an effect on the share price of an issuer, or perhaps even a sector. The analyst in such cases may not be an insider for the purposes of the insider dealing legislation.

(g) *Lack of investor knowledge or experience.* The DP15 analysis under this head recognises that some of the conflicts of interest which analysts may experience only become a problem in practice through investors' lack of experience or knowledge. This may not affect all investors. Institutional investors might be able to read research more critically through their knowledge of the conflicts of interest which the analyst faces. For example, a retail investor might not appreciate that a "hold" or "neutral" rating from the analyst might mean "sell". Retail investors might also not understand that by the time research reaches them institutional investors will already have acted on it and that prices may have adjusted to take account of it. Retail investors must as a result be long-term investors rather than short-term speculators.

(h) *Monitoring of analysts.* A poorly performing analyst may persist as an analyst for longer than he ought if investment firms do not monitor effectively the quality of the research he produces. Similarly, a good analyst might not receive sufficient credit for the same reason.

(i) *Qualifications.* There is no regulatory requirement for a minimum educational standard for analysts. Analysts are not subject to the Approved Persons regime.[35] Regulatory standards of this type might assist in an improvement in the standard of analysts should this be considered necessary.

DP15 was followed in February 2003 with the publication of Consultation Paper 171, *Conflicts of Interest: Investment Research and Issues of Securities.* This provided a feedback statement to DP15 and also raised additional concerns. The practices of "spinning" and "laddering"[36] had not been analysed in DP15, but were included in CP171. The Consultation Paper affirmed the tentative conclusion advanced in DP15 that similar conflicts of interest to those identified in the US could occur in the UK.

The draft rules published for consultation in CP 171 were based on three key messages. Firstly, the UK's principle-based approach to regulation provides the correct framework for addressing conflicts of interest. The US system is a great deal more prescriptive in its approach, but it is not considered necessary to mimic this in the UK. Secondly, despite this support for the principle-based approach, there is a need for a clearer regulatory line on acceptable standards of conduct. Thirdly, the UK's approach should be as close as possible to emerging regulatory responses in the US and EU.

4–017 However, consistency does not necessarily mean an identical approach: "We doubt, for example, whether sell-side funding of independent research for retail investors—a feature of the disciplinary settlement in the US—is a necessary step for the UK market".[37] In addition, there are decisions to be made later in 2003 on the implementation of the Market Abuse Directive which will clearly have an impact on the UK regulatory approach in this area. And the draft revised Investment Services Directive includes "investment

---

[35] See the following two modules of the FSA's *Handbook of Rules and Guidance* for further details of the applicable standards for Approved Persons: Statements of Principle and Code of Practice for Approved Persons (APER) and the Fit and Proper Test for Approved Persons (FIT).

[36] "Laddering" involves the investment bank allocating shares in an IPO to clients in exchange for the clients supporting the issue through later deals in the secondary market.

[37] *ibid.,* paras 1.6 and 4.43–4.46.

research and financial analysis" within its scope where provided by a regulated firm.

Respondents also made the point to the FSA that any regulatory response to conflicts of interest in the UK investment analyst market should recognise that UK analysts' research is generally consumed by institutional investors, whereas in the US there are many more retail research consumers. Institutional investors should be better able to understand that conflicts exist and should be able to assess in that light the extent to which the research can be taken at face value.[38] However, edited research emanating from investment bank analysts might yet find its way to unsophisticated UK retail consumers through the media and web-based distribution channels.[39] At bottom, though, "both institutional and retail consumers should be able to operate on the basis that the research that they see is at least factual and objective".[40]

It is clear that the FSA regards firms' internal systems and controls as crucial to limiting the impact of analysts' conflicts of interest. Decisions on what stocks are covered for research, what is written and when should not be made under management control of the investment banking, equity sales or trading divisions of the firm.[41] Analysts' compensation and reward structures should not be based on contribution to profits on specific investment banking deals, or for it to be determined by managers in investment banking, equity sales or trading. The FSA does, however, recognise that the expertise of analysts may on occasion be legitimately used elsewhere in the firm, but reminds firms that they must tightly control the process by which analysts are taken "over the wall". However, it would be going too far to use analysts in a marketing capacity, meaning that analysts should not be used in pitches for new investment banking mandates or in the active marketing of new issues.[42]

4–018 The firms' systems and controls should in addition ensure that the firm does not offer or accept any inducement to produce favourable research in order to retain or secure any business or information from a subject company. Firms should not cede editorial control for research reports to subject companies. If a firm finds itself unable to resolve differences of opinion with the subject company, the only realistic option may be to cease coverage of the stock—a decision which should be disclosed to investors.

The FSA proposes to introduce a "quiet period"—a period of 30 days from the time a prospectus is published during which no research could be produced on the company by the lead or co-manager of the issue, or by any member of the underwriting syndicate.[43] No "quiet period" is proposed for secondary issues, but any firm publishing research around the time of a secondary issue would need to justify the publication, and show that it did not

---

[38] *ibid.*, para.3.4.
[39] *ibid.*, para.3.6.
[40] *ibid.*, para.4.2.
[41] *ibid.*, para.4.6.
[42] *ibid.*, para.4.7.
[43] *ibid.*, para.4.18.

contain any information designed to condition the market in favour of the issue.

The FSA proposes that analysts should be prohibited from dealing in the securities of the sectors they cover, including derivatives based on those securities. Analysts should similarly not be permitted to disclose research recommendations to other persons in order to encourage them to deal.[44]

4–019 A requirement for prominent disclosure is also included in CP171. This is consistent with the approach being taken in the US. The UK disclosures would include:

(a) an explanation of the ratings or recommendations given, together with the spread of the firm's ratings or recommendations;

(b) a statement of whether the firm has had any investment banking mandates or managed the issue of securities for the subject company in the last 12 months, or whether such deals are expected in the next six months;

(c) a statement whether the firm makes a market in the company's shares or acts as corporate broker;

(d) a three-year historical chart showing price movements against recommendations, including the points where the ratings or price targets changed—designed to show the analyst's track record in covering the security concerned;

(e) a statement whether the analyst or any associate of his has a financial interest in the securities of the subject company[45]

(f) a disclosure of any material shareholding of the firm in the subject company or of the company in the firm.[46] The materiality threshold was left open for consultation, though 1 per cent was floated as a possibly appropriate threshold. In addition, other holdings and positions may be included in the disclosure requirement—for example, the firm's holdings in the subject company's debt instruments, or short positions in securities. Such disclosures would be necessary to give investors "the full picture of the firm's potential conflict of interest".[47]

The FSA proposes some tightening of the existing prohibition on firm's dealing ahead of published research.[48] This would involve deleting the exceptions

---

[44] "Laddering" involves the investment bank allocating shares in an IPO to clients in exchange for the clients supporting the issue through later deals in the secondary market, paras 4.21 and 4.22.

[45] This would not of course be necessary if the proposal to prohibit such dealings were accepted.

[46] CP171, para.4.26.

[47] *ibid.*, para.4.28.

[48] COB, 7.3.

that presently allow a firm to "deal ahead" where: (a) it believes that the research report will not materially move the price of the security concerned; (b) it merely anticipates customer demand; or (c) if it has disclosed in the research report that it has or may have dealt.[49]

The FSA has concluded that the practices known as "spinning" and "laddering" contravene the FSA's Principles, meaning that firms carrying on such activities could be subject to discipline. Existing rules in the Conduct of Business Sourcebook deal with the practices through requirements on firms to manage their conflicts of interest.[50] Guidance is proposed to make clearer the standards firms are expected to meet in this area.[51]

The FSA proposes new guidance to help a firm acting for an issuer to manage conflicts of interest arising between the issuer and: (a) itself—*i.e.* the firm's own interest in receiving an allocation of securities; (b) itself—in facilitating its ability to distribute the securities; (c) the interests of its investment customers in receiving suitable investments; and (d) itself—in securing future investment banking mandates.

Bundling and Soft Commission Arrangements

The Myners Review

When the *Myners Review*[52] was published, one recommendation in particular **4–020** attracted a great deal of attention from the industry. The *Review* noted that the management fee which UK pension funds pay to their investment manager is subject to scrutiny by the trustees and their investment consultants.[53] Logically therefore, competition around the management fee should lead to pressure on investment managers to keep their fee as low as possible. However, the Review also noted that investment managers incur commission charges when they transact deals in securities as agent for their customers. The Review saw two differences in the way in which the commission costs are treated compared with the management fee. First, although the Review recognises that there is disclosure of the commission costs, that disclosure is not as transparent as it should be to the customer. Secondly, the firms which provide the execution services for the investment manager (and who are remunerated by the payment of commission) are selected by the manager acting as agent and without reference to the customer. Some, but not all managers had put in place methods by which they could assess the quality of the execution services they received for their commission.

---

[49] CP171, para.4.36. See COB, 7.3.4R(1), (4) and (5).
[50] COB, 7.1.
[51] CP171, para.5.8.
[52] *Institutional Investment in the United Kingdom: A Review* (HM Treasury, 2001).
[53] *ibid.*, para.5.102.

In addition to providing trade execution, the brokers to whom commission is paid may be providing goods or services back to the investment manager in exchange for the commission paid. Some of these goods and services, for example research, are, in effect, tools of the manager's trade. It enables them to carry out the contract it with its customer. So, as Myners puts it, ". . . the manager outsources a business input to the sell-side with the cost charged directly to the client".[54] Myners considered that this arrangement was not in the interests of the investment managers' customers. Competitive distortion was likely to occur because these costs "will not be scrutinised by the client and are not a direct charge to the fund manager's profit".[55] Myners recommended that:

> "Clients' interests would be better served if they required fund managers to absorb the cost of any commissions paid, treating these commissions as a cost of the business of fund management, as they surely are. Fund managers would of course seek to offset this additional cost through higher fees; this would be a matter for them to agree with their clients. Under this system, the incentives would be different. Institutional clients would see more clearly what they were actually paying to have their funds invested. Incentives for them to manage costs would apply equally to all costs, as opposed to acting on some more than on others, as a present. Fund managers would choose which services to buy and which to provide themselves".[56]

Paul Myners concluded that if investment managers were to absorb the costs of commission, then "current inefficiencies and complexities associated with practices such as soft commission and commission recapture would be likely to cease".[57] So the bundling and softing problem would, according to the *Review*, be solved through a bundling solution—the commission costs would be bundled with the investment manager's other business costs (and profit) and charged through the management fee.

4–021   After the *Myners Review* was published the Fund Managers' Association[58] commissioned a piece of research from Professors Richard A Brealey and Anthony Neuberger of the London Business School.[59] This report concluded that a requirement for investment managers to absorb commission costs could itself lead to other incentive problems. The report therefore concludes

---

[54] *Institutional Investment in the United Kingdom: A Review* (HM Treasury, 2001), para.5.107.
[55] *ibid.*, para.5.107.
[56] *ibid.*, para.5.108.
[57] *ibid.*, para.5.113.
[58] The Fund Managers' Association has since merged with the Association of Unit Trusts and Investment Funds to form the Investment Management Association (IMA).
[59] *The Treatment of Investment Management Fees and Commission Payments: An Examination of the Recommendations contained in the Myners Report*, Fund Managers' Association, October 2001.

that "it would be inappropriate to try to enforce a move to all-inclusive fees, though we would hope that both plan sponsors and fund managers would regard such fees as an option that deserves serious consideration".[60] Indeed, the report suggests that there is probably no fee structure which would completely align the interests of the investment manager with those of its client.[61] An all-inclusive fee, such as Myners recommended, would, for example, leave the investment manager with an incentive to trade too little, whilst it is arguable that the present arrangement means that (some) investment managers may be incentivised to trade too much (so as to generate softed and bundled services).

However, the report strongly recommends increased transparency as a means to enable investment management clients to monitor the activities of their managers.

FSA's Consultation Paper 176, Bundled Brokerage and Soft Commission Arrangements

In July 2001, HM Treasury announced that the FSA would bring forward a **4–022** piece of work, which was already planned, to look at "soft commission" practices. This review would also look at "bundled" or "full service" brokerage arrangements. In April 2003, the FSA published its paper *Bundled Brokerage and Soft Commission Arrangements* (CP176).[62]

Before proceeding to look at the content of CP176 it is important to distinguish between soft commission ("softing") and "bundled" brokerage ("bundling") under the present regulatory system. Both softing and bundling are arrangements under which a broker provides goods or services to an investment manager in exchange for execution of deals in securities. Softing, however, generally involves the broker arranging for the provision of goods and services by a third party.[63]

It is possible though for there to be a softing arrangement with a broker for its own proprietary goods and services—the hallmark of softing is *agreement*. The definition of the term in the FSA's *Handbook of Rules and Guidance* states that a "soft commission agreement" is: "an agreement in any form under which a firm receives goods or services in return for designated investment business put through or in the way of another person". If there is a soft

---

[60] *ibid.*, p.4, para.5.

[61] *ibid.*, p.29, paras 49–57. The point is that ideally the fund manager should have the same incentives to deal with his customer's money as the customer himself. A customer should be willing to spend up to £1 to generate £1 profit. However, a fund manager's fee gives him only a fraction of any upside, so he will never be willing to spend the optimal amount.

[62] CP176, available on the FSA's website.

[63] Softing—the provision of an effective rebate on the "hard" commission paid by the investment manager to the broker, grew up in the 1970s as a means by which brokers could compete with each other in spite of the minimum commissions agreement which existed at that time. Its continued persistence despite the ending of minimum commissions must be questionable.

EFFICIENCY, CONFLICTS OF INTEREST AND GOVERNANCE

commission agreement in place, it must be reduced to writing.[64] Bundled brokerage arrangements do not usually entail an express agreement that the bundled goods and services are provided in return for any particular volume of deals for execution. Nor is there any agreement in advance to provide any quantity of bundled goods and services.

4–023 Various other regulatory consequences flow from the existence of a soft commission arrangement, including a requirement to make prior and periodic disclosure.[65] The investment manager's client must agree that soft commission agreements may be entered into on his behalf.[66] Given that relationships with brokers are arranged by the investment manager on a "house" basis, and that the soft benefits received are generally used for the benefit of all the investment manager's customers, it is questionable whether getting consent is effective. It could be said that, in most cases, where the investment manager engages in softing it is done for all customers.

Both softing and bundling arrangements are also subject to Conduct of Business Rules on "inducements". These rules require that firms are not allowed to give or receive any inducement "which is likely to conflict to a material extent with the firm's duty to its customers".[67]

CP176 is concerned only with the goods and services which the investment manager receives back from the broker in exchange for commission flow. It does not deal with the wider question raised in the *Myners Review* of whether managers should absorb the cost of dealing commission. The CP suggests that as much as 40 per cent of the £2.3 billion annual commission payments made by managers to brokers is actually spent on services additional to trade execution, both bundled and softed.[68] Around 10 per cent of all trades were found to be "soft". Most soft commission credits (around 50 per cent–57 per cent) were spent on market information technology, including market pricing and information services. Then followed research and analysis into companies and markets (25 per cent–30 per cent) and computer hardware and software (14 per cent–17 per cent).[69]

4–024 CP176 suggests that bundling and softing provide for incentive misalignments on the part of managers "to make trading decisions, or to engage in dealing arrangements, that do not necessarily serve the best interests of their customers".[70] In particular, the practices have the following effects:

(a) *Opacity.* Managers are enabled through softing and bundling practices to finance some of their business expenses by making opaque charges to

---

[64] COB, 2.2.8(1)R.

[65] *ibid.*, 2.2.16R and 2.2.18R.

[66] This is the cumulative effect of COB, 4.2.10R, 4.2.11E and para.15 of 4.2.15E—at least at the time the initial customer agreement is concluded.

[67] See COB, 2.2.3R.

[68] CP176, para.3.1.

[69] *ibid.*, para.3.10.

[70] *ibid.*, para.3.15.

96

their clients. The management fee itself is fully visible and indeed is hotly negotiated with institutional clients both at the inception of the investment management arrangement and periodically thereafter. However, although the management fee is subject to competitive pressure, the additional fee represented by commission payments is not. This finding matches Myners' own. The argument here is that managers are not incentivised to seek value-for-money for the softed and bundled goods and services they receive.

(b) *Over-consumption.* The goods and services which are provided to the manager in exchange for commission payments are, because of the opacity, not subjected to full scrutiny by clients. Thus investment managers may buy more of the softed and bundled goods and services than they actually need to meet their business needs. For example, managers may be in possession of more market information terminals than they actually need. This does not suggest that "surplus" terminals gather dust in a cupboard, or are used for purposes unconnected with client portfolio management. The issue is simply whether, if the manager were required to pay for them himself, the same number of terminals would be used— or would managers make better use of a smaller number of terminals?

More controversially, investment managers may receive more investment research than they need.

Economic reports commissioned by the FSA provide some evidence of this—it is reported that 31 per cent of managers interviewed by the researchers said that they would spend less on the additional goods and services if they could no longer acquire them through softing.[71]

(c) *Excessive dealing.* Softing and to a lesser extent bundling[72] involve a commitment for the manager to provide an expected volume of deals to justify the goods and services being received through the auspices of the broker. Therefore a manager may be motivated to trade securities by the need to generate the expected dealing volume, instead of for legitimate investment management reasons. It is in practice extremely difficult to second-guess a manager's trading decisions, so any excessive dealing would be almost impossible to detect by the customer (or, indeed, the regulator).

(d) *Quantity of trading decisions and execution.* Even if there is no excessive dealing in total, there may be an incentive to place trades with a broker who might not provide best execution. For example, a broker may provide excellent research but may still not provide best execution.

---

[71] *ibid.*, para.3.18.
[72] Although, as noted above, bundling would become "softing" if there were an agreement for the provision of goods or services in exchange for execution deals, it is of course evident that a manager will cease eventually to receive "bundled" goods and services from a broker if the manager does not deal at all through the broker concerned.

It is arguable that managers who succumb to the incentive misalignments noted would thereby suffer inferior performance and thus lose their clients to rival managers. The FSA however point to the difficulty in that there are many factors which affect performance, and isolating the effect on performance of a specific factor such as broker commission costs would be extremely difficult to do. Investment management customers are therefore unlikely to be able to use performance as a means of spotting the effects of incentive misalignment. So for example, a manager who refused to engage in softing or bundling (assuming that to be possible) may not stand head and shoulders above the softers and bundlers. He may be a poor manager, or he may simply be unlucky over some period.

CP176 does point to other economic considerations. Bundling for example may provide positive benefits—the cost of the bundled package may be less than if the bundled goods and services were purchased separately.

4–025   Importantly, the CP176 analysis leads to the conclusion that different regulatory treatment for softing and bundling may not be justified.[73]

CP176 concludes[74] that the misalignment of incentives between firms and customers "is likely to be a cause of material disadvantage". This is likely to be greater for retail as against institutional consumers, given that retail consumers' monitoring of fund management costs is inherently weak. The existing regulatory regime is believed insufficient to address the interest misalignments.

The FSA's proposed solution to the identified incentive misalignments is made up of two parts:

(a)   *Limitation of goods and services which may be softed or bundled.* Economic research done for the FSA suggests that there is little justification for softing or bundling goods and services for which demand is reasonably predictable. Thus, the investment manager should be able to estimate with reasonable certainty in advance how much of such goods and services he will need over a future period. It follows therefore that there is no reason why he should not pay for the goods and services himself. Because the cost of the goods and services can be forecast, the manager will be able to incorporate them into his management fee. Conversely, the likely volume needed of some other goods and services may not be so easily estimated in advance. Execution itself is of course the principal one—a manager is most unlikely to know with any degree of precision how many deals he will need to transact over a future period. The number of deals will depend on economic and market changes among other things.

The FSA therefore proposes to restrict the range of goods and services which can be acquired in exchange for dealing commission. It seems

---

[73] CP176, para.3.38.
[74] *ibid.*, paras 3.47–3.48.

that the limitation of permitted goods and services would include market pricing and information services, for example screens. This part (a) would thus impact more heavily on softing than on bundling. Most bundled goods and services, principally investment research, are produced by brokers incidentally to their execution services. They tend therefore to be closely related to trade execution. Note though that economic research done for the FSA suggests that the volume of required investment research is not necessarily closely related to the need for execution services.[75] This part of the policy proposal therefore seems to represent a form of "proximity test".

(b) *Limiting the cost-pass-through for remaining bundled and softed goods and services.* Under this part of the proposal, the FSA proposes that where goods and services are able to be softed and bundled (*i.e.* they survive the proximity test set out in (a)), and where they are additional to trade execution, the fund manager would be required to "determine the cost of those [goods and] services and rebate an equivalent amount to his customers' funds".[76] The intention here is to allow the manager to continue to charge clients' for execution services, but anything additional to that which is in fact paid for from commission must then be reimbursed to the client. This in turn means that the cost of additional goods and services received from the broker must be paid for by the manager himself in the first instance.

The FSA gives some fairly high level ideas about how the additional goods and services might in practice be valued, though more work would be needed on this. Softed goods and services are relatively easily valued because they have a market price. Bundled goods and services, however, do not. It is possible that brokers may assist in the process of valuing the additional goods and services through "unbundling"—breaking down the cost of the various services which are presently bundled. CP176 does not mandate any unbundling by the broker, but the FSA recognises that market forces may effectively bring it about. In any event the FSA will need to produce a further Consultation Paper to take forward any preferred policy options which might result from CP176. The FSA is required to consult on the draft rules. CP176 is set at a principle level, and no draft rules were included. Policy option (b) will only succeed, of course, to the extent that commissions charged by brokers reduce by the value of the goods and services received by the fund manager. If commissions do not reduce in line with the reimbursements made to client portfolios by the investment manager, and if the manager is able to pass

---

[75] *An Assessment of Soft Commission Arrangements and Bundled Brokerage Services in the UK*, OXERA, March 11, 2003, published on the FSA's website. See para.164. However, see also para.290 suggesting that there may be other factors which would suggest that investment research might reasonably continue to be bundled or softed.

[76] CP176, para.4.14.

on absorbed costs through an increase in management fee, the customer would effectively be paying more—the precise opposite of the purpose of the policy.[76a]

The FSA considers the impact of the policy options set out in CP176 on the market for investment research. The options effectively treat bundled and softed research in the same way, so that any incentive, which may exist at present, for managers to prefer bundled research over softed research would disappear. Such a preference may arise from the fact that softed goods and services are subject to requirements for prior and periodic disclosure.[77]

Best Execution

4–026 The FSA published a Discussion Paper on Best Execution in April 2001,[78] and followed it with a Consultation Paper in October 2002.[79] The intention of this strand of regulatory work is to modernise the concept of "best execution" so as to keep up with market developments, particularly given the growth of execution venues now available. The policy proposals set out in CP154 are four-fold—restructuring the best execution obligation; provision of information on firms' execution arrangements; review of execution arrangements and monitoring execution quality.

It is, however, likely that an outcome on Best Execution will need to await development of the revised Investment Services Directive currently under negotiation in Brussels. The revised directive will allow for the creation of secondary legislation under the so-called "Lamfalussy process". It is important to avoid putting the UK industry through two rule changes in quick succession, so it does make sense to await European developments.

Restructuring the best execution obligation

4–027 There is a perception that best execution is all about achieving the lowest cost for deals done for clients. But the FSA points out that price, though significant, is not the only matter which must be borne in mind. Minimising relevant costs is also crucial. From the customer's perspective, the overall net result is the important matter. The current best execution rule includes an "evidential provision" that where securities are traded on SETS, the firm satisfies the best execution obligation by executing the order through SETS.[80] Given the development of new trading venues, the FSA proposes to remove the reference to SETS from the rules. Of course, firms will still need to con-

---

[76a] Though these may be benefits derived from a reduction in unnecessary consumption.
[77] COB, 2.2.16R–2.2.18R.
[78] Discussion Paper 5, *Best Execution*.
[79] CP154, *Best Execution*.
[80] COB, 7.5.6E(3).

*sider the prices available on the main markets available to them. However, the FSA feels that a fixed benchmark does not provide any incentive for a firm to seek out the best deals for its customers.

Provision of information on firms' execution arrangements

In DP5 the FSA raised the possibility of requiring firms to maintain access to a minimum number of execution venues. The FSA states in CP154 that this proposal is unlikely to proceed. Instead, greater reliance on disclosure is proposed, with firms required to provide information to their customers on their execution arrangements. This should be a help to customers in deciding between the execution services on offer from different firms, thereby enabling them to make an informed choice.   **4–028**

Review of execution arrangements

The FSA proposes that firms should be required through rules to review their execution arrangements regularly, thereby prompting firms to make changes where necessary to improve the process.   **4–029**

Monitoring execution quality

The FSA proposes also to require firms to monitor their execution perform-ance. Some firms, particularly large firms, already do undertake such moni-toring. The FSA expressed interest in whether a more standardised approach would be desirable.   **4–030**

Polarisation

What is polarisation?

The polarisation regime was introduced into the UK's financial regulatory system as a result of Professor Jim Gower's report,[81] which also led to the Financial Services Act 1986 heralding the modern era in UK financial regu-lation. The purpose of polarisation was clarificatory—Gower felt that the status of some financial advisers was unclear as a matter of agency law. In agency law, an agent must act in his principal's best interests—and because of that, agents owe a series of strict fiduciary duties and duties of care to their   **4–030A**

---

[81] *Review of Investor Protection*, January 1984, Cmnd. 9125.

principals. It is possible for an agent to be the customer's agent, thereby owing those duties to the customer as his "client", or he could be agent for the product provider, in which case its client-facing duty of care is more limited and its fiduciary duty minimal or non-existent (though regulation can change the nature of the legal duties). The difficulty for the customer lay in finding out the status of the agent.[82] Many occupied an ambiguous position.

Gower's suggested solution involved eliminating the ambiguity. If agents were required to be unambiguously the agent of either the customer or the product provider, the customer would know where he stood. The polarisation principle requires just that—an adviser who advises private customers must either be "tied", advising on the products of the adviser's group,[83] or an "independent intermediary" acting on the customer's behalf and in the customer's best interests.[84] Note though that polarisation applies only in respect of "packaged products", which are defined in the *Handbook Glossary* as:

"(a) a life policy;
 (b) a unit in a regulated collective investment scheme;
 (c) an interest in an investment trust savings scheme;
 (d) a stakeholder pension scheme;

whether or not (in the case of (a), (b) or (c)) held within a PEP or an ISA."

Polarisation means that a product provider is faced with a number of potential distribution channels for his packaged products:

(a) *Independent financial advisers (IFAs)*. IFAs are able to advise on the products of any product provider;

(b) *Direct sales force (DSF)*. The product provider can employ his own sales force, advising only on his own products. The advisers may be remunerated either on a salaried or commission basis (or a combination of salary and commission).

(c) *Appointed representatives (ARs)*. An appointed representative is a person who has an arrangement with an authorised person, whereby the authorised person agrees to accept responsibility for the AR's regulated activities. This enables businesses, which are not themselves primarily

---

[82] See CP121, *Reforming Polarisation: Making the Market Work for Consumers*, FSA, January 2002, para.2.5.

[83] See COB, 5.1.7R(1). A tied adviser may also now advise on an "adopted packaged product", another provider's product, which has been adopted into his product range by his employing product provider.

[84] *ibid.*, 5.1.16R.

engaged in financial services business (for example, estate agents) to agree to distribute the products of a particular product provider.[85]

(d) *Direct sales*. The product provider may himself place advertisements in newspapers, television or elsewhere, inviting would-be investors to invest in packaged products.

4–030B Polarisation effectively requires that the product provider bears responsibility for its direct sales ((d), above) and for the advice given by members of its direct sales forces and appointed representatives ((b) and (c)). The IFA is, however, responsible for the advice it gives to the exclusion of the product provider.

Moreover the IFA's duty of loyalty is owed to its customer, to the exclusion of any product provider. COB, 5.1.6R states that:

"An independent intermediary must act in the best interests of its private customers when it gives advice on investments which are packaged products".

A provider, in contrast, does not have any such duty, and its marketing activities are limited to its own products. COB, 5.1.7R(1) states:

"A provider firm must . . . take reasonable steps to ensure that neither it, nor any of its employees or representatives gives advice on investments to a private customer about the purchase of a packaged product unless the product is:

(a) issued by the firm itself or by another member of its marketing group; or

(b) an adopted packaged product."

An "adopted packaged product" is a stakeholder pension product which is not produced by the firm or in the firm's marketing group, but by another producer (whether a firm or not). The product must have been formally adopted by the selling product provider.[86]

---

[85] Appointed representatives, as exempt persons, may only carry on certain prescribed activities without triggering the need to become authorised themselves. Those activities are: (a) arranging deals in investments; (b) safeguarding and administering investments; (c) advising on investments; and (d) agreeing to do any of the activities comprised in (a) to (c). See the Financial Services and Markets Act 2000 (Appointed Representatives) Regulations 2001 (SI 2001/1217).

[86] The process for adoption is at COB, 5.1.4R.

Regulatory reform

4–031 The polarisation regime was considered by the Director-General of Fair Trading to be "significantly anti-competitive" in a report produced in August 1999.[87] It was therefore decided that the FSA would review the application of the rules and their effect.

An interim review by the FSA in March 2001 saw some changes to the polarisation regime, namely:

(a) *Direct offer advertising*. Such advertising was removed from the scope of the polarisation rules; and

(b) *Product adoption*. This enabled product providers to "adopt" stakeholder pension products of other product providers into their product ranges.

In January 2002, the FSA published further proposals for changing the polarisation regime, stating that, had it not existed already, it would be difficult to justify introducing such a regime under the regulatory framework applied through the Financial Services and Markets Act:[88]

> "Based on our research, we do not believe that polarisation is delivering today sufficient consumer benefits to justify it as a continuing intervention in the market"[89]

The FSA accepted that the regime has catalysed the development of the independent financial adviser sector—which is considered to be a benefit to consumers in selecting the best product for their needs and desires.

4–032 The proposals in CP121, if implemented, will effectively dismantle the polarisation regime, allowing for a new middle ground "multi-tied" adviser who would be tied to more than one product provider. This would add a new distribution channel to the extant list of IFAs, direct sales forces, appointed representatives and direct sales. This new channel, called provisionally a "distributor firm" would fall short of being an IFA, but would permit advice to be given on the packaged products of more than one company or group. Thus the product provider would not necessarily be accepting responsibility for the advice given by the distributor firm. In addition, the reforms would enable product providers to "adopt" any other provider's packaged product into its product range—at the moment this can only happen with stakeholder pension products.

---

[87] In fact the Director-General found the rules to be "significantly anti-competitive" as long ago as 1987, before they were brought into force.

[88] CP121, para.1.4.

[89] *ibid.*

To the extent that distributor firms replace direct sales forces and appointed representatives, the customer will potentially get a better range of products—and the tied routes will also offer more products through the adoption process. It is possible that the IFA sector might shrink, but research indicates that only 20 per cent of products are presently distributed through IFAs—and IFAs also tend to service wealthier customers anyway, who are often more sophisticated that the average. The likely effect of the changes would therefore seem to be to increase the choice of product for the majority of customers.

In addition, CP121 suggested:

"... that firms who wish to use the 'independent' description should be remunerated only by fee or on the basis of a 'defined payment agreement' with the customer".[90]

The "defined payment system" as explained in CP121 required the adviser to negotiate a fee with the customer, meaning that, if he did receive commission for products sold, he would not be allowed to keep it.[91] If the adviser wished to call himself "independent", he would not be able to receive commission.

However, on October 28, 2002, the FSA announced that it would not proceed with the proposals for a "defined payment system". Instead, a "menu system" would be adopted. This would require the adviser to provide a document to the consumer, "in the early stages of the sales process", which would set out[92]:

4–033

- An outline of the services the adviser is offering;

- For independent advice, the option of paying by fee and a fee scale;

- Where offered, the option of paying by commission and, for a range of popular products, the commission that the adviser normally charges, set alongside average rates charged in the market.

The FSA will consult on draft rules for the "menu". This approach would be adopted across all advice channels, not just the independent sector.

On November 21, 2002, FSA Chairman Howard Davies announced the decision of the FSA Board to proceed with the abolition of polarisation.[93]

---

[90] *ibid.*, para.4.30.

[91] He would need to: (a) rebate the commission into the customer's investment product; (b) offset the commission received against payment due; or (c) pay any excess commission directly to the customer. Any fee conditional on the purchase of a product would be regarded as commission.

[92] See FSA Press Notice FSA/PN/103/2002, issued October 28, 2002.

[93] See FSA Press Notice FSA/PN/115/2002, issued November 21, 2002.

On January 20, 2003, the FSA published draft rules to give effect to the depolarisation policy.[94]

The *Sandler Review*

Overview

4–034 Following a recommendation made by Paul Myners in his 2001 *Review*,[95] Mr Ron Sandler was asked by HM Treasury to carry out a review of "capital and information flows around personal investment products".[96] Ron Sandler's report, *Medium and Long-Term Savings in the UK, A Review* was published by HM Treasury in July 2002. Its remit was to:

> ". . . identify the competitive forces and incentives that drive the industries concerned, in particular in relation to their approaches to investment, and, where necessary, to suggest policy responses to ensure that consumers and the investment needs of the economy are well served."[97]

The *Sandler Review* found that the retail savings industry is characterised by complexity and opacity. Complexity was found in the charging structures of products and also in the number of product types and products within those types (the *Sandler Review* points to the fact that there are around 1,600 unit trusts/ICVCs on offer). The *Review* also refers to the wide use of technical terminology which may well be incomprehensible to the average retail investor. Opacity is found in the wide price disparity between similar or identical products. Sandler suggested also that commission-driven selling is a problem, with advisers recommending products based on the commission on offer, instead of for reasons of suitability for the investor.

Sandler says that retail investors are deterred from buying long-term savings vehicles by their complexity and opacity, and also by the fact that the benefit of the product is far in the future—consumption now is preferable to setting money aside for the future. Buying savings products is a very rare event for most retail investors, and the intervals between purchases means that most investors develop no particular expertise in the field of retail finance. A general lack of interest in savings products deters investors from monitoring the on-going performance of savings products after purchase, suggesting that poor products persist longer in the market than they should.

4–035 These various factors conspire to create a market in which consumers are generally weak and Sandler suggests that "the regulatory regime, which has a

---

[94] CP166, Reforming Polarisation: Removing the Barriers to Choice (January 2003).
[95] *Institutional Investment in the United Kingdom: A Review*, HM Treasury, March 2001.
[96] See *Myners Review*, para.9.65.
[97] *Productivity in the UK: Enterprise and the Productivity Challenge*, HM Treasury, June 2001.

THE SANDLER REVIEW

considerable impact upon industry behaviour, is fundamentally a response to consumer weakness".[98]

An assessment of the regulatory regime as such was outside the scope of the *Sandler Review*. However, regulation was considered to the extent that it has an economic effect on the market for retail products. Sandler says that regulation is necessary to deal with the problem of "weak consumers". So the fact that the FSA's *Conduct of Business Sourcebook* (COB) entails some increase in firms' costs is not an argument *per se* against the existing regime. Ron Sandler's particular concern was to see whether he could identify any instances of unnecessary costs triggered by regulation, whether greater efficiencies are possible. He was much influenced by the fact that, in fulfilling their COB requirements to "know your customer"[99] and to make "suitable" recommendations[1] to private customers, many investment advisers claim to be constantly looking over their shoulder, concerned that a case might be made that they have mis-sold products. This, Sandler concludes, causes many advisers to create elaborate and costly records to justify the advice given, even though there is no specific requirement for such detailed records in COB.

Importantly, Professional Indemnity Insurance (a regulatory requirement) is difficult for IFAs to obtain, because the insurers are concerned at the indeterminate nature of the risk of an adviser being disciplined for mis-selling or required to carry out costly remedied action of some sort—in short there is a perceived problem in understanding what the applicable standards are. The FSA published a note in April 2003 (revised in July 2003) to advise the industry on the definition of "mis-selling" with the intention of defusing this situation.[2] The note pointed out that a precise definition of mis-selling is well nigh impossible:

> "[I]t would not be practicable or ultimately desirable for the FSA to provide an exhaustive set of specifications by way of safe harbour. If those specifications were to be exhaustive, they would be bound to be very lengthy, detailed and prescriptive. A central aspect of the FSA's regulatory regime is the responsibility of firms' senior management to run their business in a way that meets our requirements and hence to decide what systems and controls to adopt to ensure they write good quality business which meets customers' needs."[3]

The note helpfully explained that complaints about investment performance are not, on their own, treated as mis-selling complaints. However, the

4–036

---

[98] *Sandler Review*, p.5, para.22.

[99] COB, 5.2.

[1] COB 5.3.

[2] *FSA advises industry on definition of mis-selling*, see Press Notice on the FSA website, *www.fsa.gov.uk*. This was followed by a revised version, *Clarifying "Mis-selling": A note by the FSA*, published in July 2003.

[3] July 2003 note, p.3.

FSA does expect that firms will "keep a record of . . . advice given and the reasons for it. Keeping adequate records will both help firms to demonstrate compliance and lessen the need for regulatory attention and intervention". And "in assessing any individual case, the FSA will seek to proceed on the facts, rather than on the unsupported assertions of the customer or the firm".[4]

The increasing cost of compliance contributes to a selling problem for the less-well-off in that companies find it uneconomic to service investors whose savings potential is below a certain critical threshold. This in turn denies those investors the opportunity to make optimal investment decisions, and some may not save at all unless stimulated to do so by an investment adviser. Sandler's proposed solution was for simpler products which could attract less regulation as to their distribution, and this is described more fully in paras 4–037 *et seq.*

The *Sandler Review* made a number of recommendations for the future regulation of "with-profits" life insurance products. The *Review* was most concerned at the opacity of these products—particularly arising from the fact that the return on with-profits contracts arises from four distinct elements: the underlying investment return of the assets held in the life fund; the smoothing of the return, up or down depending on economic conditions; the returns (losses) enjoyed (suffered) from participation in the product provider's own business activities; and the charging of costs.

Simpler products

4–037   Although there are many recommendations in the *Sandler Review* which, if implemented, would impact on investment managers, the recommendation for simpler products has attracted the greatest publicity and would seem likely to create the greatest change to the shape of the retail investment product regime. In fact, in making his recommendation, Ron Sandler was picking up on a thread in the FSA's Consultation Paper 121, *Reforming Polarisation: Making the market work for consumers*, published in January 2002. In CP121 the FSA acknowledged the argument that regulatory costs are increasing and that some consumers are becoming uneconomic to advise.[5] Sandler attempted to quantify this statement, concluding that firms find it uneconomic to service customers who cannot afford to save more than £70 per month or make a lump sum of at least £8,500.[6] The FSA said that "[f]urther consideration could be given to the potential benefits to consumers of a broader range of benchmarked or 'safe haven' products that were relatively easy to understand and suitable for certain clearly defined basic purposes.

---

[4]   July 2003 note, p.4.
[5]   CP121, para.5.20.
[6]   *Sandler Review*, para.5.11.

Such consideration should be based on the relative risk of consumer detriment from the availability or not of such benchmarked products".[7] The implication from CP121 was that the lower risk products could be sold by a different type of intermediary, with reduced training and competence requirements. Thus, the reduced compliance cost for sales of the simplified products would make it economically feasible to reach less-well-off consumers.

The *Sandler Review* concluded:

"The Review therefore recommends the introduction of a suite of simple and comprehensible products. The features of these would be sufficiently tightly regulated to ensure that, with certain additional safeguards, a consumer could be sold these products safely without regulated advice".[8]

The Review stated explicitly that product regulation is intended to substitute for regulation of advice in respect of these "stakeholder" products.[9] Note that the term "stakeholder" should not be confused with "stakeholder pensions"—a product which has existed for some time already. However, conscious that even these products may not be automatically suitable for every retail consumer—some consumers need "specific and tailored advice"—the *Review* recommended "a simple and clear warning process at the point of sale to allow consumers themselves to conduct some basic suitability tests". It seems that this is intended to avoid, for example, customers tying money into a pensions product which they might need to access on a shorter time horizon. It may be observed also that some customers would benefit from reducing their debt levels instead of making payments to savings products, even if they are within the "stakeholder" target group.

The *Sandler Review* recommended that "stakeholder" products should **4–038** include at least the following: a mutual fund or unit-linked life fund; a pension product; and a with-profits product.[10] The *Review* left open whether a pure protection life product should be included.

The *Sandler Review* made a number of recommendations on the product regulation to be applied to the simpler products it wished to see developed. There would be no initial charge; annual charges should be regulated—a 1 per cent charge cap is suggested as a starting point, though the *Review* acknowledged that setting this limit would be controversial and moreover would directly relate to the likely success of the product—they can only be

---

[7] CP121, para.5.24.
[8] para.10.12.
[9] The FSA has more regulatory tools available to it than product regulation and regulation of advice. See the list set out in *A New Regulator for the New Millennium*, FSA, January 2000, Ch.3.
[10] The contemplated with-profits product would however have to have to be a 'new style' product—*i.e.* it would include the product improvements which the Review recommended for with-profits products.

successful if product providers are prepared to manufacture them, which will only occur if it is cost-effective to do so. Ideally, there should be no early surrender charges for "stakeholder" products, but the *Review* was willing to accept imposition of a "limited and defined financial penalty".

The *Sandler Review* recommended that the investment risk of "stakeholder" products should be limited.[11] It was accepted that the products needed to be exposed to some equity risk. However, the product should provide "a high level of diversification of risk". This would be achieved by requiring first that the underlying fund must have a minimum component of fixed income securities, and secondly, that the equity investments should not be invested in a single market or sector.

4–039 Sandler recommended that the industry should be consulted on the detail of the product regulation to be applied to "stakeholder" products and in response the Treasury and Department of Work and Pensions jointly issued a Consultation Document in February 2003, *Proposed Product Specifications for Sandler "Stakeholder" Products*.

The Treasury Consultation Document reflects the Government's desire not to "over-specify", and to apply a "relatively simple framework of key requirements to secure consumer protection and to permit product innovation to meet consumer interests".[12] Minimal standards, rather than a one-size-fits-all approach, is the preferred Treasury outcome—recognising that the target market of the new products will not be homogeneous. Indeed, the Treasury Document indicated that the target investors for the "stakeholder" products amount to a significant proportion of the UK's adult population, perhaps a more significant number of investors than Sandler had foreseen.[13]

Each of the "stakeholder" products will be regulated as to their simplicity, risk-control and charges.

Unitised product

4–040 The unitised product will embrace both unit linked life insurance and authorised collective investment schemes (unit trusts and investment companies with variable capital). The Government do not consider that the different tax treatments applicable to these investments should affect this decision—the important point is that both product types serve the same retail market.

The issues for regulation arising for the unitised product are: (a) risk; and (b) flexibility to allow for industry innovation. Trackers as currently structured are unlikely, according to the Treasury, to provide an adequate risk limitation—tracking an index still leaves open the possibility of market risk affecting the index. So the proposed solution is to set a maximum level of

---

[11] para.10.36.
[12] Treasury Consultation Document, para.36.
[13] *ibid*., paras 44 and 45.

equity exposure. In its Consultation Document the Treasury proposes a 60 per cent maximum for equity exposure in the unitised products. A minimum equity investment level was considered but the Treasury proposes not to apply such a threshold.

The Treasury does not propose any requirements for the "grade" of fixed income securities, on the ground that lower-grade securities might be negatively correlated with other securities in the portfolio, such that their inclusion would lower overall portfolio risk. The Treasury does, however, recognise that ". . . without additional restrictions there is the danger that this part of the portfolio could be invested in, for example, highly correlated Eastern European junk bonds".[14]

The Treasury recognises that its proposed maximum equity exposure limits might not provide sufficient regulation—for example the product could invest the fixed income portion in "highly correlated junk bonds" and invest the equity portion in "a small number of technology shares". Such a product would not be lower risk. So an additional diversification requirement may be needed. There is a question as to how this should be implemented—the Treasury sees this as a choice between a higher level principle based approach on the one hand or a set of quantitative limits on the other.

The Treasury asks for views on the appropriate charge cap. The 1 per cent cap recommended by Ron Sandler provides therefore an opening gambit, but it does seem that the Government will require some persuasion to move away from that figure. In support of the 1 per cent charge, the Treasury points to the "stakeholder pension experience"—there are 40 registered providers of the product and over 1.2 million products have been sold. However, of course, there is an automatic demand created for stakeholder pension products in that, generally speaking, employers who have more than five employees are required to offer a stakeholder product to their staff if they do not otherwise provide pension benefits. The new "stakeholder" products will not have any such inbuilt demand.

4–041

With-profits product

The Treasury recognises the benefits of inter-generational smoothing provided by the with-profits model. Nevertheless, to be included in the "stakeholder" suite of products changes are necessary to improve clarity and transparency. Although it has yet to decide, the Treasury is attracted to the product improvements which the *Sandler Review* recommended. It is possible that only the "improved" products will be allowed as Sandler "stakeholder" products. However, the Treasury is content to await the outcome of FSA work in this area. The product improvements comprise:

4–042

---

[14] *ibid.*, para.65.

(i) *100/0 fund structure*. Under this structure, 100 per cent of the fund's declared surplus is distributed to policyholders. Returns to shareholders are thus funded by an explicit charge to the fund. At present fund surpluses can be allocated to shareholders of the life company as well as to policyholders.

(ii) *Explicit management charging*. Sandler recommended the establishment of a separate management company to provide management of the fund. The fund would be charged explicitly for this management.

(iii) *Separate smoothing account*. The *Sandler Review* recommended that a separate smoothing account be established. In the long term the balance on the smoothing account should be zero. When in deficit, the firm's capital would be called upon.

(iv) *Market value adjusters ("MVAs")*. MVAs are used "to ensure that those leaving at a particular time do not take more than a fair share of the assets of the fund, to the detriment of those remaining in the fund".[15] Sandler recommended that MVAs should be permitted only in circumstances where there had been a significant change in the value of the underlying assets since the setting of the redemption value or, alternatively, where a high volume of redemptions has taken place.

The Treasury are working on the assumption that the charging structure of the with-profits product could follow that for the unitised product, based on the belief that the costs should be comparable. However, the with-profits product will offer additional features—smoothing and, possibly, guarantees. The Treasury is therefore interested in views on the appropriate charging structures for these extra features.

The risk control measures taken for the with-profits product will need to bear in mind that the smoothing feature itself cushions policyholders from risk. Despite this, the Treasury suggests that it might be appropriate to apply the same risk controls as are proposed to apply to the unitised product—a 60 per cent maximum equity exposure plus additional diversification requirements across firms, sectors and industries.

Pension product

4–043 The existing "stakeholder pension product" meets the requirements for a Sandler "stakeholder" product, except that the existing product is not controlled for risk. The Treasury is not attracted to the idea of running the two "stakeholder" products alongside each other—it would lead to unnecessary complication. Existing "stakeholder pensions" could be required to offer a

---

[15] Treasury Consultation Document, para.95.

Sandler "stakeholder" product fund link. Alternatively, the existing product could be simply brought within the new "stakeholder" range. This is the Treasury's preferred option. Limits on investment would however be applied.

Other products

The Consultation Document asks for views on whether various other products might be brought into the "stakeholder" range: a guaranteed investment product; term assurance; deposits; annuities; a financial health-check; the Child Trust Fund.

4–044

Feedback to CP121

CP121 asked:

4–045A

> "What criteria should be set for the products able to be sold by the lower tier of adviser in any differentiated advice structure?"

The feedback to CP121[16] indicated some support for the idea of a lower-tier of adviser as a means of increasing access to financial services. There was a degree of consensus about what such advisers should be able to do. First, they should not be restricted to selling part of the range of regulated products. The consumer's first priority might be debt counselling rather than investment. The advisers should thus be able to advise on debt, bank accounts, credit cards and also on standard repayment mortgages. They should be able to ensure that consumers have considered the need to take appropriate insurance. This should extend to home and contents insurance, term assurance and perhaps private medical assurance.[17]

FSA's Discussion Paper 19—Options for regulating the sale of "simplified investment products"

Discussion Paper 19 (DP19) was published by the FSA in January 2003, and sets out the options which the FSA believes it has for the regulation of the "stakeholder" products. This is necessarily a conceptual level view, given that the regime for the products has yet to be firmed up by the Treasury. DP19 is concerned with how the FSA might be able to fulfil Ron Sandler's expectation that the "stakeholder" products could be subjected to a less onerous regulatory regime for retail distribution.

4–045

---

[16] CP166, *Reforming Polarisation: Removing the Barriers to Choice*, FSA, January 2003, Annex D.
[17] *ibid.*, Annex D, para.D175.

EFFICIENCY, CONFLICTS OF INTEREST AND GOVERNANCE

Three options are canvassed in DP19:

4-046 **Option 1 ("Self Help")**—proposes lifting of the *Conduct of Business Source-book* requirements for "know your customer" and "suitability". This would make the customer responsible for deciding whether the product being marketed to him meets his needs and wishes. There would, of course, be requirements for appropriate disclosure to the customer, and the disclosure would be accompanied by a warning that the information provided "was in general terms and applicable to all consumers".[18] It is proposed that consumers should "self-certify that they have understood both the information . . . and the consequences of buying solely on the strength of that information".[19]

4-047 **Option 2 ("Guided Self-Help")**—builds on the approach in Option 1 and proposes in addition a series of "filter questions" "which seek to identify those who should not be thinking about buying an investment product in the first place and directing them elsewhere".[20] This recognises that even heavily regulated products will not be suitable for every retail investor.

4-048 **Option 3 ("Focussed Advice")**—proposes retaining "a limited assessment of individual suitability" in respect of the "stakeholder" products. This would need to fall short of a full review of the customer's circumstances (that would not represent any relaxation of the present selling requirements). The FSA recognises that this would present difficult choices for the regulator.[21]

It is clear that Options 1–3 would provide, in varying degrees, for reductions in compliance costs. Option 1 is the most favourable in this regard, with Options 2 and 3 following in turn. The FSA expressed an initial preference for Option 2, but remains open to persuasion.[22]

Hedge Funds: Marketing, Regulation and Short Selling

Introduction

4-049 The appropriate regulation of hedge funds is a long-running and complex issue which was elevated to crisis proportions by the near collapse of Long-Term Capital Management (LTCM) in 1998. For the UK, there are three

---

[18] DP19, para.4.16.
[19] *ibid.*, para.4.17.
[20] *ibid.*, para.4.19.
[21] *ibid.*, para.4.25.
[22] *ibid.*, para.5.8.

principal issues (and many subsidiary ones) wrapped up in the "hedge fund question". First, there is a question of systemic stability—can the failure of a large, highly-leveraged hedge fund bring about a collapse or paralysis of the financial markets? LTCM allegedly threatened this, but the fund was bailed out by a consortium of its counterparties, facilitated by the New York Federal Reserve Bank. Secondly, the UK is home to a significant and growing number of hedge fund managers and this raises questions about their regulation. At the moment, they fall to be regulated in exactly the same way as any other "conventional" asset manager, so the regulatory interest lies in whether hedge fund management requires a different regulatory approach. In particular, would managers who run "conventional" funds alongside hedge funds should be subject to any different rules. Thirdly, there is a question of retail accessibility—should hedge funds, or products linked to them, be freely marketed to or invested in, by retail investors? This turns on the meaning of "protection".

Hedge funds and their regulation are a truly international subject, and many other jurisdictions have been carrying out their own reviews. It is interesting to note, however, that the regulatory issues raised by hedge funds differ from jurisdiction to jurisdiction. The Securities Exchange Commission (SEC) in the US has shown much interest in hedge funds over the last several years, culminating in a public hearing held in Washington in May 2003 and the SEC Paper of October 2003 (see also Chapter 6). However, it is clear that some of the issues raised in the US debate arise from the interaction of hedge funds with existing US regulation—in particular with various exemptions from regulation provided in US Securities law. Because the existence of hedge funds impacts differently on different regulatory regimes, some regulators might be looking at increasing regulation, whilst others at the same time may be looking at reducing regulation. This may be inevitable when a new product type emerges within a jurisdiction, and has to be fitted into the product structures and regulation which have been designed with other purposes in mind.

In August 2002, the FSA published a Discussion Paper, *Hedge Funds and the FSA*,[23] which tackled two of the three questions referred to above: first, whether the regulation applied to hedge fund managers under the present regime was appropriate, and secondly, whether hedge fund products should be opened to greater retail marketing. A Feedback Statement[24] was published in March 2003. These papers will be referred to where appropriate in the discussion below.

It is important to realise that the offshore location of hedge funds **4–050** means that the FSA does not regulate the funds themselves, even though it might regulate the manager of the fund. Hedge fund managers have a

---

[23] DP16, available from the FSA website.
[24] Feedback Statement 16, *Hedge Funds and the FSA: Feedback Statement on DP16*, available from the FSA website.

EFFICIENCY, CONFLICTS OF INTEREST AND GOVERNANCE

firm/customer relationship with hedge funds that they manage. The hedge fund is a customer of the manager in the same way as any other customer. Financial regulation in the UK does not usually require firms to accept responsibility for the actions of their customers.

Definition

4–051   The term "hedge fund" refers to a loose and variable set of investment strategies which are more easily defined by what they are not, than by what they are. In the UK at least, regulated collective investment schemes offer two fundamental product features for investors—diversification and management. They are managed baskets of shares. The product offers the retail investor the opportunity to get access with his limited resources to a "professional" portfolio which he could not hope to recreate cost-effectively himself from the underlying investments. These products will be referred to as UK retail "investment entities".

Hedge funds are not UK retail investment entities under this definition. Instead, they take market exposure in a wide variety of ways—typically through use of derivatives, cash borrowing and short selling. Particular strategies have developed within this "hedge fund" class, such as arbitrage funds look for pricing anomalies in the capital markets and seek to profit from them. The infinitesimally small sizes of some of the pricing anomalies in turn means that such strategies frequently require significant leverage to make them profitable. Other strategies seek to remove directional market risk entirely from a portfolio, so that the profits (or losses) of the portfolio closely reflect the manager's ability (or otherwise) in stock selection. Managers of this type typically use short selling and derivatives products to operate their strategies.

The looseness with which the term "hedge fund" is used, even by those in the industry suggests that the term is largely useless for regulatory purposes (though some might say that it equates with the "offshore fund" concept of a decade or two ago). Indeed, the term seems primarily to be used as a marketing tool, capitalising on the genre's "masters of the universe" image so as to entice investors into the funds.[25]

4–052   Given that hedge funds are often not retail investment entities, as they have historically been perceived in the UK, it may be more appropriate to consider hedge funds as trading entities, much in the same way as, for example, a pharmaceutical or oil company. A principal difference, of course, lies in the fact that the hedge fund does not produce any goods or services as an output.

---

[25] There is some evidence that investors are "irrationally" affected by the names of an investment funds—see P. Raghavendra Rau *et al.*, *Changing names with style: Mutual fund name changes and their effects on fund flows*, available on the Purdue University website, *www.purdue.edu* (an unpublished working paper).

However, it is certainly consistent with the view that hedge funds are best thought of as a securitised version of banks' trading desks.

Systemic risk issues—the LTCM effect

Hedge funds typically domicile themselves in tax-efficient jurisdictions such as the Cayman Islands. It is certainly not desirable to establish such a fund in, for example, the UK. However, although the fund is offshore, it is quite common for hedge fund managers to be established in the UK. Applications for authorisation as hedge fund managers[26] have proved a staple activity for the FSA's Authorisations Division for some time. The fund's investors have their relationship with the hedge fund through the fund itself, often through the mediation of the fund's administrator. The administrator is also unlikely to be based in the UK.

4-053

The LTCM fund, Long-Term Capital Portfolio LP, was established as a partnership in Cayman in early 1994. The manager of the fund, Long-Term Capital Management LP, was a Delaware limited partnership with its main offices in Connecticut. The managers also had an office in London. LTCM's principals included two Nobel laureates, Myron Scholes and Robert Merton, and that fact, together with the fund's spectacular performance record in 1995–1997, meant that LTCM was very much a "hot property", with potential investors clamouring to be allowed to invest. As the President's Working Group Report put it, "Overall, the distinguishing features of the LTCM fund were the scale of its activities, the large size of its positions in certain markets and the extent of its leverage, both in terms of balance-sheet measures and on the basis of more meaningful measures of risk exposure in relation to capital".[27]

As reported by the President's Working Group, LTCM had, just before its near-collapse in August 1998, positions with gross notional amounts of $1,400 billion made up of contracts on futures exchanges ($500 billion); swaps contracts ($750 billion) and options and other OTC derivatives ($150 billion). A number of the fund's futures positions represented more than five per cent of the open interest in the contracts concerned and in some cases amounted to more than 10 per cent. The fund also had outlandish positions in some specific securities. At the same time the fund's balance sheet included $125 billion in assets. With an equity capital of $4.8 billion this implies a balance-sheet leverage ratio in excess of 25 to 1. This degree of leverage implied a great deal of risk.

---

[26] In fact the managers seek authorisation as investment managers in the same way as any other investment manager. There is no separate regulatory category of "hedge fund manager".

[27] *Hedge Funds, Leverage, and the Lessons of Long-Term Capital Management, Report of the President's Working Group on Financial Markets*, April 1999, p.11.

4-054   LTCM's risks were crystallised by the unusual market conditions following Russia's declaration of a rouble devaluation and debt moratorium in
mid-August 1998:

> "Russia's actions sparked a 'flight to quality' in which investors avoided
> risk and sought out liquidity. As a result, risk spreads and liquidity pre-
> miums rose sharply in markets around the world. The size, persistence,
> and pervasiveness of the widening of risk spreads confounded the risk
> management models employed by LTCM and other participants. Both
> LTCM and other market participants suffered losses in individual mar-
> kets that greatly exceeded what conventional risk models, estimated dur-
> ing more stable periods, suggested were probable . . . Finally, the 'flight
> to quality' resulted in a substantial reduction in the liquidity of many
> markets, which, contrary to the assumptions implicit in their models,
> made it difficult to reduce exposures quickly without incurring further
> losses."[28]

The fund held capital of $4.8 billion at the start of 1998, but that reduced to
$4.1 billion by July. Losses of $1.8 billion in August 1998 reduced the capital
base to $2.3 billion, implying a capital loss over the year to date of around
50 per cent. The fund now badly needed to reduce its positions or to
increase in capital, or some measure of each. Reducing the positions was
problematic, however, due to their size. Attempts to raise additional capital
were unsuccessful. The fund teetered on the brink of failure.

The firms who would most suffer in the event of LTCM's collapse were the
fund's counterparties and creditors. A meeting brokered by the New York
Federal Reserve Bank resulted in the creation of a consortium of LTCM
counterparties who were willing to recapitalise LTCM through investments
of around $3.6 billion. In return the consortium members received a 90 per
cent equity stake in LTCM's portfolio together with operational control.
Thus, as the President's Working Group Report puts it, "The responsibility
and burden of resolving LTCM's difficulties remained with the counterparties that had allowed the hedge fund to build up its positions in the first
place".

It seems that part of the problem with LTCM's activities arose from an
absence of scrutiny by the fund's investors and counterparties of the fund's
activities. A minimal level of disclosure was tolerated because of the reputation of the fund's principals, its impressive track record, and the opportunity
for the investors and counterparties to profit from the fund—in other words
investors and counterparties were just grateful to be allowed to be involved.

4-055   Had LTCM defaulted, counterparties would have moved to limit their
exposures as quickly as possible, in a market that was already suffering from

---

[28] *Hedge Funds, Leverage, and the Lessons of Long-Term Capital Management, Report of the
President's Working Group on Financial Markets*, April 1999, p.12.

a substantial reduction in liquidity. It seems likely this would have resulted in a substantial loss to the counterparties—the President's Working Group reports that LTCM itself estimated that the top 17 counterparties would have suffered losses potentially between $3 billion and $5 billion in aggregate. The consortium firms estimated their losses as being $300 million to $500 million each.

The President's Working Group estimated[29] that three consequences would have occurred on a default by LTCM. First, the sudden liquidation and closing out of positions could have had caused significant movements in market prices and rates which would have affected the market value of the positions held by other market participants. Secondly, a sudden reappraisal of credit risks, together with an increase in uncertainty could have exacerbated the general decline in market liquidity making it more difficult for market participants to manage risks. Thirdly, firms with exposures to LTCM could have found their own credit standing under threat, with a consequential risk in their own costs of obtaining funds.

It seems that risk management weaknesses at LTCM were not unique to that manager. In addition, the President's Working Group Report makes clear that, although some hedge funds are highly leveraged institutions, not all hedge funds are, and not all highly leveraged funds are hedge funds. LTCM had at the end of 1997 total assets of $129 billion, which made it significantly larger than any other reporting hedge fund family at that time. At the end of 1998, the five largest commercial bank holding companies had total assets ranging from $261.5 billion to $617.7 billion. The replacement value of their derivatives positions may have been as high as $61.6 billion. The figures for investment banks were also significant. However, these other organisations differed from hedge funds in having more diverse sources of revenue and funding sources, making them better able to deal with periods of market uncertainty, though they may also have higher fixed costs and more illiquid assets.

The President's Working Group pointed to better credit discipline and better counterparty information as being key to problems of the sort LTCM created, which might have gone on to destabilise markets, had the consortium solution not been found.

The President's Working Group made the following important findings:

- "[T]he main limitation on the LTCM Fund's overall scale and leverage was that provided by its managers and principals"[30];

- There were risk management failures at LTCM and also by the counterparties. Importantly, although there were sound risk management policies

4–056

---

[29] *ibid.*, p.20.
[30] *ibid.*, p.15.

in place, "the pressure to generate profit seems to have caused actual practice to deviate from those policies"[31];

- Financial firms simply did not understand the risk profile of LTCM and what would have happened to market liquidity if the fund collapsed;

- The favourable economic times caused market participants to "take their eye off the ball", granting very liberal credit terms;

- The counterparties relied in part on collateralisation as a safeguard for their involvement with LTCM. However, collateral arrangements did not adequately deal with the extraordinary shocks which the market faced in September 1998. Any liquidation of collateral would therefore take place in a declining market;

- There were difficulties with transparency and the adequacy of disclosure by highly leveraged institutions to investors, creditors and counterparties. Many of the counterparties did not establish meaningful limits on their exposures to the fund.

Following the LTCM event, greater attention seems to have been paid to exposures by both the hedge funds and, importantly, their counterparties. However, markets sometimes have short memories, and it will be important for regulators world-wide to be vigilant to conditions which might suggest a slackening-off of desirable standards. Should that happen, the solution may well be some form of more direct regulatory intervention than has been considered necessary hitherto.

Regulation of hedge fund managers in the United Kingdom

4–057   Hedge funds themselves do not establish in the United Kingdom, essentially for tax reasons—a UK-domiciled hedge fund would be liable for corporation tax on income and capital gains. It would also be directly affected by any subsequent changes in UK governmental policy, whether or not specifically aimed at hedge funds as such. Hedge fund administration is largely an offshore activity also. However, despite the absence of the funds and administrators, the UK does host many hedge fund managers and applications for hedge fund manager authorisation remains a staple part of the work of the FSA's Authorisations Department.

Hedge fund managers typically seek authorisation from the FSA for the regulated activities of "managing investments" and "advising on investments". As with all applications for authorisation, the FSA will ensure that the applicant manager meets the threshold conditions for authorisation,

---

[31] *Hedge Funds, Leverage, and the Lessons of Long-Term Capital Management, Report of the President's Working Group on Financial Markets*, April 1999, p.30.

120

which include the requirement that the person is a "fit and proper" person to be authorised.[32]

Once authorised, a hedge fund manager is required to follow the same rules as any other investment manager. The FSA's rules on "Senior Management Arrangements, Systems and Controls" apply to hedge fund managers (as to all firms), and those rules require that a firm "must take reasonable care to establish and maintain such systems and controls as are appropriate to its business".[33] This applies a high level standard for hedge fund managers.

More detailed standards apply as set down in the *Conduct of Business Sourcebook* (COB). In DP16 the FSA asked whether these generally applicable standards are appropriate for hedge fund management, or whether different (higher or lower) standards should apply. The general consensus was that the existing COB rules were appropriate for hedge fund management. The FSA agreed: "We have no plans at present to introduce rules specifically to regulate hedge fund management".

The retail marketing of hedge funds

In many jurisdictions around the world, hedge funds have not been readily saleable to retail investors. There has been a recent trend among regulators to question all aspects of the regulation of hedge funds, including their marketability to retail investors. This was one of the issues which the FSA raised in its Discussion Paper 16, where the question was asked, "Do respondents believe that hedge funds, or certain types of hedge funds, can be suitable products to be marketed and sold to the retail sector?"[34]

4–058

The issue—whether hedge funds should be allowed to market themselves more aggressively to the retail market—is intimately connected with the perceived meaning of "consumer protection". The Financial Services and Markets Act 2000[35] requires the FSA to have regard to the following when regulating for the protection of consumers:

(a) the differing degrees of risk involved in different kinds of investment or other transaction;

(b) the differing degrees of experience and expertise that different consumers may have in relation to different kinds of regulated activity;

(c) the needs that consumers may have for advice and accurate information;

---

[32] See Sch.6 to the Financial Services and Markets Act 2000 and the Threshold Conditions ("COND") Module of the FSA's Handbook of Rules and Guidance.

[33] SYSC, 3.1.1R.

[34] DP16, Question 2, p.25.

[35] See s.5(2).

(d) the general principle that consumers should take responsibility for their decisions.

The argument for retail hedge fund investment as put forward by hedge fund industry is that hedge funds have the potential to turn in positive performance even in a falling market. This is of course due to the ability of hedge fund managers (not shared typically by the managers of retail investment products) to take positions which take advantage of falling markets or which are not dependent on "market direction" at all. Short selling, for example, involves the manager acquiring a security which he does not own, or which he is obliged to return to another, and then selling it. If the value of the security sold later declines, the manager can buy it back at the lower price, making a profit from the difference. Thus, short selling is similar in economic effect to a put option, where the buyer of the option has the right to sell the underlying at a specified (strike) price. If the price falls below the strike price, the option holder is in profit.

4–059 The hedge fund industry argues that it is not in keeping with any idea of consumer protection to deny retail consumers the opportunity to invest in hedge funds. Such a policy means that the vast majority of retail investors will be fully invested into retail investment entities as these have been defined above in paras 4–051, *et seq.* This means that in adverse market conditions, retail consumers are consigned to sinking ships. Pursuing the metaphor, hedge funds are more like submarines with the ability to fall or rise. In addition, it could be argued that restricting the promotion of hedge funds is not in keeping with the principle that consumers should "take responsibility for their decisions".

However, hedge funds are marketable to retail investors in the UK to some extent. Their marketability is derived from the nature of the fund. If structured as a closed-ended company, the entity takes its marketability from the regime for companies. If it falls within the definition of a "collective investment scheme", then its marketability is as for any other unregulated collective investment scheme. Hedge funds do not often domicile themselves in the UK, essentially for tax reasons, so whether structured as company or as a scheme, the vehicle itself will be offshore.

A detailed discussion of the regime for the marketing and selling of securities is outside the scope of this Chapter. However, some general points may be worthwhile. Taking closed-ended company securities first, the contents of prospectuses and listing particulars is largely outside the FSA's remit—art.73 of the Financial Promotions Order[36] provides an exemption from the financial promotion regime, which is provided for in the Financial Services and Markets Act 2000, material which forms part of a prospectus for the public offer of unlisted securities. Art.71 of the same Order performs the same

---

[36] Financial Services and Markets Act 2000 (Financial Promotion) Order 2001 (SI 2001/3591).

function for Listing Particulars. Of course, the FSA is able to regulate the activities of persons authorised by it in the activity of arranging deals in such investments.

It is not possible, under present rules, for hedge funds to be admitted to the **4–060** Official List for trading in the UK. Funds of hedge funds, however, can be admitted to the List. This is because investment companies are required to invest "with the object of spreading investment risk and managing its portfolio . . .".[37] This requirement for risk spreading is effectively taken to mean that an investment company must be an "investment entity". The "trading" nature of a hedge fund means that it is regarded as falling outside the definition of "investment company", for example, through being a short-seller.[38] A fund of hedge funds, conversely, does satisfy the definition of an "investment company" providing it is structured as a long-only investor in a portfolio of underlying hedge funds.[39] Several funds of hedge funds were admitted to the Official List in 2001. They were, in addition, qualifying investments for the purposes of the Individual Savings Account Regulations[40] and can thus be held in ISAs by retail investors.

Turning to collective investment schemes, hedge funds are outside the scope of schemes which the FSA is willing to authorise or which are covered by the UCITS Directive. The FSA is able to permit authorised collective investment schemes to be marketed to the general public as a whole. However, unauthorised schemes are precluded by the FSMA from being so widely marketed.[41] Unregulated schemes may be marketed by FSA firms in accordance with the *COB Sourcebook*. Annex 5 of Chapter 3 of COB[42] states that such schemes may be marketed to:

- a person who is already a participant in an unregulated scheme of the type to be promoted, or has been within the last 30 months;

- a person for whom the firm has taken reasonable steps to ensure that investment in the scheme is suitable, but only where the person is an established or newly accepted customer of the firm or the firm's group;

- a person eligible to participate in a scheme constituted under the Church Funds Investment Measure 1958, s.24 of the Charities Act 1993 or s.25 of the Charities Act (Northern Ireland) 1964;

- an eligible employee (as defined) but only where the scheme is within the class specified;

---

[37] See the definition of "investment company" in the Listing Rules, para.21.1(f).
[38] See DP16, *Hedge Funds and the FSA* para.4.15.
[39] *ibid.*, para.4.16.
[40] SI 1998/1870.
[41] Financial Services and Markets Act 2000, s.238(5).
[42] See COB, 3.11.2R.

EFFICIENCY, CONFLICTS OF INTEREST AND GOVERNANCE

- a person admitted to membership of Lloyd's or a person entitled or bound to administer his affairs, where the scheme is established for the sole purpose of underwriting Lloyd's insurance business;

- an exempt person under the Financial Services and Markets Act 2000, other than one exempted only by s.39 if the promotion relates to the regulated activity in respect of which the person is exempt.

- a market counterparty or an intermediate customer—thus a firm may promote unregulated schemes to a private customer who has been classified as an "expert private customer".[43]

Unauthorised persons are able to promote unregulated schemes if they can rely on the exemptions set out in the Financial Services and Markets Act 2000 (Promotion of Collective Investment Schemes) (Exemptions) Order 2001. This enables promotion to be made to, *inter alia*, sophisticated investors. Note though that promotion to "high net worth" investors, another class of exemption, is generally not possible because the exemption is limited to schemes which invest "wholly or predominantly in the shares and debentures of an unlisted company".[44] Hedge funds would tend to invest in other instruments.

4–061 In addition to marketing, it is useful to remember that hedge funds can be recommended to retail consumers on the advice of an authorised financial adviser. Such advice must be consistent with the FSA rules which require that retail financial advisers must "know their customer"[45] and recommend only "suitable" investments in the light of that knowledge.[46]

From the description above, it is clear that limited marketing is possible, particularly where there is an intermediary of some kind standing between the investor and the product provider—either through advising the investor or else accepting responsibility for his status as sophisticated. This is logical—after all, institutions are free to invest into unregulated schemes, subject of course to any limits contained in the fund's own constitution. It is clear though, that for completely unregulated schemes such as hedge funds, marketing is extremely limited. Thus there is a trade-off between product regulation and marketability. At the moment there is no middle ground between fund authorisation (often with marketing possible to the whole of the EEA) and non-authorisation (marketing extremely limited). This will change to some extent with the introduction by the FSA of the new concept of "Non-Retail Schemes". At the time of writing this is merely a proposal.[47] However,

---

[43] See COB, 4.1.9R.
[44] Financial Services and Markets Act 2000 (Promotion of Collective Investment Schemes) (Exemptions) Order 2001, art.21(6).
[45] COB, 5.2.
[46] *ibid.*, 5.3.
[47] See the FSA's Consultation Paper 185, *The CIS Sourcebook—A New Approach*, May 2003.

124

it is most likely that a regime for such schemes will survive consultation and become part of the FSA rules. As their name implies, Non-Retail Schemes will be marketable only to non-retail investors. However, it seems that a retail investor may be able to invest, providing he has been classified as an "expert private investor".[48]

From CP185, it seems that funds of hedge funds will be possible as "non-retail" schemes, and also that it will be possible to construct some single manager hedge funds within this regime. However, limitations are proposed (*i.e.* some product regulation will be applied), and this would seem to preclude many hedge fund strategies from the regime.

Nonetheless this development will allow institutional investors a half-way house between investing in authorised, fully retail-saleable schemes on the one hand, and investing in a completely unregulated scheme on the other. The FSA is therefore proposing to take on some of the "due diligence" currently left entirely to the investor. That may well enable wider investment into hedge funds by cautious institutional investors. In addition, some institutional funds are precluded by the fund constitution from investing into unauthorised schemes and of course these "non-retail" schemes would be authorised. A greater universe of funds will therefore be available to such investors.

4–062

The "non-retail" schemes will also match developments elsewhere in Europe. Taking Ireland as an example, the Central Bank of Ireland announced in December 2002 the introduction of "Funds of Unregulated Funds Schemes".[49] To qualify for authorisation, these schemes have a minimum subscription of €12,500.[50] The French Commission des Operations de Bourse has announced a regime to regulate the retail marketing of funds of unregulated schemes, as has the German Finance Ministry. It seems that there is an international trend towards introducing regimes for the retail marketing of such funds. Most, however, do not permit the free marketing of the funds to the general public. Some regimes stratify would-be investors through a minimum subscription requirement. Others require some measure of sophistication on the part of the investor. The FSA's development of "non-retail funds" is therefore very much in tune with developments internationally.

Some hedge fund practitioners may express some disappointment that the UK regime does not permit marketability for hedge fund products on a par with other authorised funds. There is certainly an argument that funds of hedge funds are "investment entities" and could therefore be given greater

---

[48] Note that the intention with these schemes is not just that they cannot be marketed otherwise than to "non-retail" investors, such investors are precluded from making any investment in the scheme. CP185 states "The [Authorised Fund Manager] would be under an obligation to take reasonable steps to ensure that only [permitted] investors become holders in the fund": see CP185, para.5–53.

[49] Central Bank of Ireland, NU Series of Notices, Notice NU 25.1.

[50] *ibid.*, para.4.

marketability. This contention, however, may require testing before it is accepted. Is it the case that such funds of funds provide a similar diversification to "conventional" funds or funds of funds, or is there a greater concentration of risks possible? For example, if the hedge funds underlying the fund of funds take similar positions could the risk position of the fund of hedge funds become dangerously concentrated?[51] Or, alternatively, if the underlying funds take opposite positions, could these simply cancel out—meaning that the fund of fund's position is zero? These questions need to be considered before the analogy with "investment entities" can be accepted. Further details of the "non-retail" funds regime, and other CIS regulatory proposals will be included in *CIS Reform*, paras 4–068, *et seq*.

4–063   In addition, one should not understate the implications of the introduction of "non-retail funds". Hitherto the FSA has only had to consider in authorisation, the merits of a relatively narrow range of product structures and operations. So for the first time, the FSA will be considering the merits of funds of hedge funds and possibly certain types of single manager hedge fund, among others.

If funds of hedge funds prove to be retail investment entities, there would seem to be no reason why they should not be added to the existing range of widely marketable collective investment schemes within the UK. Single manager funds, however, are manifestly not retail investment entities. Any wider retail marketing for single manager funds would need to take place, it is submitted, in the context of a fundamental structural change to the regime for the marketing of retail investment products generally. Simply adding them to the existing regime for UK authorised schemes would be confusing for investors. Single manager funds span a wide range of risk-and-return possibilities. It is possible for a hedge fund to fail spectacularly and in a very short period—rather like a trading company in fact. In January 2003 a Japanese hedge fund called "Eifuku" collapsed over a period of one week in relatively calm trading conditions. It was reported[52] that the manager of the fund had assets of at least $1.4 billion but concentrated in only a few positions.

In the interests of allowing consumers to take responsibility for their own decisions, it might be possible to create a regime for some types of non retail investment entity—these products would not be "baskets of shares" with which retail investors were familiar. They could be hedge funds, but the difficulty in defining what is meant by the term "hedge fund" means that other products would need also to be in prospect. It would probably not be appropriate for retail investors to put a significant proportion of their savings into any one of these products, so great attention would be needed to developing appropriate disclosures and warnings.

---

[51] See by way of comparison the current problems with UK-based split-capital Investment Trusts.
[52] Henry Sender and Jason Singer, A Betting Man and His Fund's Hard Fall, *The Wall Street Journal*, April 11–13, 2003.

In its Feedback Statement to DP16, the FSA indicated that there has not **4–064** been any significant demand for hedge fund products, either from product providers, retail investment advisers or indeed from retail customers.[53] A further issue must therefore be whether the introduction of retail hedge fund vehicles would be met with any demand. The indications are that the introduction of any such regime would result in a gradual take-up rather than a sudden rush.

Before leaving the subject of retail hedge fund marketability, it is worth mentioning that the subject is unlikely to leave the international agenda quickly. A recent European Directive amending the UCITS Directive includes a requirement for the European Commission to produce a report, to be forwarded to the European Parliament and Council, reviewing the application of the UCITS Directive. The report must:

".... review the scope of the Directive in terms of how it applies to different types of products (*e.g.* institutional funds; retail-estate funds; master-feeder funds and hedge funds); the study should in particular focus on the size of the market for such funds, the regulation, where applicable of these funds in the Member States and an evaluation of the need for further harmonisation of these funds."[54]

The Report must be produced no later than February 13, 2005.

Short selling

In October 2002 the FSA published a Discussion Paper on short selling.[55] **4–065** This followed a great deal of press comment in the summer of 2002 which alleged that the depth of the bear market had been exacerbated by the activities of short-sellers. In addition, as stated by the FSA in its Paper, the markets have moved on since the last review of short-selling in 1996/7, and for that reason also it appeared to be time to look again at the practice. It is worth pointing out that, although hedge funds received some bad press coverage in this context, hedge funds are by no means the only short-sellers in the market.

The FSA summarised the arguments for and against the practice. Critics of short-selling claim it leads to increased share price volatility, and forces share prices to lower levels than would be reached otherwise. In extreme cases, a dramatic fall in the share price might cause companies difficulties, perhaps by undermining commercial confidence or making fundraising more difficult.

---

[53] *Hedge Funds and the FSA: Feedback Statement on DP16*, para.3.6.
[54] European Parliament and Council Directive 2001/108, O.J. L41, 13.2.2002, Art.2(b).
[55] DP17, *Short Selling*, FSA (October 2002).

On the other hand, proponents of short selling believe it is a necessary and desirable practice, which promotes liquidity and accelerates price corrections in over-valued stocks. Indeed, some people believe that short sellers actually stabilise prices in falling markets by covering their short sale positions (*i.e.* buying the stock for delivery). The point was also made that, even if short-selling itself were banned, the same effect could be achieved by dealing in futures or options. Did this mean that all other forms of bear trading should be banned as well?

4–066   The FSA stated in its Discussion Paper that its initial position was "[w]e do not consider that banning short selling or imposing constraints on its operation are either necessary or desirable".[56] This remained the FSA's view after the consultation exercise was completed.[57]

The FSA proposed three general options for increased transparency. Two of them were general disclosure-based options. Option 1 suggested that short sale transactions would be marked at the point of trade, with regular reporting to the FSA itself and to the exchanges. The information would then be published at intervals, in aggregated form. Option 2 would entail short positions to be aggregated by security in derivatives and cash equities.

Option 3 entailed the publication of securities lending data, already held by CRESTCo. The FSA was suggesting that the lending data might be used as a proxy for short selling.

4–067   In addition to the three general transparency options, the FSA also put forward three more targeted options. Option 4 entailed short sellers disclosing to the shorted company its short positions in the company's stock above a set threshold. Option 5 proposed that those taking uncovered short positions should disclose those positions. Option 6 concerned a proposed obligation on company directors to disclose short positions taken by them in the stock of the firms on whose boards they sit.

The FSA opted for Option 3 alone, stating that:

> "We believe that publication of stock borrowing data is a cost-effective way of improving market transparency. While the data may not be a good proxy for short selling, we believe the information is useful of itself to warrant publication. Provided sufficient customer confidentiality protections are put in place, publication should not harm legitimate commercial interests. We also believe that regular publication can, over time, provide a broad indication of short selling trends".[58]

---

[56] DP17, *Short Selling*, FSA (October 2002), para.2.7.
[57] See Feedback Statement 17, *Short Selling*, FSA (April 2003).
[58] *ibid.*, para.3.33.

CIS Reform

Introduction

The FSA published in Consultation Paper 185 a substantial rewrite of its **4–068** existing rules governing the authorisation and operation of collective investment schemes ("the CIS rules").[59] At the time of writing the proposals in CP 185 remain subject to consultation.

Various reasons are given for the decision to rework the CIS rules. European developments, such as the amendments to the UCITS Directive[60] have influenced policy thinking generally in this area and also the likely development of simplified products following the recommendations of the *Sandler Review*.[61] The existing rules were in any event rolled forward from the FSA's predecessor regulatory organisations and thus are based on the perceived regulatory needs of more than a decade ago. Arguably much of this goes back much further, to the Prevention of Fraud (Investments) Act 1958, and its predecessor legislation first introduced shortly after the 1929 stock market crash. Importantly, the FSA notes that its research indicates that "our product regime, unlike that in many other jurisdictions, did not reflect the different needs and risk profiles of CIS market participants". It is possible therefore that institutional investors are not as well served by the present regime as they might be.

CP185 sets out a complex scheme of regulatory change. The most important changes are described below.

Categorisation of retail funds

Various categories of authorised collective investment scheme ("AUT") are **4–069** allowed under the present rules. Such schemes can be securities schemes; money market schemes; futures and options schemes; geared futures and options schemes; property schemes; warrant schemes, feeder funds; or fund of funds schemes. CP185 proposes to simplify this regime to allow for first, "UCITS schemes" and, second, "Non-UCITS schemes". It is intended that firms will be able to target both these types of scheme at UK retail investors. A further scheme type, "Non-retail schemes" will, as their name implies, be available only for non-retail investors. This contraction of scheme types will accommodate the existing schemes—it does not imply a reduction in the variety of schemes. For example, the new regime will continue to allow for fund of funds schemes although the specific regime currently applied to them will

---

[59] CP185, *The CIS Sourcebook—A New Approach*, May 2003.
[60] European Parliament and Council Directives 2001/107 and 2001/108.
[61] See paras 4–034 to 4–048, above.

EFFICIENCY, CONFLICTS OF INTEREST AND GOVERNANCE

not continue. Indeed, the proposals are intended to introduce flexibility by eliminating the need to pigeonhole schemes into narrow categories.

Non-UCITS retail schemes will have investment policies which are different to those provided for in the UCITS directive. However, a requirement for a prudent spread of risk remains.[62] These schemes would not qualify for passporting under the UCITS directive and so will not be generally marketable elsewhere in the EEA.[63]

Limited redemption

4–070   CP185 proposes to allow operators of non-UCITS funds to restrict the right of unit holders to redeem their investment immediately.[64] Thus redemption may be limited to once in six months for funds where the FSA believes investors would be willing to accept less than immediate access[65] to their money, specifically funds which invest substantially in property or which have an objective to provide a specified return over a period.

The FSA intends that there should be disclosure of limited redemption arrangements before point of sale.[66]

Non-retail schemes

4–071   Non-retail schemes have already been referred to above in the discussion on hedge funds. However, the proposal to introduce a regime for non-retail schemes goes wider than hedge funds. A fuller analysis is therefore appropriate.

Although the non-retail schemes will be subject to some product regulation, there is acceptance that investors in these funds will not require the same level of protection as retail investors. Such investors will need to accept a higher degree of risk and also will be expected to have a greater degree of experience and expertise than retail customers. The applicable product regulation will be much lighter than that applied to retail schemes.

The authorised manager of a non-retail fund will be required to "take all reasonable steps to ensure that ownership of units in that scheme is only recorded in the register for . . . market counterparties and intermediate customers".[67] Thus, expert private customers, classified as intermediate

---

[62]   Draft rule 5.6.3R.

[63]   See draft rule CIS, 5.6.2R(1).

[64]   The FSA's interprets the UCITS directive to mean that limitation of redemption is not possible for UCITS funds, see CP185, para.4.19.

[65]   Present rules require that an investor must be able to sell units at least twice per month.

[66]   CP185, para.5.33.

[67]   Draft rule CIS, 8.1.2R. See also 8.5.14R where the obligation to be willing to effect the sale of units only applies in relation to qualifying investor.

130

CIS REFORM

customers under COB, 4.1.9R would be able to invest in the non-retail schemes. In addition to restricting the eligibility of investors, CP185 also proposes that the *Conduct of Business Sourcebook* should be amended to "prohibit promotion of these funds to clients falling outside the market counterparties and intermediate customer classification".[68]

Non-retail funds will not be subject to detailed rules on investment and borrowing powers, as are retail funds. Instead, draft rule 8.4.3R requires that the authorised fund manager:

    "... must take reasonable steps to ensure that the scheme property of the authorised fund provides a spread of risk, taking into account the investment objectives and policy of the scheme as stated in the most recently published prospectus and in particular any investment objective as regards return to the unit holders (whether through capital appreciation or income or both)".

It seems that the spread of risk must be in relation to both the capital and income of the scheme. In turn this seems to mean that "non-retail" funds must be "retail investment entities" as that term has been used in this Chapter.[69] So this would enable funds of hedge funds to be authorised, but many single manager funds may not satisfy the spread of risk test, much in the way that they are considered not to satisfy the requirement for spread of risk in the Listing Rules. CP185 specifically invites opinion on whether more guidance is needed to illustrate how diversification of risk may be provided. It is likely that the potential providers of hedge fund products will wish to seek further clarifications.

Financial and commodity derivatives will be allowed in the portfolios of non-retail schemes. CP185 suggests that this "together with our borrowing proposals means that these authorised funds could provide some of the characteristics that are currently present in some (unauthorised) hedge funds". However, the scheme's derivatives liability "should at all times be limited to the net assets of the fund, in order to prevent the fund's liabilities exceeding its net assets".[70] The non-retail schemes will be able to short-sell.

The new funds will be able to invest 100 per cent of their assets in foreign, development or untenanted real estate. However, a single real estate investment by the scheme would be unlikely to meet the requirement for a spread of risk.

4–072

4–073

Precious metals will be a permitted investment for the non-retail funds. Commodities contracts will also be permitted providing they are normally and regularly traded on a regulated market. The intention is to exclude all other non-financial assets. In addition, where the asset underlying a derivative or

---

[68] CP185, para.5.54.
[69] See paras 4–051 and 4–059.
[70] *ibid.*, para.5.56.

commodity contract is subject to physical delivery, the authorised scheme manager must ensure that he can readily close out the transaction.[71]

Borrowing is to be permitted for the non-retail funds up to 100 per cent of the net asset value of the property. The manager must take reasonable care to ensure that arrangements are in place to enable borrowing to be closed out to ensure that the 100 per cent limit is not breached.

4–074   Non-retail funds will be allowed to provide for limited redemption where this is allowed for by the fund's constituting instrument and where it is properly disclosed in the scheme prospectus. Intriguingly, the draft rules contain, as guidance, a requirement to consider "the reasonable expectations of the target investor group", indicating that disclosure is not the end of the story.[72] The guidance gives the example of a fund aiming to invest in "large property developments". In such a case it is reasonable to restrict redemption, essentially because the investors will understand the difficulties of quicker redemption in such cases—the illiquidity of the real estate investment would make it difficult to secure quick sale to release redemption proceeds. Even if it is possible in fact, a quick sale may not be achieved at the most advantageous price.

Retail funds are subject to considerable prescription in the way units in the fund are priced and valued. However, for the non-retail funds no prescription is proposed over the general requirement that the price must be related to net asset value. This is a statutory requirement for authorised funds.[73] The method of pricing must be set out in the prospectus. Prices will need to be published "in an appropriate manner".[74] This means that the frequency of pricing can be linked to the frequency of dealing. However, a rule is proposed to require the authorised fund manager to provide an indicative price on the request of the unit holder. This is linked to the possibility of limited redemption. If redemption were say, monthly, with monthly pricing to match, a unit holder would need to rely on potentially out-of-date information to make his decision to deal. So the ability to ask for an indicative price would enable the investor to base his decision to deal on current information.

As with a retail scheme, the depositary of a non-retail scheme will undertake the safekeeping of the scheme property.[75] The FSA perceives a need to ensure that the authorised scheme manager complies with the various rules on valuation, pricing, income calculation and investment and borrowing requirements. In retail schemes this oversight function is the responsibility of the depositary. For non-retail schemes, CP185 proposes that the oversight function may be exercised by another authorised person who is independent of the manager, provided that that person has "appropriate experience and

---

[71] Draft rule CIS, 8.4.8R(2).
[72] *ibid.*, 8.5.15G.
[73] Financial Services and Markets Act 2000, s.243(10)(a).
[74] Draft rule CIS, 8.5.12R(10).
[75] *ibid.*, 8.5.6R(1).

expertise" to do so.[76] The FSA believes that this separation of the oversight function may lead to increased competition in the market for those services.

CP185 proposes a simplified approach to charges. The types of charge **4–075** which might be levied and their level must be disclosed in the scheme instrument and in the non-retail scheme prospectus.[77]

The authorised scheme manager will be required to prepare reports and accounts for the non-retail scheme.[78]

Conclusion

This Chapter has presented a series of issues with which the investment man- **4–076** agement industry is concerned to varying degrees. These are not the only challenges facing the industry from regulation—the Chapter has ignored many FSA initiatives which impact generally across the financial sector. Space does not allow for a discussion of the extensive European agenda for regulatory change set down in the Financial Services Action Plan.

While it is difficult to draw a common thread through even the subjects aired in the Chapter, three overarching themes are suggested.

Economic efficiency

Questions and perceptions of economic efficiency feature in many of the **4–077** subjects discussed.

Paul Myners' *Review* points to problems with the way in which investment management is carried on, and asserts that a better deal can be achieved for investors through, for example, paying less attention to benchmarks between fund managers, and more attention to the liabilities of pension funds.

Polarisation is a matter of efficiency in the market for retail financial advice. Reform of polarisation should enable the majority of retail investors to get access to a wider range of investment products. The *Sandler Review* is concerned with efficiency in the retail investment market. The FSA's root and branch review of the regime for authorised collective investment schemes is also undoubtedly a question of efficiency.

The regulatory concern over hedge funds is also a matter of efficiency— in particular in ensuring that a range of funds is available to retail investors which meets the FSA's statutory objective to secure "the appropriate degree of protection for consumers", particularly in light of the statutory requirement to have regard to "the general principle that consumers should take responsibility for their decisions".

---

[76] *ibid.*, 8.5.7R(1).
[77] *ibid.*, 8.5.17G.
[78] *ibid.*, 8.3.6R.

CONCLUSION

Conflicts of Interest

4–078   Conflicts of interest are at the root of the concerns which the FSA's work on investment research, best execution and bundling and soft commissions are intended to address.

Corporate Governance

4–079   Governance as an issue underlies a great deal of the FSA's work since its inception—the development of Senior Management Responsibilities is perhaps the clearest example of that. Corporate governance is an important thread of Paul Myners' prescriptions for the investment management industry, and improved governance is the perceived solution to the spate of corporate scandals which has occurred in the US of which Enron is perhaps the leading example. It is likely that attention to corporate governance will remain a strong feature of regulatory change. Indeed, the FSA's work on Operational Risk is another pointer in that direction.[79]

---

[79] CP142, *Operational Risk Systems and Controls*, July 2002. See also the Feedback Statement, published in March 2003 and a further Policy Statement, *Building a Framework for Operational Risk Management: the FSA's Observations*, published in July 2003.

134

CHAPTER 5

CUSTODY—THE REGULATORY AND LEGISLATIVE REGIME

Nick Doe, Ernst & Young

Introduction and Definitions

The regulation of custody was introduced in 1997 when the activities of safe-guarding of investments and associated administration became authorised investment business under the Financial Services Act 1986. The regulatory regime introduced by the Self Regulating Organisations at that time has been integrated into Chapter 9 of the Conduct of Business section of the *FSA Handbook*, consolidating and standardising the approach. **5–001**

The current rules are underpinned by the Investment Services Directive, Art.10 and Principle 10 of the Financial Services Authority Principles for Businesses, both of which require a firm to provide adequate protection for investors' assets when entrusted to it.

The COB rules give effect to Financial Services and Markets Act 2000, ss.129–131. These sections and the COB rules also cover client money protection, mandates over client's assets, and collateral arrangements, not covered within the scope of this Chapter.

Safe custody investments

Custody is regulated where it applies to "safe custody investments". These are designated investments, defined in the Financial Services and Markets Act as follows: **5–002**

(a)   life policy;

(b)   share;

(c)   debenture;

(d)   government and public security;

(e) warrant;

(f) certificate representing certain securities;

(g) unit;

(h) stakeholder pension scheme;

(i) option (including a commodity option and option on a commodity future);

(j) future (including a commodity future and a rolling spot forex contract;

(k) contract for differences (including a spread bet and a rolling spot forex contract);

(l) rights to or interests in investments in (a) to (k).

In addition to being designated investments, to be a "safe custody investment", the following criteria must apply:

- the asset must not be the property of the firm;

- the firm, or any nominee company controlled by the firm or by its associate, must have accepted accountability for it;

- The asset must have been paid for in full by the client.

An asset ceases to be a safe custody investment when the firm has disposed of it in accordance with a valid instruction.

The investments can be in physical or dematerialised form, for example, securities within CREST. When safe custody investments are disposed of in accordance with a valid instruction by or on behalf of a client, they cease to be safe custody investments and are no longer covered by the custody rules.

Custody assets

5–003 "Custody assets" are a wider category of assets including both designated investments held for or on behalf of a client and any other asset, which is or may be held with a designated investment held for or on behalf of a client. This slightly confusing wider definition is intended to apply the custody rules in a manner appropriate to the nature and value of any assets held alongside designated investments as part of a portfolio for which the firm has accepted responsibility from the client. For example, works of art, jewellery and other physical assets would be required to be held with appropriate security when part of the overall investor's portfolio, but would not require the additional protection of the sections of the custody rules designed for designated investments and set out below.

INTRODUCTION AND DEFINITIONS

Safeguarding and administration

To require regulation, a custody service must be performed in respect of **5–004** designated investments and must consist of:

(a)   the safeguarding of assets belonging to another; and

(b)   the administration of those assets,

or arranging for one or more other persons to carry on that activity, where:

- the assets consist of or include any designated investment; or

- the arrangements for their safeguarding and administration are such that the assets *may* consist of or include designated investments, and have been held out as ones under which designated investments would be safeguarded and administered.

Safeguarding alone, such a pure safekeeping service performed by most banks within safe deposit boxes within its vault, is not custody requiring regulation. However, where safeguarding is performed in conjunction with administration, the overall activity becomes subject to regulation. Administration is defined as consisting of the following functions:

(a)   arranging settlement;

(b)   monitoring and processing corporate actions;

(c)   client account administration, liaison and reporting, including valuation and performance measurement;

(d)   ISA or PEP administration;

(e)   investment trust savings scheme administration.

These activities bring what would otherwise be pure safeguarding within the scope of custody regulation. However, they stop short of activities which would bring them under the heading of regulated investment management, which involve the exercise by the firm of material discretion over transactions in the investments.

Arranging custody

In addition to the performing of custody by a firm, the arrangement of **5–005** custody is also subject to the rules contained within COB 9. This covers the situation where a firm undertakes to arrange with an authorised custodian for the clients' assets to be safeguarded and administered. However, if

137

all the firm does is simply put the client in touch with a custodian who then makes arrangements directly with that firm, the rules do not apply to the introducing firm.

Exemptions

5–006 The custody rules do not generally apply to the following circumstances:

- Assets held for affiliated companies, unless the firm has been notified that the designated investment belongs to a client of the affiliated company.

- Assets held by an *operator* of a collective investment scheme in connection with that scheme.

- Assets temporarily held by a Personal Investment Firm provided that the firm:

    (a) keeps the asset secure, records it as belonging to that client, and forwards it to the client or in accordance with the client's instructions, as soon as practicable after receiving them;

    (b) retains the asset for no longer than the firm has taken reasonable steps to determine is necessary to check for errors and to receive the final document in connection with any series of transactions to which the documents relate; and

    (c) makes a record, which must then be retained for a period of three years after the record is made, of all the designated investments handled in accordance with (3)(a) and (b) together with the details of the clients concerned and of any action the firm has taken.

- Delivery versus payment transactions through a commercial settlement system.

The Legal Pre-Requisites and Regulatory Requirements

Client agreements

5–007 Before providing a custody service firms must ensure that a client agreement has been entered into with the customer setting out the terms and conditions of the service. The conduct of business rules are prescriptive as to the minimum items of information to be contained in such a contract. These include:

1 arrangements for registration of investments if not in the client's name;

THE LEGAL PRE-REQUISITES AND REGULATORY REQUIREMENTS

2   the extent of the firm's liability if a custodian defaults (a firm cannot disclaim responsibility for losses arising from default by its own nominee company or an affiliated company) for losses arising from fraud, wilful default or negligence by the firm;

3   the circumstances in which a firm can exercise its right to realise a safe custody investment for the purposes of collateral to meet the client's liabilities;

4   arrangements for the claiming and receiving of dividends, interest payments and other entitlements accruing to the client;

5   arrangements for handling takeovers and other corporate actions and for exercising voting, conversion and subscription rights;

6   arrangements for the distribution of entitlements to shares and any other benefits arising from corporate events where client's balances have been pooled;

7   arrangements for the provision of information to the client relating to investments held in custody;

8   the frequency of issue of statements to the client and the basis on which the assets shown on the statement are to be valued;

9   the fees and costs for the safe custody service (unless they have been notified to the client elsewhere); and

10 if pooling of investments of a number of clients is to take place, an explanation of the effects of pooling, for example that individual entitlements may not be identifiable and that in the event of an unreconcilable shortfall after the failure of a custodian, more clients may be required to share in that shortfall in proportion to their original share of the assets in the pool.

Custody and sub-custody agreements

Where firms arrange to pass clients' investments to a custodian (or a custodian delegates their responsibilities to a sub-custodian), this arrangement also is required to be covered by written terms including: **5–008**

1   confirmation that the title to the safe custody investment does not belong to the firm or to an affiliated company;

2   that the custodian will hold the safe custody investment separately from any designated investment belonging to the firm or the custodian;

3   that the custodian will deliver to the firm a statement as at specified dates of amounts and descriptions of all safe custody investments;

139

4　　that the custodian will not claim any lien, right of retention or sale over any safe custody investment, except with the client's consent or to meet any unpaid charges in respect of the safe custody service;

5　　arrangements for registration or recording of the safe custody investments, if not in the client's name;

6　　that the custodian is not permitted to withdraw any safe custody investment except on the firm's instructions;

7　　procedures and authorities for the passing of instructions from the firm to the custodian;

8　　arrangements for the claiming and receiving of dividends, interest payments and other entitlements accruing to the client; and

9　　the extent of the custodian's liability in the event of the loss of a safe custody investment caused by the fraud, wilful default or negligence of the custodian, or an agent appointed by him.

Segregation of safekeeping investments from the firm's assets

5–009　Safe custody investments must be segregated from the designated investments owned by the firm. If investments are placed with a custodian/sub-custodian, it must be clear that such investments belong to a client and should be segregated from the firm's own investments. This requirement includes ensuring that the title of any account held with a custodian makes clear that it is an account for safe custody investments belonging to one or more clients of a firm.

Registration

5–010　Registration of the legal title to safe custody investments must be made in the name of:

1　　the client (or the underlying client of an authorised person);

2　　a nominee company controlled by the firm, an affiliate, a recognised or designated investment exchange, or a custodian;

3　　a custodian, if the investment is subject to law or market practice of a jurisdiction outside the United Kingdom (provided this is in the client's best interests) and the firm has notified the client in writing;

4　　the firm (again if outside the United Kingdom and in the client's best interests), provided the client has been notified and, if a private customer, has given prior written consent; or

THE LEGAL PRE-REQUISITES AND REGULATORY REQUIREMENTS

5   any other person in accordance with the client's specific written instruction (provided that that person is not an associate of the firm if the client
is a private customer).

Adequate investigations must be made of the market concerned, if outside
the United Kingdom, including the obtaining of the appropriate legal
opinion.

Due diligence assessments on custodians and sub-custodians

Firms holding safe custody investments with a custodian or recommending **5–011**
custodians to private customers must carry out appropriate due diligence on
that custodian before appointment and on an ongoing basis, taking account
of the following:

1   expertise and market reputation;

2   arrangements for holding and safeguarding investments;

3   the legal position in the event of the insolvency of the custodian;

4   current industry standard reports;

5   the regulatory status of the custodian;

6   the custodians capital or financial resources;

7   the custodians credit rating; and

8   any other activities undertaken by the custodian and any affiliated
company.

Reconciliation

Fundamental to the protection of safe custody investments within the FSA   **5–012**
rules is the requirement for reconciliation of the records held by the firms
against information supplied by independent sources. The rules differentiate
between the reconciliation required for assets held with custodians (or in
dematerialised form) and those held physically by the firm.

In the case of assets held with custodians or in dematerialised form the
firm must reconcile its own records of safe custody investments with statements obtained from the custodians or from the person who maintains the
record of dematerialised legal entitlement. This reconciliation must be performed as frequently as is necessary to ensure the accuracy of the records, but
no less than once every 25 business days. The frequency of reconciliation is
determined at the firm's discretion in the light of the volume of transactions

occurring on accounts and other factors which might affect the accuracy of records. However, the FSA would expect a firm to set the frequency at a level which would prevent difficulties in investigating any exceptions arising from the reconciliation and in resolving them on a timely basis.

The rules recognise that it may be problematic to obtain statements of client's entitlements from unit trust managers, operators of ICVC's or administrators of offshore mutual funds. In this case the rules allow reconciliations of such holdings to be performed only as often as the statements are received but no less than once in every six months.

5–013   In the case of assets held physically by a firm, a reconciliation must be carried out no less than every six months (or twice in a period of 12 months but at least five months apart). It should involve a count of all investment physically held and a reconciliation of the result of that count with the firm's record of client holdings. It should also involve a reconciliation between the firm's record of client holdings and its record of the location of safe custody investments.

The guidance attached to the rules require a firm to ensure that the physical reconciliation is carried out by somebody who is independent of the production or maintenance of the records being reconciled.

The reconciliation must be performed as soon as reasonably practicable after the date to which it relates and will normally be expected to be completed within 25 business days of the date to which the statements relate.

5–014   The reconciliation method can consist of either:

- a total count of all investments as at the same date; or

- a count of a particular safe custody investment (stock line) as at the same date provided that all safe custody investments are counted and reconciled during a period of six months.

The latter method, known as the "rolling stock method", is conditional upon the FSA receiving written confirmation from the firm's auditor that appropriate systems and controls are in place adequately to perform this method.

Rectification and restitution

5–015   Where a reconciliation has been performed of assets held with third parties or directly by the firm, any discrepancies must be corrected promptly and a shortfall made good where there are reasonable grounds for concluding that the firm is responsible for that shortfall. If it is justifiably concluded that another person is responsible for the shortfall, the firm is not required to make it good. However, it is expected to take reasonable steps to resolve the position with the other person.

Notification requirements

If a firm fails to carry out any reconciliation requirement in accordance with the rules, or fails to comply with the requirement to correct discrepancies or make good shortfalls, it must notify the FSA in writing without delay. **5–016**

Record keeping

Proper records must be kept of all custody assets held or received by a firm. These must be maintained for a period of three years after the date when they were made. The records must separately identify any safe custody investments used in stock lending activity. **5–017**

Statements

Statements must be provided to clients, no less frequently than annually, listing all custody assets held for the client for which the firm is accountable. The rules prescribe the content of the client's statements and require that they are despatched within 25 business days of the date on which they are prepared. **5–018**

It is possible for custody statements to be provided as part of other statements provided by the firm, for example in respect of discretionary investment management, provided they are prepared in relation to the same date and delivered to the client within a reasonable period of one another. If a firm provides a range of safe custody services for a private customer which result in statements being produced by more than one system, the due date must be the same and the statements must be despatched within one week of each other, unless each statement makes clear that it relates to a particular service.

Issues for Consideration

The boundary between custody and pure safekeeping

The custody rules pose a problem in respect of the boundary between pure safekeeping of investments and safeguarding and administration. This turns on the inclusion within the rules of the definition of custody assets which embraces assets held alongside safekeeping investments (namely designated investments) and widens the scope of the rules considerably where firms are responsible for a client's entire portfolio. **5–019**

When custody became regulated in 1997 it was not intended to cover activities such as safekeeping services operated by banks. However, where such a service ends and safe custody in a regulated sense begins can be difficult to maintain. For example, in a private banking environment where banking and asset management are complimentary services provided to customers, the assets held may well be kept in the same safe and so share certificates held originally for safekeeping purposes would move into the regulated regime simply on the basis of the firm agreeing to carry out certain administrative services not previously comprehended in the relationship with the client. Examples of this could include undertaking to arrange for the collection of dividends or the transfer of securities into the firm's own CREST account or nominee for the purposes of facilitating the sale of investments.

Likewise, maintaining policy documents in safekeeping could become authorised custody in the event that administrative services are developed around those documents. Examples could include the buying of life policies for investment purposes, accompanied by an arrangement whereby the bonus is paid or accumulated and further investments made, supported by an administrative service providing valuations and periodic statements. Although such an arrangement might be intended to operate as an investment account, the holding of the policy documents would count as safekeeping of designated investments and therefore the custody rules would apply, requiring amongst other things, periodic reconciliation of policy documents which might not fully reflect the client's total investment.

5–020 It is hard to imagine that the FSA would choose to make technical distinctions between the accountability of firms for assets held as pure safekeeping investments and assets held as safe custody investments, particularly in view of the wider definition of custody assets and the difficulty in drawing boundaries around its meaning. Firms should not lose sight of the requirement of FSA Principal for Business 10 (Clients Assets) which states "a firm must arrange adequate protection for client's assets when it is responsible for them". This is very widely drawn and does not necessarily relate to the narrow definition of safekeeping investments.

Value-added services

5–021 With regard to firms authorised to conduct custody activities, many will find that their business is simply safekeeping and administration as defined by the rules. However, this is a somewhat artificial distinction when set alongside the role of a trustee/depository for collective investment schemes where safekeeping and administration of investments is combined with regulatory oversight of the investments undertaken by the schemes concerned. The rules on client agreements set out above provide that details should be supplied for arrangements of the provision of information on safe custody investments held by the firm or its nominee. Firms may wish to consider enhancing their basic custody service with monitoring services around areas such as investment strategy and limits. The increased concentration of the investment

ISSUES FOR CONSIDERATION

management industry and the development of boutique firms will be likely to lead to an increased demand for such services.

Consolidation of the custody industry

Consolidation also affects the custody industry itself. The FSA will be con- **5–022** cerned at the increasing concentration of custodial services and the globali-sation of the institutions involved, in terms of the impact on the UK investment management industry should one institution fail.

Presently, firms are required to carry out due diligence on potential custo-dians and overseas jurisdictions before appointing or recommending a custo-dian. In addition to these requirements, firms are required to notify customers, and to give them the opportunity to opt out, before recommend-ing a custodian within the same corporate group as themselves. It is likely that the globalisation of custody services, which has an identical effect in terms of group risk, will be subject to regulatory attention in the near future.

Passporting of custody services

Custody is the regulatory responsibility of the home state regulator and **5–023** therefore the FSA have responsibility for oversight of activities conducted in an EEA host state by a UK firm. This responsibility is likely to reinforce the FSA's interest in concentration within the custody industry, in the light of its responsibility for UK firms spanning a variety of European jurisdictions.

Responsibility of the custodian for corporate actions

Custodians generally arrange for corporate events to be responded to on **5–024** behalf of their underlying clients. As stated above, the FSA rules require that a client agreement should give details of arrangements for dealing with takeovers, voting rights, conversion and subscription rights. However, the rules are unclear as to the level of accountability of the custodian for the proper exercise of these entitlements and for the exercise of their administrative responsibilities.

It is true that authorised custodians will be subject to the requirements of the FSA Principles for Business covering Skill, Care and Diligence (2) and Management and Control (3). However, in order to differentiate themselves from their competitors, custodians are increasingly likely to rely on the qual-ity of their service standards around both their basic and their value-added services.

In addition to the processing of corporate actions, the availability of a range of banking services, the operation of accounts in foreign currencies, and the provision of stock borrowing and lending facilities, it is likely that custodians will enhance their services by the offering of, for example, regulatory oversight facilities as described above. An illustration of the feasibility of such additional services can be found in paras 5–025 *et seq.*, below, which set out the responsibilities of trustees and depositaries for authorised collective investment schemes operating in the UK. It is notable that for corresponding investments in European jurisdictions, the role is already performed by the designated "custodian".

The trustee/depository as custodian

5–025   The FSA's custody rules provide that where a trustee or depository acts as custodian for a trust or collective investment scheme and the trust for the scheme is established by a written instrument, then only certain rules will apply. This is subject to the trustee/depository having satisfied itself that the constitution of the scheme will provide protection at least equivalent to the custody rules. In such cases, only the rules regarding segregation, registration and recording, holding, stock lending, reconciliation and records will apply. However, when the trustee/depository arranges for or delegates the provision of custody to another person they must also carry out appropriate due diligence assessment of that person, disclose the relevant risks to their customers and arrange for a custodian agreement to be put in place containing the details set out above.

The basis for the deregation from the full extent of the custody rules when applied to trustees and depositories of authorised collective investments is to be found in the FSA's Collective Investment Schemes Sourcebook. Here, both in respect of authorised unit trusts and ICVC's, particular duties are placed on the trustee / depositary. Broadly, these are as follows:

1   the duty to ensure that the manager/ACD is managing the scheme in accordance with the Trust Deed or Instrument of Incorporation;

2   ensuring that the limitations on investment and borrowing powers are adhered to;

3   ensuring that appropriate procedures and methods are adopted to calculate prices accurately at each valuation point;

4   ensuring that the manager/ACD maintains sufficient records with regard to pricing;

5   ensuring that appropriate provisions are made for tax on the scheme including stamp duty reserve tax;

6   informing the FSA of any circumstances where there is no longer certainty that the scheme is being managed in accordance with the duties of

the manager/ACD or that decisions about the constituents of the scheme's property are not in accordance with the rules on investment and borrowing powers;

7   ensuring that all income due to the scheme is collected and all claims for repayment of tax are made;

8   taking into custody all deeds or other documents of title representing the scheme property;

9   exercising all rights (including voting rights attaching to the scheme property); and

10   executing all documents to ensure that transactions for the scheme are properly entered into.

The above statement of responsibilities amply illustrates the additional services to which reference was made above when discussing the role of the custodian in regulatory oversight. The FSA rules place a requirement on regulated firms to ensure that compliance monitoring is undertaken on a risk based approach. The limited resources available to perform this provide a strong argument for regulated firms to utilise delegated compliance monitoring resources of the custodian, trustee or depositary, not only for collective investments but for directly managed funds. This blurring of the distinction between trustee and custodian is in line with the approach adopted in Continental European regimes with for example, UCITS schemes able to be marketed into the UK.

Custody in a dematerialised environment

The move to dematerialised title in both equities and units has produced both benefits and disadvantages in respect of the role of the custodian.   **5–026**

The existence of settlement systems such as CREST and EUROCLEAR have enabled the transfer of both tangible and intangible securities to be handled in very similar ways, namely by a form of book entry rather than physical delivery of the stock. However, the existence of these systems has produced corresponding difficulties for the custodian particularly in respect of their obligations to reconcile assets and deliver statements to their clients. The development of the dematerialised systems have not been accompanied by effective obligations on managers of collective investments or portfolio managers to produce statements to a frequency corresponding to that of the reconciliation obligations on the custodian. Consequently, the rule requiring custodians to reconcile dematerialised assets is a somewhat unsatisfactory compromise and allows reconciliations to be performed less frequently than monthly in the event that it proves difficult to obtain statements from asset managers.

CUSTODY—THE REGULATORY AND LEGISLATIVE REGIME

Should there prove to be an increased move towards the trustee/ custodian model referred to above, a necessary pre-requisite of this would be co-ordination of the rules affecting the provision of information between different service providers in the market. This would enable accuracy of records, efficiency of reconciliation, and the avoidance or prompt rectification of discrepancies.

Custody in a material environment

5–027 With the increased move towards demateralisation of securities, it can be easy for regulated firms to lose sight of the strict requirements for physically held assets. The sheer time-consuming nature of conducting a physical count of securities places burdens on firms and the time taken to investigate reconciliation differences can be significantly longer than the time taken for dematerialised investments.

In many cases stock certificates are out-of-date or stock lines have been sub-divided. Company names may have changed or corporate events may have altered the entitlement of the client to securities without corresponding changes to the paper records.

The physical location of the assets may be problematic, as not all firms will possess vaults of adequate size and vaults may well be in a number of locations.

5–028 Significant effort will be required to coordinate the physical count and to ensure that it is supervised at all locations by the person independent from the creation of the relevant records. These difficulties will apply whether the firm adopts the total count or rolling stock line basis of reconciliation. Should firms decide to adopt the latter approach, it should not be forgotten that prior approval is required from the firm's auditor to the systems and controls enabling each stock line to be counted separately at least once within a six month period. Notification to the FSA is also required.

Regardless of the choice of approach adopted by firms, the firm's auditors will be required on an annual basis to certify to the FSA that the firm has complied with the customer asset rules. It is therefore prudent for firms to satisfy their auditors in any event with regard to their systems and controls over customer assets and their process for controlling reconciliation and the resolution of discrepancies.

Sub-custody

5–029 The requirements for agreements when a firm passes customer safe custody investments to a custodian are set out above. The same requirements apply in the event that a custodian makes arrangements for assets in particular jurisdictions to be held by sub-custodians in those jurisdictions. Agreements must

148

ISSUES FOR CONSIDERATION

be in place covering the specified items and the custodian must undertake due diligence with regard to their sub-custodian and the jurisdiction in which they operate. The criteria for carrying out the risk assessment on the custodian are set out above. It is a requirement of the rules that this assessment is made in respect of the continued appointment of a custodian/sub-custodian periodically as often as is reasonable in the relevant market, taking account of the current legal requirements and the custodial practices of that jurisdiction.

Practical arrangements for conducting this due diligence review will vary. In some jurisdictions it will be possible to use local agencies to perform the assessment on behalf of the firm or custodian. Local branches of the firm performing the assessment may well be suitable to carry this out. In other instances, where for example, an emerging market is involved, the risks attached to that jurisdiction may justify direct visits from the firm/custodian to perform the due diligence personally. Firms should develop a risk-based monitoring programme to ensure that visits/reviews of the appropriate frequency and nature are performed. The results of these visits should be maintained for review and to demonstrate compliance to the FSA.

Future developments

The above review of the regulatory regime for custody in the UK has pointed towards probable changes in the approach in the future. These changes centre mainly on the enhancement of the custodians' role to provide regulatory oversight services for the benefit of firms and in support of the FSA's supervision of the market. In addition to their response to regulatory developments it is likely that firms providing custody will wish to differentiate themselves from their competition both in terms of service standards and in the delivery of enhanced services to their clients. The high-volume, low-cost basic custody service is unlikely to prove profitable without the addition of such value-added additional services. The current boundaries, where they exist, between trustee/depositary services, third-party administration services (transfer agency) and custody are likely to become less significant in the marketplace going forward.

5–030

As indicated above, it is also likely that the FSA will endeavour to limit the concentration of risk with particular custodian firms. Should such firms be providing significant other services to the market, as is already the case in respect of third-party administration, it is likely that additional safeguards and higher supervisory and prudential requirements will be applied.

Finally, it is clear that the overall regulatory burden applicable to custody and the provision of services associated with it will continue to increase rapidly. This is not surprising but is notable in the light of custody only becoming a regulated activity in 1997.

CHAPTER 6

US REGULATION OF INVESTMENT MANAGEMENT

Michael McDonough and Maureen Magner, Dechert LLP, London

Introduction

6–001 The US Securities and Exchange Commission ("SEC"), under the Investment Advisers Act of 1940 (the "Advisers Act"),[1] regulates persons classified as "investment advisers" when they provide investment advice or investment management services (discretionary and non-discretionary) to clients. The US Congress passed the Advisers Act in the wake of the stock market crash of 1929 and the depression of the 1930s as a measure to achieve high ethical standards in the securities industry, and to mitigate and eliminate fraud or deceit by an adviser on any existing or prospective client.[2] The Advisers Act seeks to achieve these goals by exposing actual and perceived conflicts of interest that might cause an adviser to render less than disinterested advice to its client.[3]

The Adviser's Act supplements a series of other US federal statutes regulating the securities industry.[4] It requires registration of certain advisers who must then comply with a range of rules and regulations on matters such as record-keeping, advisory contracts, advertising, custody of client funds and assets, proxy voting, *etc.* The Advisers Act also imposes an "antifraud" provision upon all investment advisers, regardless of whether they are required to register with the SEC.[5]

This Chapter provides a general overview of who must register with the SEC as an investment adviser, exemptions and exceptions from such registration,

---

[1] 15 U.S.C., § 77a *et seq.* All citations to Sections and Rules are to sections of the Advisers Act and rules thereunder unless otherwise specified.
[2] *Securities and Exchange Commission v Capital Gains Research Bureau, Inc.*, 375 U.S. 180 (1963) (considering the history and purpose of the Advisers Act).
[3] *ibid.*
[4] The Act was preceded by the Securities Act of 1933, the Securities Exchange Act of 1934, the Public Utility Holding Company Act of 1935, the Trust Indenture Act of 1939, and the Investment Company Act of 1940.
[5] Investment Advisers Act of 1940, Section 206. See "Anti-Fraud" section at para.6–016.

INTRODUCTION

and the regulatory requirements and responsibilities of a registered adviser. It does not describe every requirement to which an investment adviser may be subject. US fiduciary duties are dealt with in Chapter 9, and futures management in Chapter 12.

US Federal vs State Regulation

In 1996, the US Congress enacted the National Securities Market Improve- **6–002** ment Act of 1996 ("NSMIA"), which allocated regulation of investment advisers between the SEC and the US states.[6] The SEC has exclusive juris- diction over the following: (i) advisers with managed assets of at least $30 million or advisers with at least $25 million who choose to register with the SEC[7]; (ii) advisers to US registered investment companies[8]; (iii) non-US advisers[9]; (iv) advisers located in states that do not regulate investment advisers (currently, Wyoming and the US Virgin Islands)[10]; (v) advisers that are excluded from the definition of "investment adviser" under Section 202(a)(11); (vi) nationally recognised statistical rating Organisations ("NRSROs")[11]; (vii) advisers that anticipate being eligible for SEC registra- tion within 120 days of filing their application[12]; (viii) pension consultants to plans with at least $50 million in assets[13]; (ix) advisers that are affiliated with, and have the same principal office and place of business as, one of the fore- going[14]; and (x) advisers providing investment advise to clients exclusively through an interactive website.[15]

States have exclusive jurisdiction over advisers with less than $25 million in assets under management that are not otherwise eligible to register with the SEC. A state is prohibited from applying its registration and licensing laws to investment advisers (including its "supervised persons", *i.e.* partners, direc- tors, officers and employees of the adviser) that are registered under the Advisers Act or excepted from the definition of "investment adviser" under the Advisers Act.[16] Further, where an adviser is not registered with the SEC (*e.g.* in reliance on an exemption) or excepted from the definition of "invest- ment adviser" a state may not impose its registration or licensing laws on the

---

[6] National Securities Markets Improvements Act of 1996 ("NSMIA"), Pub.L. No. 104–290, 110 stat. 3416 (1996).
[7] Investment Advisers Act of 1940, Section 203A(a)(1)(A); Rule 203A-1.
[8] *ibid.*, Section 203A(a)(1)(B).
[9] Rules Implementing Amendments to the Investment Advisers Act of 1940, Investment Advisers Act Release No.1633, 1997 WL 253350 (May 15, 1997) ("Release 1633").
[10] Release 1633.
[11] *ibid.*, Investment Advisers Act of 1940, Rule 203A-2(a).
[12] *ibid.*, Rule 203A-2(d).
[13] *ibid.*, Rule 203A-2(b).
[14] *ibid.*, Rule 203A-2(c).
[15] *ibid.*, Rule 203A-2(f).
[16] *ibid.*, Section 203A(b)(1).

adviser if it does not have a place of business within the state and has had fewer than six clients who are state residents during the last 12 months.[17]

An adviser must be aware that although state investment adviser statutes no longer apply to SEC-registered advisers, other state laws, including other state securities laws, still apply. In addition, state laws may require an SEC-registered adviser to: (i) comply with state anti-fraud prohibitions; (ii) provide the state regulator with a copy of its SEC registration; and (iii) pay state licensing and renewal fees.

Who Must Register Under the Advisers Act

6–003   Any investment adviser engaging in US interstate commerce (*e.g.* telephone calls or faxes to or from the US) must register with the SEC unless it is: (i) excluded from the definition of "investment adviser" as defined pursuant to Section 202(a)(11), (ii) exempt from registration, or (iii) prohibited from registration.[18]

Definition

6–004   The Advisers Act defines "investment adviser" to mean, in part, any person who (i) for compensation; (ii) is engaged in the business of; (iii) providing advice to others or issuing reports or analyses regarding securities.[19] A person must satisfy all three heads of the definition to be an "investment adviser". Each head is separately and generally discussed below.

For compensation

6–005   "Compensation" includes the receipt of any economic benefit, whether in the form of an advisory or other fee, a commission, or any combination thereof.[20] The compensation element is satisfied if a single fee is charged for multiple services, including investment advice or the issuing of reports or

---

[17] *ibid.*, Section 222(d); Release 1633.
[18] *ibid.*, Section 203(a).
[19] *ibid.*, Section 202(a)(11).
[20] *SEC v Fife*, 311 F.3d 1 (1st Cir. November 6, 2002) (providing advice on the understanding that successful investment will yield a future commission satisfies the "compensation" element); In *Re Alexander v Stein*, Investment Adviser Act Release. No.1497 (June 8, 1995) (diverting client funds for personal use satisfies the "compensation" requirement); Applicability of the Investment Advisers Act of 1940 to Financial Planners, Pension Consultants, and Other Persons Who Provide Others with Investment Advise as a Component of Other Financial Services, Investment Advisers Act Release No.1092 (October 8, 1987) ("Release 1092").

WHO MUST REGISTER UNDER THE ADVISERS ACT

analyses concerning securities within the meaning of the Advisers Act.[21] Additionally, indirect receipt of a fee (*e.g.* a fee or commission received from someone other than the recipient of the advice) also satisfies the compensation element.[22] For example, if an adviser receives a commission from a third party for sale of an investment product to a client, that commission may satisfy the compensation requirement.[23]

Engaged in the business

There is no formula for determining when a person may be deemed to be "engaged in the business" of giving advice. Providing advice need not be a person's sole or principal business activity or represent a specific percentage of such person's business activity.[24] Rather, determining whether a person is "engaged in the business" is based on the surrounding facts and circumstances of the situation.[25] Factors considered in making such a determination include: (i) whether the person holds himself out as an investment adviser or as one who provides investment advice; (ii) whether the person receives compensation for providing advice about securities; and (iii) the frequency of the advice provided.[26] Generally a person providing advice about specific securities will be considered "engaged in the business" unless the person renders specific advice rarely or on an isolated occasion.[27]

6–006

Advice about securities

A person is deemed to be providing advice about securities when they provide advice about securities specifically or generally.[28] Moreover, the SEC staff has determined that advice about the following is considered to be "advice about securities": (i) market trends[29]; (ii) the selection and retention of other advisers[30]; (iii) the advantages of investing in securities versus other types of investments[31]; (iv) providing a selective list of securities data even if no advice

6–007

---

[21] Release 1092; Financial Planning and Advisory Services, SEC No-Action Letter, (December 11, 1979).

[22] Kenisa Oil Company, SEC No-Action Letter (May 6, 1982).

[23] Warren M. Linvingston, SEC No-Action Letter (March 8, 1990).

[24] Release 1092.

[25] *ibid.*

[26] Release 1092; *Zinn v Parish*, 644 F.2d 360 (7th Cir. 1981).

[27] *ibid.*

[28] *ibid.*

[29] Maratta Advisory, Inc., SEC No-Action Letter, (July 16, 1981); Dow Theory Forecasts, SEC No-Action Letter (February 2 1978);

[30] Capital Asset Program, SEC No-Action Letter (December 1, 1974).

[31] *ibid.*

is provided as to any one security[32]; (v) asset allocation[33]; and (vi) statistical or historical data, unless the advice is no more than an objective report of facts on a non-selective basis.[34]

Advice about commodities is not advice about securities.[35] Also, the SEC staff does not believe that the Advisers Act applies to persons whose activities are limited to advising issuers concerning the structuring of their securities offerings.[36]

Although the Advisers Act only refers to the giving of "advice", it is in practice assumed to extend to both advisory and discretionary management, and the distinction between advice and discretion made in the UK is unfamiliar to US practitioners.

Exclusions from registration

6–008 Certain entities, which include, among others, brokers and dealers, are excluded from the definition of "investment adviser" and are thus not subject to the Advisers Act provisions. Brokers and dealers that are registered with the SEC under the Securities and Exchange Act of 1934 ("Exchange Act") are excluded from the Advisers Act if the advice given is incidental to the conduct of their business as brokers or dealers, and they do not receive any "special compensation".[37] The SEC staff has stated that a registered representative of a broker-dealer can rely on the exception if the broker-dealer: (i) gives advice within the scope of employment and incidental to the employer's activities as a registered broker-dealer; and (ii) receives no special compensation for the advice.[38]

A non-US broker or dealer who is not registered under the Exchange Act and who provides investment advice and brokerage research to US persons would be required generally to register under the Advisers Act.[39] However, the SEC staff may respond favourably to no-action requests where a non-US broker-dealer is not registered under the Exchange Act but meets the requirements of Section 202(a)(11)(C) (registered broker-dealer exemption from adviser registration) and meets certain conditions in Rule 15a-6 under

---

[32] RDM Infodustries, Inc., SEC No-Action Letter (March 25, 1996) (providing information about securities in a report does not constitute providing advice about the securities if: (i) the information is readily available to the public in its raw state; (ii) the categories of information presented are not highly selective; and (iii) the information is not organised or presented in a manner that suggests the purchase, holding, or sale of any security.

[33] Maratta Advisory, Inc., SEC No-Action Letter (July 16, 1981).

[34] *ibid.*; Bridge Data Co., SEC No-Action Letter (May 31, 1975).

[35] Robert R. Champion, SEC No-Action Letter (September 22, 1986).

[36] Applicability of the Advisers Act to Financial Advisors of Municipal Securities Issuers, Division of Investment Management, SEC Staff Legal Bulletin No. 11 (September 19, 2000).

[37] Investment Advisers Act of 1940, Section 202(a)(11)(C).

[38] Institute of Certified Financial Planners, SEC No-Action Letter (January 21, 1986).

[39] Citicorp, SEC No-Action Letter (September 14 1986).

the Exchange Act (which exempts non-US broker-dealers from registration under the Exchange Act where their activities are limited to those permitted by Rule 15a-6).[40] For example, the SEC staff did not a require a non-US broker-dealer to register as an investment adviser where the non-US broker-dealer furnished research reports to major US institutional investors, in a manner not designed to induce transactions in the securities covered by the report or otherwise result in transactions being executed through the non-US broker-dealer.[41]

Exemptions from registration

The Advisers Act provides six voluntary registration exemptions, (though an adviser eligible for such exemptions can nonetheless register with the SEC if it so wishes).[42] An adviser exempt from registration is not subject to the Advisers Act's record-keeping rules or SEC examination, but is subject to the Advisers Act's anti-fraud provisions.[43]   **6–009**

The most common exemption from registration used by investment advisers is the "fewer than 15 clients" exemption. This *de minimis* exemption permits an investment adviser to have up to 14 clients without being required to register with the SEC.[44] An investment adviser with its principal place of business outside of the US, need only count its US clients in determining whether it has reached the 14-client limit.[45] Moreover, all investment advisers may count a corporation, general partnership, limited partnership, limited liability company, or trust (that receives investment advice based on its investment objectives rather than the individual investment objectives of its shareholders, partners, limited partners, members, or beneficiaries) as a single client. For example, a manager may count an investment company, including a hedge fund, as one client.[46] To rely on the *de minimis* exemption,

---

[40] Securities Exchange Act Release No. 27017 (July 11, 1989); Charterhouse Tilney, SEC No-Action Letter (July 15, 1993); James Cape & Co. Limited, SEC No-Action Letter (December 6, 1989).

[41] Charterhouse Tilney, SEC No-Action Letter (July 15, 1993); James Cape & Co. Limited, SEC No-Action Letter (December 6, 1989).

[42] A firm might register voluntarily to gain a competitive advantage in attracting capital for its investment vehicle. For example, a hedge fund manager registered as an adviser pursuant to the Advisers Act may (subject to a number of further requirements) accept ERISA assets that exceed the 25 per cent plan asset limit typically adhered to by managers. Moreover, a manager would be able to give assurances to its US investors that it is regulated and monitored by a suitable and well-respected regulatory agency. An assurance of this sort is requested more frequently in the US financial market in light of recent large scale frauds.

[43] See "Anti-Fraud" Section at para.6–016.

[44] Investment Advisers Act of 1940, Rule 203(b)(3)-1.

[45] *ibid.*, Rule 203(b)(3)-1(b)(5).

[46] The SEC staff in its recent report "Implications of the Growth of Hedge Funds" (the "Report"), proposed amending the *de minimis* exemption to require hedge fund managers to "look through" their hedge fund clients and count each investor in a hedge fund as a client for purposes of the 15-client threshold. If adopted, this will result in a registration

US REGULATION OF INVESTMENT MANAGEMENT

an investment adviser must comply with certain conditions, which include ensuring that it does not "hold itself out" in the US as an investment adviser.

Advisory affiliates

6–010 Previously, the SEC staff took the position that a non-US investment adviser could avoid the purview of the Advisers Act if the firm formed a separate and independent subsidiary to provide investment advise to US clients. Such subsidiaries were subject to strict conditions which included, among other things, that the subsidiary was adequately capitalised and did not share investment advisory personnel with the non-US investment adviser.[47] These conditions caused difficulty for non-US investment advisers who did not want to assign senior personnel to be employed exclusively by their US registered subsidiary. This in turn led, in some instances, to a reduction in the quality of the services provided by the relevant US adviser to its US clients.

In *Uniao de Bancos de Brasileiros SA ("Unibanco"),*[48] and in related SEC no-action letters,[49] the SEC staff relaxed this position by adopting a "conducts and effects" approach to the extraterritorial application of the Advisers Act.[50] Unregistered affiliates(s) may now provide advisory personnel to assist a registered affiliate as "participating affiliates" provided, among other things, that: (i) an unregistered adviser and its registered affiliate are separately organised; (ii) the registered affiliate is staffed with personnel (located in the US or abroad) who are capable of providing investment advice; (iii) all personnel involved in US advisory activities must be deemed "associated persons" of the registered affiliate[51]; and (iv) the SEC must have adequate access to trading and other records of the unregistered adviser and to its personnel,

---

requirement for most hedge fund managers in the US and for any non-US hedge fund manager with more than 14 US investors. For example, if a non-US hedge fund manager advises or sub-advises one hedge fund with more than 14 US investors then the manager would be required to register with the SEC as an investment adviser. A copy of the Report is available on the SEC's website at *http://www.sec.gov/news/studies/hedgefunds0903.pdf.*

[47] Richard Ellis, SEC No-Action Letter (September 17, 1981).

[48] Uniao de Bancos de Brasilerios, S.A., SEC No-Action Letter, (July 28, 1992) ("*Unibanco*").

[49] *Unibanco* involved an unregistered parent sharing employees with a registered subsidiary. Subsequent SEC no-action letters concluded that the same principles apply to sharing advisory personnel between sister companies or affiliates. See, *e.g.* Mercury Asset Management plc, SEC No-Action Letter (April 16, 1993) ("*Mercury*"); Kleinwort Benson Investment Management Limited, SEC No-Action Letter (December 15, 1993)("*Kleinwort*"); Murray Johnstone Holdings Limited, SEC No-Action Letter (October 7, 1994) ("*Murray Johnstone*"); and Royal Bank of Canada, SEC No-Action Letter (June 3, 1998) ("*Royal Bank*").

[50] The scope of SEC enforcement activities under the Advisers Act would be limited to those advisory activities that are either conducted in the United States or have effects in the United States.

[51] In *Unibanco*, the SEC staff defined "associated persons" as including "research analysts and other employees of Unibanco whose functions or duties relate to the determination of which recommendations UC may make to its United States clients." *Kleinwort* and subsequent letters restated and expanded the definition as follows: "[E]ach employee of the Participating

156

WHO MUST REGISTER UNDER THE ADVISERS ACT

to the extent necessary to enable the SEC to monitor and police conduct that may harm US clients or markets.

Adviser Registration Process

Filing Form ADV

Investment advisers required to register with the SEC must file a registration **6–011** statement known as "Form ADV" with the SEC. Form ADV is primarily a disclosure document which gives information to the SEC and US states, as applicable, for administrative and regulatory purposes and gives information to advisory clients for disclosure purposes. Investment advisers required to register only with certain US states rather than with the SEC generally, will use Form ADV for their US state registration(s). Form ADV covers the investment adviser, its employees and others that the investment adviser controls. As long as the advisory activities of an employee are undertaken on behalf of the registered adviser, the employee is not required to register individually as an investment adviser or an investment adviser agent.[52]

Form ADV, Part I

Part I of Form ADV is primarily for SEC use, and must be filed electronically **6–012** with the SEC through the IARD, a website created by the National Associa- tion of Securities Dealers Regulation, Inc. ("NASDR"). Part I requires a variety of information about an adviser's business, including the persons who own or control the adviser and whether the adviser or certain of its personnel have been sanctioned for violating the securities laws or other laws.

Form ADV, Part II

Part II of Form ADV is primarily intended for client use. It is a written dis- **6–013** closure statement (or a written brochure) that provides information about business practices, fees, services, types of clients and investments, trading strategies, and conflicts of interest that the adviser may have with its clients. Part II cannot yet be filed electronically through the IARD, although such

---

Affiliate, including research analysts, who (i) provides advice to . . . United States clients; or (ii) has access to any information concerning which securities are being recommended to . . . United States clients prior to the effective dissemination of the recommendations." See, also, *Murray Johnstone; Royal Bank*.

[52] Investment Advisers; Uniform Registration, Disclosure, and Reporting Requirements; Staff Interpretation, Investment Advisers Act Release No.1000, (December 3, 1985) ("Release 1000"); Ms. Corinne E. Wood (April 17, 1986).

electronic filing is being proposed. See further under "Brochure Rule" at para.6–033 below.

Investment advisers are required to deliver a copy of a current Part II (or a brochure containing at least the information required by Part II) to prospective clients at least 48 hours before entering into an advisory agreement or at the time of entering into the agreement if it is terminable by the client without penalty for five days.[52a] Part II must be offered annually to clients and maintained in updated form on the adviser's premises for SEC inspection.[52b]

SEC response

6–014   Within 45 days after filing Form ADV, the SEC must either grant the adviser's registration by order, or institute proceedings to deny registration.[53] The SEC may deny registration where the applicant has been convicted of any felony involving the purchase or sale of securities, or other felony involving theft, larceny, forgery, etc.[54] If the SEC staff have questions or problems with an ADV filing, they typically will call or write to the investment adviser. The Staff may request that the adviser agree to delay the effectiveness of its ADV so that any problems can be resolved.

Updating Form ADV

6–015   To keep its registration in good standing, an investment adviser must amend its Form ADV at least annually, within 90 days after the end of the investment adviser's fiscal year, and more frequently in the case of certain more significant information changes.[55] Failure to update a Form ADV may result in disciplinary, administrative, injunctive, or criminal action against the investment adviser by the SEC and/or a state.[56] Additionally, a materially misleading Form ADV could be the basis for a client asserting a claim against the investment adviser for fraud.

[52a] Investment Advisers Act of 1940, Rule 204-3.
[52b] *ibid.*
[53] *ibid.*, Section 203(c)(2).
[54] *ibid.*
[55] *ibid.*, Rule 204-1 and General Instructions to Form ADV.
[56] See *e.g.* Re C&G Asset Mgmt., Inc., Investment Advisers Act Release No.1536 (November 9, 1995) (failure to amend Form ADV promptly to disclose NASD disciplinary actions against adviser and affiliates).

Ongoing Requirements for a Registered Investment Adviser

Anti-fraud

Section 206 contains a general anti-fraud provision under which many investment adviser activities, some of which are discussed more fully below, are regulated.

6–016

Section 206 provides that is shall be unlawful for *any* investment adviser (whether exempt from registration or not): (i) to employ any devise, scheme, or artifice to defraud any client or prospective client; (ii) to engage in any transaction, practice, or course of business which operates as a fraud or deceit upon any client or prospective client; (iii) acting as principal for his own account or as broker for another client, knowingly to sell any security to or purchase any security from a client, or to effect any security transaction no behalf of the account of a client, without previously disclosing the details of the transaction to the client and obtaining the client's consent thereto (except when a client deals with a customer of a broker-dealer and the broker-dealer is not also acting as investment adviser in relation to the transaction); or (iv) to engage in any act, practice, or course of business which is fraudulent, deceptive or manipulative.

Principal transactions

An investment adviser must not, as principal for its own account, knowingly buy any security from a client, or sell any security to a client, without: (i) disclosing to the client the capacity in which it is acting in writing and before completion of the transaction, and (ii) obtaining the client's consent to each such transaction.[57] Client consent may be obtained either prior to execution of the transaction or prior to the settlement of the transaction.[58] A "blanket" disclosure and consent normally is not sufficient absent specific relief granted by the SEC.[59] These requirements also apply where an adviser's affiliate, for example a broker-dealer under common control with the adviser, acts as a principal in transactions with the adviser's clients.[60]

6–017

---

[57] Investment Advisers Act of 1940, Section 206(3).

[58] Interpretation of Section 206(3) of the Investment Advisers Act of 1940; Release No.1732 (July 17, 1998) ("Release 1732").

[59] Re Stephens, Inc. Investment Advisers Act Release No.1666 (September 16, 1997) (finding that although the investment adviser had obtained written blanket consents to principal trades from clients, such blanket consents do not satisfy the requirements of Section 206(3)).

[60] Merrill Lynch Trust Company, FSB, SEC No-Action Letter (July 6, 2000); Re Calamos Asset Mgmt., Inc., et al., Investment Advisers Act Release No.1594 (October 16, 1996); Re Concord Investment Co., Investment Advisers Act Release No.1585 (September 27, 1996); Re Clariden Asset Mgmt. (New York) Inc., et al., Investment Advisers Act Release No.1504 (July 10, 1995); Re Credit Suisse Asset Mgmt., Inc., Investment Advisers Act Release No.1452 (November 16, 1994); Re Piper Capital Mgmt., Inc., Investment Advisers Act Release No.1435 (August 11, 1994); Interplan Securities Corp., SEC No-Action Letter, (February 23, 1978); Hartzmark & co., Inc., SEC No-Action Letter (November 11, 1973).

Agency cross-transactions

6–018 An investment adviser is also generally prohibited from taking part in agency cross-trades, *i.e.* acting as broker for both its advisory client and the counterparty to the brokerage transaction.[61] However, the SEC provides a safe harbour from this prohibition if the adviser meets all the following conditions: (i) the client executes a written consent prospectively authorising such transactions; (ii) the adviser makes full written disclosure to the client of the capacity in which it is acting, and its possible conflict of loyalty and responsibility; (iii) the adviser sends the client written confirmation of each agency cross transaction; (iv) the adviser sends the client on an annual basis a statement of all agency cross transactions for the year; and (v) all disclosure statements advise the client that it can revoke the authority it has granted to the adviser under at any time.[62]

The safe harbour does not relieve advisers of their responsibility to act in the best interests of their clients, including fulfilling their duty to obtain best price and execution for any transaction.[63]

Cross-trades

6–019 Effecting cross-trades between clients, where a third-party broker is used, is not specifically addressed by the Advisers Act, but is subject to the anti-fraud provisions of the Advisers Act.[64] Cross-trades involve potential conflicts of interest, and thus many advisers follow the methodology required by a rule under the Investment Company Act of 1940, as amended (the "Investment Company Act") when a client is an investment company.[65]

Aggregation of client orders

6–020 An investment adviser may aggregate or "bunch" orders for the purchase or sale of securities on behalf of two or more of its accounts, so long as the bunching is done for the purpose of achieving best execution and no client is systematically advantaged or disadvantaged by the bunching.[66] Investment

---

[61] Release 1732. In the UK, agency cross trades are not afforded any special treatment, but are covered by the general conflict of interest provisions in FSA, COB 7.1.

[62] Investment Advisers Act of 1940, Rule 206(3)-2.

[63] *ibid.*, Rule 206(3)-2(c).

[64] Renberg Capital Management, Inc. and Daniel H. Renberg, Investment Advisers Act Release No.2064 (October 1, 2002).

[65] Investment Advisers Act of 1940, Rule 17a-7.

[66] Pretzel & Stouffer, SEC No-Action Letter, (December 1, 1995). The approach to aggregation is very similar to the UK. See FSA, Rule COB 7.7.

ONGOING REQUIREMENTS FOR A REGISTERED INVESTMENT ADVISER

advisers must have procedures in place to ensure clients are treated fairly and equitably in the aggregation/bunching process.[67]

Advertising

The anti-fraud provisions of the Advisers Act apply with respect to both existing and prospective clients. Under these provisions, an investment adviser, registered or required to be registered, is prohibited from using any advertisement that contains any untrue statement of material fact or is otherwise misleading.[68] Additionally, an advertisement may not: (i) use testimonials[69]; (ii) refer to past specific recommendations that were profitable unless an adviser includes a list of all recommendations made during the past year[70]; (iii) represent that any graph, chart, or formula can in and of itself be used to determine which securities to buy or sell[71]; (iv) advertise any report, analysis, or service as free, unless it really is free.[72] Advertisements containing performance information must not be misleading. The SEC considers an advertisement containing performance information misleading if it implies, or if a reader would infer from it, conclusions about an adviser's competence or possible future investment results that would be unwarranted if the reader knew all of the facts.[73] Advisers must retain all advertisements, and create and retain for SEC inspection documents necessary to substantiate any performance information contained in their advertisements.[74]

6–021

Custody of client assets

Investment advisers with "custody" over client assets are required under Rule 206(4)-2 to implement a set of controls designed to protect those client assets from being lost, misused, misappropriated or subject to an adviser's financial services.[75] The SEC recently amended Rule 206(4)-2 (the "Custody Rule") and such amendments were effective as of November 5, 2003 with a

6–022

---

[67] SMC Capital Inc., SEC No-Action Letter (September 5, 1995); Pretmel & Stoofer Chartered, SEC No-Action Letter (December 1, 1995).

[68] Investment Advisers Act of 1940, Rule 206(4)-1(a)(5).

[69] *ibid.*, Rule 206(4)-1(a)(1).

[70] *ibid.*, Rule 206(4)-1(a)(2).

[71] *ibid.*, Rule 206(4)-1(a)(3).

[72] *ibid.*, Rule 206(4)-1(a)(4).

[73] Edward F. O'Keefe, SEC No-Action Letter (April 13, 1978); Anametrics Investment Management, SEC No-Action Letter (May 5, 1977); Clover Capital Management, Inc., SEC No-Action Letter (October 28, 1986).

[74] Investment Advisers Act of 1940, Rule 204-2(a)(16).

[75] *ibid.*, Section 206(4)-2.

compliance date of April 1, 2004.[76] The amended definition of "custody" and ensuing requirements for an adviser with "custody" of client funds and/or securities are generally discussed below.

Definition of custody

6–023 The term "custody" is defined as "holding, directly or indirectly, client funds or securities, or having any authority to obtain possession of them". For example, an investment adviser is deemed to have custody of client assets if it:

(i) has "possession of client funds or securities" (inadvertent receipt is excluded so long as the investment adviser returns the assets to the sender within three business days of receiving them);

(ii) has any arrangement (including a general power of attorney) under which it is authorised or permitted to withdraw client funds or securities maintained with a custodian upon instruction to the custodian (*e.g.* to instruct the custodian to pay fees to the adviser); and

(iii) acts in any capacity that gives it or its supervised person legal ownership of or access to clients funds or securities.[77]

Example (ii) clarifies that custody includes: (1) powers of attorney giving an adviser authority to, (a) sign checks on a client's behalf, (b) withdraw funds or securities from a client's account, or (c) dispose of client funds or securities except for authorised trading purposes; and (2) cases in which an adviser is "authorized to deduct advisory fees or other expenses directly from a client's account".[78] Prior SEC staff no-action letters allowed advisers who automatically deducted their fees to avoid being deemed to have custody under certain conditions.[79] These letters were expressly withdrawn upon adoption of the amended Custody Rule.[80]

The SEC refused to remove direct billing arrangements from the scope of the amended Custody Rule on the grounds that defining "custody" broadly serves "the remedial purposes of the rule". However, the SEC revised Form ADV, Part 1, Item 9, to allow advisers having custody solely as a result of automatic deduction of advisory fees to tick "no" in response to questions on

---

[76] *Final Rule: Custody of funds or Securities of Clients by Investment Advisers*, Investment Advisers Release No.2176 (September 25, 2003) ("Adopting Release"). See also, *Proposed Rule: Custody of Funds or Securities of Clients by Investment Advisers*, Investment Advisers Act Release No.2044 (July 18, 2002) ("Proposing Release"). See also SEC staff responses to questions about the amended Custody Rule at *www.sec.gov/divisions/investment/custodyfaq-htm*.

[77] Investment Advisers Act of 1940, Rule 206(4)-2(c).

[78] See *Adopting Release*, above, para.6–022, n.76.

[79] See, *e.g.* Investment Counsel Association of America, Inc., SEC No-Action Letter (June 9, 1982); John B. Kennedy, SEC No-Action Letter (June 5, 1996); Securities America Advisors Inc., SEC No-Action Letter (April 4, 1997).

[80] See Adopting Release, above, para.6–022, n.76.

whether the adviser or a related person has custody of client assets and noted that "an adviser that has 'custody' for purposes of rule 206(4)-2 may not necessarily have custody for other purposes".[81] In any event, advisers who have direct billing relationships with a client whose advisory contract states that the adviser will not have custody may wish to consider revising or clarifying such advisory contracts.

Custody rule requirements

Use of qualified custodians—The amended Custody Rule, with limited exceptions, requires advisers having custody of client funds and securities to maintain such assets with "qualified custodians".[82] Qualified custodians include banks and savings associations,[83] broker-dealers,[84] futures commission merchants,[85] and non-US financial institutions that customarily hold financial assets for customers.[86]

    6–024

Qualified custodians must either: (1) maintain a separate account for each client under that client's name[87]; or (2) place such funds and securities under the adviser's name, as agent or trustee for the adviser's clients, in accounts containing only that adviser's clients' funds and securities.[88] Promptly upon opening an account with a qualified custodian on a client's behalf, the adviser must provide notice to client, in writing, containing: (1) the name of the custodian; (2) the address of the custodian; and (3) the manner in which the funds or securities are maintained.[89] Similar notice is required for any changes to this information.

Advisers meeting the definition of qualified custodian may hold client assets themselves provided they comply with the account statement requirements

---

[81] *ibid.*

[82] Investment Advisers Act of 1940, Rule 206(4)-2(a)(1).

[83] *ibid.*, Rule 206(4)-2(c)(3)(i): "A bank as defined in Section 202(a)(2) of the Advisers Act or a savings association as defined in Section 3(b)(1) of the Federal Deposit Insurance Act that has deposits insured by the Federal Deposit Insurance Corporation under the Federal Deposit Insurance Act".

[84] *ibid.*, Rule 206(4)-2(c)(3)(ii): "A broker-dealer registered under Section 15(b)(1) of the Securities Exchange Act of 1934, holding the client assets in customer accounts". As a result of the inclusion of broker-dealers within the definition of "qualified custodian" under the amended Custody Rule, the SEC noted that the exemption for broker-dealers contained in the Custody Rule would no longer be necessary. See "Adopting Release" at para.6–010.

[85] Investment Advisers Act of 1940, Rule 206(4)-2(c)(3)(iii): "A futures commission merchant registered under Section 4f(a) of the Commodity Exchange Act, holding the client assets in customer accounts, but only with respect to clients' funds and security futures, or other securities incidental to transaction in contracts for the purchase or sale of a commodity for future delivery and options thereon".

[86] *ibid.*, Rule 206(4)-2(c)(3)(iv): "A foreign financial institution that customarily holds financial assets for its customers, provided that the foreign financial institution keeps the advisory clients' assets in customer accounts segregated from its proprietary assets".

[87] *ibid.*, Rule 206(4)-2(a)(1)(i).

[88] *ibid.*, Rule 206(4)-2(a)(1)(ii).

[89] *ibid.*, Rule 206(4)-2(a)(2).

US REGULATION OF INVESTMENT MANAGEMENT

and any "custody rules imposed by the regulators of the advisers' custodial functions".[90] Moreover, advisers having an affiliate which is a qualified custodian may place client assets with that affiliate.[91]

6–025　**Account statement delivery and surprise audits**—The old Custody Rule required advisers with custody to send each client quarterly statements and engage an independent accountant to conduct an annual Surprise Audit of client assets.[92] Under the amended Custody Rule, advisers that have a reasonable basis for believing that clients receive quarterly account statements *directly* from the qualified custodian are no longer subject to the surprise audit requirement.[93] The quarterly statements must identify all funds and securities in the account at the end of the period, must set forth all account transactions during the period and may be delivered electronically.[94] In response to industry comment, the amended Custody Rule allows clients to appoint an independent representative to receive their account statements.[95]

Some advisers choose not to disclose to qualified custodians the identity of their clients, or the underlying investors in their pooled investment vehicles, "to prevent a potential competitor from having access to their clients" or to "protect the privacy of certain well-known clients".[96] Under these circumstances, an adviser may send the required quarterly account statements itself, rather than relying on the custodian. However, these advisers are subject to an annual surprise audit.[97] The surprise audit must be conducted in accordance with the same audit standards currently in existence and the auditor must file a certificate with the SEC within 30 days following completion of the audit.

In the case of a pooled investment vehicle, the adviser may avoid the surprise audit and account statement delivery requirements if the pooled

---

[90] Adopting Release, above, para.6–022, n.76, at text following n.23.

[91] *ibid.*

[92] See Investment Advisers Act of 1940, Rule 206(4)-2(a)(4) and (5).

[93] Adopting Release, above, para.6–022, n.76. An adviser may form a "reasonable belief" if the qualified custodian provides the adviser with copies of the account statements sent to clients.

[94] Investment Advisers Act of 1940, Rule 206(4)-2(a)(3).

[95] An "independent representative" is a person that: "(i) acts as an agent for an advisory client, including in the case of a pooled investment vehicle, for limited partners of a limited partnership (or members of a limited liability company, or other beneficial owners of another type of pooled investment vehicle) and by law or contract is obliged to act in the best interest of the advisory client or the limited partners (or members or other beneficial owners; (ii) does not control, is not controlled by, and is not under common control with [the adviser]; and (iii) does not have, and has not had within the past two years, a material business relationship with [the adviser]." Rule 206(4)-2(c)(2).

[96] See Proposing Release, above, para.6–022, n.76.

[97] Investment Advisers Act of 1940, Rule 206(4)-2(a)(3)(ii). The auditor must also file a certificate with the SEC within 30 days following completion of the audit "stating that it has examined the funds and securities and describing the nature and extent of the [audit]; and . . . upon finding any material discrepancies during the course of the [audit, the auditor must notify the SEC] within one business day of the finding." Rule 206(4)-2(a)(3)(ii)(B) and (C).

ONGOING REQUIREMENTS FOR A REGISTERED INVESTMENT ADVISER

investment vehicle is subject to an annual audit, the results of which are distributed to investors within 120 days following the end of the pooled investment vehicle's fiscal year.[98] The provision relating to delivery of audited financials includes no explicit reference to use of an "independent representative" and may be read to require delivery directly to investors. Advisers for pooled vehicles which do not timely deliver audited financials to investors, are subject to all of the reporting requirements, including account statement delivery and, if the adviser itself sends account statements, the surprise audit.[99] Delivery to the fund is insufficient. Account statements must be delivered directly to the investors or their independent representatives.[1]

Elimination of balance sheet requirement—Currently, an adviser with custody must include a balance sheet audited by an independent accountant with Part II of Form ADV.[2] Form ADV, Part II, Item 14 has been amended to eliminate this requirement for advisers registered or registering only with the SEC.[3] The SEC indicated that the balance sheet may give investors an imperfect picture of the financial health of the advisory firm.[4] Additionally, because Rule 206(4)-4 requires advisers to disclose any financial condition reasonably likely to impair the adviser's ability to meet its contractual commitments to its clients,[5] the SEC concluded that balance sheet disclosure is unnecessary.[6] The text of the revised form limits this relief to advisers who are registering or registered only with the SEC. This clearly allows states to require advisers registered with them to provide a balance sheet. It is unclear whether advisers registered both with the SEC and Non-US regulatory authorities would be required to provide an audited balance sheet.

6–026

Exemptions from the Custody Rule—The amended Custody Rule provides exemptions for advisers with respect to: (i) registered investment companies[7]; (ii) shares of open-end mutual funds (for which advisers may use the mutual

6–027

---

[98] Adopting Release, above, para.6–022, n.76.
[99] Adopting Release, above, para.6–022, n.76. See also, Investment Advisers Act of 1940, Rule 206(4)-2(a)(3)(iii).
[1] Investment Advisers Act of 1940, Rule 206(4)-2(a)(3)(iii).
[2] See Form ADV, Part II, Item 14. Advisers which require prepayment of more than $500 in fees per client six or more months in advance (as well as those which are not registering or registered only with the SEC) must continue to provide an audited balance sheet, *ibid.*
[3] See amendment to Part 279, amending Item 14 of Part II by adding ("unless applicant is registered or registering only with the Securities and Exchange Commission" after the words "client funds and securities").
[4] See Adopting Release, above, para.6–022, n.76 at n.59.
[5] See 17 CFR 275.206(4)-4.
[6] See Adopting Release, above, para.6–022, n.76.
[7] Investment Advisers Act of 1940, Rule 206(4)-2(b)(4). The SEC reasoned that the strict requirements of section 17(f) of the Investment Company Act of 1940 and related rules render compliance with the amended Custody Rule superfluous.

165

fund's transfer agent, even where that transfer agent is not a qualified custodian)[8]; and (iii) certain privately offered securities, provided that a limited partnership (or limited liability company or other type of pooled investment vehicle) may only rely on this exemption if it is audited annually and distributes audited financial statements to all limited partners (or members or other beneficial owners) within 120 days of the end of its fiscal year.[9]

Solicitations

6–028 It is unlawful for any adviser required to be registered with the SEC to pay a cash fee (directly or indirectly) to a third party (a "solicitor") unless the arrangement complies with a number of conditions: (i) the solicitor is not a "bad boy" *i.e.* not subject to court order or administrative sanction; and (ii) such cash fee is paid pursuant to a written agreement to which the adviser is a party. If the solicitor is not an officer, employee, or partner of the adviser and is not controlled by the adviser, the written agreement required above must: (i) describe the solicitation activities to be undertaken; and (ii) require the solicitor, at the time of solicitation, to provide the client with a copy of the adviser's "brochure" and the separate disclosure agreement. This separate disclosure agreement must describe, among other things, any affiliation between the solicitor and the adviser, the terms of the solicitor's compensation, and the difference, if any, in the adviser's advisory fee that is attributable to the solicitation arrangement.[10]

Disclosure of material financial and disciplinary information

6–029 The Advisers Act requires all investment advisers to disclose certain material financial and disciplinary information to their clients.[11] Rule 206(4)-4 provides that it is a fraudulent, deceptive or manipulative act, practice, or course of business within the meaning of Section 206(4) of the Advisers Act for any investment adviser to fail to disclose to any client or prospective client all material facts with respect to:

(i) A financial condition of the adviser that is reasonably likely to impair the ability of the adviser to meet its contractual commitments to clients if the adviser has discretionary authority (expressed or implied) *or*

---

[8] *ibid.*, Rule 206(4)-2(b)(1).
[9] *ibid.*, Rule 206(4)-2(b)(3).
[10] *ibid.*, Rule 206(4)-3.
[11] *ibid.*, Rule 206(4)-4.

ONGOING REQUIREMENTS FOR A REGISTERED INVESTMENT ADVISER

custody over client assets *or* requires prepayment of advisory fees of more than $500 from each client, six months or more in advance[12]; or

(ii) Any legal or disciplinary event that is material to an evaluation of the adviser's integrity or ability to meet contractual commitments to clients. The Rule further creates a rebuttable "presumption of materiality" for certain defined legal or disciplinary events involving the adviser or any *management person* of the adviser, including certain specified criminal judgments, certain findings in federal and state administrative proceedings, and certain self-regulatory organisation findings and sanctions.

Proxy voting

Rule 206(4)-6 provides that its is a fraudulent, deceptive, or manipulative act, practice or course of business, for an investment adviser registered or required to be registered to exercise voting authority with respect to client securities, unless the adviser: (i) adopts and implements written policies and procedures that are reasonably designed to ensure that the investment adviser votes proxies in the best interest of clients and which address material conflicts of interest that may arise between interest of the investment adviser and those of its clients; (ii) describes its proxy voting policies and procedures to its clients and provides copies of such policies and procedures to its clients upon request[13]; and (iii) discloses to clients how they may obtain information on how the investment adviser voted their proxies.

6–030

Supervision

Advisers have a continuing responsibility to comply with the Advisers Act, and this duty includes the supervision of and responsibility for anyone acting in their behalf.[14] Under the Advisers Act, a person (*e.g.* an adviser or an officer of the adviser) will not be deemed to have failed to supervise a person if: (i) the adviser had established procedures designed to prevent the conduct; and (ii) the person reasonably discharged its supervisory duties, and had no reason to believe that the procedures were not being followed.[15]

6–031

---

[12] This Rule would require an adviser facing bankruptcy to either immediately resolve the issues that would be causing it to declare bankruptcy or to notify its clients of its financial instability.

[13] The SEC has clarified that the description may be provided in From ADV and that it only need be a general summary of the proxy voting process. *Proxy Voting by Investment Advisers*, Investment Advisers Act Release No.2106 (January 31, 2003).

[14] Investment Advisers Act of 1940, Section 203(e)(6). See TBA Financial Corporation (December 7, 1983).

[15] Investment Advisers Act of 1940, Section 203(e)(6). See Western Asset Management Co. and Legg Mason Fund Adviser, Inc., Investment Advisers Act Release No.1980 (September 28, 2001).

Insider trading and use of confidential information

6–032 Advisers must establish, maintain, and enforce written policies and procedures reasonably designed to prevent the misuse of material, nonpublic information by the adviser or any of its associated persons.[16]

Brochure rule

6–033 Advisers must generally provide clients with a written disclosure statement containing information about background and business practices. This statement is generally known as the adviser's "brochure". The brochure may be either (i) Part II of Form ADV[17]; or (ii) a written document containing at least the information required by Part II of Form ADV.[18] The Brochure must be delivered at least two days before the advisory contract is entered into, or at the time the contract is entered into if the client can terminate the contract within five days thereafter.[19]

Satisfaction of the brochure delivery requirement does not necessarily satisfy an adviser's full disclosure obligation under the anti-fraud rules.[20] For example, an investment adviser should make full and fair disclosure of all material facts necessary for informed decision-making by clients, irrespective of wither such disclosure is called for by a specific item in Form ADV. An adviser must also ensure that it does not omit material facts from its brochure.

An adviser need not offer or deliver a written disclosure statement in connection with entering into either an advisory contract with a US-registered investment company or any contract for impersonal advisory services.[21]

Record keeping

6–034 The SEC generally requires a registered investment adviser to maintain extensive books and records, including (i) "typical accounting records" that any business would normally keep; and (ii) certain additional records the SEC

---

[16] Investment Advisers Act of 1940, Section 204A. See Re Gabelli & Co. Inc., Investment Advisers Act Release No.1457 (December 8, 1994).

[17] See "Adviser Registration Process" at para.6–011.

[18] Investment Advisers Act of 1940, Rule 204-3(a).

[19] *ibid.*, Rule 204-3(b)(1).

[20] *ibid.*, Rule 204-3(e); Re Aetna Capital Management, Inc., et al, Investment Advisers Act Release No.1379 (August 19, 1993).

[21] Investment Advisers Act of 1940, Rule 204-3(b)(2); Rule 204-3(g)(1) ("Contract for impersonal advisory services" means a contract under which investment advice is provided solely by means of oral statements or written materials which do not purport to meet the investment needs of specific individuals or statistical information not expressing any opinions about the investment merit of particular securities).

believes are necessary in the light of the adviser's fiduciary duty.[22] There are special record-keeping rules for non-US resident investment advisers.[23]

"Typical accounting records" include: (i) all cheque books, bank statements, cash reconciliations, and cancelled cheques[24]; (ii) all written agreements entered into by the investment adviser with any client or otherwise relating to the adviser's business (such as rental and service agreements, mortgages, employment contracts, and contracts for investment advisory services)[25]; (iii) all bills or statements relating to the adviser's business[26]; and (iv) all trial balances, financial statements, and internal audit working papers relating to the adviser's business.[27]

Further record keeping requirements include: (i) a record of the personal securities transactions of the adviser and its employees[28]; (ii) a memorandum of each order given by the investment adviser for the purchase or sale of any security and any instruction from the client concerning such purchase or sale[29]; (iii) the originals of all written communications received and copies of all written communications sent by the adviser relating to any recommendation made or proposed to be made, any advice given or proposed to be given, any receipt, disbursement or delivery of funds or securities, or the placing or executing of any order to purchase or sell any security[30]; (iv) a copy of all circulars, advertisements, newspaper articles, etc. sent to 10 or more persons[31]; (v) a list of all the client accounts over which the investment adviser has authority[32]; (vi) a copy of each written statement given to any client in compliance with the brochure rule[33]; (vii) each client's acknowledgement of receipt of a solicitation agreement[34]; and (viii) all documents necessary to demonstrate the calculation of any performance advertising.[35]

Other record-keeping requirements, may also be applicable. For example, **6–035** an investment adviser who has custody or possession of securities or funds of any client[36] must keep additional records regarding that activity.[37] An investment adviser who renders any investment supervisory service (*i.e.* the giving of continuous advice as to the investment of funds on the basis of the individual needs of each client) or management service must keep additional

---

[22] *ibid.*, Rule 204-2.
[23] *ibid.*, Rule 204-2(j).
[24] *ibid.*, Rule 204-2(a)(4).
[25] *ibid.*, Rule 204-2(a)(10).
[26] *ibid.*, Rule 204-2(a)(5).
[27] *ibid.*, Rule 204-2(a)(6).
[28] *ibid.*, Rule 204-2(a)(12).
[29] *ibid.*, Rule 204-2(a)(3).
[30] *ibid.*, Rule 204-2(a)(7).
[31] *ibid.*, Rule 204-2(a)(11).
[32] *ibid.*, Rule 204-2(a)(8).
[33] *ibid.*, Rule 204-2(a)(14).
[34] *ibid.*, Rule 204-2(a)(15).
[35] *ibid.*, Rule 204-2(a)(16).
[36] See "Custody" section, at para.6–022.
[37] Rule 204-2(b).

records regarding that activity which now includes records of each proxy statement received pertaining to client securities, each vote cast with respect to such securities, any document material to its proxy voting decisions, its proxy voting policy and each written client request for information on how the adviser voted its proxies.[38]

All books and records required to be kept must be maintained and preserved in an easily accessible place for a period of not less than five years, the first two years in an appropriate office of the investment adviser.[39] Records may be kept on film or computer.[40] If kept on film or computer the investment adviser must, among other things, store a duplicate copy of the record on any medium allowed by Rule 204-2.[41] In the case of records on electronic storage media, the investment adviser must also establish and maintain procedures which (i) reasonably safeguard such records from loss, alteration, or destruction; (ii) limit access to the records to properly authorised personnel and the SEC; and (iii) reasonably ensure that any reproduction of a non-electronic original record on electronic storage media is complete, true and legible when retrieved.[42]

An investment adviser is exempt from the above record-keeping rules if the adviser is a broker-dealer keeping the same records pursuant to Rules 17a-3 and 17a-4 of the 1934 Act.[43]

Form 13F disclosure

6–036 An SEC-registered investment adviser that exercises investment discretion over at least $100 million in "Section 13(f) securities" must periodically file Form 13F with the SEC.[44] "Section 13(f) securities" generally include equity securities that trade on either the New York or American Stock Exchange, or that are quoted on the NASDAQ National Market System.[45] Form 13F must be filed electronically, via the SEC's Electronic Data Gathering, Analysis and Retrieval ("EDGAR") system, within 45 days after the end of the relevant calendar quarters. Form 13F reports must identify, among other things: (i) the name of the issuer; (ii) the number of shares owned; and (iii) the fair market value, as of the end of the quarterly filing period, of the reported securities.

---

[38] *ibid.*, Rule 204-2(c).

[39] *ibid.*, Rule 204-2(e).

[40] *ibid.*, Rule 204-2(g).

[41] *ibid.*

[42] *ibid.*

[43] Investment Advisers Act of 1940, Rule 204-2(h).

[44] *ibid.*, Section 13(f) of the Exchange Act; rule 13f-1(a) under the Exchange Act.

[45] "Section 13(f) securities" also include certain equity options and warrants, shares of closed-end investment companies, and some convertible securities. Shares of open-end investment companies are not "Section 13(f) securities", *ibid.*, Rule 13f-1(c).

Advisory Contracts

The Advisers Act also sets out certain provisions which must not (or must be) included in an advisory contract.[46]

6–036A

Restrictions on performance-based fees

An adviser is prohibited from entering into a contract with a client when the adviser's remuneration varies with the adviser's success in managing the client's assets *i.e.* a fee based on a share of the capital gains or appreciation of a client's funds.[47] This general prohibition, however, does not prohibit an investment advisory contract, which provides for compensation based upon a percentage of assets under management. [48] Moreover, this prohibition does not apply to an investment advisory contract with: (1) a registered investment company; or (2) certain other entities with assets exceeding $1 million, which imposes a type of performance fee knows as a "fulcrum fee".[49] This fee must be based on the asset value of the funds under management over a "specified period" and must increase or decrease proportionately with the "investment performance" of funds under management in relation to an "appropriate index of securities prices".[50] In addition, performance fees are permitted for certain advisory contracts with business development companies, "qualified purchaser"[51] private investment companies, and non US residents.[52]

6–037

An adviser may also enter into a performance fee contract with certain "qualified clients".[53] A qualified client is defined as: (i) a natural person or company that has at least $750,000 under management with the adviser immediately after entering into the contract; (ii) a natural person or company that the adviser reasonably believes has a net worth of more than $1.5 million at the time the contract is entered into, or is a "qualified investor"; or (iii) a natural person who is an officer, director, trustee, or general partner (or a person serving in a similar capacity) of the adviser, or an employee who participates in investment decisions of the adviser and has done so for at least 12 months.[54]

---

[46] *ibid.*, Section 205.
[47] *ibid.*, Section 205(a)(1).
[48] *ibid.*, Section 205(b)(1).
[49] *ibid.*, Section 205(b)(2).
[50] *ibid.*, Section 205(b)(2). Rules 205-1 and 205-2 define the terms in the text. The SEC has published a release discussing factors that investment companies considering entering into a fulcrum fee should consider. Investment Advisers Act Release No.113 (April 18, 1972).
[51] "Qualified purchaser" generally means certain investors who have prescribed net worth or level of sophistication.
[52] *ibid.*, Section 205(b)(3)–(5).
[53] *ibid.*, Rule 205-3.
[54] *ibid.*, Rule 205-3(d)(1).

Assignments of advisory contracts

6–038   Advisory contracts must contain a provision prohibiting their assignment without the client's consent.[55] An assignment generally includes any direct or indirect transfer of an advisory contract by an adviser or any transfer of a controlling block of an adviser's outstanding voting securities.[56] A transaction that does not result in a change of actual control or management of the adviser (*e.g.* a corporate reorganisation) would not be deemed to be an assignment for these purposes.[57] If the adviser is established as a partnership, each of its advisory contracts must provide that the adviser will notify the client of a change in the members of the partnership.[58]

Hedge clauses

6–039   The Advisers Act voids any provision of a contract that purports to waive compliance with any provision of the Advisers Act.[59] An adviser that includes any such provision in a contract misleads its clients in violation of the Advisers Act's anti-fraud provisions, by implying that a legal right or remedy under the Advisers Act is not available.[60]

Pre-paid fees

6–040   The SEC interprets the anti-fraud provisions of the Advisers Act as requiring an adviser receiving its fee in advance, to give a client terminating a contract a *pro rata* refund of pre-paid fees (less reasonable expenses),[61] unless the adviser is to receive a pre-determined amount upon termination for services already performed, and the client is provided with adequate disclosure.[62]

SEC Inspections

6–041   Section 204 of the Advisers Act grants the SEC a general inspection power over investment advisers. Inspections are usually confidential[63] and are

---

[55]   *ibid.*, Section 205(a)(2).

[56]   *ibid.*, Section 202(a)(1).

[57]   *ibid.*, Rule 202(a)(1)-1. See also, *Zurich Insurance Company, Scudder Kemper Investments*, SEC No-Action Letter (August 31, 1998) (stating that the adviser must itself evaluate whether a particular transaction involves a change of actual control or management).

[58]   *ibid.*, Section 205(a)(3).

[59]   *ibid.*, Section 215(a).

[60]   Opinion of the General Counsel, Investment Advisers Act Release No.58 (April 10, 1951).

[61]   National Regulatory Services, SEC No-Action Letter (December 2, 1992).

[62]   BISYS Fund Services, Inc., SEC No-Action Letter (September 2, 1999).

[63]   Section 210(b) of the Advisers Act prohibits the SEC or the SEC staff from disclosing publicly either the existence of an examination or investigation conducted under the Act, or the results of or any facts ascertained during an examination or investigation.

performed by personnel in the Commission's various Regional Offices. Inspections are typically supervised by the SEC's Office of Compliance, Inspections and Enforcement. There are three types of inspections: (i) routine inspections, (ii) sweep examinations and (iii) cause examinations.

The SEC staff conducts an on-site routine inspection examination of each SEC registered adviser approximately every five years. Sweep examinations are conducted by SEC staff from time-to-time and consist of a series of limited on-site exams intended to evaluate a perceived problem or area of concern (*e.g.* soft dollar, best execution practices, performance issues, and proxy voting). Cause examinations may be based on receipt of a client complaint or competitor, press reports of problems, rumours, or anonymous tips.

Inspectors generally look for evidence of, among other things, the following: (i) front-running client trades, (ii) engaging in brokerage practices that are not in the client's interest (*e.g.* failure to obtain best execution, improper use of soft dollars, unsuitable recommendations); (iii) deceptive advertising, (iv) ineligibility for SEC adviser registration (*e.g.* whether the adviser really manages $25 million of client assets); (v) inadequate internal controls; (vi) improper custody of client cash or securities; and (vii) improper recordkeeping.

There are generally three possible results from an examination: (i) the SEC **6–042** staff finds no problems and sends the adviser a letter stating that the inspection is finished (this is rare); (ii) The SEC staff sends a "deficiency letter" informing the adviser of any violations or possible violations found and requests that the adviser promptly take any necessary corrective steps and notify the SEC staff of the corrective actions taken; or (iii) the SEC staff commences an enforcement proceeding (this is not a common first step).

CHAPTER 7

SOME CONTRACTUAL ISSUES

Dick Frase, Dechert LLP, London

7–001   This Chapter discusses some selected contractual issues, relating to investment management agreements and other financial services contracts.

The Investment Mandate

7–002   Key elements of the mandate are found in the clauses which deal with the investment objectives, the restrictions on the objectives, and the extent of the discretion granted to the manager to achieve them.

Objectives and restrictions

7–003   The objectives and restrictions (sometimes also described as the "guidelines") set the precise scope of the investment mandate, in terms of what the manager can and cannot invest in. Their content is ultimately a commercial matter which, when formulated contractually, can vary from a simple one line statement ("the objective of the life fund is capital appreciation") to several pages of prescriptive requirements (as typically with a pension scheme with a very precise mandate to fill).

Objectives

7–004   Typically, the objectives will address the main investment classes to be covered (equities, bonds, derivatives, foreign exchange, etc) the possibility that ancillary classes of investment may be used (a securities mandate for instance may provide that derivatives may be used for efficient portfolio management) and any specific benchmarks or performance targets. Benchmarks and targets are usually included as a yardstick for performance rather than as a guarantee that the target will be achieved; and should be construed accordingly.

THE INVESTMENT MANDATE

Restrictions

Restrictions are usually treated as separate from the objectives, and operate   **7–005**
formalistically as restrictions on the objectives themselves. They may be
expressed in terms of a straight prohibition (defining the general scope of the
mandate again) or the particular proportion of investments which may be
made in a particular investment category, which goes to risk spreading rather
than scope. Standard risk spreading restrictions would be that no more than
X per cent of the portfolio may be invested in any one sector, no more than
X per cent of the portfolio in any one corporate issuer, and no more than X
per cent of the portfolio may be exposed to any one counterparty.

The fact that the main objectives exclude (by implication) all assets which
are not covered by the objectives is usually seen as a scope issue rather than
a formal restriction.

The FSA's requirements in this area are orientated towards ensuring that
any limits or restrictions are properly disclosed. Thus, COB, 4.2.15E(4)
requires the agreement to state any restrictions on the types of designated
investment in which the customer wishes to invest and the markets on which
the customer wishes transactions to be executed; or to state that there are no
such restrictions.

Modern agreements often contain a list of permissions specifically autho-   **7–006**
rising the manager to do certain specialised activities unless otherwise agreed.
This is largely a response to the very formalised and case-specific requirements introduced over the years by the regulators. Under Current FSA-rules,
statements are required on the following matters:

- that the services may include advice on or executing transactions in unregulated collective investment scheme, if this is the case[1];

- that the firm may enter into transactions for the customer, where the
  customer will incur obligations as an underwriter or sub-underwriter, if
  this is the case[2];

- where the client is a private customer:

  - details of how the firm may undertake stock lending activity with or
    for the private customer[3];
  - details of any contractual rights to realise the private customer's
    assets[4];

- where the firm is acting as a discretionary manager, details of:

  - any restrictions on the value of any one investment; and

---

[1] COB, 4.2.15E(17).
[2] *ibid.*, 4.2.15E(18).
[3] *ibid.*, 4.2.15E(19).
[4] *ibid.*, 4.2.15E(20).

SOME CONTRACTUAL ISSUES

- the proportion of the portfolio which any one investment or any particular kind of investment may constitute; or
- a statement that there are no such restrictions[5]

- where the firm is acting as a discretionary manager:

  - if the firm may commit the customer to supplement the funds in the portfolio, including borrowing on his behalf, that this is the case, the circumstances in which it may do so; any limits, and any circumstances in which such limits may be exceeded[6]
  - if the firm may commit the customer to underwrite securities, any restrictions on the categories of securities which may be underwritten and any financial limits on the underwriting.[7-8]

Residual discretionary powers

7–007   The objectives and restrictions are the main ways by which the scope of the mandate is defined. Once this has been established, a discretionary manager's residual authority needs to be defined, and this is usually drawn as widely as possible.

Such a manager will typically be stated to have complete discretion for the account of the customer and without prior reference to the customer to buy, sell, retain, exchange or otherwise deal in investments and other assets, effect transactions on any markets, negotiate and execute counterparty and account opening documentation, take all day-to-day decisions and otherwise act as the manager judges appropriate, etc. This residual authority is often expressed to be subject to any particular instructions from the client. It is normally implicit that any such instructions would have to be both reasonable and within the scope of the mandate. See the discussion of "Instructions" at para.7–011, *et seq.*, below.

The FSA rules expressly state that, in the case of a discretionary manager, the agreement must describe the extent of the discretion to be exercised.[9]

The portfolio

7–008   The FSA requires an advisory or discretionary manager to specify the initial value and composition of the managed portfolio.[10] This identification might

---

[5]   COB, 4.2.16E(1).
[6]   *ibid.*, 4.2.16E(4).
[7-8] *ibid.*, 4.2.16E(5).
[9]   COB, 4.2.16E(1).
[10]   *ibid.*, (8)(b)–(c)

be a significant issue in certain circumstances, such as where the firm is only given discretionary management power over a part of the client's portfolio, but has custody of the whole portfolio. However, where the client controls his own assets, he is usually in a better position to determine the portfolio content than the firm. In such cases the contractual description may not be much more than a variation on the theme of "such assets as are made available by the client", and the substantive identification and valuation of the assets will be by the client or its custodian.

The assets comprising the portfolio may be referred to in the contract by a variety of terms such as "investments", "securities", "funds", etc. Usually these terms are interchangeable, and the portfolio should be recognised as containing whatever it actually contains. The use of the term "investment", for instance, is not normally taken literally, otherwise the service might be construed as limited to FSMA-defined investments, or as excluding risk management activities.

Where the manager is not providing a custody service it is normal for the agreement to state expressly that the manager will not hold any client money or other assets. This helps to avoid any confusion as to the services it is providing, and marginal uncertainties such as whether new money might in some circumstances be paid to the manager for onward transmission to the custodian. If this were possible, it could cast the manager in a quasi-custody role and potentially bring the client money rules into play.

Commencement of the Mandate

In simple one-off or occasional transactions such as execution brokerage, the **7–009** time at which a particular mandate commences is rarely an issue, since it normally results from a very specific instruction—buy this stock—sell that stock—and so on.

In continuous investment management the date of commencement is more significant. The firm may assume some or all of its responsibilities:

- when it is appointed to manage the assets;

- when it receives control over (some or all of) the client's assets;

- when it actually starts to manage (some or all of) the assets; or

- (in advisory management) when it first starts to give advice on the portfolio as a whole.

In the case of discretionary management, the discretionary management service cannot begin until the client has either granted the manager power to give directions to the client's custodian and to instruct executing brokers to buy and sell the client's assets or, (where the manager acts as custodian) delivered the assets to the manager.

There is an issue as to how soon and in what manner the management powers should be exercised. For instance, if the client's portfolio consists initially of cash there is a question as to how quickly the cash should be invested. It is increasingly considered that if the firm anticipates a long period—say several months—before the portfolio is fully invested, this ought to be disclosed to the client up front. The firm is being paid to manage the assets, not sit on them and do nothing. At the same time, cash holdings may be justifiable if they are part of a deliberate strategy, as where markets are falling. In other situations, such as large synthetic credit derivative portfolios, a run-up of several months may be needed in order to build the portfolio in the right way and in accordance with the mandate, and some sort of bridging finance may be used to avoid involving the end-investors in this process.

7–010   In derivatives trading moreover, significant cash holding is often the norm. A futures account is always, in a sense, a cash account, which the manager uses to move in and out of the market and provide cash margin to cover its positions, with each position being reconverted to cash when it expires or is closed out.

In the case of a fund launch there is a further timing issue. To ensure fair treatment for all investors, initial subscriptions must be made available for investment at the same time on the first dealing day. Most launches are based on cash subscriptions; but where there is in specie subscription this too must be valued and made available for investment at the same time. Similar timing issues arise where funds are merged. In each case the object is to make sure that the date when the investor commits his cash or assets for investment matches with the date when the assets are actually available for management by the firm.

Client's Instructions

7–011   The FSA rules now require any firm providing an advisory or discretionary management service to include in the agreement a section describing arrangements for the giving and acknowledging of instructions.[11]

The term "instructions" can be somewhat vague, as it can cover both the main management mandate itself and also the giving of ad hoc instructions on particular matters within the scope of the main mandate. This discussion is primarily concerned with ad hoc instructions within the main mandate.

---

[11] COB, 4.2.15E(8)(a). For a specimen provision see the IMA standard terms, cl.G20.

Acceptance of instructions

A firm may accept its instructions explicitly, by a general indication of agreement[12], or by conduct. The fact that the firm has begun to act in the way requested by the instructions is an extremely strong indication of acceptance.

7–012

In continuous service situations, the firm's freedom to accept or reject instructions may be limited to the initial phase of the service where the terms of its mandate are being established. Thereafter the firm may be under a general obligation to accept instructions which relate to the detail of a mandate it has already agreed to perform.

To give some examples in the brokerage market, a client who gives a broker a one-off instruction to execute a trade "at best", would normally be entitled to instruct the broker to change this to a limit order, provided the trade remained unexecuted. The change relates to the details of how the existing instruction is to be performed, rather than the giving of a completely new instruction. Similarly a futures broker which has opened a position by executing a trade, is probably under an implied obligation to accept instructions to close that position; but is not obliged to accept instructions to open a completely new position.

Brokerage and investment banking firms often put clauses in their contracts which say that they are under no obligation to accept new instructions, and such a clause should be interpreted in the light of the principles described above.

Inadequate or ambiguous instructions

In some cases the client's initial instructions on a matter may be too vague to be acted on, and below a minimum threshold will not amount to instructions at all. A client who says "I need some help with my financial affairs" is not giving an instruction, but merely initiating preliminary discussions or an invitation to treat; even if such discussions eventually lead to the giving of formal advice or executing a transaction.

7–013

If the instructions are clear on the face of it, but ambiguous in the sense that they are capable of more than one interpretation, and the firm interprets them in good faith and in a reasonable manner, its actions based on that

---

[12] In *Bertram, Armstrong and Co v Hugh Godfray* [1830] 1 Knapp 381; 12 E.R. 364, PC, the Argentinean branch of a UK broker received written instructions to sell Argentinean government bonds if they reached 85. The broker replied that the price had now fallen to 75, and added: "We do not despair nevertheless, as we expect that on the news of the prosperous state of this country, and the expulsion of the Spaniards from South America, they will take favour at home. Should they again revive to your limits we will keep your order in view." This reply was held to amount to a direct acceptance of the client's instructions. See also *Pankhurst v Gardner & Co* (1960) 25 D.L.R. (2d) 515.

SOME CONTRACTUAL ISSUES

interpretation should be treated as properly authorised, even if the firm's interpretation was not the one intended by the client.[13]

Even where the instructions are patently inadequate, the firm may be justified in going ahead and acting on them if the circumstances so require.[14] But the firm will be liable if it puts an unreasonable interpretation on its instructions.[15] In *European Asian Bank AG v Punjab and Sind Bank*,[16] an issuing bank which failed precisely to follow instructions from a buyer to open a documentary credit was held to be in the same position as an agent who fails to follow his instructions. Goff L.J. said:

"... the principle [under discussion] presupposes. . .that a party relying on his own interpretation of the relevant document must have acted reasonably in all the circumstances in doing so. If instructions are given to an agent, it is understandable that he should act on those instructions without more; but if, for example, the ambiguity is patent on the face of the document it may well be right (especially with the facilities of modern communications available to him) to have his instructions clarified by the principal, if time permits, before acting upon them."

Ambiguity is not the same as brevity or lack of detail. The fact that instructions are couched in very brief or general terms is not necessarily a sign that they are incomplete or inadequate. The client may intend the firm to exercise a significant discretion as to how the instructions are performed. Or he may intend them to be carried out in accordance with usual practice, or a prior course of dealing.

7–014   In one instance vagueness may be said to have resulted from the instructions which clients were invited to give by their own stockbrokers. In the retail advisory brokerage market there is or was a long-standing practice of asking a client to give instructions as to his attitude to risk by ticking boxes on short *pro forma* forms indicating whether he wanted a high, medium or low

---

[13] See *Ireland v Livingston* (1872) 27 L.T. 79 (client's instructions for shipping a cargo of sugar from Mauritius to Britain unclear; firm's interpretation held to be reasonable); *Dixon v Hovill* (1828) 4 Bing. 665 (insurance broker); *Enlayde v Ltd v Roberts* [1917] 1 Ch.109, *per* Sergeant J. at 120 (firm acted reasonably in interpreting instructions in accordance with usual practice of insurance brokers); *Midland Bank v Seymour* [1955] 2 Lloyds Rep. 147 at 153 and 168 (bank's interpretation of ambiguous instructions from a buyer to open a documentary credit held reasonable); *Mitchell v Newhall* (1846) 15 M. & W. 308; 4 Ry. & Can. Cas. 300; 15 L.J. Ex. 292; 7 L.T.O.S. 88; 10 Jur. 318; 153 E.R. 867 (order to buy shares which had not yet been issued was properly interpreted as authority to purchase letters of allotment for such shares).

[14] *Weigall & Co v Runciman & Co* (1916) 115 L.T. 61 (insurance broker had been instructed to obtain insurance cover by a specified deadline, and did not have time before that deadline to clarify the instructions with its client)

[15] *Wiltshire v Sims* (1808) 1 Camp. 258; 170 E.R. 949, NP (instruction to broker to sell securities was (under usual practice) authority to sell for cash and could not be interpreted as giving the broker authority to sell to a buyer on credit); *R v Clowes and Another (No 2)* [1994] 2 All E.R. 316, CA; *Bertram, Armstrong & Co v Godfray* (1830) 1 Knapp 381; *the Hermione* (1922) 126 L.T. 701.

[16] [1983] 1 W.L.R. 642 at 656.

180

CLIENT'S INSTRUCTIONS

risk approach to his investment strategy. This left the firm with a very wide discretion as to how it interpreted this tick box response.

The SFA concluded that this was unsatisfactory, and in 1993 it announced[17] that where the customer ticked the low risk box:

". . . if this is the only information about a customer's investment objectives, SFA would expect all transactions to be made on 'low risk' criteria. It would not be clear, without further information from the customer, that he was willing for his portfolio as a whole to be managed on a low risk basis, with some of the individual transactions being made on a 'higher risk' basis."

In truth, this was not so much a resolution of the issue as a "default" interpretation which would apply if the broker failed to clarify what it meant by high/low/medium risk. In response to this, firms increasingly began to publish policy statements which described the way they would interpret these risk categories, and their approach to risk and management style generally. The client's risk instructions could then be said to have been given on a properly informed basis.

Unreasonableness

If, after the initial mandate has been established, the client gives supplementary instructions which appear to be part of the initial instructions, but are patently unreasonable, the firm should be able to decline to follow them, on the grounds either that its original commitment cannot have been intended to include an undertaking to follow unreasonable instructions, or that that an unreasonable instruction cannot come within the scope of the service it has agreed to provide in the first place. In such circumstances the firm should notify its client that it considers his instruction unreasonable and does not accept it—otherwise, its silence might still be construed as acceptance of the instruction.

7–015

A contractual formulation of this principle might be on the following lines:

"The firm will not be obliged to act on any instructions it considers unreasonable or improper, whether because of the absence of, or inadequate, authority, the firm's exposure to credit risk or other liability, impracticability of execution, conflict with applicable law or regulation, or otherwise."

---

[17] SFA Briefing No.5, May 1993, p.5.

SOME CONTRACTUAL ISSUES

Instructions which are likely to be treated as unreasonable or impossible would include:

- an instruction to a discretionary or advisory manager not to make a loss, or to make a particular level of profit, to sell out at the top of the market, or to buy at the bottom of the market, when the firm had, at most, only contracted to *try* to do these things;

- an instruction to perform an illegal act[18];

- an instruction to a member of the London Stock Exchange ("LSE") to do something on the LSE which is contrary to the LSE's rules[19];

- a refusal by a client to pay an increased rate of margin (properly called for by the broker in accordance with its contractual rights), or to give instructions to close out or transfer the open positions to another carrying firm[20];

- an instruction to close one side of a hedged futures position without providing the margin requested by the firm to cover the resulting open position.[21]

Where the client has made it impossible for the firm to carry out its mandate this may also, in the circumstances, constitute appropriate or necessary grounds for the firm terminating the service, even though it has not completed performance of the promised service.[22]

Firm unable to obtain instructions

7–016   Where an unforeseen event arises which makes the client's initial instructions impractical or inappropriate for some reason, the firm may need to seek fresh instructions. Where the firm cannot obtain such fresh instructions (as where it is unable to contact the client) it may be justified in doing nothing.

On the other hand, it may also be justified in taking some positive action, particularly if it has a general idea of what is in the client's interests, or what

---

[18] *Cohen v Kittell* [1889] 22 Q.B.D. 680.

[19] *Cuncliffe-Owen v Teather & Greenwood* [1967] 1 W.L.R. 1421.

[20] *Samson v Frazier, Jelke & Co* [1937] 2 All E.R. 588; see also *Morten v Hilton, Gibbes & Smith* Financial Times, July 3, 1908; [1937] 2 K.B. 176n, HL.

[21] *SNW Commodities v Falik* [1984] 2 Lloyd's Rep. 224.

[22] See *Underwood, Son and Piper v Lewis* [1894] 2 Q.B. 306; 64 L.J.Q.B. 60 (solicitor entitled to terminate his retainer if he is hindered or prevented from conducting the action by his client). In *the Hermione* (1922) 126 L.T. 701 at 705 (Hill J.), Hill J. said: "[the firm's] only alternative, if they thought [their client] was a wholly unreasonable man, would seem to me to be to communicate with him and the other people for whom they were acting and say 'Well, we cannot go on; we must cease to act as your agent'".

the client might want to do.[23] Any actions taken in this way should of course be in good faith and drawn to the client's attention as soon as possible. In this situation, an agent which is unable to communicate with its client when a commercial necessity arises can exercise the authority of an agent of necessity.

The need to act urgently in response to unforeseen events is often an issue in futures broking. In particular, the firm may need to be able to close out a client's positions in a falling market for the firm's own protection.[24] In the case of options exercise, the firm might anticipate a failure by its client to give instructions by an express contractual provision such as:

> "It is your responsibility to give us instructions to exercise an option. If no instructions are received, we will use reasonable efforts to protect your position and to exercise the option if any value attaches thereto",

but the same or a similar authority may be implied in any event for the reasons given above.

---

[23] See *Weigall & Co v Runciman & Co* (1916) 115 L.T. 61, where an insurance broker needing to place insurance within a specified time could not place it on the exact terms required by his instructions and was unable to obtain fresh instructions in the time available. The broker was held to be justified in obtaining cover on terms which a reasonably competent broker would have chosen in such circumstances: *i.e.* as close as it could reasonably get to the required terms of cover.

[24] In *Morten v Hilton, Gibbes & Smith, Financial Times* July 3, 1908; [1937] 2 K.B. 176n, HL, (cited in *Samson v Frazier, Jelke & Co* [1937] 2 All E.R. 588) a broker was rolling over a spot unsettled securities position for a client, Mr Morten, who would not close the account or give security or transfer the account to another broker. Instead he alleged, wrongly, that the brokers had agreed to carry over his account beyond March. The brokers closed the account in two lines of stock (Rio Tinto and Hudson's Bay) on March 11, but carried over the balance of his holdings. When the client repudiated both these pieces of business they closed the whole account, and succeeded in an action for the differences. Lord Loreburn L.C. said: "When these things were done the brokers were under the personal liability for the bargains they had made, and were left without any instructions whatever as to what they should do, except the demand that they should continue liability on Mr Morten's behalf, which, like sensible men, they refused to do. In these circumstances, the appellant's counsel . . . urged that the brokers, although entitled to close the whole account at the proper day in March, were not entitled to close part of it and carry over the remainder . . . I am not satisfied that the account was one, and indivisible. Even if it were, I think the brokers, left without proper instructions, would be entitled to do what was reasonable in their own interests and those of their principal, which were largely identical, and, in such a situation as the principal had here created, their action, if in good faith, ought not to be lightly condemned."

Compare *Prager v Blatspeil, Stamp & Heacock Ltd* [1924] All E.R. 524 where agents bought furs for clients. Due to the outbreak of the Great War it became impossible to send the furs to the clients, or communicate with them. The agents took it upon themselves to sell the furs. Held, there was no commercial necessity for the sale of the furs as they could have been placed in storage, at minimal cost, and the agents had not acted in good faith).

SOME CONTRACTUAL ISSUES

Timeliness

7–017 A firm is normally under a general obligation to act in a *timely manner*.[25] This is similar to the commonly implied term that a contract must be performed within a reasonable time. This timeliness principle applies both to investment decision making and the subsequent implementation of such decisions. In advisory services it also applies, in theory, to the provision of the advice, but there is likely to be a good deal more leeway as to the precise timing of such advice.

The implications of failing to act in a timely manner are usually incremental. For instance, a short delay is often of no real importance, but may become increasingly serious as the delay continues. Where a firm is culpably slow in doing something this would normally amount to negligent performance. But beyond a certain point, it may amount to complete non-performance.[26]

Timeliness is not the same as saying that "time is of the essence." The main reason for including a "time of the essence" provision is in counterparty contracts where, as soon as the time for performance is past, the firm wants to know that it is free to terminate the contract for repudiatory breach. This is important if, for instance, the firm is involved in a series of physical delivery back-to-back trades in the oil or metals markets, where all the trades in the chain need to be performed at the same time, and the same underlying asset needs to be delivered all the way down the chain.

Delegation

Authority to delegate

7–018 Where a firm (a principal firm) undertakes to provide an agency service, and wants to appoint another firm (a sub-firm) to perform part of the service, the

---

[25] See *Varden v Parker* (1798) 2 Esp. 710; *Potter v Equitable Bank* (1921) 8 Ll. Rep. 291 at 332; *Turpin v Bilton* (1843) 5 M. & G. 45 (insurance broker obtaining cover); *London Borough of Bromley v Ellis* [1971] 1 Lloyds Rep. 97 (insurance broker obtaining cover); *Volkers v Midland Doherty* (1985) 17 D.L.R. (4th) 343 (CAN) (stockbroker executing order).

[26] See *Turpin v Bilton* (1843) 5 Man. & G. 455 (insurance brokers liable for unreasonable delay in obtaining insurance where client suffers uninsured loss as a result—thereafter the delay could not be remedied in respect of that loss); *Reggentin v Beecholme Bakeries Ltd* [1968] 2 Q.B. 276, CA (solicitors liable for delay when client's action struck out for lack of prosecution); and *Midland Bank Trust v Hett Stubbs & Kemp* (solicitors forgot to register an option for several years—seriousness of the failure ultimately depended on whether or not the omission could be remedied. Once the property had been transferred in disregard of the option the failure was irretrievable).

In *Volkers v Midland Doherty* (1985) 17 D.L.R. (4th) 343 (CAN), a broker was instructed to buy stock at the market price first thing in the morning. When the market opened the broker delayed the purchase because he was waiting for the arrival of the trader he usually dealt with. One and three quarter hours after the market had opened, and before the trader had arrived, the securities were suspended. The broker was liable to the client for the resulting loss of profits.

DELEGATION

general rule is that it must have its client's authority do this. The assumption is that if the client chose the principal firm personally to provide the service, it is entitled to expect that it is that firm which will do this. This can be an important issue in investment management, so an express power of delegation is normally included in management agreements. In the absence of an express provision, authority to delegate may be implied where:

- the firm's client knew that it intended to delegate, and this was to be expected in the circumstances[27-28];

- such delegation is necessary or usual in the ordinary course of business[29];

- it is necessary to delegate because of unforeseen circumstances; or the nature of the mandate is such that it will have to be performed by a sub-firm.[30]

Delegation of trade execution by a manager to brokers is intrinsic to the investment management process and will be readily inferred into a conventional investment management mandate, both as a common practice and because it is apparent with specialist managers that they do not have the resources to broke or execute trades themselves. Similarly, it has been held that a trustee may employ brokers to invest its assets if in doing so it follows the usual course of business adopted by ordinary prudent people.[31]

Conceivably trade execution could be seen, not as the manager delegating to the broker, but as the manager appointing the broker on behalf of the client. However, in discretionary management, the task of executing is usually considered to be given in the first instance to the manager as part of its mandate, so the appointment of a broker to execute a particular trade is more normally seen as delegation.

The power of a manager to delegate the main management service to another person will often depend on the facts. If the manager has held itself out as personally providing the main management service it would, as indicated above, be prudent for it to include an express power to delegate as described above. Arguably, authority to delegate to another company in the same group would be more readily implied than authority to delegate the management role to an unconnected third party. Authority to delegate the main management role would also probably be implied where it was reasonably apparent that the manager might do this, as where the manager did not possess an in-house management capacity, or held itself out as specialising in the selection and appointment of sub-managers (raising an inference that it would apply this skill in providing the service).

[27-28] *Quebec & Richmond Railway Co v Quinn* (1858) 12 Moo. P.C. 232.
[29] *Solley v Wood* (1852) 16 Beav. 370; *Wray v Kemp* (1884) 26 Ch.D. 169.
[30] *De Bussche v Alt* (1878) 8 Ch.D. 286 at 310–311.
[31] *Speight v Gaunt* (1883) 9 App. Cas. 1 and *Jobson v Palmer* [1893] 1 Ch.71.

SOME CONTRACTUAL ISSUES

Liability for sub-firms

7–019   In some cases the manager does not delegate to another person but recommends or arranges the appointment of another person by its client. The manager arranging the appointment of a custodian by its client would fall into this category. The substantive services are provided to the client directly by the sub-firm, and the role of the principal firm is simply to arrange this.[32] A principal firm in this position is sometimes described as an "appointing agent". In such cases the appointing firm's obligation may be limited to making the appointment with reasonable care and skill.[33]

If a manager or other principal firm delegates the performance of the main service it has contracted to provide, *prima facie* the firm has hired a third party to discharge the firm's own obligations, rather than to substitute for the firm's obligations, and the principal firm remains liable for the sub-firm's performance. It is, however, very common for firms to qualify or vary this principle contractually. A principal firm which does not wish to be held liable for the failings of its sub-firm may cover itself by an exclusion clause, as in the *Calico Printers* case,[34-35] where Barclays was held not liable for the failings of its sub-firm because of an exclusion clause. In the case of a manager's delegation to executing brokers, such a qualification is likely to be implied as a matter of course.

Firm's obligation to supervise delegates

7–020   As noted, firms are reluctant to accept responsibility for the conduct of sub-firms over which they have no real control, such as unconnected executing brokers or custodians. In such situations a second level of liability may be established by the contract under which the firm does not accept liability for the faults of its sub-firms but does agree to take reasonable care to supervise them.

The regulators have paid some attention to the supervisory aspect of delegation. IMRO took the view[36] that a client would expect, and be entitled to expect, that a firm delegating investment management functions would take reasonable steps to ensure the performance of those functions. What is reasonable would depend on the circumstances, but would normally involve: (1)

---

[32]   See *e.g. de La Bere v Pearson* [1908] 1 K.B. 280; [1904–7] All E.R. Rep. 755.

[33]   In *Thomas Cheshire v Vaughan Bros. & Co* [1920] 3 K.B. 240 at 259, Atkin L.J. suggested *obiter* that the appointing agent would only be liable if he failed to exercise reasonable care in selecting the sub-agent. (All the parties had in fact proceeded on the assumption that the principal firm would be liable for any negligence of the sub-firm.)

[34-35]   *Calico Printers' Association Ltd v Barclays Bank Ltd* (1931) 145 L.T. 51.

[36]   IMRO Reporter, November 1996, Issue 16.

DELEGATION

clarifying the functions to be delegated, almost certainly on the basis of a written agreement; (2) vetting the delegate[37]; (3) monitoring the delegation (which may in appropriate circumstances include visits by the delegator, reports from the delegate, and access to the delegate's records); and (4) taking appropriate remedial action including in an extreme case withdrawing the delegation in the interests of the ultimate client.

The FSA rules discuss the concept in much more generalised terms which cover any form of outsourcing generally. SYSC, 3.2.4 states that a firm should take reasonable care to supervise the discharge of outsourced functions by its contractor and obtain sufficient information from its contractor to enable it to assess the impact of outsourcing on its systems and controls. SYSC, 3.2.3 says that a firm should assess whether a delegate is suitable to carry out the delegated function, there should be arrangements to supervise the delegation, and if cause for concern arises there should be appropriate follow-up action.

The FSA has also issued a consultative paper CP142 and a Feedback paper **7–021** on operational risk systems and controls. This contains proposed guidance on, among other things, SYSC, 3.2.4 and outsourcing. This guidance is expected to come into force some time in 2004. In paragraph 3.9 of the Feedback paper the FSA commented that, where a firm relies on a third-party report on the sub-firm's performance, senior managers should satisfy themselves that the report is suitably independent and objective and covers all the issues they would wish to see addressed. It adds that: "the use of these reports does not mean that the firm is absolved of the responsibility to maintain any other oversight. Also, the outsourcing firm should not normally have to forfeit its right for itself or its agents to gain access to the premises of the third party supplier".

These are sensible principles, though they seem more orientated to issues such as administration and compliance outsourcing than the delegation of specialist investment management functions, and are not designed to be applied to "delegation" by a manager to executing brokers. In view of this, the IMRO statement summarised above still provides useful guidelines for the delegation of investment management responsibilities.[38]

---

[37] Vetting would involve taking reasonable steps to: (a) assess the delegate's honesty, competence and solvency; (b) identify key business risks arising from the functions being delegated and ensuring that a proper standard of care is exercised by the delegate in these areas; (c) ensure that any assets held by the delegate are properly safeguarded; (d) check that the delegate has adequate internal controls and compliance; and (e) make a record of the steps the firm has taken to this effect.

[38] Thought note that the IMRO guidance is orientated towards the investment decision-making process rather than delegation to executing brokers.

187

SOME CONTRACTUAL ISSUES

Client/sub-firm privity

7–022   Usually, the sub-firm will not have any contractual liability to the client because there is no privity of contract between them.

Whether there is privity depends on the (objectively assessed) intention of the parties. The mere fact that an agent (the principal firm) itself appoints an agent (the sub-firm) is not enough in itself to make the sub-firm the agent of the principal firm's client. In *Calico Printers' Association v Barclays Bank*,[39] Wright J. said:

> "To create privity it must be established not only that the principal contemplated that a sub-agent would perform part of the contract, but also that the principal authorised the agent to create privity of contract between the principal and the sub-agent".

Relevant factors might include whether the sub-firm takes instructions from or otherwise deals directly with the client. But such privity is generally difficult to establish. The fact that the client specifically requests the firm to instruct a particular sub-firm,[40] or the sub-firm has power to commit the client in contracts with third parties, or to exercise a discretion on its behalf, or the client's name has been disclosed to the sub-firm, or the client has authorised the delegation,[41] does not in itself establish privity. In *Henderson v Merrett*[42] where Lloyd's members' agents placed their clients on syndicates operated by other managers (sub-agents) by entering into sub-agency agreements with those sub-agents, and the sub-agency agreement expressly stated that the sub-agent would act as the sub-agent for the agent's clients and had power to commit them to contracts of insurance, there was still held to be no privity of contract.

7–023   Where there is no agency and the parties deal with each other on a principal to principal basis, it is normally self-evident that there is no privity, even though the substantive effect may be similar to a chain of agency relationships.

A similar concept is to be found in the parallel FSA scheme where an authorised firm (the sub-firm) dealing with an agent (the principal firm) is entitled to treat the principal firm as its customer to the exclusion of the underlying client. FSA COB, 4.1.5R(1) says that if a firm ("F") is aware that a person ("C1") with or for whom it is conducting designated investment business, or related ancillary activities, is acting as agent for another person ("C2") in relation to that business, C1, and not C2, is the client of F in respect

---

[39] (1931) 145 L.T. 51 at 55.

[40] See *Mackersy v Ramsays* (1843) 9 C.L. & F. 818 at 845 and the judgment of Wright J. in *Calico Printers Association v Barclays Bank* 145 L.T.R. 51 at 55–56.

[41] *New Zealand & Australian Land Co v Watson* (1881) 7 Q.B.D. 374.

[42] [1994] 3 All E.R. 506, HL at 537–541.

of that business (provided that avoidance of duties which F would otherwise owe to C2 is not the main purpose of the arrangements between the parties).

While the Contracts (Rights of Third Parties) Act 1999 could in principle overcome the absence of privity, it is normally excluded as a matter of course in any proposed firm/sub-firm agreements, not least because of its unpredictable effects.

In summary, the only sure way to establish privity with the sub-firm is for the client to be explicitly included as a party to the written contract with the sub-firm, either on its own (with the principal firm being appointed separately to act as the client's agent in operating the contract), or in addition to the principal firm. **7–024**

This strict approach to privity is very desirable from the sub-firm's point of view to ensure certainty as to who is authorised to give it instructions, which has power to agree a variation of the contract and so on, and to avoid the risk of receiving conflicting instructions from the principal firm and the ultimate client. However, from the client's point of view it can give rise in extreme cases to what is politely described as a legal lacuna. This occurs if the client has no right of action against the sub-firm because there is no privity, and no right of action against the principal firm because the principal firm has not itself breached any obligation it owes to the client and has excluded any liability to its client for the acts of the sub-firm.

Sub-firm's liability in tort

It is possible, in the absence of privity of contract, for the sub-firm to be liable to the client on the grounds that it owes the client a *Hedley Byrne* duty of care. The courts are often unenthusiastic about taking such a step, on the grounds that it overrides the privity concept and the contractual intention of the parties, though this consideration is perhaps more relevant to counterparty or arms length contracts, as distinct from a service relationship, where the lacuna described above could otherwise create a serious problem. **7–025**

Thus, in *Henderson v Merrett*[43], sub-firms were held to owe their ultimate client a duty of care. The House of Lords found that the sub-firms held themselves out as possessing special skills, and that the clients were relying on them to use those skills in the clients' interest. In such a situation there was nothing inconsistent in holding the sub-firms liable both to the principal firm and the principal firm's client. Similarly, in *Jones and Marsh McLennan v Crawley Collosso*[44] a US broker instructed a London correspondent to effect insurance for the US broker's client, Mr Jones. The London correspondent had no contractual relationship with Mr Jones, but was held to owe him a

---

[43] *ibid.*
[44] Lloyds List August 1, 1996.

duty of care because it was aware that the services it was providing were for that particular client's benefit.

Where the client has a cause of action against both the firm and the sub-firm, generally speaking, the question for each firm will be what acts of negligence can be attributed to it, as distinct from the other firm. It will then need to be decided whether the firm's own negligence was the sole cause, or an effective or dominant cause of a particular loss. Two or more firms may also be jointly responsible for the same loss, in which case liability can be apportioned between them under the Civil Liability (Contribution) Act 1978.

Advisory delegation

7–026 Delegation issues are less relevant to an advisory service since advice in itself does not have the power to change the clients' legal position. Advice cannot take effect at one remove from the client in the way agency can. It must reach the client to be operative. Typically a sub-firm appointed to give advice will give this to the principal firm, which it then uses as the basis for its own advice to the client. The firm is in effect adopting the sub-firm's advice as its own. The position is broadly similar in tort, with the firm discharging its duty of care by appointing a delegate to provide the promised advice.[45]

Delegation by fund vehicles

7–027 The same contractual delegation principles apply in the case of appointments made by an investment fund vehicle, such as a unit trust or open-ended investment company (an "OEIC"). For persons investing in the fund, their contractual relationship is with the unit trust trustee or as shareholders in the OEIC. The manager is appointed as a separate exercise by the trustee or the OEIC. The manager's client is the trustee or OEIC, not the underlying investor, and there is no privity of contract between the investors and the manager.

The interposition in the chain of delegation of, in one case a trust, and in the other a corporate entity make it relatively unlikely that the investor would have a tortious claim directly against the manager, particularly in the case of an OEIC, where the corporate veil interposes between the investor and the OEIC's business activities, and the investor does not have any interest in the underlying assets of the OEIC. As regards the position of unit trusts, a

---

[45] *Luxmoore May v Messanger May Baverstock* [1990] 1 W.L.R. 1009, CA [1990] 1 All ER 1067, CA (Messanger May assumed a personal duty of care to the client and could discharge this by seeking and transmitting the advice of a consultant acting as an independent contractor provided that advice was not itself negligent).

DELEGATION

somewhat analogous situation may have occurred in *White v Jones*,[46-47] where a solicitor was held liable (in tort) to the beneficiaries of a will made by the solicitor's client. However, this was a controversial decision and, even if it were accepted as a general authority beyond the particular facts, it only allows for "look through" liability where there is a lacuna in the law which cannot otherwise be remedied.

Know Your Customer and Suitability

One of the basic factors affecting the way a firm provides its services is its knowledge of its client's personal circumstances and the way it acts on this knowledge. These are particular aspects of the general legal duty of reasonable care and skill, and will as such be much affected by the individual facts of the case.

7–028

They have received particular regulatory attention in relation to private clients through the FSA's private client "know you customer" and "suitability" rules,[48] which are now very detailed. This discussion is limited to a few general principles on these topics.

Know your customer

Where a firm has actual knowledge of the client's affairs it will normally be under a duty to take account of this if relevant.[49] Where it passes information provided to it by the client on to a third party who it knows will rely on it, it owes a general obligation to its client to do so in an accurate manner.[50] It may also be under a duty to act where it has actual knowledge that information provided to it by the client to be passed on is wrong.[51]

7–029

Whether the firm is under an obligation actively to elicit information from the client about his circumstances is quite a different matter, and depends on the overall scope of the service. If a firm has held itself out as offering a

---

[46-47] [1995] 2 A.C. 207, HL.

[48] COB, 5.2 and 5.3.

[49] See *e.g. Brown v KMR Services Ltd; Sword-Daniels v Pitel and Others* [1994] 4 All E.R. 385. In *Transportation Agency Ltd v Jenkins* (1972) 223 E.G. 1101 (Kerr J.) a conveyancing solicitor knew his clients intended to use the property they were buying as a restaurant, but failed to point out that the premises were subject to a covenant prohibiting cooking. In *McCann v Western Farmers Mutual Insurance Co* (1978) 87 D.L.R. (3d) 135 (CAN) a broker insuring premises on terms which excluded business use was held liable because he knew that the premises were used for business purposes.

[50] *O'Connor v BDB Kirby & Co* [1972] 1 Q.B. 90, CA at 101, *per* Megaw L.J.

[51] See *Dunbar v A&B Painters Ltd* [1985] 2 Lloyds Rep. 616 (insurance proposal form contained misrepresentations on matters which were within the insurance broker's actual knowledge).

particular type of portfolio management service, but is not offering to advise the client on whether or not the service is suitable to the client's personal circumstances, this does not in itself give rise to an obligation to advise the client whether the service is suitable to his personal circumstances. The position may be different if the firm is, say, actively recommending such a service to private investors as a proactive face-to-face exercise.

The nature of any such obligation will ultimately depend on the scope of the service which the firm has agreed to provide. A service such as investment management often carries with it a "normal scope", outside of which the firm is not obliged to provide services. If, however, the firm steps out the normal scope of its service and agrees to provide an additional service, it will assume any additional "know your customer" or "suitability" duties which attach to that additional service. Thus, in *Fine's Flowers Ltd v General Accident Assurance Co of Canada*,[52] an insurance broking case, the court held that: (a) the service provided by the average insurance broker does not involve deciding what sort of insurance the client should take out; but (b) if the broker contracts to provide this service it cannot do this properly without knowing the client's circumstances.

Suitability

7–030   Suitability considerations may follow both from the customer information available and the nature of the services themselves. So:

- an investment manager acting for a private customer will have a general obligation to make investment decisions which are suitable to a private customer's agreed investment objectives;

- a firm which advises a private customer on what those objectives should be will also need to take account of information about the client, such as available assets and attitude to risk; and

- a firm which advises a private customer on his financial affairs generally will need to take account of all relevant personal financial circumstances.

To advise on suitability the firm will often need to know the client's attitude to risk. This may reflect both his personal circumstances and preferences. Is the client risk averse, or is he willing to take a greater amount of risk in return

---

[52] (1977) 81 D.L.R. (3d) 139 at 149, *per* Wilson J.A., Blair J.A. concurring (CAN). If "the client gives no . . . specific instructions but rather relies upon his agent to see that he is protected and, if the agent agrees to do business with him on those terms, then he cannot afterwards, when an insured loss arises, shrug off the responsibility he has assumed. If this requires him to inform himself about his client's business in order to assess the foreseeable risks and insure his client against them, then this he must do."

for a chance of greater profits? To a cautious private customer a direct investment in domestic equities may be relatively risky compared with government bonds, while to a more aggressive investor they may be at the lower end of the risk scale. And the investor's attitude may also vary depending on the purpose of a particular transaction. A private customer may be happy with a medium risk profile on his securities portfolio, but want to take a much more cautious approach where his personal pension arrangements are concerned.

The regulatory concept of suitable advice was considered in *Morgan Stanley UK Group v Alfio Puglisi Cosentino*.[53] Morgan Stanley was held to have failed in its obligation to consider the suitability of two investments it had recommended to Mr Puglisi, who was accepted as being a private customer.

The first investment was in Morgan Stanley's Foreign Exchange Global Trading Fund. This carried too high a risk to be consistent with the client's investment objectives, nor was there any suggestion that those objectives had been revised to allow the investment to take place. The customer was familiar with speculative foreign exchange contracts but not with the special characteristics of the firm's Foreign Exchange Global Trading Fund which included a very high leverage. The terms of the fund only allowed it to be sold to authorised firms, business and expert investors, and persons for whom after due enquiry, the fund was considered suitable. Mr Puglisi was not a business customer. The firm might have been able to categorise Mr Puglisi as an expert customer under the SFA rules if it had carried out a proper assessment, but it had not done so. And Longmore J. found that the firm had not considered the suitability of the transaction. It was not sufficient for the firm to say that Mr Puglisi's experience of swap transactions with Italian banks made the fund a suitable investment for him,[54] especially when the prospectus itself imposed severe restriction on the persons to whom shares in the fund should be offered.

The second investment was in a repo product called PERLS. The firm made available a short term loan facility to Mr Puglisi to finance a long term investment by him in its PERLS product. Longmore J. said that the PERLS were not a suitable investment for Mr Puglisi because:

"(1) the investment he made of $10 million . . . was considerably greater than any investment he had made hitherto with Morgan Stanley; (2) the structure of the investment is, or was, such that it was relatively illiquid, but the structure of the borrowing arrangement was such that every six months Mr Puglisi was at risk of having to find money from his resources to repurchase the entire investment without any commitment from Morgan Stanley for continuing finance."

---

[53] unreported, January 29, 1998 (Longmore J.).
[54] More of an expert customer test in any event.

Risk Warnings

Risk warnings in agreements and prospectuses

7–031 It is increasingly common to include risk warnings in investment management agreements and prospectuses, whether or not the warnings are required under the FSA rules. It is sometimes difficult for a firm to judge the significance of such warnings from an investor's point of view. While some warnings appear extremely obvious, verging on the banal (investments may go down in value as well as up), the level of sophistication of the investors being addressed is clearly relevant to this.

Risk warnings are generally considered to be legally effective as disclosures/disclaimers. Indeed, at one level they may not appear to be substantially different from the ordinary disclosures and statements contained elsewhere in the agreement or prospectus. Nevertheless, case law and regulation support the idea that there is a meaningful distinction between merely describing a particular factual situation and actively warning a client about certain aspects of the intended investment approach, and the risk warnings section is often one of the more accessible sections of the document.

Risk warnings in private client advice

7–032 An obligation to warn of risk can also form part of an advisory service, particularly where the advice is being provided to unsophisticated private clients.

In such circumstances a firm will generally be under an obligation to warn its client of material risks if it knows or should know that the client is unaware of or unfamiliar with the risks. The less sophisticated or experienced the client, the more significant this is likely to be.[55] Conversely, a firm is not under an obligation to issue warnings about matters which are, or might reasonably be expected to be, obvious or self-evident to a client.[56]

There may also be an obligation to warn of risks which are unusual or exceptional to the transaction itself, and sometimes even where the risk involved falls outside the scope of the advice being provided by the firm.[57] It

---

[55] *Boyce v Rendells* (1983) 268 E.G. 268, CA (law firm had general duty to call attention to and advise on any particular risks which should be obvious to the adviser but which the client, a layman, might not appreciate); *Morris v Duke-Cohan & Co* (1975) 119 S.J. 821 (law firm failed to warn client of the risk of exchanging contracts before the prospective purchaser of the client's existing property has paid a deposit); *Re a Solicitor Ex p Incorporated Law Society*; *Income Trust Co v Watson* (1984) 26 B.L.R. 228 (Ontario High Court) (law firm liable for failing to warn a lender of the risk of lending money on the security of a mortgage which could not be registered).

[56] See *Ginora Investments Limited v James Capel & Co Ltd* February 10, 1995, discussed at para.7–034.

[57] *Boyce v Rendells* (1983) 268 E.G. 268, CA, at 402–403: "If, in the course of taking instructions, a professional man like a land agent or a solicitor learns of facts which reveal to him as

RISK WARNINGS

has been held that an insurance broker should generally warn a client if a policy includes a new or unusually onerous term.[58] Solicitors should warn the client if a contract he intends to enter into contains any unusually onerous provisions.[59]

PIA Regulatory Update No.85; dated March 2001, discussing the marketing of derivative-linked investments and hedge funds by financial planning advisers to private customers, commented on this in some detail:

7–033

> "A complicated product structure makes it very difficult for investors to form a view as to the risk profile of a product. Even if an investor is able to understand the mechanics of the product, they may not be able to quantify the risk or to form a reasonable assessment of risk, or to be able to make any sensible assumptions about risk before the purchase decision. PIA considers the onus is clearly on firms to provide an explanation of risk in terms that investors will understand. This will require the firm to make an assessment of the product, its risk profile and the types of risk to which investors may be exposed . . . for example, the product might have a high likelihood that the investor will face a shortfall, but the likely shortfall might be relatively small. Another product might have a high likelihood of returning capital in full, but where any losses would be significant. Such characteristics should be clearly explained to investors."

In addition to these general principles, the FSA regulatory scheme treats certain investments as involving particular risks for retail clients, and requires prescribed warnings to be given.[60] The broad assumption tends to be that the client should normally be able to understand the implications of basic securities investment, but needs a special warning of the consequences of, say, investing in derivatives (because of the high gearing involved, and in particular the fact that the client may lose more than his original investment) or warrants (which can also be risky from a gearing point of view, particularly if they are sold as if they were ordinary securities).

---

a professional man the existence of obvious risk, then he should do more than merely advise within the strict limits of his retainer. He should call attention to and advise upon the risks". *Yager v Fishman & Co and Teff and Teff* [1944] 1 All E.R. 552 (solicitor under no duty to advise a client not to exchange contracts before the mortgage was arranged, there being a presumption that a solicitor is not obliged to advise on business matters as part of his normal service, but *should* warn his client of the risks involved); *Chatterton v Gerson* [1981] Q.B. 432 at 443 (medical practice duty to warn the patient on the inherent risks and side-effects of the treatment).

[58] *King (or Fiehl) v Chambers & Newman (Insurance Brokers) Ltd* [1963] 2 Lloyds Rep. 130.
[59] *Stannard v Ulithorne* (1834) 10 Bing. 491.
[60] See COB, 5.4.3R (Requirement for risk warnings) which applies to private customers and refers specifically to warnings about warrants or derivatives; non-readily realisable investments; penny shares; securities which may be subject to stabilisation; stock lending activities; and security or investment trust savings schemes.

Some risk warning cases

7–034   In *Brown v KMR Services Ltd; Sword-Daniels v Pitel and Others*[61] a Lloyd's members' agent made certain generalised risk disclosures to a private investor. These were to the effect that membership of Lloyd's involved unlimited liability, and that insurance was a risk business which could result in losses as well as profits. But it also left him with the impression that when losses did occur they were small and easily containable. Gatehouse J. held that a further risk warning should have been made on the lines that, while the syndicates in question usually produced excellent profits in catastrophe-free years, sooner or later a major catastrophe was certain to occur and when it did the loss could be very serious; that if more than one occurred in any one year, however unlikely that might seem on past history, such syndicates might go through their own reinsurance protection; that the danger to names would be that much greater; and that personal stop-loss protection was not the answer.

A second, more sophisticated, claimant was held to be in a similar position because the firm had not given him the risk information which he needed to make a properly informed decision; and without that information his position was no different from that of the wholly inexperienced client. His relative sophistication was, however, taken into account in assessing the measure of loss, where he was awarded 70 per cent of his actual losses, on the grounds that it was reasonable to assume that if he had known the true position he would still have invested 30 per cent of his portfolio in the high risk, ultimately loss-making, syndicates.

In *Ginora Investments Limited v James Capel & Co Ltd*[62] Capel, a corporate finance adviser, was held to have an obligation to advise a bidder on the level of risk inherent in a proposed hostile bid for a target company. However it was also obvious that its client's board knew perfectly well that, by embarking on a hostile bid, they were incurring an element of risk as to what they might find when they opened the target's door and walked in. An obligation to advise on this downside element of a hostile bid would be an obligation to advise its client of what it already knew. Capel owed its client no such obligation. It was inherent in the client's willingness to proceed by way of a hostile bid that it was prepared to run risks of this sort, and Capel owed the client no obligation to remind it of such risk.

In *Bankers Trust v PT Dharmala Sakti Sejahtera,*[63] economic projections included in Bankers Trust's research material were held by Mance J. to be based on self-evidently uncertain assumptions and factors which the research identified. An express "health warning" was unnecessary.

---

[61] [1994] 4 All E.R. 385.
[62] Unreported, February 10, 1995.
[63] Unreported, December 1, 1995.

The Trade Execution Process

UK regulatory discussion of trade execution has historically focused on the **7–035** obligations of the executing broker-dealer, assessed on a trade by trade basis. The position of the investment manager is dealt with only briefly. In the investment contract it takes a simplistic form—either that the firm will provide best execution (according to the FSA definition in COB 7.5) or that it will not. While this approach has proved adequate in the past, it seems unlikely that it will do so for the future. Already there is a tendency for a firm dealing with intermediate customers to disapply best execution, and then in the next breath describe exactly what quality of execution it will provide on common law " reasonable care and skill basis"—*e.g.* "the best price reasonably obtainable in the circumstances". Best execution is, of course, another formation of the obligation of reasonable care and skill, so why is it now such a contentious issue?

Under FSA rules an investment manager is *prima facie* responsible for best execution in the same way as an executing broker. But the rules also provide under COB 7.5.4(3) that the best execution rule does not apply if the firm relies on another person to whom it passes a customer order for execution to provide best execution and has taken reasonable care to ensure that the other person will do so. Managers who are not themselves brokers will almost invariably need to rely on this exemption, though there is a tendency to regard it as a form of best execution in itself, rather than an exemption from the best execution rule *per se*.

Historically, best execution has not been seen as a major issue for managers because the emphasis was on the exercise of investment judgement rather than trade execution. The new business and regulatory interest in trade execution as a distinctive part of the investment management process means that the manager's obligations in this area now need to be given more consideration. For example:

- The accumulation of detailed regulatory pronouncements on best execution, often with a domestic equity market focus, means that the regulators' rules on this topic, originally a codification of the general obligation of care and skill, have become increasingly formulaic, in ways which are not always suited to different markets.

- In the FSA rule, best execution is broadly synonymous with best price, assessed on a trade by trade basis. This, while appropriate if the subject is looked at from the broker's point of view, does not reflect the range of other considerations which a manager will take into account when selecting its executing brokers, and the fact that, because it has delegated execution to the broker, it will normally have to evaluate that execution quality on an *ex post facto* basis.[64]

7–036 Factors such as this have led the FSA to consider, in Consultative Paper 154, whether the best execution concept may need to be subsumed in a wider concept which encompasses the full trading process. For a further note on this see Chapter 4, para.4–026.

As already mentioned, the current tendency is to divide the investment management service into two sequential phases. The first is the process by which an investment decision is made, and the second the process by which it is implemented. Decision-making is the more glamorous function, seeking to add value to client portfolios by choosing the investments to be made. The subsequent implementation of the decision, though much less central to the investment management role, also seeks to add value by achieving the most efficient means of trade execution. Neither process can be treated as reducible to a predictable mathematical formula, but needs to be assessed "in the round", combining fundamental "service/duty" concepts with monitoring of historic data to manage ongoing trading policies and procedures.

The implications of this have been considered in more detail in the US, and it is possible that much of this could be applied as a gloss on the COB 7.5.4(3) exemption.

7–037 A recent SEC list of factors to be taken into account in evaluating best execution included:

- level of commissions;

- speed of trade;

- size of order;

- trading characteristics of the security;

- availability of accurate information affecting choices as to the most favourable market centre;

- availability of technical aids to process such information;

- cost and difficulty of achieving an execution in a particular market centre.

A particularly useful overview of the process has been set out by the Association for Investment Management and Research (AIMR) a US-based trade organisation, in its "Trade Management Guidelines", (the "Guidelines") published in November 2001.

---

[64] Of course, if the exemption in COB, 7.5.4(3) is interpreted sensibly, this should not happen.

The Guidelines are described as seeking to establish recommended best practice for investment management trading or how firms can consistently work towards best execution for their clients. Best execution is defined as "well informed trade execution decisions made with the intention of maximizing the value of client portfolios under the particular circumstances of the time." The Guidelines stated that best execution:

- is intrinsically tied to the portfolio decision value and cannot be evaluated independently;

- is a prospective, statistical concept that cannot be known with certainty *ex ante*;

- has aspects that may be measured and analysed over time on an *ex-post* basis even though accurate measurement on a trade-by-trade basis may not be feasible; and

- is interwoven into complicated, repetitive, and continuing practices and relationships that depend on trust and fidelity.

Thus, the emphasis is not on trade by trade monitoring but on quality of oversight of the trading function and monitoring procedures overall. The guiding principle is that "what gets measured gets managed".

The Guidelines suggest that a firm should have established trade management policies and procedures. To do this it should:

- Establish a trade management oversight committee for developing, evaluating and where necessary changing order-routing and related compliance practices and monitoring compliance practices within the firm. The committee should also consider wider issues such as changes in market forces, availability of risk capital, market fragmentation, liquidity, and so on.

- Establish firm wide trade management policies.

- Develop trade management procedures that describe the firm's policy, which should include procedures for identifying and managing actual and potential conflicts of interest, reviewing the quality of brokers' services and monitoring soft commission practices.

- Implement a trade measurement process to analyse trading costs and execution trends with reference to the manager's client base, changing conditions in the market and available trading venues in a way which facilities comparison:
  - period to period;
  - against appropriate objectives and benchmarks (such as peer group performance);
  - by broker, trading venue and trading method.

SOME CONTRACTUAL ISSUES

7–038   The firm should establish clear firm-wide guidelines on broker selection together with an approved brokers' list, based on recommendations and actual experience. To do this it should assess broker ability to meet its clients' needs on an ongoing basis. Relevant factors are:

- The broker's ability to minimise total trading costs while remaining financially sound. A broker should be able to:
    - maintain and commit adequate capital when necessary to complete trades;
    - respond during volatile market periods; and
    - minimise the number of incomplete trades.

- The broker's level of trading expertise, which should enable it to:
    - handle a high volume of transactions without undue market impact;
    - complete trades;
    - maximise the opportunity for price improvement;
    - execute a trade quickly;
    - maintain the anonymity of an investment manager;
    - search for and obtain liquidity to minimise market impact;
    - exert the necessary efforts to satisfy trading needs in a diligent and consistent manner;
    - act with integrity;
    - account for its trade errors and correct them in a satisfactory manner;
    - accommodate unusual market conditions; and
    - engage in after-hours and cross-border trading, when required.

- The broker's infrastructure, which should enable it to provide the following (where relevant to the service):
    - order entry systems;
    - adequate lines of communication;
    - timely order execution reports;
    - an efficient and accurate clearance and settlement process; and
    - capacity to accommodate unusual trading volume.

- The broker's ability to provide the following ad hoc information or services:
    - suggestions that improve the quality of trade executions;
    - proprietary research;
    - third-party research;
    - visits with research analysts;
    - access to broker staff; and
    - access to issuers and their road-shows.

- The broker's ability to provide ancillary services. A firm should where necessary check the usefulness of such services against any prejudice to its

200

fiduciary duties and ability to deliver best execution to its clients. Such ancillary services may involve:

- executing unique trading strategies;
- executing and settling difficult trades;
- handling client-directed brokerage and softing arrangements including commission recapture and step-outs;
- custody services;
- sponsoring wrap programmes (fees for advisory services not based directly on client transactions, such as advice on the selection of other advisors);
- participation in underwriting syndicates and initial public offerings.

Based on these principles, the firm should develop an approved brokers' list and brokerage target allocation plan, together with a budget for broker remuneration. Performance should be monitored against budget. The firm should also where appropriate consider alternative trading options in the light of, *e.g.* technology developments and market changes.

The firm should also monitor and evaluate its brokers' actual performance and execution quality. Appropriate methods might include:

- quarterly brokerage reports covering:

  - commission summaries;
  - transaction reports;
  - failed trades;

- information on the broker's financial condition such as audited financial statements;

- feedback from staff such as individual managers, analysts, and back office staff with significant broker contact;

- evaluation of broker performance against the firm's measurements of its total trading costs.

Liability

The general rule is that an agent such as a manager is not liable to third parties for the obligations of its principal.[65] In some cases the agent may have personal liability, but this is normally only an issue for broker-dealers because of their dual agency and own-account capacities.[66]

7–039

---

[65] *Bowstead & Reynolds on Agency* (15th ed. 2001), Article 99; *Montgomerie v UK Mutual S Assn Ltd* [1891] 1 Q.B. 370.

[66] See *e.g. E Bailey & Co Ltd v Balholm Securities Ltd* [1973] 2 Lloyds Rep. 404 (Kerr J.) (futures broker incurring personal liability to market counterparties); *Moore v Moore* (1611) 1 Bulst.

SOME CONTRACTUAL ISSUES

Where the agent acts within the scope of its actual authority, there is also an implied term in the agency contract that it will be entitled to an indemnity from its principal for any liability it incurs to third parties in so doing.[67] This right to an indemnity is almost always reinforced by an express term in the relevant agreement.

Where the client is contracting in its capacity as a trustee, it will typically want to limit its liability under this indemnity to the value of the assets of the trust from time to time. This may in turn involve the firm seeking further assurances from the trustee as to how the trust assets will be dealt with.

7–040   The contract also normally includes a related clause, stating that the manager is not liable to the client for any loss the client incurs in connection with the management services.

In both cases it is normal to include or negotiate a carve out under which there will be no right to an indemnity where the firm has acted improperly or negligently,[68] and the firm will be liable for loss to the client resulting from the firm's own negligence or deliberate misconduct.

This carve-out is particularly relevant when juxtaposed with a contractual indemnity. An unqualified indemnity, by its very nature, merely looks to compensate the loss of the indemnified party, without taking account of factors which would be brought into account in an ordinary claim for damages, such as contributory negligence or a failure to mitigate on the part of the indemnified party.

7–041   The underlying principle is that investment and other losses are for the client's account, unless they have been caused by the actual misconduct of the firm. A shorter way of describing the same concept is to say that the firm's exclusion of liability and indemnity apply in relation to all losses incurred in the *proper* performance of its duties. In other words, if the firm has acted improperly, the contractual situation will be reassessed.

The carve-out for the firm's own negligence or deliberate misconduct can be expressed in several ways. Common terms for the "deliberate misconduct" concept are "bad faith" and/or "wilful default". "Negligence" is usually described as such, though occasionally the term "gross negligence" is substituted.

There is no definitive ruling on the meaning of "gross negligence" and its interpretation must depend on its context. In case law the general rule appears to be that it is the same as ordinary negligence. In *Wilson v Brett*[69]

169; *Cropper v Cook* (1868) L.R. 3, CP 194 (stockbroker incurring personal liability on contract under market usage); *Anglo Overseas Transport Co Ltd v Titan Industrial Corp (United Kingdom Ltd)* [1959] 2 Lloyds Rep. 152 (freight forwarder incurring personal liability under trade usage for dead freight when customer provides insufficient cargo).

[67] *Bowstead & Reynolds on Agency* (15th ed. 2001), Article 64; *Warlow v Harrison* (1859) 1 E. & E. 309 at 317 (auctioneer); *Cropper v Cook* (1868) L.R. 3, CP 194 (broker).

[68] See *e.g. Capp v Topham* (1805) 6 East. 392 (solicitor not entitled to fees for a prosecution which he had carried out so negligently that the case was lost).

[69] (1843) 11 M. & W. 113 at 115.

LIABILITY

Rolfe B famously described gross negligence as no more than "negligence with a vituperative epithet". In *Pentecost v London District Auditor*[70] the application of a test of gross negligence or ordinary negligence by a District Auditor was held to produce the same result. Lynsky J. said,[71]

"Epithets applied to negligence, so far as the common law is concerned, are really meaningless. Negligence is well known and well-defined. A man is either guilty of negligence or he is not guilty of negligence. Gross negligence is not known to the English common law so far as civil proceedings are concerned."[72]

More recently, in *Armitage v Nurse*,[73] Millett L.J. said,

7–042

"it would be very surprising if our law drew the line between liability for ordinary negligence and liability for gross negligence. In this respect English law differs from Civil law systems, for it has always drawn a sharp distinction between negligence, however gross, on the one hand and fraud, bad faith and wilful misconduct on the other. .... we regard the difference between negligence and gross negligence as merely one of degree. English lawyers have always had a healthy disrespect for the latter distinction."

It is suggested that in a conventional financial services contract, negligence and gross negligence are both purposively intended to indicate the obverse of "reasonable care and skill", so that there is no reason (absent special circumstances to the contrary) to distinguish gross negligence from negligence. Cases where the concept of gross negligence has been upheld as a separate standard tend to be based on more distinctive situations and facts. For instance, a chargee, whose duties of care to the chargor are normally of a strictly limited nature, might exclude any liability to the chargor for the way the chargee enforced its security "other than in the case of wilful default or gross negligence". The standard for deciding whether a director should be disqualified from acting as a director is gross negligence rather than negligence, to indicate the seriousness of the disqualification.[74] In *Great Scottish*

---

[70] [1951] 2 K.B. 759.

[71] *ibid.*, at 764.

[72] In the same case Lord Goddard C.J. said at 766. "The use of the expression 'gross negligence' is always misleading. Except in the one case when the law relating to manslaughter is being considered, the words 'gross negligence' should never be used in connection with any matter to which the common law relates because negligence is a breach of duty, and, if there is a duty and there has been a breach of it which causes loss, it matters not whether it is a venial breach or a serious one".

[73] [1998] Ch. 241; [1997] 3 W.L.R. 1046; [1997] 2 All E.R. 705 at 712, CA.

[74] See *Re Bath Glass Ltd* [1988] B.C.L.C. 329 at 333, 4 BCC 130 at 133, *per* Peter Gibson J. (ordinary commercial misjudgment is not sufficient to justify disqualification of a director) and *Re D'Jan of London* [1994] 1 B.C.L.C. 561; [1993] B.C.C. 646 (Absence of gross negligence on the

SOME CONTRACTUAL ISSUES

and Western Railway Company Ltd. v British Railways Board[75] Neil L.J. distinguished cases where the negligence/gross negligence distinction had been held to be meaningless on the facts. The case concerned a claim by a railway company under a haulage contract with the British Railways Board. The term gross negligence in the haulage contract appeared in close proximity to the words "wilful neglect",[76] and it was held that the two terms should be construed ejusdem generis as both describing the same extreme concept of negligence.

This is of course an English law analysis, and gross negligence is perhaps most commonly found in agreements governed by US law, where the statutory scheme and related contract law have evolved differently. Thus, in *Red Sea Tankers Ltd v Papachristidis (The Hellespont Ardent)*,[77] where the court accepted that gross negligence represented a different standard from negligence, the contract in question was governed by New York law and Mance J. reached this conclusion on the basis of a review of New York statute[78] and case law. He characterised "gross negligence" as serious negligence amounting to reckless disregard of or indifference to an obvious risk.

Conflicts of Interest

7–043 It is standard in UK management and broker-dealer agreements to include a disclaimer of liability for conflicts of interest, followed by a list of general situations in which such a conflict might arise. This is at one level a reflection of City drafting practice. At a slightly deeper level it reflects the FSA requirement that the contract should state, when a material interest or conflict of interest may or does arise, the manner in which the firm will ensure fair treatment of the customer under COB, 7.1.3R[80] (though there are so many ways this might be achieved that the statement is liable to be very generally worded). At a third level it is an important and direct response to a whole

---

part of a negligent director cited as reason for the court exercising its discretion under s.727 of the Companies Act 1985, where the director had acted honestly and reasonably, to relieve him from liability).

[75] unreported, April 5, 1993, CA.
[76] "The Board . . . will not be liable . . . for any damage to or any loss of any property owned leased or hired by [the Railway Company] except to the extent that such loss or damage . . . was caused wholly by the gross negligence or wilful neglect of the Board" perhaps this sort of restriction explains why US commercial cases so often resort to charges of fraud and breach of fiduciary duty.
[77] [1997] 2 Lloyd's Rep. 547.
[78] The judgment noted that "under New York law it is contrary to public policy for a party to contract out of liability for wilful misconduct or gross negligence," and that New York case law defined gross negligence as "conduct that evinces a reckless disregard for the rights of others or "smacks" of intentional wrongdoing." On the other hand US statute and regulation offer financial services customers a range of courses of action which are not available in the UK.
[79–80] COB, 4.2.15E(13).

CONFLICTS OF INTEREST

series of issues relating to fiduciary duty. The rest of this section outlines a "current practice" understanding of the relevant fiduciary issues. For a more detailed discussion of this from a regulatory point of view, see Chapter 9.

The nature of the fiduciary relationship

A fiduciary is not a trustee, but has a special relationship of trust and confi- **7–044**
dence[81] with its client, which gives it special influence over the client's affairs and a corresponding "duty of loyalty" to the client. There is a vulnerability[82] on the part of the beneficiary which results in reliance or dependence[83] on the fiduciary. Thus the client relationship described in Chapter 2 will also normally also give rise to a fiduciary relationship.

Firms making investment decisions or implementing trades for a client, and in some cases giving a client advice, are all liable to stand in a fiduciary relationship to that client.[84] The granting of control over, carrying with it the *de facto* power to dispose of, financial assets, will also usually give rise to a fiduciary duty.[85] Advice as usual is more nebulous, and even professional expert advice does not necessarily have the same fiduciary effect.[86] The most relevant factor with is the extent of the advisee's dependence on, and trust in, the advice and the adviser.[87]

Fiduciary duties are sometimes confused with other duties arising from the same facts, such as care and skill. The one key obligation which arises from the duty of loyalty, and which does not arise from any other legal obligation, is the fiduciary's duty to deal properly with any conflicts of interest.

This can be divided into: (a) the fiduciary's duty not to put its personal **7–045**
interest ahead of its clients (a firm/client conflict); and (b) its duty not unduly to favour one client's interest over another (a client/client conflict). Within

---

[81] *Bristol & West Building Society v Mothew (t/a Stapley & Co)* [1996] 4 All E.R. 698, CA at 711–712, *per* Millett L.J. A fiduciary is: "someone who has undertaken to act for or on behalf of another in a particular manner in circumstances which give rise to a relationship of trust and confidence."

[82] *LAC Minerals Ltd v International Corona Resources Ltd* [1990] Fleet Street Reports 441 (CAN); *Frame v Smith* (1987) 42 D.L.R. (4th) 81 at 98–99; *Hospital Products Ltd v US Surgical Corp* (1984) 55 A.L.R. 417 at 488, *per* Dawson J.: "inherent in the nature of the [fiduciary] relationship itself is a position of disadvantage or vulnerability on the part of one of the parties which causes him to place reliance upon the other and requires the protection of equity."

[83] *e.g. Lloyds Bank v Bundy* [1975] 1 Q.B. 326 at 341; *Coleman v Myers* [1977] 2 N.Z.L.R. 225 (dependence on information and advice).

[84] The fiduciary "undertakes to act on behalf of or for the benefit of another, often as an intermediary with a discretion or power which affects the interest of the other who depends on the fiduciary for information and advice": "Fiduciary Duties and Regulatory Rules" (1995) Law Com. No. 236.

[85] In *Hancock v Smith* (1889) 41 Ch.D. 456, CA, it was held that when a client delivered share certificates with instructions to sell the relationship became a fiduciary one.

[86] *Burns v Kelly Peters & Associates Ltd* [1987] 16 B.C.L.R. (2d).

[87] *Tate v Williamson* (1866) 2 Ch. App. 55.

SOME CONTRACTUAL ISSUES

this broad concept the duty to avoid a secret profit may need separate consideration, since it has been held to exist even where there is no other substantive form of conflict.[88] In *LAC Minerals Ltd v International Corona Resources Ltd*[89] La Forest J. said:

"Compendiously [the fiduciary's obligation] can be described as the fiduciary duty of loyalty and will most often include the avoidance of a conflict of the common law encompasses this duty and interest and a duty not to profit at the expense of the beneficiary."

Another rather legalistic concern (to be found in Law Commission Consultation Paper No.124 (May 1992) on fiduciary duties) is that the duty of loyalty requires the fiduciary to utilise all the knowledge it possesses, including imputed knowledge, in the service of its client, even where this would require it to breach its duties to other clients, or where the individual employee dealing with the client has no personal knowledge of the matter in question. This has not, however, received much support from recent case law.[90]

Managing the conflict

7–046   Currently the main ways of dealing with a conflict of interest appear to be:

- Full disclosure and fully informed consent on a case-by-case basis.

- Express or implicit contractual disclosure and express or implicit contractual consent.

---

[88]   *Boardman v Phipps* [1966] 3 All E.R. 721 and *Regal (Hastings) Limited v Gulliver* [1967] 2 A.C. 134.

[89]   [1990] Fleet Street Reports 441 at 454 (CAN).

[90]   See *e.g. Kelly v Cooper* [1992] A.C. 205, PC; *Prince Jefri Bolkiah v KPMG* [1999] 2 A.C. 222, HL (effectiveness of a Chinese wall concerned with actual not imputed knowledge), *per* Lord Millett: "There is no cause to impute or attribute the knowledge of one partner to his fellow partners. Whether a particular individual is in possession of confidential information is a question of fact which must be proved or inferred from the circumstances of the case". See also *North & South Trust Co v Berkeley* [1971] 1 All E.R. 980 (Lloyds' brokers in breach of their duties to the insured, but not bound to disclose information to the insured obtained while acting for the underwriter); *Hilton v Barker Booth & Eastwood (A firm)*, *The Times* June 6, 2002, CA (solicitor who acted for more than one party to a transaction might be obliged to disclose information from one of them to the other. However the solicitor's retainer must be subject to an implied exclusion from any general duty of disclosure of that which they were legally obliged to treat as confidential. As a result of this he might be in breach of a duty to warn his client that he could not act properly for him; but was not also in breach of a duty to disclose to the client what he knew of the other client/party to the transaction).

206

CONFLICTS OF INTEREST

- Managing the client relationship by means such as objective impartiality and control of information flows,[91] so that a substantive conflict does not, as a matter of fact, arise.

The FSMA regime tracks these various "common law" options and puts the onus on the firm to ensure that the client receives fair treatment in such circumstances. Notably, it does not limit the firm's options to the extreme position of having to make either full disclosure or ceasing to act. COB 7.1.3 provides a high level summary of conflict principles which by virtue of its generalised nature helps to circumvent some of the more arbitrary conclusions which can result when extracting general principles from individual case law. It is widely used nowadays as the yardstick for fiduciary duties in the financial services industry.

Full disclosure and informed consent

The customer may consent to the particular conflict provided he has knowl-   **7–047**
edge of the material facts and his consent is therefore given on a properly informed basis. This has been described as "full, fair and complete" disclosure of all material facts[92] and is to be distinguished from the mere disclosure of an interest in general terms.[93]

This is the traditional view of how a conflict should be handled and some cases have suggested that it is the only way.[94] The practical point is perhaps that informed consent is the only *completely* certain way of resolving a conflict. This does not mean that other resolutions are not possible.

In many unexceptional modern business situations, fully informed disclosure may be simply unrealistic. The increasingly complex nature of financial services and the business conglomerates that provide them are capable of generating a potentially never-ending series of disclosures throughout the firm/client relationship.[95] Theoretical client/client conflicts start as soon as a firm has more than one client. An SEC Special Study of Securities Markets in the 1960s[96] observed that:

> ". . . total elimination of all [conflicts of interest]..would involve complete segregation of functions . . . would have to involve fragmentation

---

[91] Strictly speaking the fiduciary duty arises in equity, not the common law.
[92] *Parker v McKenna* (1874) L.R. 10 Ch. 96; *Dunne v English* (1874) C.R. 18 Eq. 524.
[93] *Dunne v English* (1874) C.R. 18 Eq. 524 at 533, *per* Sir George Jessel; *New Zealand Netherlands Society v Kuys* [1973] 1 W.L.R. 1126 at 1131–1132, *per* Lord Wilberforce.
[94] *e.g. Harrods v Lemon* [1931] 2 K.B. 157 CA. Contrast *SCF v Masri* [1986] 1 Lloyds Rep. 293.
[95] On the other hand, the recent divestment by international accounting firms of their "added-value consultancy arms, under pressure from the SEC, suggests that setting up a large and multifunctional business which generates a continuous flow of multiple conflicts is not a defence in itself.
[96] "Special Study of Securities Markets" (1963), Part 1, p.440.

of the business to a point where ... each investor would have his own broker who would not be permitted to act for any other customer or for himself"

Disclosure and consent in the service contract

7–048 In recent years there has been increasing reliance on a contractual analysis in dealing with conflicts. Fiduciary duties arise as a matter of law not contract,[97] but the relationship which gives rise to them can be created by contract, and must be looked at subject to the contract terms[98]:

> "The existence and scope of [the fiduciary duties of agents] depends upon the terms on which they are acting ... the scope of the fiduciary duties owed ... are to be defined by the terms of the contract of agency".[99]

In particular, where a disclosure is included in the fiduciary's service contract with its client, the client may be regarded as having consented to the matter disclosed.[1] Recent case law and discussion has encouraged the use of contractual disclosures, which list on a non-exclusive basis the "normal" conflicts which may occur in the ordinary course of business. These disclosures, of their nature, will deal with generalised situations. For instance, the possibility of the firm making a "secret profit" is regularly addressed by a provision that it will not be obliged to disclose or account for any fees or commissions which it might earn from third parties.

The client's consent may also be via an implied contractual term as well as to an express one. In other words, a client's agreement to an obvious conflict may be implied on the basis of market and regulatory usage and practice[2]; or on a "common sense" or "obvious" basis.[3]

---

[97] Dowrick, "The relationship of principal and agent" (1954) 17 M.L.R. 24.

[98] *Prince Jefri Bolkiah v KPMG* [1999] 2 A.C. 222, HL.

[99] *Kelly v Cooper* [1993] A.C. 205, PC at 214, *per* Lord Browne-Wilkinson.

[1] *Aston v Kelsey* [1913] 3 K.B. 314; *Kelly v Cooper* [1992] A.C. 205, PC.

[2] In *SCF v Masri* [1986] 1 Lloyds Rep. 293, pp. 299 and 302, a future's broker's general right to act as both principla and agent in the same market was accepted by the court. The brokers were entitled to trade on their own behalf as a matter of market practice and "the tiny scale on which they did so avoided any risk of conflict". In *Jones v Canavan* [1972] 2 N.S.W.L.R. 236 (AUS) it was held that an agent's fiduciary duties regarding conflict of interest could be modified by a reasonable usage.

[3] *i.e.* it is necessary to make sense of the agreement. This may be because such a term is needed to give business efficacy to the contract. Without it the contract would not work, or would be a nonsense. It is assumed that the parties would not have intended to enter into a contract which was a nonsense. See *The Moorcock* (1889) 14 P.D. 64. A term may also be implied because it represents an obvious inference from the express and other implied terms. As such it may be described as an unexpressed intention which was (by inference) in the minds of both parties at the time the contract was entered into. See *Reigate v Union Manufacturing Co (Ramsbottom) Ltd* [1918] 1 K.B. 592, CA.

CONFLICTS OF INTEREST

In *Kelly v Cooper*[4] the Privy Council held that there must, on a common **7–049** sense basis, be an implied term allowing an estate agent to act for several clients who were vendors in the same market, without requiring it to disclose information to one vendor about the activities of the others. Lord Browne-Wilkinson said:

> ". . . it is [estate agents'] business to act for numerous principals; where properties are of a similar description, there will be a conflict of interest between the principals each of whom will be concerned to attract potential purchasers to their property rather than to that of another. Yet, despite this conflict of interest, estate agents must be free to act for several competing principals, otherwise they will be unable to perform their function. . . . Since the plaintiff was well aware that the defendants would be acting also for other vendors of comparable properties and in so doing would receive confidential information from those other vendors, the agency contract between the plaintiff and the defendants cannot have included either (a) a term requiring the defendants to disclose such confidential information to the plaintiff or (b) a term precluding the defendants acting for rival vendors or (c) a term precluding the defendants from seeking to earn commission on the sale of the property of a rival vendor."

Similarly, large accountancy firms are entitled to act as auditors for clients which are in commercial competition with each other. The identity of the audit clients is publicly acknowledged and the clients are taken to consent to the auditors acting for competing clients. This would include consenting to instructions which were a natural extension of the audit function.[5]

Using the contract to define the scope of the service

A firm's role as fiduciary may be separated as a matter of fact from other **7–050** activities carried on in an arm's length capacity with the same person:

> "If a solicitor is actually engaged to conduct or is conducting for his client an action, say, for slander and, while the action is pending, meets his client in the hunting field and bargains and buys from him a horse, each party relying on his own knowledge of horseflesh, that transaction will stand on the same footing as a transaction between strangers."[6]

---

[4] [1993] A.C. 205, PC, at 214–215.
[5] *Prince Jefri Bolkiah v KPMG* [1999] 2 A.C. 222 *per* Millett L.J., HL.
[6] *Allison v Clayhills* (1907) L.T. 709 at 711, *per* Parker, J. See also *Eagle Trust plc v SBC Securities Ltd and SBCI Bank Corporation Investment Banking Ltd* [1995] B.C.C. 231 at 249, *per* Arden J.: "An underwriter does not in my judgment take on underwriting obligations in the course of carrying out his duties as financial adviser and accordingly he cannot be treated as

A switch from a fiduciary to an arm's length relationship also occurs when the firm ceases to act for the client. In *Macoun v Erskine, Oxenford & Co*[7] a broker who had closed out a defaulting client's positions and then sold them, was entitled immediately to repurchase the securities concerned, so long as it had put the securities through the market as a bona fide commercial transaction. The client relationship had terminated at the point the shares were sold, and the broker was entitled to make the repurchase provided it was not so much a part of the original sale that the market maker who bought and sold back the shares took no risk.

It follows from this that it ought in principle to be possible to structure a relationship, or particular aspects of a relationship, so that they contain no fiduciary elements. The service contract is a good place to set out these demarcation lines, and the more specific the provision the more effective it is likely to be. A purely interpretative provision such as the following may still be effective to eliminate marginal uncertainties such as a duty to utilise confidential information provided by other clients:

"Neither the relationship between us nor the services we provide will give rise to any fiduciary or equitable duties on our part which would prevent or hinder us from performing such services or generally acting in the manner contemplated in this Agreement, whether acting as principal or agent in doing business for or with you, or doing business with associates, connected customers, and other investors."

7–051   It is much more questionable whether the authorities can be used to justify a provision which simply seeks to operate as an exclusion clause, such as:

"Neither the relationship between us, nor the services we provide, nor any other matter, will give rise to any fiduciary duties on our part."

If, as a matter of fact, the contractual obligations and surrounding factual matrix *do* import fiduciary duties, a clause which simply denies this is likely to be set aside as a mere "failed relabelling" exercise. See the unsuccessful attempt to recharacterise a fiduciary relationship as a counterparty relationship in the *Glynwill* case.[8] See also the further discussion of this topic in Chapter 9.

---

having some hybrid character of a 'financial adviser/underwriter' when selecting sub-underwriters". In *Aas v Benham* (1891) 2 Ch.244, a case on partnership duties, Lindley L.J. said at 255: "if [a partner] avails himself of [partnership information] for any purpose which is within the scope of the partnership business, or of any competing business, he must account to the firm . . . but there is no principle or authority which entitles the firm to benefits derived by a partner from the use of information for purposes which are wholly without the scope of the firm's business".

[7] [1901] 2 K.B. 493.
[8] *Glynwill Investments NV v Thompson McKinnon Futures Limited*, unreported, February 13, 1992, Simon Tuckey Q.C. This important case was first discussed in an article by the author in J.I.B.F.L., December 1992, pp.572–580.

CONFLICTS OF INTEREST

Impartial treatment(1): the firm clears its mind

Where a generalised disclosure is insufficient to deal with the particular facts, **7–052**
the firm may still be able to manage the conflict in such a way that the COB,
7.1.3 principle of fair treatment is met.

One way of doing this is for the relevant individual within the firm to put
out of his mind the matter giving rise to the conflict, so that he may, on behalf
of his firm, still properly discharge its fiduciary duties. This loosely equates
with the FSA concept of an "independence policy".

In *Spector v Ageda*[9] Megarry J. commented that while it was undesirable
for a solicitor to act for both parties to a contract, it was still possible, in the
absence of personal interest, in the vast majority of cases, for the solicitor to
discharge his duty of acting impartially in the interests of each of his clients.
(However, where one of the parties was the solicitor himself his position
would normally be impossible.)

The controversy over whether packaged product salesmen should be remu- **7–053**
nerated by a commission paid by the product provider or a fee paid by the
client is an instance of the sort of situation where this issue arises. In stock
and futures broking in contrast it has always been accepted that an advisory
broker can be paid by a trade-based commission. The broker's commission is
paid by the client directly as a disclosed part of the execution costs, and is not
wrapped up in an oblique way with the investment itself, as is the way with
life product sales.

This stockbroker or futures broker conflict is dealt with primarily by the
broker's duty not to churn its client's account. In churning cases, the predominate purpose of the broker's advice ceases to be to the benefit the client
and becomes the maximisation of the number of trades executed in order to
maximise brokerage commission.

Another example is an agency cross, where the firm (broker or manager)
crosses a trade between two clients rather than putting the trade through the
market. It is generally considered that if the cross is made at a price which is,
or is reasonably believed to be, as good as the clients would have got in the market, this is an appropriately objective market standard for conflict purposes.[9a]

Where an "impartial treatment" arrangement works, it is because the stan- **7–054**
dard of care the firm follows (and internal procedures are very important
here) is sufficiently objective and discrete to be identified and followed in its
own right. The individual representing the firm must be able to put to the
back of his mind any conflicts between: (a) the client's interests; and (b) his
own interests or the interests of his firm. But in some situations this approach
may not be possible. This is most likely where the individual employee's duty

---

[9] [1973] Ch.30 at 47.
[9a] In *Jones v Canavan* [1972] NS.W.L.R. 236, an agency cross which had been done in accordance with market practice and by reference to market price was upheld, even though disclosure had been made, Jacobs J.A. commenting at 245 that there was no real conflict involved.

211

SOME CONTRACTUAL ISSUES

goes beyond mere impartial adherence to a market standard and involves actively promoting his client's interests as against those of another client or the firm itself.

For example, an individual adviser would have real difficulty in achieving a common objective standard where he was acting for both buyer and seller on a corporate acquisition, and the terms of engagement required him actively to negotiate the best price he could for each client as against the other. In such a situation the adviser's duty to negotiate the highest price for the seller conflicts inexorably with his duty to negotiate the lowest price for the buyer. He could of course propose what he considers to be a medium price and invite both parties to accept it but this would involve not performing his mandate but changing the terms of his engagement.

This situation was contemplated in *North and South Trust Co v Berkeley*[10]:

"... [an expert witness] assures me that part of the training of the broker is to act properly in the dual capacity, and that he has never known insurance brokers to use their dual position improperly. But how do you train anyone to act properly in such a situation? What course of action can possibly be adopted which does not involve some breach of the duty to one principal or the other?. . .neither skill nor honesty can reconcile the irreconcilable."

Impartial treatment(2): Chinese walls

7–055   One of the surest ways of ensuring that the client is treating the client fairly, and is not prejudiced by the conflict, is for individual representatives of the firm not to have any *actual* knowledge of the matters giving rise to the conflict. The firm can then be sure that the actual service rendered to the client is not affected by the conflicting interests to which the firm itself is subject.

The arrangements used to limit the movement of information must overcome a legal presumption that information moves within a firm. The burden of proving that the information has not moved is on the firm. Not only must an individual firm representative not have the relevant knowledge at a particular point in time, the firm must be able to show that he cannot be expected to acquire such knowledge in the course of his employment.[11]

As to whether the firm can demonstrate that effective arrangements are in place, the circumstances in *Rakusen v Ellis, Munday & Clarke*[12] provide a useful reference point. In that case an early version of a Chinese wall was accepted as effective in circumstances where the firm concerned was operating as two

---

[10] [1971] 1 W.L.R. 470 [1971] 1 All E.R. 980.
[11] See, *e.g. Harrods v Lemon* [1931] 2 K.B. 157, CA; *Rakusen v Ellis, Munday & Clarke* [1912] 1 Ch. 831, CA; *Supasave Retail v Coward Chance* [1991] 1 All E.R. 668.
[12] [1912] 1 Ch.831, CA.

212

independent businesses with separate principals, no clients in common, and no material knowledge about each others' clients or client matters.[13]

The wall probably does not need to be effective against deliberate or dishonest disclosure, only against accidental or inadvertent disclosure. At first instance in the *Bolkiah* case, the court was not prepared to impute to KPMG or their staff anything other than an honest intention not to disclose.[14]

Confidentiality

Confidentiality is such a natural adjunct to a fiduciary relationship it is often assumed that it is another aspect of fiduciary duty. But a conflict can exist without any confidential information being involved, and a duty of confidentiality can arise in a non-fiduciary situation.   **7–056**

Firms normally owe a duty of confidence to their clients as a matter of contract,[15] but the same duty may also arise in the course of arms length contracts, or non-contractual situations such as pre-contractual dealings or where the duty is owed to former clients or business partners. A standard arms-length example is where the parties to a proposed company sale and purchase exchange confidential information about the business to be sold.[16]

Nature of confidential information

Confidential information includes trade secrets, personal confidences, government information and artistic and literary confidences. Trade secrets are the class of confidential information associated with business and commerce and consist of items or collections of information which because of their inaccessibility to the rest of the market, give a competitive advantage to the firm which owns or uses them. In investment management, typical examples of confidential information would be a proprietary trading strategy or risk   **7–057**

---

[13] In practice of course many modern conglomerates will not be able to achieve this level of client segregation. Factors such as different businesses and principal staff will be relevant to, say, the segregation of investment management and banking businesses within the same group. A Chinese wall established for a more specific purpose, such as keeping a particular piece of price-sensitive confidential information away from the firm's investment managers, will operate on a more limited footing.

[14] This point was not pursued before the House of Lords, who gave their judgment on the assumption that accidental or inadvertent disclosure was the only material concern.

[15] Thus there is an implied term in a banking context that a banker shall not without the consent of its customer disclose to any other person any document or other information obtained in the course of the relationship.

[16] *LAC Minerals Ltd v International Corona Resources Ltd* [1990] Fleet Street Reports 441 at 450 (CAN). "While both of them were seriously and honestly engaged in preparing a deal . . . LAC and the other party would both have a duty towards each other not to hurt each other as the result of any information that was exchanged."

model, or non-public information about the client's or manager's actual positions or trading intentions.

Confidences are enforced by an action for breach of confidence in which the claimant must demonstrate that the information imparted was confidential. This usually involves showing that:

(1) the information provided by the confidant was non-public and confidential[17];

(2) the information was imparted by the confidant in a manner which imposed a duty on the recipient to respect the confidentiality of the information. A reasonability test is used to decide whether the information was imparted in circumstances such that a duty of confidence arises[18]; this may be because there is an express agreement for confidentiality, or because the information was imparted for a particular or limited purpose only[19]; and

(3) the recipient has breached his duty of confidence (often shown by the fact that the recipient has made an unauthorised use of the information).[20] Unauthorised use can include using the information itself or disclosing the information to a third party in a way which is outside the scope of the purpose for which it was provided by the confidant. There will be some exceptions to this, as where the recipient is under a legal duty to disclose, under the money laundering regulations for instance, or where disclosure is in the public interest.

Confidential information is only protected as between the confidants and the recipients of the information from such confidants. It does not affect an independent discovery of the same information. A trade secret is only susceptible to protection for as long as it remains confidential.

Duties of loyalty and confidence to former clients

7–058 In the case of a former client, the fiduciary duty of loyalty comes to an end with the retainer and thereafter there can be no conflict of interest.[21]

---

[17] Where the information is a mixture of public and confidential information the confidential element may still be protected provide it can be identified as such: *Seager v Copydex Ltd* [1967] 1 W.L.R. 923, CA.

[18] *Coco v AN Clark (Engineers) Ltd* [1969] R.P.C. 41.

[19] *ibid.*, at 47, *per* Megarry J.

[20] "The relevant question to be asked is what is the confidee entitled to do with the information, and not to what use is he prohibited from putting it. Any use other than a permitted use is prohibited and amounts to a breach of duty: "*LAC Minerals Ltd v International Corona Resources Ltd* [1990] Fleet Street Reports 441 at 449, 451, *per* La Forest J.

[21] *Macoun v Erskine, Oxenford & Co* (1901) 2 K.B. 493; *Prince Jefri Bolkiah v KPMG* [1999] 2 A.C. 222, HL.

CONFIDENTIALITY

In contrast, the firm's duty of confidentiality continues in relation to information imparted during the retainer. The duty is not to misuse the information. This means that, absent the client's consent, the firm must not make use of the confidential information or cause others to make use of it otherwise than for the client's benefit.

This distinction was summarised by Millett L.J.[22]:

> "[T]he Court's intervention [to protect a past client] is founded not on the avoidance of any perception of possible impropriety but on the protection of confidential information. . . . It is otherwise where the court's intervention is sought by an existing client, for a fiduciary cannot act at the same time both for and against the same client. . . . His disqualification has nothing to do with the confidentiality of client information. It is based on the inescapable conflict of interest which is inherent in the situation."

7–059 A firm must not make use of a former client's confidential information or cause others to do so other than for that client's benefit or with the client's consent. The test is: (a) was the firm in possession of information which was confidential to the past client; and (b) was or might such information be relevant to the matter on which it is instructed by a current client?

It appears from this that where there are a series of occasional contacts as distinct from a continuous retainer the client may be a "past client" in the gaps between contacts. In the gaps, the only opportunity which the firm has to abuse the relationship is by breach of confidentiality. It is not in a position to influence the client's actions because the client has not instructed it to do anything.

Default and *Force Majeure* Clauses

7–060 A default clause is regularly used in counterparty contracts and broking contracts where the firm incurs liability on behalf of the customer and holds customer's assets—usually in the form of collateral. Default by the customer will typically trigger a right to terminate the contract immediately and special rights such as the ability to net off different debits and credits against each other and to enforce security rights against the client's assets or collateral account.

Purely management agreements, without any custody element, do not normally need to include a default clause. This is because: (a) the agreement is frequently terminable at will; and (b) the manager does not typically trade with or carry any market liability for the client, or have security over or

---

[22] In *Prince Jefri Bolkiah v KPMG.*

215

recourse against its client's assets. Its financial exposure to the client is limited to any accrued but unpaid management fees.

In futures management this position is different because the futures broker is on risk to its market counterparties for all the client' open futures positions and contractual provision is always made for calling an event of default against the client for, say, non-payment of a margin call or simply for the firm's own protection in a falling market, together with associated powers to close out positions and realise and apply collateral are major issues. Even if such a clause were not included, it may be inferred as an implied term on grounds of market efficacy.[23]

7–061   *Force majeure* clauses are important in counterparty transactions, where they help to mitigate the absolute performance obligations which would otherwise apply. They are much rarer in management agreements because they are much less relevant. Most of the firm's duties are already qualified rather than absolute and, in residual cases, what appear in normal circumstances to be absolute duties may end up being qualified by a *force majeure* situation. For example, if a manager breaches its investment restrictions purely because of movements in market prices, this is clearly beyond its control, and would generally be interpreted as requiring the firm to make adjustments to bring the portfolio back within the relevant investment limits, rather than as constituting an automatic breach of mandate in itself.

Having said this, both event of default and *force majeure* clauses are included in investment management agreements from time to time because of particular circumstances and/or as a matter of preference.

Termination

Contractual duration

7–062   It is very common for investment management and broking contracts to state that they are terminable at will by both parties, but there are many variations on this. For instance, the manager may want an initial guaranteed period in which it can demonstrate its ability to manage the portfolio, while the client my want a guaranteed period of notice where the firm terminates, in order to have time to find a replacement manager.

---

[23] *SNW v Falik* [1989] 2 Lloyd's Rep. 224 (Webster J.).

FSA requirements

Under FSA requirements the customer agreement should outline:
7–063

- How it may be terminated,[24] including statements:
    - that termination will be without prejudice to the completion of trans-actions already initiated, if this is the case;
    - that the customer may terminate the terms of business by written notice to the firm and when this may take effect;
    - that if the firm has the right to terminate the terms of business, it may do so by notice given to the customer, and specifying the minimum notice period, if any; and
    - of any agreed time after which, or any agreed event upon which, the terms of business will terminate.

A normal legal agreement would cover these sorts of issues as a matter of course, but in the past in some markets documentation has been sketchy or even non-existent. The absence of a termination agreement would not have mattered much for an LSE commission broker executing trades and giving one-off advice as and when instructed. It becomes more of an issue when the same broker starts managing its client's portfolio, and the duration of the service moves from being "one-off or occasional," to "continuous".

The FSA also states that the agreement should describe the way in which transactions in progress are to be dealt with upon termination.[25] Usually this is dealt with on the basis that any outstanding/pipeline trades will be com-pleted and the manager's outstanding fees and expenses met.

If the manager is providing custody the process is more complicated. The firm will usually have included a contractual right to deduct amounts owing to it from the custody assets, and an agreement to transfer the balance of the portfolio in accordance with the manager's instructions. It will also normally have a right to reimbursement of costs incurred in the transfer process, or in maintaining the portfolio if the client fails to give transfer instructions.

Termination of specific task mandates

In the absence of express agreement, the parties' right to terminate is still **7–064**
likely to be at will. However, if the client has promised to allow the firm to earn the fee which will result from completing a particular task or mandate, it may be liable for that fee if it terminates prematurely.

---

[24] COB, 4.2.15(23).
[25] COB, 4.2.15(24).

Where the firm's mandate involves the performance of a specific engagement or project (more common in corporate finance and broking than in investment management) the general rule is that the firm is expected to finish the business for which it has been engaged.[26] In line with other skilled judgment services, this obligation is normally a qualified one, and the firm will usually be able to terminate early for good cause and on reasonable notice, as where it becomes apparent that the task cannot be completed for reasons beyond the firm's control.[27] If the retainer is protracted, and breaks occur, this may be construed as justifying termination at any one of such breaks.[28]

Relevant considerations for the calculation of "reasonable notice" include: the extent to which services undertaken remain unperformed; the importance to the client of those unperformed services; the extent to which the client is dependent on the firm to provide those services; the availability of alternative service providers with comparable skills; the time frame required for obtaining such alternative services; any indebtedness between the parties which needs to be unwound; and any custody or collateral arrangements which need to be unwound to complete the termination.

---

[26] See *Re Homer and Haslam* [1893] 2 Q.B. 286 at 298, CA.

[27] *Re Hall and Barker* (1878) 9 Ch. D. 538; *Underwood, Son and Piper v Lewis* [1894] 2 Q.B. 306; 64 L.J.Q.B. 60; *Bauman v Hulton Press Ltd* [1952] 2 All E.R. 1121; *Martin-Baker Aircraft Co Ltd v Murison* [1955] 2 Q.B. 556; *Decro-Wall International SA v Practitioners in Marketing Ltd* [1971] 1 W.L.R. 361 at 376–377. The very simplest example would be an agency broker who is unable to find a counterparty to fill his client's order.

[28] *Re Hall and Barker* (1878) 9 Ch. D. 538.

CHAPTER 8

JUDGMENT AND IMPLEMENTATION—A COMMENTARY

Dick Frase, Dechert LLP, London

The concepts of judgment and implementation have been identified in Chapter 2 as key components of a client relationship. Here we look at them in a little more detail.

8–001

The Exercise of Skilled Judgment

The dependence service which underlies both discretionary and advisory management, as well as one-off or occasional investment advice, is the exercise of skilled judgment on the customer's behalf. It leads (in the case of discretionary management) to a decision to deal on behalf of a client or (in the case of an advisory service) the provision of advice to the client, in each case based on the underlying investment judgment.

8–002

As noted in Chapter 2, the framework within which client services are provided (and to which the regulatory system is applied) is one of qualified rather than absolute duty. The firm is instructed to use its judgment to decide on the sales and purchases which will be good for its client. It is not liable to account for the success or failure of those decisions on a strict liability basis.

The nature of discretionary management

The judgment exercised by a firm with a discretionary mandate is "at large"—the firm does not need to refer its decisions to its client or obtain any client sign-off before it executes them. The relationship is an agency one and the concepts used are generally recognisable from agency law, where they equate in agency terminology with the agent being given an "authority to act" by its principal. One difference of emphasis is that much of agency law is focused on what we have called here the "implementation process",

8–003

219

without this necessarily being distinguished from the "judgment process" which immediately precedes it.

As with other agency relationships, this means that the discretionary manager has an absolute duty to keep within the scope of the authorities given to it by its client. The most important of these is the manager's duty to adhere to the investment objectives and restrictions agreed with its client. A manager whose mandate forbids it from investing in equities will be strictly liable for any loss which results from making an investment in equities in breach of that restriction, though it might expect to be able to set off against this any profits which it also made for the client from the same breach.

It is important to be able to recognise the difference between an objective which lays down a parameter which must not be crossed, and the different ways in which a firm might seek to achieve that objective. A failure to keep within the scope of the investment mandate is to be distinguished from a negligent performance of that mandate.

8–004 Breach of mandate is much less likely with an open-ended or generalised objective, such as "maximising capital growth". Of course, if the firm follows a strategy designed to generate income rather than capital, this will breach its absolute duty to concentrate on capital growth. But this aside, the level of risk appropriate to the mandate, whether the investment strategy should be long term or short term, which investments and markets should be invested in, and whether the manager should use leverage to gear up on its market exposure, are all issues which go to the level of skill which the firm is bringing to bear in performing its mandate, and not to whether or not it is acting within the scope of the mandate itself.

A breach of strict duty will be more easily established where the client has set out its investment objectives and restrictions in detail, giving detailed requirements as to matters such as the permitted exposure to particular types of investment, markets, asset classes, and leverage.

The nature of advice

8–005 Skilled judgment, provided in the form of an advisory service, has historically been viewed as an aspect of the law of professional negligence, and examined by reference to the particular profession concerned, rather than to any general concept of advice.[1] The advice concept is accordingly discussed here at a relatively theoretical level.

---

[1] See the standard textbooks such as *Charlesworth & Cain on Negligence.*

Advice as a concept

Historically, advice has not been seen as a distinctive legal area, though it **8–006** is to be found in aspects of agency law,[2] professional negligence, and misrepresentation.

The dictionary definition of advice is wide enough to include almost any form of communication. Here we are concerned with a narrower framework, within which advice is a particular channel for the provision of a skilled judgmental service. Relevant heads of advice for this purpose, as found in the Shorter Oxford English Dictionary, are: "consider, reflect . . . deliberate upon . . . recommend, offer counsel . . .".

Examples of skilled advice provided as a service in the financial markets are:

- a corporate finance firm, advising a business client on a particular financial project or general business strategy);

- the sales desk at a broking firm, advising a client on the merits of the securities of a particular issuer;

- a broker advising a client on the best method of executing an order. However, in routine execution situations the individual actually employed by a broking firm to execute client orders is typically not held out as providing a skilled advisory service. At most the broker should only be liable for any actual misrepresentations he makes, and on which the client relies on to the client's detriment;

- a retail financial adviser, advising a private client on how to arrange his personal financial affairs;

- an investment management adviser, advising a client on asset allocation, how to construct an investment portfolio, or on portfolio objectives and strategy[3];

- an advisory investment manager, providing day-to-day advice on potential new transactions;

- a boutique specialist, advising a corporate treasurer on its currency or interest rate risk management activities.

Advice involves the firm communicating, not to a third party, on behalf of **8–007** the client, but to the client itself. The firm's exercise of judgment, on which the client relies, is a rather opaque service, usually mixed up with a range of

---

[2] Notwithstanding the absence of the fundamental agency power to alter the principal's legal relations.

[3] This level of advice is common to both advisory and discretionary investment managers.

other, internal, often informal, communications between the firm and its client. Such communications may be:

- persuasive: "you should [do this];" or "you ought [to believe this];" or "it is in your interests [to do this]",

- factual: "this is [how it is]"; statements of intention: "I will [do this]"; or "I intend [to do this]"; or

- compulsory or mandatory: "you must [do this]" or "you will [do this]".

Financial service advice is generally regarded as persuasive rather than factual or mandatory. It is this which gives it its distinctive advisory quality and encourages the client to rely on it. Thus, Rand J in *J R Moodie Co Ltd v Minister of National Revenue*[4] said:

> "The word "advice" in ordinary parlance means primarily the expression of counsel or opinion, favourable or unfavourable, as to action, but it may, chiefly in commercial usage, signify information or intelligence."

But however intense the persuasive element, it is up to the recipient to decide whether or not he follows the advice. Unlike discretionary or other agency services, advice cannot, of its nature, compel the client to follow it; and a communication which is mandatory (such as a tax bill or a court summons) is not advisory.

This means among other things that an advisory manager does not have the same absolute duty as a discretionary manager to keep within the terms of its client's investment objectives. If the firm makes a recommendation which falls outside the agreed objectives and the client accepts it, then *prima facie* the client has sanctioned a variation of the objectives. But this may not always be the case. An inexperienced private customer is likely to assume that any advice given will be within the agreed investment mandate. In such circumstances, if what is being proposed is in effect, change to the mandate the firm must specifically draw this to the client's attention for the client's consent to the change to be valid.[5]

---

[4] [1950] 2 D.L.R. 145 (CAN) at 148.

[5] In *Brown v KMR Services Ltd; Sword-Daniels v Pitel and Others* [1994] 4 All E.R. 385 (Gatehouse J.) a private client was assured that his agent would follow a safety-first conservative approach in recommending the portfolio, and ensure that every syndicate was low risk. Despite this, in his first year of underwriting £80,000 out of his £190,000 of allocated premium was placed with high risk syndicates. The agent was aware of the high-risk nature of the business it was doing for the client but did not warn him to this. Without such a warning the client's agreement to the allocations in the year was an uninformed agreement, and did not constitute valid consent to what amounted to a change of his investment objectives.

Nature of persuasive advice

To be persuasive, a statement may be either subjectively intended, or objectively likely, to persuade or influence[6] the recipient. There is a flavour of these alternatives in the dictionary reference to advice as "given or offered".[7] The subjective intention of the firm (to influence or not to influence the client) is a relevant factor, but the predominant issue is whether the advice is actually, objectively, likely to influence the decisions or actions of that client. The firm is expected to use reasonable efforts to recognise when its communications to the client are likely to have this effect.

The persuasive effect is usually based on a profession of special skill or knowledge. This both encourages the recipient to rely on the advice and makes it reasonable to hold the firm responsible for this. Thus, sales puffs and hyperbole tend not to qualify as strict sense advice because, though intended to be persuasive, they are unlikely, in themselves, to imply that some special skill has been applied in making them.[8]

To be of any practical significance the persuasion must also be of a material nature. In other words it must represent some material exercise of judgment or discretion by the firm. A trivial or unimportant communication (including advice on matters which are common knowledge and which therefore does not reflect any special skill) will tend not to qualify for a range of reasons. Trivial advice, or advice on a trivial matter, is not something which should be relied on for a substantive purpose. There is a strong inference that the adviser will not have assumed responsibility for such advice. Its persuasive effect is weak. It may be sales hyperbole. The client may know about it already. The client would not be expected to rely on it as the basis for a major decision. Insofar as it does have an effect this will probably be corrected, balanced or superseded by other, more substantive, communications between the firm and its client.

The FSA definition of investment advice in the Regulated Activities Order (RAO)[9] takes a broadly similar line to this, but narrows the scope of the regulated activity by tying it to advice given: (a) to a potential investor; (b) on the merits of buying or selling a particular investment or the exercising of a right to buy or sell conferred by such an investment. An investment manager's advice to a potential client on the general terms of a proposed

8–008

8–009

---

[6] These two terms are treated as aspects of a single concept, and not as separate heads or alternatives. One or the other may predominate depending on the circumstances. But influential communications tend to be persuasive, and persuasion tends to influence the recipient. "Influence" is perhaps more orientated towards the recipient's point of view than is "persuasion".

[7] *The Shorter Oxford English Dictionary* (1993 ed.) also describes "persuasion" in both subjective and objective terms: "(1) the action or an act of persuading or trying to persuade; something tending or intended to induce belief or action . . .".

[8] The position may be different if the sales puff is directed at a client who lacks the expertise to recognise this, and may reasonably be expected to treat the statement as skilled advice.

[9] art.53.

investment strategy or mandate would not therefore be investment advice within the meaning of the RAO, though it would still be a skilled financial advisory service. Similarly, in RAO terms, a corporate finance adviser advising a corporate client on how to raise money in the capital markets would not be giving advice because it would not be advising a potential investor.

The strength of the advice

8–010　Part of the firm's discretion is as to how persuasive to be—the strength with which it puts it advice to its client. The persuasive element can be strong, weak, or middling. It can vary from mild suggestion, through encouragement and coercion, to the apparently mandatory—"it is *essential* that you must not miss this opportunity".

There must be actual reliance. A client who pays no attention to advice, or knows it to be untrue, cannot be said to have relied on it. The advice will have had no causative effect for which the firm can be held responsible. This could be the case if the client knows more about the subject matter of the advice than the adviser.[10] It may also be the case where both the individual representing the firm and the client with whom he is dealing know that the operative advice, on which the client will rely, will actually be given by a different adviser (either another individual within the same firm who specialises in such matters, or a different advisory firm independently instructed by the client).[11]

In advisory services actual reliance takes place when the client makes a decision to act on the advice. This contrasts with a discretionary management, where reliance takes place as soon as the firm is granted authority and control over the client's portfolio. Of course, it might be that the strength of an advisory service is such that the client will do whatever the firm recommends, in which case the service is almost (but not quite) the same as a discretionary service.

Implicit advice and advice by conduct

8–011　People often assume that advice only arises where there is an explicit statement by the adviser to the recipient such as, "I advise you to invest in US Treasuries". This is of course the clearest and most readily identifiable form

---

[10]　*e.g. Ginora Investments Limited v James Capel & Co Limited*, unreported February 10, 1995 (Rimer J.).

[11]　*e.g. Attwood v Small* (1838) 6 Cl. & Fin. 232, HL. For a retail financial example see the practice where an introducer has initial discussions with a private client about his financial needs and then refers him to a specialist financial adviser (possibly elsewhere in the same firm) for a substantive advisory service.

THE EXERCISE OF SKILLED JUDGMENT

of advice. However, advice may also be implicit, from the firm's words or conduct.[12] Often it is a combination of both.

An apparently impartial communication is more likely to be treated as containing implicit advice where the recipient is an unsophisticated investor, and vice versa.[13]

A recommendation can include describing something in negative terms so that its opposite seems especially attractive.

A description by a firm of the services which it is able to provide, particularly to an inexperienced client, may amount to advice to the client to instruct the firm to provide those services. An exploratory conversation with a client may involve presumptions or inferences which lead the client in a particular direction, again amounting to a substantive originating recommendation.

8–012

Implicit advice and advice by conduct may also alter the persuasive or influential quality of the advice given. Apparently low-key, equivocal or neutral statements may, because of their context, amount to implicit persuasion.

Nor does advice have to be given verbally. It may consist of or be supplemented by other forms of communication and conduct such as pictures, diagrams and other visual images; even physical gestures and body language. The mere despatch of a particular prospectus by a broker to a client may (in the circumstances) amount to a recommendation of the shares promoted in the prospectus, without any express verbal endorsement by the broker. A gesture of approval or enthusiastic manner may supplement a verbal communication to the same effect as a verbal recommendation.

The Basics of Implementation—Agency and Principal Dealing, and Arranging

Closely allied with the exercise of skilled judgment is the implementation of the resulting investment decisions by performance in the market. It involves the firm either effecting a change to its client's legal rights and obligations in relation to a third party, or replicating the effects of such a change. This may involve the firm:

8–013

- Making a legally binding commitment as agent on behalf of its client with a third party such as a broker or (where the firm itself enters the market directly) with a market counterparty. This is the norm for most investment managers.

---

[12] In *SBCI Bank Corporation Investment Banking Ltd*, *Independent*, September 28, 1994, a bank was treated as having advised a borrower to change insurers. The bank had not expressly advised the borrower to do this and the actual advice had emanated from the borrower's broker and solicitor but its actions had lead the borrower reasonably to believe that she should do so and that the broker's advice was given on its behalf.

[13] *e.g. Bankers Trust v PT Darmahla*, unreported, December 1, 1995.

225

- Making the commitment as principal in its own right with the third party, on terms that it will be replicated by a matching contract between the firm and its client. This is more common in principal broker markets such as the UK futures markets.

- Making the arrangements for such a commitment, but leaving the final commitment to be made by the client direct with the third party (arguably implementation could also extend to something rather less conclusive, such as receiving and transmitting communications between a client and a third party, if this had a significant implementory effect).

- Performing/completing on behalf of the client a commitment which has already been entered into between the client and third party (usually by one of the above means).

The relationship of implementation to discretion and advice

Discretion

8–014 **Consensual content**—Discretion and implementation both have their roots in the legal concept of a strict sense agency relationship. They depend on the existence of an authority from the client to act for him in a particular way. They are thus inherently consensual and contract-based. The client authorises the firm to exercise discretion and implement transactions for him. The firm agrees to do so.

8–015 **Ability to change the client's legal position**—Once the discretionary nature of the firm's authority is established, the judgment involved in its implementation, and the related power to change the client's legal position, passes entirely from the client to the firm.

Client dependence is axiomatic to such a service. The "strength" of that reliance or the firm's discretion is not really an issue—it simply depends on the scope of the authority granted.

8–016 **Operative effect**—Another reason why implementation is intrinsic to this exercise of judgment is because the firm's judgment does not have any operative effect until it is actually *implemented* as a trading decision in the market.[14] At any time prior thereto its judgments are only internal to the firm, in the nature of provisional conclusions, and capable of being changed or abandoned at any time.

---

[14] Of course if the firm's decision is that no transaction should be entered into there will be nothing to implement, but it is difficult to envisage a discretionary service which did not involve the implementation of at least *some* transactions.

Advice

Consensual content—In an investment management arrangement any advice given will normally form part of the consensual contractual service. But advice can arise in other situations, as where an adviser makes an unsolicited approach to a client, or where a manager and a potential client are in pre-contractual discussions. In such situations advice is not dependent on any consensual arrangement, but can be completely ad hoc and unsolicited.

8–017

Ability to change the client's legal position—In contrast to the exercise of a discretion, the giving of advice is not an agency function, and does not in itself change the client's legal position. Rather it seeks to *persuade* the client to act on the advice and the final decision remains with the client.

As a result of this, advice is not uniform in its effect. Its "strength" varies according to its persuasiveness, as does the level of client dependence on the advice. (A similar point arises in relation to implementation by arranging—see para.8–027 below.)

8–018

Operative effect—The exercise of skilled judgment involved in advice is operative *as soon as it is given* to the client, irrespective of whether the client then: (a) instructs the adviser to implement it; (b) accepts the advice but instructs a third party to implement it; or (c) never accepts it at all. In practice of course, the chance of advice being acted on will be increased where the adviser firm is standing by ready to implement it if so instructed.

8–019

Dependence in implementation transactions

An investment manager normally deals exclusively as agent on behalf of its customer. Sometimes however, it may deal as an arm's length counterparty, or sit somewhere between the agency and counterparty extremes. This sort of situation is most likely to arise where the firm also does business as a broker dealer.

8–020

The fact that the firm may have described itself as an agent or as a principal is not in itself conclusive.[15] A putative agent may turn out to be an own account trader.[16] A firm which contracts with its customer as a principal

---

[15] See *Glynwill Investments NV and Proxyward Limited v Thomson McKinnon Futures Limited* ("*Glynwill*"), unreported, February 13, 1992, *Garnac Grain Co Inc v HMF Fairclough Ltd* [1968] A.C. 1130, 1137, *per* Lord Pearson; *Curtain Dream plc* [1990] B.C.L.C. 925; *Re George Inglefield Limited* [1932] 1 All E.R. 244 at 251.

[16] *Branwhite v Worcester Works Finance Ltd* [1968] 3 All E.R. 104 (no agency between car dealer & finance company).

may still have a duty to act in that customer's interests, executing at the best market price available, and avoiding conflicts of interest.

Various factors give a pointer to whether the relationship is a client or counterparty one:

- Does the firm deal in its own or its client's name when contracting with the third party?

- Is service or counterparty terminology used? Does the firm deal "for or on behalf of" the customer or does it deal "with" him, or buy or sell "from or to" him?[17]

- Was the customer's order filled by the broker selling to him at a price which the customer did not have an opportunity to accept or reject?[18]

- Does the firm expect to be given an agency-style indemnity by its customer if it incurs a loss while performing his duties?

- Does the firm take any market risk, or does it eliminate this by dealing back to back with its customer's order?[19]

- What is the customer's expressed intention?[20] Does the firm negotiate an individual price with the customer, or does the customer rely on the firm to decide the price at which the trade should be executed?[21]

- Is commission charged, or does the firm make its money by taking a turn between the prices at which it buys and sells?[22]

- Is there privity of contract between the customer and the counterparty?[23]

- Does the customer look to the firm, or to some other counterparty with which the trade was executed, for performance?

---

[17] See *Glynwill*, above, para.8–020, n.15.

[18] *ibid.*

[19] In *Glynwill* a foreign exchange trader which dealt, and held itself out as dealing, on a principal basis, was found to have a fiduciary relationship with its customer. The judge said "as an intermediary trading on a principal to principal basis [the brokers] would take no market risk because they only dealt back to back with their client's order . . . there would be a sale by [the brokers] to the client at a price which it had never been able to consider in circumstances where the seller has taken no risk, knows the buyer's position and is also making a commission on the transaction".

[20] In *Glynwill* the customer said that he preferred using brokers rather than dealing direct with traders because they could be relied on to deal at the best price.

[21] See *Glynwill*.

[22] *Woodward v Wolfe* [1936] 3 K.B. 529 at 533; *Erskine Oxenford & Co v Sachs* [1901] 2 K.B. 504 at 511; *Re Glynwill*.

[23] *Robinson v Mollett* (1875) L.R. 7 HL 802.

Methods of implementation

Agency execution

Agency implementation is well known and its qualities well-established. **8–021** Generally, the firm:

- has its client's authority to act on his behalf in dealings with a third party;

- executes a contract with the third party which is binding on its client;

- may (in some circumstances) also be able to make representations to the third party which are binding on its client—*i.e.* for which its client is liable;[24]

- is a party to the contract between its client and the third party;

- (usually) is not liable to the third party for its client's performance;[25]

- may still be able to bind its client even when it exceeds its authority (under the doctrines of apparent authority, agent of necessity or ratification).

Similar agency powers may give a firm authority to dispose of its client's assets or money to the extent that they are under the control of the firm, whether or not it has authority to do so.

Agency implementation is prevalent in investment management services provided by specialist managers and in agency stockbroking. In the case of investment management, the manager normally has an agent's powers and control over its client's portfolio, coupled with a discretion as to which deals to execute on a day to day basis for the portfolio.

The contract-based nature of implementation, in particular agency implementation, is often taken for granted.[26] However, a firm may also assume an implementation role as a non-contractual agent if there is no consideration.[27]

---

[24] See *e.g. Sollitt v Broady* C.L.W. June 5, 2000, the Litigation Letter July 2000, CA (law firm making an admission of liability on behalf of its client after proceedings had begun had apparent authority to do so and could therefore bind its client. The client could not resile from the admission because the other party would have suffered serious prejudice due to reliance on the admission).

[25] Unless it steps outside its agency role to guarantee its client's performance in some way. In some markets there may be a usage that a broker stands as guarantor for its principal, or has joint liability with him. In shipping broker cases, much importance was historically attached to the wording used to describe the capacity in which the broker signed the contract.

[26] In *Kelly v Cooper* [1993] A.C. 205. PC at 213–214; Lord Browne-Wilkinson took it for granted that: "Agency is a contract made between principal and agent . . . like every other contract the rights and duties of the principal and agent are dependent upon the terms of the contract between them."

[27] See *e.g. General Accident Fire & Life Assurance Corp Ltd v Tanter (The Zephyr)* [1985] 2 Lloyds Rep. 529 at 537, *per* Mustill L.J.

This is known as a gratuitous agency.[28] But even where there is no contract, consent of some sort is still normally essential.[29] In a few very limited situations (apparent authority, necessity, estoppel, ratification, and agency by operation of law) a form of agency may arise without the principal's consent, though even then usually only as an adjunct to a genuine and pre-existing agency relationship.[30]

Apparent authority

8–022 A firm acting as agent normally has legal power to commit its principal to a contract with a third party, even if it does not have actual authority from the principal to do so, if that action is within the scope of the firm's authority which the agent appears to have.[31] It "appears" to have such authority from the third party's point of view. The agent will, as between it and its principal, be in breach of duty to its principal.

Apparent authority is based on estoppel principles.[32] For it to apply, there must be some (direct or indirect) representation or holding out by the principal. An unsupported representation by an agent that he has authority

---

[28] The gratuitous agent must show a standard of care appropriate to such an agent. *Chaudhry v Prabhakar* [1989] 1 W.L.R. 29, CA, *per* Stuart-Smith L.J. A gratuitous relationship can also arise in a social context, though it may be that the nature of agency will itself tend to establish a business relationship. In *Chaudhry v Prabhakar* Stuart-Smith L.J. said: "where, as in this case, the relationship of principal and agent exists, such that a contract comes into existence between the principal and a third party, it seems to me that, at the very least, this relationship is powerful evidence that the occasion is not purely a social one, but, to use Lord Reid's expression, is in a business connection. Indeed the relationship between the parties is one that is equivalent to contract . . . save only for the absence of consideration." The gratuitous agent was held to owe an agency duty in relation to the purchase of a second-hand car for a friend, and also a *Hedley Byrne* duty in relation to statements he made about the car's condition.

[29] In *Garnac Grain Co In v HMF Faure & Fairclough Ltd* [1968] A.C. 1130 at 1137, Lord Pearson said: "The relationship of principal and agent can only be established by the consent of the principal and the agent."

[30] Thus, an agency of necessity may arise as a special authority to act where a firm needs to take immediate action to protect its client's interests, even though it has no actual instructions to do so. The FTSE index enters a volatile period with prices falling rapidly. A futures broker knows that its client has written several FTSE put options which will be badly affected by the falling prices. The broker is unable to contact its client for instructions. It may be justified in taking steps to protect its client's position such as establishing a hedge, without obtaining instructions. (On another view such action is covered by the firm's implied authority.)

[31] *Freeman & Lockyer v Buckhurst Park Properties (Mangel) Ltd* [1964] 2 Q.B. 480 (company director acting with apparent authority to bind the company: very close to usual authority). Even the fact that the agent is acting fraudulently will not alter this. See *Hambro v Burnand* [1904] 2 K.B. 10 (insurance agent underwrites for client in breach of fiduciary duty for his own benefit but in the ordinary course of business at Lloyds and so within actual authority. Counterparty had no knowledge of this. The contract was binding); *Navarro v Moregrand Ltd* [1951] 2 T.L.R. 674 (agent letting flat for principal demanded and paid an illegal premium to his principal (apparent authority) which was recoverable by the tenant from the principal).

[32] See *e.g. Freeman & Lockyer v Buckhurst Park Properties (Mangel) Ltd* [1964] 2 Q.B. 480.

THE BASICS OF IMPLEMENTATION

is not enough, in itself, to create such authority.[33] The representation may be express, or of a general nature. It may be implied by a course of dealing, or by permitting the agent to act in a particular way in the conduct of the principal's business, or (in the case of a disposal of the principal's property) by entrusting the agent with indicia of title, such as share certificates and share transfer forms. It may also arise by virtue of the agent's usual or incidental authority, rather than express instruction or action by the principal himself.[34]

The third party must have relied on the representation. Entering into a contract in reliance on the representation of authority is normally enough.[35] If the third party does not know, and is not on notice, that the agent is acting as agent, or does not believe that the agent has the necessary authority, it may not be in a position to hold the principal liable.

Riskless principal implementation

In some cases a firm deals partly or wholly as a principal, but not for its own account. The economic benefit and burden of the trade is passed through to the client, and the firm is still under a duty to act for the client's benefit. Typically, on this model: **8–023**

- the firm has its client's authority to deal with a third party;

- the firm executes a contract between the third party and the firm, which is binding on the firm but not the client;

- the firm has both authority from and an obligation to its client to create, on the establishment of its contracting with a third party, a replicated contract with the client;[36]

- the firm has full rights and obligations as a principal to: (a) the contract with the third party; and (b) the matching contract with its client;

---

[33] See *Armagas Ltd v Mundogas SA (The Ocean Frost)* [1986] A.C. 717 at 730–735; but contrast *Furst Energy (UK) Ltd v Hungarian International Bank Ltd* [1993] 2 Lloyds Rep. 194.

[34] See *Whitehead v Tuckett* (1812) 15 East. 400 at 411 where an instance of apparent authority was described as a holding out to the world.

[35] *Freeman & Lockyer v Buckhurst Park Properties (Mangel) Ltd* [1964] 2 Q.B. 480; *Arctic Shipping Co Ltd v Mobilia AB (The Tatra)* [1990] 2 Lloyds Rep. 51 at 59. In *Farquharson Brothers & Co v King & Co* [1902] A.C. 325 at 341.

[36] To do this the firm may: (a) agree with its client that, when the firm executes a contract with a third party, an identical matching contract will automatically come into existence between the firm and the client; or (b) it brokes and matches the precise price individually acceptable to both clients (by the use of two telephones at once or some similar method). In (a) the firm has a strict-agency discretion to alter its principal's relationships with another, albeit that that other is the "agent" itself.

231

- the firm retains virtually all the service duties owed to a client by a firm exercising a discretion in the interests of the client other than the "duty" to execute as an agent. In particular, it can be expected to have a duty to go into the market for price discovery purposes and to pass the benefit of the price it obtains through to the client by way of the matching contract.

In securities and futures broking, this arrangement is often known as "riskless principal"[37] trading. The broker contracts as principal but not for its own account. It merely fronts a trade between the two substantive counterparties. The same model is used for futures clearing at the London Clearing House, and by some clearing and settlement firms. It may also suit a client who do not wish to disclose his identity to the counterparty, or a counterparty which prefers the broker's credit risk to that of its clients, or wants to ensure that mutual set off is available.[38]

This sort of arrangement has long been recognised in futures and commodities trading,[39] though the duty to act in the client's interest may not always have been fully appreciated by the firms involved. For a recent case on this point see *Glynwill Investments NV and Proxyward Limited v Thomson McKinnon Futures Limited*.[40] The FSA recognises the concept in general terms in its definition of a customer's order in the best execution rule.[41] As recently as 2001 the SFA considered it necessary to put out a special board notice,[42] directed at principal market practices on the LME, stressing the fact that an LME firm could still be in the position of accepting an order for execution *on behalf* of a customer in circumstances where it was dealing with the customer principal to a principal.[43]

---

[37] In FSA's capital adequacy rules it is described as a "matched principal" transaction.

[38] See *The Hong Kong and Shanghai Banking Corporation v Kloeckner & Co AG* (1989) 2 Lloyds Rep 323 (Hirst J.) at 324, where Kloeckner fronted contracts for a company called Gatoil with the general oil market by means of back to back contracts.

[39] In *Woodward v Wolfe* [1936] K.B.D. 529 at 533, the court identified such an arrangement on the Liverpool Cotton Exchange, saying that the broker, acting as its client's agent, executed a binding contract with a third party in the market, and then, because the rules of the market required it to do so, issued a "form" of contract between it and its client as direct contractors. In *E Bailey & Co v Balholm Securities* [1973] 2 Lloyds Rep. 404 at 408, *per* Kerr J. brokers dealt in the market as principals by concluding contracts of purchase and sale in their own name, but were held to be acting as agent for their client as principal.

[40] Unreported, February 13, 1992. First discussed in "Fiduciary Duties and the Financial Markets", Dick Frase, J.I.B.F.L. December 1992 and subsequently in Law Commission Consultation Paper No.124 at para.2.4.7.

[41] An "order" includes both an order to a firm to effect a transaction as agent and any other order to effect a transaction in circumstances giving rise to similar duties to those of an agent.

[42] SFA Board Notice 578 of March 16, 2001.

[43] The SFA Notice said that the exact duties would reflect the terms of the contract between the customer and the firm, the course of dealings including for instance statements made by an account executive in discussion with the customers, and the customs and practices of the market. This in turn reflected the fact that, under LME practice, metals brokers could deal both with the their customers either on a riskless principal or an own-account counterparty basis so that the position effectively had to be looked at on a trade-by-trade basis.

Generally, under this riskless principal model: **8–024**

- The agent's right to an indemnity from its principal is replaced by the firm's right to require performance from its client under the matching contract.

- The client's liability for the firm's actions will, in principle, depend solely on the internal agreement between them, and does not (in contrast to agency) include actions outside the scope of that agreement but within its apparent authority.

- The client has no contractual or other legal rights against the third party. If the firm becomes insolvent the client will not be able to look to the third party for performance.

- From the third party's point of view its rights and obligations relate to the firm alone. In contrast to agency dealing, the client will be unaffected by the default of the third party, and equities or rights of set-off which the third party is entitled to raise in relation to the contract cannot be asserted against the client.

This is a model which has developed, not so much by evolution from general legal principles, but because it has been designed to achieve a particular commercial effect. If the replication between the two contracts is not exact, the economic effect may be quite different.

The client is exposed to the credit risk of the firm, as distinct from that of the third party. But if the terms of the trade state that firm's performance is conditional on the third party's performance, the client is exposed to a double credit risk.

If the terms of the two contracts are not an exact match, the result may be closer to hedging than riskless principal execution. And in theory, if the principal to principal structure is not completely clean, the contract might acquire an agency quality—for instance if the firm holds the benefit of its transaction with the counterparty on trust for the firm's client, the client may have equitable rights against the counterparty.

Own account order execution

Here, the client places an order with the firm, which the firm agrees to fill for the benefit of the client. The firm then elects to fill the order off its own book, instead of executing it in the market. An example would be an integrated securities house where the broking division wants to fill a client's order by executing with the proprietary trading division. This practice, once considered invalid in law, is now usually accepted, subject to various controls and standards. **8–025**

JUDGMENT AND IMPLEMENTATION—A COMMENTARY

Typically the arrangement involves the following:

- The firm has its client's authority to fill an order by taking the other side of the order itself (implicitly on terms no less beneficial to the client than open market execution).

- The firm estimates the price at which the order could be placed through a third party, but does not offer the fill to the market (or perhaps offers it only on a limited basis).

- The firm takes the other side of the order.

- Firm and client are liable to each other for performance under the contract and to no one else.

- The firm is still liable for the way in which it determines the terms of the trade; i.e. it retains the service duties of exercising a discretion in the interests of the client.

The general principle, it is submitted, is that for this form of client service to be valid, the firm must provide execution at a price equivalent to the "best" reasonably available on the market. The firm is expected to access the market for price discovery (this may, depending on what is considered acceptable in market practice terms, involve actually going into the market, or perhaps just checking the current market prices) and contract with its client at a price which is objectively fair. Often this means a price comparable to the best price currently available.[44]

8–026   If there is no suitable market price to refer to, either as a direct match or as a marker or reference price, the firm will have to make its own price. In such a situation the duty of a firm providing an order execution service is probably to make a price which is reasonable in the circumstances. But it may be that, in the particular circumstances, such a "service' cannot properly be provided on anything other than an arm's length counterparty basis.

It is evident that this arrangement is close to, and liable to be confused with, the situation where a broker-dealer adopts a purely market-making role (for whatever reason), offering to buy from or sell to a client on terms of the broker-dealer's own choosing, off its own book and on a purely counterparty basis. This is particularly so where the firm has (or has had) a trading relationship with the customer in both a service and counterparty capacity.

---

[44] Consistent with *Moody v Cox & Hatt* [1917] 2 Ch.71 and the trustee "fair dealing rule" In *Coles v Trecothick* (1804) 9 Ves. 234 at 247, Lord Eldon V.C. said that for a trustee to buy property from a beneficiary the court would need to be satisfied that the beneficiary was a willing seller and that there was no fraud, no concealment, and no advantage taken by the trustee of information acquired by him in the character of trustee.

234

Arranging

It is possible for a firm to achieve the substantive effect of implementation **8–027** without itself contracting as either agent or principal. This concept was given prominence by the Financial Services Act 1986, which first introduced the idea of a firm arranging a transaction between its client and a third party as a distinctive and authorisable activity. The current definition is in art.25(1) of the RAO, and corresponds broadly to the Investment Services Directive activity of receiving and transmitting orders. The discussion which follows is, however, based on common law principles rather than these particular regulatory definitions.

Under implementation by arranging:

- The firm is not an agent in the strict legal sense. It may have its client's authority to negotiate with a third party but is not authorised to make any contractual commitments on behalf of or with the client. Nor does it have authority to implement riskless principal type commitments.

- Any contract resulting from the arrangements is entered into between the client and the third party. The firm is not a party to the contract, and so has no rights or liabilities under the contract. An agent in contrast often has rights under the contract against its client's counterparty, and is also sometimes treated as having responsibility for its client's performance. A principal trader always has such rights and liabilities.

- The firm's service duties depend on the extent to which it is responsible for the client's entering into the contract. The final act of executing the contract will always be that of the client. However, if the "strength" of the arrangements made by the firm are such that the primary reason for the client entering into the contract is the firm's judgment that it should do so, the firm will have all the normal service duties that go with an agency trade. If on the other hand, the firm merely relays instructions from the client, its role will be merely administrative.

The concept of arrangement is thus a fluid one and, like advice, can operate at a number of different levels. The "strength" of the implementation will vary, according to the nature of the arranging. Several related acts of "arrangement", individually of a minor nature, may need to be looked at together to establish their overall, cumulative effect.

A "mere introducer",[45] which puts two parties in touch with each other and leaves them to deal or not, as they choose, is at the lowest end of any arranging scale, exercising no judgment or discretion for either party. Special

---

[45] Not to be confused with the regulatory concepts of an introducing broker or an introducer to a product provider, both of which potentially involve substantive advisory and arranging services.

service-type duties should be very limited indeed.[46] Similarly, purely administrative arranging is unlikely to constitute any form of skilled judgmental service.

8–028   A substantive element of arranging may also involve a firm making representations or similar statements on its client's behalf, in the course of negotiations with a third party. If the third party subsequently enters into a contract with the client in reliance on those statements, and the statements prove to be wrong or misleading, the client will be liable to the third party for this.[47]

As noted above, where the firm's actions are the predominant cause of the client executing the contract, the arranging has had a causative or operative effect, equivalent to full agency or principal execution. This is probably most common in the retail products market, where for instance an adviser arranges for its client to buy an investment product by drawing the product to his attention, helping the client to fill in and sign an application form, and forwarding this, together with the client's cheque, to the product provider. The service is usually accompanied by advice, both generally and in FSA terms, and the arranging typically consists of implementing the transaction which results from this advice.

While a conventional, agency or principal, execution service will also include elements of arranging, these would normally be treated as subsumed within the main agent/principal execution function.[48]

---

[46] In *Morgan v Elford* (1876) 4 Ch.352, Elford, a merchant and commission agent, who occasionally sold mines, was asked by Morgan to introduce a buyer for Morgan's anthracite mine. It was held *per* James L.J. at 384 that the introduction subsequently made did not involve any fiduciary relationship.

[47] There is some doubt as to whether this is best treated as governed by agency or tort. The tortious concept of servants and independent contractors does not really fit the situation and it is suggested that the agency concepts of actual and apparent authority are most appropriate.

[48] art.28 of the RAO provides that a firm which arranges a transaction to which it intends to be a party, whether a principal or as agent, is excluded from the regulatory definition of "arranging".

CHAPTER 9

INVESTMENT MANAGEMENT AND FIDUCIARY DUTIES

Stuart Willey, Financial Services Authority

Introduction

This Chapter considers whether, and to what extent, investment managers are **9–001** fiduciaries. It also considers how the various incidents of a fiduciary's duty are identified and applied through the conduct of business rules made by the FSA under the Financial Services and Markets Act 2000 (FSMA). The interaction between the way the common law recognises and applies fiduciary duties, the obligations expressed in the regulatory scheme established under FSMA, and the terms on which a firm engages contractually with a client, raises a complex set of legal and regulatory issues, some of which have yet to be tested by the courts or by the specialist Tribunal established under FSMA. There are relatively few direct precedents in the investment management context indicating how intensely fiduciary duties will be applied or whether attempts by firms to avoid fiduciary duties through the use of contractual exclusion clauses will always be successful. The regulatory scheme does not overtly apply or even use the express language of fiduciary duties and it continues to be necessary to refer to common law authorities in establishing the scope of their application. The combination of the common law and the regulatory scheme results in investment managers being subject to different layers of accountability and scrutiny derived from fiduciary duties and conduct of business requirements imposed under FSMA.

An analysis of fiduciary duties, in the regulatory context at least, is normally concerned with identifying conflicts of interest between a fiduciary and a person entitled to the benefit of the duty—the beneficiary—and examining whether those conflicts are avoided or, alternatively, managed in a fair way. The prevalence of potentially unresolved fiduciary duties within financial services businesses became more intense and urgent following the onset of the "Big Bang" deregulation in the City from 1986 onwards. In particular, Big Bang involved a dismantling of controls on securities firms which had previously prevented them from acting in more than one capacity or being owned

237

by non-securities businesses. Deregulation resulted in the introduction of multi-functional conglomerates offering a full range of services which in turn gave rise to a range of new potential conflict situations. Investment and commercial banks, in particular, are involved both in assisting corporate clients to raise finance in the capital markets whilst at the same time acting in an advisory capacity for other clients and undertaking asset management.

The open architecture of financial institutions ushered in by the deregulation of the 1980s has come in for renewed scrutiny in consequence of the financial scandals which have unfolded in the wake of the collapse of Enron and WorldCom. These events have caused governments in the US and in Europe to reassess fundamentally standards of corporate governance and financial reporting and the means of enforcing those standards. The centrality of a company director's fiduciary duty has been re-stated. The need for an external auditor's duty to the company to be free of conflict has been reasserted and buttressed by a variety of new regulatory devices. Standards of financial reporting are to be more proactively monitored. Sarbanes-Oxley in the US has been followed by the Higgs and Smith reports in the UK. To add to this, the investigations undertaken by the New York Attorney-General and the SEC have led to serious allegations of malpractice among US investment banks. These allegations have included the misuse of company research by institutions which are active in the capital markets on behalf of the companies for which they maintain analysis and the improper allocation of IPO opportunities.

9–002 More recently mutual investment fund managers also have fallen under suspicion of allowing the funds under their management to be traded by "late traders" and so-called "market timers" to the detriment of the average buy and hold investor. At the same time there has been a continued focus on the extent to which investment managers obtain valuable "soft commissions" in return for the execution of trades in the investments they manage. Generally, the allegations levelled at investment banks, and now investment fund managers, are testing some of the assumptions which underpinned the impetus to deregulation in the 1980s.[1] Elements of the corporate governance reforms and the re-examination of how governments and regulatory agencies are responding to the malign consequences of un-controlled conflicts within financial institutions and audit firms, arguably, amount to "re-regulation". It remains to be seen how far this will go.

This Chapter suggests that investment managers, whether acting for institutional or private clients, should be characterised as "fact-based" fiduciaries who are subject to the overriding duty of client loyalty which flows from the special relationship of trust and confidence which exists between an investment manager and its client—a relationship which is the hallmark of a fiduciary relationship. It is suggested the origin of the fiduciary relationship lies

---

[1] Which for example in the US included the partial repeal of the Glass Steagall Act.

INTRODUCTION

in the degree of control over the client's property which is ceded to the manager coupled with the basic undertaking to use skill, care and expertise in the management of that property to advance the financial interests of the client. This Chapter considers how fiduciary duties play out in the business and regulatory environment, and the effectiveness of contractual terms which seek to limit or exclude fiduciary duties.

The proper characterisation of a firm carrying on financial services business as a fiduciary is obviously important from the point of view of ascertaining whether, in any given circumstance, it is open to a party to expect another person to observe standards of conduct which are different and beyond those which are enforceable through the more conventional remedies of negligence and breach of contractual obligation. Drawing this distinction may also be important because the remedies which are available to persons who can show that they have suffered loss as a result of a breach by a fiduciary are different and in some instances more easily obtainable than under alternative common law principles. For example, the court can apply more favourable rules as to remoteness and causation of loss. In *London Loan & Saving Co v Brickenden*[2] the court stated that when a fiduciary commits a breach of its duty by non-disclosure of material facts, it cannot be heard to maintain that disclosure would not have altered the decision to proceed with the transaction—once the court has determined that the non-disclosed facts were material, speculation as to what other course the claimant would have taken had there been no breach of duty becomes irrelevant. However more recent authority suggests that the court is likely to limit the approach in *Brickenden* to cases where the breach of fiduciary duty can be regarded as equivalent to fraud.[3]

Are Investment Managers Fiduciaries?

The answer to this question must primarily be drawn from the common law rather than the overlay of regulatory duties imposed under FSMA. Neither the statutory scheme nor the FSA's rules and guidance *expressly* apply fiduciary status to investment managers or any other investment professionals. The regulatory scheme does though, as is explained below, create a number of obligations which are of a similar kind and acknowledges the existence of conflicts which arise for persons acting in a fiduciary capacity. As a result an analysis of how fiduciary principles apply to investment managers can appear somewhat piecemeal.

In *Bristol & West Building Society v Mothew*[4] Millett L.J. defined a fiduciary as follows:

9–003

---

[2] [1934] D.L.R. 465, PC.
[3] *Swindle v Harrison* [1997] 4 All E.R. 705; and see also *Nationwide Building Society v Balmer Radmore (a firm) and related actions* [1991] All E.R. (D) 95.
[4] [1998] 1 Ch., p.18.

239

INVESTMENT MANAGEMENT AND FIDUCIARY DUTIES

"A fiduciary is a person who has undertaken to act for or on behalf of another in a particular matter in circumstances which give rise to a relationship of trust and confidence. The distinguishing obligation of a fiduciary is the obligation of loyalty. The principal is entitled to the single-minded loyalty of his fiduciary".

This formulation accords with that given by Finn:

"A person will be a fiduciary in his relationships with another when and insofar as that other is entitled to expect that he will act in that other's interests or (as in a partnership) in their joint interests, to the exclusion of their several interests".[5]

9–004 One further guiding principle is that where parties are in a contractual relationship, the terms of the contract will influence and determine the scope and nature of the fiduciary duties which may be owed by one party to another.[6] This is something which is particularly important in the context of attempts by investment managers and others to limit or exclude their exposure to fiduciary duties, a matter which is considered below.

In the case of an investment management agreement, there are, it is suggested, two powerful factors which sustain a presumption that the investment manager will act in a fiduciary capacity and owe fiduciary duties to its client. The first is the existence of a custodial relationship between the manager and client where the manager is entrusted with assets belonging to the client and where, through the relationship of custody, the manager (or his nominee) comes to hold legal title but with the client retaining a beneficial interest at least for so long as the custodial relationship subsists. The second factor is the unilateral power conferred on the manager to take decisions which affect the value of the assets in its possession and of which its client is the beneficial owner. This is a discretion which the manager is expected to exercise for the benefit of the client. It seems to coincide and to fit more or less exactly with the so called "discretionary theory" which explains the application of fiduciary duties as described by Penner:

"The force of the discretionary theory lies in its pointing out that in certain legal arrangements, the essence of the arrangement is that one person, the principal, relies on the expertise or the capacity for action of another, the fiduciary, and it is impossible to specify in advance how that expertise or capacity for action ought to be exercised, besides simply requiring that it be exercised for the benefit of that other. If the law is to allow such arrangements . . . then the fiduciary must take the interests of the other party to be the sole guiding consideration in his exercise of his

---

[5] Finn, *Fiduciary Obligations* (1997).
[6] *Kelly v Cooper* [1993] A.C. 205.

240

discretion. Otherwise, the arrangement simply will not work; that is, if the law will not recognise that such a duty can be undertaken, then this discretion-conferring undertaking cannot operate, for it would not serve the advantage of A to confer a discretion on B to effect A's position if B could not be required to exercise that discretion solely in A's best interests. Therefore, if the law wishes to provide for this sort of arrangement, it must impose fiduciary obligations where this sort of arrangement is entered into. According to this theory of fiduciary obligations, a fiduciary duty can be strictly defined as the duty of the fiduciary to exercise a discretion solely in the best interests of his principal, in circumstances where one person, the fiduciary, has agreed to undertake *legal* powers to effect the *legal* position, *i.e.* the legal rights and duties or powers, of another the fiduciary's principal and the fiduciary has a discretion in the way he will exercise those legal powers."[7]

This seems to offer a compelling and satisfactory basis for asserting the existence of fiduciary duties owed by an investment manager to its client. The essence of the investment management agreement is an undertaking by the manager to exercise discretion over the composition of the client's portfolio which is entrusted to the manager's custody and care. It is an arrangement in which, and whether within wide or circumscribed parameters, the value of the client's assets are more or less wholly to be determined by the manager's decisions, which are expected to be taken in the client's interest. It accordingly is a relationship of "trust and confidence" of a kind to which fiduciary duties attach.

One aspect of how fiduciary duties should be properly characterised is concerned with establishing whether a fiduciary has a duty to act *positively* in the interests of the beneficiaries of the duty and not merely a duty to *avoid* situations of conflict. Lionel Smith has argued[8] that a fiduciary's duty should properly be seen as a positive duty to advance the interests of the beneficiary. On this basis the no-conflict rule should be viewed as an added layer of protection to prevent the fiduciary being found in a position in which the fiduciary might subordinate the beneficiary's interests to those of his own:

> "I would argue that the heart of the fiduciary obligation is the surveillance and the justiciability of motive. Whatever powers a fiduciary has, he must exercise them (or not exercise them) with a particular motive. He must act (or not act) in what *he perceives to be* the best interests of the beneficiary."[9]

9–005

---

[7] J E Penner in *Breach of Trust* (Birks and Pretto ed., Hart Publishing 2002), Ch.8, p.245.
[8] Lionel Smith, "The Motive, Not the Deed" in *Rationalising Property, Equity and Trusts: Essays in Honour of Edward Burn* (Joshua Getzler ed., Butterworths 2003), Ch.4.
[9] *ibid.*, p.73.

Smith goes onto argue, however, that the fiduciary duty is not one which will invariably cause the fiduciary to act (or not act) in particular way but rather it controls the decision making process and obliges the fiduciary to act with a particular motivation.[10] Establishing whether the fiduciary has acted with proper motive becomes the key to determining whether the relevant obligations have been satisfied.

The formulation of the idea that investment management firms, when acting as fiduciaries, have a *positive* duty to advance the interests of their clients and beneficiaries and not merely a duty to avoid conflict and self-profit, is a powerful one.

9–006   The identification of fiduciary duties seems to be most straightforward in the context of a bilateral discretionary management agreement between a particular client (whether institutional or private) and a management firm—all the necessary attributes of discretion and trust are present. This is demonstrated in the claims considered in *Ata v American Express Bank Limited*[11] where the court proceeded on the common assumption that the claimant being the client under a discretionary management agreement with the bank was able at least to advance claims based upon breach of fiduciary duty by the bank when acting as manager under the discretionary management agreement. Indeed the claim (which the court in the event rejected) was essentially that the bank had failed as fiduciary to advance the interests of the claimant by closing-out certain foreign currency derivative positions.

Some further consideration is needed, however, in the case of collective investment schemes such as a unit trust or investment company. In such cases the relationships are more complex. The investor's interest in the fund assets is not direct but will be an interest in a pooled collection of assets and will take the form of a security—a unit or share. For example in the case of a unit trust, the management company will normally be both the founder and promoter of the scheme and also the first and primary investment manager appointed to operate and manage the assets of the scheme in accordance with the trust deed. In a unit trust it is possible to view the trustee and the unit trust manager as sharing trust or trust-like duties, with the manager agreeing to manage the assets in accordance with the trust deed and for the benefit of the unit holders. In this scenario it may be argued that the manager owes fiduciary duties to the fund investors as well as the trustee:

"Whilst it cannot be characterised as a trustee, its activities as fund manager are most likely to be accepted by the court as establishing a fact-based fiduciary. The manager has control of properties belonging to others, although it does not hold their title. It is undertaking activities in the interests of other persons, the unit-holders. It is the holder of power that can unilaterally affect the interests of the unit-holders. In a

---

[10]   *ibid.*, p.77, n.1.
[11]   *The Times*, June 26, 1998 (Court of Appeal).

commercial sense the unit-holders are in a vulnerable position for they have no right to interfere with the management of their own money ... Moreover, it is their confidence in the manager's investment expertise that attracts investors to become unit-holders. These common factors alone should satisfy all tests for establishing a fiduciary relationship in the management activities of the manager."[12]

This analysis is consistent with the "discretionary theory" described above. It is the combination of the vulnerability of the investor, the control over assets and the manager's wide power to affect the value of the investor's property which brings the fiduciary relationship into existence. This is also the conclusion reached by the current authors of Collective Investment Schemes: The Law and Practice.[13] Given that an investment manager would not fall within one of the established categories of "status-based" fiduciary to the extent that it matters, the manager is a "fact-based" fiduciary.

In the case of an investment company there will, on the reasoning set out above, normally be a fiduciary relationship between the company and a third party investment manager. The company will hold the benefit of this relationship for the investing shareholders. In this sense the fiduciary duty is more indirect but arguably no less intense.

Comparison With Other Investment Firms

More generally, the categorisation or identification of financial services firms as fiduciaries is not by comparison always as straightforward. In part this derived from the labels which firms apply to themselves in acting as principal with or as agent for counterparties and clients. For the most part a search for firms acting in a fiduciary capacity will involve the identification of agency relationships which will often attract fiduciary obligations.[14]   **9–007**

For example, where a firm is a member of, and acts under the rules of, an exchange or market, where ostensibly the rules of the exchange require firms to deal with each other as principal, difficulties can arise where firms, as well as acting as principal and for their own account deal on the exchange to fulfil the orders of their clients. In these circumstances, firms may well wish to view their dealings with clients as invariably involving them acting as principal such that the customer effectively deals *with* the firm, for example, for the purchase of securities or commodities rather than by way of an agent-principal arrangement where the latter acts *for* its client.

---

[12] Kam Fan Sin, *The Legal Nature of the Unit Trust* (Clarendon Press, Oxford, 1997), pp.171–173.

[13] *Collective Investment Schemes: The Law and Practice* (Sweet and Maxwell, 2003), para.A4. 231.

[14] Although not every agent is necessarily a fiduciary, see *Bowstead and Reynolds on Agency* (7th ed.), para.6–036.

243

INVESTMENT MANAGEMENT AND FIDUCIARY DUTIES

In *Glynwill Investments NV v Thompson McKinnon Futures Limited*,[15] the court considered the position of a firm acting as a foreign exchange dealer where it effectively filled clients' orders by entering the market and dealing with other market makers and where it felt able to apply a mark up to the price it obtained and which it accordingly charged to it customer. The customer bringing the claim contended that the relationship between it and the firm was in fact analogous to one of principal and agent. The firm relied on the terms of its contract which specified that it was acting as principal throughout. The Judge however looked at the substance of the relationship including the facility for the firm to charge commission on deals and concluded that the trading relationship was one of principal and agent. Accordingly, the claimant was entitled to recover the amount of mark up which had been applied by the defendant to its order.

9–007A   Very similar issues have arisen in connection with firms trading on the London Metal Exchange (LME). The rules of the LME stipulate that firms when dealing on exchange do so as principal. The regulators have had cause, however, to remind firms that categorising customers as persons who deal with them as principal for the purposes of the LME rules does not mean that they may not also incur fiduciary type duties to the extent that their dealings fall within the pattern of principal and agent. Consistent with the approach of the court in *Glynwill*, the regulators look to the substance of the relationship subsisting between the firm and client rather than the label which the firm may have used in it contract.[16] The manner in which the firm solicits its business, the basis on which it charges and the expectations which it may generate are all matters which may point to a proper characterisation of the relationship as being one in which fiduciary duties arise. For this purpose it is immaterial that the firm may act in principal capacity. Whether and to what extent a firm owes agency type duties in any particular transaction may be determined by:

(a)   the written terms of business between the customer and firm;

(b)   the course of dealings between the firm and customer relevant to the transaction including, for example, statements made by an account executive in discussion with the customer; and

(c)   the customs and practice of the market.

The regulators went on to say that in the metals market a range of business is undertaken *some* of which involves pure principal dealing between firms and customers and some of which is the provision of services on a basis which gives rise to agency type obligations. These obligations may arise even

---

[15]   Unreported, February 13, 1992, Mr Simon Tuckey Q.C.
[16]   SFA Board Notice No.578, The Customer Relationship and other Conduct of Business Requirements for Firms Engaged in Metals Business.

COMPARISON WITH OTHER INVESTMENT FIRMS

where the transfer of title to metal is on a principal-to-principal basis. The decision in *Glynwill* in consistent with the later decision of the Commercial Court in *Brandeis Brokers v Black*[16a] a case concerning an LME member firm dealing effectively as a risk-less principal but where the Court was satisfied that it had incurred fiduciary duties to its client including a duty not to make an undisclosed profit in its dealings with customers.

For further analysis of the different capacities in which a firm may execute a customer trade see the discussion of "implementation" in Chapter 8.

What Fiduciary Duties Do Investment Managers Owe?

The Law Commission summarised the fiduciary's duties as follows[17]:   **9–008**

- the "no conflict" rule: a fiduciary must not place himself in a position where his own interest conflicts with that of his beneficiary or customer, the beneficiary;

- the "no profit rule": a fiduciary must not profit from this position as fiduciary; the undivided loyalty rule;

- this includes the proposition that the fiduciary must not place himself in the position in which his duty towards one customer conflicts with a duty that he owes to another;

- the duty of confidentiality, a fiduciary must not use confidential information obtained from a client for his own benefit or for the benefit of another.

And consistent with the arguments canvassed by Smith there may be added a fifth—a positive duty to advance the interests of the beneficiary or customer within the scope of the duties the firm has assumed.

These fiduciary duties are available to be called upon by a relevant beneficiary—the individual or corporate client of the discretionary portfolio manager, the unit or shareholder in a collective investment scheme whether constituted as a unit trust or investment company. The overriding fiduciary duty is loyalty requiring the fiduciary to put his client's interests above those of his own. This has some obvious application in the case of an investment manager who may also be entering the market to execute trades on behalf of itself or on behalf of other clients. The duty of loyalty also speaks directly to situations in which the manager or an affiliate may become a counterparty to deals in the assets being managed. An investment manager in breach of any such obligation may be called upon by a court to account to the beneficiary,

---

[16a] [2001] 2 All E.R. (Comm) 980.
[17] Law Commission Report, para.1.4.

INVESTMENT MANAGEMENT AND FIDUCIARY DUTIES

to disgorge any profit or advantage which the manager may have secured for his own or an affiliate's benefit.

Fiduciary Duties under FSMA

9–009 The enforcement of fiduciary duties as such is primarily a matter of private law but fiduciary type duties are also to be found in the regulatory scheme established under FSMA. One purpose of statutory intervention in the field of investment business was to provide a framework in which adequate and appropriate protection can be secured for investors[18] in the face of the challenges presented by the new architectures of financial conglomerates. Accordingly some of the territory occupied by the, relatively, new "conduct of business rules" is the same as is covered by conventional legal duties and remedies including, for example, negligence by professionals and obligations generated by persons who act in a fiduciary capacity.

It is important to establish whether regulatory duties and fiduciary duties are congruent or whether they collide with each other and, if so, what the consequences might be. This involves predicting whether the courts will be prepared to define and interpret the standards required of fiduciaries by taking account of, and if appropriate internalising, the standards of conduct required by regulatory agencies operating with statutory authority. Any commentary in this area must acknowledge the work of the Law Commission which following a consultation in 1992 reported in 1995 on the interaction between fiduciary duties and regulatory rules.[19]

FSMA contains few provisions that apply directly to firms. Rather, it is for the most part an enabling statute that confers powers and establishes the framework for the regulation of financial services.

9–010 The regulatory provisions applicable to investment managers and which refer to or otherwise touch on the responsibilities of fiduciaries are for the most part to be found in the rules and guidance issued by the FSA. This material exhibits three characteristics:

- the substance of a fiduciary duty may be incorporated in a regulatory requirement;

- conflicts arising from the duty may be capable of management through disclosure and by obtaining prior consent;

- the extent of a duty may be modified or limited.

---

[18] Particularly the non-professional consumer—the so called "private investor".

[19] Fiduciary Duties and Regulatory Duties, Consultation Paper No.124, May 1992; Report Law Com. No.236, December 1995.

246

In the case of authorised collective investment schemes, the FSA acknowledges that its scheme of regulation for managers and trustees sits within a wider legal framework with specific reference to fiduciary duties. CIS 7.7.1 provides:

> "The guidance in CIS 7.8.2 G (Valuation and pricing) and the rest of CIS 7 relate to the powers and duties of the manager and the trustee. In addition, both the manager and trustee have fiduciary duties under the general law relating to trusts, and powers and duties under other chapters of this sourcebook and the trust deed."

The FSA's Principles for Businesses

The FSA's Principles for Businesses contain a series of high level statements which are applicable to all firms. These overarching standards incorporate several fiduciary type duties: **9–011**

- a firm must conduct its business with integrity;

- a firm must observe proper standards of market conduct;

- a firm must pay due regard to the interests of its customers and treat them fairly;

- A firm must manage conflicts of interest fairly, both between itself and its customers and between a customer and another client.[20]

Some of the Principles for business have universal application (for example—conducting business with integrity) whilst others are coloured by the status of the firm's client. So for example in relation to conflicts of interest, the obligation is in respect of the firm and its "customers" a term which is defined as meaning private customers and intermediate customers. Although most of the Principles have relatively limited application in the context of inter-professional business carried on with other market-counterparties, a regulated collective investment scheme is treated for all purposes as a "private customer" and an unregulated scheme as an "intermediate customer".[21] The result of this classification is that the FSA's Principles apply to investment management carried on in relation to collective investment schemes. The manager of such schemes must look upon the fund (and collectively thereby its participants) as a person to whom it owes the duty of fair treatment; the manager must fairly manage conflicts of interest arising between itself and the scheme. Individual portfolio managers will also be

---

[20] Principles 1, 5, 6 and 8.
[21] See *FSA Glossary* definitions.

INVESTMENT MANAGEMENT AND FIDUCIARY DUTIES

likely to be acting mainly for persons who are classified as "customers" and hence the same analysis will apply.

Contravention of an FSA's Principle does not give rise to a civil cause of action for damages under s.150[22] of the FSMA but it may enable the FSA to exercise a range of powers including obtaining an injunction or an order for restitution.

FSA Rules—Single Capacity for Certain Investment Managers

9–012 Article 6 of the UCITS Directive as first enacted provided that no management company may engage in activities other than the management of unit trusts and investment companies.[23] The UCITS Directive is concerned with the authorisation and operation of investment funds which are to be available to the general public. The intention behind Article 6 was to ensure that the entirety of the fund manager's business is regulated and that the scope for conflicts of interest to arise be restricted. This provision has been somewhat relaxed by the later Management Directive which permits a management company to carry individual portfolio management and to provide investment advice as a non-core activity[24] and this remains an example of the use of legislation to force single capacity on investment firms on the basis that firms might otherwise be unable adequately to avoid or manage conflicts.[25]

The FSA has implemented the single capacity rule in respect of managers of Unit Trusts in rule CIS 16.5.1:

"A firm which is the manager of an AUT which is a UCITS scheme must not engage in any activities other than:

(1) Acting as manager of

    (a) a Unit Trust; or

    (b) an open ended investment company or any other body corporate whose business consists of investing its funds with the aim of spreading investment risk and giving its members the benefit of the results of the management of its funds by or on behalf of that body; or

    (c) Any other collective investment scheme under which the contributions of the participants and the profits or income out of which payments are to be made to them are pooled; or

---

[22] PRIN, 1.1.7 G.
[23] UCITS Directive 85/611.
[24] See Directive 2001/108, Art s5.2 and 5.3.
[25] See "Towards An (sic) European Market for the Undertakings for Collective Investment in Transferable Securities: Commentary on the provisions of Council Directive 85/611/EEC of 20 December 1985", para.38.

248

FSA RULES—SINGLE CAPACITY FOR CERTAIN INVESTMENT MANAGERS

(2) Acting as the director of an ICVC; or

(3) Activities for the purposes or in connection with those in (1) or (2)".

This rule will be amended upon the implementation of the Management directive which will widen the scope of the activities which may be undertaken by a management company acting for a UCITS scheme, nevertheless the principle of restricting the capacity of such firms is a means of preventing undesirable conflicts arising remains.

Secret Profits

If investment managers are properly viewed as acting in a fiduciary capacity on behalf of their clients whose assets they manage, then there may be a breach of the "no secret-profit" rule to if the investment manager, as a consequence of dealing in the assets under his management, is able to generate streams of profit or income for his own rather than the fund's or customer's benefit. This analysis, in part, explains the FSA's approach to controlling the receipt of so called "soft commissions" by firms which deal as agent on behalf of their customers. **9–013**

Investment managers will normally charge the dealing costs associated with fund transactions directly to the investment fund. This will include the commissions and mark up paid to executing brokers. Prior to the reforms of the UK securities market in 1986, executing brokers were required to charge minimum commissions for executing deals. This lead to executing brokers competing for business by offering a range of other services beyond mere execution. The costs of these additional services were, notionally at least, included within the commissions charged for trade execution. This practice developed so that investment managers could secure a range of valuable services to support the infrastructure of their investment management business including, for example, information services, screens and valuable research provided either by the broking house itself or by a third party. The amount of soft commission obtainable on trade execution placed by an investment manager with a broker is in proportion to the amount of business placed through the broker. Under soft commission arrangements, the credits generated for the investment manager can be used to obtain services from third party sources including the providers of information screens and independent research. As is explained in Chapter 4, UK practices have developed in a very similar way to the "soft dollars" arrangements in the US.

A different model has existed in relation to trade execution carried out by investment banks offering full service broking. Under these arrangements, the broker will, in return for commission paid for the execution of deals, receive not only the execution services but also a range of other services

INVESTMENT MANAGEMENT AND FIDUCIARY DUTIES

including access to the brokers analysts and other services which are either provided by the broking firm itself or normally by another group firm.

9–014   The FSA has characterised the provision of soft commission and bundled services as effectively being a "rebate" on the commission charged by the broker for trade execution. This rebate can therefore be viewed as a form of "secret profit" which, without more, offends against the principles applying to the investment manager as fiduciary. The FSA's analysis of these arrangements, however, has tended to emphasis the malign effects of these practices on the *competitiveness* of investment managers and the services they provide. This builds upon the critique offered by Myners in his report published in 2001.[26] The FSA's analysis of bundling and soft commission is brigaded under four headings:

(i)   Opacity—bundling and softing enable investment managers to finance some of their management expenses by charging their customers in a way which is opaque thus making it difficult for customers to identify which additional services are being brought with their money or how much they are paying for them—customers do not have enough information to judge whether they are getting good value for money.

(ii)   Over consumption of additional services—since investment managers are not paying for the services they receive by way of bundled services and soft commission they may "over-consume" those services, *i.e.* they may buy more of the goods and services than they need for efficient operation.

(iii)   Excessive dealing—there is an incentive for investment managers to undertake volumes of trading that may be motivated by a desire to obtain particular quantities of additional services rather than to improve the performance of their customers' assets.

(iv)   Quality of trading decisions and execution—An investment manager may select brokers who offer generous bundling and softing terms but inferior execution quality such as wider dealing spreads or higher commission rates. There is a disincentive for investment managers to consider other trade execution options.[27]

Currently, the FSA's rules impose certain controls on investment managers who may operate with soft commission agreements. The rules do not address the position of managers dealing with integrated investment houses offering bundled services. The soft commission rules require:

---

[26]   Institutional investment in the United Kingdom: A Review: HM Treasury—March 2001.
[27]   FSA consultative paper 176 bundled brokerage and soft commission arrangements—April 2003, paras 3.15–3.22.

SECRET PROFITS

- a soft commission arrangement to be in writing;

- to be used only to acquire certain goods and services that will enhance the provision of the firms investment services to its customers;

- the broker must agree to provide best execution;

- the firm must obtain the customers prior consent to softing and be given periodic disclosure of the commissions paid and the value of the softed services received.[28]

There are, arguably, three particular features of the FSA's current approach which suggest that the fiduciary duty of the investment manager is not being properly addressed and managed. First, there is the lack of any analogous requirements relating to the provision of "bundled services" to an investment manager by full service brokers. Secondly, it is notable that the soft commission rules do not apply to an investment manager acting for authorised investment funds sold on a retail basis to the general public—unit trusts and open ended investment funds. In part this is explicable because of the practical impossibility of applying the consent rule and the obvious inability of the manager to disaggregate benefits received on the soft commission and bundled arrangements depending upon whether any particular client in a fund had in practice consented to such arrangements.[29] Third, there is the evidence brought forward by the FSA to show that disclosure by investment managers of soft commission arrangements may be inadequate to impress upon the customer the value to the investment manager of the services supplied along with execution. Accordingly it is difficult for the customer to judge fully the relative value of an investment manager's services and if necessary choose alternative cheaper services.

The FSA proposes to strengthen its rules in the following ways: **9–015**

- further restricting the kind of goods and services which can be purchased via bundled services and soft commission. In particular this would prohibit market pricing and information systems (including information screens);

- the cost of services acquired should be determined and an equivalent amount should be rebated to the customer (accordingly only the actual cost of trade execution would be charged to the portfolio).[30]

---

[28] See COB, 2.2.8R—2.2.12R. Essentially therefore the current regulatory approach is one which relies upon prior disclosure of the softing arrangements and the requirement to obtain the clients prior consent.

[29] See COB, 10.

[30] FSA CP176, paras 4–13—4.20.

251

INVESTMENT MANAGEMENT AND FIDUCIARY DUTIES

The second of these, rebating the value of soft commissions and bundled services, appears directly to address the fiduciary's duties to account for profits generated in carrying out the client's business.

FSA Rules—Self-Dealing in Fund Assets

9–016 One obvious way in which an investment manager might infringe the fiduciary's duty of loyalty to a beneficiary client is through dealing as principal with the client's property. This is controlled in the case of a manager of an authorised fund through rules limiting the circumstances in which a manager or an associate can deal in the fund property. The FSA's rules provide that a manager must take reasonable steps to ensure that it does not:

(1)   place cash with an affected person;

(2)   borrow money from an affected person;

(3)   buy and sell scheme property from to an affected person.[31]

For this purpose an "affected person" includes the manager (and trustee and depositary) and any person who is an associate of the manager (or trustee or depositary) and "associate" means:

an affiliated company of the manager ("A");

an appointed representative of A or of any affiliated company of A;

any other person whose business or domestic relationship with A or his associate might reasonably be expected to give rise to a community of interest between them which may involve a conflict of interest in dealings with third parties.[32]

The rule is qualified to the extent that a transaction can be shown to be at "arm's length" which is expressed as being "at least as favourable to the [fund] as would any comparable arrangement effected on normal commercial terms negotiated at arm's length between the affected person and an independent party".[33] This provision is then further refined by mandating the requirement for an independent valuation of the property which is the subject of the transaction or, if appropriate best execution on a recognised exchange.

9–017 It would presumably be arguable that the FSA's requirements fall short of the highest standards of conduct which could be expected of fiduciary—that

---

[31] See for example CIS 7.6.3 R (Conflicts of interest) in relation to the authorised corporate director of an investment company with variable capital.

[32] *FSA Glossary*.

[33] CIS 7.6.3 R (2).

the fiduciary (and its associates) should avoid dealings in the beneficiary's property altogether.[34] This is an example of how the very highest standards which could be expected of a fiduciary are modified by the statutory scheme of regulation. As suggested below it is very likely that that the court will recognise the efficacy of this and other similar provisions. It is consistent with the extent to which the courts have been willing to give effect to contractual clauses which modify the normal effect of a fiduciary duty.

Other investment managers not subject to the particular requirements imposed upon managers of authorised investment schemes are subject to the "fair treatment rule" in the FSA's conduct of business rules.

If a firm has or may have:

(1) a material interest in a transaction to be entered into with or for a customer; or

(2) a relationship that gives or may give rise to a conflict of interest in relation to a transaction in (1); or

(3) an interest in a transaction that is, or may be, in conflict with the interest of any of the firm's customers; or

(4) customers with conflicting interests in relation to a transaction; the firm must not knowingly advise, or deal in the exercise of discretion, in relation to that transaction unless it takes reasonable steps to ensure fair treatment for the customer.[35]

For the purposes of this rule, a firm may manage a conflict of interest by taking one or more of the following reasonable steps: **9–018**

(1) disclosure of an interest to a customer;

(2) relying on a "policy of independence";

(3) establishing internal arrangements (Chinese walls);

(4) Declining to act for a customer.[36]

The FSA rules contain an evidential provision giving examples of material interest or conflicts of interest that a firm should disclose under COB 7.1.4 E (1):

(1) dealing in investments as principal (unless the firm is acting as a market maker);

---

[34] *Boardman v Phipps* [1967] 2 A.C. 46.
[35] COB, 7.1.3 R.
[36] *ibid.,* 7.1.4 E.

INVESTMENT MANAGEMENT AND FIDUCIARY DUTIES

    (2)   dealing in investments as agent for more than one party;

    (3)   a recommendation to buy or sell a designated investment in which one of the firm's customers has given instructions to buy or sell;

    (4)   a recommendation to buy or sell a designated investment in which the firm has respectively a long or short position;

    (5)   acting as a broker fund adviser.[37]

In disclosing an interest to a customer, a firm should:

    (1)   disclose to the customer, either orally or in writing, any material interest or conflict of interest it has, or may have, whether generally or in relation to a specific transaction, before it advises the customer about the transaction or before it deals on behalf of the customer in the exercise of discretion in relation to the transaction; and

    (2)   be able to demonstrate that it has taken reasonable steps to ensure that the customer does not object to that material interest or conflict of interest.[38]

9–019   If it is not practical for a firm to make prior disclosure of a conflict or to obtain the client's consent to acting it *may* demonstrate that it has taken reasonable steps to ensure fair treatment for its customers by relying on a policy of independence. If a firm relies on a policy of independence, that policy should:

    (1)   require the relevant employee to disregard any material interest or conflict of interest when advising a customer or dealing for a customer in the exercise of discretion;

    (2)   be recorded in writing by the firm and made known to the relevant employee;

    (3)   be disclosed to a private customer stating that the firm may have a material interest or conflict of interest relating to the transaction or service concerned.[39]

        A firm may also manage a conflict of interest by establishing and maintaining a Chinese Wall.[40] If a firm determines that it is unable to manage a conflict of interest using one of the methods described above, it should decline to act on behalf of the customer.[41]

---

[37] COB, 7.1.5 E.
[38] *ibid.*, 7.1.6 G.
[39] *ibid.*, 7.1.7 G.
[40] *ibid.*, 7.1.8 G.
[41] *ibid.*, 7.1.9 G.

An institutional or private client investment manager may be within a group which may generate analysis and research on issues whose securities the manager may hold or consider buying. This may mean that a manager receiving such research will have to consider whether it is possible to act upon it before it is received by the persons for whom it is primarily intended.[42] Equally, this may mean that the manager must not receive the report until the firm within the group producing it has allowed the firm's clients the opportunity to deal on the strength of the report.

FSA Rules—Priority and Aggregation of Orders

A firm must execute customer orders and own account orders in designated **9–020** investments fairly and in due turn.[43] This does not however preclude a firm from, for example:

(1) executing:

    (a) a prior own account order ahead of a subsequent current customer other than in the same designated investment or a related designated investment; or

    (b) a current customer order when the person dealing for the customer nether knew nor ought reasonably to have known of an earlier unexecuted current customer order;

(2) postponing execution of a current customer order when the firm has taken reasonable steps to ensure that execution of another customer order ahead of that customer order is likely to improve the terms on which the current customer order is executed (in which case the firm should ensure that the customer whose customer order is being executed ahead of that other customer is also being treated fairly);

(3) treating the life fund as if it were a customer to the extent that the firm is an insurance company dealing for the account of its life fund;

(4) treating the investment trust or scheme as if it were a customer to the extent that the firm is dealing for the account of an investment trust or a collective investment scheme that is a body corporate, which in either case is in the same group as the firm;

(5) treating an employee (or close relative) of the firm or of its associate, or a trustee acting on his behalf, as if he were a customer, or

---

[42] *ibid.*, 7.3.3 R.
[43] *ibid.*, 7.4.3 R.

INVESTMENT MANAGEMENT AND FIDUCIARY DUTIES

(6) treating the firm's occupational pension scheme as a customer to the extent that the firm is dealing for the account of its occupational pension scheme.

When a firm aggregates a customer order with an own account order, or with an order from a market counterparty, or with another customer order, and subsequently allocates the designated investments concerned, it must do so in accordance with a written policy on allocation that is consistently applied and that fulfils the requirements of this section.[44]

A firm may not aggregate a customer order with an own account order, or with an order from a market counterparty, or with another customer order, unless:

(1) it is likely that the aggregation will not work to the advantage of each of the customers concerned; and

(2) it has disclosed either orally or in writing to each customer concerned, either specifically or in the terms of business, that the effect of

(3) aggregation may work on some occasions to its disadvantage.

9–021 When a firm has aggregated a customer order with an own account order, or with an order from a market counterparty, or with another customer order, and part or all of the aggregated order has been filled, it must promptly allocate the designated investments concerned.

To allocate promptly, a firm that has aggregated an order under COB, 7.7.4 R should complete the allocation of the designated investments concerned within one business day of the transaction. But this period is five business days if:

(1) only intermediate customers are concerned; and

(2) each of them has agreed to such an extension;

and three business days if:

(3) the aggregated order relates to one or more ISAs or PEPs; and

(4) the firm can show that it is necessary to execute those transactions in that way in order to serve its customers' best interests.

All transactions in a series of transactions, all of which are executed within the one business day, may be treated as having been executed at the time of the last transaction, so long as a record of the time that each individual

---

[44] COB, 7.4.4 R.

256

transaction was executed is made, such as by means of a time stamp. If such a series of transactions occurs over more than one business day, then the requirement for timely allocation in COB, 7.7.5 R (and (1), (2) or (3) as appropriate) will apply separately in relation to each business day in which any such transaction is executed.

Duty of Care—Investment Managers As Fiduciaries

Professional investment managers are very likely to owe a duty of care to those whose assets they manage. This duty may be derived from common law principles which may enable a client to bring an action in negligence or may be derived from the terms of the manager's contractual retainer. From the client's point of view, important questions are likely to be concerned with identifying the class of persons to whom such a duty is owed and the extent of the duty after taking account of the investment management agreement which may limit or exclude duties.[45]

9–022

The manager will in the first instance owe duties to the party with whom it contracts to provide its services and may owe concurrent duties of care which sound in negligence. The FSA rules modify and extend this where managers manage collective schemes by stipulating that the manager must treat a regulated or unregulated fund as its private or as its intermediate customer.[46] This may mean that fund investors may have rights of action under FSMA to bring actions for breaches of rule based obligations or, alternatively, such rights may reside in the trustee of a fund on behalf of fund investors.

For the purpose of this Chapter the relevant and perhaps more interesting question is whether, in addition, common law liabilities arising in contract negligence and statute, it is also possible to identify a separate strand of liability derived from the investment manager's fiduciary status. Is it possible to establish a *fiduciary duty of care* which may be actionable by reference to rules of causation and limitation which may in the circumstance be more favourable for the claimant? This question might also be relevant in determining in any case whether contractual terms have been effective to limit or exclude the manager's duty and liability.

It is suggested that an investment manager would normally fall with the third category of fiduciary identified by Birks where the fiduciary is to be regarded as subject to the obligations to act with positive altruism combined

9–023

---

[45] For example in December 2001 the trustee board of the Unilever pension fund announced that it had reached a settlement with Merrill Lynch Investment Advisers (formerly Mercury Asset Management). The amount of the settlement was reported to be £70m and arose from allegations that Mercury had been negligent in the manner in which it had acted in respect of one of its mandates with apparent lack of controls which led to investment decisions which were not in line with the contemplated risk profile of a section of the fund.

[46] See *FSA Glossary* definitions

with disinterestedness[47] but this does not, as Birks argues, mean that the such a person is also to be regarded as being subject to a "fiduciary" duty of care. Support for this view can be derived from the *Mothew* case[48] where Millet L.J. said that not every breach of duty by a fiduciary was breach of fiduciary duty. In particular it was inappropriate to say that trustee or fiduciary who failed to use proper skill and care in the discharge of duties was in breach if fiduciary duty :

> "That leaves those duties which are special to fiduciaries . . . The distinguishing feature of a fiduciary is the obligation of loyalty. The principal is entitled to the single minded loyalty of his fiduciary".

So in *Mothew* the solicitor's negligence in failing to inform the building society that that the borrower would breach a condition of the loan, though negligent, was not also to be characterised as a breach of fiduciary duty. To the extent that duties of care can be modified or excluded through contractual terms leads to an analysis in which the contractual scope of the duties assumed by a professional is paramount irrespective of whether the professional is also properly regarded as a fiduciary with an overriding duty of loyalty to the client:

> "The liability of a fiduciary for the negligent transaction of his duties is not a separate head of liability but the paradigm of the general duty to act with care imposed by law on those who take it upon themselves to act or advise others. Although the historical development of the rule of law and equity have in the past caused different labels to be stuck on different manifestations of the duty, in truth the duty of care imposed on bailees, carriers, trustees, directors, agents, and other is the same duty: it arises from the circumstances in which the defendants were acting, not from their status or description. It is the fact that they have assumed responsibility for the property or affairs of others which renders them liable for the careless performance of what they have undertaken to do."[49]

This approach to the characterisation of the fiduciary's duty of care does not find universal support. Some commentators view a "fusion" of the various doctrines of duty derived from common law with those derived from equity as reprehensible.[50] It seems nevertheless clear that the court will be

---

[47] Professor Birks, "The Content of Fiduciary Obligations", Cohen Lecture, 2000.
[48] *ibid.*, n.X.
[49] *Henderson v Merrett Syndicates* [1994] 3 All E.R. 506 at 544, *per* Lord Browne-Wilkinson.
[50] See for example Getlzler, "Legislative incursions into the modern trust doctrine in England: The Trustee Act 2000 and the Contracts (Rights of Third Parties) Act 1999" (2002) *Global Jurists Topics*: "Millett L.J. in *Mothew* and *Armitage* does lay down very clearly that any objective duty of care a trustee might have sounds in tort or contract, and the trustee may cut

DUTY OF CARE—INVESTMENT MANAGERS AS FIDUCIARIES

reluctant to super-impose upon a professional investment manager some additional duty or standard of care which goes beyond what, in the circumstances, may be warranted by the application of conventional duties derived from tort and contract. A duty of care implying special standards of diligence or probity in investment decisions is unlikely to be identified as within the "core" fiduciary duties which flow from the central duty of disinterested loyalty. Although it may be possible to identify aspects of a fiduciary's duty which can suggest an obligation *positively* to advance the beneficiaries interests[51] it seems that breaches of duty by investment managers will invariably be determined by reference to conventional principles of negligence and the contractual setting.

In the regulatory context investment managers are subject to some specific **9–024** obligations which are directed to the suitability of the transactions which are effected for the customer's benefit. These protections are applicable in the case of private customers and require a firm to "know its customer" and to take reasonable steps to ensure that transactions for a client's portfolio are suitable having regard to what the firm knows about the customer (or ought reasonably to know). Where a manager is managing a pooled fund on behalf of several clients then the transactions must be suitable having regard to the stated investment objectives of the fund.[52] The requirement for best execution of transactions for a customer or for a managed fund is also a relevant aspect of the investment manager's duty of care.[53]

The Modification of Fiduciary Duties Through Contract

The FSA's rules acknowledge a variety of means by which a firm may fairly **9–025** manage a conflict of interest both arising between itself and a client and between different clients of the firm. In some instances the conflicts may be managed through the use of a structural device within the firm such as a Chinese Wall or alternatively, through adequate disclosure to the client of the material facts giving rise to the conflict and obtaining the client's consent. The use of suitable contractual provisions may not however be practicable particularly in the case of the management of pooled funds where it is not normally possible for the manager to act differently in relation to trading

---

this back by indemnity or exemption clauses at the time of constitution of the trust along the lines of obligational duties grounded in contract or tort. The exemption clause is effective unless the trustee advertently relies on the clause when attempting some wrongdoing. This new doctrine was as much an assertion of policy to protect trustees as doctrinal restatement of the law."

[51] In *ATA v American Express Bank Limited* (*ibid.*, n.10) the argument that the bank had acted in breach of its fiduciary duty by failing to exercise its discretion to close out certain open positions.

[52] COB 5.2.R and 5.3.5 R.

[53] *ibid.*, 7.5.3 R.

INVESTMENT MANAGEMENT AND FIDUCIARY DUTIES

decisions depending on whether a particular underlying client has or has not consented to a particular course of action. The Law Commission's study on fiduciary duties was particularly concerned about the relationship between fiduciary duties at common law and the extent to which they were capable of modification through contractual provisions and the extent to which a court would take into account the existence of regulatory requirements established under the statutory framework for investor protection.

Of particular importance to the Law Commission's final view was the decision in 1993 of the Privy Council in *Kelly v Cooper*.[54] In this case the plaintiff complained that his estate agent had not acted in accordance with its fiduciary duty in failing to pass on to him information concerning another transaction in which the agent was involved and which would have enabled him to have a stronger bargaining position with ultimate purchaser of his property.

The Privy Counsel laid particular emphasis on the scope and extent of the contractual relationship between the claimant and the defendant estate agent, and held that in this case the extent of the fiduciary's duties should be defined and limited by reference to the terms of that contractual relationship, including for this purpose its implied terms. In the course of his judgment Lord Browne-Wilkinson referred to the Australian case of *Hospital Products Limited v United States Surgical Corporation*[55] where Mason J. said:

> "That contractual and fiduciary relationships may co-exist between the same parties has never been doubted. Indeed, the existence of a basic contractual relationship has in many situations provided a foundation for the erection of a fiduciary relationship. In these situations it is the contractual foundation which is all important because it is contract that regulates the basic rights and liabilities of the parties. Fiduciary relationship, if it is to exist at all, must accommodate itself to the terms of the contract so that it is consistent with, and conforms to, them. The fiduciary relationship cannot be superimposed upon the contract in such a way as to alter the operation which the contract was intended to have according to its true construction."

9–026   Applying that principle in this case, the Privy Council concluded that the estate agent had not committed any breach of fiduciary duty.

Kelly v Cooper was followed by a further Privy Council decision, *Clarke Boyce v Mouat*.[56] In this case the claimant and her son were advised by a firm of solicitors concerning a transaction by which the son was able to borrow

---

[54] [1993] A.C. 205.
[55] (1984) 156 C.L.R. 41.
[56] [1994] 1 A.C. 428.

260

money on the basis of a mortgage offered by the claimant on her property. The son's business failed with the result that the claimant was left with the liability of repaying the mortgage. She brought an action against the solicitors alleging that they had acted negligently and in breach of contract in failing to ensure that she received her own independent advice and that in breach of their fiduciary duty they had failed to decline to act for her or to advise her adequately of the need to obtain independent legal advice.

The Privy Council held that there was no general rule of law that a solicitor could never act for both parties in a transaction where their interests might conflict. A solicitor was entitled to act for both parties in such a transaction provided he obtained the informed consent of both parties. For this purpose informed consent means consent given in the knowledge that there is a conflict between the parties and that as a result the solicitor might be disabled from disclosing to each party the full knowledge which he possessed as to the transaction or might be unable to give advice to one party which conflicted with the interests of the other provided the parties were content to proceed on that basis a solicitor could properly act for both parties. In determining whether a solicitor had obtained informed consent it was essential to determine precisely what services were required by the parties. A solicitor might be under no duty whether before or after accepting instructions to proffer unsought advice on the wisdom of the transaction.[57]

9–027 Both *Kelly* and *Clarke Boyce* suggest that in determining the extent of any fiduciary duties assumed by a person a court will look at the factual and contractual circumstances surrounding the relationship between the putative fiduciary and beneficiary. This is not, however, merely a matter of disclosing the potential for conflicts of interest to arise but there must be, in the sense described by Lord Jauncey in *Clarke Boyce*, informed consent.

The effectiveness of contractual terms which seek to limit or exclude a party's liability for breach of duty (whether in contract or negligence) is effected by the application of two statutory schemes, the Unfair Contract Terms Act 1977 ("UCTA") and the Unfair Terms in Consumer Contracts Regulations 1999 ("UTCCRs"). Both of these pieces of legislation are primarily concerned with contracts made with consumers. Section 3 of UCTA is a wide provision, controlling the use of duty limiting clauses where a party deals on another party's standard terms of business or deals as consumer. Such duty limiting clauses are subjected to a test of reasonableness. The UTCCRs apply to contracts with consumers which contain terms which have not been individually negotiated. Such terms will be unfair, and potentially unenforceable, if contrary to the requirement of good faith it causes a significant imbalance in the party's rights and obligations arising under the contract to the detriment of the consumer. For this purpose, a term is to be regarded as not having been individually negotiated where it has been drafted

---

[57] [1993] 4 All E.R. at 268.

INVESTMENT MANAGEMENT AND FIDUCIARY DUTIES

in advance and the consumer has not therefore been able to influence the substance of the term.[58]

Both UCTA and the UTCCRs may therefore have a considerable impact on the ability of investment managers to limit the extent of their fiduciary duties where the investment management agreement between the client and manager is not individually negotiated but on standard terms.

9–028 The FSA's rules relating to the exclusion of liability say that a firm must not in any written or oral communication to a private customer seek to exclude or restrict or to rely on any exclusion or restriction of any duty or liability unless it is reasonable for it to do so. A firm cannot however rely upon a contractual provision to exclude liability which it may have incurred to a customer under the regulatory system.[59]

The first FSA rule (no unreasonable exclusion of liability) mimics the effect of the UCTA and the UTCCRs mentioned above but with the added consequence that the FSA may use its enforcement powers to prevent a firm from relying on a clause which might unreasonably limit the extent of a fiduciary duty owed to a private customer. The second rule more simply prohibits the contracting out of any regulatory duty which is owed to a private customer.

Section 253 of the FSMA provides that any provision of the trust deed of a unit trust is void in so far as it would have the effect of exempting the manager or trustee from liability for any failure to exercise due care and diligence in the discharge of his functions in respect of the scheme. The duty of care imposed upon trustees by the Trustee Act 2000 applies to the trustee of a unit trust scheme. The effect of s.253 of FSMA is to prevent the drafter of a trust deed for a unit trust scheme taking advantage of para.7 of Sch.1 to the Trustee Act 2000 which permits the duty of care to be excluded by express provision.[60]

9–029 The general position (derived from *Kelly*, etc.) appears to be that attempts by firms to limit or exclude liabilities which would otherwise result from conduct which does not comply with the standards of a fiduciary may through the use of appropriate contractual terms be successful. However there is a hierarchy of tests which a contracting party will have to satisfy. This begins in the case of contracts between professional parties with the need for clarity and informed consent. If professional parties deal on the basis of standard terms contracts which are not individually negotiated then s.3 of UCTA will require that an exclusion clause satisfies the test of reasonableness.

Private customers and consumers benefit from a range of controls which may also allow a court to review the *fairness* of any duty limiting or exclusion clause. Private customers will also benefit from the prohibition contained in

---

[58] Unfair Terms in Consumer Contracts Regulations 1999 (SI 1999/2083), reg.5.
[59] *ibid.*, 2.5.3 and 2.5.4 R.
[60] The duty of care in s.1 of the Trustee Act is not disapplied in the case of authorised unit trust schemes by s.37 of the Act.

THE MODIFICATION OF FIDUCIARY DUTIES THROUGH CONTRACT

the FSA's rules on exclusion and duty limiting clauses. Generally, the existence and content of the statutory scheme for the regulation of investment managers is likely to be relevant if the court is required to assess the "reasonableness" of a particular contractual provision which is intended to limit or exclude liability. The extent to which the FSA rules accommodate fiduciary duties is likely to be persuasive.

CHAPTER 10

US APPROACH TO FIDUCIARY DUTIES: GENERAL LAW, THE INVESTMENT ADVISERS ACT, THE INVESTMENT COMPANY ACT, AND ERISA

John F. Cacchione, Esq., Dechert LLP, Philadelphia

10–001 In the United States, a significant component of the law of investment management involves the statutory imposition of fiduciary duties on primary actors in the investment management industry—particularly investment managers and members of the boards of directors of collective investment vehicles. The US Investment Advisers Act of 1940 (the "Advisers Act"), the US Investment Company Act of 1940 (the "ICA"), and, where applicable, the US Employee Retirement Income Security Act of 1974 ("ERISA") create additional layers of fiduciary duties beyond what is typically required under state law. This Chapter examines the general fiduciary law of the States and then looks at additional duties of particular relevance to investment managers under the Advisers Act, the ICA, and ERISA. It concludes with a discussion of fiduciary duties under the state law of business entities and some of the supplemental duties imposed by the ICA on directors and officers of investment companies.

Introduction to the Law of Fiduciaries in the United States

Preliminary note on the federal nature of the US legal system

10–002 The system of government in the United States is a federal one, and the US Constitution delegates certain powers to the national government[1] while reserving the remaining powers "to the States respectively, or to the people".[2] As a result, several areas of regulation fall within the respective purviews of both the national and state governments. For the purposes of economic and

---

[1] See generally US Const. Art. I, § 8.
[2] US Const. amend. X.

264

INTRODUCTION TO THE LAW OF FIDUCIARIES IN THE UNITED STATES

commercial regulation, the most important delegated power is the power of the US Congress (the national legislature) to regulate interstate commerce.[3] This power has been liberally interpreted over the years, allowing national regulation of "the use of the channels of interstate commerce", "the instrumentalities of interstate commerce, or persons or things in interstate commerce", and "those activities having a substantial relation to interstate commerce, *i.e.*, those activities that substantially affect interstate commerce".[4] In enacting the various securities laws, Congress repeatedly references use of the mails[5] and use of means or instrumentalities of interstate commerce to emphasise its authority to legislate in this area.[6]

Because of this structure, general fiduciary law, whether common law or statutory law, is typically a matter of state jurisdiction. Similarly, state law generally governs the chartering and regulation of corporate bodies and other associations formed as business entities.[7] The fiduciary duties imposed on investment managers and members of the boards of directors of collective investment vehicles by the national securities laws (particularly, for purposes of this Chapter, the Advisers Act and the ICA and, where applicable, by ERISA) are additional duties designed to supplement applicable state-imposed fiduciary duties.

---

[3] See US Const. art. I, § 8, cl. 3 (vesting in Congress the power "[t]o regulate commerce with foreign nations, and among the several States, and with the Indian tribes").

[4] *United States v Lopez*, 514 U.S. 549, 558–59 (1995) (citation omitted).

[5] The national government's exclusive right to regulate the mails derives from Article I, Section 8, clause 7 of the US Constitution, which grants Congress the power "[t]o establish Post Offices and post Roads."

[6] See, *e.g.*, Securities Act of 1933 § 5 (registration of securities offerings) [hereinafter Securities Act]; Securities Exchange Act of 1934 §§ 12(g) (registration of securities), 15(a)(1) (registration of brokers and dealers) [hereinafter Exchange Act]; ICA § 7 (restrictions on transactions of unregistered investment companies); Advisers Act § 203 (registration of investment advisers); see also ERISA § 2(a) (listing the congressional findings of fact prompting adoption of ERISA which include *inter alia* "that [employee benefit plans] have become an important factor in commerce because of the interstate character of their activities, and of the activities of their participants, and the employers, employee organizations, and other entities by which they are established or maintained; [and] that a large volume of the activities of such plans is carried on by means of the mails and instrumentalities of interstate commerce").

[7] This is not to say, however, that the national government is not permitted to charter corporate bodies. On the contrary, recognition of the national government's right in this regard is long standing. *See M'Colloch v Maryland*, 17 U.S. 316, 424 (1819) (Marshall, C.J.) ("After the most deliberate consideration, it is the unanimous and decided opinion of this court, that the act to incorporate the Bank of the United States is a law made [by Congress] in pursuance of the constitution, and is a part of the supreme law of the land."). To this day, national banks are still chartered by the national government. *See* 12 U.S.C.A. § 21 (West 2001) (establishing procedures for the incorporation of national banks). This state of affairs exemplifies the non-exclusive jurisdiction of the national government and the state governments with respect to matters not explicitly and exclusively delegated to either. Clearly, the US constitutional and legal system recognises the national government and the respective state governments as dual sovereigns. See above, para.10–002, text accompanying nn.2–3.

265

Agency and the general law of fiduciaries

10–003 At the most fundamental level, fiduciary duties arise out of agency relationships. While the precise contours of what constitutes an agency relationship are typically determined under each state's common law, the general definition of "agency" is reasonably straightforward:

> "The term "agency" means a fiduciary relationship by which a party confides to another the management of some business to be transacted in the former's name or on his or her account, and by which such other assumes to do the business and render an account of it. It has also been defined as the fiduciary relationship which results from the manifestation of consent by one person to another that the other will act on his or her behalf and subject to his or her control, and consent by the other so to act."[8]

The party acting for, or on behalf of, another is the "agent", and the person for whom, or on whose behalf, the agent acts is referred to as the "principal".[9] The principal-agent relationship is contractual, and the principal and the agent must agree upon, and consent to, the scope and extent of the agency relationship created.[10] Often, the principal's maintenance of some degree of control over the agent's actions is the most critical characteristic of the relationship.[11]

With respect to matters within the scope of the agreement, the agent is a fiduciary of the principal, bound, therefore, "to exercise the utmost good faith, loyalty, and honesty to the principal". The agent's status as a fiduciary, however, does not generally extend to matters outside the scope of the agency.[12] In addition to the duties of good faith, loyalty, and honesty, the agent, by virtue of its status as a fiduciary, also bears the duty "to make full disclosure to the principal of all material facts relevant to the agency",[13] the duty "to keep records and render to the principal an account of all transactions within the scope of the agency",[14] and the duty to obey the principal's "reasonable instructions and directions with regard to the manner of performing a service that he or she has contracted to perform and to adhere faithfully to them in all cases where they ought properly to be applied".[15] In upholding its duties, the agent "owes to the principal the use of such skill as is required to accomplish the object of the employment", and the agent must

---

[8] 3 Am. Jur. 2d *Agency* § 1 (2002) (footnotes omitted).
[9] *ibid.*
[10] *ibid.*, § 15.
[11] *ibid.*, § 2.
[12] *ibid.*, § 205.
[13] *ibid.*, § 206.
[14] *ibid.*, § 207.
[15] *ibid.*, § 213.

INTRODUCTION TO THE LAW OF FIDUCIARIES IN THE UNITED STATES

exercise "reasonable care, diligence, and judgment".[16] If the agent fails to do so, the agent may be held liable for any resulting losses or damages to the principal.[17]

Thus, in a celebrated 1928 opinion for the New York Court of Appeals, Chief Judge Benjamin Cardozo (later a Justice of the United States Supreme Court) explained what it means for someone to be a fiduciary of another and what the quality of a fiduciary's duties are:

10–004

> "Many forms of conduct permissible in a workaday world for those acting at arm's length, are forbidden to those bound by fiduciary ties. A [fiduciary] is held to something stricter than the morals of the marketplace. Not honesty alone, but the punctilio of an honor the most sensitive, is then the standard of behavior."[18]

Fiduciary Duties of Investment Advisers

As explained above,[19] Congress, in adopting the Advisers Act and the ICA, sought, among other things, to establish for, and apply to, investment advisers fiduciary standards even stricter than those ordinarily imposed by state law. The material which follows explains how these two laws amplify and augment investment advisers' fiduciary duties to their clients.

10–005

Fiduciary duties under the Advisers Act

One of the central underlying notions of the Advisers Act is that an investment adviser is a fiduciary.[20] As such, an investment adviser owes its clients "more than mere honesty and good faith alone" and is prohibited from overreaching and from taking unfair advantage of its clients' trust.[21] An investment adviser must always be aware of the possibility of providing its clients with advice that is less than disinterested.[22] Even when an investment adviser intends a client no harm and even if the client suffers no harm, an investment adviser can be faulted for a breach of its fiduciary duties.[23]

10–006

Neither the Advisers Act nor the rules of the US Securities and Exchange Commission (the "SEC") thereunder explicitly state that investment advisers

---

[16] *ibid.*, § 210.
[17] *ibid.*
[18] *Meinhard v Salmon*, 164 N.E. 545, 546 (N.Y. 1928).
[19] See above, para.10–002, n.7.
[20] See Robert E. Plaze, *The Regulation of Investment Advisers by the Securities and Exchange Commission*, Investment Adviser Regulation, Course of Study January 30–31, 2003 (ALI-ABA 2003) [hereinafter cited as Plaze, *Regulation of Investment Advisers*].
[21] *ibid.*
[22] *ibid.*
[23] *ibid.*

are fiduciaries with fiduciary duties to clients.[24] Moreover, the investment adviser's fiduciary duties are not a product of the language of the contract between an investment adviser and its client, and the scope of the fiduciary relationship cannot be narrowed by negotiation.[25] Instead, the very nature of the relationship between investment adviser and client gives rise—by operation of law—to the investment adviser's fiduciary duties.[26]

This concept is "embodied in the anti-fraud provisions of the Advisers Act" (which provisions make the fiduciary duties enforceable) and otherwise indirectly incorporated into the Advisers Act.[27] The anti-fraud provisions of the Advisers Act appear in Section 206 as follows:

"It shall be unlawful for any investment adviser, by use of the mails or any means or instrumentality of interstate commerce, directly or indirectly —

(1) to employ any device, scheme, or artifice to defraud any client or prospective client;

(2) to engage in any transaction, practice, or course of business which operates as a fraud or deceit upon any client or prospective client;

(3) acting as principal for his own account, knowingly to sell any security to or purchase any security from a client, or acting as broker for a person other than such client, knowingly to effect any sale or purchase of any security for the account of such client, without disclosing to such client in writing before the completion of such transaction the capacity in which he is acting and obtaining the consent of the client to such transaction . . . ; [or]

(4) to engage in any act, practice, or course of business which is fraudulent, deceptive, or manipulative."[28]

---

[24] See Plaze, *Regulation of Investment Advisers*, above, para.10–006, n.20.

[25] *ibid*.

[26] See Arleen W. Hughes, Exchange Act Release No.4048 (February 18, 1948) ("The very function of furnishing investment counsel on a fee basis—learning the personal and intimate details of the financial affairs of clients and making recommendations as to purchases and sales of securities—cultivates a confidential and intimate relationship and imposes a duty upon the [investment adviser] to act in the best interests of her clients and to make only such recommendations as will best serve such interests.").

[27] Plaze, *Regulation of Investment Advisers*, above, para.10–006, n.20; see also *SEC v Capital Gains Research Bureau, Inc.*, 375 U.S. 180, 191–92 (1963): "The Investment Advisers Act of 1940 thus reflects a congressional recognition 'of the delicate fiduciary nature of an investment advisory relationship,' as well as a congressional intent to eliminate, or at least expose, all conflicts of interest which might incline an investment adviser—consciously or unconsciously—to render advice which was not disinterested. It would defeat the manifest purpose of the Investment Advisers Act of 1940 for us to hold, therefore, that Congress, in empowering the courts to enjoin any practice which operates 'as a fraud or deceit,' intended to require proof of intent to injure and actual injury to clients." (footnotes omitted).

[28] Advisers Act § 206.

An investment adviser's fiduciary duty (and the prohibitions of Section 206) give rise to several obligations, namely, fully disclosing conflicts of interest, providing suitable advice to the client, having a reasonable basis for recommendations to the client, seeking "best execution" for client trades, and voting proxies in the client's best interests.[29] Each of these obligations will be discussed in turn.

10–007

Full disclosure of conflicts of interest

As a fiduciary, an investment adviser must consider as its paramount concern, and, therefore, work solely to promote, the best interests of its clients.[30] As a result, the investment adviser should never be in a position where its position and a client's position are in conflict, unless the adviser has already disclosed the conflict to its client and received from the client its informed consent to the conflict: The duty of loyalty owed to clients requires the investment adviser "to disclose all material circumstances fully and completely".[31]

10–008

Suitable advice

An investment adviser's fiduciary duty to its client requires that the investment adviser provide investment advice which is suitable to its client.[32] To do so, an investment adviser must inquire into its client's financial circumstances, investment experience, and investment objectives and reasonably determine that its advice to the client is suitable in light of the foregoing.[33]

10–009

Reasonable basis for recommendations

An investment adviser's recommendations to a client must have a reasonable, independent basis.[34]

10–010

---

[29] See Plaze, *Regulation of Investment Advisers*, above, para.10–006, n.20.

[30] See Arleen W. Hughes, Exchange Act Release No.4048 (February 18, 1948) (stating that an investment adviser requests and receives from its clients "the highest degree of trust and confidence on the representation that [the investment adviser] will act in the best interests of [its] clients").

[31] *ibid.*

[32] See Suitability of Investment Advice Provided by Investment Advisers, Advisers Act Release No.1406 (March 16, 1994): "Investment advisers are fiduciaries who owe their clients a series of duties, one of which is the duty to provide only suitable investment advice." (footnotes omitted).

[33] *ibid.*, reflecting the SEC's view that investment advisers should consider the factors listed.

[34] See Alfred C. Rizzo, Advisers Act Release No.897 (January 11, 1984).

Best execution

10–011 An investment adviser must typically obtain "best execution" for its client's trades.[35] This requires the investment adviser "to execute securities transactions for clients in such a manner that the client's total cost or proceeds in each transaction is the most favorable under the circumstances".[36] In assessing the scope and quality of the broker's services and in reaching a conclusion that best execution has been obtained, the investment adviser should consider, among other things, "the value of research provided as well as execution capability, commission rate, financial responsibility, and responsiveness to the [investment adviser]".[37] Since this is not an exhaustive list of factors, investment advisers often take into account additional considerations, such as the broker's effectiveness in clearing and settling trades.[38] Given the flexibility inherent in best execution evaluation, the SEC tends to be liberal when examining an investment adviser's practices, focusing primarily on the adviser's institution of adequate internal controls for monitoring execution activity and the consistency of the investment adviser's disclosure to clients with its actual procedures.[39]

An important sub-issue which arises when considering an investment adviser's best execution is that of "soft dollars". The term "soft dollars" refers to an investment adviser's purchase of research products and other services (such as performance measurement services, fundamental research, economic analysis, and publications) with client brokerage commissions.[40] The use of soft dollars emerged when brokerage commission rates were fixed by the New York Stock Exchange (and competition among brokers was, therefore, not based on the price for their services). But, despite the fact that commissions have not been fixed since 1975, the use of soft dollars has endured.[41] Because the benefits of soft dollars received by an investment adviser as a result of the execution of client transactions can inure to an investment adviser and not to its clients, "[a] legal analysis of an adviser's soft dollar practices must be placed in the context of an adviser's duty of best execution and its duty of loyalty".[42]

In response to investment advisers' fears of being held to have breached their fiduciary duty to clients if they selected a broker which did not charge

---

[35] Interpretive Release Concerning the Scope of Section 28(e) of the Securities Exchange Act of 1934 and Related Matters, Exchange Act Release No.23170 (April 23, 1986) (hereafter referred to as Section 28(e) Interpretive Release) [citing Kidder Peabody & Co., Inc., Advisers Act Release No. 232 (October 16, 1968)].

[36] Kidder Peabody & Co., Inc., Advisers Act Release No.232 (October 16, 1968).

[37] Section 28(e) Interpretive Release, above, para.10–011, n.35.

[38] See Clifford E. Kirsch, *Investment Adviser Regulation: A Step-by-Step Guide to Compliance and the Law* (2003 rev.) 12–2 [hereinafter cited as Kirsch, *Investment Adviser Regulation*].

[39] *ibid.*, 12–3.

[40] *ibid.*, 13–2.

[41] *ibid.*

[42] *ibid.* 13–3.

the lowest available commission but from which the investment adviser received soft-dollar research products or services, Congress, in 1975, adopted Section 28(e) of the Securities Exchange Act of 1934 (the "Exchange Act").[43] Section 28(e) is a "safe harbour" precluding liability for investment advisers whose activities are covered by its terms.[44] Section 28(e) provides:

"No person using the mails, or any means or instrumentality of interstate commerce, in the exercise of investment discretion with respect to an account shall be deemed to have acted unlawfully or to have breached a fiduciary duty under State or Federal law unless expressly provided to the contrary by a law enacted by the Congress or any State . . . solely by reason of his having caused the account to pay a member of an exchange, broker, or dealer an amount of commission for effecting a securities transaction in excess of the amount of commission another member of an exchange, broker, or dealer would have charged for effecting that transaction, if such person determined in good faith that such amount of commission was reasonable in relation to the value of the brokerage and research services provided by such member, broker, or dealer, viewed in terms of either that particular transaction or his overall responsibilities with respect to the accounts as to which he exercises investment discretion."[45]

Thus, there are four elements to the applicability of the safe harbour: (i) provision of the research products and services by the broker effecting the transactions; (ii) provision of such products and services to a person with investment discretion; (iii) a good-faith determination by the recipient that the commissions paid to the broker are reasonable relative to the value of the research products and services received; and (iv) inclusion of the research products and services within the meaning of "brokerage and research services" in Section 28(e).[46] The term "brokerage and research services" includes all of the following: advice about securities; "analyses and reports concerning issuers, industries, securities, economic factors and trends, portfolio

10–012

---

[43] *ibid.*, 13–4.

[44] *ibid.*

[45] Exchange Act § 28(e)(1). Despite references to "dealers" in the statute, the SEC has interpreted Section 28(e) as generally applying not to principal transactions (which are executed for "markups" or "markdowns" on a principal basis), but only to broker transactions (which are executed for a "commissions" on an agency basis) and to certain approved classes of riskless principal transactions. See Commission Guidance on the Scope of Section 28(e) of the Exchange Act, Exchange Act Release No.45194 (December 27, 2001) (explaining that the Section 28(e) safe harbor is available "for research and brokerage services obtained in relation to commissions paid to a broker-dealer acting in an 'agency' capacity", as well as markups, markdowns, commission equivalents, or other fees paid for "Eligible Riskless Principal Transactions"); see also Kirsch, *Investment Adviser Regulation*, 13–5, above, para.10–011, n.38. There are numerous other interpretive questions that arise in Section 28(e). See Kirsch, *ibid.*, 13–5 to 13–10.

[46] Kirsch, *Investment Adviser Regulation*, 13–4 to 13–5, above, para.10–011, n.38.

271

US APPROACH TO FIDUCIARY DUTIES

strategy, and the performance of accounts"; and the effecting of securities transactions and the performance of incidental functions thereto (such as clearance, settlement, and custody).[47]

Section 28(e) also mandates that persons making use of soft dollars disclose their soft-dollar policies and procedures to clients.[48] The SEC holds the position that an investment adviser has a fiduciary duty to disclose *all* of its soft-dollar arrangements, whether within the Section 28(e) safe harbour or not,[49] and that failure to disclose the receipt of products or services purchased with client commission dollars and "[c]onduct outside the safe harbour of Section 28(e) may constitute a breach of fiduciary duty as well as a violation of specific provisions of the federal securities laws, particularly under the [Advisers Act] and the [ICA] and of [ERISA]".[50]

One should also note that investment advisers who are Fiduciaries of Plans subject to ERISA (as described below[51]) making use of soft dollars are required at all times to remain within the safe harbour of Section 28(e) when managing the assets of such Plans, unless otherwise duly directed by another Plan Fiduciary to obtain brokerage services from one or more designated broker-dealers.[52]

Proxy voting

10–013 An investment adviser to whom a client has delegated authority to vote proxies must vote such proxies in the client's best interest, regardless of the investment adviser's own interests.[53]

Additional duties under the ICA

Section 36

10–014 Section 36 of the ICA imposes fiduciary duties on investment advisers of registered investment companies. As it can with respect to directors (and offi-

---

[47] Exchange Act § 28(e)(3).

[48] *ibid.*, § 28(e)(2).

[49] See SEC Inspection Report on the Soft Dollar Practices of Broker-Dealers, Investment Advisers and Mutual Funds (September 22, 1998) [hereinafter cited as SEC Soft Dollars Inspection Report].

[50] Section 28(e) Interpretive Release, above, para.10–011, n.35; see also Plaze, *Regulation of Investment Managers*, above, para.10–006, n.20.

[51] See below, paras 10–017, *et seq.*

[52] See Statement on Policies Concerning Soft Dollar and Directed Commission Arrangements, DOL ERISA Tech. Rel. 86–1 (May 22, 1986); see also SEC Soft Dollars Inspection Report, above, para.10–012, n.49.

[53] See Plaze, *Regulation of Investment Managers*, above, para.10–006, n.20.

272

cers) of registered investment companies,[54] the SEC can also institute suits in federal court against investment advisers of registered investment companies if the investment adviser engaged in the last five years, or is about to engage, in any act or practice which constitutes "breach of fiduciary duty involving personal misconduct in respect of any registered investment company".[55] Courts are given broad injunctive powers where such breaches of fiduciary duty are proven. Those who breach this fiduciary duty may be temporarily or permanently enjoined from positions as investment advisers, directors, officers, etc. with registered investment companies, or, alternatively, courts may fashion "such injunctive relief against such person as may be reasonable and appropriate under the circumstances".[56]

Section 36(b) of the ICA imposes another duty on investment advisers of registered investment companies. Specifically, it provides that:

> "the investment adviser of a registered investment company shall be deemed to have a fiduciary duty with respect to the receipt of compensation for services, or of payments of a material nature, paid by such registered investment company, or by the security holders thereof, to such investment adviser or any affiliated person of such investment adviser."[57]

Actions alleging breach of this duty may be brought either directly by the SEC or derivatively by any shareholder of the investment company on the investment company's behalf.[58]

According to seminal case law, the test of whether an investment adviser has violated its duty under Section 36(b) "is essentially whether the fee schedule represents a charge within the range of what would have been negotiated at arm's-length in the light of all of the surrounding circumstances".[59] Therefore, violations of Section 36(b) are found when the investment adviser charges "a fee that is so disproportionately large that it bears no reasonable relationship to the services and could not have been the product of arm's-length bargaining".[60] Furthermore, the courts have set forth a series of factors for use in applying this test:

10–015

(a) the nature and quality of the services provided by the investment adviser to the shareholders of the investment company;

(b) the profitability of the investment company to the investment adviser;

---

[54] See below, para.10–032.
[55] ICA § 36(a).
[56] *ibid.*
[57] *ibid.* § 36(b).
[58] *ibid.*
[59] *Gartenberg v Merrill Lynch Asset Mgmt., Inc.*, 694 F.2d 923, 928 (2d Cir. 1982).
[60] *ibid.* (citations omitted).

(c)   "fall-out" benefits, *e.g.* profits of an affiliate of the investment adviser resulting from trading with the investment company;

(d)   economies of scale as reflected in a fee schedule providing for progressively lower advisory fee rates with rising amounts of assets of the investment company under the investment adviser's management;

(e)   a comparison of the investment adviser's fees with those of other investment advisers managing the assets of investment companies with similar objectives and strategies; and

(f)   the "independence and conscientiousness" of the directors in evaluating the fee schedule.[61]

Section 15(c)

10–016   As described below,[62] Section 15(c) of the ICA imposes on directors of registered investment companies the duty to request and evaluate from their investment advisers "such information as may reasonably be necessary to evaluate the terms" of the advisory contracts with such investment advisers. Section 15(c) reciprocally imposes on investment advisers of registered investment companies the duty to furnish such information to the directors.

Fiduciary Duties Under ERISA

General introduction to certain principles of ERISA

Plans and fiduciaries

10–017   Congress enacted ERISA primarily in order to provide additional protections for many types of employee benefits. Thus, ERISA creates the regulatory framework applicable to employee benefit plans and other similar kinds of plans, typically established (or "sponsored") by employers for the benefit of their employees (collectively, "Plans" and each a "Plan"). ERISA imposes a variety of fiduciary duties on any individual or entity considered under the statute to be a "fiduciary" of a Plan (a "Fiduciary"). As set forth in ERISA, a Fiduciary of a Plan is a person or entity that:

---

[61]   See, e.g. *Krinsk v Fund Asset Mgmt., Inc.*, 875 F.2d 404, 409 (2d Cir. 1989); *Kalish v Franklin Advisers, Inc.*, 742 F. Supp. 1222, 1228 (S.D.N.Y. 1990). In light of this guidance from the courts, investment company directors should consider these factors when evaluating an investment adviser's fee schedule while considering whether to enter into, or renew, an advisory contract with the investment adviser pursuant to Section 15(c) of the ICA. See below, para.10–033.

[62]   See below, para.10–033.

FIDUCIARY DUTIES UNDER ERISA

(a) exercises any discretionary authority or discretionary control respecting management or disposition of the Plan's assets;

(b) either renders investment advice for a fee or other compensation, direct or indirect, with respect to any moneys or other property of the Plan or has any authority or responsibility to do so; or

(c) has any discretionary responsibility in the administration of the Plan.[63]

A Plan may only be established pursuant to a written instrument, and the instrument must provide for one or more "Named Fiduciaries" who jointly or severally have the authority to control and manage Plan operation and administration.[64] The term "Named Fiduciary" is defined to include a Fiduciary named in the Plan instrument or, pursuant to a procedure specified in the Plan, identified as a Fiduciary either by a person who is an employer or employee organisation with respect to the Plan or by such an employer and such an employee organisation acting jointly.[65] Every Plan is required to:

(a) provide a procedure for establishing and carrying out a funding policy and method consistent with the objectives of the Plan and of ERISA;

(b) describe any procedure under the Plan for allocation of responsibilities for Plan operation and administration (including any procedure for the allocation of fiduciary duties among the Plan's Fiduciaries);

(c) provide a procedure for amending the Plan and for identifying the persons who have the authority to amend the Plan; and

(d) specify the basis on which payments are made to and from the Plan.[66]

Generally, the assets of a Plan must be held in trust by one or more trustees who are either named in the Plan instrument or appointed by a Named Fiduciary.[67] The trustees, who are themselves Fiduciaries, have exclusive authority and discretion to control the Plan's assets, except to the extent that:

(a) the Plan expressly provides that the trustees are subject to the direction of a Named Fiduciary who is not a trustee, in which case the trustees will be subject to the proper directions of such other Named Fiduciary

---

[63] See ERISA § 3(21)(A). The definition also explicitly excepts from status as a Fiduciary a registered investment company and its investment adviser and principal underwriter (except insofar as any of them maintain Plans for their own employees), in instances where money or other property of a Plan is invested in the registered investment company; *ibid.*, § 3(21)(B). Additionally, a Plan may provide that "any person or group of persons may serve in more than one fiduciary capacity with respect to the Plan": *ibid.*, § 402(c)(1).

[64] ERISA § 402(a)(1).

[65] *ibid.*, § 402(a)(2).

[66] *ibid.*, § 402(a).

[67] *ibid.*, § 403(a).

made in accordance with the Plan's terms and not contrary to ERISA; or

(b) authority to manage, acquire, or dispose of the Fund's assets is delegated to one or more investment managers.[68]

10–018 The term "investment manager" is defined to include any Fiduciary:

(a) that has the power to manage, acquire, or dispose of any asset of a Plan;

(b) that:

  (i) is registered as an investment adviser under the Advisers Act;
  (ii) is a state-registered investment adviser meeting certain conditions;
  (iii) is a bank; or
  (iv) is an insurance company qualified under the laws of at least two states to manage, acquire, or dispose of any asset of a Plan; and

(c) that has acknowledged in writing that it is a Fiduciary with respect to the Plan.[69]

Thus, fiduciary responsibilities of a Plan initially fall to its Named Fiduciaries, but Named Fiduciaries can appoint or otherwise engage others in various capacities. With each appointment or delegation of authority, however, the appointee or delegatee becomes a Fiduciary.

One other point merits notice: Regulations adopted under ERISA by the US Department of Labor (the "DOL") require that the indicia of ownership of any assets of any Plan be maintained within the jurisdiction of US district courts.[70] Generally, plans investing in foreign property comply with this rule by "either bring[ing] the actual indicia of ownership (*e.g.*, stock certificate, bond, property title, or currency) back to the United States, or arrang[ing] for such indicia of ownership to be maintained by certain entities that are subject to the jurisdiction of the US district courts".[71]

"Plan assets"

10–019 "Integral to ERISA's requirements is an understanding of the concept of plan assets. Preservation of plan assets is an underlying theme of the statute".[72] The discussion above indicates that persons with discretion over "plan assets" are considered Plan Fiduciaries. Therefore, one must under-

---

[68] ERISA § 403(a).
[69] *ibid.*, § 3(38).
[70] See Labor Reg. § 2550.404b-1(a).
[71] Susan P. Serota, "Overview of ERISA Fiduciary Law", in *ERISA Fiduciary Law* 9 (Susan P. Serota ed. 1995), p.16 [hereinafter cited as Serota, Overview].
[72] *ibid.*

stand when assets are considered "plan assets". The DOL describes "plan assets" in Regulation 2510.3-101 as follows:

> Generally, when a plan invests in another entity, the plan's assets include its investment, but do not, solely by reason of such investment, include any of the underlying assets of the entity. However, in the case of a plan's investment in an equity interest of an entity that is neither a publicly-offered security nor a security issued by an investment company registered under the Investment Company Act of 1940 its assets include both the equity interest and an undivided interest in each of the underlying assets of the entity, unless it is established that—
>
> (i)   The entity is an operating company, or
> (ii) Equity participation in the entity by benefit plan investors is not significant.
>
> Therefore, any person who exercises authority or control respecting the management or disposition of such underlying assets, and any person who provides investment advice with respect to such assets for a fee (direct or indirect), is a fiduciary of the investing plan".[73]

The Regulation, however, also explains what constitutes "significant" equity participation: "Equity participation in an entity by benefit plan investors is 'significant' on any date if, immediately after the most recent acquisition of any equity interest in the entity, 25 percent or more of the value of any class of equity interests in the entity is held by benefit plan investors".[74] For this purpose, the term "benefit plan investors" includes:

> not only ERISA plans, but also IRAs [*i.e.*, individual retirement accounts], other qualified plans that may not be subject to ERISA (such as a plan covering only self-employed persons [and] state and local benefit plans excluded from coverage under ERISA), and even foreign pension plans. Benefit plan investors also include any entity whose underlying assets include plan assets by reason of a plan's investment in such entity.[75]

---

[73] Labor Reg. § 2510.3-101(a)(2). The Regulation goes on to provide exceptions for investments by a Plan in entities meeting conditions for classification as "venture capital operating companies" or "real estate operating companies"; *ibid.*, § 2510.3-101(d), (e).

[74] *ibid.* § 2510.3-101(f)(1). The Regulation continues: "For purposes of determinations pursuant to this paragraph (f), the value of any equity interests held by a person (other than a benefit plan investor) who has discretionary authority or control with respect to the assets of the entity or any person who provides investment advice for a fee (direct or indirect) to with respect to such assets, or any affiliate of such a person, shall be disregarded".

[75] Serota, Overview, above, para.10–018, n.71, p.18; see also Labor Reg. 2510.3-101(f)(2).

Thus, the Regulation essentially creates a system of "look-throughs" to determine whether assets are "plan assets": If 25 percent or more of any class of equity interests in a collective investment vehicle (other than a registered investment company) is beneficially owned by Plans, then the assets of the collective investment vehicle themselves constitute "plan assets." Such collective investment vehicle would then itself become a benefit plan investor, and its investment in any other collective investment vehicle would be counted toward the latter's own less-than-25 percent limit.

10–020   Often, collective investment vehicles simply decide not to allow benefit plan investors to hold 25 percent or more of any class of their outstanding equity securities. Assuming all other regulatory requirements are satisfied, this strategy precludes the collective investment vehicle from holding "plan assets" and keeps such vehicle and its affiliates (typically including its investment adviser) from being considered Fiduciaries with respect to assets of the Plans investing in the vehicle and from having to adhere to all of the fiduciary duties otherwise imposed by ERISA.

Section 404(a) and fiduciary duties under ERISA

10–021   Section 404(a) imposes fiduciary duties on Fiduciaries. Specifically, it requires that a Fiduciary discharge its duties with respect to its Plan "solely in the interest of the participants and beneficiaries" and:

> "(A) for the exclusive purpose of:
>
> > (i)   providing benefits to participants and their beneficiaries; and
> > (ii) defraying reasonable expenses of administering the plan;
>
> (B)   with the care, skill, prudence, and diligence under the circumstances then prevailing that a prudent man acting in a like capacity and familiar with such matters would use in the conduct of an enterprise of a like character and with like aims;
> (C)   by diversifying the investments of the plan so as to minimise the risk of large losses, unless under the circumstances it is clearly prudent not to do so; and
> (D)   in accordance with the documents and instruments governing the plan insofar as such documents and instruments are consistent with the provisions of [ERISA]."[76]

Each of these fiduciary duties will be discussed briefly below. It is worthwhile to note, however, that while these fiduciary duties largely parallel the

---

[76] ERISA § 404(a)(1).

FIDUCIARY DUTIES UNDER ERISA

duties of trustees under state common law of trusts, Congress has modified the basic common law to further its policies under ERISA.[77]

"Solely in the interest"/"exclusive purpose"

The duty that a Fiduciary investing the assets of a Plan act "solely in the **10–022** interest" of the Plan's participants and beneficiaries and for the "exclusive purpose" of providing benefits and defraying reasonable expenses of the Plan "codifies the common law requirement that a trustee act with undivided loyalty to the beneficiaries".[78] A Fiduciary would violate this duty of loyalty if it were to invest the Plan's assets so as to advance the Fiduciary's own interests (or those of others, *e.g.* friends, clients, affiliates, etc.) to the detriment of those of the Plan's participants and beneficiaries—regardless of whether the Fiduciary's intent is good or evil, honest or dishonest.[79] Case law and a DOL opinion, however, permit a Fiduciary to derive ancillary benefit from investments or transactions with assets of the Plan so long as the Fiduciary "reasonably conclude[s] after a careful and impartial investigation that the actions best promote the interests of the participants and beneficiaries" of the Plan.[80]

---

[77] See *Eaves v Penn*, 587 F.2d 453, 457 (10th Cir. 1978): "The above provisions [in ERISA § 404(a)] embody a carefully tailored law of trusts, including the familiar requirements of undivided loyalty to beneficiaries, the prudent man rule, the rule requiring diversification of investments and the requirement that fiduciaries comply with the provisions of plan documents to the extent that they are not inconsistent with [ERISA]."; Lee H. Robinson, "Investment Management by Fiduciaries", in *ERISA Fiduciary Law 117* (Susan P. Serota ed. 1995), p.121 [hereinafter Robinson, *Fiduciaries*]: "[F]iduciary standards [adapted from the common law of trusts] are to be interpreted bearing in mind the special nature and purpose of employee benefit plans. . . . [J]udges enforcing ERISA must be guided not only by the principles of trust law, but also by Congress' departure from the absolute common law rule against fiduciaries' dual loyalties.". But see *ibid.*, at p.122: "Nevertheless, some courts have indicated that ERISA fiduciaries will generally be judged by a higher standard than existed under common law" (emphasis added) (citing *Donovan v Mazzola*, 716 F.2d 1226, 1231–32 (9th Cir. 1984)).

[78] Robinson, *Fiduciaries*, above, para.10–021, n.77, p.118.

[79] *ibid.*, pp.118–19.

[80] *ibid.*, pp.119; see also *Donovan v Bierwirth*, 680 F.2d 263 (2d Cir. 1982): "Although officers of a corporation who are trustees of its pension plan do not violate their duties as trustees by taking action which, after careful and impartial investigation, they reasonably conclude best to promote the interests of participants and beneficiaries simply because it incidentally benefits the corporation or, indeed, themselves, their decisions must be made with an eye single to the interests of the participants and beneficiaries."; *Bussian v RJR* Nabisco, Inc. 223 F.3d 286 (5th Cir. 2000) (citing *Donovan v Bierwirth*); Ralph Katz, DOL Adv. Op. 85–036A (October 23, 1985): "[I]t would not be inconsistent with the requirements of sections 403(c) and 404 of ERISA for plan fiduciaries to select an investment course of action that reflects non-economic factors [from the standpoint of the Plan], so long as application of such factors follows primary consideration of a broad range of investment opportunities that are, economically, equally advantageous."

279

The "prudent man" test

10–023 The duty to act with the utmost "care, skill, prudence, and diligence"[81] similarly codifies the "prudent man" standard of the common law of trusts, although adaptation to the realm of ERISA allows a Fiduciary of a Plan to invest the Plan's assets in stock of the employee-sponsor of the Plan even though such action would likely be precluded under trust law because of the conflict of interest between the Plan's sponsor and its participants and beneficiaries.[82]

As mentioned above,[83] Section 403(a) vests Plan trustees (who are Fiduciaries) with "exclusive authority and discretion to manage and control the assets of the plan". Section 403(a)(2), however, provides that trustees may delegate management of the Plan's assets to professional investment managers (who are also themselves Fiduciaries) appointed by the Named Fiduciary. The benefit to trustees of the appointment of professional investment managers is that, under Section 405(d), the trustees are no longer responsible (or liable) for the investment of the Plan's assets.[84] This is important because "[i]t is now well established that nonprofessional trustees are held to the same standards as professional investors when measuring the prudence of an investment or investment course of action".[85] Of course, the Named Fiduciary is itself subject to the prudent man standard in selecting investment managers and in monitoring their performance, and the Named Fiduciary and the trustees remain responsible (and liable) for decisions regarding the determination of the investment objectives, guidelines, and restrictions to which the investment managers must adhere.[86]

Irrespective of whether a Plan's assets are being managed by the Plan's trustees or professional investment managers, the Fiduciaries managing the assets are subject to the prudent man standard. In Regulations, the DOL has established a "safe harbour" whereby the Fiduciary will be automatically deemed to be investing in accordance with the prudent man standard if such Fiduciary:

> "(i) Has given appropriate consideration to those facts and circumstances that, given the scope of such fiduciary's investment duties, the fiduciary knows or should know are relevant to the particular investment or investment course of action involved, including the role the investment or investment course of action plays in that

---

[81] ERISA § 404(a)(1)(B).

[82] *ibid.* § 408(c)(3).

[83] See above, para.10–017, n.67.

[84] ERISA § 405(d)(1): "[N]o trustee shall be liable for the acts or omissions of [the] investment manager or managers, or be under an obligation to invest or otherwise manage any asset of the plan which is subject to the management of such investment manager."

[85] Robinson, *Fiduciaries*, at 2003 Cum. Supp. 102, above para.10–021, n.77.

[86] *ibid.* p.123.

portion of the plan's investment portfolio with respect to which the fiduciary has investment duties; and

(ii) Has acted accordingly."[87]

The Regulation proceeds to set forth a non-exclusive list of factors to be considered by the Fiduciary, including a determination that the investment will further the Plan's objectives, the risk of loss and the opportunity for gain associated with the investment, the diversification of the portfolio, the liquidity and current return of the portfolio relative to the Plan's anticipated cash flow requirements, and the projected return of the portfolio relative to the Plan's funding objectives.

Diversification

Like the "solely in the interest"/"exclusive purpose" and "prudent man" tests, **10–024** the duty to diversify investments to minimise the risk of large losses represents the codification of the common law of trusts. Determining whether a Plan's investments are sufficiently diversified requires a facts-and-circumstances analysis, and factors to consider in such an analysis include the Plan's purposes, the amount of the Plan's assets, general financial and industrial conditions, types of investment vehicles, diversification across geographical location and industry, and maturity dates (if any) of securities in the portfolio.[88] Congress's addition of the words "unless under the circumstances it is clearly prudent not to do so" at the end of its statement of the diversification duty in Section 404(a)(1)(C) constitutes a modification of the common law of trusts. The result is that "in an action for plan losses based on breach of the diversification requirement, the plaintiff's initial burden will be to demonstrate that there has been a failure to diversify. The defendant then is to have the burden of demonstrating that this failure to diversify was prudent".[89]

Compliance with plan documents

Finally, the duty to invest in accordance with Plan documents insofar as such **10–025** documents are consistent with ERISA is a codification of "the common law rule that fiduciaries must comply with the governing plan documents to the extent that it is legal to do so".[90] A Fiduciary, therefore, must obtain, read, and understand the governing documents of the Plan in order to comply with

---

[87] Labor Reg. § 2550.404a-1(b)(1).
[88] Robinson, *Fiduciaries*, above, para.10–021, n.77, p.133.
[89] H.R. Conf. Rep. No. 1280, 93d Cong., 2d Sess. 304 (1974), reprinted in 1974 U.S.C.C.A.N. 5038, 5084.
[90] Robinson, *Fiduciaries*, above, para.10–021, n.77, p.135 (citing *Eaves*, 587 F.2d at 457).

its fiduciary duty.[91] Although ERISA provides no definition of "plan documents", the trust agreement, the plan instrument (as described in Section 402(a)[92]), and any investment management agreement with a professional investment manager would be considered plan documents.[93]

Liability for breach of fiduciary duty

10–026 Section 409 provides that a Fiduciary found to have breached its fiduciary duty is personally liable for losses to the Plan resulting from the breach, and such Fiduciary must restore to the Plan any profit of the Fiduciary resulting from its use of the Plan's assets.[94] Section 409 also permits a court to enter against a Fiduciary that has breached its fiduciary duty "such other equitable or remedial relief as the court may deem appropriate, including removal of such fiduciary".[95]

In certain circumstances, a Fiduciary with respect to a Plan can also be held liable for breaches of fiduciary duty by *another* Fiduciary with respect to such Plan. Specifically, Section 405(a) states:

> "in addition to any liability which he may have under any other provision of this part, a fiduciary with respect to a plan shall be liable for a breach of fiduciary responsibility of another fiduciary with respect to the same plan in the following circumstances:
>
> (1) if he participates knowingly in, or knowingly undertakes to conceal, an act or omission of such other fiduciary, knowing such act or omission is a breach;
>
> (2) if, by his failure to comply with section 404(a)(1) [the section providing for the four types of fiduciary duties imposed by ERISA[96]] in the administration of his specific responsibilities which give rise to his status as a fiduciary, he has enabled such other fiduciary to commit a breach; or
>
> (3) If he has knowledge of a breach by such other fiduciary, unless he makes reasonable efforts under the circumstances to remedy the breach."[97]

---

[91] Robinson, *Fiduciaries*, above, para.10–021, n.77, p.135 (citing Eaves, 587 F.2d at 457).
[92] See above, para.10–017.
[93] Robinson, *Fiduciaries*, above, para.10–021, n.77, pp.135–136.
[94] See ERISA § 409.
[95] *ibid.*
[96] See above, para.10–021, n.76.
[97] ERISA § 405(a).

Fiduciary Duties Under the State Law of Business Entities

As described above,[98] business corporations, partnerships, limited liability **10–027** companies, and business trusts are, as a practical matter, creatures of state law, and state statutes typically establish the framework for due formation and legal operation of business entities. Despite the existence of various statutes governing the different types of business entities, notions of fiduciary duty are often analogous. Therefore, for purposes of simplification, the present discussion will be limited to fiduciary duty in the corporate context, focusing on the duties of directors and officers.

By their very nature, the positions of director and officer bestow upon their holders duties with respect to the management of corporate affairs and the custody and use of corporate assets.[99] Furthermore,

> "[t]he directors and officers of a corporation in charge of its management are, in the performance of their official duties, under obligations of trust and confidence to the corporation or its stockholders and must act in good faith and for the interests of the corporation or its stockholders, and within the scope of their authority."[1]

Additionally, because it is generally accepted that the relationship of directors and officers to the corporation and its shareholders is fiduciary in nature, directors and officers are:

> "required to act in the utmost good faith, and in accepting the office [of director or officer], they impliedly undertake to give to the [corporation] the benefit of their care and best judgment and to exercise the powers conferred solely in the interest of the corporation or the stockholders as a body or corporate entity, and not for their own personal interests.[2]

Thus, "fiduciary duties" are imposed on directors and officers, and directors and officers may be held liable for breaches of their duties, even in the absence of bad faith, dishonesty, or injury to the corporation's shareholders.[3] The two primary fiduciary duties of directors and officers are the "duty of care" and the "duty of loyalty", both of which are discussed briefly below.

Fiduciary duties are similarly imposed on individuals or groups owning a majority of the outstanding stock of a corporation. Such majority stockholders, simply by voting their stock, can elect the corporation's directors and can effectively "control and direct the action of the corporation" in every

---

[98] See above, para.10–002, n.7 and accompanying text.
[99] See 18B Am. Jur. 2d Corporations § 1684 (1985).
[1] *ibid.* (footnotes omitted).
[2] *ibid.* (footnote omitted).
[3] *ibid.*

way.[4] Even though minority stockholders may receive notice of the times and places of meetings of directors and meetings of stockholders, it is the majority stockholders who "determine the policy to be pursued and manage and direct the corporation's affairs, and the minority must submit to their judgment so long as the majority act in good faith and within the limitation of the law".[5] Thus, the corporate law of nearly every state considers individual controlling shareholders and groups of shareholders "acting together to exercise control" fiduciaries of the corporation, of minority shareholders, and, if present, of other majority shareholders.[6] Such fiduciary duties of majority shareholders are comparable to the fiduciary duties of directors and officers.[7]

Duty of care

10–028 One of the two primary fiduciary duties of directors and officers is the duty of care. The duty of care encompasses several related concepts. It requires that directors use due care and be diligent in managing and administering corporate affairs and in using and preserving corporate assets.[8] Additionally, directors must exercise ordinary skill in the conduct of their duties and act with reasonable intelligence.[9]

In any given situation, whether a director or officer has exercised due care is a fact-intensive inquiry; there is no specific standard that can be applied because certain behavior in one set of circumstances may exhibit due care but, in another set of circumstances, the same behavior may not.[10] As a result, it is often said that a director or officer must exercise "ordinary care", *i.e.* "such care as a prudent man should exercise in like circumstances and charged with a like duty".[11]

Because there could be unfortunate or unprofitable results from a decision made after the exercise of due care, reasonable diligence, and good faith and because courts are reluctant to second-guess the decisions of corporate directors and officers in the context of litigation years after such decisions are made, the "business judgment rule" has been developed as a critical part of state corporate law.[12] The business judgment rule generally provides that corporate transactions free of self-dealing or other personal interest will not be judicially voided or enjoined on the grounds that the directors failed to perform their duties satisfactorily. Under the business judgment rule, directors will not be found liable for damages resulting from the transaction, unless the

---

[4] 18A Am. Jur. 2d Corporations § 762 (1985).
[5] *ibid.* (footnotes omitted).
[6] *ibid.*
[7] *ibid.*
[8] See 18B Am. Jur. 2d Corporations § 1695 (1985).
[9] *ibid.*
[10] *ibid.*, § 1696.
[11] *ibid.*
[12] *ibid.*, §§ 1704–1705.

directors: (i) failed to exercise due care; (ii) authorised the transaction despite the fact that they did not reasonably believe (or could not have reasonably believed) that the transaction was in the best interests of the corporation; or (iii) did not act in good faith.[13]

Duty of loyalty

The other primary fiduciary duty of directors and officers is the duty of loyalty. This duty requires that a director or officer must act at all times in the best interests of the corporation and its shareholders; in doing so, the director or officer must remain personally uncompromised by monetary gain.[14] A director's or officer's responsibility as a fiduciary "is not limited to a proper regard for the tangible balance sheet assets of the corporation, but includes the dedication of his uncorrupted business judgment for the sole benefit of the corporation in any dealings which may adversely affect it".[15] Indeed, the duty of loyalty continues to apply in full force to directors or officers of a corporation serving also as directors or officers of a subsidiary of a corporation.[16]   **10–029**

The duty of loyalty does not, however, legally prevent a director or officer from being involved with business transactions independent from, even if similar to, those of the corporation, so long as the director or officer acts in good faith and does not obstruct the corporation's own business.[17] Additionally, transactions between a director or officer and the corporation are generally not prohibited outright, but a director or officer who personally enters such a transaction has a "heavy burden" when demonstrating that he has not breached his duty of loyalty.[18] Of course, a director or officer can neither engage in a business competing with the corporation nor "divert to himself business opportunities in which the corporation has an interest or expectancy."[19]

Additional Obligations of Boards of Directors Under the ICA

In 1935, Congress commissioned the SEC to conduct a study and prepare reports for it on the state of the investment management industry.[20] The SEC did so and recommended that Congress address abuses by industry actors   **10–030**

---

[13] *ibid.*, § 1703.
[14] *ibid.*, § 1711.
[15] *ibid.*
[16] *ibid.*
[17] *ibid.*
[18] *ibid.*
[19] *ibid.* (footnote omitted).
[20] See ICA § 1(b).

US APPROACH TO FIDUCIARY DUTIES

that compromised the integrity of the industry and injured individual investors. Congress responded by enacting the ICA, which generally requires registration of investment companies[21] and limits the array of available investments for investment companies.[22] The ICA also, among other things, imposes additional regulation on both the structure and certain activities of boards of directors of investment companies[23] and additional duties and obligations on investment company directors beyond what is otherwise required by applicable state law.[24]

Composition of boards of directors and the qualifications of board members

10–031 Because investment companies are very often formed under the aegis of the investment adviser which will manage the assets of the investment company,[25]

---

[21] See ICA § 8. Certain investment companies may be exempt from registration if they meet the requirements of Section 6 of the ICA.

[22] *ibid.*, § 12.

[23] The ICA defines the term "investment company" to mean:

> any issuer which —
>
> (A) is or holds itself out as being engaged primarily, or proposes to engage primarily, in the business of investing, reinvesting, or trading in securities;
>
> (B) is engaged or proposes to engage in the business of issuing face-amount certificates of the installment type, or has been engaged in such business and has any such certificate outstanding; or
>
> (C) is engaged or proposes to engage in the business of investing, reinvesting, owning, holding, or trading in securities, and owns or proposes to acquire investment securities having a value exceeding 40 per centum of the value of such issuer's total assets . . . on an unconsolidated basis.

ICA § 3(a)(1). The ICA provides numerous specific exclusions from this definition. See generally *ibid.*, § 3(b)–(c). Among the most commonly encountered are the "private funds" exclusions in Section 3(c)(1) and 3(c)(7). Section 3(c)(1) excludes funds which are beneficially owned by no more than 100 persons and privately placed; Section 3(c)(7), adopted in 1996, excludes funds which are offered solely to "qualified purchasers" (*i.e.* individuals and entities with very high amounts of net worth) and privately placed.

[24] As noted above, para.10–002, business enterprises are typically organized under state law. In this respect, investment companies are no different from other business enterprises. *Kamen v Kemper Fin. Servs., Inc.*, 500 U.S. 90, 98 (1991): "The presumption that state law should be incorporated into federal common law is particularly strong in areas in which private parties have entered legal relationships with the expectation that their rights and obligations would be governed by state-law standards. Corporation law is one such area." (citations omitted); *Burks v Lasker*, 441 U.S. 471, 478–79 (1979): "'Corporations are creatures of state law,' and it is state law which is the font of corporate directors' powers. . . . Federal regulation of investment companies and advisers is not fundamentally different in this respect. [Investment companies], like other corporations, are incorporated pursuant to state, not federal, law. . . . The ICA does not purport to be the source of authority for managerial power; rather, the Act functions primarily to 'impos[e] *controls and restrictions* on the internal management of investment companies.'" (emphasis in original) (citations omitted).

[25] See *Kamen*, 500 U.S. at 93 (noting that investment companies "typically are organized and underwritten by the same firm that serves as the company's 'investment adviser'").

286

Congress sought to provide a measure of independent oversight over the general management of the investment company. To do this, Congress included Section 10(a) in the ICA. Section 10(a) straightforwardly declares, "No registered investment company shall have a board of directors more than 60 per centum of the members of which are persons who are interested persons of such registered investment company".[26] The operative term in Section 10(a) is "interested person", which is intricately defined with respect to an investment company in Section 2(a)(19)(A) to include the following:

"(i)   any affiliated person[27] of such company,

(ii)   any member of the immediate family of any natural person who is an affiliated person of such company,

(iii)   any interested person of any investment adviser[28] of or principal underwriter for such company,

(iv)   any person or partner or employee of any person who at any time since the beginning of the last two completed fiscal years of such company has acted as legal counsel for such company,

(v)   any person or any affiliated person of a person (other than a registered investment company) that, at any time during the 6-month period preceding the date of the determination of whether that person or affiliated person is an interested person, has executed any portfolio transactions for, engaged in any principal transactions with, or distributed shares for—

(I)   the investment company;

(II)   any other investment company having the same investment adviser as such investment company or holding itself out to investors as a related company for purposes of investment or investor services; or

(III) any account over which the investment company's investment adviser has brokerage placement discretion,

---

[26] ICA § 10(a).

[27] For purposes of the ICA, "affiliated person" means: "(A) any person directly or indirectly owning, controlling, or holding with power to vote, 5 per centum or more of the outstanding voting securities of such other person; (B) any person 5 per centum or more of whose outstanding voting securities are directly or indirectly owned, controlled, or held with power to vote, by such other person; (C) any person directly or indirectly controlling, controlled by, or under common control with, such other person; (D) any officer, director, partner, copartner, or employee of such other person; (E) if such other person is an investment company, any investment adviser thereof or any member of an advisory board thereof; and (F) if such other person is an unincorporated investment company not having a board of directors, the depositor thereof"; ICA § 2(a)(3).

[28] The definition of the term "interested person" with respect to an investment adviser is in most respects parallel to the definition of the term with respect to an investment company. See ICA § 2(a)(19)(B).

(vi) any person or any affiliated person of a person (other than a registered investment company) that, at any time during the 6-month period preceding the date of the determination of whether that person or affiliated person is an interested person, has loaned money or other property to —

(I) the investment company;

(II) any other investment company having the same investment adviser as such investment company or holding itself out to investors as a related company for purposes of investment or investor services; or

(III) any account for which the investment company's investment adviser has borrowing authority, [or]

(vii) any natural person whom the Commission by order shall have determined to be an interested person by reason of having had, at any time since the beginning of the last two completed fiscal years of such company, a material business or professional relationship with such company or with the principal executive officer of such company or with any other investment company having the same investment adviser or principal underwriter or with the principal executive officer of such other investment company:

Provided, That no person shall be deemed to be an interested person of an investment company solely by reason of (aa) his being a member of its board of directors or advisory board or an owner of its securities, or (bb) his membership in the immediate family of any person specified in clause (aa) of this proviso".[29]

In addition to mandating that at least 40 percent of the directors of an investment company not be interested persons, the ICA also contains provisions governing the election of directors. Section 16(a) generally requires that directors be elected by shareholders. It does, however, permit directors to fill vacancies in their number without requiring a shareholder vote, so long as at least two-thirds of the sitting directors after the appointment of any director were elected by shareholder vote. Section 9(a) prohibits the election or appointment of any person as a director if that person has been either convicted, within the previous 10 years, of any of certain felonies or misdemeanours arising out of securities, commodities, or banking transactions or permanently or temporarily enjoined from acting in any of a number of capacities in the securities, commodities, or banking industries, including the capacities of broker, dealer, and investment adviser.

---

[29] ICA § 2(a)(19)(A).

Section 36(a)

Section 36(a) of the ICA expressly authorises the SEC to institute suits in federal court against a registered investment company's directors and officers,[30] for any act or practice in which the director or officer either has engaged in the last five years or is about to engage, which constitutes "breach of fiduciary duty involving personal misconduct in respect of a registered investment company".[31] The ICA bestows upon courts the same broad injunctive powers in remedying such breaches of fiduciary duties by directors and officers as are bestowed with respect to the breaches by an investment company's investment adviser, *viz.*, the temporary or permanent injunction of directors and officers from positions as directors, officers, investment advisers, etc. and the right to craft such relief "as may be reasonable and appropriate in the circumstances".[32]

10–032

Duties regarding the advisory contract with the investment adviser

Contracts between registered investment companies and their investment advisers must be in writing. The contracts must precisely describe the compensation to be paid to the investment adviser; initially have a term no longer than two years (and must thereafter be subject to annual renewal by the registered investment company's board of directors or the vote of its shareholders); provide for termination at any time, on no more than 60 days notice to the investment adviser and without penalty to the registered investment company, either by the board of directors or by vote of the shareholders; and provide for automatic termination in the event of its assignment.[33] Additionally, when initially entering into the contract or when subsequently renewing it, a majority of the non-interested directors must vote to approve the contract at a meeting called for the specific purpose of voting on such approval.[34] Moreover, Section 15(c) of the ICA imposes on directors the duty to request and evaluate such information from the investment adviser as may be reasonably necessary to evaluate the terms of the contract.[35]

10–033

---

[30] And, among others, investment advisers; *ibid.*, § 36(a). See above, paras 10–014—10–015.
[31] ICA § 36(a).
[32] *ibid.*
[33] *ibid.*, § 15(a).
[34] *ibid.*, § 15(c).
[35] Section 15(c) also imposes on the investment adviser the duty to furnish such information to the directors.

Some other obligations of directors

10–034 Despite the fact that boards of directors delegate investment management authority to investment advisers pursuant to advisory contracts, boards of directors remain ultimately responsible for the overall management of the investment company and its compliance with applicable laws and regulations. Therefore, directors must maintain continual oversight over the activities of the investment adviser to make certain, for example, that the general investment restrictions applicable to all registered investment companies[36] and the specific investment policies of the directors' investment company[37] are respected.

Generally, the non-interested directors, subject to subsequent ratification by shareholders, must also appoint the independent accountants for the investment company.[38] The expertise of such independent accountants is, in turn, useful to the directors in meeting the directors' own duty to value accurately securities owned by the investment company.[39]

---

[36] See generally *ibid.*, § 12.
[37] Changes in a registered investment company's investment policies must be authorised by vote of its shareholders. See ICA § 13.
[38] *ibid.*, § 32(a).
[39] *ibid.*, § 2(a)(41).

CHAPTER 11

DEVELOPMENTS IN INVESTMENT MANAGEMENT ACCOUNTABILITY—BENCHMARKS, PERFORMANCE TARGETS AND INTERNAL CONTROLS

Helen Parry, London Metropolitan University and Duncan Black, Dechert LLP, London

"The shape of asset management has been changing substantially. Corporate power has moved very significantly over the past twenty years from the management of the company to the institutional investor. Equally significant is very open competition for the management of funds. End investors are more likely to change mandates for management of funds in the light of performance against agreed benchmarks and the insidious extension of liability for professional negligence under judge made law leaves fund managers open to claims where funds under management do not perform according to benchmarks especially if the agreed investment strategies are not scrupulously followed."[1]

The Case of Unilever and Mercury Asset Management

Introduction

When the news first broke of the impending court action for breach of contract being brought by Unilever against Mercury Asset Management ("MAM"),[2] many in the city were gloomily predicting that it would be the first in an avalanche of lawsuits that would brought by disgruntled trustees unhappy with their investment managers' performance.

11–001

---

[1] Bob McDowall, "Investor relations—a growing concern?", *www.it-director.com* March 15, 2003.
[2] By the time the case came to court Mercury had been taken over by Merrill Lynch and the defendant named in the claim was Merrill Lynch Investment Managers.

Many were rather startled by the fact that the parties had failed to resolve the situation through mediation and had felt compelled to seek resolution in the courts thereby provoking considerable media interest.

Throughout the period of the trial, the business press was breathless with reports of this unholy catfight between the two women at the centre of the dispute: Carole Galley, the star investment manager at MAM, dubbed "the Ice Maiden", and Wendy Mayall, the chief investment officer at Unilever. It seemed at times that there was more interest in the contents of Ms Galley's wardrobe and jewellery box, than they were in the internal systems and controls in place at MAM.[3]

The performance target

11–002 MAM had been investment manager to a sizeable portfolio of Unilever's £4 billion Superannuation Fund (the "Fund") since 1987. In January 1997 a revised contract was entered into for the management of the portfolio, with new investment objectives and guidelines. Performance was linked to a benchmark made up of a composite of market indices. The objective was to outperform the benchmark by 1 per cent over three years, and the agreement stated that "In normal circumstances the return will be expected to be no more than 3 per cent below the benchmark in any period of four successive quarters."

In the context of peer group benchmarking, the intended 1 per cent outperformance return would place MAM in the upper quartile of its peer group, while 3 per cent underperformance would put it in the bottom group.[4]

The dispute arose when MAM failed to fulfil its performance target, and, instead of sitting comfortably near the top of the investment management league tables, actually found itself scraping along the bottom. In particular, there was significant underperformance in the UK Equity component of the portfolio, managed by Alistair Lennard, against the FTSE All Share Index.

11–003 The FTSE All-Share is a capitalisation weighted index[5] which represents 98–99 per cent of UK market capitalisation and is the aggregate of the FTSE 100, FTSE 250 and FTSE Small cap Indices.[6] It was reported that in 1997 and early 1998, instead of outperforming the FTSE All Share Index, the UK

---

[3] Carol Galley was known as the "Ice Maiden" because of her reputation for being rather harsh with underperforming chief executives, ousting Sir Rocco Forte as head of his family hotels group: "'Here sit those two,' said the Ice Maiden. 'Many a chamois have I crushed. Millions of Alpine roses have I snapped and broken off; not a root have I spared. I know them all, and their thoughts, those spirits of strength!' and again she laughed. 'Here rolls another avalanche,' said those in the valley.'" *The Ice Maiden*, Hans Christian Andersen.

[4] Market Monitor, "Unilever's war drags on", *www.euromony.com*, December 2001.

[5] Most indices weight companies on market capitalisation. If a company's market capitalisation is £1,000,000 and the value of all the stocks in the index is £100,000,000, the company would be worth 1% of the index.

equity portfolio was the worst performer among 1600 UK funds.[7] The FTSE index had made exceptional gains at this time and critically had a weighting of 60 per cent of the composite benchmark which was based on US and UK shares.[8] Specifically, the FTSE All Share Index rose by 31 per cent per year during the period in question, whereas the portfolio rose by only 20.6 per cent.[9] Unilever claimed damages of £110 million; which was the extra amount that would have been earned if MAM had passively tracked the index.

The Investment management agreement

The investment management agreement between Unilever and MAM pro- **11–004** vided that, in carrying out its duties, MAM should comply with the terms of the agreement including the specific restrictions set out in the Investment Guidelines and Annexes attached to the agreement. There was no absolute guarantee that the downside tolerance would not be exceeded, but it was agreed that MAM had to exercise the highest standards of care and expertise in carrying its obligations under the agreement. This extended to an obligation to use the highest standards of care in managing the assets with the object of achieving the target return and not breaching the downside tolerance, and contrasts with the more usual formula of "reasonable" care and skill (See Chapter 2, qualified duties, para.2–018, *et seq.*).[10]

The claim: too many eggs in the wrong basket

Unilever alleged that MAM had failed to structure the portfolio consistently **11–005** with Unilever's investment objectives, in that the portfolio was highly concentrated, unbalanced and not properly diversified so as to limit the risk of underperformance. In particular it was alleged that the UK equities fund sector, which accounted for 60 per cent of the £1 billion portfolio managed by MAM was concentrated in too few stocks, with a disproportionate exposure to certain sectors and under-representation in others. Furthermore, the UK

---

[6] The FTSE 100 is comprised of the 100 highest capitalised blue chip companies representing approximately 80% of the UK market. The FTSE 250 is comprised of mid-capitalised companies not covered by the FTSE 100, representing 18% of UK market capitalisation. The FTSE Small Cap is comprised of companies with the smallest capitalisation.

[7] "The Ice Maiden keeps her cool under fire" The Telegraph-online, November 6, 2001.

[8] "Financial Services: suing fund managers", Cameron McKenna Law-Now archive, January 22, 2003.

[9] "MAM sued over Unilever pension", *Independent* online, October 16, 2001.

[10] See also Christa Band, "Negligence actions against fund managers" *In-House Lawyer*, February 2002.

equities fund was underweight in big stocks. Companies worth less than £400 million[11] accounted for eight of the 39 holdings in its portfolio.[12]

It was further claimed that MAM had disregarded controls on investment which had been portrayed as being mandatory while being treated in practice as discretionary.[13] It was further claimed that Mr Lennard ignored MAM's investment policies and that nobody stopped him. An expert witness called by Unilever provided in written evidence released by the judge that "there was little, if any, evidence of responsible and controlling management by more senior executives in MAM".[14]

Pitch and switch

11–006 It was further claimed that Carol Galley at MAM, while representing that she would be looking after the account herself, had in fact handed it over to Mr Lennard, a junior colleague, and that for two years did not disclose this fact to Unilever—a case of so called "pitch and switch".

In order to win a case in such circumstances, a plaintiff would need to prove that a breach of the terms of the contract caused the loss. In this case the damages were claimed to be the difference between the level of return achieved by the fund and that which would have been achieved had the fund been managed to the high standard allegedly required.

Problems with the portfolio

11–007 The critical decision appears to have been taken in 1995 when it was alleged that Mr Lennard sold out all of the banking stocks and concentrated the fund into UK property and industrial and construction stocks. Other investment managers had preferred banking, pharmaceuticals and insurers.[15]

Market conditions played a significant part in the problem with Lennard's investment strategy.

1997 saw a significant rise of the dollar and pound sterling against the mark.[16] This had a negative effect on the price of the industrials into which Lennard had placed 45 per cent of the UK equity fund. At the same time, he had taken the wrong view on the banking sector which he is reported to have seen as overvalued. The dotcom bubble was in full swing and would continue

---

[11] "MAM sued over Unilever pension", *Independent* online, October 16, 2001.
[12] "Galley Battles Unilever court storm", *Evening Standard*, November 9, 2001.
[13] "Unilever v Merrill Lynch", Take Stock Nicholson Graham Jones, May 2002.
[14] "Expert says Mercury Chiefs lost control", *www.telegraph.co.uk*, November 30, 2001.
[15] "Unilever goes to court over pensions", BBC online, October 15, 2001.
[16] "International Capital Markets: Developments prospects and Key Policy Issues", IMF, September 1997.

to rise steeply for the next few years and banking shares did particularly well during this time. Other factors were the addition of new banking shares into the FTSE All-Share Index caused by demutualisations in the building society sector, including Alliance and Leicester, the Woolwich and the Halifax.[17]

MAM's defence

MAM's main defence was to claim that Unilever was aware of the strategy that they had adopted and that they had raised no objections.[18] Carole Galley alleged that Ms Mayall had failed to read the detailed documentation concerning MAM's investment strategy.[19] Mr Lennard further argued Unilever had actually proposed a draft agreement that would allow Mr Lennard to concentrate its equity portfolio in a smaller number of stocks. Up to the end of 1996 MAM had been allowed a maximum of 5 per cent of the portfolio in one company's shares, but Unilever considered changing this to 8 per cent which would have allowed MAM to hold just 12 stock lines in its stock portfolio.[20] Ms Galley argued that it was acceptable for Lennard to run a higher risk profile than his colleagues provided he was monitored and managed. She pointed out that investment management is about judgment and that one has sometimes to take on board more risks to outdo the pack.[21]

MAM claimed that Mr Lennard's approach was consistent with house style, and that this kind of strategy had allowed the Unilever fund to make an extra £126 million over the returns that would have been generated in the period between 1988 and 1995.

11–008

The settlement

According to press reports MAM settled the suit without accepting any liability and agreed to pay an amount which has been reported to be approximately £70 million. This has been seen by commentators, such as Professor John Coffee, as very favourable to Unilever, given that it amounts to more than 50 per cent of the claim.[22]

Since the Unilever case it has been reported that MAM has faced the threat of lawsuits from other clients such as Sainsburys, Astra Zeneca, the Co-op

11–009

---

[17] *Independent* online, November 4, 2001.
[18] *ibid.*
[19] Richard Nothedge, "Star turns take stage in £130million Unilever drama", *The Scotsman* online, November 11, 2001.
[20] "Lennard says portfolio risk levels were higher", *The Scotsman* online, November 15, 2002.
[21] Paul Armstrong, "Galley battles Unilever court storm", *Evening Standard*, November 9, 2001.
[22] James Paton, "Does litigation cross borders?", Reuters, December 6, 2001.

and Surrey County Council[23] and may have provided an undisclosed sum to Sainsbury's,[24] although Astra Zeneca is reported to have dropped its claim.[25]

Another development that may encourage more such claims against investment managers in the future is the fact that an insurance product is being marketed for trustees who take legal action against a third party.

The Legal Basis For Claims Against Investment Managers

Negligence suits arising from the collapse of Confederation Life—another case of too many eggs in one basket?

11–010 Although there have been no direct precedents involving pension fund trustees suing investment managers for failure to reach a benchmark performance target, and the *Unilever* case itself did not provide one, there are a number of cases involving issues related to liability for breach of contract, negligence and negligent misrepresentation in the financial services context which may be helpful in considering such potential liability.

There are cases featuring *inter alia* investment advisers and stockbrokers,[26] commodity brokers,[27] financial advisers for packaged products,[28] trustees,[29] valuers[30] and auditors.[31]

The two cases summarised below both resulted from the collapse of Confederation Life and illustrate the duties of an advisory investment manager, including in particular its duty to keep the client's portfolio under review and be proactive in initiating action where necessary.

Royal Court; Voisin v Matheson Securities

11–011 In *Royal Court; Voisin v Matheson Securities*,[32] a case which went to the Court of Appeal in Jersey, Matheson Securities were acting as investment

---

[23] "Pension fund sues Merrill—Council Staffs mismanaged £300 million", *www.forums. transanationale.org*, November 8, 2002.

[24] Jill Treanor, "Merrill stumps up to end Sainsbury pension fund row", *www.money.guardian. co.uk*, August 6, 2002.

[25] Patrick Tooher, "Atrazeneca abandons fund writ", *Mail on Sunday*, March 2, 2003.

[26] *Voisin v Matheson Securities (CI) Ltd*, (CA), Jer July 24, 2000, (1990–2000) 2 I.T.E.L.R. 907; *Dixon & Org v Jefferson Seal Ltd* 1997 J.L.R. 20.

[27] *Stafford and Comstock Ltd. v Conti Commodity Services Ltd.* [1981] 1 Lloyd's Rep. 466; *Merrill Lynch Futures Inc v York House Trading Court of Appeal* (1984) 81 L.S.G. 2544.

[28] *Primavera Allied Dunbar Assurance Plc* [2003] Lloyd's Rep. P.N. 14; *Loosemore v Financial Concepts* [2001] Lloyd's Rep. P.N. 235; *Investors Compensation Scheme Ltd v West Bromich Building Society (No.2)* [1999] Lloyd's Rep. P.N. 496; *Hale v Guildarch* [1999] P.N.L.R. 44.

[29] *Nestle v National Westminster Bank Plc* [2000] W.T.L.R. 795.

[30] *Banque Bruxelles Lambert SA v Eagle Star Insurance Co Ltd* [1995] Q.B. 375.

[31] Mark Milner, "Deloitte & Touche negligent in Barings audit" *Guardian*, June 12, 2003.

[32] 1999 J.L.R. 177.

advisers and stockbrokers to a private trust of which Michael Voisin was the main trustee. The investments were in corporate bonds, selected because the client had specified that he wanted a higher return on trust investments than could be obtained by using gilts. He was however risk adverse. A pattern emerged that the investments would be switched if problems arose.

Such a problem did arise with some Eurobonds issued by Confederation Life, a Canadian insurance company. At the time the bonds were bought the insurance company apparently had large assets and a high credit rating. However, later it emerged that the company's assets were less than they seemed and the credit rating of the bonds was downgraded.

Confederation Life had concentrated its assets in real estate throughout the 1980s and early 1990s. By 1993 71 per cent of the company's assets were in real estate. Between 1990 and 1993 rental values fell from $208 per square foot to $129 per square foot. A $200 million property portfolio that Confederation had assembled for various pension funds lost 34 per cent of its value during the same period.

Matheson did not become immediately aware of this downgrade because it **11–012** was mistakenly not noted in the daily report on which it relied, and the lead market maker did not pass on news of it. When the defendant did become aware of the problem it attempted to determine whether there was any opportunity to sell the bonds on the market, but apparently there was not. Matheson then informed its client of what had happened and told it that none of the bonds could be sold. Confederation subsequently became insolvent and Federal officials shut the company down. The liquidators, KPMG, estimated losses at $1.3 billion and the whole of the client's investment was lost. The trustees brought an action for professional negligence against Matheson, submitting that there was no system in place to allow for proper monitoring of the markets and that it had been agreed that Matheson would tell the plaintiff of anything that affected the valuation of the bonds and that it had not done so.

Matheson at first instance submitted that there was an appropriate system of monitoring in place in that there was monitoring of price, both absolute and relative to gilts; scrutiny in the press daily, preparation of a weekly valuation report for the portfolio, discussions with the consultant who represented the trust, and discussions with the market in general.

Matheson won the argument at first instance.

It was held that Matheson owed a duty of care to its client to exercise the **11–013** skill and diligence that a reasonably competent and careful stockbroker would use. It was not necessary that the investment advisers it employed should possess the highest degree of expertise possible, and liability would not be imposed merely because loss resulted form what turned out to have been errors in judgment, so long as that judgment had been exercised according to their standard of care.

It was held further that there was a system in place appropriate to Matheson's duty of care to the trust. The system was not perfect but it was adequate. Matheson was let down by an error in the report and the failure of the market makers to let them know of the problems with the bonds. It was reasonable for Matheson to rely on these sources which it saw as the tools of its trade.

As there was no possibility of selling the holding there was no action that Matheson could have taken and therefore no causal link between the failure to inform the plaintiff of the problems with the bonds and the loss sustained. Negligence had not been proved.[33]

Negligence found on appeal

11–014 However, on appeal, the Court of Appeal found for the client, holding that Matheson had placed a high level of reliance on an informal arrangement between itself and the market maker as a means of obtaining information which did not amount to an adequate level of monitoring. It was also found that Matheson was negligent in relying on casual exchanges of information between dealers in the market and failing to monitor market information systems, and that stockbrokers offered the service of monitoring of portfolios as a means of generating fees and transactions commissions. Matheson had offered such services and failed to meet its attendant responsibilities.[34]

Dixon, Richardson and Reed Investments Limited v Jefferson Seal Limited[35]

11–015 This was the second case to come before the Jersey High Court following the collapse of Confederation Life; the plaintiffs brought an action against their stockbrokers for negligent investment advice. The defendant stockbroker was to provide them with advice as to which investments would be suitable for them. The plaintiff had little knowledge of the markets and was risk averse, not interested in capital growth but with earning interest.

The defendant advised the purchase of Confederation Life bonds which gave a relatively high return. When the defendant subsequently learned of the troubles that were besetting Confederation Life, it did not pass this information on to its client, and it further did not recommend selling the bonds.

In the ensuing action for negligence, expert evidence was brought by both sides. The plaintiffs argued that the information available even before the insolvency made it plain that it was not a suitable low risk investment and the defendant had failed in their duty to inform them of the subsequent developments thereby depriving them of the opportunity to sell the bonds. The

---

[33] *Voisin and Abacus (C.I.) Limited (as Trustees of the prior Settlement) v Matheson Securities (Channel Islands) Limited* [1999] J.L.R. 177.
[34] See para.11–009, n.25, above.
[35] [1997] J.L.R. 205.

plaintiffs' expert witness attested to the fact that the defendant's failure to keep appropriate records showed that its business methods were inadequate.

The defendant broker was found to be negligent as it owed a duty of care to the plaintiffs to exercise that skill and diligence which a reasonably competent and careful stockbroker would use. It was not necessary that the defendant should possess the highest degree of expertise possible and liability would not be imposed merely because loss resulted from what turned out to have been errors of judgment so long as that judgement had been exercised according the relevant standard of care. **11–016**

On the evidence presented, the court found that the defendant had failed to meet requisite standard of care. In particular it had failed to ensure that its recommendations were suited to the clients' needs and to keep continually under review the clients' investments in the light of those requirements.

The defendant was liable to repay to the client the losses incurred as a result of its negligence.

In order to ascertain whether the appropriate level of care had been exercised it was sufficient that a number of experts in the field of giving investment advice could testify to the existence of an accepted standards of conduct. Where, as in this case, the experts disagreed, although negligence was not established merely by the defendant's failure to meet the standard of a particular body of opinion within its profession, the disagreement of the experts did not prevent the court analysing the conflicting evidence and reaching a conclusion. **11–017**

Commodity brokers cases

The issue of the nature of evidence that would be required to prove a case of negligence in the context of commodity futures broking was also raised in the cases of *Stafford and Comstock Ltd., v Conti Commodity Services Limited* and *Merrill Lynch Futures Inc. v York House Trading*.[36] **11–018**

In both of these cases the brokers were found not to have been negligent. The plaintiffs had in both cases raised the issue of *res ipsa loquitur*, arguing that because so may of the trades carried out on their behalf by their brokers were unsuccessful the doctrine should be applied as evidence of negligence. But this argument was rejected in both cases on the basis that it was quite inappropriate in the context of such unpredictable and risky markets.

It was found in *Stafford* that a broker could not always be right in the advice that it gave in relation to so wayward and rapidly changing a market as the commodities futures market, an error of judgement, if there had been one, was not necessarily negligent and losses made on the commodity market did not of themselves provide evidence of negligence on the part of the

---

[36] See para.11–010, n.27, above.

The trustee and the share index—the Nestle judgement

11–019 In the much criticised case of *Nestle v the National Westminster Bank*,[37] the Court of Appeal held that although the bank had failed in its duties as trustee to review trust investments, and had failed to take legal advice on the scope of its powers, it was not liable to a plaintiff who had failed to prove loss as a result of the defendant's breach of duty.

The facts were that the bank acted as sole trustee of the will of N who died in 1922. It managed the investments first for N's widow and two sons to provide annuities as expressly required by the will, and then for the two sons. From time to time the investment strategy was changed to provide the sons with income to meet their particular tax requirements. In 1986 G, the granddaughter of N and the sole remaining beneficiary, became absolutely entitled. At that time the trust fund was worth £269,203. If it had kept pace with the ordinary share index since 1922 it would have been worth £1,800,000. G issued proceedings for negligence.

The High Court found against the plaintiff, holding that the bank had adhered to standards of prudent investment management and was entitled to be judged by the prevailing investment orthodoxies of the time.

11–020 The standard of care to be borne by a trustee was to act with the care of an ordinary prudent individual acting for someone for whom he felt morally bound to provide. A trustee's duties towards investments were extremely flexible. If the trustee had acted prudently in the interests of the beneficiaries from time to time it was not negligent if the investments failed to keep pace with market indices.

On appeal, Dillon and Legatt L.J. were very critical of the bank, concluding that there was not much for the bank to be proud of in administering the Nestle trust. It was inexcusable that they took no steps at any time to seek legal advice as to the scope of their power to invest in ordinary shares; and they had erroneously interpreted the trust deed as restricting them to banking and insurance shares. But they even suggested that no testator in the light of the example of the Nestle trust would choose the bank for the effective management of an investment. The court still found that there had been no breach of trust, holding that the plaintiff had failed to prove that she had suffered loss as a result of the bank's breaches of duty. The trustees were entitled to balance the fund between income generation and capital growth and were not obliged to rebalance the fund annually or make constant changes.

---

[37] [1994] 1 All E.R. 118.

Inactivity and poor diversification held not imprudent

It was found that inactivity and poor diversification were not imprudent and that the major long-run equity index was an inappropriate benchmark for how the equities in the fund might have been expected to fare. **11–021**

Legatt L.J. was influenced by the notion that safety and inactivity, especially in the context of an investment manager in the 1950s, were paramount and overriding considerations, and that active investment management might have been seen as speculative.

Commentators have suggested that this may have been an inappropriate approach. Stephen Lofthouse[38] cites the views of John Maynard Keynes from a work of 1924 proposing that investment management should be driven by an active investment policy and goes on to cite other sources from as far back as 1904 which put the case for balanced distribution of assets of not placing too many eggs in one basket. He concludes that:

> "It would seem that during the life of the portfolio under consideration, theory, popular financial writing and common practice would have suggested broad diversification by sector to reduce risk, and the portfolio was inadequately diversified. The inactive stance, instead of being prudent behaviour, increased risk by making returns dependent on a small section of the market instead of the entire market."[39]

Lofthouse goes on to consider the conundrum of how to prove that a loss has been caused by this bad management. The usual method is by reference to a benchmark index. The plaintiff preferred to measure the portfolio's performance against the BZW equity index, which was the only market capitalisation weighted index with a dividend yield available for the period since 1918. It is very similar to the FTSE All-Share index. **11–022**

Dillon L.J. had three arguments against using this index (which in Lofthouse's view were erroneous): (1) most growth unit trusts failed to beat the BZW index; (2) because the composition of the index was frequently changed it was hard to beat; and (3) the fund was not large enough to include substantial holdings in all the leading equities.

Lofthouse concludes by proposing that diversification is essential for a prudent trustee, and that, while the Court of Appeal rejected the use of a standard index of long term equity returns, their technical objections seemed incorrect, and that, on the contrary, a comparison with such an index would be an appropriate measure.

---

[38] Stephen Lofthouse, "Nestle v National Westminster Bank PLC: Flawed Reasoning", 4 [1997] *Private Client Business*, 1997, 232–243.
[39] *ibid.*

11–023   It has also been suggested by Watt and Stauch that the decision in *Nestle* was influenced by the *"deep seated judicial reluctance to review the decision-making essential to trustee investments."*[40]

They consider that the Court in *Nestle* wrongly conflated the breach and loss stages in determining trustee liability for imprudent investment in cases of express trust, and prefer the approach of Brightman J. in *Bartlett v Barclays Trust Co. (No.1)*:

"The questions that I must ask myself are:

(1) what was the duty of the bank?
(2) was the bank in breach of duty and if so in what respect?
(3) If so, to what extent is the bank liable to make good that loss?"[41]

The Trustee Act 2000 and investment managers

11–024   Some of the difficulties surrounding the Nestle litigation may well be unlikely to reoccur as the new Trustee Act 2000 (the TA) provides a modern statutory basis for matters such as the duty of care and the powers of the trustee to invest. The TA follows a Law Commission Consultation Paper published in 1999 and addresses the fact that trusts today operate in very different circumstances in terms of the appropriate regime of investment for trust funds.[42] Traditional notions of trust fund investment were inherently conservative and did not countenance the need for growth and the meeting of inflationary pressures. This conservative approach can be seen clearly in the attitude of the judges in the *Nestle* case.

The new TA provides that a trustee should:

". . . exercise such care and skill as is reasonable in the circumstances, having regard in particular to:

(a) any special knowledge or experience that he has or holds himself out as having, and
(b) if he acts as trustee in the course of a business or profession, to any special knowledge or experience that it is reasonable to expect of a person acting in the course of that kind of business or profession."[43]

It further provides that:

---

[40] Gary Watt and Marc Stauch, "Is There Liability for imprudent Trustee Investment?", [1998] *Conveyancer and Property Lawyer Conv.*, Sep/Oct, 352–361.
[41] [1980] Ch.515 at 530H.
[42] Law Com. (No.260).
[43] s.1.

THE LEGAL BASIS FOR CLAIMS AGAINST INVESTMENT MANAGERS

"subject to the provisions of this Part, a trustee may make any kind of investment that he could make if he were absolutely entitled to the assets of the trust."

The TA gives trustees power to delegate their powers of investment to investment managers[44] imposing on them a statutory duty to ensure that this power is exercised with reasonable skill and care. The new regulation may affect investment managers. A breach may give rise to a negligence claim, against the trustee of its failure to meet its obligations under the TA or against the manager if it fails to meet the trustee's specified requirements.

11–025

The TA further provides that all relationships with agents must be governed by a written agreement[45] and that investment manager policies must be guided by written policy statements governing the way they carry out their duties for the trustees. The investment management agreement must contain a clause requiring investment managers to comply with the written policy statement (including compliance with any revisions subsequently introduced).[46] The investment manager must comply with the restrictions and duties set out in the TA.

Restrictions and duties on trustees under the TA

The duties include:

- ensuring that standard investment criteria relating to suitability and diversification are complied with when making any investment;[47]

11–026

- considering these standards investment criteria when deciding whether to vary investments;[48]

- ensuring that the policy statement will lead to investment management functions being exercised in the best interests of the trust[49];

- appointing a qualified custodian in writing where bearer securities are involved (unless the trust deed says otherwise)[50];

- if the trustees choose to use the new statutory power to delegate to an investment manager, the terms of delegation can be expected to impose on the investment manager an obligation to comply with the restrictions and duties set out in the TA.

---

[44] s.11(1).
[45] s.15(1).
[46] s.15(2).
[47] s.4(3)(a) and (b).
[48] s.4(2).
[49] s.15(3).
[50] s.18.

DEVELOPMENTS IN INVESTMENT MANAGEMENT ACCOUNTABILITY—BENCHMARKS

The *Myners Review*

11–027 Further developments in the field of pension fund management have been highlighted by the *Myners Review*.[51]

This report has proposed a duty of care for pension fund trustees in the following terms:

"... there should be a legal requirement that where trustees are taking a decision, they should be able to take it with the skill and prudence of someone familiar with the issues concerned."

This would mean that trustees would need to develop expertise or delegate the decision to an organisation which does have the skill and expertise required. This might generate business for specialist investment management providers, adding to the possible boost to such business given by the new powers to delegate in the TA.[52] Furthermore, trustees will now automatically have full investment powers which they may not have had before if they were under restrictions imposed by the 1961 Trustee Investments Act.[53] They also are obliged to seek advice and review their investments.[54] See further the discussions of this topic in Chapters 4 and 13.

Conclusion

11–028 It is evident that the law is slowly catching up with the realities of the contemporary investment management, and trustees and those to whom trustees delegate the job of managing portfolios must do more than simply preserve the book value of the fund. The impact of the *Unilever* case will no doubt be seen in the form and content of investment management contracts.

Investment managers will have to ensure that they have systems in place to provide that portfolios are suitable and well diversified and that the risk management regimes and monitoring regimes that they have in place are adequate to deal with the challenges of the contemporary financial markets and more demanding clients.

Part of the reported case against MAM was that, in addition to the inappropriate concentration in the portfolio, there were inadequate risk management systems in place. In his evidence during the case, Mr Lennard is reported to have admitted to the court that MAM did not have quantitative

---

[51] See Ch.4, paras 4–002—4–013.

[52] Robert Smeath, "The Trustee Act 2000 and Investment Managers", [2001] P.C.B. 6, 369–371 and "Trustee Act 2000-Implications for Investment Managers" *www.elexia.com* February 2003.

[53] This does not apply to occupational pensions schemes authorised unit trusts and schemes under the Charities Act 1933.

[54] s.5.

304

CONCLUSION

risk management procedures to help investment managers check whether levels of sector and stock bets were appropriate to meet client performance targets. Instead, they held "brainstorming" sessions to see how portfolios would behave in different circumstances.[55] Furthermore, Paul Harwood, who took over the running of the account from Mr Lennard, is reported as describing the portfolio as being beyond the limits of prudent risk management.[56]

However in a reported interview with Pamela Shimell,[57] Brian Fullerton, **11–029** Merrill Lynch Investment Manager's Global Director of Risk Management, in discussing Merrill's quantitative tools for risk management, makes it clear that whatever was the case at MAM in 1996, risk management systems have now moved on at Merrill Lynch.[58]

Trustees of pension schemes may wish to consider what practical steps they can take to safeguard their position in the light of recent developments. In particular, in drafting contractual terms, they should incorporate terms that cover risk management and performance very clearly and ensure that the trustees' attitude to risk is taken into account. The contract should set out clearly how the investment manager plans to meet performance targets and what level of care it will take to try to do so.

---

[55] Ian Watson, "Lennard points finger at Galley in Mercury case", *www.scotsman.com*, November 14, 2001.

[56] "Some investments 'not prudent,' court is told", *ibid.*, November 22, 2001.

[57] Author of "The Universe of risk—How top business leaders control risk and achieve success" (Prentice Hall), December 2001.

[58] Pamela Shimell, "What's the next big thing for business?", *www.pearson.co.uk*.

CHAPTER 12

US REGULATION OF MANAGED FUTURES—COMMODITY TRADING ADVISORS AND COMMODITY POOLS

Susan C. Ervin, Dechert LLP, Washington DC

12–001 Investment managers seeking to take advantage of the growing array of futures and other derivative products on behalf of an investment fund being offered in the US or to US persons must consider the likelihood that this activity will trigger the application of US regulatory requirements. This Chapter explores the US regulatory framework applicable to investment management activity involving futures contracts and other derivative products, with a view toward identifying the most significant regulatory constraints. It looks in particular at the regulatory regime applying to Commodity Trading Advisers and Commodity Pool Operators.

The Regulatory Landscape for Derivatives

Introduction

12–002 The US Commodity Futures Trading Commission (CFTC) administers the Commodity Exchange Act (CEA), a federal regulatory framework governing transactions in the US futures markets. Under this framework, funds that engage in futures transactions are "commodity pools", subject to a distinct set of rules and requirements imposed upon the fund manager or "commodity pool operator". Advisers to such funds and to other types of investors in the futures markets are "commodity trading advisors", also subject to special rules and requirements. To add to the complexity, some types of derivatives are regulated by the US Securities and Exchange Commission (SEC), while other classes of derivatives, including the burgeoning swaps market, are largely unregulated.

306

Regulated versus unregulated derivatives

Broadly speaking, there are three main categories of derivatives for regula-   **12–003**
tory purposes: (1) futures contracts and related instruments regulated by the
CFTC; (2) securities options and related instruments regulated by the SEC;
and (3) unregulated, or largely unregulated derivatives such as swaps. This
chapter will focus principally upon the special regulatory requirements applicable to investment management activity involving futures contracts and
other similar derivative products regulated by the CFTC. While hedge funds
and other investment vehicles are subject to SEC regulation, as discussed in
Chapter 6, when futures transactions are added to an investment portfolio,
the separate regulatory framework of the CFTC must be addressed.

Terminology—commodities, derivatives, futures and options

Futures contracts, now commonly traded in public marketplaces, are one of   **12–004**
the oldest forms of derivative transactions. They are designed to enable a
business to hedge a price exposure efficiently by entering into a futures position that is equal and offsetting to an inventory of a particular commodity or
some other commodity exposure. A futures position, by increasing (or
decreasing) in value to the extent that the price of the relevant commodity
decreases (or increases), offsets losses incurred by holding the actual commodity. Futures and commodity options entail the use of "leverage",
whereby a small margin deposit secures a hedge position which protects the
value of a much larger "cash" or actual commodity position, thus providing
an economical form of insurance against price movements. In the US, futures
margins tend to be quite low as compared to securities margins, often as little as two or three per cent of the value of a futures contract, resulting in the
potential for highly leveraged portfolios.

A commodity option is a transaction whereby a party obtains, in consideration for a premium payment, the right but not the obligation to purchase
or sell a specified commodity at a specified price at a future time. Commodity options also include options on futures contracts. Commodity options are
regulated by the CFTC. The SEC, however, regulates securities options which
are options on individual securities, groups of securities, or securities indices.

Under the CEA, a "commodity" is not itself a futures contract or a derivative but a separate source of value—a good, service or interest—on which a
futures contract may be based. The CEA definition of the term "commodity" is nearly all-inclusive, encompassing the traditional agricultural commodities (wheat, cotton, rice, and the like) as well as "all other goods and
articles, except onions . . . and all services, rights, and interests in which contracts for future delivery are presently or in the future dealt in". Consequently, the term "commodity" covers the universe of tangible and intangible
sources of value, ranging from stock indices, interest rates, and the Consumer

Price Index to "hard" or "physical" commodities such as corn, soybeans, silver, and heating oil.[1]

12–005 Derivatives are contracts or interests derived from the price of a commodity. Unlike the term "commodity", which is defined in the CEA and has regulatory significance, the term "derivative" is fundamentally a market term, without fixed meaning or legal significance in the US. The term "derivatives" potentially includes all interests and instruments, whether or not traded on organised futures or securities exchanges, that are contracts creating rights and obligations based upon the performance of some underlying instrument, investment, currency, product, index, right, service, or rate. The term "derivatives" is often used interchangeably (but inaccurately) with "commodities", and funds that trade in derivatives (whether commodity futures or option contracts traded on futures exchanges or over-the-counter (OTC) products, such as swaps) are widely known as "commodity funds". Derivatives include many types of instruments in addition to futures and commodity options, and the regulatory implications for a collective investment vehicle engaging in derivatives depend greatly on the exact type of derivative transaction undertaken.

CFTC and SEC regulatory oversight

12–006 The potential for dual or multiple regulatory overseers over derivatives activity is an important aspect of US investment management activity involving derivatives. The SEC regulates the US securities markets; the CFTC regulates the US futures markets; and the 50 individual states, except to the extent pre-empted from doing so by federal statute, may regulate securities and futures activities within their borders. Consequently, a money manager may, through a single investment fund or account, engage in activity that is regulated by the SEC, the CFTC and one or more of the individual states.

Key parties in the marketplace

12–007 A prospective investor who seeks to enter the futures markets has several routes available. The investor might establish an account directly with a futures broker, which will either place orders in the futures markets as directed by the investor or make investment decisions for the investor pursuant to a power of attorney. The investor might also avail himself of the

---

[1] Section 1a(3) of the Commodity Exchange Act, 7 U.S.C. § 2. The broad view of the scope of the term "commodity" stated in the text has long been taken by the CFTC. However, others read the term "commodity" to include only those products which futures contracts actually are or have been traded. See P. Johnson and T. Hazen, *Commodities Regulation* (3rd ed., Aspen Law & Business, 1998), para.1–02.

advice of a commodity trading advisor (CTA). The "commodity pool" is another, increasingly popular route by which a customer may access the futures markets, being set up as a professionally managed, generally limited liability vehicle by which an investor may access the services of one or more CTAs as well as, potentially, one or more securities investment advisers.

Commodity trading advisors

CTAs provide advice about futures transactions (including commodity options) and the futures markets, make discretionary investment decisions pursuant to a power of attorney from their client, or invest in a commodity pool advised by one or more other CTAs. They are the futures markets equivalent of an investment manager, and are modeled to a large degree on the concept of "investment adviser" in the Investment Advisers Act of 1940.

12–008

Commodity pools

Commodity pools are at the centre of the CFTC's regulation of investment vehicles. In practice, the typical commodity pool is not purely or even primarily a vehicle for participation in the futures markets. Most often, a commodity pool is a fund that pools the assets of multiple investors and invests those assets in an eclectic mix of traditional and non-traditional investments. These investments might include, for example, futures contracts, forward contracts, options, swaps, repurchase agreements, interests in hedge funds, currencies, real estate, and equity and debt securities. Nonetheless, the springboard for CFTC regulation of the entity remains the fund's futures activity, including transactions in futures contracts and commodity options. The term "commodity pool" is often used interchangeably with other terms such as "commodity fund" or "managed futures fund".

12–009

"Commodity pool" is not defined by statute and in the absence of a governing definition, the meaning and scope of the term has generated controversy. The CEA does define the term "commodity pool operator" ("CPO"), essentially as any person operating a business in the nature of an investment trust which has the purpose of trading in futures contracts or commodity options and who solicits or accepts funds or property in connection with that business.[2] Following this approach, the CFTC has by rule defined the term "commodity pool" to mean "any investment trust, syndicate, or similar form of enterprise operated for the purpose of trading in commodity interests", with commodity interests defined to include futures contracts and

---

[2] Section 1a(4) of the CEA, 7 U.S.C. § 2.

commodity option contracts.[3] As construed by the CFTC, commodity pools include pooled investment vehicles engaging to any significant extent in futures or commodity options, even where they also invest in securities or other investment products, and even where these other investments constitute the primary content of the portfolio.

Commodity pool operators

12–010 Under the CEA, regulatory requirements are imposed not upon the commodity pool but upon the CPO of the pool. Under the CEA, the CPO is the person who bears direct regulatory responsibility for the pool and generally is the creator and manager of the pool. Typically, the pool operator is responsible for marketing the pool and soliciting investors, for hiring and managing trading advisors and investment advisers for the pool, and for obtaining brokerage services for the pool. The CPO may itself manage the pool's futures and commodity option transactions or it may retain independent advisors to do so. In many cases, the CPO engages multiple trading advisors, each of whom is allocated a portion of the pool's assets to invest in futures and, potentially, other investments.

Futures commission merchants and introducing brokers

12–011 Futures commission merchants (FCMs) are the futures equivalent of securities broker-dealers. They are the only category of CFTC registrant permitted to solicit and accept customer accounts and orders and to receive and hold customer funds for futures trading. FCMs are permitted to provide trading advice to their customers in a manner incidental to their business. Introducing brokers (IBs) are permitted to solicit and accept customer accounts but may not handle customer funds.

Floor brokers and floor traders

12–012 Floor brokers execute customer orders on exchange floors; floor traders enter orders for their own accounts. Both types of floor professionals must be registered with the CFTC.

---

[3] CFTC Rules, 4.10(d)(1) and 4.10(a).

Regulation of Commodity Trading Advisors

"Commodity trading advisor" is defined in the Commodity Exchange Act as including persons who, for compensation or profit, engage in the business of advising others, directly or through publications or electronic media, on the trading, or advisability of trading, futures contracts or commodity options, or who issue analyses or reports concerning such transactions. **12–013**

Generally, a person acting as a CTA must register, pursuant to Section 4m(1) of the CEA, in order to conduct its business, unless subject to an exclusion or exemption from registration, and must comply with disclosure, recordkeeping and other requirements established by CFTC rules. Providing advice for compensation or profit includes acting as an advisor to a commodity pool, as well as exercising discretionary authority over accounts in which futures contracts or commodity options are traded and giving advice through written publications, such as newsletters, or electronic media.

Exclusions and exemption from the CTA definition

Incidental futures advice by banks, brokers and others

Certain persons are excluded by statute from the CTA definition provided that they are rendering trading advice in a manner solely incidental to the conduct of their business or profession. These potentially excluded persons are: any bank or trust company or any person acting as an employee thereof; any news reporter, news columnist, or news editor of the print or electronic media, or any lawyer, accountant, or teacher; any floor broker or futures commission merchant; the publisher or producer of any print or electronic data of general and regular dissemination, including its employees; the fiduciary of any defined benefit plan that is subject to ERISA; any contract market or derivatives transaction execution facility; and such other persons not within the intent of this paragraph as the Commission may specify by rule, regulation, or order. **12–014**

The CFTC staff has emphasised that the term "solely incidental" must be interpreted in the context of the business concerned and has given a specific interpretation of its application to bank advisory services. In CFTC Letter No.83–2,[4] the CFTC staff identified certain factors, which if found to exist, would allow a bank providing certain financial futures advisory services to be excluded from the broad statutory CTA definition. Those factors were:

(a) the bank's financial futures advisory service would be offered in connection with its rendition of other commercial banking services, but

---

[4] [1982–1984 Transfer Binder] Comm. Fut. L. Rep. (CCH) 21,788 (March 18, 1983).

not offered to persons to whom the bank otherwise provided only depository services;

(b) the bank would limit its trading advisory activities to hedging programmes using financial futures contracts;

(c) the bank would not actively market the service; and

(d) revenues from the service would constitute a minimal percentage of the bank's consolidated revenues and also of its banking revenues, separately stated.

The CTA definition and its exclusions are closely patterned after the definition of "investment adviser" in the Investment Advisers Act of 1940[5] (the "IA Act"). However, the CTA definitional exclusions, unlike the investment adviser exclusions, are all qualified by the statutory "solely incidental" clause. In contrast, not all of the exclusions set out in the IA Act are modified in the same way. For example, certain banks are outside the definition of "investment adviser" under the IA Act, even if the bank provides investment advice continuously as a part of the financial services it offers.[6]

Section 4m(3) exclusion for SEC-registered investment advisers not primarily acting as CTAs

12–015   Section 4m(3) of the CEA creates a broad exemption from CTA registration for SEC-registered investment advisers providing commodity trading advice that is ancillary to their securities advisory business. Under this provision, SEC-registered investment advisers are exempt from registration as CTAs if their business "does not consist primarily" of acting as a CTA and they do not act as CTAs to any investment trust, syndicate, or similar form of enterprise "that is engaged primarily in trading in any commodity for future delivery on or subject to the rules of any contract market or registered derivatives transaction execution facility". Thus, an SEC-registered investment adviser may provide futures trading advice that is incidental and secondary to its securities advice without CTA registration.

"15 person" exemption

12–016   Section 4m(1) of the CEA[7] provides CTA registration relief for any CTA "who, during the course of the preceding twelve months, has not furnished

---

[5] 15 U.S.C. § 80b-1 *et seq.*
[6] IA Act § 202(a)(11), 15 U.S.C. § 80b-2(a)(11).
[7] 7 U.S.C. § 6m(1).

commodity trading advice to more than fifteen persons and who does not hold himself out generally to the public as a commodity trading advisor".[8] The exemption is self-executing.[9] US and non-US persons are counted.[10] In addition, in determining whether a CTA meets the "no more than 15 persons" restriction in Section 4m(1), the CFTC historically had "looked through" artificial legal entities that are collective investment vehicles to count the individual participants therein.[11] However, the CFTC has recently adopted a rule to codify the application of this exemption and to clarify that for this purpose, legal organisations generally will be counted as one person.[12] New Rule 4.14(a)(10) provides that a general partnership, corporation, limited partnership, limited liability company, trust or other legal organisation that receives commodity interest trading advice based on its investment objectives rather than the individual investment objectives of its shareholders, partners, limited partners, etc. shall be one person.

Rule 4.14(a)(8)

"CFTC Rule 4.14(a)(8) provides an exemption from CTA registration **12–017** for financial advisers who also fall within the definition of a CTA, provided they satisfy certain conditions.[13-14] Persons eligible for relief under Rule 4.14(a)(8) include:

(1) *Investment Advisers.* Persons who are registered as IAs under the IA Act.

---

[8] This section also exempts from registration the following persons in addition to the small, "private" CTA described above. Those persons are: (1) persons also in cash market business—persons who also operate in the cash markets of certain agricultural commodities listed in Section 2(a) of the CEA (now Section 1a) and who provide advice in a manner that is solely incidental to their business; and (2) nonprofit, voluntary membership, general farm organisations—certain non-profit, voluntary membership, general farm organisations, who provide advice on the purchase or sale of any of the agricultural commodities listed in Section 2(a) of the CEA (now Section 1a) and who do so in a manner solely incidental to the operation of the general farm organisation.

[9] CFTC Letter No.91-9, [1992–1994 Transfer Binder] Comm. Fut. L. Rep. (CCH), undated, para.24.189.

[10] *ibid.*

[11] CFTC Letter No.96-43, [1994–1996 Transfer Binder] Comm. Fut. L. Rep. (CCH), (May 14, 1996), para.26.713; CFTC Letter No.95-39, [1994–1996 Transfer Binder] Comm. Fut. L. Rep. (CCH), December 5, 1994, para.26.380.

[12] 68 FR 47221 (August 8, 2003).

[13-14] Note generally that a number of other persons are eligible for relief under paras (a)(1) to (7) of Rule 4.14. Those persons include: Persons involved in cash market transactions in a commodity as a dealer, processor, broker or seller, if the commodity trading advice is solely incidental to the conduct of the primary business (Rule 4.14(a)(1)); nonprofit, voluntary membership, trade associations or farm organisations, if the commodity trading advice is solely incidental to the conduct of the primary business (Rule 4.14(a)(2)); associated persons of CFTC registrants, exempted as to advice provided in connection with employment as such (Rule 4.14(a)(3)); registered CPOs, exempted as to advice provided in connection with and

US REGULATION OF MANAGED FUTURES—COMMODITY TRADING ADVISORS

(2) *Banks.* Persons who are excluded from the definition of the term "investment adviser" pursuant to the provisions of Sections 202(a)(2) and 202(a)(11) of the IA Act".[15]

12–018   *Eligibility Criteria.* As recently revised by the CFTC, the eligibility criteria for Rule 4.14(a)(8) relief from registration are that the registered investment adviser (or bank) is not otherwise holding itself out as a CTA and that its commodity trading advice is solely incidental to its business of providing securities or other investment advice to one of the following types of entities:

Qualifying entities as defined in CFTC Rule 4.5 for which a notice of eligibility has been filed;

Collective investment vehicles that are excluded from the definition of "commodity pool" under CFTC Rule 4.5(a)(4);

Commodity pools that are organised and operated outside of the US, its territories and possessions, which are not marketed to US persons or from the US and which will have only Non-US person beneficial interest holders, with the exception of the pool's operator and advisor, and their principals;

A commodity pool operator who has claimed exemption from registration under Rule 4.13(a)(3) or 4.13(a)(4).

In order to claim the exemption, the investment adviser (or bank) must file a notice with the Commission containing certain identifying information and representations with respect to the manner in which it will provide commodity interest trading advice to the Rule 4.5 trading vehicle.[16] As noted above, CEA Section 4m(1) provides CTA registration relief for any CTA "who, during the course of the preceding twelve months, has not furnished commodity trading advice to more than fifteen persons and who does not hold

---

directed solely to, and for the sole use of, the pools for which the CPO is registered (Rule 4.14(a)(4)); certain CPOs exempt from registration, provided that the advice is provided solely to, and for the sole use of, pools for which the CPO has obtained an exemption from CPO registration (Rule 4.14(a)(5)); and introducing brokers, exempted as to advice provided in connection with introducing broker business (Rule 4.14(a)(6)).

[15] 15 U.S.C. §§ 80b-2(a)(2) and (a)(11). Section 202(a)(2) defines the term "bank" to include banking institutions organised under the laws of the United States, a member bank of the Federal Reserve System, or any other banking institution or trust company, whether incorporated or not, doing business under the laws of any State or of the United States, a substantial portion of the business of which consists of receiving deposits or exercising fiduciary powers similar to those permitted to national banks under the authority of the Comptroller of the Currency, and which is supervised and examined by a State or Federal authority having supervision over banks, and which is not operated for the purpose of evading the provisions of the IA Act.

[16] See Rule 4.14(a)(8)(11).

314

himself out generally to the public as a commodity trading advisor". In adopting Rule 4.14(a)(8), the Commission made clear the effect of that rule on Section 4m(1). Specifically, the Commission stated:

> "[T]he relief provided by § 4.14(a)(8) is [not] mutually exclusive from that provided by Section 4m(1)—that is, depending on the nature of its activities a CTA may be exempt from registration as such under either or both provisions. Thus, the fact that a CTA who is claiming an exemption under § 4.14(a)(8) has more than 15 clients for the purpose of that rule will not affect the CTA's ability to claim an exemption under Section 4m(1) for a different set of clients—*i.e.*, clients who are other than § 4.5 trading vehicles."[17]

Rule 4.14(a)(9) exemption for CTAs providing standardised, impersonal advice

CFTC Rule 4.14(a)(9) provides an exemption from registration for CTAs who provide standardised commodity trading advice by means of media such as newsletters, pre-recorded telephone newslines, websites, and non-customised computer software.[18] The exemption exempts CTAs who are not engaged in specified types of advisory activities. To qualify for the exemption, the CTA must not engage in any of the following activities[19]: **12–019**

(a)   directing client accounts; or

(b)   providing commodity trading advice based on, or tailored to, the commodity interest or cash market positions or other circumstances or characteristics of particular clients.

CTAs satisfying the conditions of Rule 4.14(a)(9) are not required to register with the CFTC and are also exempt from the various regulatory requirements set forth in the CEA and CFTC rules that, by their terms, apply only to registrants or persons required to be registered. For example, an exempt CTA is not subject to the Disclosure Document requirements of Rule 4.31.

---

[17]   52 Fed. Reg. 41975, 41978 (November 2, 1987).

[18]   65 Fed. Reg. 12938 (March 10, 2000).

[19]   A 2001 CFTC staff letter advised that an internet service and software programme that makes recommendations with respect to natural gas purchases or sales over a period of 12 months is exempt under Rule 4.14(a)(9) since the "system's recommendations will be the same from one client to the next, regardless of the particular attributes of each client". CFTC Letter No.01-64, [2000–2002 Transfer Binder] Comm. Fut. L. Rep. (CCH) (June 14, 2001), para.28.577. In another recent letter, the staff stated that a website that presents opinions on the 25 most highly capitalised non-tech stocks (at no cost) and monitors a "model hypothetical hedge-type account" (for a fee, but not client-specific) would not be covered by Rule 4.14(a)(9) because managed accounts would also be promoted on the website. CFTC Letter No. 01-35, [2000–2002 Transfer Binder] Comm. Fut. L. Rep. (CCH) (March 12, 2001), para.28.525.

US REGULATION OF MANAGED FUTURES—COMMODITY TRADING ADVISORS

However, exempt CTAs would remain subject to the anti-fraud prohibition of Section 4o of the CEA, Rule 4.30, which bars CTAs from handling clients' funds, and Rule 4.41, which prohibits deceptive advertising and requires certain representations to accompany presentations of simulated or hypothetical performance results.

Regulatory requirements applicable to CTAs

12–020 Applicants for registration as a CTA, the applicant's principals, and applicants for registration as salespersons ("associated persons") of a CTA must file with the National Futures Association (NFA) information concerning their employment and disciplinary histories and fingerprint cards for fitness screening through the Federal Bureau of Investigation database. The CTA applicant and any associated person must also pass the National Commodity Futures Examination ("Series 3") or other applicable proficiency test. Upon registration and periodically thereafter, each registered CTA and associated person thereof must attend ethics training, as more fully discussed in para.12–027 below. If required to register, a CTA is subject to the CFTC's regulatory provisions relating to disclosure, recordkeeping, advertising and customer funds, discussed below, unless specifically exempted from such requirements.

Rule 4.31: disclosure requirements

12–021 CTAs seeking to enter into agreements to manage accounts for clients must, at or before: (i) the time of solicitation, or (ii) entry into the agreement, whichever is earlier, deliver or cause to be delivered to the prospective client a Disclosure Document for the trading programme pursuant to which the trading advisor seeks to direct the client's account or to guide the client's trading. This requirement applies to a CTA who is seeking to enter into an agreement to direct the client's futures account or to guide the client's futures trading by means of "a systematic program that recommends specific transactions".[20] A CTA may deliver the Disclosure Document to a prospective client in paper form or by electronic means (*e.g.*, by download from the CTA's website to the prospective client's computer), provided that the prospective client has given informed consent to receive required materials electronically. An electronically-delivered Disclosure Document must present information in the same format and order as specified in CFTC rules and must reflect the same differences in emphasis and prominence that would exist in the paper document.[21] The CTA may not enter into an agreement to guide or direct a client's account unless he first receives from the prospective

---

[20] Rule 4.31(a).
[21] 62 Fed. Reg. 39104, 39109 (July 22, 1997).

client a signed acknowledgment confirming that the client has received a Disclosure Document for the trading programme pursuant to which the CTA will direct or guide trading in the account. In the case of an electronically delivered Disclosure Document, the acknowledgment may be obtained electronically, using a unique identifier (such as a "PIN" number) to confirm the identity of the prospective client.[22]

Possible Rule 4.7 exemption—If a CTA is dealing with an investor with substantial resources or other specified indicia of sophistication, as provided in Rule 4.7, the CTA may be exempt from the disclosure requirements, set forth above. For a discussion of the Rule 4.7 exemption, see the discussion below at para.12–037.   **12–022**

Rule 4.33: recordkeeping requirements

General recordkeeping and access requirements—The recordkeeping obligations applicable to CTAs are set forth in Rule 4.33 and Rule 1.31. Generally, books and records must be kept current and accurately, and within the United States. Records must be kept for five years and be readily accessible during the first two years of the five-year period. If the CTA does not maintain its original records within the United States because its main office is located elsewhere, the books and records must be made available to a Commission representative within 72 hours at a place in the United States specified by the Commission representative. Records required to be maintained concerning clients include: **12–023**

(a) Name and address of each client.

(b) From each client, a signed and dated acknowledgment that the client has received a Disclosure Document explaining the trading programme which the CTA will use in directing or guiding trading in the client's account.

(c) For each client, powers of attorney, and other documents needed to authorise the CTA to trade on behalf, or guide the trading in the account, of the client.

(d) All other written agreements entered into by the CTA and with the client.

(e) A master list of all client accounts in commodity interests that the CTA exercises trading authority over, and all transactions effected therein.

---

[22] *ibid.*, at 39115.

US REGULATION OF MANAGED FUTURES—COMMODITY TRADING ADVISORS

(f) Confirmations—copies of each confirmation of a client transaction in futures or commodity options received from an executing futures commission merchant.

(g) Monthly statements—copies of monthly statements received from futures commission merchants.

(h) Copies of any brochure, report, letter, advertisement, or other written or oral presentation, including radio, television and seminar presentations, distributed to clients and prospective clients, with the date first distributed noted on the document or medium.

Books and records required to be maintained relating to the CTA, and trading in proprietary or principal accounts include:

12–024
(a) An itemised daily record of each transaction in commodity interests listing transaction date; quantity; specific commodity interest; price or premium; delivery month; exercise date (options); put or call (options); strike price (options); underlying contract for future delivery; futures commission merchant carrying the account; introducing broker, if any; whether the contract was purchased, sold, exercised, or expired; and gain or loss realised.

(b) Records of the commodity interest transactions (*e.g.* trade confirmations, monthly statements, purchase and sale statements) received from a futures commission merchant (FCM), relating to the personal account of the CTA, or relating to a personal account of a principal of the CTA.

If a CTA is dealing with highly accredited investors as specified in Rule 4.7, the CTA may be exempt from certain recordkeeping requirements. Rule 1.31 now permits most required records to be maintained in micrographic or electronic form.

Rule 4.30: solicitation of funds in client's name

12–025
Rule 4.30 expressly prohibits a CTA from soliciting, accepting or receiving from clients or prospective clients cash, securities or any other property in the CTA's name (or extending credit in lieu thereof), to purchase, margin, guarantee or secure futures or commodity option contracts.

REGULATION OF COMMODITY TRADING ADVISORS

Relief from certain disclosure and recordkeeping requirements under rule 4.7

Rule 4.7 provides an exemption from the disclosure requirements of Rule **12–026** 4.31 and the recordkeeping requirements of Rule 4.33 applicable to CTAs providing commodity trading advice to Qualified Eligible Persons (QEPs) as defined in Rule 4.7(a). To claim relief under Rule 4.7, CTAs are required to file a notice of claim for exemption containing specified representations. CTAs who file the notice required by Rule 4.7(d) obtain relief from complying with the specific requirements of Rules 4.31, 4.34, 4.35 and 4.36 which, *inter alia*, prescribe the contents of CTA Disclosure Documents, and the specific requirements of Rule 4.33, concerning recordkeeping.

(a) Disclosure relief is subject to the caveat that any brochure, report or other disclosure provided to clients must be accurate and contain sufficient facts so that the information presented is not materially misleading. In addition, in standardised language, the brochure must inform the recipient that the brochure or other writing has not been filed with the CFTC.[23]

(b) General relief from Rule 4.33 is granted, except that the CTA must maintain at its main business office all the books and records prepared in connection with its services as a CTA of the QEC clients, including, without limitation, documents establishing that such clients are QECs. All such records are subject to inspection by the CFTC and other regulatory authorities in accordance with Rule 1.31.

CFTC Regulation of Commodity Pool Operators

Registration of the commodity pool operator

Unless it is within one of the registration exemptions discussed in **12–027** para.12–034 below, the operator of a fund deemed to be a commodity pool under US law must register with the CFTC as a CPO. Applicants for registration as a CPO, the applicant's principals, and applicants for registration as salespersons ("associated persons") of a CPO must file with the NFA, which processes registration applications pursuant to delegated authority from the CFTC, information on their employment and disciplinary (civil and criminal) histories, together with fingerprint cards for fitness screening through the Federal Bureau of Investigation criminal database. Also, a CPO applicant and any associated person of the applicant must pass the National Commodity Futures Examination (the "Series 3" examination) or other applicable proficiency test.

---

[23] See Rule 4.7(c)(1) for the required standardised language.

Ethics training

12–028 Upon registration, and periodically thereafter, each registered CPO and associated person thereof must attend ethics training. This requirement is set forth in a Statement of Acceptable Practices issues by the CFTC in October 2001.[24] The Statement lists the following topics as ones which an ethics training programme should address:

- an explanation of the applicable laws and regulations and rules of self-regulatory organisations or contract markets and registered derivatives transaction execution facilities;

- the registrant's obligation to the public to observe equitable principles of trade;

- how to act honestly, fairly and with due skill, care and diligence in the best interest of customers and the integrity of the markets;

- how to establish effective supervisory systems and internal controls;

- obtaining and assessing the financial situation and investment experience of customers;

- disclosure of material information to customers; and

- avoidance, proper disclosure and handling of conflicts interest.

Subsequently, the NFA issued an Interpretive Notice to provide additional guidance concerning the ethics training obligations of commodity professionals. The Interpretive Notice explains that all firms should have written procedures which outline their ethics programme. Acceptable procedures will address the topics that will be included in the training programme, who will provide the training, the format of the training, the frequency with which the employees will receive the training, and how the firm will document that it has followed its procedures. The Notice recommends that each firm ascertain that the selected provider of the ethics training is qualified and has three years of relevant industry experience or similar experience. The ethics training may be provided through a variety of media and formats and the training programme should be responsive to the type and size of the firm's business. NFA stresses that maintaining documentation of the ethics training programme is critical since it enables the NFA Member to be certain it is implementing the policies it has deemed necessary and appropriate for its business.

---

[24] CFTC Rules, Pt 3, App. B.

Disclosure document

Content and delivery requirements. Each CPO (including persons registered as **12–029** CPOs or persons required to be registered as such) soliciting prospective investors must, absent an exemption, provide each prospective participant, and file with the NFA and the CFTC, a Disclosure Document containing information specified in CFTC rules.[25] The Disclosure Document must include information concerning such matters as the principal risk factors relevant to investment in the pool; the business background of the CPO and its principals; the CPO's and the pool's historical performance results; fees to be incurred by the pool; conflicts of interest on the part of the CPO, CTAs and other commodity professionals who will provide services to the pool; and material legal proceedings against the CPO, CTAs for the pool and other relevant persons during the past five years. The CPO may not accept or receive funds, securities or other property from a prospective pool participant unless it first receives from the prospective participant a signed acknowledgment confirming that the prospective participant has received the Disclosure Document for the pool.

Electronic delivery. A CPO may deliver the Disclosure Document to a prospective pool participant by electronic means (*e.g.* by download from the CPO's website to the prospective participant's computer), provided that the prospective participant has given informed consent to receive required materials electronically. An electronically delivered Disclosure Document must present information in the same format and order as specified in CFTC rules and must reflect the same differences in emphasis and prominence that would exist in the paper document.[26] In the case of an electronically delivered Disclosure Document, the acknowledgment may be obtained electronically, using a unique identifier (such as a "PIN" number) to confirm the identity of the prospective participant.[27]

Two-part disclosure rules. NFA rules require the CPO of a pool which is required to register its securities under the Securities Act of 1933 ("publicly offered pool") to use a two-part Disclosure Document format.[28] The first part of the Disclosure Document must contain the specific information items required by CFTC Rules 4.24 and 4.25 but summary performance information required by Rule 4.25(c)(5) may be included in the Statement of Additional Information ("SAI"), if the CPO prepares an SAI. The first part of the Disclosure Document must also contain any other information that the SEC or state securities administrators require to be included in the first part of a

---

[25] The NFA reviews all Disclosure Documents filed by privately offered commodity pools as well as Disclosure Documents filed by CTAs. The NFA has also been delegated responsibility for processing all notices, statements and claims filed under Rules 4.5, 4.7, 4.12(b), 4.13, 4.14(a)(8) and CFTC Advisory 18-96.

[26] 62 Fed. Reg. 39104, 39109 (July 22, 1997).

[27] 17 C.F.R. § 4.21(b).

[28] 63 Fed. Reg. 58300 (October 30, 1998).

two-part disclosure document, and such other information as is necessary to understand the fundamental characteristics of the pool or to keep the Disclosure Document from being misleading. The first part of the Disclosure Document may not contain any other information, must be written using plain English principles, and must be delivered at or before the time of solicitation. The SAI must be delivered to prospective participants by the CPO of a public pool prior to the CPO's acceptance or receipt of funds from such participants.

Profile disclosure document rule. The CFTC also permits the use of "profile" disclosure documents analogous to the profile prospectuses permitted for registered investment companies.[29] These rules permit a CPO to deliver a short document, containing key information about a commodity pool, to a prospective participant prior to delivery of the pool's Disclosure Document. The profile document is required to comply with NFA requirements as to form and content, including a requirement that it state that an investment in the pool may not be made until after the prospective participant has received the full Disclosure Document. Under NFA Compliance Rule 2-35(d),[30] the profile document is required to include key data concerning the investment, such as the risks of participating in commodity pools and any risks specific to the particular pool; a break-even analysis reflecting all fees and expenses of the pool; a discussion of the pool's trading strategy; any conflicts of interest material to the pool; a summary of any material actions against the CPO and its principals within the past five years; a brief description of the pool's redemption policies; and the performance of the offered pool.

Periodic account statements and annual reports

12–030   Absent exemption, CPOs must provide each pool participant with an account statement at least quarterly (monthly for pools with net assets exceeding $500,000) and an annual report within 90 calendar days after the end of the pool's fiscal year. Financial statements in annual reports must be prepared in accordance with generally accepted accounting principles (GAAP) and certified by an independent financial accountant. The annual report also must be filed with the CFTC.[31]

---

[29] See 65 Fed. Reg. 58648 (October 2, 2000), amending CFTC Rules 4.2, 4.21, 4.26 and 4.38.
[30] *NFA Rulebook*, para.5148. The *NFA Rulebook* can be accessed online at *www.nfa.futures.org*.
[31] 17 C.F.R. § 4.22.

Recordkeeping requirements

Generally, CPOs must make and keep specified books and records at their main business office and make them available for inspection by the CFTC and the United States Department of Justice.[32] For each fund operated, the CPO must make and keep records that include the following: an itemised daily record of each commodity interest transaction for the pool; a journal of original entry of all receipts and disbursements of money, securities and other property; general ledgers of all asset, liability, expense and income accounts; transaction confirmations, purchase and sale statements and monthly statements received from futures commission merchants; canceled checks and bank statements; and all other records, data and memoranda prepared or received in connection with the operation of the pool.[33]

12–031

The CPO is also required to maintain records concerning its own futures transactions and other transactions in which it engages, including: an itemised daily record of each commodity interest transaction of the CPO and each principal of the CPO; transaction confirmations, purchase and sale statements and monthly statements furnished by an FCM to the CPO relating to the CPO's personal account and to each principal of the CPO relating to a personal account of the principal; and books and records "of all other transactions in all other activities in which the pool operator engages."[34] Most records may be maintained on either micrographic or electronic storage media.[35]

Structural requirements of organisation and operation

The CFTC imposes few structural constraints upon commodity pools and no restrictions upon the range of investment activity in which they may engage. There are three basic requirements established by CFTC rules relating to the structure and operation of commodity pools:

12–032

- *Legal separation of commodity pool operator and the commodity pool.* CFTC Rule 4.20(a)(1) requires that a CPO operate a commodity pool as a separate legal entity from the CPO. Rule 4.20(a)(2) provides that

---

[32] The CFTC staff has permitted books and records to be kept at alternate locations in some cases. See *e.g.* CFTC Letter No.98-27, [1996–1998 Transfer Binder] Comm. Fut. L. Rep. (CCH) (March 24, 1998), para.27.304 (permitting a CPO located in California to maintain its books and records at the New York office of its parent company); CFTC Letter No.98-23 [1996–1998 Transfer Binder] Comm. Fut. L. Rep. (CCH) (March 24, 1998), para.27.300 (permitting a CTA to maintain its books and records at its parent company's office).

[33] 17 C.F.R. § 4.23(a).

[34] 17 C.F.R. § 4.23(b).

[35] 17 C.F.R. § 1.31.

the CFTC may exempt corporations from this requirement in certain circumstances.

- *Funds and property to be received in the pool's name.* CFTC Rule 4.20(b) requires that all funds, securities and property received by the CPO from existing or prospective pool participants for purchase of pool interests or as assessments on pool interests be received in the pool's name.

- *Maintenance of the integrity of pool property.* Rule 4.20(c) bars the CPO from commingling the property of any pool that it operates with the property of any other person.

Commodity pools are not subject to any investment restrictions under US law by virtue of their commodity pool status. The CEA imposes no restrictions upon the types of investments a commodity pool may make, the degree of leverage (gearing) of such investments, or the fund's ability to invest in futures contracts on, or engage in it, spot or forward transactions in, physical commodities or other non-financial products. As discussed below, the volume of futures transactions to be undertaken by a pool may affect the CPO's duty to register. Otherwise, provided that full disclosure is made, required records maintained, and the integrity of the pool's property preserved in accordance with the strictures discussed above, a commodity pool may engage in any type of business or investment activity.

Potential investors

12–033 The CEA also imposes no restrictions upon the types of investors who may participate in a commodity pool. However, the accreditation level of the pool's investors will affect the availability of the "sophisticated investor" registration exemption discussed below. Further, under the federal securities laws, unless the fund's securities have been registered with the SEC, the fund will be required to be offered in accordance with provisions of the securities laws with respect to non-public offerings. In addition, if the fund is offered pursuant to the CFTC's Rule 4.7, investor qualification criteria for Qualified Eligible Persons (QEPs) must be satisfied. As discussed below, this exemption applies to a CPO whose pool offering is limited to non-US investors and to specified categories of high net worth institutions and individuals satisfying the CFTC criteria for QEP status.

Exemptions from CPO requirements

New CPO registration exemptions

Although, as noted above, the CFTC has taken a very inclusive view of the reach of the "commodity pool" definition, it has recently adopted rules that substantially reduce the regulatory implications of that characterisation. In August 2003, the CFTC created two broad new exemptions from CPO regulation: one based upon compliance with quantitative constraints upon the volume of a pool's futures transactions, and the other upon the relatively high level of sophistication of the pool's investors.[36] The first of these exemptions responds to long-standing requests that the agency recognise a *de minimis* exemption from CPO registration for the operators of funds that trade a relative small volume of futures contracts. A new limited futures trading exemption has been codified as CFTC Rule 4.13(a)(3). The new exemption is available with respect to pools that are sold pursuant to an exemption from registration under the Securities Act of 1933 (1933 Act), that are not marketed to the public in the US, whose investors are limited to accredited investors, and that satisfy one of two alternative quantitative restrictions. To meet the quantitative conditions of this new exemption, the pool may not: (i) commit more than five per cent of its assets to establish futures or commodity option positions, or; (ii) hold futures and commodity option positions that have a notional value that exceeds 100 per cent of the pool's liquidation value. At all times, the pool must satisfy one but not both of the specified trading limits.

12–034

A second new exemption is based upon the presumed sophistication of investors who are "Qualified Purchasers" as defined in Section 2(51)(A) of the Investment Company Act of 1940 or who satisfy other specified accreditation benchmarks. Under this exemption, a CPO would not be required to be registered in order to operate a pool offered pursuant to an exemption from registration under the 1933 Act and not marketed in the US, and whose investors are limited to persons reasonably believed to be QEPs within the categories specified in Rule 4.7(a)(2), which includes Qualified Purchasers. Institutional investors in such pools would be required only to be accredited investors or QEPs within any of the categories of QEPs set forth in CFTC Rule 4.7.

To take advantage of either the limited futures trading or sophisticated investor exemptions, the CPO must file a notice with the NFA and provide written disclosure to prospective pool participants concerning the nature of the exemption. The CPO operating an exempt pool would be precluded from marketing the pool to potential investors as a vehicle for trading in futures or options markets.

---

[36] 68 FR 47221 (August 8, 2003).

Mutual funds and other regulated investment vehicles

12–035 CFTC Rule 4.5 excludes from regulation as CPOs the operators of specified "qualifying entities" which are subject to the supervision of other US regulators. To qualify under Rule 4.5, the investment vehicle must be operated by a qualifying regulated person and the investment vehicle must be one of four types of regulated entities. Qualifying regulated persons are defined in Rule 4.5(a)(1)-(4) as including:

(a) an investment company registered as such under the Investment Company Act of 1940;

(b) an insurance company subject to regulation by any state;

(c) a bank, trust company or any other such financial depository institution subject to regulation by any state or the United States; and

(d) a trustee of, a named fiduciary of (or a person designated or acting as a fiduciary pursuant to a written delegation from or other written agreement with the named fiduciary), or an employer maintaining a pension plan that is subject to Title I of the Employee Retirement Income Security Act of 1974 (ERISA).

Qualifying entities operated by such persons are defined in Rule 4.5(b)(1)-(4) to include:

(a) with respect to an investment company, the registered investment company itself;

(b) with respect to an insurance company, a separate account established and maintained or offered by an insurance company pursuant to the laws of any state or territory of the United States, under which income gains and losses, from assets allocated to such account, are credited to or charged against such account, without regard to other income gains, or losses of the insurance company;

(c) with respect to a bank, trust company, or other financial depository institution, the assets of any trust, custodial account or other separate unit of investment for which it is acting as a fiduciary and for which it is vested with investment authority; and

(d) with respect to a trustee or named fiduciary (or a person acting as a fiduciary pursuant to delegation by the named fiduciary) of a pension plan, and subject to the proviso specified in Rule 4.5(a)(4) [discussed at para.12–036, below], a pension plan that is subject to Title I of ERISA.

The CPO seeking exclusion from commodity pool regulation must disclose in writing to prospective and existing participants that the entity is operated by a person who has claimed the exclusion and who is therefore not subject to registration or regulation as a CPO. The CPO also must file a notice of eligibility with the Commission prior to the date upon which such person intends to operate the qualifying entity pursuant to the Rule 4.5 exclusion.

Rule 4.5 also excludes completely from the commodity pool definition (*i.e.* without the necessity of filing a notice of eligibility with the CFTC or compliance with Rule 4.5(c)), the following types of pension and welfare plans: **12–036**

(a) a non-contributory plan, whether defined benefit or defined contribution, covered under Title I of ERISA;

(b) a contributory defined benefit plan covered under Title IV of ERISA; *provided, however,* that with respect to any such plan to which an employee may voluntarily contribute, no portion of an employee's contribution is committed as margin or premiums for futures or options contracts;

(c) a plan defined as a governmental plan under Section 3(32) of Title I of ERISA; and

(d) any employee welfare benefit plan that is subject to the fiduciary responsibility provisions of ERISA.

Pools restricted to "Qualified Eligible Persons"

CFTC Rule 4.7 provides an exemption from many of the CFTC's disclosure, reporting, and recordkeeping requirements to registered CPOs offering pool participations only to investors who qualify as QEPs. The QEP standards are designed to assure that the investor has sufficient financial resources and sophistication to warrant waiver of such obligations. The exemption differs from the CPO registration exemption discussed above in that it is available only to *registered* CPOs and is available with respect to pools offered to any categories of QEPs.   **12–037**

Generally, QEPs include:

(a) **Persons not required to satisfy the portfolio requirement**—These include FCMs registered pursuant to Section 4d of the CEA[37]; brokers and dealers registered pursuant to Section 15 of the Securities Exchange Act of 1934[38];   **12–038**

---

[37] 7 U.S.C. § 6d.
[38] 15 U.S.C. § 78o (1999).

certain registered CPOs, CTAs and investment advisers; "Qualified Purchasers" as defined in Section 2(51)(A) of the Investment Company Act of 1940; "knowledgeable employees" as defined in 17 C.F.R. § 270.3c-5; CPOs, CTAs, or investment advisers of the exempt pool, their principals and qualifying employees thereof; trusts whose settlor and trustee are QEPs[39]; and Non-US persons.[40]

12–039 **(b) Persons subject to the portfolio requirement**—A second category of QEPs consists of persons whom the CPO reasonably believes, at the time of sale to that person of a participation in a Rule 4.7-exempt pool, own securities and other investments with an aggregate market value of at least $2,000,000 or have had on deposit with an FCM within the preceding six months at least $200,000 in exchange-specified initial futures margins and commodity option premiums, *and* who are within specified categories of "accredited investors" as defined in Rule 501 of SEC Regulation D, including:

(1) an investment company registered under the Investment Company Act of 1940;

(2) a bank or savings and loan association acting for its own account or the account of a QEP;

(3) an insurance company acting for its own account or for the account of a QEP;

(4) a plan established and maintained by a state, its political subdivisions, or agency or instrumentality of a state or its political subdivisions, for the benefit of its employees, if such plan has total assets in excess of $5,000,000;

---

[39] CFTC staff have stated that "the assets of a revocable grantor trust may be treated as belonging to the grantor for the purposes of determining whether the grantor has sufficient net worth, meets the Portfolio Requirement and thus qualifies as a QEP . . . . Moreover, because [the grantor] qualifies as a QEP, the [t]rust also is a QEP under Rule 4.7(a)(2)(ix)." CFTC Letter No.0169, [Current Transfer Binder] Comm. Fut. L. Rep. (CCH) (July 2, 2001), para.28.596.

[40] For purposes of Rule 4.7 QEP definition, the following persons are defined as "Non-United States persons": (1) a natural person who is not a resident of the United States; (2) a partnership, corporation, or other entity, other than an entity organised principally for passive investment, organised under the laws of a foreign jurisdiction; (3) an estate or trust, the income of which is not subject to US income tax regardless of source; and (4) a pension plan for the employees, officers, or principals of an entity organised and with its principal place of business outside the United States. A "United States person" also does not include an entity organised principally for passive investment such as a pool, investment company or other similar entity, *provided* that units of participation in the entity held by US persons represent in the aggregate less than 10% of the beneficial interests in the entity, and that such entity was not formed principally for the purpose of facilitating investment by US persons in an entity with respect to which its CPO is claiming an exemption from the CFTC's pool regulations by virtue of its participants being non-United States persons.

CFTC REGULATION OF COMMODITY POOL OPERATORS

(5) an employee benefit plan within the meaning of ERISA, *provided* that the investment decision is made by a plan fiduciary, as defined in Section 3(21) of such Act, which is a bank, savings and loan association, insurance company, or registered investment adviser; or that the employee benefit plan has total assets in excess of $5,000,000; or, if the plan is self-directed, that investment decisions for, or the decisions as to the types of investment alternatives under the plan, are made solely by persons that are QEPs;

(6) a private business development company as defined in Section 202(a)(22) of the Investment Advisers Act of 1940;

(7) an organisation described in Section 501(c)(3) of the Internal Revenue Code, with total assets in excess of $5,000,000;

(8) a corporation, Massachusetts or similar business trust, or partnership, other than a pool, which has total assets in excess of $5,000,000, and is not formed for the specific purpose of participating in the exempt pool;

(9) a natural person whose individual net worth, or joint net worth with that person's spouse, at the time of his purchase in the exempt pool exceeds $1,000,000;

(10) a natural person who had an individual income in excess of $200,000 in each of the two most recent years or joint income with that person's spouse in excess of $300,000 in each of those years and has a reasonable expectation of reaching the same income level in the current year;

(11) a pool, trust, insurance company separate account or bank collective trust, with total assets in excess of $5,000,000, not formed for the specific purpose of participating in the exempt pool, and whose participation in the exempt pool is directed by a QEP;

(12) except as provided *or* the governmental entities referenced in sub-para.(4) above, if otherwise authorised by law to engage in such transactions, a governmental entity (including the United States, a state, or a foreign government) or political subdivision thereof, or a multinational or supranational entity or an instrumentality, agency, or department of any of the foregoing.

To claim the Rule 4.7 exemption, a CPO must file a notice with the CFTC. Rule 4.7 exempts the CPO of a qualifying pool from making the specific required disclosures (*e.g.* past performance history, discussion of the principal risk factors of the pool, description of the investment programme and use of the proceeds of the offering, conflicts of interest, litigation history, etc.), permits reporting to investors on a quarterly in lieu of monthly basis and in streamlined form, and reduces applicable recordkeeping requirements. CPOs

US REGULATION OF MANAGED FUTURES—COMMODITY TRADING ADVISORS

who obtain relief pursuant to Rule 4.7 remain subject to the duty to disclose all material information and to the antifraud prohibitions of Section 4o of the CEA.[41] Rule 4.7 requires that a standardised disclosure concerning the exempt status of the pool be provided to prospective pool participants either in an offering memorandum for the pool or, if no offering memorandum is provided, in the subscription agreement for the pool.

Rule 4.12(b): pools primarily engaged in securities transactions

12–040 Rule 4.12(b) provides narrower exemptive relief than Rule 4.7 but is available to a broader range of investment vehicles. As the rationale for Rule 4.7 relief is the presumed sophistication of the pool's participants, the predicate for the Rule 4.12(b) exemption is that the fund's primary investment activity is in securities, that the fund's futures activity is limited and incidental to its securities trading activities, and that compliance with applicable securities requirements can therefore be relied upon in lieu of compliance with certain CFTC requirements. Rule 4.12(b) relief is available to registered CPOs who operate pools which: (1) are offered and sold pursuant to the Securities Act of 1933 or an exemption therefrom; (2) are generally and routinely engaged in the buying and selling of securities and securities derived instruments; (3) do not commit more than ten percent of the fair market value of their assets to establish commodity futures or option positions; and (4) will trade commodity futures and options in a manner solely incidental to their securities trading. To obtain Rule 4.12(b) relief, the CPO must file a written claim for exemption identifying the CPO and the pool for which relief is being claimed and containing representations that the pool will be operated in accordance with the requirements of the rule.

If a pool qualifies for exemption under Rule 4.12(b), the CPO may with respect to that pool: (1) use an offering memorandum prepared in accordance with the Securities Act of 1933 or a relevant exemption therefrom, supplemented by certain, but not all, disclosures otherwise required by the CFTC; (2) provide a quarterly statement indicating the net asset value of the pool as of the end of the reporting period and the change in net asset value from the end of the previous reporting period, in lieu of the prescribed account statement; (3) provide in lieu of the prescribed annual report a certified annual report which contains, at a minimum, Statements of Financial Condition and of Income (Loss); and (4) claim exemption from certain recordkeeping requirements.[42] The disclosure relief available under Rule 4.12(b) includes

---

[41] 7 U.S.C. § 6o.
[42] Specifically, the requirements of Rule 4.23(a)(10) and (a)(11), which relate to Statements of Financial Condition and Statements of Income (Loss).

330

CFTC REGULATION OF COMMODITY POOL OPERATORS

relief from providing certain past performance disclosures otherwise required by Rule 4.25.

Rule 4.13: non-profit and small pools

Rule 4.13(a)(1) and (2) provide exemptive relief from the CPO registration requirement for two categories of persons: (1) persons operating on an uncompensated (directly or indirectly) basis only one commodity pool at a time, who are neither required to register with the CFTC in another capacity nor affiliated with a person required to so register and who conduct no advertising in connection with the pool; and (2) persons who receive in the aggregate not more than $400,000 in total gross capital contributions for units of participation in all pools operated, none of which pools may have more that 15 participants. Rule 4.13(a)(5) requires that prior to soliciting pool participants, the pool operator claiming the Rule 4.13 exemption deliver a statement to any prospective participant containing prescribed language to the effect that the CPO is not required to register, and has not registered with, the CFTC, and that the CPO is not required to deliver a Disclosure Document, periodic account statements, or annual reports to pool participants. The pool operator claiming exemption under Rule 4.13(a)(1) and (2) must file this statement with the CFTC and the NFA and is required to provide each pool participant with monthly statements for the pool received from its FCM and to maintain and make available to the CFTC its books and records.

12–041

Selected CFTC/NFA Compliance Considerations Relevant to CPOs and CTAs

In addition to the specific disclosure, reporting and recordkeeping duties that may apply to CPOs and CTAs, certain supervisory and compliance duties are common to CPOs and CTAs.

12–042

Duty to supervise registered persons

CFTC 166.3 requires that each person registered under the CEA, except associated persons who have no supervisory duties, must diligently supervise the handling by its officers, partners, employees and agents of all commodity interest accounts carried, operated, advised or introduced by the registrant and all other activities relating to its business as a CFTC registrant. Although there is no express duty in the CFTC's rules to have written supervisory procedures, such procedures are recommended as a general matter and are required in certain specific areas by NFA rules.

12–043

331

NFA Compliance Rule 2-9 places a continuing responsibility on every Member firm diligently to supervise its employees and agents in all aspects of its futures activities. NFA leaves the exact form of supervision to the Member, thereby providing the Member with flexibility to design procedures that are tailored to the Member's own situation.

NFA members are required to complete a self-examination checklist on an annual basis which reflects many of the basic elements of a compliance programme. Other NFA Compliance Rules impose specific supervisory duties. Rule 2-8 contains detailed requirements regarding the supervision of discretionary accounts. Rule 2-29(e) requires each member to adopt and enforce written procedures regarding communications with the public, including advance review and approval of all promotional material by an appropriate supervisory person. Rule 2-30(h) requires each member to adopt and enforce procedures regarding customer information and risk disclosure.

Account opening procedures

No suitability requirement

12–044   CFTC rules do not require customer suitability determinations with respect to recommended futures transactions. This is due to the profile of the typical futures trader, the high level of potential risk in futures trading generally, and the risk disclosures mandated by CFTC rules. Unlike securities, which vary widely in risk, *e.g.* from investment grade-government and corporate bonds to "hot" issues, "penny" stocks, and junk bonds, all futures contracts have essentially the same high level of potential risk. In *Phacelli v ContiCommodity Services, Inc.*,[43] the CFTC ruled that a commodity broker did not violate CEA Section 4b (antifraud prohibition) merely because he failed to determine whether a customer was suitable for futures trading. However, the CFTC emphasised that several courts had treated "over-reaching" conduct (*e.g.* taking advantage of exceptionally gullible customers) and misrepresentations that futures trading is suitable for a particular customer as conduct equivalent to fraud, which thus may be actionable under the CEA. The CFTC also noted in *Phacelli* that it may consider the characteristics and circumstances of the complainants in evaluating assertions that they have been misled or otherwise defrauded and that "an individual's duties under the law may vary according to the characteristics of the particular customer being solicited".

---

[43] [1986–1987 Transfer Binder] Comm. Fut. L. Rep. (CCH) (September 5, 1986), para.23.250.

SELECTED CFTC/NFA COMPLIANCE CONSIDERATIONS

NFA "know your customer" requirement

NFA rules impose the general requirement that NFA members "observe high **12–045**
standards of commercial honor and just and equitable principles of trade in
the conduct of their commodity futures business" (NFA Rule 2–4). In addition, NFA Rule 2–30, often referred to as the "know your customer" rule,
requires members to obtain certain specified information (such as income,
net worth and prior investment and futures trading experience) from customers at or before opening an account. Under NFA's interpretation of this
rule, members are required in appropriate cases to disclose that futures
trading is too risky for a particular customer.

Customer agreements

The CFTC does not specify by rule the content of an account agreement **12–046**
between a customer and an FCM or an IB or even require that there be such
a written agreement. However, all firms use their own standard customer
agreements as a matter of sound business practice, and such agreements typically grant firms important rights concerning the treatment of customer
positions and funds. Customer account agreements are also generally used to
fulfill the requirement of CFTC Rule 1.37 that the FCM keep a record of the
name, address and principal occupation of the account owner as well as the
name of any other person guaranteeing or exercising any trading control with
respect to such account.

Restrictions on advertising

NFA Rule 2-29 ("Communications with the Public and Promotional Mater- **12–047**
ial") prohibits various forms of misrepresentation and other inappropriate
forms of solicitation activity, such as "high-pressure approach[es]" and statements that futures trading is appropriate for all persons. NFA Rule 2-29(e)
requires that each NFA member adopt and enforce written procedures for
supervision of its associates and employees for compliance with this rule,
including procedures for prior review and approval of all promotional material by an officer, general partner, sole proprietor, branch office manager or
other supervisory employee other than the individual who prepared such
material.

In addition to the general antifraud prohibitions set forth in Sections 4b
and 4o of the CEA, CPOs, CTAs and their principals are subject to the specific advertising restrictions of CFTC Rule 4.41. Under Rule 4.41, any CPO,
CTA (and any principal thereof), whether registered or exempt from registration, is generally prohibited from advertising in a manner which employs

333

US REGULATION OF MANAGED FUTURES—COMMODITY TRADING ADVISORS

"any device, scheme or artifice to defraud" participants or clients or prospective participants or clients or involves any "transaction, practice or course of business which operates as a fraud or deceit" upon any client or participant or prospective client or participant. In addition, Rule 4.41(b) requires that advertising that includes the performance of simulated or hypothetical accounts must contain a cautionary statement stating, among other things, that hypothetical or simulated performance results are subject to certain limitations and are also "designed with the benefit of hindsight".[44]

Antifraud provisions specifically applicable to CTA, and CPOs

12–048 Section 4o of the CEA,[45] expressly prohibits a CTA or CPO, or an associated person thereof, from engaging in fraudulent behaviour.

Section 4o

12–049 Section 4o(1) of the CEA provides as follows:

"It shall be unlawful for a commodity trading advisor, associated person of a commodity trading advisor, commodity pool operator or associated person of a commodity pool operator by use of the mails or any means or instrumentality of interstate commerce, directly or indirectly

(a) to employ any device, scheme, or artifice to defraud any client or participant or prospective client or participant; or

(b) to engage in any transaction, practice, or course of business which operates as a fraud or deceit upon any client or participant or prospective client or participant".

Subsection (2) of Section 4o prohibits any CTA or CPO, or person associated therewith, from representing or implying, based on the registrant's registration status with the Commission or otherwise, that the CTA, CPO or associated person, "has been sponsored, recommended, or approved, or that such person's abilities or qualifications have in any respect been passed upon, by the United States or any agency or office thereof".

---

[44] See Rule 4.41(b) for statement quoted in full. See also NFA Compliance Rule 2-29(c), *NFA Rulebook*, para.5147.20 and NFA's Interpretive Notice on Rule 2-29, *NFA Rulebook*, para.9003, concerning hypothetical performance results.
[45] 7 U.S.C. § 60.

334

Rule 4.15

A person who is exempted from registration by operation of 17 C.F.R. Part 4, including Rules 4.13 and 4.14, remains subject to the antifraud provisions of Section 4o of the CEA.

12–050

CHAPTER 13

INVESTMENT MANAGEMENT AND OCCUPATIONAL PENSION SCHEMES

Andrew Powell and Fraser Sparks,
Hammonds, London

Introduction

13–001   As a consequence of the relatively small pension provided by the State, private pension provision in the UK is big business. Whether a personal pension or an occupational pension, many individuals are saving towards their retirement (although, generally speaking, people need to be saving more). The management of these pension funds is also big business and, with the current trend towards defined contribution/money purchase pension schemes where the individual can control (to a certain extent) where their pension is being invested, individuals are becoming more sophisticated and more demanding of their investment managers.

There are many types of pension arrangement but by far the most common are those approved by the Inland Revenue as exempt approved pension schemes for the purposes of the Income and Corporation Taxes Act 1988. If a pension scheme is approved in this way, subject to certain limitations, payments into the pension scheme and investment growth within the pension scheme will not be subject to either income or capital taxes.

As with most forms of investment, the investment of pension scheme assets is currently going through a period of change. Gone are the days when it did not matter a great deal how assets were invested and the only question was how big the returns would be. In today's financial climate, pension scheme investment is being scrutinised as never before. Negative returns are commonplace and trustees of occupational pension schemes are expected to make complex strategic investment decisions which will have a real impact on whether the scheme is continued by the employer and could affect whether employees will actually receive the benefits the scheme was designed to provide (although trustees are bound to consult with their sponsoring employer in setting an investment strategy and, generally, they will have to seek advice from a regulated investment consultant).

336

INTRODUCTION

There is a great deal of legislation and regulation controlling the invest- **13–002** ment of pension scheme assets (including financial services provisions) and the effects of this legislation will be considered in this Chapter. For reasons we will come back to, occupational pension schemes are established by way of trust and so, in addition to the legislative controls on occupational pension scheme investments, centuries-old trust law principles developed in the context of private trusts are now having an effect on the investment of hundreds of billions of pounds worth of assets.

To complete the regulatory picture of the investment of pension scheme assets, occupational pension schemes now have an investment code of best practice which is intended to work in a similar way to the Combined Code of the Committee on Corporate Governance.[1] Currently, it is not a legal requirement to comply with this code. However, the Government expects occupational pension scheme trustees to disclose the extent to which these principles have been followed (and the reasons for not following the principles) on a voluntary basis. If the pensions industry does not adopt this approach on a voluntary basis, the Government has said it will legislate to make this disclosure exercise a legal requirement.

This Chapter will concentrate on investment management issues (both the **13–003** legislative controls and the practicalities) for large, self-administered occupational pension schemes and, in particular, defined benefit arrangements. However, consideration will also be given to issues which are relevant to defined contribution pension schemes (both occupational and insurance policy based arrangements) and, to a lesser degree, to small self-administered schemes ("SSASs").

Before going into the detail of these issues, it is important to understand the different types of pension arrangement available.

Benefit structure

Pension schemes will either provide benefits on a defined contribution or a **13–004** defined benefit basis. In defined contribution schemes (sometimes called money purchase schemes), an individual will build up a fund of money generated by contributions and investment growth and, when the individual retires, they will use the accumulated fund to purchase an annuity. In this type of arrangement, the investment risk rests with the individual and they are at the mercy of short-term fluctuations in the market. To decrease the risk from short-term fluctuations, as individuals approach retirement they will often go through a process of moving their fund away from investments such as

---

[1] The Combined Code was published in 1998 by the London Stock Exchange following the reports of the Cadbury, Greenbury and Hempel committees. All UK incorporated companies which are listed on the London Stock Exchange must disclose in their annual reports the extent to which they have complied with the Combined Code.

337

equities and into fixed interest investments which better match the cost of annuities. Personal pension schemes, stakeholder arrangements and a growing number of occupational pension schemes operate on a defined contribution basis.

In a defined benefit pension scheme, the investment risk rests with the sponsoring employer because, regardless of the contributions paid by the employees and the investment returns achieved by the fund, the scheme provides a guaranteed level of retirement income. The defined benefit provided by the scheme can take various forms, although the traditional benefit structure will be one where the individuals accrue a fraction, say, $\frac{1}{60}$ of their final pensionable salary for each year of service with the employer (a "final salary scheme"). An alternative form of defined benefit scheme will base the benefits not on individuals' final salary but on their average salary over the period of their membership of the scheme.

For a defined benefit occupational pension scheme to comply with legislation, it must, to some degree, pre-fund the promised benefits. This requires the employers participating in a defined benefit pension scheme to pay contributions into the scheme which, broadly speaking, are intended to be sufficient to provide the benefits promised. This method allows the employer to spread the cost of providing pensions for its workforce over a long period of time but it also puts the focus on the investment returns the pension scheme is able to achieve and, consequently, the management of the scheme's assets. If sufficient investment returns are achieved, a surplus of assets will be generated which may allow the employer to suspend its contributions to the scheme. Of course, if investment returns are sufficiently poor, the employer's obligation to fund the scheme may become unsustainable and lead to the scheme being wound up.

13–005 A tension has developed between the investment requirements of a pension scheme and the desire to control payments required by pensions legislation (the "minimum funding requirement"). This can be seen most plainly in the investment philosophy that is adopted.

The need to match assets to liabilities on the basis required by the statutory minimum funding requirement calls for a particular investment strategy which may not fit with the basis recommended by the actuary, on the assumption that the pension scheme will not be wound up. However, to adopt an investment strategy which moves away from the matched approach called for by the minimum funding requirement would run the risk of short-term financial volatility which has a real and immediate impact on sponsoring employers (short-term deficits on the minimum funding requirement basis can trigger a requirement for immediate contributions from the sponsors). A similar distortion can be caused by the need to control the expression of the value and cost of the pension promise in sponsoring employers' accounts.

INTRODUCTION

Personal pension plans and stakeholder arrangements

Personal pension plans differ from occupational pension schemes because **13–006** they are established by way of individual policies with an insurance company. Even where an employer has established a group personal pension plan with an insurer, this will be made up of a series of individual policies. These arrangements are established on a defined contribution basis and have the advantage of portability, *i.e.* an individual leaving the employment of a particular employer can easily take the insurance policy with him or her when changing jobs.

A new form of pension scheme recently introduced by the Government is the stakeholder arrangement. This type of arrangement provides benefits on a defined contribution basis and must comply with various regulatory restrictions, particularly with regard to ongoing management charges and exit charges if an individual stops contributing to the policy.[2] A stakeholder pension scheme must be registered with the Occupational Pensions Regulatory Authority ("OPRA") and, although it is possible for this type of pension arrangement to be established as a trust based arrangement (similar to an occupational pension scheme), by far the majority are established as contract based arrangements (akin to a personal pension plan).

Generally speaking, these type of bundled arrangements raise few investment issues that are driven by statutory concerns. However, where these arrangements are used to provide an alternative to state pension provision, there are restrictions on the way that assets may be dealt with. Moreover, there are specific rules relating to the solvency of the institutions providing the product and requirements as to disclosure etc.

Occupational pension schemes

According to the National Association of Pension Funds, there are estimated **13–007** to be 103,165 "live" occupational pension schemes in the UK.[3] Occupational pension schemes are those established by employers primarily to provide pensions for their employees in retirement. However, these arrangements have developed far beyond simply providing a retirement pension. An occupational pension scheme will often be used as the vehicle for providing redundancy benefits, lump sum payments on death and ill-health benefits.

The term "occupational pension scheme" is, in itself, used to describe different types of arrangement and this type of scheme may provide benefits on either a defined contribution or a defined benefit basis. There is currently a trend for employers to switch to defined contribution pension schemes, not

---

[2] The Welfare Reform and Pensions Act 1999 and the Stakeholder Pension Schemes Regulations 2000 (SI 2000/1403).
[3] The NAPF Yearbook 2003.

339

only because of recent poor investment returns but because of regulatory and accounting issues which discourage arrangements where the investment risk lies with the employer.

They may be wholly insured with an insurance company, in which case the trustees of the pension scheme will hold an insurance policy providing the benefits payable by the pension scheme, or they may be self-insured, in which case the trustees will invest their scheme's assets to provide the benefits payable by the pension scheme. The advantage of being self-insured is that, obviously, none of the pension scheme's assets are making a profit for an insurance company.

Small Self Administered Schemes (SSASs)

13–008 Until 1973 the Inland Revenue treated directors who, broadly speaking, controlled five per cent or more of a company's share capital as self-employed and, consequently, they were not permitted to join the company's occupational pension scheme. The Finance Act 1973 changed the test for controlling directors and allowed them to join the company's self-administered occupational pension scheme. However, the Inland Revenue recognised the scope for controlling directors to manipulate their pension benefits and imposed certain restrictions on small schemes where the people who control the company also control the pension scheme and are the members of the scheme. The main provisions controlling SSASs are set out in the Retirement Benefits Schemes (Restriction on Discretion to Approve) (Small Self-administered Schemes) Regulations 1991[4] and the Inland Revenue's practice notes on the approval of occupational pension schemes.[5]

Broadly, a SSAS is a self-administered occupational pension scheme with fewer than 12 active members (*i.e.* members who are currently accruing benefits under the scheme) and those members are connected with each other, the trustees or an employer in relation to the scheme. As explained later in this Chapter, there are special investment provisions which apply to SSASs.[6]

The proposed changes to the tax structure for exempt approved pension schemes, recently published by the Inland Revenue, may have a profound effect on these arrangements as may the proposals for a more stringent duty of care in respect of investment decisions.[7]

---

[4] SI 1991/1614.
[5] IR12 (2001).
[6] See para.13–100 below.
[7] "Simplifying the taxation of pensions: increasing choice and flexibility for all" published by HM Treasury and the Inland Revenue in December 2002 and the Government's response to Paul Myners' review of institutional investment "Familiar with the Issues Concerned": A Consultation Document, issued by the Department for Work and Pensions, February 2002.

340

INTRODUCTION

Tax treatment

The relatively low State pension and the corresponding prevalence of private **13–009** pensions have already been mentioned. To encourage employees to save for their retirement and employers to contribute to their employees' retirement, various tax reliefs are available. The extent to which relief is available will depend on the type of pension scheme and whether or not it has been granted approved status by the Inland Revenue under the Income and Corporation Taxes Act 1988. For a pension scheme to be treated in this way, it must comply with various Inland Revenue limits which, for example, control the amount an employee may contribute to a pension scheme in any one tax year and the amount of earnings an employee may use for the purpose of calculating his contributions and pension.

In addition to Inland Revenue approved arrangements, employers may establish unapproved pension schemes for their senior executives who earn in excess of the Inland Revenue's earnings limit. These arrangements may be established on a funded basis (a Funded Unapproved Retirement Benefits Scheme or FURBS) or on an unfunded basis (an Unfunded Unapproved Retirement Benefits Scheme or UURBS).

Application of trust law

For an occupational pension scheme to be eligible for approved status with **13–010** the Inland Revenue, it must be established by way of irrevocable trust. This ensures that the pension scheme's assets are held separately from those of the employer (they are under the control of the pension scheme's trustees) and the pension scheme cannot be used by the employer in order to avoid tax, other than in the provision of pension benefits. It is also possible to establish stakeholder pension schemes under trust.

Consequently, trust law and equity principles apply to occupational pension schemes (and stakeholder pension schemes established under trust) which will affect the manner in which trustees exercise their duties and the extent of their powers. Of particular relevance to the investment of pension scheme assets is the level of expertise which trustees are deemed to have. Regardless of the type of trust, save for professional trustees (*i.e.* people carrying out the business of trusteeship), trustees will be viewed as volunteers and will not be taken to have any particular degree of knowledge on matters such as investments. However, following Paul Myners' review of institutional investment, steps are being taken to raise this duty of care so that trustees will be judged against a person familiar with the issues concerned.[8]

---

[8] See para.13–037 *et seq.* below.

341

Pension scheme investments

13–011 The law and practice of pension scheme investments is complex and applies different principles depending on the type of pension scheme in issue. However, it is important to understand this area of law and practice because of the sheer magnitude of pension scheme investments. Occupational pension funds in the United Kingdom have assets in excess of £776 billion with an annual investment income of £21 billion. Members of the National Association of Pension Funds alone currently control approximately 20 per cent of the shares on the London stock market.[9]

Particular Investment Vehicles

Common investment funds

13–012 A common investment fund is used where the trustees of more than one exempt approved pension scheme wish to pool their investments in order to achieve economies of scale with regard to investment returns and administrative expenses. In addition, by participating in a common investment fund, smaller pension schemes will be able to access particular types of investment which may not be viable for it individually (generally, because of diversification issues). Common investment funds will also be allowed to submit centralised repayment claims on behalf of the participating pension schemes.

A common investment fund is not a separate legal entity and the participating schemes remain the beneficial owners of their respective shares in the assets within the fund. It is transparent for tax purposes and thus the pension scheme exemptions from income tax and capital gains tax apply in the same manner as if the assets were held directly.

The Inland Revenue's pension schemes section will view a common investment fund on a tax transparent basis provided that the share of each scheme participating in the fund is identifiable at all times.[10] Further, Inland Revenue guidelines state that, for a common investment fund to be acceptable, it must meet the following requirements:

(a) all of the participating pension schemes must be sponsored by the same employer or by employers within the same group of companies;

(b) the participating pension schemes must be exempt approved or in the process of receiving such approval;

---

[9] The NAPF Yearbook 2003; these figures are attributed to various sources. However, falls on the equity markets and an unwillingness for pension schemes to rebalance their investments between equities and fixed interest products may have lowered this figure to nearer 15–17%.

[10] IR12 (2001), para.17.12 and Inland Revenue Pension Schemes Office Manual, para.17.1.72.

PARTICULAR INVESTMENT VEHICLES

(c) the documentation governing the common investment fund should:

   (i)   set out the rights and obligations of each participant and of the administrator of the common investment fund;

   (ii) set out the method by which the fund's assets and liabilities are apportioned between the participants;

   (iii) identify those pension schemes participating in the common investment fund; and

   (iv) require the prior approval of the Inland Revenue for further pension schemes to participate;

(d) each participating pension scheme must retain its entitlement to, and the power to withdraw, its share of the assets;

(e) proper accounts must be kept of the common investment fund's assets and liabilities which identify the increase or decrease in the value of each participating pension scheme's interest in the fund; and

(f) the common investment fund should not subject the assets of the participating schemes to any trusts in addition to those which govern those schemes.[11]

It is not necessary for the participating pension schemes to place all of their assets within the common investment fund and this provides participating schemes with even greater flexibility. Although the exact role of the fund's administrator will depend on the common investment fund in question, generally it will review the performance of the investment managers and disseminate information to the participating schemes.

13–013

The exact relationship between the participating pension scheme trustees, the common investment fund administrator and the investment managers must be ascertained clearly in order to avoid potential financial services issues. As we have already seen, occupational pension scheme trustees may only delegate investment decisions (which relate to regulated activities for the purposes of the FSMA) to an investment manager who is authorised or exempt from authorisation under the FSMA. For a common investment fund to be viable, from the point of view of costs, the group of employers will probably want to avoid the need for the administrator to be authorised or exempt in this way and, as such, the participating pension schemes must be careful not to delegate their investment decision making powers to the administrator. However, any discretion to make investment decisions may be delegated to investment managers "by or on behalf" of pension scheme trustees[12] and investment managers may be appointed "by or on behalf" of pension scheme trustees.[13] It follows that, in a common investment fund

---

[11] IR12 (2001), para.17.12 and Inland Revenue Pension Schemes Office Manual, para.22.4.22.

[12] Pensions Act 1995, s.34(2); para.13–045, below.

[13] Pensions Act 1995, s.47(2); para.13–053, below.

343

established by way of a contract between the participants, the administrator will appoint investment managers on behalf of the participants and will delegate those trustees' investment discretions to the investment managers on their behalf.

If a common investment fund is established on this basis, the trustees of the participating pension schemes will also be able to avoid being treated as managing investments by way of business because they will not be making routine or day to day investment decisions.[14] A further financial services issue which should be taken into account when establishing a common investment fund is that a common investment fund will generally fall within the definition of a collective investment scheme.[15] However, there are certain exemptions from the collective investment scheme requirements which are likely to be relevant to common investment funds. A common investment fund will not be a collective investment scheme for the purposes of the FSMA if:

(i) each participating scheme can withdraw its own property at any time;

(ii) the common investment fund is not operated "by way of business". This phrase is not defined in this context and the FSA has confirmed it will give the phrase its "actual meaning". If the common investment fund is administered in-house and the administrator is not being paid for its services this exemption is likely to apply; or

(iii) each participating trustee is a corporate trustee in the same group as the administrator.[16]

If the arrangement falls within the definition of a collective investment scheme, the administrator will have to be authorised under the FSMA.

13–014 Although one of the conditions laid down by the Inland Revenue for a common investment fund to be acceptable is that it should not subject the assets to an additional trust, the Inland Revenue does allow common investment funds to be established by way of a bare trust or nomineeship. Broadly speaking, a bare trust is a trust where the trustee (here, the trustee of the common investment fund) holds the property for the benefit of the beneficiaries (i.e. the trustee boards of the participating pension schemes) absolutely.

In this way, the beneficiaries may require the trustee to convey the property in a particular manner and the trustee must act in accordance with the beneficiaries' instructions. Translating these provisions into the context of a common investment fund operated by way of a trust, the participating trustee boards must be capable of directing the trustee of the fund to take certain

---

[14] See para.13–029, below.
[15] Financial Services and Markets Act 2000, s.235.
[16] Article 3 of, and paragraphs 1, 4 and 10 of the Schedule to, the Financial Services and Markets Act 2000 (Collective Investment Schemes) Order 2001, art.3 and Sch., paras 1, 4 and 10. Also, para.6.9.3G of the draft perimeter guidance on activities relating to pension schemes (CP179) issued by the Financial Services Authority.

steps (this will probably be dealt with in the trust deed establishing the arrangement) and of withdrawing their assets from the trust at any time. This approach does have certain advantages over a contractual common investment fund, most notably that the trustee of the fund may appoint investment managers centrally and the arrangement has an appearance of a centralised investment fund with centralised ownership of assets.

Establishing a common investment fund under a bare trust will involve the trustees of the participating pension schemes delegating their investment powers to the common investment fund trustee. This will be possible under the Pensions Act 1995 and the FSMA only if the common investment fund trustee is either authorised under the FSMA or delegates all routine and day-to-day investment management decisions to investment managers. The same provisions regarding collective investment schemes will apply to a trust-based common investment fund and, consequently, the trustee will need to be authorised under the FSMA in any event unless one of the exemptions set out above can be used.

As the participating pension schemes remain the beneficial owners of the **13–015** assets they put into a common investment fund, the transfer of UK assets into a fund in return for an issue of units attracts only nominal fixed-rate stamp duty (currently £5). Similarly only fixed-rate stamp duty arises on a transfer of assets out of a fund back to the relevant participating pension scheme. Further, since an arrangement between exempt approved pension schemes is specially exempted from constituting a unit trust for stamp duty reserve tax purposes, no liability to stamp duty reserve tax arises on the surrender of units within the common investment fund.[17] Stamp duty reserve tax may, however, become payable on the transfer of units and it is advisable that units should only be surrendered for cash or in specie rather than by way of a transfer.

From a practical point of view, each pension scheme participating in the common investment fund must have a similar Statement of Investment Principles, at least to the extent that they place assets within the fund. However, it is possible, by having more than one investment mandate and allowing participating trustees to invest more heavily in one mandate than another, to allow participating pension schemes to have different asset allocation policies. The common investment fund document should require participating pension schemes to withdraw their assets from the fund if their Statement of Investment Principles means that it is no longer appropriate for those assets to be commingled within the fund.

---

[17] Finance Act 1999, Sch.19, para.16.

Unit trusts

13–016 A unit trust is a collective investment scheme based on trust law. A trustee holds the assets on trust for the unit-holders whose share in the assets underlying the trust is calculated by reference to the number of units they hold out of the total number of units in issue.

Unit trusts are widely used in the retail sector of the financial services industry and such arrangements will generally be authorised by the Financial Services Authority (and are thus known as "authorised unit trusts"). Authorised unit trusts are treated as if they are companies for tax purposes,[18] but they are exempted from tax on chargeable gains[19] and are subject to corporation tax on income at the reduced rate of 20 per cent. This tax is not recoverable by any investing pension scheme.

The trustees of a pension scheme are able to invest in such authorised unit trusts alongside other investors they so wish. However, a different form of unit trust is also open to pension schemes (and other, sophisticated investors), namely an "unauthorised unit trust". As the name suggests, these unit trusts are not authorised by the Financial Services Authority but this only means they are not authorised for sale to the general public.

13–017 An unauthorised unit trust continues to be treated as a trust for tax purposes. If the unit trust is established as an "exempt unauthorised unit trust" such that only bodies which are themselves exempt from capital gains tax on investments (such as approved pension schemes) are able to become unit-holders, then no liability to capital gains tax arises to the trustee on the disposal of any assets held within the trust.[20] In order to ensure the availability of this exemption is not prejudiced, the unit trust manager must seek confirmation from the trustees of any prospective pension scheme investor that it is wholly exempt from capital gains tax.

Although the trustee of an exempt unauthorised unit trust remains subject to tax on any income that arises, any distributions made to unit-holders are to be treated as having been made after deduction of such tax and pension funds are able to reclaim any tax treated as having been deducted from any distributions made to them. Accordingly, effective tax transparency is achieved by pension funds holding units in an exempt unauthorised unit trust (provided that all income arising to the unit trust in any period is distributed to unit-holders).

As the unit trust (whether authorised or unauthorised) is a collective investment scheme for the purposes of the FSMA, the administrator of the trust is required to be authorised. As well as investing in third-party operated unit trusts, it is also possible for a group of pension schemes to work together (most commonly where they are sponsored by the same employer or by employers

---

[18] Income and Corporation Taxes Act 1988, s.468.
[19] Taxation of Chargeable Gains Act 1992, s.100(1).
[20] *ibid.*

PARTICULAR INVESTMENT VEHICLES

within the same group of companies) and form their own exempt unauthorised unit trust. This can provide similar practical benefits as forming a common investment fund.

Dealings in unit trusts (whether authorised or unauthorised) may be subject to stamp duty reserve tax, resulting an *ad valorem* charge of up to 0.5 per cent when the unit-holder trustees either surrender (for cash or in specie) or transfer units. This issue has not been resolved and is currently under consideration by the Stamp Office.

Pension fund pooling vehicles ("PFPVs")

PFPVs are unauthorised unit trusts to which the tax rules usually applicable to such unit trusts have been disapplied. Regulations made in 1996 provide that unit trusts registered with the Inland Revenue and duly approved as PFPVs are to be treated as wholly transparent for tax purposes. These Regulations disapply the income tax, capital gains tax and stamp duty provisions which apply to unauthorised unit trusts.[21] Instead, participating pension schemes are treated, for the purposes of income and capital gains taxes, as if they own a share of the PFPV's assets directly and the pension scheme exemptions from such taxes arising in relation to scheme investments apply accordingly.

13–018

With regard to stamp duty, units in a PFPV are not treated as stock for the purposes of stamp duty on transfers or as chargeable securities for the purposes of stamp duty reserve tax (since, as is the case for common investment funds, a PFPV is expressly excluded from constituting a unit trust scheme for these purposes). In this way, UK assets can be transferred into PFPVs without incurring a charge to stamp duty or stamp duty reserve tax.

Although the participants in the PFPV must be exempt approved pension schemes (or the overseas equivalent), there is no requirement that the trustees or the sponsoring employers belong to the same corporate group. However, if the trustees are not all corporate trustees within the same group as the trustee of the PFPV, the trustee of PFPV will have to be authorised under the FSMA as the PFPV will fall within the definition of a collective investment scheme, unless another exemption can be used.[22]

Because of this flexibility, PFPVs make ideal vehicles for pension funds of companies within the same group if there is a possibility that any of the employer companies or any of their businesses may be demerged or otherwise sold outside the group. In this way, the assets of the original pension funds

13–019

---

[21] Income Tax (Pension Funds Pooling Schemes) Regulations 1996, Capital Gains Tax (Pension Funds Pooling Schemes) Regulations 1996 and The Stamp Duty and Stamp Duty Reserve Tax (Pension Funds Pooling Schemes) Regulations 1996.

[22] See para.13–013, above.

347

can be easily divided and transferred if necessary to new pension schemes by a simple transfer of units in the PFPV.

The main disadvantage with the PFPV, however, is that there are a number of strict statutory conditions that need to be met before the Inland Revenue is able to approve a unit trust vehicle as a PFPV and these can be administratively burdensome. In particular, it is necessary for the trustee of a PFPV to agree a method with the Inland Revenue for allocating income to the participating pension schemes.

Open-ended investment companies ("OEICs")

13–020 OEICs are similar to authorised unit trusts and the same direct and stamp duty reserve tax analysis applies to them.[23]

They are established as a corporate entity but the Companies Act 1985 does not apply to them. Unlike a company, the OEIC is open-ended because it can expand or contract depending on demand by issuing or buying back its shares. As an OEIC is a corporate entity, there is no need for a trust and the assets belong beneficially to the OEIC.[24]

OEICs are collective investment schemes and can only exist as an investment authorised by the Financial Services Authority. They must have an authorised corporate director and an authorised depository responsible for scheme property

In the context of pension schemes, OEICs may provide a special class of share which is only open to tax exempt investors.

Trustees' Investment Powers

General provisions

13–021 As a consequence of occupational pension schemes being established by trust, the investment powers of trustee boards will depend greatly on the provisions of the pension schemes' trust deed. In the unlikely event that the trust deed contains no express investment power, trustees will be able to rely on the statutory power contained in the Pensions Act 1995 (the "Pensions Act") which permits them to make an investment of any kind as if they were absolutely entitled to the assets of the scheme.[25] This statutory power is subject to any express restrictions contained in the trust deed.

Although the Pensions Act permits trustees to make an investment of any kind, the term "investment" is not defined in that Act. The leading authority

---

[23] See paras 13–016 *et seq.*, above.
[24] Financial Services and Markets Act 2000, s.236(2).
[25] Pensions Act 1995, s.34(1).

on the meaning of the words "invest" and "investment" is the case of *Re Wragg*,[26] which dates back to 1919. The judgment contains the following paragraph:

> "Without attempting to give an exhaustive definition . . . the words 'to invest' when used in an investment clause may safely be said to include as one of its meanings 'to apply money in the purchase of some property from which interest or profit is expected and which property is purchased in order to be held for the sake of the income which it will yield'."

Unfortunately, this case has been taken by some to mean that assets purchased by trustees for reasons other than deriving an income are not investments. If this point is accepted, a specific power would be required in a pension scheme's trust deed allowing the trustees to purchase assets to achieve a capital gain. This interpretation does not follow from the comments made in *Re Wragg* as it is clear from the quote set out above that this is just one of the meanings of "to invest" and it seems likely that, if the term was to be interpreted today, it would include assets purchased for capital gains.[27] Consequently, while a specific power to purchase assets which are not income producing puts the matter beyond doubt, the absence of this power should not be taken to be a decisive barrier to pension scheme trustees purchasing such assets.

However, it is clear that, for pension scheme trustees to participate in a common investment fund or to purchase units in a unit trust, a specific power in the trust deed is required. This follows from the general trust law principle that trust assets should not be blended with other assets and, with regard to common investment funds, the requirements of the Inland Revenue. **13–022**

The Pensions Act 1995

We have already seen that the Pensions Act contains a default power of investment permitting occupational pension scheme trustees to invest the trust assets as if they were absolutely entitled to those assets. In addition, the Pensions Act sets out overriding provisions regarding the matters occupational pension scheme trustees must consider when exercising their investment powers. Importantly, these provisions also apply to an investment manager to whom those powers have been delegated. **13–023**

The trustees and investment managers must have regard to the need for diversification of investments (to the extent this is appropriate to the circumstances of the scheme), to the suitability to the scheme of investments of the

---

[26] [1919] 2 Ch.58, Lawrence J.
[27] See comments in *Marson v Morton* [1986] 1 W.L.R. 1343 and Report of the Pension Law Review Committee.

INVESTMENT MANAGEMENT AND OCCUPATIONAL PENSION SCHEMES

description proposed and also to the suitability to the scheme of the proposed investment itself.[28] Although this process is likely to be at the forefront of pension scheme trustees' minds when they make investment decisions, it may be more difficult for investment managers to consider the circumstances of particular pension schemes when considering how to exercise the powers delegated to them.

Trustees are required, before making any investment (other than narrower-range investments not requiring advice[29-30]) and at such intervals thereafter as they decide to be appropriate, to obtain and consider written advice on the question of whether the investment is satisfactory in light of the principles outlined above.[31] If this written advice would constitute a regulated activity under the Financial Services and Markets Act 2000 ("FSMA"), it must be obtained from a person authorised under the FSMA or exempt from such authorisation. In other circumstances, the advice must be obtained from a person the trustees reasonably believe to be "qualified by his ability in and practical experience of financial matters and to have the appropriate knowledge and experience of the management of the investments of trust schemes".[32]

13–024   Section 35 of the Pensions Act requires the trustees of an occupational pension scheme (save for, broadly speaking, wholly-insured arrangements and small self-administered pension schemes[33]) to prepare, maintain and revise from time to time a written statement of principles which will govern investment decisions for the purposes of the pension scheme (the "Statement of Investment Principles").[34] The statement must cover the following:

(a)   the trustees' policy for complying with the requirements for diversification and suitability of investments and also the statutory minimum funding requirement (s.56 of the Pensions Act);

(b)   the kinds of investments to be held;

(c)   the balance between the different kinds of investments;

(d)   risk;

---

[28]   Pensions Act, s.36(2).

[29-30]   Trustee Investment Act 1961 Sch.1, Pt I sets out the narrower-range investments as follows: Defence Bonds, National Savings Certificates and Ulster Savings Certificates, Ulster Development Bonds, National Development Bonds, British Savings Bonds, National Savings Income Bonds, National Savings Deposit Bonds, National Savings Indexed Income Bonds, National Savings Capital Bonds, National Savings FIRST Option Bonds, National Savings Pensioners Guaranteed Income Bonds; in deposits in the National Savings Bank, and deposits in a bank or department.

[31]   Pensions Act 1995, s.36(3) and (4).

[32]   ibid., s.36(6).

[33]   Full details of the schemes to which Pensions Act 1995 s.35 does not apply are set out in Occupational Pension Schemes (Investment) Regulations 1996 (SI 1996/3127), reg.10.

[34]   Also, see Occupational Pension Schemes (Investment) Regulations 1996 (SI 1996/3127), Pt III.

350

(e)   the expected return on investments;

(f)   the realisation of investments;

(g)   the extent (if any) to which social, environmental or ethical considerations are taken into account in the selection, retention and realisation of investments; and

(h)   the trustees' policy (if any) in relation to the exercise of the rights (including voting rights) attaching to investments.

Section 35(4) of the Pensions Act specifically prohibits any restriction in a pension scheme's trust deed or the Statement of Investment Principles from being placed on the trustees' power of investment by reference to the consent of the employer. However, before the Statement of Investment Principles is prepared or revised, the trustees must consult with the employer. The trustees must also obtain written advice on the suitability of the statement from a person reasonably believed by the trustees to be qualified by his ability in and practical experience of financial matters and to have the appropriate knowledge and experience of the management of the investments of pension schemes.

Restrictions: employer-related investments

In order to maintain the independence of an occupational pension scheme,   **13–025**
the Pensions Act restricts the extent to which pension scheme trustees may invest in employer-related investments.[35] Section 40(2) of the Pensions Act defines "employer-related investments" as:

"(a)   shares or other securities issued by the employer or by any person who is connected with, or an associate of, the employer,

(b)   land which is occupied or used by, or subject to a lease in favour of, the employer or any such person,

(c)   property (other than land) which is used for the purposes of any business carried on by the employer or any such person,

(d)   loans to the employer or any such person, and

(e)   other prescribed investments."

The Investment Regulations[36] set out the "other prescribed investments" which include:

---

[35] Pensions Act 1995, s.40.
[36] Occupational Pension Schemes (Investment) Regulations 1996 (SI 1996/3127), Pt II.

INVESTMENT MANAGEMENT AND OCCUPATIONAL PENSION SCHEMES

(a) the proportion attributable to the pension scheme's resources of any investments which would have been employer-related investments if they had been made directly by the pension scheme;

(b) any guarantee of, or security given to secure, obligations of the employer or a person connected with or an associate of the employer shall be an employer-related investment. Any guarantee or security given shall be treated as an investment equal to the amount of the obligations guaranteed or secured; and

(c) a loan where the repayment depends on the employer's actions or situation (unless the intention behind the loan was not to provide financial assistance to the employer).

The Pensions Act does not prohibit pension scheme trustees from entering into employer-related investments, but it does limit the extent to which the trustees may do so. Regulation 5 of the Investment Regulations states that not more than five per cent. of the current market value of the resources of a scheme may at any time be invested in employer-related investments and none of the resources of a scheme may at any time be invested in any employer-related loan. However, no scheme resources may be invested in any employer-related investment if it would involve the trustees entering into a transaction at an undervalue within the meaning of the Insolvency Act 1986.[37]

13–026 It is important to note that the five per cent limit is an ongoing limit, so that the test applies not only when the trustees enter into an employer-related investment but during the whole time such investments are held. Therefore, if an employer-related investment is held by the trustees of a pension scheme, frequent checks on the value of the employer-related investment would need to be made.

There are certain employer-related investments to which this restriction does not apply,[38] including:

(i) where pension scheme resources are placed in an account with a person permitted to accept deposits;

(ii) where the resources derive from additional voluntary contributions by members and they have provided written agreement to the investment; and

(iii) where a debt is owed by the employer to the pension scheme by virtue of the Pensions Act.

---

[37] Insolvency Act 1986, s.238(4): essentially, a person enters into a transaction at an undervalue if he or she receives no consideration or the value of the consideration received is significantly less than the consideration provided by that person.

[38] Investment Regulations, reg.6.

The restrictions set out in reg.5 of the Investment Regulations do not apply to pension schemes where each member is a trustee of the scheme or where the rules require the consent of each member to be obtained before an employer-related investment is entered into. Although this provision will not be relevant for most pension schemes, it is a very important provision for small self-administered schemes.[39]

If a pension scheme breaches the employer-related investment restrictions, the trustees will be liable to a penalty imposed by OPRA if they have failed to take all reasonable steps to ensure compliance with the restrictions. In addition, any trustee who agreed to make an investment which contravenes this restriction will be guilty of a criminal offence and liable for a fine and/or imprisonment. Clearly, these provisions are taken extremely seriously, although an extreme breach of the Pensions Act would be necessary in order to incur a prison sentence.

Restrictions: financial services issues

Although the basic premise is that pension scheme trustees have the power to make investments as if they were absolutely entitled to the pension scheme's assets, in addition to any restrictions that may be set out in the trust deed, the trustees must comply with the FSMA.

13–027

It is highly unlikely that a board of pension scheme trustees will either be authorised under the FSMA or exempt from such authorisation and, consequently, they must take care not to breach the provisions of the FSMA by undertaking regulated activities by way of business. Until recently, there was no guidance from the Financial Services Authority (the "FSA") on how FSMA and the associated regulations applied to pension schemes. Fortunately, draft guidance was issued for consultation in April 2003 which sets out a proposed appendix to the FSA's authorisation manual.[40] Although the guidance has not been finalised, it seems unlikely that it will be changed significantly.

The functions of an occupational pension scheme trustee will undoubtedly involve undertaking regulated activities and so the question is whether a trustee is carrying an a regulated activity by way of business. In the context of occupational pension schemes, the test for determining whether an activity is being carried on by way of business will differ depending on the particular activity.

---

[39] See para.13–100, below.
[40] "The Authorisation Manual—Draft perimeter guidance on activities related to pension schemes": CP179.

INVESTMENT MANAGEMENT AND OCCUPATIONAL PENSION SCHEMES

Managing investments

13–028 Taking s.22 and Sch.2 to the FSMA together with the Regulated Activities Order ("RAO")[41] managing investments belonging to another by way of business, in circumstances involving the exercise of discretion, is a specified activity under the FSMA if the assets consist of, include or may include any investment which is a security or a contractually based investment. Consequently, decisions regarding investments in, for example, real property and deposits will not fall within this regulated activity.

Notwithstanding that occupational pension scheme trustees are the legal owners of the scheme's assets, for the purposes of FSMA the trustees will be regarded as managing investments "belonging to another".[42] One consequence of this is that, where members are able to choose how their pension fund is invested, the trustees will not be managing investments if they must follow the members' instructions.[43] In this situation, the FSA takes the view that a member is managing their own investments and, as such, the member will not be conducting the regulated activity of managing investments belonging to another.

Although there is an exclusion in the RAO for the activity of managing assets by a person acting as a trustee, this will not apply in the context of an occupational pension scheme where the activity is being carried on by way of business.[44] The test for whether trustees of an occupational pension scheme are managing assets of that scheme "by way of business" is set out in Art.4 of the Business Order.[45] Article 4 provides that occupational pension scheme trustees will be managing the assets of their scheme by way of business unless they fall within one of the following exceptions.

Routine and day-to-day decisions

13–029 Occupational pension scheme trustees will not be carrying on the regulated activity of managing assets by way of business if all "routine and day-to-day decisions" concerning the management of the pension scheme's securities and contractually based investments are taken on behalf of the trustees by a person who is authorised under the FSMA, exempt from such authorisation or an overseas person. Therefore, to avoid the need for authorisation under the FSMA, occupational pension scheme trustees must ensure that all such decisions are delegated to their investment managers in accordance with the Pensions Act (see below).

---

[41] Financial Services and Markets Act 2000 (Regulated Activities) Order 2001 (2001/544), art.37.

[42] FSA's draft guidance, para.6.6.4G.

[43] Other issues connected with offering members a choice of investments are discussed in paras 13–048 *et seq.*, below.

[44] Regulated Activities Order, art.66(3).

[45] The Financial Services and Markets Act 2000 (Carrying on Regulated Activities by Way of Business) Order 2001 (2001/1177).

354

TRUSTEES' INVESTMENT POWERS

This can cause issues for trustees who wish to purchase units in a unit trust or shares in an open-ended investment company without using an investment manager. In this situation, trustees will need to ensure that they are not making the relevant decisions on a routine or day-to-day basis.

The FSMA does not provide any information on what constitutes a "routine or day-to-day decision" and until the FSA's draft guidance was published there was no explanation of what this phrase means in practice.[46]

According to the FSA's draft guidance,[47] to determine whether a decision is routine or day-to-day, the nature and the context of the decision must be considered. Consequently, decisions that may be routine or day-to-day in respect of one pension scheme may not be in respect of another pension scheme. The draft guidance also states that decisions may become routine or day-to-day if they are decisions in relation to which the trustees are regularly involved. Unsurprisingly, in the FSA's view, day-to-day decisions will generally be those which need to be made on a daily basis or very frequently and routine decisions are those "regularly made in the course of a standard procedure". In addition, the significance of the decision must be considered.

Clearly, it is difficult to give a precise definition of "routine or day to day decisions" and the FSA stresses in its draft guidance that "the treatment of particular decisions will depend on their individual circumstances". The draft guidance lists certain decisions which, in the FSA's view, will or will not generally be treated as routine or day-to-day: **13–030**

(a)   decisions which will not generally be routine or day to day are those:

- about the adoption of a statement of investment principles[48];
- about the formulation of an asset allocation policy, including prescribing the basis for rebalancing;
- about the appointment of investment managers[49]; and
- which require consulting the trustees in exceptional circumstances only (for example where the investment manager has a conflict of interest); and

(b)   decisions which will generally be routine or day-to-day are those:

- about the buying or selling of particular securities or contractually based investments which an investment manager would be expected to make;

---

[46] The Financial Services Act 1986 used the phrase "day-to-day decisions" and the Securities and Investment Board had issued guidance on the meaning of "day-to-day decisions" (SIB Guidance Release 2/88). However, this guidance ceased to have effect when the FSMA came into force.

[47] Draft para.6.7.7G *et seq.*

[48] See paras 13–023 *et seq.* above.

[49] In the FSA's view, the appointment and removal of investment managers could itself amount to managing investments if it is part of a strategic decision to change the general allocation of the pension scheme's assets (draft para.6.6.8G).

355

INVESTMENT MANAGEMENT AND OCCUPATIONAL PENSION SCHEMES

- about which annuities to purchase in order to provide pensions from the scheme; and
- making recommendations to investment managers with a force amounting to a direction.

Article 4(6) of the Business Order provides that decisions made by trustees of an occupational pension scheme regarding investing in, broadly speaking, private equity, will not constitute routine or day-to-day decisions provided that the decision is taken in line with advice from an authorised, exempt or overseas person. This exception relates to the purchase of units in a collective investment scheme or of corporate shares or debentures where the primary purpose is to acquire and hold non-traded shares or debentures.[49a]

Small self-administered schemes

13–031 This exception applies to two different types of small pension schemes:

(a) The first type of pension scheme is one which has no more than 12 members who are all trustees (other than those who are incapable of acting or unfit to act as trustee). It must be a requirement of the scheme that all routine or day-to-day decisions regarding the management of securities and contractually based investments held for the purposes of the scheme are taken by all or a majority of the members or an authorised or exempt person.

The Inland Revenue requires this type of small pension scheme to have a trustee who is not a beneficiary under the scheme (called a "pensioneer trustee"). Obviously, a pensioneer trustee will not be able to take part in routine or day-to-day decisions if this exception is to be relied upon. Pensioneer trustees are required to monitor the pension scheme's investments to ensure that any investments are permitted by the Inland Revenue. The FSA's draft guidance states that it is possible for pensioneer trustees to monitor investments, object to investments and give a view as to whether a particular investment is permitted without making a routine or day to day investment decision.[50]

(b) The second type of pension scheme is one which has no more than 50 members and all contributions to the scheme must be used in the acquisition of a life policy in respect of the life of each member. The only investment management decision regarding securities and contractually

---

[49a] The FSA issued an update on the progress of CP 179 in February 2004 which indicated hat the business test may revert to "day-to-day" (as it was in the Financial Services Act 1986). The FSA's update also mentioned that the Treasury Department is considering extending Art.4(6) of the Business Order to cover all pooled arrangements, whether relating to private equity or otherwise.

[50] Draft paras 6.7.5G and 6.7.6G.

356

based investments must be choosing the life policy and each member must be able to select the life policy that will apply to him or her.

It is important to note that the business test in art.4 of the Business Order only applies to the management of assets held for the purposes of the pension scheme. Consequently, the trustees of an occupational pension scheme will not be subject to the business test in art.4 when, for example, they decide which annuity to purchase for a member which will be held in the member's own name rather than as an asset of the pension scheme. In this situation, trustees would be subject to the business test in art.3.

Other regulated activities

Where the trustees of an occupational pension scheme carry out regulated activities other than the management of assets in the circumstances where art.4 of the Business Order applies,[51] whether or not they are acting by way of business will be determined in accordance with the general business test in art.3 of the Business Order. Article 3(1) states that a person will not be regarded as carrying on a regulated activity by way of business unless he carries on the business of engaging in one or more of those activities. In the FSA's opinion, this business test would apply where a person provides a service on a regular basis in return for reward of some kind. However, the existence of a reward of some kind may not result in an activity being carried on by way of business where the carrying on of the activity does not represent the carrying on of a business comprising that activity.

13–032

From the FSA's draft guidance, it is difficult to see how occupational pension scheme trustees (other than professional trustees) would be regarded as carrying out any of their duties "by way of business" under art.3 provided they do not hold themselves out as someone whose business it is to carry on that regulated activity. Even where there is some doubt over whether or not a trustee is acting in the course of business, the usual activities carried out by trustees are unlikely to be regulated activities. For example:

Dealing

Notwithstanding the trust structure of occupational pension schemes, the FSA regards pension scheme trustees as dealing in investments as principal.[52] However, trustees will fall within exclusions to this regulated activity if they do not hold themselves out as someone whose business involves buying

13–033

---

[51] The list of relevant regulated activities is set out in art.3(2) of the Business Order.
[52] FSA's draft guidance, para.6.4.2. It is interesting to compare this to the FSA's view of the management of assets where pension scheme trustees are taken to be managing investments belonging to another.

INVESTMENT MANAGEMENT AND OCCUPATIONAL PENSION SCHEMES

securities or life policies with a view to selling them or deals in contractually based investments only through an authorised or exempt person.[53]

Arranging

13–034 Occupational pension scheme trustees will not be considered to be carrying out the regulated activity of arranging transactions in respect of scheme assets because they are a party to the transaction. This exclusion applies even where the members are taking the investment decisions and instructing the trustees how they wish to proceed. Even where the transaction is not in respect of scheme assets, the trustees may be able to rely on an exclusion where the transaction is with or through an authorised or exempt person.[54]

Advising

13–035 To be carrying out the regulated activity of advising on investments, those investments must be specified investments. As an interest under an occupational pension schemes is not a specified investment for the purposes of the FSMA, any advice to a member with regard to his or her interest under the occupational pension scheme will not constitute a regulated activity.

Financial promotion

13–036 Section 21 of the FSMA prohibits an unauthorised person, acting in the course of business, from communicating an invitation to engage in investment activity. As mentioned above, is seems unlikely that pension scheme trustees will be acting on the course of business when issuing information to their scheme members. In any event, for these purposes, an investment activity does not include interests under the trusts of an occupational pension scheme.[55] In addition, art.54 of the Financial Promotion Order[56] disapplies the restrictions contained in s.21 of the FSMA in respect of any communication between a trustee and the beneficiaries that relates to the management of the trust fund and the FSA's draft guidance confirms that this provision applies to pension schemes.[57] Notwithstanding these technical arguments, as a breach of these provisions is a criminal offence, in practice many pension scheme trustees take the precaution of arranging for the information to be reviewed by a person who is authorised for that purpose under the FSMA.

---

[53] Regulated Activities Order arts 15 and 16.
[54] *ibid.*, arts 28 and 29.
[55] Financial Services and Markets Act 2000 (Financial Promotion Order 2001) art.4 and Sch.1, para.27(2).
[56] The Financial Services and Markets Act 2000 (Financial Promotion) Order 2001.
[57] Draft para.6.14.5G.

Duty of care

Although occupational pension schemes are established as trusts, the invest-   **13–037**
ment of pension scheme assets is one area where the difference between the
law applying to pension schemes and private trusts is growing. The investment principles that have developed out of the *Myners' Review* of institutional investment and the proposed increase of the duty of care required of
pension scheme trustees will take this difference to a new level.

The current duty of care: the prudent man

At present, the basic principle when investing assets is that pension scheme   **13–038**
trustees (as with any other trustees) must take "such care as an ordinary prudent man would take if he were minded to make an investment for the benefit of other people for whom he felt morally bound to provide".[58] This (rather
low) duty of care follows from the traditional view that the office of trustee
is a voluntary office and, as such, trustees should be viewed in much the same
way as an ordinary person investing their own money.

However, in the context of sophisticated trusts, such as pension schemes, it
seems that this duty of care must be extended. The *Goode Report* suggested
adding that a trustee should "use such additional knowledge and skill as the
trustee possesses or ought to possess by reason of the trustee's profession,
business or calling".[59] This would certainly raise the duty of care required to
be exercised by a professional trustee, which is logical. Professional trustees
will be paid to be trustees of a particular private trust or pension scheme on
the basis that they have a degree of expertise which will be beneficial to the
members of the trust. To judge professional trustees against the prudent man
test does not seem to fit with the rationale for appointing a professional
trustee. At least one case has considered this point and concluded that a professional trustee should be judged against the degree of skill which it professes
to have.[60]

The duty of care should also be viewed in the light of the requirements of
the Pensions Act with regard to the choice of investments.[61] The Pensions Act
states that, before investing in any manner, the trustees must obtain and consider written advice as to whether the investment is satisfactory having regard
to the need for diversification, the suitability of the investment to the scheme
and the scheme's Statement of Investment Principles. Where the trustees have
sought investment advice, they would need good reasons for not following

---

[58] *Learoyd v Whiteley* (1887) 12 App. Cas. 727, *per* Lindley L.J.
[59] *The Report of the Pension Law Reform Committee* (chaired by Professor Roy Goode), 1993.
[60] *Bartlett v Barclays Bank Trust Co Ltd* [1980] Ch.515. Also, see the Department for Work and
Pensions consultation document, "Familiar with the issues concerned" (February 2002).
[61] Pensions Act 1995, s.36; see paras 13–023 *et seq.*, above.

that advice even if the decision ultimately made would have been one that an ordinary prudent man could have made had he not had the benefit of that advice. It follows that the duty of care required of pension scheme trustees should take account of this requirement to obtain advice. Consequently, it is at least arguable that the duty of care for occupational pension scheme trustees has already been raised from the original prudent man test to the following:

> "In investing trust assets, an occupational pension scheme trustee must exercise such care as an ordinary prudent man would take if he were minded to make an investment for the benefit of other people for whom he felt morally bound to provide and to use such additional knowledge and skill as the trustee possesses or ought to possess by reason of the trustee's profession, business or calling or by reason of proper advice obtained in accordance with the Pensions Act.

Notwithstanding the suggestion that the duty of care has been strengthened from the original "prudent man" test, in practice it seems likely that trustees who satisfy the investment provisions set out in the Pensions Act and act in accordance with proper professional advice will have complied with their duty of care.

The *Myners' Review* proposed duty of care: the prudent expert

13–039 One of the particular concerns highlighted by the *Myners' Review*[62-63] was the lack of investment knowledge of pension scheme trustees. In preparing the review, a survey of pension scheme trustees was conducted which showed that 62 per cent of trustees have no investment qualifications and 54 per cent of pension schemes did not have an investment sub-committee.

Occupational pension scheme trustees are responsible for the investment of hundreds of billions of pounds worth of assets and it is difficult to argue that the people ultimately responsible for these investments, *i.e.* the trustees, do not need a degree of investment knowledge. *The Myners' Review* was concerned that the current duty of care (even when taking into account the knowledge and experience the trustees actually have or ought to have by virtue of their profession) places no duty or legal incentive on trustees to gain expertise beyond that they already possess. The review was troubled by the proposition that, at present, trustees can satisfy their duty of care simply by obtaining advice and information and doing the best they can.

The *Myners' Review* proposed that trustees should assess the effectiveness of their contribution to meeting the objectives of the scheme, ensure that decision-making structures assist the efficient running of the scheme and that

---

[62-63] "Institutional investment in the UK: a review", published in March 2001.

responsibilities between the trustees are correctly allocated. However, the main thrust of the *Myners' Review* on this subject was that the duty of care should be raised to provide for a legal requirement that, where trustees take a decision, they should be able to take it with the skill and care of someone familiar with the issues concerned. If they do not feel they possess this level of skill and care, the trustees should either acquire it or delegate the decision to a person or organisation whom they believe does possess this skill and care. (The ability of trustees to delegate their duties effectively is considered in more detail below and, as we shall see, the main problem for trustees in delegating investment decisions concerning issues with which they are not familiar is that they may remain responsible for the decision taken by the delegate.) This higher duty of care is based on the "prudent expert" test contained in the United States of America's Employment Retirement Income Security Act 1974 (ERISA).

The *Myners' Review* reported that many respondents to the consultation **13–040** exercise argued there was no need to raise the duty of care as pension scheme trustees were required to obtain proper advice and this use of advisers "dealt satisfactorily with trustees' lack of investment understanding".[64] The review was not satisfied with this reasoning and argues that the trustees should be in a position to "critically examine the information on which [the advice] is based".[65] The reasoning behind this was that, as the trustees are legally responsible for their decisions, they should understand the nature of what they are deciding.

The *Myners' Review* was also concerned that the methodology behind the investments would not develop as the trustees would not feel they have the expertise to change investment direction and the advisers would feel they lacked the power to make such decisions. In this way, pension schemes will continue investing in the same asset classes and ignoring alternatives, particularly private equity.

The *Review's* logic is that, if pension scheme trustees have a greater understanding of investment issues, pension schemes will invest in previously under-researched asset classes which will provide greater opportunities for enhanced returns. This seems unlikely. Even if the "prudent expert" test is introduced so that pension scheme trustees making decisions regarding investments are familiar with the issues, why would trustees suddenly begin to explore unchartered asset classes? More than previously, the onus of making prudent investment decisions would rest with the trustees who, by the nature of what they are trying to achieve, are unlikely to seek out high risk investments. Pension scheme trustees have no incentive to obtain record-breaking investment returns but they do have an incentive to avoid record-breaking losses. Although the sponsoring employer will undoubtedly want to see a good rate of return to minimise the amount of money it needs to pay

---

[64] *The Myners' Review*, p.6.
[65] *The Myners' Review*, p.7.

INVESTMENT MANAGEMENT AND OCCUPATIONAL PENSION SCHEMES

into the pension scheme, it is unlikely to want the trustees to pursue a high risk strategy whereby its contributions to the scheme might be dramatically increased. This seems to be the real reason behind the apparent inertia to invest differently; the first trustees to break away from tradition will be watched closely and will feel open to criticism if they get it wrong.

13–041 The trustees cannot ignore the fact that, in a balance of cost final salary occupational pension scheme, the employer is the person who picks up the bill. The Pensions Act states that nothing in the pension scheme's trust deed or the Statement of Investment Principles may impose any restrictions on any power to make investments by reference to the consent of the employer[66] but occupational pension scheme trustees should consider the wishes of the employer. As trustees, they must act in the best interests of the members and these interests will not be served by following an investment strategy so risky that the employer decides it cannot accept that risk and winds up the pension scheme. Consequently, any decision to explore new asset classes must be made in consultation with the employer and the trustees would need to consider very carefully if they are acting in the members' best interests by going against the wishes of the employer.

The Government's proposals

13–042 The Government has accepted the need to modify the duty of care owed by pension scheme trustees with regard to investment decisions, although its reasoning for doing so is to ensure that:

> "the investment decisions made about pension fund assets are taken by those with sufficient skill and information to make them effectively; and those responsible for decisions in law are those taking them in fact".[67]

The Government recognises that pension scheme trustees should not be required to be investment experts and should be entitled to make use of the expertise of others but does acknowledge the need for trustees to be able to evaluate advice and exercise their own judgment when considering and acting upon advice. The 2004 Pensions Bill[67a] requires trustees to have knowledge and understanding appropriate for the purpose of enabling them to exercise properly their functions as trustees.

Myners was only asked to review investment matters and, when reading his report, it must be remembered that pension scheme trustees exercise many important functions other than the investment of assets. That is not to say

---

[66] Pensions Act 1995, s.35(4).
[67] "Familiar with the Issues Concerned": A Consultation Document, issued by the Department for Work and Pensions, February 2002.
[67a] As published on February 10, 2004.

362

TRUSTEES' INVESTMENT POWERS

that investment decisions are not important but a balance must be struck. The Government's proposals, while very similar to those of the *Myners' Review*, appear to have shifted emphasis very slightly so that the importance is not so much on making investment decisions but in understanding the advice obtained from professional advisers.

The Government's proposed standard of care is for pension scheme trustees to act "with the care, skill, prudence and diligence under the circumstances then prevailing that a prudent person acting in a like capacity and familiar with such matters would use in the conduct of an enterprise of like character and with like aims". There will be no statutory definition of "familiar" as the Government is of the opinion that to do so would restrict the flexibility of the standard of care and, consequently, this will be a question for the courts to decide. In addition, the Government proposes to apply the statutory standard of care set out in the Trustee Act 2000 to pension schemes so that:

(i) where a pension scheme trustee has, or holds himself out as having, any special knowledge or experience, he must exercise such care and skill as in reasonable in the circumstances; and

(ii) where a pension scheme trustee acts in the course of a business or profession, he must exercise such care and skill as is reasonable in the circumstances having regard to any special knowledge or experience that it is reasonable to expect of a person acting in the course of that kind of business or profession.

It is arguable that these provisions will simply confirm the current common law position.

These proposals have been taken forward by the Government's White **13–043** Paper[68] which proposes legislation to require trustees to be "familiar with the issues or have relevant knowledge across the full range of their responsibilities". As part of the drive to reduce the quantity of pensions legislation, the statutory duty will be supported by a "code of practice" issued by the occupational pensions regulator to give trustees guidance on how the regulator believes the statutory principle should be complied with.

EU Pensions Directive

The European Union has recently published its Directive "on the activities **13–044** and supervision of institutions for occupational retirement provision".[69] The

---

[68] "Simplicity, security and choice: Working and saving for retirement—Action on occupational pensions", June 2003 (Cm 5835). The timetable set out in the White Paper suggests that this legislation will be introduced in Spring 2005.
[69] Directive 2003/41 of the European Parliament and of the Council, June 2003, and published in the Official Journal of the European Union on September 23, 2003.

INVESTMENT MANAGEMENT AND OCCUPATIONAL PENSION SCHEMES

Directive sets the "prudent person rule" as the "underlying principle for capital investment". However, the prudent person rule will not require any changes in the UK, particularly as the proposed new duty of care for all matters dealt with by occupational pension scheme trustees is more onerous.

Delegating Decision-Making Powers

Power to delegate

13–045   The first place to look when determining the ability of occupational pension scheme trustees to delegate their powers is the trust deed and rules. Any restrictions on this ability to delegate will be of particular relevance to investment managers and they will usually require the trustees to warrant that there are no restrictions on the power to delegate which would prevent the trustees entering into the investment management agreement.

Although most pension scheme trust deeds will contain a specific power allowing the trustees to delegate their powers and setting out the manner in which this can be achieved, the Pensions Act contains a default power in respect of investment decisions. Section 34(2) of that Act provides that any decision about investments may be delegated "by or on behalf" of the trustees to an investment manager who is either authorised under the FSMA or exempt from such authorisation. In addition, s.47 provides that for every occupational pension scheme with assets which include investments (as defined in s.22 of the FSMA 2000) there shall be appointed an investment manager.

If the trustees delegate their investment discretion in accordance with s.34(2), they will not be responsible for the acts or defaults of the investment manager provided the trustees (or the people making the delegation on behalf of the trustees) have taken all reasonable steps to satisfy themselves that the investment manager has the appropriate knowledge and experience for managing the pension scheme's investments, is carrying out his work competently and is complying with the Pensions Act requirement to have regard to the need for diversification and the suitability of the investment to the pension scheme.[70]

13–046   Section 34 goes on to provide that pension scheme trustees may not delegate any decision about investments in any other way save for (subject to any restriction in the pension scheme's trust deed):

(a)   authorising two or more trustees to make investment decisions on behalf of the full board of trustees; and

---

[70]   Pensions Act 1995, s.34(4).

364

(b) delegating their discretion to an investment manager who is not authorised or exempt from authorisation under the FSMA (such as a manager based overseas) but only if giving effect to this decision would not constitute a regulated activity for the purposes of the Act.

However, if pension scheme trustees delegate their investment discretion in one of these two ways, the entire trustee board will remain liable for the acts and defaults of the delegates in the same way that it would have been liable for them if they had been if the acts and defaults of the trustee board.

Investment sub-committees

As part of the suggestion that pension scheme trustees' duty of care with **13–047** regard to investment decisions should be raised, the *Myners' Review* wanted to ensure that the people making investment decisions are familiar with the issues involved.[71] One of the ways in which the review envisages trustees complying with the higher duty of care is for them to delegate investment decisions to an investment sub-committee of trustees. However, under the current law, the full board of trustees will remain liable for any investment decisions taken by a sub-committee of trustees. This could discourage trustees from setting up this type of sub-committee as, even if they have no particular investment knowledge, they may well want to be present when decisions are made the consequences of which they will be liable for.

It is at least arguable that pension scheme trustees who have considered their duty not to make decisions concerning issues with which they are not familiar and have taken steps to ensure that such decisions are delegated to an appropriately constituted sub-committee should not remain liable for the acts or defaults of that sub-committee. This is an issue on which the Department for Work and Pensions has sought consultation[72] and it will be interesting to see if the policy of encouraging trustees to delegate decisions concerning issues with which they are not familiar will include excluding their liability for these decisions.

---

[71] See paras 13–029 *et seq.*, above.
[72] The Department for Work and Pensions consultation document, "Familiar with the issues concerned" (February 2002), asked the questions "Knowing that pension scheme trustees make decisions both individually and collectively, should the new standard of care apply to individual trustees, any trustee sub-committee that exists, or to the trustee board collectively? Should the new standard apply also to independent pension scheme trustees?".

Defined contribution arrangements—member choice

13–048 A common element of modern defined contribution (or money purchase) occupational pension schemes (and also additional voluntary contribution arrangements within defined benefit pension schemes) is a certain degree of member choice with regard to the investment of their "individual pension account". In accordance with Inland Revenue restrictions, these accounts are purely notional and are intended only to allow investment returns to be apportioned between the members. Contributions made by the employer in respect of each member and the contributions by each member will be separately recorded, together with the investment choice selected by each member. The trustees will then be able to apportion investment returns to each member and calculate the value of the notional individual pension accounts on the same basis that would apply if members had a legal interest in only their individual account rather than the scheme as a whole.

Trustees of pension schemes offering a choice of investments will select a range of investment options from which the members may choose how to invest their account. Frequently, there is also a "default option" which will be applied for those members who do not inform the trustees of their investment choice.[73] Clearly, the decision as to which options should be available is an investment decision, although probably not a routine or day to day decision, and, in setting the options, the trustees must obtain and consider proper written advice.[74]

An important issue for occupational pension scheme trustees to consider is whether granting members investment choices in this way is a delegation of their investment decision making power. If it is a delegation, it would be prohibited by the Pensions Act which provides that pension scheme trustees may only delegate investment decisions to a sub-committee or an investment manager.[75] So how can members be offered investment choices? The answer is to do so in a way which does not delegate the trustees' investment power. There are at least three schools of thought on this issue:

(1) Compulsory directions

13–049 The first suggestion is to require the trustees to act on the choices made by the members. The argument is that, by requiring the trustees to act on the members' instructions, this removes any element of discretion from the trustees' duties with the consequence that they have no investment decision to delegate.

This argument seems flawed as the power of investment still rests with the trustees. The are delegating that power to members and simply requiring the

---

[73] The *Myners' Review* (Ch.6) considered the issues to be borne in mind in setting the investment options and the use of default options.

[74] Pensions Act 1995, s.36(3); see para.13–023, above.

[75] *ibid.*, s.34; see paras 13–045 *et seq.* above.

trustees to follow this direction does not remove the element of delegation (on the contrary, it seems to affirm it). This suggestion also begs the question of what action the trustees may take if it transpires one option is no longer suitable. Although the trustees could withdraw the option and prevent further contributions being invested, if the trustees felt it appropriate, they could not transfer assets previously invested in that option to another option without being directed to do so by the members because they restricted themselves to following the members' directions.

(2) Limited investment power

An alternative suggestion is to draft the trust deed so as to restrict the **13–050** trustees' investment power. If the trustees' investment power is restricted in this way so that it does not to apply to those assets which members have chosen to invest in the options selected by the trustees, the trustees have no power to invest these assets and, consequently, they cannot be said to have delegated that power.

The restriction would have to be carefully drafted so as to apply only where members have actually made use of the options. This will ensure that the trustees retain the power to invest in a default option where members have failed to make a positive election. In addition, the trustees may wish to have a limited investment power in respect of those assets which members have chosen to invest in the available options in order to permit the trustees to intervene where a particular option is no longer suitable.

(3) The overall suitability test

Finally, it is suggested that, for trustees to be said to have satisfied their duty of **13–051** care with regard to investments, all of the options must be suitable for all of the members. If this is the case, whichever options are selected by a member will be an investment decision a prudent person would have taken with the result that the trustees cannot be criticised in respect of any particular choice.

This approach fails to acknowledge that the trustees have still delegated their investment power. Further, if, for example, the options include (as is likely) an equity fund, it may not be within the range of reasonable decisions a prudent person would make for a member who is only a year away from retirement to invest their entire fund within this option.

Whichever approach is adopted to justify allowing members to select how their pension fund should be invested from a range of options, it must be recognised that some residual duties remain with the trustees. They have a duty to ensure the options provided are suitable for the members and must discharge their duty of care in selecting and maintaining the availability of the options. Further, the Myners' Principles for defined contribution pension schemes[76] state that, where investment options are given to the members, they

---

[76] See paras 13–070 et seq., below.

should be given sufficient information to allow them to make an appropriate choice. Although the Myners' Principles set out best practice only, it seems possible that, in the future, a member may seek to claim compensation from the pension scheme trustees for failing to provide information which would have prevented the member from making an inappropriate investment decision and suffering financial loss.

13–052 In addition to the legal issues relating to the method by which members are able to choose how their pension account should be invested, providing these options raises financial services issues about which the trustees must be aware. In particular, by offering these investment options, occupational pension scheme trustees must take care not to breach the financial services requirements relating to financial promotion.[77]

Bringing these strands together, the trustees of an occupational pension scheme providing defined contribution benefits who wish to allow the scheme's members a degree of choice with regard to the investment of their pension fund must:

(a) ensure that the structure of the arrangement is such that they are not delegating their investment power to the members;

(b) select appropriate options for the members, acting on the written advice of their investment advisers, and review regularly the suitability of these options; and

(c) provide the members with sufficient information to allow them to make an appropriate choice while being careful not to breach the requirements of the FSMA.

Appointment of investment managers and custodians

13–053 The Pensions Act prescribes the manner in which certain "professional advisers" are appointed by occupational pension scheme trustees. These requirements are set out in s.47 of the Pensions Act and the Scheme Administration Regulations.[78] The term "professional adviser" includes investment managers and custodians and a failure to comply with s.47 when appointing these professional advisers will leave any trustee who places reliance on the skill or judgement of the professional adviser open to a financial penalty.

Section 47(2) of the Pensions Act requires that occupational pension schemes which have assets consisting of investments (as defined in FSMA, s.22) must appoint an investment manager. As with the power of delegation, the investment manager must be appointed "by or on behalf" of the trustees.

---

[77] These issues have already been discussed at para.13–036, above.
[78] The Occupational Pension Schemes (Scheme Administration) Regulations 1996 (1996/1715).

However, there are some exceptions to this requirement and schemes where an investment manager is not required include:

(a) wholly-insured pension schemes (*i.e.* a scheme where all of the benefits are secured by way of an insurance policy);

(b) unapproved pension schemes;

(c) public service pension schemes;

(d) unfunded occupational pension schemes;

(e) schemes with less than two members; and

(f) schemes providing death benefits only.[79]

The appointment of professional advisers must be made in writing and the contract must specify the date the appointment is take effect, the person to whom the adviser is to report and the person from whom the adviser should take instructions. The investment adviser must then acknowledge the appointment within one month. In addition, a professional adviser who is subject to the rules of the FSA (the "FSA Rules") regarding conflicts of interest must confirm in writing that the trustees will be notified in writing of any conflicts of interest to which the adviser may be subject in relation to the pension scheme. Any other professional adviser must confirm to the trustees in writing that it will notify the trustees of any conflict of interest in relation to the pension scheme as soon as the adviser becomes aware of its existence.

The Pensions Act also sets out basic requirements for removing a professional adviser and for the resignation of a professional adviser. In practice, these situations will be governed by the terms of the contract and will build on the requirements of the Pensions Act.

Appointment of investment managers

In accordance with the requirements of the Pensions Act, all investment management agreements ("IMAs") with occupational pension scheme trustees must be made in writing and before entering into the IMA, the pension scheme trustees and the investment manager will need to ensure that the trustees have the powers which they are purporting to delegate to the investment manager. Although the trustees will be able to check their trust deed and rely on professional advice in this regard, the investment manager is likely to require an express warranty to this effect. In some circumstances, it may be appropriate to append the text of the trustees' investment power to the IMA. The investment manager should also request sight of the pension

13–054

---

[79] Scheme Administration Regulations, reg.3(3).

INVESTMENT MANAGEMENT AND OCCUPATIONAL PENSION SCHEMES

scheme's Statement of Investment Principles[80] as this may include self-imposed restrictions on the trustees' investment powers. The investment manager may also require the Statement of Investment Principles to be appended to the IMA and for the IMA to require the trustees to consult with the investment manager before any changes to the statement are made. The investment manager may wish to have the ability to terminate the IMA if it does not approve of the any revisions to the Statement of Investment Principles but whether such a provision is included in the IMA will depend on the negotiating position of the parties.

The IMA should also set out the customer classification for the pension scheme trustees. According to the FSA Rules, pension scheme trustees will be "intermediate customers" if the trust has (or has had in the previous two years) at least 50 members and assets under management of at least £10 million. If the trustees fail to meet those criteria, they will be "private customers" for the purposes of the FSA Rules and a full customer agreement will be required. Even if trustees fall within the definition of an intermediate customer, they may seek to be treated as a private customer for the purposes of the IMA but this is likely to be resisted by the investment manager.

13–055 A specimen document for IMAs involving discretionary investment management has been produced by the Investment Managers' Association[81] and is known as FMA1 should not be seen as an industry standard; indeed according to the Allocation it is only available to its members. Depending on the negotiating position on the parties, the trustees should not accept an IMA simply because it reflects the provisions of FMA1 or reject it because it does not. As an example, FMA1 does not reflect the requirements of s.47 of the Pensions Act so as to include the effective date of the appointment, and the name of the person from whom the investment manager should take instructions and to whom the investment manager should report.

Occupational pension scheme trustees must ensure that any IMA they enter into includes an express contractual requirement for the investment manager to comply with the requirements of the Pensions Act and, in particular, s.36 (diversification and suitability of investments).[82] If it does not, the trustees cannot rely on s.34 of the Pensions Act and they will be responsible for the acts or defaults of the investment manager. If the IMA allows the investment manager to sub-delegate investment decisions, trustees will also want to ensure that the sub-delegation agreement meets the requirements of s.34 so that they can rely on their statutory protection in respect of the acts or defaults of the sub-delegate.

The extent to which the investment manager will be liable for the acts or defaults of the sub-delegate will be a matter for negotiation. FMA1 provides

---

[80] See paras 13–023 *et seq.*, above.
[81] "FMA" refers to the Fund Managers' Association. In 2002 the Fund Managers' Association merged with the Association of Unit Trusts and Investment Funds to form The Investment Management Association.
[82] See paras 13–045 *et seq.*, above.

that the investment manager would remain liable for acts or defaults if the sub-delegate is an "associate" *(i.e.* someone connected with the investment manager) but does not ordinarily provide for the investment manager to remain liable for acts or defaults if it employs an associate as an agent.

By virtue of s.49 of the Pensions Act, pension scheme trustees must gener- **13–056** ally only keep money with a "deposit taker" within the meaning of the FSMA if certain requirements are met. Consequently, the trustees must determine whether the investment manager or other person who will hold their cash is a "deposit taker" and, if it is not, suitable provisions must be inserted into the IMA in order to comply with the Scheme Administration Regulations.[83] The provisions of the Pensions Act requiring "proper advice" to be given in writing[84] should also be included if there are to be any circumstances in which advice will be given by the investment manager.

In accordance with the FSA Rules, FMA1 uses the concept of "best execution". The FSA Rules state that to provide best execution a firm must take reasonable care to ascertain the best price available to the customer and to execute the customer order at a price no less advantageous to the customer, unless reasonable steps have been taken to ensure it would be in the customer's best interests not to do so.[85] FMA1 defines best execution as the method whereby the investment manager seeks to achieve the best terms for its customer. Although it is generally possible for investment managers to agree with intermediate customers that the duty of best execution shall not apply to the IMA, the FSA Rules prohibit any such agreement where the customer is the trustee of an occupational pension scheme.

FMA1 requires the investment manager to set out its policy with regard to soft commissions and to list any soft commission agreements relevant to the IMA. Soft commission is paid where the investment manager agrees to place business with a particular firm in return for a service which could improve the overall level of performance provided by the investment manager to its clients. This practice is becoming increasingly uncommon and, notwithstanding that pension scheme trustees could negotiate a requirement for the investment manager to account for soft commissions received in respect of the pension scheme, in light of the Myners Principles[86] soft commission arrangements seems likely to be removed from pension scheme IMAs in most circumstances.

The IMA clauses likely to be subject to the most negotiation are those **13–057** relating to liability and indemnity. Pension scheme trustees should look for a provision requiring the investment manager to maintain adequate and suitable insurance cover where appropriate. Any indemnity to be provided by the trustees to the investment manager should be subject to a cap to prevent the pension scheme trustees from becoming personally liable under the terms of

---

[83] Occupational Pension Schemes (Scheme Administration) Regulations 1996 (SI 1996/1715).
[84] Pensions Act 1995, s.36(7); see para.13–023 above.
[85] FSA Handbook COB, 7.5.
[86] See paras 13–070 *et seq.*, below.

371

an IMA. It is common for indemnities to be limited to the value of the pension scheme's assets from time to time.

However, if the pension scheme trustees have entered into more than one IMA and each includes an indemnity limited to the value of the pension scheme's assets, the trustees may still find themselves having to meet the indemnity out of their own pockets if they do not have an indemnity themselves from the employer sponsoring the scheme.[87] It is for this reason that, in circumstances where more than one investment manager is being appointed, pension scheme trustees should argue strongly for the indemnity to be limited to the value of the pension scheme's assets being managed by that investment manager from time to time. Investment managers often resist this limit on the indemnity on the basis that the trustees could simply avoid the indemnity by moving their assets to a different manager. In practice, a compromise will have to be reached based on the parties' relative negotiating positions.

Investment mandates

13–058 When an investment manager is appointed, the pension scheme trustees need to set that manager a mandate as to how the pension scheme's assets should be invested. In addition, the pension scheme trustees will generally set the investment manager a benchmark against which their investment returns will be judged. For example, for an active manager, the investment management agreement may set the manager the target of outperforming the benchmark by one per cent over a rolling three-year period. However, mandates expressed in this way can discourage investment managers from diverging from the benchmark to any material degree thereby limiting the scope for the scheme's investments to outperform the market, which was probably the rationale for using an active manager in the first place. It is unlikely this level of performance will be guaranteed by the investment manager but it must invest the pension scheme's assets in a manner which is appropriate to achieve this level of return.[88] The alternative to active management is passive management where the investment mandate will be for the manager to track a given benchmark. As there is no out-performance requirement, the costs of passive management will be less than for an active manager, but the tendency will be slightly to under-perform the benchmark.

There are various different approaches which can be adopted with regard to investment mandates. For example, an investment manager may be appointed under a "balanced management" mandate whereby the manager will balance the assets under its control between different asset classes to achieve capital growth and income. More complex arrangements will involve

---

[87] See para.13–062 below.

[88] This issue was at the centre of *Unilever v Mercury Asset Management* (unreported as the case was ultimately settled). See Ch.11 (the case of Unilever and Mercury Asset Management).

the appointment of a number of investment managers, each with a very specific investment mandate. For example, one manager may be appointed to invest in fixed interest investments while the other managers invest against equity benchmarks. It is important in arrangements such as these that the pension scheme trustees (or, more commonly, their investment advisers) look at the overall asset allocation and risk to ensure that the pension scheme's assets are being invested appropriately.

Of course, the more complex the investment mandates, the more the investment managers are likely to charge. It may also be more costly to comply with the Myners' Principles on shareholder activism and reviewing the investment managers' performance.

Appointment of custodians

Whereas the investment manager will decide how to invest a pension scheme's **13–059** assets, the custodian will normally be the legal owner of those investments. Although it is possible for the investment manager to act as the custodian, this is becoming rare because of the requirements of the FSA Rules in such circumstances. There are various alternative ways of appointing a custodian and FMA1 allows for these alternative approaches.

If the investment manager uses a nominee custodian there is unlikely to be a direct contractual relationship between the pension scheme trustees and that custodian. Rather, the IMA will require the investment manager to take responsibility for the nominee exercising its functions properly. The alternative to this would be for the pension scheme trustees to appoint their own custodian by way of a separate custodian agreement. In this situation, the investment manager will be given the identity of the custodian in order to manage the investments. Finally, there may be a tripartite agreement between the pension scheme trustees, the investment manager and the custodian. Here, all parties will have contractual rights and obligations against each other.

Transition management

The trustees of an occupational pension scheme may decide from time to **13–060** time that they wish to alter the allocation of assets between their investment managers or to appoint different investment managers or, quite possibly, a combination of the two. The management of this process will be vital in order to minimise the costs of achieving the transition. For example, the costs connected with selling unwanted assets and purchasing new assets can be avoided by appointing a transition manager to oversee the process so as to avoid stocks being sold which another investment manager subsequently purchases. Generally, a transition manager will only be required where the value of the assets involved is significant as, clearly, there will be more scope to reduce the costs of the transition.

The first task of a transition manager will be to identify those stocks and securities which are the subject of the transition. The transition manager will then obtain "wish lists" from the investment managers who will be investing the pension scheme's assets after the transition is completed. These wish lists will set out the stocks and securities the managers would ideally hold when the transition process has been completed. The stocks and securities which are subject to the transition will be transferred to the transition manager's account and the transition manager will then compare those stocks and securities with the stocks and securities set out in the wish lists.

At this stage, the transition manager will know exactly what stocks and securities it has and what stocks and securities it needs to end up with. By comparing the two, the transition manager can minimise costs which could arise because of bid/offer spread, transfers (custody fees and commissions) and tax. In addition to these direct savings, by structuring the transition in this way, particularly where the value of the assets involved is significant, the transition manager can minimise the impact of the transition on the market which could, in turn, have a detrimental effect on the price at which the pension scheme's assets are sold or purchased. A particularly effective way of minimising costs is to use "crossing", where transactions are undertaken with other investors away from the open market. These transactions will usually be at the mid-market price and will generate only low levels of commission. As crossing transactions are completed away from the open market, the indirect costs associated with market impact are greatly reduced.

13–061   During the transition process, the pension scheme trustees will want to ensure that they are still exposed to the market so that they will benefit from any increases in the market during the transition process. How this exposure will be achieved will need to be discussed with the transition manager at the outset and it may be appropriate to make use of arrangements such as hedge funds and phasing the transition through futures contracts.

Perhaps the most important issue when a transition is being prepared is to ensure that all relevant responsibilities have been assigned to a particular party. The danger is that a particular matter will be forgotten and, as responsibility for that matter will not have been assigned, it will not be dealt with. Depending on the size of the fund being restructured, it may also be important to keep the transition confidential as it will be market sensitive information. In this situation, for the transition manager to provide best execution, it should complete the trades associated with the transition in same manner as it would for an ongoing mandate. Investment managers will often have a separate team dealing with transition management to protect this confidential information and to avoid any conflicts of interests with other clients.

Trustee Protection

Occupational pension scheme trust deeds will often contain express exonera-   **13–062**
tion and indemnity provisions to protect pension scheme trustees. Typically,
the exoneration clause will purport to absolve the trustees from any liability
in respect of their actions as trustees (save for liability as a consequence of
wilful default). The indemnity provisions will generally allow the trustees to
claim any costs they have incurred by virtue of their office as trustees from
the pension scheme or, to the extent this is not possible, from the employer.
However, due to the potentially far-reaching effect of these provisions, they
are limited by legislation. For example, pension scheme trustees may not be
indemnified out of the pension scheme's assets in respect of penalties
imposed by the OPRA.[89] This prohibition extends to insurance premiums
where the policy covers such penalties.

In the context of investment management, although pension scheme
trustees will probably delegate all routine and day-to-day investment decisions to investment managers, it does not follow that, by delegating these
powers, the trustees absolve themselves from their duty of care in relation to
the investment of their pension scheme's assets. Section 33 of the Pensions
Act states that liability under any rule of law to take care or exercise skill in
the performance of any investment function cannot be excluded or restricted
by any instrument or agreement. Consequently, any provision in a pension scheme trust deed purporting to exonerate trustees from any liability in
relation to investment decisions will not be effective.

However, as we have already seen,[90] pension scheme trustees will not be
responsible for the acts or defaults of investment managers in the exercise of
discretions delegated to them in accordance with s.34(2) of the Pensions Act
if steps have been taken to satisfy the trustees (or the person delegating the
discretion on their behalf) that the investment manager has the appropriate
knowledge and experience for managing the investments of the pension
scheme and that the investment manager is exercising the discretion competently and in accordance with the Pensions Act. In addition, notwithstanding
s.33 of the Pensions Act, it is possible for the trustees to exclude or restrict
their liability for the acts or defaults of an investment manager to whom discretion to make investment decisions has been delegated where this does not
constitute a regulated activity under the FSMA, provided they have taken the
same protective steps that apply where the investment manager is conducting
a regulated activity.[91]

In the Government's consultation paper on proposals to increase the duty
of care required of pension scheme trustees, it is suggested that s.33 should
be extended to those matters which will be subject to the new duty of care.

---

[89] Pensions Act 1995, s.31.
[90] See para.4.1 above.
[91] Pensions Act 1995, s.34(5) and (6).

However, the consultation paper reflected the current protections where investment decisions have been delegated to an investment manager provided the increased duty of care had been exercised in the selection and monitoring of the person appointed.[92]

The *Myners' Review* and the Government's Response

The Myners' Review of Institutional Investment in the UK

13–063 The *Myners' Review* has already been considered in this Chapter and Chapter 4 with regard to the duty of care pension scheme trustees must exercise when making investment decisions.[93] However, the scope of the review was much wider than this point.

The Treasury Department commissioned the review as part of the 2000 Budget to consider "whether there were factors distorting the investment decision-making process of institutions".[94] The review was specifically asked to consider institutional investment in private equity and whether there were any unnecessary barriers to this type of investment. With regard to the investment of occupational pension schemes' assets, the main proposals made by the *Myners' Review* are as follows:

Trustee expertise

13–064 This Chapter has already considered the proposals to increase the duty of care required to be exercised by pension scheme trustees in making investment decisions. As part of this proposal, the review recommended that trustees should be paid (unless there is a specific reason why this is not necessary), more investment should be made in training trustees and pension schemes should establish an investment sub-committee. In addition, the sponsoring employer should provide in-house staff to assist the trustees with their investment responsibilities.

With regard to investment decision making by pension scheme trustees, the review recommended that the trustees should:

- set out explicitly an overall investment objective for the scheme which represents their best judgement of what is necessary to meet the scheme's liabilities;

---

[92] "Familiar with the Issues Concerned": A Consultation Document, issued by the Department for Work and Pensions, February 2002; see para.13–039 *et seq.* above.
[93] See paras 13–039 *et seq.* above.
[94] *Myners' Review*, p.4.

THE MYNER'S REVIEW AND THE GOVERNMENT'S RESPONSE

- set objectives for their investment managers that are coherent with the scheme's aggregate investment objective; and
- set out explicitly what decision is being taken by whom.[95]

Investment restrictions

The *Review* suggested that pension scheme trust deeds and the Statement of Investment Principles should not contain any restrictions on the use of particular types of investment or asset classes.

13–065

Investment consulting

The *Myners' Review* was concerned about the lack of competition in the investment consulting industry which provides advisory services to pension schemes, and recommended that contracts for actuarial services should be separated from investment consulting and the investment consultants should be formally assessed. It also recommended that trustees ensure the investment consultants have sufficient expertise to provide the advice being sought.

13–066

Shareholder activism

The Review also concluded that the US approach to shareholder activism should be introduced to the United Kingdom.

The review found that institutional investors in the US were, to a greater degree than in the UK, protected from the poor performance by the companies in which they invest because investment managers are expected to intervene in companies where there is a reasonable expectation that doing so will increase the value of the investment.

As an initial step to tackle this issue, the review suggested that trustees should include this principle of intervention in investment management mandates. However, the *Review* also suggested that, in time, the principle should be more fully set out in legislation. This approach was endorsed by the Government in its consultation document "Encouraging Shareholder Activism" published in February 2002 which proposed introducing an express statutory duty of intervention. For further discussion of this topic see Chapter 4.

13–067

Issues regarding conflicts of interest and insider knowledge were considered by the Government and dismissed as barriers to activism. In the Government's opinion, investment managers could cope with these issues by "Chinese walls" to ensure that information obtained as a result of activism is

13–068

---

[95] The *Myners' Review*, Recommendations: Investment decision-making by trustees.

377

INVESTMENT MANAGEMENT AND OCCUPATIONAL PENSION SCHEMES

isolated. Finally, the Government accepted the cost of intervening may not always justify the benefits to be gained. In these circumstances, no intervention should take place.

The Government's proposals have not been embraced widely. For example, the Investment Managers Association, in its response to the Government's consultation document on shareholder activism, criticised the Government's proposed duty as being "extremely vague" and said that it would "encourage litigation as a means of seeking clarification". The Association also pointed out that, while the US Department of Labor's bulletin and the Government's consultation paper recognise that intervention should only take place where there is a reasonable expectation of enhancing the value of the investment, the Government's proposed duty of intervention does not depend on whether it is likely to have a positive effect. In the Association's opinion, as envisaged by the *Myners' Review*, the duty of activism should not be included in legislation at this time and should only be included in the future after reviewing how practices have changed in the meantime.

Principles

13–069 The main outcome of the *Myners' Review* was two sets of principles (one for defined benefit pension schemes and one for defined contribution pension schemes) which set out the *Review*'s suggested best practice for effective decision making. The *Review* recommended that trustees disclose the steps they have taken to implement these principles in the Statement of Investment Principles (which would be sent to all members). Initially, the Review recommended that this information should only be provided on a voluntary basis. However, if this voluntary approach does not result in sufficient disclosures, the review suggested consideration be given to compulsion.

The Government's proposals

13–070 The Government announced in the 2001 Budget that it intended to take forward all of the recommendations made by the *Myners' Review*. The Government has issued various consultation papers in addition to its formal response to the review and its proposals regarding the duty of care to be exercised by those trustees undertaking investment functions have already been considered.[96]

---

[96] See para.13–042, above.

378

Revised Myners Principles

Following consultation on the principles of best practice put forward by the **13–071** *Myners' Review*, the Government has amended the principles slightly. The Government agreed that, initially at least, there should be no statutory requirement to disclose against these principles, but the position may change if it transpires that disclosures are not being made voluntarily. The Government has instituted a two year review period, commencing in March 2003, over which to assess the extent to which the "Myners Principles" have been adopted voluntarily. The principles are as follows:

Principles for defined benefit pension schemes

Effective decision-making

Decisions should be taken only by persons or organisations with the skills, **13–072** information and resources necessary to take them effectively. Where trustees elect to take investment decisions, they must have sufficient expertise and appropriate training to be able to evaluate critically any advice they take.

Trustees should ensure that they have sufficient in-house staff to support them in their investment responsibilities. Trustees should also be paid, unless there are specific reasons to the contrary.

It is good practice for trustee boards to have an investment subcommittee to provide the appropriate focus.

Trustees should assess whether they have the right set of skills, both individually and collectively, and the right structures and processes to carry out their role effectively. They should draw up a forward-looking business plan.

Clear objectives

Trustees should set out an overall investment objective for the fund that: **13–073**

- represents their best judgement of what is necessary to meet the fund's liabilities given their understanding of the contributions likely to be received from employer(s) and employees; and

- takes account of their attitude to risk, specifically their willingness to accept underperformance due to market conditions.

Objectives for the overall fund should not be expressed in terms which have no relationship to the fund's liabilities, such as performance relative to other pension funds, or to a market index.

Focus on asset allocation

13–074 Strategic asset allocation decisions should receive a level of attention (and, where relevant, advisory or management fees) that fully reflect the contribution they can make towards achieving the fund's investment objective. Decision-makers should consider a full range of investment opportunities, not excluding from consideration any major asset class, including private equity. Asset allocation should reflect the fund's own characteristics, not the average allocation of other funds.

Expert advice

13–075 Contracts for actuarial services and investment advice should be opened to separate competition. The fund should be prepared to pay sufficient fees for each service to attract a broad range of kinds of potential providers.

Explicit mandates

13–076 Trustees should agree with both internal and external investment managers an explicit written mandate covering agreement between trustees and managers on:

- an objective, benchmark(s) and risk parameters that together with all the other mandates are coherent with the fund's aggregate objective and risk tolerances;

- the manager's approach in attempting to achieve the objective; and

- clear timescale(s) of measurement and evaluation, such that the mandate will not be terminated before the expiry of the evaluation timescale for underperformance alone.

The mandate and trust deed and rules should not exclude the use of any set of financial instruments, without clear justification in the light of the specific circumstances of the fund.

Trustees, or those to whom they have delegated the task, should have a full understanding of the transaction-related costs they incur, including commissions. They should understand all the options open to them in respect of these costs, and should have an active strategy—whether through direct financial incentives or otherwise—for ensuring that these costs are properly controlled without jeopardising the fund's other objectives. Trustees should not without good reason permit soft commissions to be paid in respect of their fund's transactions. [97]

---

[97] As a result of this principle, a joint working party made up of members of the Investment Management Association and the National Association of Pension Funds have drawn up a Pension Fund Disclosure Code (published in May 2002) "to assist pension fund trustees' understanding of the charges and costs" being levied. However, adherence to this code is entirely voluntary.

THE MYNER'S REVIEW AND THE GOVERNMENT'S RESPONSE

Activism

The mandate and trust deed should incorporate the principle of the US **13–077**
Department of Labor Interpretative Bulletin on activism. Trustees should
also ensure that managers have an explicit strategy, elucidating the circumstances in which they will intervene in a company; the approach they will use
in doing so; and how they measure the effectiveness of this strategy.

Appropriate benchmarks

Trustees should: **13–078**

- explicitly consider, in consultation with their investment manager(s),
  whether the index benchmarks they have selected are appropriate; in particular, whether the construction of the index creates incentives to follow
  sub-optimal investment strategies;

- if setting limits on divergence from an index, ensure that they reflect the
  approximations involved in index construction and selection;

- consider explicitly for each asset class invested, whether active or passive
  management would be more appropriate given the efficiency, liquidity
  and level of transaction costs in the market concerned; and

- where they believe active management has the potential to achieve higher
  returns, set both targets and risk controls that reflect this, giving the managers the freedom to pursue genuinely active strategies.

Performance measurement

Trustees should arrange for measurement of the performance of the fund **13–079**
and make a formal assessment of their own procedures and decisions as
trustees. They should also arrange for a formal assessment of performance
and decision-making delegated to advisers and managers.

Transparency

A strengthened Statement of Investment Principles should set out: **13–080**

- who is taking which decisions and why this structure has been selected;

- the fund's investment objective;

- the fund's planned asset allocation strategy, including projected investment returns on each asset class, and how the strategy has been arrived at;

- the mandates given to all advisers and managers; and

- the nature of the fee structures in place for all advisers and managers, and
  why this set of structures has been selected.

381

INVESTMENT MANAGEMENT AND OCCUPATIONAL PENSION SCHEMES

Regular reporting

13–081 Trustees should publish their Statement of Investment Principles and the results of their monitoring of advisers and managers. They should send key information from these annually to members of these funds, including an explanation of why the fund has chosen to depart from any of these principles.

Principles for defined contribution pension schemes

Effective decision-making

13–082 Decisions should only be taken by persons or organisations with the skills, information and resources necessary to take them effectively. Where trustees elect to take investment decisions, they must have sufficient expertise and appropriate training to be able to evaluate critically any advice they take.

Where scheme members are given a choice regarding investment issues, sufficient information should be given to them to allow an appropriate choice to be made.

13–083 Trustees should ensure that they have sufficient in-house staff to support them in their investment responsibilities. Trustees should also be paid, unless there are specific reasons to the contrary.

It is good practice for trustee boards to have an investment subcommittee to provide appropriate focus.

Trustees should assess whether they have the right set of skills, both individually and collectively, and the right structures and processes to carry out their role effectively. They should draw up a forward-looking business plan.

Clear objectives

13–084 In selecting funds to offer as options to scheme members, trustees should:

- consider the investment objectives, expected returns, risks and other relevant characteristics of each fund, so that they can publish their assessments of these characteristics for each selected fund; and

- satisfy themselves that they have taken their members' circumstances into account, and that they are offering a wide enough range of options to satisfy the reasonable return and risk combinations appropriate for most members.

Focus on asset allocation

13–085 Strategic asset allocation (for example for default and lifestyle options) should receive a level of attention (and, where relevant, advisory or management fees) that fully reflects the contribution they can make to achieving investment objectives. Decision-makers should consider a full range of investment opportunities, not excluding from consideration any major asset class, including private equity.

Choice of default fund

Where a fund is offering a default option to members through a customised **13–086** combination of funds, trustees should make sure that an investment objective is set for the option, including expected returns and risks.

Expert advice

Contracts for investment advice should be open to competition, and fee **13–087** rather than commission based. The scheme should be prepared to pay sufficient fees to attract a broad range of kinds of potential providers.

Explicit mandates

Trustees should communicate to members, for each fund offered by the **13–088** scheme:

- the investment objective for the fund, its benchmark(s) and risk parameters; and

- the manager's approach in attempting to achieve the objective.

These should also be discussed with the investment manager concerned, as should a clear timescale(s) of measurement and evaluation, with the understanding that the investment mandate will not be terminated before the expiry of the evaluation timescale for underperformance alone.

Trustees, or those to whom they have delegated the task, should have a full understanding of the transaction-related costs they incur, including commissions. They should understand all the options open to them in respect of these costs, and should have an active strategy—whether through direct financial incentives or otherwise—for ensuring that these costs are properly controlled without jeopardising the fund's other objectives. Trustees should not without good reason permit soft commissions to be paid in respect of their fund's transactions. As a result of this principle, a joint working party made up of members of the Investment Management Association and the National Association of Pension Funds has drawn up a Pension Fund Disclosure Code (published in May 2002) "to assist pension fund trustees' understanding of the charges and costs" being levied. It should be noted that adherence to this code is entirely voluntary.

INVESTMENT MANAGEMENT AND OCCUPATIONAL PENSION SCHEMES

Activism

13–089 The mandate and trust deed should incorporate the principle of the US Department of Labor Interpretative Bulletin on activism. Managers should have an explicit strategy, elucidating the circumstances in which they will intervene in a company; the approach they will use in doing so; and how they measure the effectiveness of this strategy.

Appropriate benchmarks

13–090 Trustees should:

- explicitly consider, in consultation with their investment manager(s), whether the index benchmarks they have selected are appropriate; in particular, whether the construction of the index creates incentives to follow sub-optimal investment strategies;

- if setting limits on divergence from an index, ensure that they reflect the approximations involved in index construction and selection;

- consider explicitly for each asset class invested, whether active or passive management would be more appropriate given the efficiency, liquidity and level of transaction costs in the market concerned; and

- where they believe active management has the potential to achieve higher returns, set both targets and risk controls that reflect this, giving managers the freedom to pursue genuinely active strategies.

Performance measurement

13–091 Trustees should arrange for measurement of the performance of the funds and make a formal assessment of their own procedures and decisions as trustees. They should also arrange for a formal assessment of performance and decision-making delegated to advisers and managers.

Transparency

13–092 A strengthened Statement of Investment Principles should set out:

- who is taking which decisions and why this structure has been selected;

- each fund option's investment characteristics;

- the default option's investment characteristics, and why it has been selected;

- the agreements with all advisers and managers; and

- the nature of the fee structures in place for all advisers and managers, and why this set of structures has been selected.

Regular reporting

Trustees should publish their Statement of Investment Principles and the results of their monitoring of advisers and managers. They should send key information from these annually to members of these funds, including an explanation of why the fund has chosen to depart from any of these principles.   **13–093**

Ethical and Socially Responsible Investments

The requirement for occupational pension scheme trustees to prepare, maintain and revise a Statement of Investment Principles has already been referred to but it is important to note the requirement for that statement to include the extent (if any) to which social, environmental or ethical considerations are taken into account in the selection, retention and realisation of investments.[98] This requirement is important because of the general trust law proposition that, in the context of a trust providing financial benefits for its beneficiaries, the best interests of those beneficiaries are normally their best financial interests.   **13–094**

To what extent, then, can trustees of occupational pension schemes take into account social, environmental and ethical considerations when setting their investment policy? This issue will be of more importance to certain employers than others. For example, a cancer research charity is unlikely to want its pension scheme trustees to invest in tobacco companies and a children's charity is unlikely to want its pension scheme trustees to invest in publishers of, say, pornography.

Probably the most high-profile court case on this subject is *Cowan v Scargill*,[99] in which Arthur Scargill argued that the trustees of the Mineworkers' Pension Scheme should be able to set an investment policy which excluded overseas investments and investments in energies which were in direct competition with coal. The then Vice Chancellor, Sir Robert Megarry, was of the opinion that, when the purpose of a trust is to provide financial benefits for the beneficiaries, the best interests of the beneficiaries are normally their best financial interests and he held that the trustees of the pension scheme in question could not be doing their best for the beneficiaries of that scheme by prohibiting a wide range of investments permitted by the terms of the trust.

Although this view reflects the current law, it is perhaps an extreme example and, over the years, it has become widely accepted that trustees can take into account non-financial criteria in setting investment strategies. In the case   **13–095**

---

[98] Occupational Pension Schemes (Investment) Regulations 1996 (SI 1996/3127).
[99] [1984] All E.R. 750.

of *Martin v City of Edinburgh District Council*,[1] it was held that the most profitable investment of assets is only one of a number of matters to be considered by trustees in securing the best interests of the beneficiaries. There is also the case of *Bishop of Oxford v The Church Commissioners*,[2] in which Vice Chancellor Nicholls (as he then was) commented that the starting point for trustees must be that investments should be chosen on the basis of well-established investment criteria but this did not mean that "trustees who own land may not act as responsible landlords or those who own shares may not act as responsible shareholders". However, trustees should not invest in a manner which conflicts with the purpose of the trust and they should not use their trust assets to make "moral statements".

When the Government introduced the requirement that pension scheme trustees should disclose in their Statement of Investment Principles the extent to which social, ethical and environmental considerations have been taken into account, the Green Paper stated:

"The Government believes that, subject to the overriding requirement of trust law in respect of the beneficiaries, trustees should feel able to consider moral, social and environmental issues in relation to their investments. We believe it is right that all trustees should consider how far such issues should affect the way they invest the assets of the pension fund".[3]

Despite the Government's stated beliefs, it did nothing to alter the law in this area, save for the addition of the disclosure requirement.

13–096 Even if there is an express provision in the terms of the trust allowing trustees to consider non-financial aspects of investments, the matter will not be put beyond doubt. For example, if the investment provisions of the pension scheme's trust deed explicitly state that the trustees should take into account "such ethical, environmental and social considerations as the trustees deem to be appropriate when setting their investment strategy", notwithstanding that the trustees would clearly have a power to take these matters into consideration, they would remain subject to their overriding duty to act in the best interests of the members. Consequently, these clauses are relatively uncommon in occupational pension schemes. However, if the investment power, for example, states that no investment may be made in tobacco companies, then the trustees would be bound to abide by this restriction. Again, this type of provision is uncommon and is likely to remain so following the comments of the *Myners Review* on general restrictions to trustees' investment powers which were discussed earlier in this chapter.

---

[1] Court of Session, Edinburgh [1988] S.L.T. 329, [1989] P.L.R. 9.
[2] [1993] 2 All E.R. 300.
[3] Department for Social Security Green Paper: "A New Contract for Welfare: Partnership in Pensions" published in 1988 (Cm 4179).

So where does this leave pension scheme trustees who wish to invest taking into account ethical, environmental or social considerations? Trustees must always consider their overriding duty to act in the best interests of the members and remember, in the context of a pension scheme, this will normally be the financial interests of the members. However, within this duty it is likely that trustees may:

(a) consider the non-financial benefits of the members, particularly where the members value those non-financial benefits highly; and

(b) properly take account of the views of the sponsoring employer (which may involve the employer wishing its pension scheme to reflect its own views on investment policy),

but only if these considerations do not have an adverse impact on the financial returns achieved by the pension scheme. A broad brush approach would be to adopt some form of "negative screening", whereby certain investments would be covered by a blanket exclusion. Taken to its extreme, this approach leads trustees back to *Cowan v Scargill* and it is likely a more focused approach should be used. One such approach which has found support is "engagement". Engagement is the process where the companies in which pension scheme funds are to be invested are asked to explain their policy on social, environmental and ethical issues. When considering the trustees' overriding duties, it has been suggested that this approach would present the trustees with the fewest legal difficulties.

Of course, in practice, it is not often the pension scheme trustees who take **13–097** routine or day-to-day investment decisions and they can only set a general policy for their investment managers to follow. Therefore, it is important for the trustees to satisfy themselves that their investment managers have the capability to "engage" the companies in which they intend to invest in order to determine their attitude to social and other issues.[4]

In practice then, pension scheme trustees need to be wary about placing too much importance on non-financial criteria. However, to the extent they can still be said to be acting in the members' best interests and assuming there is no specific provision in the trust deed on the subject, trustees are at liberty to take into account ethical, environmental and social considerations when setting their investment strategy.

---

[4] Further information on engagement can be found in "Engaging for Success—Engagement guidance on socially responsible investment for investors and companies", published by the NAPF in association with the Institute of Business Ethics.

Other Issues

Real estate

13–098   Although the specific issues relating to the investment of pension scheme assets in real property are beyond the scope of this Chapter, it is worth noting that particular attention needs to be paid to property transactions involving trustees (whether they are trustees of a pension scheme or any other trust) in order to ensure that title is either effectively obtained by the trustees or effectively passed to the purchaser. Investments in property also cause difficulties for pension scheme trustees because of the large sums of money involved.

For smaller pension schemes, investment in property can be impractical as it would not allow the trustees to diversify their investments sufficiently. However, particularly with the recent, relatively poor performance of equity investments, pension funds have been keen to find a suitable vehicle through which they can access property investments. The obvious solution is some form of pooled arrangement and one particular method of pooling assets to invest in property which is worthy of note is the use of limited liability partnerships (or "LLPs").

If an LLP is used, the investors will be partners and will enter into a partnership deed which will set out their rights, interests and liabilities. The most important issues covered by the partnership deed are likely to be how profits and losses will be allocated and the terms on which partners can join or withdraw from the partnership. Unlike ordinary partnerships, an LLP has a separate legal identity and will hold the property investments in its own name. The partners will either pay money into the partnership to allow it to purchase property investments or transfer their own property investments into the partnership (by way of an *in specie* investment).

Although an LLP has similar filing and auditing obligations to those of a limited company, the tax advantages of this type of pooled arrangement for pension schemes are significant. LLPs are tax transparent so that any profits are taxed in the hands of the partners and, as such, pension schemes can use their status to avoid income and capital taxes on their property investments.

Insured pension schemes

13–099   There are many types of pension scheme which are used as a "wrapper" for an insurance policy. Although this Chapter has concentrated on the investment of occupational pension scheme assets through an investment manager, it is possible for an occupational pension scheme to be fully insured, *i.e.* for all of the benefits to be secured through an insurance policy. In this arrangement, the employer and member contributions are paid to an insurance company and it is then for that insurance company to invest that money (along with its other assets) so as to be able to pay the benefits promised by the pension scheme. Where this structure is adopted, many of the issues relating to pension scheme trustees which are set out in this Chapter fall away because the investment requirements of the pension scheme are placed solely in the hands of the insurance company.

Perhaps the most common arrangement whereby pensions are provided by an insurance company is a personal pension plan or a stakeholder pension arrangement. Although these arrangements will be established on a defined contribution basis, the basic structure will still be for contributions to be paid to an insurance company which will then invest those assets in order to provide an individual with a fund of money with which he or she can purchase an annuity at retirement.

Small Self-administered Schemes (SSASs)

For the most part, investment management issues are the same for SSASs as for large self-administered pension schemes. Although a SSAS may not be subject to the same restrictions on employer-related investments,[5] it will be subject to additional restrictions which are set out in the Retirement Benefits Schemes (Restriction on Discretion to Approve) (Small Self-administered Schemes) Regulations 1991.[6]   **13–100**

A full review of the restrictions on SSAS investments is beyond the scope of this Chapter, but it is worth noting that some of the restrictions require that the trustees notify the Inland Revenue of the investment (for example, if the trustees of a SSAS wish to borrow money, hold certain assets, lend money or lease assets). Another restriction worthy of note is the extent to which the trustees of a SSAS may invest in the employer. In the two years following the establishment of the SSAS, the trustees may hold no more than 25 per cent of the market value of the employer's shares and, thereafter, no more than 50 per cent.

The minimum funding requirement

The Pensions Act contains a statutory funding level (the "minimum funding requirement" or "MFR") against which occupational defined benefit pension schemes must be tested. This test is widely acknowledged to be artificial and, indeed, the Government proposes to replace this "one size fits all" approach with a scheme-specific funding test. However, even if the MFR is replaced with a scheme specific test, as with the MFR, the new test is likely to be based on a particular asset allocation between equities and fixed interest investments.   **13–101**

---

[5]   See paras 13–025 *et seq.*, above.
[6]   SI 1991/1614.

Consequently, the pension scheme's investment strategy will have a real effect on the scheme's funding level. This is an issue pension scheme trustees and employers must consider when they are setting their investment strategy.

The Sarbanes-Oxley Act of 2002

13–102 The Sarbanes-Oxley Act, which arose out of the Enron bankruptcy, concerns corporate governance in the United States of America but may have an effect on trustees of occupational pension schemes in the United Kingdom. If an occupational scheme in the United Kingdom is sponsored by a company which is either listed on a stock exchange in the United States or is owned by a company listed on a stock exchange in the United States, the trustees will need to take care not to cause the company to be in breach of this Act.

The Act contains restrictions on certain types of investments and, because of the way the Act requires pension scheme investments to be disclosed within the company's accounts, it is possible that an investment made by the pension scheme would cause the company to breach the Act. If this happened, the trustees could be liable for a criminal penalty in the United States.

APPENDIX 1

INVESTMENT MANAGEMENT ASSOCIATION: PENSION FUND DISCLOSURE CODE

(Abridged version published by kind permission of the Investment Management Association)

Introduction

This Code of Practice has been drawn up by a Joint Working Party of Members of the Investment Management Association ("IMA") and the National Association of Pension Funds ("NAPF"). The Code has been adopted by the IMA after full consultation with its Members and is strongly endorsed by the NAPF Investment Council. **App1–001**

The objective of the Code is transparency in order to assist pension fund trustees' understanding of the charges and costs levied on the pension fund assets for which they have responsibility. This will be facilitated by comprehensive, clear and standardised disclosure that will allow trustees and their advisers to monitor and compare all costs incurred during the management of the fund's assets.

The IMA has no legal authority to impose standards or reporting requirements on its Members. Neither would it wish to propose aspirational standards that few managers would be able to attain without significantly increased operational costs, or that would provide relatively little additional benefit for trustees. Instead, the Code takes a differentiated approach. In some areas the Code does not set out absolute standards, but is an approach to determining the information needs of trustees and their advisers. These needs will, of course, not be the same for every scheme. The Code also proposes a common format to suit users and providers.

Two important factors have been identified as likely to encourage compliance with the Code: **App1–002**

- the practicality of the Code for managers. Most of the reportable items specified are already available to managers, as FSA requirements or as information that managers need to demonstrate compliance with FSA Rules. It is recognised, however, that disaggregation of costs on a scheme-by-scheme basis has not hitherto been a requirement.

- the positive attitude of trustees. Trustees have an important role in compliance, by requiring information from managers that trustees need in order to carry out their responsibilities effectively.

The Code sets out minimum standards, and managers can only claim compliance with the Code if they meet all the required disclosures—they do not have the option to

INVESTMENT MANAGEMENT ASSOCIATION PENSION FUND DISCLOSURE CODE

select the sections of the Code to which they wish to adhere. A manager may, however, still be deemed to have complied with the Code in the event that particular provisions of the Code are not relevant to the business that the manager undertakes, and the manager has clearly stated and justified this position.

Background

App1–003 It has become apparent that, in the pursuit of their fiduciary obligations, trustees and their advisers are increasingly looking for numerical disclosures on costs from which they can draw conclusions as to the manner in which their assets are being managed. Equally clear is that currently there is no comprehensive, common format of numerical reporting that meets this need and that, taken out of proper context, numerical comparisons can be misleading.

In drawing up the Code, the Joint Working Party was conscious of the issues raised in the Myners Review and sought to address specific questions where appropriate. However, in the interests of promoting transparency, the Code extends beyond the disclosure of transaction costs to disclosure of all costs incurred by client portfolios, directly or indirectly, during the fund management process.

To ensure that statistics are put into appropriate context, it is necessary for trustees and their advisers to understand the rationale behind, and justification for, different costs and how these are accounted for. Consequently, there is also a need for disclosure of certain aspects of managers' trading processes, and not just of numbers alone that might be taken out of context.

App1–004 Not only are costs different for varying investment strategies, but the reliability with which different types of costs can be measured or estimated will also vary. In fact, it appears that the significance of different types of transaction costs and the reliability with which they can be measured vary inversely. Transaction costs can be categorised in increasing order of significance and decreasing order of reliability of measurement/estimation as follows: commissions, spread, market impact and opportunity costs. Consequently, the Code requires that the various types of transaction costs should be identified and assessed to the extent they can be reliably measured or estimated. Although the Code does not recommend one particular methodology above others, it does draw attention to areas where figures can be potentially misleading.

May 2002

Scope

App1–005 The Code is designed to:

- be adopted by the managers of UK pension fund mandates.

- be applied to portfolios, or portions of portfolios, consisting of listed securities (including suspended securities previously listed), derivatives (where the underlying instruments are securities, financial indices, interest rates, dividends or foreign exchange), cash and pooled funds/collective investment schemes that invest in any of the above assets.

- address all explicit costs incurred by client pension funds, including broker commissions (direct, soft and directed or recaptured), fund management and custody fees, foreign exchange charges, bank charges, taxation (stamp duty, VAT etc) and any other costs.

392

APPENDIX 1

- consider also the impact of implicit execution costs, e.g. the bid/ask spread, market impact and also opportunity costs.

The Code is limited to those custody costs borne directly by the fund, where the manager undertakes custody or has appointed custodians on behalf of clients. Withholding taxation on income is outside the scope of this Code.

In respect of those pooled funds/collective investment schemes managed by the manager or an associate, the Code provides that managers should disclose the total costs incurred by each pooled fund, in monetary terms or as a percentage of the size of the fund, whichever is the more meaningful. Attempts to attribute portions of costs to individual pension funds would be onerous and the results would not be meaningful. Although this "global" information is not currently disclosed in collective investment scheme reports and accounts, it should be readily obtainable for "in-house" managed funds and should be accompanied by appropriate commentary to put the statistics into context, e.g. where the size of the pooled fund has changed significantly during the period. The Code recognises, however, that it may not be possible for managers to obtain this level of detail from third-party funds and from investment trusts which, although they may be managed "in-house", are the responsibility not of the manager but of the relevant boards of directors. In such circumstances, the Code requires prominent disclosure of any proportion of the portfolio that is invested in assets that are not compliant with the Code and an explanation of why the manager believes it is appropriate to use such vehicles.

Disclosure Requirements

The Code only requires quantitative disclosure of costs that can be measured with certainty. For the other costs listed in Appendix 1 [*of this document*], a description of the manager's approach to handling them is required. The Code seeks to encourage disclosure of such costs without advocating any particular methodology as to how this is achieved. However, there is a requirement to state key aspects of methodology, so that informed readers can draw their own conclusions as to the usefulness of the narrative information presented. **App1–006**

It is both permissible and desirable that different house fund management styles, products and specific client requirements result in varying types of reporting. If any particular costs addressed by the Code are on occasion not relevant, or are perhaps more clearly explained by narrative rather than quantitative reporting, this should be noted in the relevant reports.

There are two distinct types of disclosure covered by the Code:

- Level One: house policies, processes and procedures in relation to the management of costs incurred on behalf of clients (see Appendix 1 [*of this document*]).

- Level Two: client-specific information (see Appendix 2 [*of this document*]). The most important requirement here is for disaggregation by counterparties to transactions, to the extent and level of detail that provide meaningful information for clients. Additional commentary should be provided when this helps to put numerical disclosure into context.

The Code sets out minimum standards, and managers can only claim compliance with the Code if they meet all the required disclosures that are relevant to the business that the manager undertakes. **App1–007**

The Code envisages that the frequency of client reporting will vary according to the type of disclosure. Level One disclosure should be updated annually, while the

393

INVESTMENT MANAGEMENT ASSOCIATION PENSION FUND DISCLOSURE CODE

quantitative client-specific Level Two disclosure should be made at least six-monthly. In the event of any material Level One changes, these should be reported promptly to clients, not left until the next annual reporting date. These frequencies mirror FSA rules that require certain transaction reports to be made at minimum six-monthly intervals and, in the case of soft commissions, at least annually. More generally, clear, consistent, consolidated reporting is regarded as critical: it will not be helpful to trustees if managers disclose the various costs listed in the Code, or comply with FSA requirements, in a number of different reports or with different reporting dates.

Managers responsible for mandates of a number of different portfolios or asset classes for one scheme, should carefully consider whether it would be more helpful to the trustees if reporting was not fully consolidated but reported at portfolio or asset class level.

Appendix 1

LEVEL ONE DISCLOSURE
MANAGER'S POLICIES, PROCEDURES AND CONTROL PROCESSES

Reporting period to which disclosure relates: | *day/month/year* | *to* | *day/month/year* |

App1–008 ***Dealing venues and methods***—description of the various dealing venues used, e.g. different types of brokers, dealing for commission and dealing net, programme trading, internal crossing, crossing networks etc. How the manager decides between these alternatives and the impact that these decisions have on client transaction costs.

Broker selection and transaction volume allocation process—manager's processes, policy on credit ratings, how brokers' relative competence is established with regard to execution, research, etc. How this results in business level targets for each broker/ dealing venue, how this is split between commission bearing, soft commission and net dealing and how progress towards and variations from these targets are monitored on an ongoing basis. Cross-reference to Level Two Disclosure, based on Appendix 2 [*of this document*].

Variations in rates of commission—manager's processes for negotiating commission rates and the impact on rates of commission in different markets, e.g. UK/overseas, bond/equity, liquid/illiquid.

Soft commissions—manager's internal policy, justification (i.e. against potential lower commissions) and control processes to ensure compliance with current FSA regulations. Any change in this policy since the last report. Cross-reference to Level Two Disclosure, based on Appendix 3 [*of this document*], and to the manager's annual soft commission disclosure.

Commission recapture—if applicable to the particular client, a description of the process. Cross-reference to Level Two Disclosure, based on Appendix 3 [*of this document*].

Dealing Efficiency Monitoring—manager's policy and procedures designed to maximise the value of client portfolios and to control transaction costs while still

394

APPENDIX 1

trading effectively. This will include policy, procedures and assumptions for assessing execution costs, including bid/offer spreads, market impact and opportunity costs, whether the manager measures these and how the results are used.

Conflicts of interest—procedures for complying with FSA requirements for fair treatment of clients in the execution of orders and allocation of trades, and procedures to identify and manage actual and potential conflicts of interest (including dealing through associates). How the manager complies with current FSA regulations on inducements. An approximate number, type and overall value of inducements logged over the period.

External and internal research—manager's policy on using external research, how the benefit of that research is assessed and how it is funded.

Access to and allocation of Initial Public Offerings and underwriting—manager's policy plus procedures for complying with relevant FSA regulations and the extent to which securing allocations of IPOs and underwriting influences trading patterns.

Custody services—where the manager appointed the custodian, an outline of the manager's selection, monitoring and review processes.

Placing of deposits—manager's policy on spreading deposits, in particular as regards placing deposits with associates, policy on credit ratings, use of money-market funds.

Foreign exchange transactions—manager's policy in spreading foreign exchange transactions, in particular as regards placing these through associates, and policy on credit ratings.

Appendix 2

LEVEL TWO DISCLOSURE

Reporting period to which disclosure relates: ⟨day/month/year⟩ *to* ⟨day/month/year⟩

Percentage of portfolio at period end not covered by the Code

e.g. in third-party collective investment schemes, investment trusts, direct property, private equity, or in commodities. An explanation as to why the manager is using such vehicles.

App1–009

Fund Management fees and any other income derived by the manager and associates

In the case of pooled funds with multiple fee scales, the fee scale borne by the particular client.

App1–010

395

INVESTMENT MANAGEMENT ASSOCIATION PENSION FUND DISCLOSURE CODE

Custody costs borne directly by the fund, and to whom paid

Transaction values/commissions paid *(see example of analysis at Appendix 3 [of this document])*

App1–011
- Transactions traded net without commission, as percentage of total transactions
- Transactions subject to commissions and fees, as percentage of total transactions
- Transactions subject to soft commissions, as percentage of total transactions
- Transactions subject to directed or recapture arrangements, as percentage of total transactions
- Total commissions incurred for the period

Underwriting/sub-underwriting commissions received

App1–012   **Stocklending** (if the manager undertakes stocklending on behalf of the client) Income to the fund and fees paid

Taxation

- VAT
- Stamp duty paid on purchases
- Any other transaction taxes or levies

Other de minimis costs, e.g. PTM levy on transaction contract notes, need not be disclosed.

396

Appendix 3

An example report

SUMMARY OF TRADING VOLUMES, COMMISSIONS AND FEES

Reporting period to which disclosure relates: day/month/year *to* day/month/year   App1–013

Counterparty	Trading volume for period			Commissions and fees paid during period			
	Total	*Traded net*	*Subject to commissions*	*Total*	*Under softing arrangements*	*Under directed or recapture arrangements*	*Other*
	£000	£000	£000	£000	£000	£000	£000
1							
2							
9							
10							
Others > 5%							
Others (total)							
Total							
% age	100%	[ ]%	[ ]%	100%	[ ]%	[ ]%	[ ]%

Disclosure is required of volumes undertaken through, and also commission paid to, different counterparties during the period. For each of these two categories, the top ten counterparties, plus any others representing over 5 per cent of the overall total, should be listed. In this regard, counterparties include brokers (any associates of the manager being clearly noted), crossing networks and as a distinct category, the total of trades internally crossed by the manager. Clearly, different counterparties may feature in the table for different disclosure elements. The proforma will need to be customised accordingly.

APPENDIX 2

INSTITUTIONAL SHAREHOLDERS' COMMITTEE

THE RESPONSIBILITIES OF INSTITUTIONAL SHAREHOLDERS AND AGENTS—STATEMENT OF PRINCIPLES

(Published by kind permission of the Investment Management Association)

1. Introduction and Scope

App2–001 This Statement of Principles has been drawn up by the Institutional Shareholders' Committee[1]. It develops the principles set out in its 1991 statement "The Responsibilities of Institutional Shareholders in the UK" and expands on the Combined Code on Corporate Governance of June 1998. It sets out best practice for institutional shareholders and/or agents in relation to their responsibilities in respect of investee companies in that they will:

- set out their policy on how they will discharge their responsibilities—clarifying the priorities attached to particular issues and when they will take action—see 2 below;

- monitor the performance of, and establish, where necessary, a regular dialogue with investee companies—see 3 below;

- intervene where necessary—see 4 below;

- evaluate the impact of their activism—see 5 below; and

- report back to clients/beneficial owners—see 5 below.

In this statement the term "institutional shareholder" includes pension funds, insurance companies, and investment trusts and other collective investment vehicles. Frequently, agents such as investment managers are appointed by institutional shareholders to invest on their behalf.

---

[1] In 1991 the members of the Institutional Shareholders' Committee were: the Association of British Insurers; the Association of Investment Trust Companies; the British Merchant Banking and Securities Houses Association; the National Association of Pension Funds; and the Unit Trust Association. In 2002, the members are: the Association of British Insurers; the Association of Investment Trust Companies; the National Association of Pension Funds; and the Investment Management Association.

APPENDIX 2

This statement covers the activities of both institutional shareholders and those that invest as agents, including reporting by the latter to their institutional shareholder clients. The actions described in this statement in general apply only in the case of UK listed companies. They can be applied to any such UK company, irrespective of market capitalisation, although institutional shareholders' and agents' policies may indicate *de minimis* limits for reasons of cost-effectiveness or practicability. Institutional shareholders and agents should keep under review how far the principles in this statement can be applied to other equity investments.

The policies of activism set out below do not constitute an obligation to micro-manage the affairs of investee companies, but rather relate to procedures designed to ensure that shareholders derive value from their investments by dealing effectively with concerns over under-performance. Nor do they preclude a decision to sell a holding, where this is the most effective response to such concerns.

App2–002

Fulfilling fiduciary obligations to end-beneficiaries in accordance with the spirit of this statement may have implications for institutional shareholders' and agents' resources. They should devote appropriate resources, but these should be commensurate with the benefits for beneficiaries. The duty of institutional shareholders and agents is to the end beneficiaries and not to the wider public.

2. Setting out their policy on how they will discharge their responsibilities

Both institutional shareholders and agents will have a clear statement of their policy on activism and on how they will discharge the responsibilities they assume. This policy statement will be a public document. The responsibilities addressed will include each of the matters set out below.

App2–003

- How investee companies will be monitored. In order for monitoring to be effective, where necessary, an active dialogue may need to be entered into with the investee company's board and senior management.

- The policy for requiring investee companies' compliance with the core standards in the Combined Code.

- The policy for meeting with an investee company's board and senior management.

- How situations where institutional shareholders and/or agents have a conflict of interest will be minimised or dealt with.

- The strategy on intervention.

- An indication of the type of circumstances when further action will be taken and details of the types of action that may be taken.

- The policy on voting.

Agents and their institutional shareholder clients should agree by whom these responsibilities are to be discharged and the arrangements for agents reporting back.

3. Monitoring performance

Institutional shareholders and/or agents, either directly or through contracted research providers, will review Annual Reports and Accounts, other circulars, and general meeting resolutions. They may attend company meetings where they may raise

App2–004

399

RESPONSIBILITIES OF INSTITUTIONAL SHAREHOLDERS AND AGENT

questions about investee companies' affairs. Also investee companies will be monitored to determine when it is necessary to enter into an active dialogue with the investee company's board and senior management. This monitoring needs to be regular, and the process needs to be clearly communicable and checked periodically for its effectiveness. Monitoring may require sharing information with other shareholders or agents and agreeing a common course of action.

As part of this monitoring, institutional shareholders and/or agents will:

- seek to satisfy themselves, to the extent possible, that the investee company's board and sub-committee structures are effective, and that independent directors provide adequate oversight; and

- maintain a clear audit trail, for example, records of private meetings held with companies, of votes cast, and of reasons for voting against the investee company's management, for abstaining, or for voting with management in a contentious situation.

In summary, institutional shareholders and/or agents will endeavour to identify problems at an early stage to minimise any loss of shareholder value. If they have concerns and do not propose to sell their holdings, they will seek to ensure that the appropriate members of the investee company's board are made aware of them. It may not be sufficient just to inform the Chairman and/or Chief Executive. However, institutional shareholders and/or agents may not wish to be made insiders. Institutional shareholders and/or agents will expect investee companies and their advisers to ensure that information that could affect their ability to deal in the shares of the company concerned is not conveyed to them without their agreement.

4. Intervening when necessary

App2–005   Institutional shareholders' primary duty is to those on whose behalf they invest, for example, the beneficiaries of a pension scheme or the policyholders in an insurance company, and they must act in their best financial interests. Similarly, agents must act in the best interests of their clients. Effective monitoring will enable institutional shareholders and/or agents to exercise their votes and, where necessary, intervene objectively and in an informed way. Where it would make intervention more effective, they should seek to engage with other shareholders.

Many issues could give rise to concerns about shareholder value. Institutional shareholders and/or agents should set out the circumstances when they will actively intervene and how they propose to measure the effectiveness of doing so. Intervention should be considered by institutional shareholders and/or agents regardless of whether an active or passive investment policy is followed. In addition, being underweight is not, of itself, a reason for not intervening. Instances when institutional shareholders and/or agents may want to intervene include when they have concerns about:

- the company's strategy;

- the company's operational performance;

- the company's acquisition/disposal strategy;

- independent directors failing to hold executive management properly to account;

- internal controls failing;

- inadequate succession planning;

400

APPENDIX 2

- an unjustifiable failure to comply with the Combined Code;
- inappropriate remuneration levels/incentive packages/severance packages; and
- the company's approach to corporate social responsibility.

If boards do not respond constructively when institutional shareholders and/or agents intervene, then institutional shareholders and/or agents will consider on a case-by-case basis whether to escalate their action, for example, by:

- holding additional meetings with management specifically to discuss concerns;
- expressing concern through the company's advisers;
- meeting with the Chairman, senior independent director, or with all independent directors;
- intervening jointly with other institutions on particular issues;
- making a public statement in advance of the AGM or an EGM;
- submitting resolutions at shareholders' meetings; and
- requisitioning an EGM, possibly to change the board.

Institutional shareholders and/or agents should vote all shares held directly or on behalf of clients wherever practicable to do so. They will not automatically support the board; if they have been unable to reach a satisfactory outcome through active dialogue then they will register an abstention or vote against the resolution. In both instances it is good practice to inform the company in advance of their intention and the reasons why.

5. Evaluating and reporting

Institutional shareholders and agents have a responsibility for monitoring and assess- **App2–006** ing the effectiveness of their activism. Those that act as agents will regularly report to their clients details on how they have discharged their responsibilities. This should include a judgement on the impact and effectiveness of their activism. Such reports will be likely to comprise both qualitative as well as quantitative information. The particular information reported, including the format in which details of how votes have been cast will be presented, will be a matter for agreement between agents and their principals as clients.

Transparency is an important feature of effective shareholder activism. Institutional shareholders and agents should not however be expected to make disclosures that might be counterproductive. Confidentiality in specific situations may well be crucial to achieving a positive outcome.

6. Conclusion

The Institutional Shareholders' Committee believes that adoption of these principles **App2–007** will significantly enhance how effectively institutional shareholders and/or agents discharge their responsibilities in relation to the companies in which they invest. To ensure that this is the case, the Institutional Shareholders' Committee will monitor the impact of this statement with a view to reviewing and refreshing it, if needs be, within two years in the light of experience and market developments.

401

INDEX

(All references are to paragraph numbers)

Account
meaning 1–004
Advice 8–005—8–012. *see also* Judgment
communications 8–007
concept, as 8–006, 8–007
conduct, by 8–011, 8–012
description of services 8–012
implementation. *see* Implementation
implicit 8–011, 8–012
meaning 8–009
nature of 8–005—8–012
persuasive, nature of 8–008, 8–009
material 8–008
special skill or knowledge 8–008
skilled, examples of 8–006
strength of 8–010
Agency
meaning 10–003
Arm's length dealings 2–001—2–004
caveat emptor basis 2–001—2–003
contractual performance 2–004
counterparty contract 2–001
examples of counterparty transactions 2–002
Arranging 8–027—8–028
definition 8–027
effect 8–028
fluidity of concept 8–027
negotiations, and 8–028

Best execution 4–026—4–030
monitoring quality 4–030

Best execution—*cont.*
provision of information on firm's execution arrangements 4–028
restructuring obligation 4–027
review of arrangements 4–029
Broking 1–027—1–029
broking advice 1–029
reasons for using 1–027
trade execution 1–028
Bundling arrangements 4–020—4–025
FSA Consultation Paper 176, 4–022—4–025
excessive dealing 4–024
limitation of goods and services which may be softed or bundled 4–025
limiting cost-pass-through for remaining bundled and softed goods and services 4–025
opacity 4–024
over-consumption 4–024
quantity of trading decisions and execution 4–024
Myners Review 4–020, 4–021

Certified high net-worth individuals
meaning 3–014
Certified sophisticated investor
meaning 3–014
Client service relationship 2–005—2–013
absolute duties 2–016, 2–017
express contractual term 2–017
care and skill 2–014—2–049

402

INDEX

Client service relationship—*cont.*
client depends on firm 2–007—2–009
discretionary management service
2–009
examples 2–009
client, meaning 2–007
client sophistication 2–035—2–040
client holding out- objective test
2–038
disclaimers 2–040
exclusion clauses 2–040
factors as indicators of 2–036
general competence, meaning 2–035
relative to particular circumstances
2–037
reliance on advice 2–039
significance 2–039, 2–040
sophistication, meaning 2–035
common practice 2–026
duration of service relationship
2–041—2–049
advisory services 2–048
categorisation of services 2–045
compensation claims 2–045
continuous 2–041
continuous advisory management
2–049
different effects in contract and tort
2–045
duration, meaning 2–041
duties of confidentiality 2–047
duty in occasional service
relationship to take account of
previous dealings 2–046, 2–047
duty to accept further instructions
from same client 2–044
duty to be proactive 2–042, 2–043
execution booking 2–048
information of progress 2–043
intermittent 2–041
intermittent advice 2–049
investment management markets
2–048, 2–049
occasional 2–041
one off event 2–041
ongoing 2–041
relationship, meaning 2–041
single event 2–041
fiduciary duty of loyalty 2–013
firm undertakes to provide service
2–006
firm's duty to act in client's interest
2–010—2–012
fiduciary duty 2–010

Client service relationship—*cont.*
firm's duty to act in client's interest—
cont.
regulatory confusion 2–012
holding out 2–028—2–034
act of performance, by 2–032
common practice 2–033
firm's promotion of itself 2–030
firm's reputation for type of
services it provides 2–031
internal intention of firm irrelevant
2–034
nature of firm's business 2–029
nature of 2–028
public standards of conduct 2–033
interface between qualified and
absolute duties 2–021, 2–022
linguistic indicators 2–005
measuring standard of skill for
qualified duties 2–023—2–027
negligence, meaning 2–024
public standards of conduct 2–027
qualified duties 2–018—2–020
absolute norm, as 2–019
bad investment, and 2–020
duty of care 2–018, 2–019
exercise of judgment 2–020
reasonable care—prudent man
standard 2–023
reasonable skill-competent firm
standard 2–024, 2–025
remuneration 2–006
scope of service 2–014—2–049
service standards 2–014—2–049
tortious concept of duty of care
2–007
Clients 1–002
corporate pension schemes 1–002
pension schemes 1–002
predominantly institutional 1–002
Client's instructions 7–011—7–017
acceptance 7–012
ambiguous 7–013, 7–014
firm unable to obtain 7–016
inadequate 7–013
timeliness 7–017
unreasonableness 7–015
Closed-ended companies 1–015
Collective investment schemes
3–004—3–007
authorisation 3–009
"bodies corporate" 3–005, 3–006
common or parallel investment
schemes 3–005

403

INDEX

Collective investment schemes—*cont.*
exclusions 3–005
fiduciary duties, and 9–006
financial promotion, meaning 3–006
key characteristics 3–004
meaning 3–004
reform 4–068—4–075
  categorisation of retail funds 4–069
  charges 4–075
  Consultation Paper 185, 4–068
  financial and commodity
    derivatives 4–072
  limited redemption 4–070, 4–074
  non-retail schemes 4–071—4–075
  pricing 4–074
  reasons for 4–068
  safekeeping of scheme property
    4–074
  spread of risk 4–072
  valuation 4–074
regulatory approach 3–007
Confidentiality 7–056—7–059
duties of loyalty and confidence to
  former clients 7–058, 7–059
nature of confidential information
  7–057
Conflicts of interest 7–043—7–055
consent in service contract 7–048,
  7–049
disclosure in service contract 7–048,
  7–049
full disclosure 7–047
impartial treatment 7–052—7–055
  Chinese walls 7–055
  firm clears its mind 7–052—7–054
informed consent 7–047
investment research, and. *see*
  Investment research
managing 7–046—7–055
nature of fiduciary relationship
  7–044, 7–045
using contract to define scope of
  service 7–050, 7–051
Custody 1–023—1–026, 5–001—5–030
administration 5–004
agreements 5–008
arranging 5–005
banking functions 1–025
boundary with pure safekeeping
  5–019, 5–020
client agreements 5–007
common asset pool 1–024
consolidation of custody industry
  5–022

Custody—*cont.*
control over arrangements 1–023
custody assets 5–003
definitions 5–003—5–006
dematerialised environment, in 5–026
depository as custodian 5–025
due diligence assessments on
  custodians and sub-custodians
  5–011
exemptions 5–006
future developments 5–030
issues for consideration 5–019—5–030
legal pre-requisites 5–007—5–018
legislative regime 5–001—5–030
material environment, in 5–027, 5–028
meaning 1–023
notification requirements 5–016
passporting of services 5–023
reconciliation 5–012—5–014
record keeping 5–017
rectification 5–015
registration 5–010
regulatory regime 5–001—5–030
regulatory requirements 5–007—5–018
responsibility of custodian for
  corporate actions 5–024, 5–025
restitution 5–015
safe custody investments 5–002
safeguarding 5–004
securities held on segregated or
  commingled basis 1–023
segregation of safekeeping
  investments from firm's assets
  5–009
standard range of services 1–026
statements 5–018
sub-custody 5–029
sub-custody agreements 5–008
trustee as custodian 5–025
typical service package 1–026
value added services 5–021
Custody assets
meaning 5–003

Default clauses 7–060, 7–061
Delegation 7–018—7–027
advisory 7–026
authority to delegate 7–018
client/ sub-firm privity 7–022—7–024
firm's obligation to supervise
  delegates 7–020, 7–021
fund vehicles, by 7–027
sub-firms, liability for 7–019
sub-firm's liability in tort 7–025

INDEX

Derivatives. *see* US regulation of managed futures

Discretionary portfolio management 3–002, 3–003
delegation 3–002
meaning 3–002
source of rights of clients 3–003

Elements of investment management 1–001—1–032

Fiduciary duties 9–001—9–029
"affected person" 9–016
bilateral discretionary management agreement, and 9–006
collective investment schemes, and 9–006
comparison with other investment firms 9–007
disclosure, and 9–018, 9–019
discretionary theory 9–004
duties owed by investment managers 9–008
duty of care—investment managers as fiduciaries 9–022—9–024
fiduciary duty of care 9–023
negligence, and 9–022—9–023
exchange, rules of 9–007
"fair treatment rule" 9–017
"fault-based" fiduciaries 9–002
fiduciary, meaning 9–003, 9–004
FSA rules—priority and aggregation of orders 9–020, 9–021
allocation of designated investments 9–021
time for allocation 9–021
FSA rules—self dealing in fund assets 9–016—9–019
FSA rules—single capacity 9–012
FSA's Principles for Business 9–011
FSMA, under 9–009, 9–010
investment managers 9–003—9–006
"late traders" 9–002
London Metal Exchange, and, 9–007A
managing conflict of interest 9–018
"market timers" 9–002
modification through contract 9–025—9–029
exclusion of liability 9–027—9–029
implied terms 9–025, 9–026
informed consent 9–027
Unfair Contract Terms Act 1977, 9–027—9–029

Fiduciary duties—*cont.*
modification through contract—*cont.*
Unfair Terms in Consumer Contracts Regulations 1999, 9–027—9–029
scope of analysis 9–001
scrutiny of financial institution, and 9–001
secret profits 9–013—9–015
excessive dealing 9–014
opacity 9–014
over consumption of additional services 9–014
proposed strengthening of FSA rules 9–015
quality of trading decisions and execution 9–014
significance 9–002
single capacity rules 9–012
soft commission rules 9–014
US approach. *see* US approach to fiduciary duties

Financial planning service 1–030—1–032
background 1–030
formal recommendation 1–032
matters accompanying 1–032
historical evolution 1–030
planning process 1–031
service 1–031, 1–032

Financial promotion
meaning 3–006, 3–008

Force majeure clauses 7–060, 7–061

Futures management 1–022
carrying broker, role 1–022

Gross negligence 7–041

Hedge funds 4–049—4–067
advice as to 4–061
baskets of shares 4–063
collapse of LTCM 4–049, 4–053—4–056
collapse of 4–063
definition 4–051, 4–052
due diligence, and 4–062
FSA Feedback Statement to DP16 4–064
greater marketability, argument for 4–062
international subject, as 4–049
limited marketing 4–061
looseness of term 4–051
marketing 4–049—4–067
non-retail 4–063

405

INDEX

Hedge funds—*cont.*
'non-retail' schemes 4–062
offshore location 4–050
regulation 4–049—4–067
regulation of managers in United
    Kingdom 4–057
retail marketing 4–058—4–064
    collective investment schemes
        4–060
    consumer protection, and 4–059
    Official List, and 4–060
    potential for positive performance
        4–058
    promotion of unregulated schemes
        4–060
short selling 4–065—4–067,
    4–049—4–067
    arguments for and against 4–065,
        4–066
    FSA proposed options 4–066,
        4–067
systemic risk issues—LTCM effect
    4–053—4–056
    absence of scrutiny 4–054
    default, effect of 4–055
    findings of President's Working
        Group 4–056
    Russian rouble devaluation 4–054
trading entities, as 4–052

Implementation 8–013—8–028
advice, and 8–017—8–019
    ability to change client's legal
        position 8–018
    consensual content 8–017
    operative effect 8–019
arranging, 8–027—8–028. *see also*
    Arranging
dependence in transactions 8–020
discretion, and 8–014—8–016
    ability to change client's legal
        position 8–015
    consensual content 8–014
    operative effect 8–016
methods 8–021, 8–022
    agency execution 8–021
    apparent authority 8–022
own account order execution 8–025,
    8–026
    "best" price 8–025
    price 8–025, 8–026
riskless principal implementation
    8–023, 8–024
    effect 8–024

Individual portfolio mandates
    1–010—1–011
existing portfolio taken over 1–011
mandate, meaning 1–010
overall strategy 1–011
statement identifying agreed
    objectives 1–010
Investment advice
meaning 8–009
Investment management accountability
    11–001—11–030
benchmarks 11–001—11–030
content of contracts 11–029
form of contracts 11–029
internal controls 11–001—11–030
legal basis for claims 11–010—11–028
    commodity brokers cases 11–019
    Dixon, Richardson and Reed
        Investments Ltd v Jefferson
        Seal Ltd 11–016—11–018
    inactivity and poor diversification
        held not imprudent
        11–022—11–024
    Myners Report 11–028
    negligence suits arising from
        collapse of Confederation Life
        11–010
    relations and duties on trustees
        under TA 11–027
    Royal Court; Voisin v Matheson
        Securities 11–011—11–015
    Trustee Act 2000 and investment
        managers 11–025, 11–026
    trustee and share index—*Nestle*
        judgment 11–020, 11–021
performance targets 11–001—11–030
practical steps to be taken by trustees
    11–030
Unilever and Mercury Asset
    Management, 11–001—11–009.
    see also
    Unilever and Mercury Asset
    Management
Investment managers 1–005—1–007
diversity of business origin
    1–005
international 1–007
    London "Big Bang" 1–007
life insurers 1–006
meaning 10–018
Investment mandate 7–001—7–010
commencement 7–009, 7–010
objectives 7–003—7–006
portfolio 7–008

406

INDEX

Investment mandate—*cont.*
residual discretionary powers 7–007
restrictions 7–003—7–006
Investment portfolio, 1–003, 1–004. *see also* Portfolio
Investment research 4–014—4–019
best execution, 4–026—4–030. *see also* Best execution
bundling arrangements 4–020—4–025
CIS reform, 4–068—4–075. *see also* Collective investment schemes
conflicts of interest, and 4–014—4–019, 4–078
analysts' compensation 4–014
analysts' true opinions 4–014
independence of analysts 4–014
spinning 4–014
undisclosed internal policies 4–014
US settlement 4–014, 4–015
changes to existing practices 4–014
corporate governance 4–079
economic efficiency 4–077
FSA's work on 4–016—4–019
analyst's portfolio 4–016
Consultation Paper 171, 4–016
Discussion Paper 15, 4–016—4–019
institutional investors, and 4–017
internal systems and controls 4–017, 4–018
knowledge not yet public 4–016
lack of investor knowledge or experience 4–016
laddering 4–019
monitoring of analysts 4–016
power of subject companies 4–016
prominent disclosure, requirement for 4–019
qualifications of analysts 4–016
quiet period 4–018
reporting structures 4–016
research recommendations, power of 4–016
reward structures 4–016
role of analysts 4–016
spinning 4–019
US approach, and 4–016, 4–017
hedge funds. *see* Hedge funds
polarisation, 4–031—4–033. *see also* Polarisation
Sandler review, 4–034—4–048. *see also* Sandler Review
soft commission arrangements 4–020—4–025

Judgment 8–001—8–012
advice, and. *see* Advice
breach of mandate, and 8–003, 8–004
discretionary management, nature of 8–003, 8–004
implementation, 8–013—8–028. *see also* Implementation
skilled, exercise of 8–002

Know your customer 7–028, 7–029

Legal nature of client services relationship, 2–001—2–049. *see also* Client service relationship
Liability 7–039—7–042
gross negligence 7–041
limitation 7–039—7–042
reasonable care and skill 7–042
Life insurers
investment managers, as 1–006
Limited partnerships 1–018

Managing investments 1–008—1–022
advisory 1–008, 1–009
discretionary 1–008, 1–009
individual portfolio mandates, 1–010—1–011. *see also* Individual portfolio mandates
proprietary strategies, 1–012—1–019. *see also* Proprietary strategies
Marketing investment products and services 3–019
common law 3–019
contract, law of 3–019
general law 3–019
misleading advertising 3–019
negligence 3–019
Myners Review 4–002—4–013
aim 4–002
bundling arrangements 4–020, 4–021
occupational pension schemes. *see* Occupational pension schemes
pension scheme trustees 4–003—4–007
advice to 4–003
asset allocation decisions 4–003
findings as to 4–003
investment objectives related to index 4–004
Issues Consultation, and 4–006, 4–007
lack of expertise 4–005
methods of running pension scheme mandates 4–004

407

INDEX

Myners Review—*cont.*
pension scheme trustees—*cont.*
  performance of scheme 4–004
  short-termism 4–005
  standard of skill and prudence
    4–005
private equity 4–013
scope 4–002
shareholder activism 4–008—4–012
  Consultation Document 4–008
  DTI White Paper 4–012
  intervention by managers 4–008
  legitimate interests 4–009
  proposed duty 4–010, 4–011
  sale of shares 4–009
soft commission arrangements 4–020,
  4–021
statistical background 4–002

Occupational pension schemes
  13–001—13–102
background 13–001, 13–002
benefit structure 13–004, 13–005
common investment funds
  13–012—13–015
  avoidance of potential financial
    services issues 13–013
  bare trust 13–014
  Inland Revenue requirements
    13–012
  stamp duty 13–015
custodians, appointment 13–059
delegating decision making powers
  13–045—13–061
  compulsory directions 13–049
  defined contribution
    arrangements—member choice
    13–048—13–052
  investment sub-committees 13–047
  limited investment power 13–050
  overall suitability test 13–051,
    13–052
  power to delegate 13–045, 13–046
employer related investments 13–025,
  13–026
  exemptions 13–026
  meaning 13–025
ethical and socially responsible
  investments 13–094—13–097
  express provision in terms of trust
    13–096
  "moral statements" 13–095
  "negative screening" 13–097
insured pension schemes 13–099

Occupational pension schemes—*cont.*
investment management, and
  13–001—13–102
investment managers, appointment
  13–053—13–058
  associate, meaning 13–055
  "best execution" 13–056
  deposit taker, meaning 13–056
  formalities 13–053, 13–054
  indemnity 13–057
  investment management agreements
    (IMAs) 13–054—13–057
  liability 13–057
  soft commissions 13–056
  "wish lists" 13–060
investment mandates 13–058
  "balanced management" 13–058
legislation 13–002
managing investments 13–028—
  13–031
  day-to-day decisions 13–029,
    13–030
  routine decisions 13–029, 13–030
  small self administered schemes
    13–031
meaning 13–007
minimum finding requirement
  13–101
Myners Review 13–063—13–093
  activism 13–089, 13–077
  appropriate benchmarks 13–078,
    13–090
  choice of default fund 13–086
  clear objectives 13–073, 13–084
  effective decision-making 13–072,
    13–082
  expert advice 13–075, 13–087
  explicit mandates 13–088, 13–076
  focus on asset allocation 13–074,
    13–085
  government's proposals
    13–070—13–093
  investment consulting 13–066
  investment restrictions 13–065
  performance measurement 13–079,
    13–091
  principles 13–069
  regular reporting 13–081, 13–093
  revised principles 13–071—13–093
  shareholder activism 13–067
  transparency 13–080, 13–092
  trustee expertise 13–064
OEICs 13–020
pension scheme investments 13–011

408

INDEX

Occupational pension schemes—*cont.*
personal pension plans 13–006
PFPVs 13–018, 13–019
real estate 13–098
regulation 13–002
Sarbanes-Oxley Act 2002, 13–102
SSASs 13–008
  restrictions 13–100
stakeholder arrangements 13–006
tax treatment 13–009
transition management 13–060,
  13–061
trust law, application 13–010
trustee protection 13–062
trustees' investment powers
  13–021—13–044
  advising 13–035
  arranging 13–034
  current duty of care 13–038
  dealing 13–033
  duty of care 13–037—13–044
  employer-related investments
    13–025, 13–026
  EU Pensions Directive 13–044
  financial promotion 13–036
  financial services issues
    13–027—13–036
  government proposals 13–042,
    13–043
  managing investments
    13–028—13–031
  Myners' proposed duty of care
    13–039—13–041
  Pensions Act 1995, 13–023,
    13–024
    Statement of investment
      principles 13–024
  prudent expert test 13–039—13–041
  prudent man test 13–038
  regulated activities 13–032
  trust deed 13–021
unit trusts 13–016, 13–017
variations on structures
  13–012—13–020
Ongoing management 1–020—1–022
day-to-day process 1–020
duration of service 1–021
futures management 1–022
scope of objectives 1–020
Open-ended companies 1–016

Pension scheme trustees
Issues Consultation 4–006, 4–007
Myners Review. *see* Myners Review

Plan assets
meaning 10–019
Polarisation 4–030A-4–033
ARs, 4–030A
direct offer advertising 4–031
DSF, 4–030A
IFAs, 4–030A
meaning, 4–030A
"menu system" 4–033
"multi-tied" advisor, proposal for
  4–032
product adoption 4–031
product provider, responsibility of,
  4–030B
regulatory reform 4–031
Portfolio 1–003, 1–004
core investments 1–003
diversified allocation 1–003
meaning 1–003
terminology 1–004
"account" 1–004
Private equity
Myners Review 4–013
Prominent disclosure
meaning 4–019
Proprietary strategies 1–012—1–019

Quiet period
common pooled fund 1–012
disclosure of objectives 1–013
legal structure for pooled investment
  funds 1–014—1–019
  closed-ended companies 1–015
  limited partnership 1–018
  open-ended companies 1–016
  unit-linked life policies 1–019
  unit trusts 1–017
meaning 4–018
parallel portfolio structure 1–012
segregated accounts 1–012

**Regulation and the promotion of
  investment management services**
  3–001—3–019
**Regulatory developments for investment
  managers** 4–001—4–079
identifiable strands 4–001
Myners Review, 4–002—4–013. *see
  also* Myners Review
**Regulatory regime for investment
  management services** 3–002—3–019
financial promotion, meaning 3–006
financial promotion restrictions
  3–008, 3–009

409

INDEX

Regulatory regime for investment management services—*cont.*
financial promotion restrictions—*cont.*
disapplication of FSA conduct of business rules 3–009
exclusions 3–009
financial promotion 3–008
section 21, FSMA 3–008
section 238, FSMA 3–009
general law on marketing investment products and services 3–019
listed closed-ended companies 3–016—3–019
applying financial promotion standards 3–017
authorised person 3–018
clear, fair and not misleading communications 3–017
communications with clients 3–017
exemptions 3–016
internal compliance function 3–018
investment advice 3–018
promotion of discretionary management and collective investment schemes compared 3–010—3–015
authorised schemes 3–012
discretionary portfolio management 3–011
types of authorised funds 3–012
purpose of management, and 3–006
unregulated schemes 3–013—3–015
"certified high net-worth individuals" 3–014
certified sophisticated investor 3–014
CIS (Promotion Order) 3–014
exclusions 3–015
Risk warnings 7–031—7–034
agreements, in 7–031
cases 7–034
private client advice, in 7–032, 7–033
prospectuses, in 7–031

Safe custody investments
meaning 5–002
Sandler Review 4–034—4–048
findings 4–034—4–036
FSA Discussion Paper 19, and 4–045—4–048
Option 1, 4–046
Option 2, 4–047
Option 3, 4–048
FSA note, and 4–035, 4–036

Sandler Review—*cont.*
overview 4–034—4–036
recommendations 4–036
simpler products, recommendation for 4–037—4–044
appropriate charge cap 4–041
diversification requirements 4–040
feedback to CP121 4–044
issues for regulation 4–040
limited investment risk 4–038
pension product 4–043
product regulation 4–038
regulation of features 4–037
Treasury Consultation Document 4–039
unitised product 4–040, 4–041
with-profits product 4–042
"weak consumers" 4–035
Secret profits
fiduciary duties, and 9–013—9–015
Shareholder activism
Consultation document 4–008
DTI White Paper 4–012
Soft commission arrangements 4–020—4–025
FSA Consultation Paper 176, 4–022—4–025
excessive dealing 4–024
limitation of goods and services which may be softed or bundled 4–025
limiting cost-pass-through for remaining bundled and softed goods and services 4–025
opacity 4–024
over-consumption 4–024
quantity of trading decisions and execution 4–024
Myners Review 4–020, 4–021
Soft dollars
meaning 10–011
Spinning
meaning 4–014
Suitability 7–030

Termination of contracts 7–062—7–064
contractual duration 7–062
FSA requirements 7–063
specific task mandates 7–064
Trade execution process 7–035—7–038
best execution 7–035, 7–036
factors 7–037
guidelines 7–038
sequential phases 7–036

410

INDEX

Unilever amd Mercury Asset Management 11–001—11–009
background 11–001
claim: too many eggs in wrong basket 11–005
investment management agreement 11–004
MAM's defence 11–008
performance target 11–002
pitch and switch 11–006
problems with the portfolio 11–007
settlement 11–009

Unit trusts 1–017, 13–016, 13–017
authorised 13–016
stamp duty reserve tax 13–017
unauthorised 13–017

US approach to fiduciary duties 10–001—10–034
additional obligations of boards of directors under ICA 10–030—10–034
composition of boards of directors 10–031
duties regarding advisory contract with investment adviser 10–033
"interested person" 10–031
obligations of directors 10–034
qualifications of board members 10–031
section 36(a) 10–032
agency 10–003, 10–004
meaning 10–003
ERISA 10–017—10–026
compliance with plan documents 10–025
diversification 10–024
"exclusive purpose" 10–022
fiduciaries 10–017, 10–018
investment manager, meaning 10–018
liability for breach of fiduciary duty 10–026
"plan assets" 10–019, 10–020
"look-throughs" 10–019
plans 10–017, 10–018
"prudent man" test 10–023
section 404(a) 10–021—10–025
significant equity participation 10–019
"solely in the interest" 10–022
federal nature of US legal system 10–002
fiduciary duties of investment advisors 10–005—10–010

US approach to fiduciary duties—*cont.*
fiduciary duties of investment advisors—*cont.*
additional duties under ICA 10–014—10–016
Advisers Act 10–006, 10–007
best execution 10–011, 10–012
full disclosure of conflicts of interest 10–008
proxy voting 10–013
reasonable basis for recommendations 10–010
registered investment companies 10–014—10–016
"safe harbour" 10–011, 10–012
"soft dollars" 10–011
suitable advice 10–009
general law of fiduciaries 10–003, 10–004
state law of business entities 10–027—10–029
directors and officers 10–027
duty of care 10–028
duty of loyalty 10–029
majority stockholders 10–027
statutes 10–001

US regulation of commodity trading advisors 12–013–12–026
disclosure requirements 12–021, 12–022
relief from 12–026
exclusions from CTA definition 12–014—12–019
banks 12–017
eligibility criteria 12–018
fifteen-person exemption 12–016
incidental futures advice 12–014
investment advisors 12–017
Rule 4.14(a)(8) 12–017—12–019
Rule 4.14(a)(a) 12–019
SEC registered advisers not primarily acting as CTAs 12–015
recordkeeping requirements 12–022—12–024
relief from 12–026
regulatory requirements 12–020—12–026
solicitation of funds in client's name 12–025

US regulation of investment management 6–001—6–040
adviser registration process 6–011—6–015

411

INDEX

US regulation of investment management—*cont.*
filing form ADV 6–011
Form ADV, Part I 6–012
Form ADV, Part II 6–013
SEC response 6–014
updating form ADV 6–015
Advisers Act 6–001
advisory contracts 6–037—6–042
assignments 6–038
hedge clauses 6–039
pre-paid fees 6–040
restrictions on performance based
fees 6–037
brochure rule 6–033
confidential information, use of
6–032
custody rule requirements
6–024—6–028
account statement delivery 6–025
elimination of balance sheet
requirements 6–026
qualified custodians, use of 6–024
surprise audits 6–025
disclosure of material financial and
disciplinary information 6–029
federal vs state regulation 6–002
Form 13F disclosure 6–036
insider trading 6–032
ongoing requirements for registered
investment adviser 6–016—6–036
advertising 6–021
agency cross-transactions 6–018
aggregation of client orders 6–020
anti-fraud 6–016—6–030
cross-traders 6–019
custody of client assets 6–022
custody, meaning 6–023
principal transactions 6–017
proxy voting 6–030
record keeping 6–034, 6–035
registration under Advisers Act
6–003—6–010
advice about securities 6–007
advisory affiliates 6–010
compensation, meaning 6–005
engaged in the business, meaning
6–006
exclusions 6–008
exemptions 6–009
investment adviser, meaning 6–004
supervision 6–031
US regulation of managed funds
12–001—12–049

US regulation of managed funds—*cont.*
CFTC regulation of commodity pool
operators 12–027—12–041
annual reports 12–030
content and delivery requirements
12–029
disclosure document 12–029
electronic delivery 12–029
ethics training 12–028
exemptions from CPO requirements
12–034—12–041
mutual funds 12–035, 12–036
new CPO registration exemptions
12–034
non-profit pools 12–041
periodic account statements 12–030
pools primarily engaged in
securities transactions 12–040
potential investors 12–033
profile disclosure document rule
12–029
"qualified eligible persons"
12–037—12–039
"qualifying entities" 12–035, 12–036
recordkeeping requirements 12–031
registration 12–027
small pools 12–041
structural requirements of
organisation and operation
12–032
two-part disclosure rules 12–029
commodity pools 12–001—12–049
commodity trading advisors
12–001—12–049
derivatives 12–002—12–012
CFTC regulation 12–006
key parties in marketplace
12–007—12–012
regulated 12–003
SEC regulation 12–006
terminology 12–004, 12–005
unregulated 12–003
key parties in marketplace
commodity pool operators 12–010
commodity pools 12–009
commodity trading advisors 12–008
floor brokers 12–012
floor traders 12–012
futures commission merchants
12–011
introducing brokers 12–011
regulation of commodity trading
advisors, 12–013—12–026. see
also

412

INDEX

US regulation of managed funds—*cont.*
regulation of commodity trading
advisors—*cont.*
US regulation of commodity
trading advisors
selected CFTC/ NFA compliance
considerations 12–042—12–049
account opening procedure 12–044
customer agreements 12–046
duty to supervise registered persons
12–043

US regulation of managed funds—*cont.*
multifraud provisions 12–048
restrictions on advertising
12–047
sales practices 12–047
section 40(1) CEA 12–049
terminology 12–004, 12–005
commodities 12–004, 12–005
derivatives 12–004, 12–005
futures 12–004, 12–005
options 12–004, 12–005